The Political Economy of the Ì

The Eurozone is not a mere currency area. It is also a unique polity whose actors span multiple levels (supranational, national, regional, sectoral) and pursue overlapping economic and political objectives. Current thinking on the Eurozone relies on received categories that struggle to capture these constitutive features. This book addresses this analytical deficit by proposing a new approach to the political economy of the Eurozone, which captures economic and political interdependencies across different levels of decision making and sheds light on largely unexplored problems. The book explores the opportunities afforded by the structure of the Eurozone, and lays the foundations of a political economy that poses new questions and requires new answers. It provides categories that are firmly grounded in the existing configuration of the Eurozone, but are a precondition for overcoming the status quo in analysis and policy.

IVANO CARDINALE is Lecturer in Economics at Goldsmiths, University of London and Life Member of Clare Hall, Cambridge. He was previously the Mead Research Fellow in Economics at Emmanuel College, Cambridge. He is developing a research programme that can be described as Structural Political Economy. This approach represents the economy at the intermediate level of aggregation, focussing on interdependent sectors that are both economic activities and socio-political groups. It uses tools of economic analysis and social theory to explore the structure of economic interests, their political representation, and the political economy paths open to societies.

D'MARIS COFFMAN is Senior Lecturer in Economics and Finance of the Built Environment, The Bartlett School, University College London, and Director of the Bartlett School of Construction and Project Management. She is a managing editor of *Structural Change and Economic Dynamics*, an associate editor of *Economia Politica: Journal of Analytical and Institutional Economics*, and senior editor of Palgrave Studies in the History of Finance. She was previously the Mary Bateson Research Fellow in History at Newnham College, University of Cambridge, and founding director of the Centre for Financial History at Newnham and Darwin Colleges (2008–2014). Her research interests include the history of British public finance, historical fiscal sociology and the origins of modern infrastructure.

ROBERTO SCAZZIERI is Professor of Economic Analysis at the University of Bologna, Italy, and Fellow of the National Lincei Academy, Rome. He is also a Senior Member of Gonville and Caius College and a Life Member of Clare Hall, Cambridge. He is a managing editor of *Structural Change and Economic Dynamics*. After receiving his undergraduate education in economics and politics at Bologna, he moved to Oxford, where he carried out research leading to a D.Phil. while also working in close contact with John Hicks. He was subsequently the founding scientific director of the Bologna Institute of Advanced Study. His research deals with the theory of production, structural dynamics, framing and cognition under fundamental uncertainty, and the political economy of structural change.

The Political Economy of the Eurozone

Edited by

IVANO CARDINALE
Goldsmiths, University of London

D'MARIS COFFMAN
University College London

ROBERTO SCAZZIERI
University of Bologna

CAMBRIDGE
UNIVERSITY PRESS

CAMBRIDGE
UNIVERSITY PRESS

University Printing House, Cambridge CB2 8BS, United Kingdom

One Liberty Plaza, 20th Floor, New York, NY 10006, USA

477 Williamstown Road, Port Melbourne, VIC 3207, Australia

314-321, 3rd Floor, Plot 3, Splendor Forum, Jasola District Centre, New Delhi - 110025, India

103 Penang Road, #05-06/07, Visioncrest Commercial, Singapore 238467

Cambridge University Press is part of the University of Cambridge.

It furthers the University's mission by disseminating knowledge in the pursuit of education, learning and research at the highest international levels of excellence.

www.cambridge.org
Information on this title: www.cambridge.org/9781107561069
DOI: 10.1017/9781316403730

© Cambridge University Press 2017

First published 2017
First paperback edition 2022

A catalogue record for this publication is available from the British Library

Library of Congress Cataloging in Publication data
Names: Cardinale, Ivano, editor. | Coffman, D'Maris, editor. | Scazzieri,
Roberto, editor.
Title: The political economy of the Eurozone / [edited by] Ivano Cardinale,
University of London, D'Maris Coffman, University of London, Roberto
Scazzieri, University of Bologna.
Description: Cambridge, United Kingdom ; New York, NY : Cambridge University
Press, 2017. | Includes bibliographical references and index.
Identifiers: LCCN 2016053239 | ISBN 9781107124011 (hardback : alk. paper)
Subjects: LCSH: Eurozone. | Finance–European Union countries. | Monetary
policy–European Union countries. | European Union countries–Economic
policy.
Classification: LCC HC241 .P61525 2017 | DDC 330.94–dc23
LC record available at https://lccn.loc.gov/2016053239

ISBN 978-1-107-12401-1 Hardback
ISBN 978-1-107-56106-9 Paperback

Contents

Figures

Tables

Contributors

IVANO CARDINALE, Lecturer in Economics, Goldsmiths, University of London, and Life Member, Clare Hall, Cambridge. Former Mead Research Fellow in Economics, Emmanuel College, Cambridge.

D'MARIS COFFMAN, Senior Lecturer in Economics and Finance of the Built Environment, The Bartlett School, University College London, and Director of the Bartlett School of Construction and Project Management. Founder and Former Director, Centre for Financial History, and Fellow, Newnham College, Cambridge (2008–2014).

LUCA EINAUDI General Director, Department for Economic Policy and Planning, Italian Prime Minister's Office. Former Senior Research Fellow, Joint Centre for History and Economics Harvard University and King's College, Cambridge, and Cambridge Endowment for Research in Finance (CERF).

MARCO FORTIS, Professor of Industrial Economics and International Trade, Catholic University of Milan; Deputy Chair of the Edison Foundation, Milan.

YUNING GAO, Associate Professor, School of Public Policy and Management, Tsinghua University, Beijing.

ALI KABIRI, Senior Lecturer in Economics, University of Buckingham, Buckingham, UK; Head of Economics, University of Buckingham, UK.

FINN MARTEN KÖRNER, PhD candidate, Department of Economics and Statistics, Chair for International Economics, Carl von Ossietzky Universität Oldenburg, Oldenburg.

MICHAEL LANDESMANN, Professor of Economics, University of Linz, and Senior Research Associate (Scientific Director 1996–2016), Vienna Institute for International Economic Studies. Fellow of the National Lincei Academy, Rome. Former Lecturer, Fellow of Jesus College, and Senior Research Officer, University of Cambridge.

JAMES MACDONALD is an independent author and former investment banker. He published *A Free Nation Deep in Debt: the Financial Roots of Democracy* (2006) and *When Globalization Fails* (2015).

DUNCAN NEEDHAM, Dean and Senior Tutor, Darwin College, Cambridge, and Director, Centre for Financial History, Darwin College.

ADRIAN PABST, Reader in Politics, University of Kent, Canterbury, UK; Visiting Professor, Institut d'Etudes Politiques de Lille (Sciences Po) and Institute of Business Studies, Moscow.

ALBERTO QUADRIO CURZIO, President of the National Lincei Academy, Rome. President of the Scientific Committee, Research Centre in Economic Analysis and International Economic Development, Catholic University of Milan. Former Professor of Political Economy, Catholic University of Milan.

ROBERTO SCAZZIERI, Professor of Economic Analysis, University of Bologna and Fellow of the National Lincei Academy, Rome; Senior Member of Gonville and Caius College and Life Member, Clare Hall, Cambridge.

HANS-MICHAEL TRAUTWEIN, Professor of International Economics, Department of Economics and Statistics, Carl von Ossietzky Universität Oldenburg, Oldenburg. President of the European Society for the History of Economic Thought (ESHET).

ALI COŞKUN TUNÇER, Lecturer in Modern Economic History, University College London. Former Research Fellow, European University Institute, Florence.

WILLIAM R. WHITE, Chairman of the Economic and Development Review Committee (EDRC), OECD in Paris. Former Head of the Monetary and Economic Department (MED), Bank for International Settlements (BIS), Basel.

Preface

The Eurozone is not a mere currency area. It is also a unique polity, whose actors span multiple levels (supranational, national, regional, sectoral) and pursue overlapping economic and political objectives. Current thinking on the Eurozone relies on received categories that struggle to do justice to these constitutive features. This volume aims to address this analytical deficit by developing new categories of analysis and policy.

The volume is divided into four parts. The historical part offers a comparative analysis of monetary unions, sovereign debt arrangements and fiscal sociologies across carefully selected case studies. The theoretical part proposes new categories that capture the overlap between economic and political domains at different levels of aggregation. The policy part explores constraints and opportunities afforded by the economic and political structure of the Eurozone as defined in the volume. The final part takes stock and lays the foundations of a political economy of the Eurozone that poses new questions and requires new answers.

The volume aims to provide categories of analysis and policy that overcome the status quo but are firmly grounded in the existing political economy of the Eurozone.

Acknowledgements

We wish to express our gratitude to the institutions that have provided the scholarly freedom and intellectual environment of which this volume is a product. In particular, Ivano Cardinale is grateful to Goldsmiths, University of London, and to Emmanuel College, Cambridge; D'Maris Coffman to the Bartlett School of Construction and Project Management, University College London, the Cambridge Endowment for Research in Finance, Judge Business School and to Newnham College, Cambridge; Roberto Scazzieri to the Department of Economics, University of Bologna, the National Lincei Academy, Rome, and to Gonville and Caius College and Clare Hall, Cambridge. We are also grateful to the Centre for Financial History, Newnham College and Darwin College, Cambridge, and to the Cambridge Research Seminar in Political Economy, Emmanuel College, Cambridge, for hosting meetings and workshops during which this project took shape, and to the Cambridge Endowment for Research in Finance (under the aegis of Cambridge Finance) and the Newnham College Senior Members Research Fund for providing research support at a critical stage of this project.

Finally and most importantly, we are grateful to the colleagues who have shared our goal to lay the foundations of a new analytical framework for understanding the political economy of the Eurozone.

1 The Eurozone as a Political Economy Field

IVANO CARDINALE, D'MARIS COFFMAN
AND ROBERTO SCAZZIERI

1.1 Introduction

The Eurozone's vicissitudes highlight multiple interfaces between economics and politics. More specifically, they reveal the manifold interdependencies at work within and across the domains of the European economy and political space.

For example, an external shock in the financial sphere (a financial crisis that started outside the Eurozone) interacted with longer-term developments in the real sphere, and especially the divergence of productive structures across different areas of the Eurozone and European Union more broadly, which resulted in the build-up of external imbalances and foreign debt positions. The ensuing crisis was also reflected in the sphere of public finance, with sovereign debt crises in several countries. The institutional architecture of the Eurozone proved unable to adequately respond to the crisis, and attempts at response caused a deep economic downturn in several Eurozone countries.

Such economic developments had dramatic effects in the political sphere, generating deep conflicts between and within countries. For example, creditor countries pushed for an 'austerity agenda' while debtor countries advocated forms of debt relief and emphasized the need to support growth. Within countries, both creditor and debtor, conflicts emerged as to which sectors or socio-economic groups (e.g. financial sector or taxpayers) should bear the burden of debt relief. Such tensions were also reflected in the electoral sphere and resulted in social unrest in some countries and widespread political instability.

In summary, the crisis has highlighted the interdependencies between different economic and political domains, as well as conflicts of interest within and across levels of aggregation (supranational, national, sectoral). Overall, the crisis has exposed serious internal tensions in the

1

constitution of the Eurozone and the EU as a whole.[1] It has also shown the need to investigate, over and above the inevitable conflicts between political economy actors, which elements of common interest underlie monetary integration.

1.2 The Eurozone as a Political Economy Field

This volume studies the Eurozone as a political economy field, by which we mean a system of interdependencies that span the economic and political spheres at different levels of aggregation (e.g. countries, regions, and sectors). The contributions in the volume show features of this field, propose analytical tools to study it, and explore policy frameworks that fit those features.

Attention for multiple levels of aggregation has key implications for how the internal differentiation of the Eurozone is understood. In fact, the latter is usually conceptualized in terms of national macroeconomies (e.g. 'Northern' vs. 'Southern' countries). This level of aggregation is associated with specific constraints for policy-making, such as the sustainability of external accounts and sovereign debt. However, exclusive focus on macroeconomies might hide from view other constraints and possibilities, and especially those which emerge at the sectoral level of aggregation. In particular, economic analysis shows that proportions between sectors must remain within a range that is compatible with the 'viability' of the system. For example, this has to

---

[1] Tuori and Tuori have highlighted the multidimensional character of the European constitution, which they describe as 'process-like' in nature, that is, 'not a temporarily and substantially clear-cut normative entity but, rather, a continuous process of constitutionalisation' (Tuori and Tuori, 2014, p. 4). This view of the European constitution also applies, with qualification, to the Eurozone, and entails the co-existence of 'a number of dimensions which evolve pursuant to diverging temporal paces' (Tuori and Tuori, 2014, p. 14). The asymmetry inherent to the European constitutional settlement reflects some of the original ('functionalist') features of that settlement (Moravcsik, 2005; Scharpf, 2010) as well as some internal transformations of European polities from classical nation states to 'sectoral states' conducive to fragmentation of national policy domains (McCormick, 2007). Responses to the Eurozone crisis reflect temporal asymmetries inherent to the European constitutionalisation process and highlight significant further steps in that process (Chiti and Teixeira, 2013; Scicluna, 2012). At the same time, those responses may have enhanced the decoupling between different policy domains within the Eurozone and jeopardized its systemic coherence (Scharpf, 2010, 2012; Iversen and Soskice, 2013; Basevi and D'Adda, 2014; Majone, 2014; Soskice, Hope and Iversen, 2016).

do with assuring that inputs are produced in sufficient quality and quantity, and at appropriate timings. Further constraints are posed if we consider interdependencies within and across countries, hence the need to import required inputs and export outputs.

The foregoing argument suggests that each level of aggregation is associated with different causal mechanisms, which often work at the same time, although some mechanisms may be more relevant than others at any given moment. In general, in order to be viable, the system must satisfy different constraints (e.g. the macroeconomic and sectoral conditions just discussed), each of which also affords different opportunities for policy. An important consequence is that, in order to understand what causal mechanisms are at work in a given situation, and to gauge constraints and opportunities for policy-making, we need analytical tools that make it possible to visualize different levels of aggregation, understand which ones are more relevant at a given moment, and understand which causal mechanisms are associated with each.

The volume tackles this problem from different perspectives and disciplinary viewpoints. For example, through the lens of comparative historical and institutional analysis, it is possible to understand the levels of aggregation and causal mechanisms that were relevant in particularly significant cases of sovereign borrowing and in previous monetary unions, as well as understand the elements of fiscal union that the latter required. Moreover, political theory can provide categories to understand the constitutional dynamics that have shaped multi-level interdependencies in the Eurozone. These categories make it possible to characterize the social structures that embed states and markets, and to study how such structures frame the forms of conflict and cooperation that take place within the economic and political spheres.

In addition to history and political theory, an important contribution to the development of appropriate categories derives from economic analysis. In fact, the modern developments of analytical traditions whose initial statements go back to Political Arithmetic, Physiocracy, and Classical Political Economy, make it possible to decompose the economy in different ways at different levels of aggregation, each of which could be suited to the causal mechanisms that are more relevant in a given situation. Such analytical tools also make it possible to consider different levels at the same time, for example by highlighting both macroeconomic and sectoral conditions. By building on these traditions, it is possible to devise analytical tools that overcome the dichotomy between micro and macro analysis, which characterizes much policy and received wisdom on the Eurozone.

Once the internal differentiation of the Eurozone is characterized at multiple levels of aggregation, it becomes clear that policies have a different impact on different parts of the Eurozone as characterized above (e.g. countries, regions, and sectors). We can expect that the political actors connected to these parts will attempt to influence policy-making in order to obtain more favourable outcomes, and that coalitions will form to support different policy measures. The complicating factor for the analysis is that coalitions are likely to depend on the issue at stake. For example, when it comes to policies concerning external imbalances, the conflict is likely to be between tradable and non-tradable sectors. When it comes to the write-off of foreign debt, the conflict is likely to be between real and financial sectors. Moreover, the two cleavages need not coincide: a given firm may well find itself in one coalition for a certain policy, and in another for another policy. A further conflict of interest may have to do with liquidity policies. In fact, not only is it unlikely that a common macroeconomic liquidity policy will fit all countries, as usually discussed; policy will also have different effects on different sectors within each country, which can result in complex coalitions at different levels.[2]

The foregoing analysis points to the potential, in a system as complex as the Eurozone, for a significant degree of fragmentation of interests. However, the volume stresses that, because of interdependencies between the constitutive parts of the system, there should also be an interest in keeping the system as a whole viable, which could result in constraints to the pursuit of sectoral interests, or even in changes in the policy stances of relevant actors once it becomes apparent that systemic viability is at risk. The category of 'systemic interest' is presented for this purpose. It is argued that the Eurozone crisis may have acted as a catalyst of systemic interest, showing the

---

[2] One important point in this connection is the configuration of cleavages within any given set of social interdependencies. Cleavages may exert a disruptive or a stabilizing influence depending on whether they are, respectively, mutually reinforcing or mutually offsetting (see, in particular, Ross, 1938; Lipset and Rokkan, 1967; Hirschman, 1968, 1970; Rae and Taylor, 1970; Rogowski, 1987; Cardinale and Coffman, 2014). Tibor Scitovsky called attention to the co-existence of cross-national and cross-sectoral patterns of interdependence during the early stages of European economic integration (Scitovsky, 1958).

unsustainability of external imbalances and the need to satisfy viability requirements at the sectoral and macroeconomic level.

The volume shows that the overlap of different divisions of interests (among sectors conceived as outlined above, and countries) and its interplay with systemic interest has great explanatory power when it comes to understanding the origins of the European Monetary System, the dynamics leading to the Eurozone crisis and the policy responses it has elicited, and the constraints and opportunities that the Eurozone faces.

The overlap of causal mechanisms and varying configurations of interests provides a theoretical rationale for a central argument of the volume, which is that, in order to be effective, policies must fit the context. For example, historical analysis of fiscal systems and monetary unions suggests that the sustainability of borrowing depends on various causal factors, and macroeconomic fundamentals may work differently depending on economic and social interdependencies as well as institutional arrangements and the availability of alternative transmission mechanisms. Moreover, the effectiveness of rules and policy arrangements varies over time and across different parts of the system. Under certain conditions, flexible rules may work better than rigid rules; more generally, monetary policy must fit the architecture of the monetary system at any given point in time.

Attention to the internal configuration of the Eurozone, and hence to differences in contexts and in the appropriateness of policy frameworks, highlights the connection between policy-making and structural change. A notable example is the restructuring of EU manufacturing that has taken place since the crisis, which is in turn likely to lead to a further reconfiguration of policy stances and of the relative weight of sectoral interests.

The foregoing discussion emphasises the opportunities and constraints afforded by the economic and institutional architecture of the Eurozone. But in order to understand the multi-layered decision-making in the Eurozone, it is necessary to also consider how political-economy actors visualize those opportunities and constraints. The volume suggests different possible origins for actors' visualizations. For example, they can result from policy beliefs, notably those deriving from policy traditions such as the ordo-liberal and neo-mercantilist views that have been particularly influential in Germany. More generally, actors' visualizations can be theorized as being influenced, yet not univocally determined, by the political economy structures within which they act. It then becomes important to study the matches and mismatches between changes in political economy structures and changes in actors' visualizations thereof.

The interplay between policy frameworks and the opportunities and constraints afforded by the economic and institutional architecture of the Eurozone is a key theme of the volume. Contributions in the volume reflect on policy frameworks that are mindful of the institutional and economic architecture of the Eurozone, recognizing interdependencies between financial and real spheres of the economy and between various parts of the system. A notable example is that of financing tools that meet both public finance and economic development objectives, and especially the stabilization of sovereign debt and the provision of systemically important infrastructure.

Taken as a whole, the volume aims to characterize the features of the Eurozone as an internally differentiated political economy field at multiple levels of aggregation; to provide analytical tools to understand these features, and especially to identify the domains, causal paths and sets of constraints and opportunities that are most relevant under given conditions; and to suggest policy frameworks that are compatible with the aforementioned features.

1.3 The Structure of the Volume

1.3.1 Comparative Historical and Institutional Perspectives

The arrangement of the volume is as follows. Part I outlines a comparative-institutional and historical framework for assessing the architecture and dynamic forces within the Eurozone. The focus of this part is on the experience of past monetary unions, on the relationship between monetary unions and federation processes, and on the conditions that led to consolidation, or disintegration, of past monetary unions.

The first chapter in this part is by D'Maris Coffman on 'Fiscal States and Sovereign Debt Markets: A New Paradigm for Apprehending Historical Structural Change'. This contribution takes the view that history is not about the past, but about thinking on the past. From this perspective, the analysis of the historical experience of sovereign bond markets illuminates similarities and differences relative to the contemporary experience, and suggests important questions concerning the latter. What historical experience highlights is that sustainable levels of sovereign borrowing are the product of different overlapping causal factors, such as macroeconomic fundamentals and policy, monetary and financial institutions, property rights and alternative transmission mechanisms. As Coffman points out, two hundred years of sovereign borrowing have supplied historians, economists and market analysts with a wealth of evidence (economic and market data, financial news and archival material) with which to debate the historical determinants of sovereign borrowing. This chapter explores the theoretical purchase of a variety of approaches, examines both causal and symptomatic elements (as defined by Schumpeter) that have been considered in those approaches, and assesses the extent to which policymakers have made use of such research findings in defence of a variety of positions. The chapter concludes with a plea for a revitalised 'fiscal sociology,' which is characterised by a 'non-Marxist structuralism', and that would be particularly attentive to sectoral interdependencies, relations between socio-economic groups, and economic dynamics. The development of sovereign debt markets since the 1688 'Glorious Revolution' has been the object of intense discussion initiated by North and Weingast's credible commitment thesis (North and Weingast, 1989; Coffman, Leonard and Neal, 2013), and remains an important area of investigation for comparative historical and institutional analysis. To properly assess that thesis it is necessary to move beyond the abstraction of the 'State' and to explore the complex web of social interdependencies supporting the State apparatus and making it more or less effective (credible) depending on historical conditions. Opening the black box of the State involves allowing for a *plurality* of causal triggers that may or may not be effective depending on the specific conditions in view. For example, property rights may or may not be central to the working of sovereign debt markets, and macroeconomic fundamentals may work differently in different historical and institutional contexts. Uncovering social interdependencies and/or cleavages calls attention to the multiple causal factors that may be relevant under different conditions. After providing a narrative account of the historical evolution of sovereign bond markets, this chapter considers the principal determinants of sovereign borrowing, which are often overlapping in practice. In this connection, Coffman warns about using historical comparison without proper attention to the specific features

of the different historical episodes and contexts. For example, in discussing the contemporary relevance of the Latin Monetary Union and
of the Scandinavian Union, she argues that in either case there was a
currency union, but there was no central monetary authority to set the
interest rate policy. Also, there was no compulsory coordination mechanism such as the one introduced with the Maastricht Treaty. In view
of these limitations, Coffman argues for the need to delve deeper into
the political economy of taxation and public borrowing in Europe past
and present. The most urgent task for the political economy of the
Eurozone is to understand the evolution of European fiscal regimes in
the post–World War II period. More research into fiscal variation
within the Eurozone is needed, but research of this type has been
actively discouraged by the fiscal rules of the Maastricht provisions.
In fact, to impose uniform fiscal rules across different member states is
to adopt a policy of indifference to how they are followed. However, a
given country's fiscal mix (the proportion of direct and indirect taxation), the economic incidence of indirect taxation (how successfully
manufacturers are able to shift the economic burden), the strategies
used by taxpayers to avoid (or, in some cases, even evade) taxation,
let alone the non-fiscal effects (from welfare effects to broader sociological phenomena) are urgent areas of study. In societies where the
state represents between a fifth and a half of the economy, it would be
unwise to neglect the ramified sociological consequences of the strategies a country uses to tax and spend. This point calls attention to the
central relevance of Schumpeterian fiscal sociology as heuristics for the
investigation of the Fiscal State issue. Fiscal sociology would contribute
to studies like those in Chapters 8 and 11.

In the following chapter ('Creating Stable Systems of Public
Finance in the United States and Germany: Lessons for the Eurozone'),
James Macdonald examines the historical experience of financial sovereignty pooling by contrasting the two cases of the United States and
Germany since the nineteenth century. The histories of the United
States and Germany are relevant because these countries are federal
systems that evolved out of independent (or nearly independent) states.
In both cases, the political systems that were initially created were
financially decentralized. And in both cases the countries found themselves moving, slowly but ineluctably, towards greater levels of centralization in response to financial crises. The financially stable federal
systems that the two countries eventually built, however, were based

on different sets of underlying principles. In the United States, fiscal union involved the federal government taking over the debts of the states. However, the amounts outstanding were not evenly distributed, as some states had borrowed using paper money that had become worthless and other states had already settled much of their debt at a discount. In any case, debt restricting as engineered by the Treasury Secretary Alexander Hamilton was a success, and it was politically achieved not through 'collective action' rules, but through the substantive economic argument that only the restructured debt would benefit from the security of the new federal tax revenues. In the end, the new consolidated debt was funded at an interest cost of around 1.5 per cent of GDP, and helped to generate a liquid market that contributed to keeping yields down and to create a large body of public creditors with a financial attachment to the federal government. The subsequent US experience shows rising levels of State and municipal debt side by side with the emergence of a federal government as 'borrower of last resort' generally unwilling to contemplate bailouts of failed States or cities. The German experience was different. At unification in 1870, Prussia dominated Germany without the need for a centralized state. At the same time, decentralization allowed Prussia to maintain a number of privileges it might otherwise have had to give up. As a result, the central State was given limited tax powers consisting mainly of customs duties, certain tolls and excises and the income from the postal system. The subsequent evolution of the fiscal state in Germany exposed the weaknesses of a system whose initial stability was achieved through flow of funds from France (indemnity after the Franco-Prussian war of 1870) and the *de facto* preponderance of Prussia within the system. Increasing levels of debt both at the central and local levels were met with further central limits on the autonomy of local government starting a process that has continued to this day. The final outcome for Germany has been a federal system operating on principles substantially different from the American one. For instead of relying on self-contained areas of responsibility working primarily through market discipline, Germany developed a complex system of overlapping responsibilities kept in balance by formal rules. In Macdonald's view, the comparative historical experience of the United States and Germany suggests that the only currently plausible solution to the Eurozone problems may be to undertake the minimum further political integration that is compatible with financial stability.

The historical experience of an important European attempt at monetary unification in the absence of political integration is examined in the chapter by Luca Einaudi ('A Historical Perspective on the European Crisis: The Latin Monetary Union'). Einaudi moves from the consideration that attempts at monetary unification have a long tradition in European monetary history. He also argues for the need to assess each attempt in the light of the specific monetary architecture in place at any given time, and of the political economy conditions making that architecture to work in particular ways depending on context. Awareness of the relationship between monetary architecture and governance structure is of critical importance in interpreting attempts at monetary unification. And it is also essential in assessing the sustainability of the current monetary union in Europe. A historical heuristic allows assessment of alternative scenarios for what concerns the relationship between monetary architecture and monetary policy, and brings to the fore their mutual fitting, or incompatibility, under given conditions. The Latin Monetary Union (LMU) had its origins in a long-term historical heritage dating back to Napoleon's monetary unification of France, Belgium, and continental Italy. Some forms of monetary uniformity had been achieved, without explicit agreement, in the years preceding the start of LMU, partly as a result of modernization processes and increasing international trade. The crisis of bimetallism associated with massive gold inflows into Europe as a result of the Californian gold rush increased pressure towards policy coordination, which ultimately led to the establishment of a Monetary Union among France, Italy, Belgium, and Switzerland with the Paris Monetary Convention of 23 December 1865. The Convention established a one-to-one fixed exchange rate among coins of the participating countries, based on the intrinsic gold and silver content of the coins. The system's architecture was a partial monetary union in which multiple exchange rates developed: fixed exchange rate between the gold coinage of member states; fixed exchange rate for 5 francs silver écus associated with upper limits on new issues; fixed exchange rate between silver divisionary coins with a ceiling on total issues; and exchange rate between banknotes and gold coins fixed in ordinary times but fluctuating in times of temporary inconvertibility. Against the background of this monetary architecture, LMU showed considerable resilience, which was partly an outcome of its flexible membership and governance. The Papal State joined after lengthy negotiations but eventually left, while Greece (which had joined in 1867) at some point had to accept inconvertibility of its paper currency and foreign control of part of its monetary issue. Difficulties were met by the tightening of existing rules and the adherence to the international gold standard. The latter decision, while increasing the stability of monetary architecture, contributed to the diminished role of LMU, whose importance had declined also as a result of the growth of forms of monetary issue different from metallic money. In conclusion, Einaudi highlights that flexibility of rules was essential in allowing the long persistence of LMU across countries at different levels of economic and financial strength. This is seen as the most enduring lesson from this historical episode. For, as Einaudi points out, '[a] monetary union seems to be a never ending construction site of reforms in order to create effective mechanisms of governance, filling gaps, adding rules and negotiating institutional expansion'. The comparative historical analysis of monetary unions provides a benchmark in terms of which to assess the architecture and governance perspectives of the Eurozone.

The following chapter by A. Coşkun Tunçer on 'Conditionality, Fiscal Rules and International Financial Control in the European Periphery before 1914' discusses the effectiveness of international financial control organisations in a number of European and Mediterranean countries in the latter part of the nineteenth century. This issue is explored in the light of the introduction of fiscal rules as means of enforcing fiscal discipline in countries affected by the recent European sovereign debt crisis. Tunçer provides a comparative assessment of multilateral enforcement bodies established in Tunisia (1869), Egypt (1876), the Ottoman Empire (1881), Serbia (1893), and Greece (1898). In particular, he highlights that the working of these bodies involved cooperation between foreign creditors and local governments as institutional changes in debtor countries (primarily for tax collection purposes) were required. In contrast to the current emphasis on international financial control as a kind of super sanction imposed by creditors on default countries, Tunçer argues that local cooperation was needed, and that the mix between foreign enforcement and local cooperation varied significantly between the different countries. For example, Egypt witnessed direct takeover of state finances by a foreign control body, Serbia and Greece had to accept international financial control of specific fiscal and monetary measures, while the Ottoman Empire, in the years before World War I, implemented through an agreement with international bodies a series of measures leading to centralization of its taxation system. The analysis of these experiences of international financial control leads Tunçer to argue that the effectiveness of control measures critically depended upon the degree of cooperation between foreign creditors and local governments. This raises the issue of the extent to which international financial control of default countries reflects the interplay of interests at the level of both the national and the international economy.

The final chapter in Part I is by Duncan Needham on 'Snakes and Ladders: Navigating European Monetary Union'. This chapter explores the competing national and sectoral interests that governed the operation of the European Monetary System in the post–Bretton Woods era and how these interests continue to shape the current policy prospects for the Eurozone. Although voluminous literature from Mundell-Fleming onwards recognized that the Eurozone is not an optimal currency area, the benefits have always been framed in terms of economic integration, especially the prospects of lower transaction costs, free movement of labour and greater economies of scale and scope. Yet, as the North American Free Trade Agreement has demonstrated, economic integration does not require monetary union. The often neglected historical and political motivations for the union must be identified and emphasized in order to make current controversies more readily comprehensible. Initial moves towards European integration were designed to prevent further wars between Germany and France. The process was accelerated by the realization, after the Suez debacle, that France and Britain were no longer world powers and that the gradual dissolution of the sterling bloc was inevitable as the central banks of British Commonwealth countries diversified their foreign currency holdings during the Arab oil crisis. The dissolution of the sterling bloc was thus important not only as a precondition for British involvement in the European monetary union but also as a relevant case study in why exchange controls, which were increasingly unrealistic in the 1970s, are even less likely to succeed today. Meanwhile, continued global influence, particularly for France, appeared to lie within a new European superstructure. From the early 1970s, closer monetary union meant limiting exchange rate fluctuations to defined ranges. By 1989, the Delors Committee had concluded that a single European market required a single European currency. It also required another political compromise to overcome German monetary objections. In 1990,

France's François Mitterrand extracted a German commitment for closer monetary union by dropping his opposition to German reunification. Although the political processes themselves were contingent and the result of a specific vision of politics shared by a particular generation of European politicians, different sectoral interests responded variously to the internal contradictions within the currency union, often in ways that proved destabilizing. Indeed, unwillingness on the part of European politicians to confront the flaws of the system helped to fuel the interest rate convergence that produced the Eurozone sovereign debt crisis. The chapter concludes with suggestions of how these conflicts might be satisfactorily resolved within the political constraints imposed by the imperative to maintain European peace.

1.3.2 Multi-Level Interdependencies

Part II outlines a conceptual framework aimed at investigating the architecture of the Eurozone across different levels of aggregation. The purpose of this part is to explore the manifold constraints and opportunities arising for Europe as we move beyond the dichotomy between micro and macro relationships and decisions, and examines the multiple interfaces between economic and political domains at different levels of aggregation.

The first chapter in this part is by Roberto Scazzieri on 'Liquidity Architectures and Production Arrangements: A Conceptual Scheme'. This contribution addresses the conceptual issue of how to understand a liquidity system (such as the Eurozone) in which debt-credit relationships develop among interdependent production and consumption activities only partially synchronized along the time dimension. The chapter starts by considering two alternative modes of connectivity, which may exist side by side within the same economic system. In the first mode, any two sectors relate symmetrically if the output of one sector is necessary to the activity of the other sector. Alternatively, the two sectors relate asymmetrically if the output of one sector is necessary to the activity of the other sector but not vice versa. In the second mode, sectors may relate sequentially across time when the activity of one sector at time t makes the activity of another sector at time $t+k$ possible (or, respectively, impossible). Endogenous liquidity constraints enter the system if interconnected production activities require intermediate stages of production (goods needed in the production of themselves or of other goods). This situation generates a structural need for liquidity, while also creating internal sources of liquidity supply. This is because long-lasting processes need liquid funds as credit to production; on the other hand, short-lasting processes make liquid funds available due to their shorter capital turnovers. As the complexity of production interdependences increases, it is more and more likely that asymmetries between time profiles will also increase. In a system of sufficient complexity, structural liquidity (Cardinale and Scazzieri, 2016) coexists with flows of funds absorbed from outside the production sphere. Relationships (and flows of funds) between the production sphere and the financial sphere are central to the transmission of impulses from one sphere to another, and make *financial architectures* into major channels of transmission of change stemming from either sphere (Hicks, 1967, 1989; Neal, 2007). This chapter argues that the interlocking between the structure of production and the flows of funds (whether endogenously or exogenously generated) is of central importance in the transmission mechanism of liquidity opportunities and liquidity constraints within the system. For any economic system in which the principal mode of connectivity is coordination between activities taking place within the same time period (horizontal interdependence), liquidity is needed to provide the initial advance for any given set of synchronised activities. After the initial liquidity supply, liquidity can be internally generated within the system *at regular time intervals*. On the other hand, if the principal mode of connectivity is coordination between activities (stages of production) carried out at different times (sequential dependence), liquidity would be needed to smooth out the differences between time profiles of different activities. In this case, liquidity is needed by different activities at different points of time. Lack of liquidity has different consequences in the two cases. In the former case, liquidity shortage generates a *macroeconomic lacking*, which may in turn be associated with generalized unemployment and/or inflationary pressure due to contraction in the overall availability of goods. In the latter case, liquidity shortage generates a *structural lacking*, which may be associated with bottlenecks affecting certain sectors and accumulation of reserves within other sectors. The two cases are clearly different and may require different financial architectures and different types of liquidity policy. In a system whose mode of connectivity is primarily of the horizontal type, liquidity is either brought into the system or taken out of it, and endogenous liquidity formation resulting from time asymmetries between different activities is to a large extent irrelevant. On the other hand, in a system whose mode of connectivity is primarily of the sequential type, a macroeconomic release or withdrawal of liquidity could be ineffective (or even counterproductive) in dealing with the stage-specific liquidity constraints and opportunities characterizing the system of debt-credit relationships. This chapter highlights the need of a structural approach to liquidity formation and absorption within the Eurozone. In particular, the chapter argues that such an approach would have far-reaching implications for the assessment of Eurozone liquidity policy. For macroeconomic expansion or contraction might have entirely different effects depending on whether macroeconomic lacking or structural lacking was at stake. There is no reason to believe that the same type of lacking would prevail across the differentiated spectrum of sub-economies within the Eurozone. This suggests that a differentiated spectrum of liquidity policies may be the most effective means of targeting the differential liquidity needs arising within and across member states.

The following chapter by Adrian Pabst ('Political Economy and the Constitution of Europe's Polity: Pathways for the Common Currency beyond Neo-Functional and Ordo-Liberal Models') addresses a complementary feature of interdependence by examining the conditions allowing existence and coordination of a plurality of decision-making centres within the Eurozone's constitutional framework. This chapter moves from the consideration that the current situation of the Eurozone can only be understood as part of the economic, political and social domain in which the European Monetary Union is inscribed. The domain in question is not limited to the set of institutions and rules within which markets, states and individuals interact, but also extends to social structures embedding both cooperation and conflict at – as well as across – different levels of interaction. The chapter addresses the political economy of the Eurozone from the point of view of the explicit or implicit constitutional dynamics that have shaped, over the years, the multi-level interdependencies characterising economic integration within and between nation states. In particular, Pabst calls attention to the fact that the Eurozone has been characterized since its inception by two important features of 'hybridity': (1) the multi-level system of economic and monetary governance that has shaped the common currency both before and after the crisis; (2) the complex and multi-layered social relationships within and across localities, regions and states. In Pabst's view, these dimensions create path dependencies whose potential outcome is fundamentally open-ended and uncertain. For path dependencies can act either as factors of inertia and even failure by slowing down crisis management and hindering crisis resolution, or as factors of transformation by pointing to alternative possibilities in relation to both the overarching institutional architecture and specific policy ideas. The constitutional approach outlined in this chapter focuses on the social interdependencies that underlie both conflict and cooperation. In Pabst's view, 'such connections are more complex than the rather homogeneous, contractual links associated with either state sovereignty or global commerce' and may suggest coordination solutions different from those that may be envisaged by solely relying on markets or states. This point of view is different from the 'ordo-liberal' approach that lies behind the architecture of the European Monetary Union and according to which a sharp distinction should be introduced between 'order' and 'process' (whereby the state defines the 'framework conditions' and the market generates, via the competitive process, a particular set of prices and allocation of commodities). The chapter then moves to considering the constitutional evolution of the European Union (and of the European Monetary Union) as a process directed by the idea of 'positive spill overs' leading from economic interdependence to legal integration, and eventually to formation of a coherent market order based on supranational rules. This approach to the constitutional order of the Eurozone (and of the European Union as a whole) has produced tensions ultimately related to a '"disembedding" of the economic field from the social field and a re-embedding of social relations in economic transactions'. In Pabst's view, the constitutional heritage of European polities may also suggest an alternative route to integration. In particular, Europe's constitutional history makes it possible to think of an alternative approach based on overlapping jurisdictions, multi-level governance, and differential treatment of distinct problem areas[3]. In policy terms, the latter approach would suggest: (1) banks recapitalisation tied to direct lending for small and medium-size producers; (2) public and private debt

---

[3] This approach builds on the historical variety of the European constitutional experience and entails moving beyond the dichotomy between the civil law and common law traditions within that experience (Grossi, 2007).

restructuring tied to a shift in government spending from consumption to investment; and (3) a targeted growth strategy centred on direct credit to producers and a European strategy for public investment in infrastructure.

The chapter by Ivano Cardinale ('Sectoral Interests and 'Systemic Interest': Towards a Structural Political Economy of the Eurozone') concludes this section of the volume. The aim of this chapter is to develop new categories for analysing the political economy of the Eurozone, which is represented as a supranational domain of decision-making (a political arena) based on a multi-layered system of economic and political interdependencies. Unlike most treatments, emphasis is put on industrial sectors and their interdependencies, rather than microeconomic agents or the macroeconomy. In particular, this contribution takes the view that industrial sectors are potential interest groups, in the sense of Truman (1962). This means that sectors may be considered as having interests in particular policies, even if it cannot be taken for granted that they have the ability or will to organise themselves to influence policy-making. The approach outlined in this chapter leads to a heuristic based on what the author calls 'political economy maps', that is, on the identification of *potential* coalitions of interest groups within and across countries, which can try to influence decision-making at both the national and supra-national levels. The construction of those maps follows the representation of the internal structure of an economic system initially conceived in François Quesnay's 1758 *Tableau Économique*, and developed by many subsequent authors (such as Leontief, 1941 and Pasinetti, 1977). This representation makes it possible to visualize the sectors behind the macroeconomy and highlights the interdependencies among those sectors. The concept of potential interest group, used in conjunction with the consideration of interdependencies between industrial sectors, allows detection of possibilities for conflict or cooperation that might otherwise go unnoticed. In particular, the chapter focusses on the technical conditions for the viability of any given system of inter-industry relationships, which allow for different proportions among industrial sectors to be compatible with the systemic goal of overall reproduction in a stationary or expanding state (Pasinetti, 1977), although – following von Neumann (1935–37) – growth will not be at the maximum rate except for a particular set of proportions. This analytical representation of the internal structure of the economy makes it possible to identify a 'systemic interest' for any given economy (this could be described as the interest to maintain the system within the range of viable sectoral proportions), while providing room for conflict concerning the specific set of proportions to be adopted. The approach of this chapter suggests a 'double shift' from the macroeconomy to an economy of industrial sectors, and from the level of the State to that of potential interest groups. The shift has far-reaching consequences for what concerns the political economy of the Eurozone. In fact, from this viewpoint, the critical issue at stake is the strength of systemic interest for the Eurozone as a whole relative to that of individual member states (or possible coalitions of them). The structural grounding of interests in sectoral interdependencies helps to envisage the likelihood of different coalitions. However, one should not overlook the strength of interdependencies external to the Eurozone, and of the possible coalitions they may suggest; nor should one ignore that interests can be visualised differently according to the representation adopted by political-economy actors. The structural heuristics outlined in this chapter aims at assessing the different schemes of interdependence 'allowed' within any given economic structure, as well as the different readings of the possibilities for conflict and cooperation that those interdependencies may suggest to actors. This assessment, as Cardinale highlights, is of critical importance to the appraisal of the Eurozone from a political economy point of view.

1.3.3 Political Economy of Structural Governance

Part III addresses core policy issues involving the political economy configuration of the Eurozone. In particular, the contributions in this part compare alternative policy options in view of the interdependence between liquidity provision, macroeconomic policy, and structural changes across different levels of aggregation within the Eurozone.

The first chapter of this part is by Finn Marten Körner and Hans-Michael Trautwein on 'German Economic Models, Transnationalization and European Imbalances'. It examines the Eurozone architecture and dynamics by focusing on the position of the German economy both within the Eurozone and within the world economy. After contrasting the 'asymmetric' and 'symmetric' explanations of the Eurozone crisis after 2009, Körner and Trautwein consider the structural position of the German economy and ask why it seems to have been 'conducive to disruptions of the international monetary order time and again'. This chapter calls attention to the existence in the economic development of the German economy since the 1950s of a persistent orientation of industrial production, macroeconomic policy and social governance that permits stylization in terms of a model characterized by the combination of ordo-liberalism and neomercantilism. Ordo-liberalism emphasizes the active role of the State in promoting markets working as close as possible to the theoretical benchmark of perfect competition. From this point of view, ordo-liberalism is opposed to stabilization policies and other forms of direct market intervention, while accepting that the State should have a central role in *Ordnung-spolitik,* that is, in the crafting and implementation of rules for the competitive working of markets. In short, ordo-liberalism (at least in its most influential formulation due to Walter Eucken, 1950) emphasizes regulatory policy but circumscribes it to the domain of formal rules and benchmarks. It is thus at odds with other approaches to State intervention that encourage a direct effective demand management (as with Keynesian policies or the policies recommended by the French regulation school). Unlike ordo-liberalism, neomercantilism is a set of practical beliefs rather than a system of fully specified and coherent theoretical principles. Its core belief is that a primary task of economic policy is to foster the domestic industries' success in international markets, thus allowing a persistent foreign account surplus. Körner and Trautwein call attention to the complementarity between ordo-liberalism and the neomercantilist attitude that has come to prevail in German policy-making over the recent past. The two mindsets (ordo-liberalism and neomercantilism) are not fully compatible with each other as far as principles are concerned. For instance, ordo-liberalism would be opposed to preferential foreign trade policy, whereas neo-mercantilism would encourage industrial policies aimed at improving national competitiveness on international markets. In practice, however, the two conceptions of economic policy have proven to be remarkably coherent from the policy-making point of view. This is partly due to the different contexts in which the two sets of principles are advocated, and to the peculiarly cyclical fashion in which their combination is made to operate across different policy domains. Thus ordo-liberal principles are advocated as a regulatory benchmark both internally and internationally in times of crisis, while neomercantilist recipes tend to prevail in practice in spite of their incompatibility with free trade principles. This chapter examines the coexistence of ordo-liberalism and mercantilism across the three most important phases in the history of post–World War II German economy (the German economic miracle period, the European Monetary System period, and the European Monetary Union period). All three phases are characterized by an export-led bias taking a different shape depending on the configuration of the international monetary system. In the first phase, the fixed exchange rates regime and the implicit undervaluation of the German Mark helped German export-led growth. In the second phase, which followed the collapse of the Bretton Woods regime, inflation targeting leading to a liquidity premium on the German Mark and relatively low interest rates relieved upward pressures on the German Mark. The third phase, which started with the introduction of the single European currency, is itself split into two sub-periods. Initially, a decline of liquidity premium led to higher costs of finance and to compensating incomes policy (wage moderation) to allow continuing export growth. Subsequently (after the 2008 financial crisis), a renewed liquidity premium, principally vis-à-vis other Eurozone economies, contributed to a strong export performance in spite of falling global demand. In the authors' view, different neomercantilist positions may be identified in each phase of the above historical trajectory. Initially the other European countries were seen as competitors for the international liquidity provided by US dollars; subsequently, the common internal market was considered as a focus for export-led growth; and finally, in the age of the European Monetary System, global competitive advantage has been facilitated by the 'protective belt' provided by weaker Eurozone countries, which was instrumental in avoiding an exchange rate appreciation detrimental to German industry. The chapter emphasizes the inherent instability of the above neomercantilist set-up, which is seen as 'not compatible with a stable and well-performing monetary union'. It is also maintained that some ordo-liberal ideas may be compatible with viable integration within the Eurozone provided fallacies of composition are avoided and the prerequisites of systemic interest are explicitly addressed.

The following chapter by Ivano Cardinale and Michael Landesmann ('Exploring Sectoral Conflicts of Interest in the Eurozone: A Structural Political Economy Approach') explores sectoral-level conflicts of interest underlying the major unresolved problems of the European Monetary Union: the build-up of external imbalances and foreign debt positions. The chapter aims to complement, and often question, the usual understanding of these problems, typically based on macroeconomic analysis involving 'Northern' versus 'Southern' countries. The authors proceed as follows. For each issue, they identify a fundamental sectoral cleavage: for what concerns developments in the real exchange rate, the conflict of interest is between tradable and non-tradable sectors, whereas with respect to the accumulation of foreign debt positions and their possible write-offs, the conflict is between financial and real sectors. The analysis highlights that, despite the conflicts of interests, sectors thus defined are interdependent, within each country and at the Eurozone level. For example, within each country the non-tradable sector's opposition to real exchange rate devaluation could be constrained by the need to ensure competitiveness of the tradable sector, which is necessary to guarantee the long-run sustainability of the external accounts of the country. At the Eurozone level, the tradable sectors of 'Northern' countries would in principle want to avoid real exchange rate appreciation relative to 'Southern' countries, which would weaken their competitive positions; however, the risk of a sharp fall in demand in the 'Southern' countries, which could occur if that real exchange rate adjustment did not take place, might lead the 'Northern' tradable sectors to moderate their aversion to policies leading to real exchange rate appreciation. The authors go on to identify situations in which such systemic interest, that is, interest in the viability of the system, may lead to changes in sectors' policy stances. In particular, they argue that the Eurozone crisis has made apparent several dimensions of systemic interest, although this was not necessarily acted upon. The authors similarly trace the processes that led to the emergence of the other policy issue, the build-up of foreign debt positions. They reconstruct the associated conflict between financial and real sectors, and the potential areas of systemic interest. They show that, in this case, it is necessary to consider an additional dimension: the interplay between sectoral interests and national governments' considerations concerning the tax burden on the national economy. The overlap of interests within sectors and across sectors and countries, and across multiple policy issues, has arguably led to a complex and often unclear articulation of interests, which may explain the prolonged periods of 'muddling through' that often characterize policy-making in the Eurozone. The authors conclude by discussing whether the attempts at crisis resolution, as influenced by the conflicts of interests analysed in the chapter, are likely to have a 'nationalist' or an 'integrationist' bias with respect to the Eurozone and European Union more broadly.

The recent Eurozone crisis had consequences on the structure of European industry with important effects on the political economy of the Eurozone. In his chapter on 'The Impact of the Economic Crisis on European Manufacturing', Marco Fortis addresses the state of Eurozone manufacturing from the perspective of the global economy. This point of view leads him to emphasize that the European Union and China are currently 'the two giants of world manufacturing', and that according to UNCTAD and WTO data, 'European Union countries are by far the most competitive in world trade'. In particular, Fortis notes that, if one considers twelve key manufacturing sectors and for each of these sectors the three most competitive economies, 'in 2013 EU countries occupied 27 of the 36 best positions: Germany had the top nine positions, Italy eight, while France, Sweden, Finland, the Netherlands and Belgium had the remaining ten best positions'. This evidence is consistent with the strong extra-EU manufacturing trade surplus of EU countries, mostly due to the trade surpluses of Germany, Italy and France. EU manufacturing is thus a strongly competitive player in the global economy, and it cannot be argued that there is a serious competitiveness problem affecting European industry. However, EU manufacturing has suffered from declining activity levels in the 2008–2013 period due to contracting internal demand. A similar contraction has affected the EU construction sector. In Fortis's view, at the root of this dynamics is the complementarity between internal and external demand for manufactures, which makes 'a strong and dynamic European domestic market' a necessary condition for long-term sustainability of a competitive position in the global economy. In fact, macroeconomic policies leading to declining internal demand within the Eurozone have led to a contraction of intra-EU trade and could trigger a 'dangerous regression' of the large single market created within the Eurozone. The contrasting dynamics of extra-Eurozone trade and intra-Eurozone trade is revealing, as it is responsible for major losses incurred by the two most important manufacturing countries within the Eurozone (Germany and Italy). In fact, Eurozone's imports from Germany had been about 30 billion euros less in 2013 relative to 2008 and Eurozone's imports from Italy about 13 billion euros less in 2013 relative to 2008. At the root of the problem is, in Fortis's view, the 'big conceptual error' of lost European competitiveness. In fact, evidence provided by international agencies shows unquestionably the strong competitive position of many Eurozone countries, even if competitiveness of the manufacturing sector does not necessarily translate into competitiveness of the corresponding national economy. For this reason, micro-industrial data on industrial competitiveness, such as those provided by UNIDO's Competitive Industrial Performance Index and by the International Trade Centre (a joint agency of the World Trade Organization and the United Nations), should be used in lieu of interviews-based qualitative competitiveness indices such as those provided by the World Economic Forum (WEF) and the Lausanne-based IMD. The contraction of domestic Eurozone demand has triggered a dynamics of the Eurozone manufacturing sector that is unrelated to manufacturing competitiveness but has had a profound impact on the internal structure of the Eurozone economy. For instance, the composition of the value added of Eurozone manufacturing has dramatically changed, as the value added of German manufacturing industry exceeds in 2014 the combined value added of the manufacturing industries of Italy, Spain, and France. This situation is strikingly different from the one in 2007, when the value added of German manufacturing was 86 billion euros less than the combined value added of Italian, French, and Spanish manufacturing industries. Fortis's contribution concludes with an in-depth overview of the impact of the Eurozone's crisis on Italian manufacturing and with a final set of remarks concerning the growing, and ultimately self-damaging, imbalances that European macro policies have created within the real economy of the Eurozone.

The following chapter is by D'Maris Coffman and Ali Kabiri on 'Fiscal Systems and Fiscal Union: Historical Variety and Policy Challenges'. This chapter assesses the variation in the fiscal systems of the constituent European states with three aims in mind. First, the data from Eurostat on tax trends within the European Union are helpful in illuminating the relevance of a closely historicized fiscal sociology. The configuration of regional, national, and sectoral interests is illustrated through the various instantiations of fiscal mixes (for example, the balance of indirect versus direct taxation, or the treatment of taxation of capital gains versus incomes), which in turn also reveal differing commitments to income redistribution, industrial policy, pricing of externalities (especially pollution), and fiscal incentives (discouraging home ownership, education, or philanthrophy and discouraging consumption, for instance, of tobacco or alcohol). The historicities of these differing solutions are crucial to understanding why fiscal reform is so elusive in many cases. Second, the chapter argues that the variety in European fiscal systems presents a significant structural challenge to fiscal union, even if the terms of the fiscal union are meant to preserve national autonomy in this regard and focus instead on outcomes. Such variation has created and will continue to create opportunities for legal and tax arbitrage, of which some are predictable and some are the unexpected consequences of ad hoc solutions in moments of crisis. The current controversy about 'tax avoidance' strategies of transnational corporations should be understood in this context, rather than simply as a populist movement or as the expression of moral anxieties. Third, the chapter aims to elaborate the political economy of taxation within the Eurozone, with special attention on the ideological contexts for the different fiscal mixes. Consensus, while not impossible, is much harder to attain when these contexts are persistently ignored, and, even more alarmingly, when the politics of comprehensive austerity across the Eurozone does violence to the specificity of particular tax systems.

The position of the Eurozone with respect to global financial flows is considered by Yuning Gao in his chapter on 'China's Investment in the Eurozone: Structure, Route and Performance'. This contribution examines the role of China as a financial and investment actor on global markets in general and vis-à-vis the Eurozone in particular. This chapter points out that the statistics on final destinations of Chinese outward direct investment show Chinese investment to have been primarily resource seeking. This is reflected in the fact that the first two largest destinations of Chinese investment have been groups of resources-exporting countries, while the third-largest destination has been the Eurozone due to large investment projects in GDF Suez (France) and Energias de Portugal. Another major route of Chinese direct investment into the Eurozone has been through the leasing and financing of infrastructural projects. In the latter connection, the most important initiative has been that of the Chinese shipping company COSCO that took a thirty-five-year lease of the main dock at the Greek port of Piraeus while pledging in return a major financial infusion to construct a new pier and upgrade the existing docks. At the same time, a consortium of Chinese banks established a fund to finance the Greek merchant shipping industry with the objective of backing Greek orders at Chinese shipyards. Against this background, Gao's analysis calls attention to the most recent developments and prospects concerning Chinese investment in the Eurozone. One important consequence of the Eurozone sovereign debt crisis has been the increase of Chinese direct investment in the United Kingdom (which contributed to making the EU the second largest destination of Chinese direct investment globally). This development took place side by side with a decline in the Eurozone share of Chinese investment in the European Union, which fell from 80 per cent in 2011 to 40 per cent in 2012. The other point worth noticing is the continuing relative lack of appeal of sovereign debt originating within the Eurozone. This is shown by the preference of China's Sovereign Wealth Fund (CIC) for long-term equity investment, and especially for investment in infrastructural and industrial projects. New financial instruments, such as European bonds issued by the European Financial Stability Facility (EFSF) or the European Stability Mechanism (ESM), may exert a certain appeal to Chinese investors, but their attractiveness should not be overestimated in view of the Chinese preference for long-term investment in infrastructural and production facilities. In conclusion, Gao's analysis comes to reinforce the point made in other contributions in this volume concerning the opportunities for an integrated European strategy aimed at the development of structural, long-term capabilities. For important financial flows from outside the Eurozone and directed at infrastructural and capability-oriented investment might well complement and strengthen European systemic initiatives in the infrastructural domain.

The following chapter by Alberto Quadrio Curzio ('Eurobonds for EMU Stability and Structural Growth') tackles the resilience and growth problems of the Eurozone by highlighting the interdependence between real and financial phenomena under conditions of structural change. A central theme of this contribution is the role that funds of accumulated wealth may have in channelling resources towards investment projects aimed at reinforcing the structural coherence of interdependent activities. This point of view leads Quadrio Curzio to examine Eurobonds as a strategic policy tool that one should assess by combining a political-institutional perspective with the analysis of conditions for a structurally integrated system at the European level. Quadrio Curzio calls attention to Jacques Delors's original Eurobond proposal in the 1993 white paper on 'Growth, Employment and

Competitiveness' (European Commission, 1993). The proposal envisaged introducing 'new facilities' such as Union bonds (with the EU budget as collateral) and Convertibles (guaranteed by the European investment Fund-EIF) as means to finance infrastructural projects deemed to be of systemic importance to the European economy in fields such as energy, transport, telecommunications and the environment. Sovereign debt stabilization had not been considered in the proposal, whose implicit feature was that sustainability of EU public finances should be addressed together with other systemic goals such as the achievement of a strong degree of interdependence between the different components of the EU economy. The subsequent, wider proposal of a Euro-Gold-Development Fund issuing Gold Eurobonds, outlined by Quadrio Curzio between 2004 and 2008, was rooted in the interdependence between Eurobonds and real guaranties (the official gold reserves of EMU's States). This proposal aimed at achieving the triple objective of lowering the cost of sovereign debts of Eurozone member states, financing merger operations within the Eurozone banking and industrial system and strengthening the internal cohesion of the Eurozone through the funding of cross-national infrastructural projects. The 2010–2015 Eurozone sovereign bond crisis triggered a shift of emphasis to Stability bonds and Rescue bonds. Eurobonds' original function of ensuring systemic cohesion in the EU single market through the building of European infrastructural networks receded to the background, and sovereign debt stabilization became the central issue. The European Stability Mechanism (ESM) established in 2012 has been so far the most important institutional development in the field of Eurozone sovereign debt crisis management. In fact, the success of its bond issues highlights the potential of a true European Financial Fund, which could undertake the function of a European sovereign fund aimed at both sovereign debt stabilization and the promotion of economic growth through funding of infrastructural projects aimed at reinforcing interdependence between the different components of the European economy. In this chapter, Quadrio Curzio outlines in detail the prospects of Euro Union Bonds, developing proposals made by himself and in 2010 and 2011 jointly with the former European Commission President Romano Prodi. The proposal moves from the belief that internal market and financial stabilization cannot by themselves achieve convergence between Eurozone member states, and that only a high-growth trajectory supported by interdependence-enhancing measures may be effective in making the structural dynamics of the Eurozone compatible with its internal cohesion. The chapter describes what could be the structure of a European Financial Fund, whose capital should consist partly of official gold reserves owned by Eurozone member states and partly of shares in companies active in the industrial and infrastructural sectors. These shares should be conferred by Eurozone member states or by private entities in which the state is the majority shareholder, such as the Kreditanstalt für Wiederaufbau (KfW) in Germany, the Caisse des Dépôts et Consignations (CDC) in France, the Cassa Depositi e Prestiti (CDP) in Italy and the Instituto de Crédito Oficial (ICO) in Spain. The proceeds from the EFF's bond issues should be used partly as a redemption fund purchasing the member states' sovereign debt according to proportions coinciding with member states' quota in the EFF. The remaining proceeds from EFF's bond issues should be used to fund industrial and infrastructural projects deemed to be of strategic importance to the overall competitiveness and cohesion of the EU economy. In the final section of his contribution, Quadrio Curzio addresses possible objections to the EFF proposal, arguing that the EFF bond issues would not mutualize sovereign debt, for which individual member states would be solely responsible, but would stabilize sovereign debt markets, making speculation more difficult. EFF's purchases of sovereign debt bonds could attract significant investment from outside the Eurozone and would likely lower the interest costs member states have to pay on sovereign debt. In the presence of convergence of debt to GDP ratios of all Eurozone member states to an agreed average ratio (not necessarily at 60 per cent level), the EFF's operations would add flexibility to the macro policy-making of member states, making it possible to balance restrictive policies in some member states with expansionary policies in others.

In the concluding chapter of Part III ('How False Beliefs about Exchange Rate Regimes Threaten Global Growth and the Existence of the Eurozone'), William White addresses a set of fundamental questions concerning the analysis of Eurozone structure and dynamics, its institutions of governance and the process of collective decision-making within it. In particular, White notes there is no consensus on which policies should be adopted, that an effective executive structure is missing and that there is no agreement on how to reach legitimate political decisions at Eurozone level. Of these three 'deficits', White argues that the one concerning lack of appropriate analytical understanding of the Eurozone is the most serious one. Indeed, he maintains that '[f]alse beliefs about the operations of the International Monetary System and the Eurozone system ... constitute a threat to the existence of the Eurozone itself.' In fact, the best approach to Eurozone structure and dynamics is by treating its economy as a complex adaptive system in which crises may be triggered by a variety of factors impossible to predict. Awareness of the 'massive interdependencies' among component parts of any given economic system and of the possibility of strongly nonlinear outcomes within them should alert economists and policy-makers about the need to identify which interdependencies are strongest under given conditions. However, complex adaptive economic systems (such as the Eurozone) are subject to structural dynamics that may alter the form and intensity of interdependence between component subsystems. Therefore, it is essential to react to instability sources by identifying the appropriate layer of complexity at which instability works, and to drop policy architectures that structural economic dynamics made defective or irrelevant. In short, as White writes, 'right' policy measures are likely to change over time, and 'it is not hard to make wrong decisions'. In the light of this analytical framework, White discusses alternative approaches to systemic crises adopted in the International Monetary System and in the Eurozone. The crucial policy alternative at the global level has been the one between fixed vs. floating exchange rate regimes. In this case, there has been a sharp difference between decisions taken at the level of the world's largest economic blocs and decisions affecting the internal structure of the Eurozone. At the global level, the choice has been to drop the fixed exchange rate regime, whereas at the Eurozone level the choice has been to introduce fixed exchange rate regimes eventually leading to monetary union. In either case, economic analysis cannot provide a 'right answer' independently of changing circumstances. In practice, choices are made by key stakeholders considering 'defining historical moments', which may suggest sharply different strategies to different actors. Memory of the 1930s Great Depression has kept the United States in the floating exchange rate camp, whereas fears triggered by the hyperinflation after World War I has made Germany to privilege stability over the growth objective. In fact, historical experience shows that both exchange rate regimes have repeatedly failed depending on changing circumstances that led to switch-overs from one regime to the other. Lack of attention to changes in the configuration of the stability vs. growth trade-off has entrenched 'false beliefs' both in the floating exchange rate and in the fixed exchange rate camp. For example, the expansionary policies of the US Federal Reserve, Bank of Japan and European Central Bank have failed to generate a sustained growth trajectory while encouraging redistribution of income away from the household sector and triggering a global expansion of liquidity that might eventually get out of control. On the other hand, reducing economic asymmetries within the Eurozone might require economic policies that could be unacceptable to countries wedded to a strong anti-inflationary target. In either case, misplaced analytical beliefs are at play. Under present circumstances, exchange rate floating is unlikely to achieve automatic adjustment of global current account imbalances, and a reversal of US monetary policy (from expansionary to contractionary) might lead to dangerous capital outflows from emerging economies with serious fiscal and current account deficits. Consequences of misplaced beliefs are also far-reaching for the Eurozone. For example, and contrary to analytical beliefs at the core of recent European policies, current account imbalances within the Eurozone have become a serious (not self-correcting) problem; austerity policies backfired through fiscal multiplier effects that made attainment of fiscal targets more difficult; and actions of the European Central Bank have proven to be to a large extent ineffective. In particular, White argues that a debt and insolvency issue is at the core of the crisis, and that provision of extra liquidity by central banks, by encouraging further debt accumulation, cannot solve the root problem. In conclusion, this chapter makes a strong case for the interconnectedness of the global and the Eurozone crises, and for the need to move beyond misplaced analytical beliefs in order to address the structural sources of the twin crises. In particular, White argues that reforming the International Monetary System in order to ensure enforcement of international discipline on key member states (the United States but also China, Germany and Japan) is needed. In line with this, European countries should give up their individual IMF membership, thereby increasing European influence at the global level and allowing a reassignment of shares to emerging countries of growing economic importance. Finally, within the Eurozone, beliefs that have governed crisis management so far should give way to a different framework acknowledging the systemic character of the crisis, the need for more symmetry between debtors and creditors and less reliance on fiscal austerity. The chapter concludes that multiple sources of instability may arise from interdependencies within the Eurozone, as well as from interdependencies within the global economy. To address those sources of instability would be a necessary precautionary measure in view of possible further turmoil in financial markets.

1.4 Framing the Eurozone

Taken in their unity, the contributions in the first three parts of the volume call attention to the Eurozone as a political economy field. Interactions within such field involve a plurality of actors at different levels of aggregation, and take place under constraints and opportunities rooted in the architecture of the Eurozone. This architecture reflects both its institutional set-up and the structural, long-term characteristics of the interdependent sub-economies within the Eurozone. A theme common to contributions in Parts I–III of the volume is that single-minded attention to microeconomic conditions and macroeconomic constraints can be misleading, especially because interdependencies between economic units may have a different character depending on which level of aggregation is considered. As a result, opportunities and constraints for the Eurozone may be different depending on the level of aggregation, and their assessment requires appropriate heuristics.

Part IV concludes the volume with an essay by Ivano Cardinale, D'Maris Coffman, and Roberto Scazzieri on 'Framing the Political Economy of the Eurozone: Structural Heuristics for Analysis and Policy'. This chapter takes stock of contributions in Parts I–III and provides a conceptual grid for addressing the Eurozone as a field straddling a variety of aggregation levels and interdependencies between different economic units. The chapter calls attention to the multiple interdependencies within the Eurozone and highlights that a plurality of causal paths may be simultaneously at work within it. As a result, the political economy of the Eurozone appears as a field open to a variety of outcomes and yet constrained by the very structure of existing interdependencies. We maintain that in-depth analysis of these interdependencies is crucial for an understanding of Eurozone's dynamics and a realistic assessment of its options.

References

Basevi, G. and D'Adda, C. (2014) 'Overview: Analytics of the Eurozone Crisis', in D. Daianu, G. Basevi, C. D'Adda and R. Kumar (eds.), *The Eurozone Crisis and the Future of Europe. The Political Economy of Further Integration and Governance*, Houndmills, Basingstoke: Palgrave Macmillan, pp. 9–22.

Cardinale, I. and Coffman, D. (2014) 'Economic Interdependencies and Political Conflict: The Political Economy of Taxation in Eighteenth Century Britain', *Economia Politica, Journal of Analytical and Institutional Economics*, 31 (3), pp. 277–300.

Cardinale, I. and Scazzieri, R. (2016) 'Structural Liquidity: The Money-Industry Nexus', *Structural Change and Economic Dynamics*, 39, pp. 46–53.

Chiti, E. and Teixeira, P. (2013) 'The Constitutional Implications of the European Responses to the Financial and Public Debt Crisis', *Common Market Law Review*, 50 (3), pp. 683–708.

Coffman, D., Leonard, A. and Neal, L. (eds.) (2013) *Questioning Credible Commitment: Perspectives on the Rise of Financial Capitalism*, Cambridge: Cambridge University Press.

Eucken, W. (1950) *The Foundations of Economics: History and Theory in the Analysis of Economic Reality*, translated by T. W. Hutchison, London, Edinburgh and Glasgow: William Hodge and Company.

European Commission (1993) *Growth, Competitiveness, Employment – The Challenges and Ways Forward into the 21st Century* (White Paper), Supplement 6/93 of the *Bulletin of the European Communities*, Luxembourg, Office for Official Publications of the European Communities.

Grossi, P. (2007) *L'Europa del diritto*, Roma-Bari: Laterza.

Hicks, J. (1967) *Critical Essays in Monetary Theory*, Oxford: Clarendon Press.

Hicks, J. (1989) *A Market Theory of Money*, Oxford: Clarendon Press.

Hirschman, A. O. (1968) 'The Political Economy of Import-Substituting Industrialization in Latin America', *The Quarterly Journal of Economics*, 82 (1), pp. 1–32.

Hirschman, A. O. (1970) *Exit, Voice, and Loyalty: Responses to Decline in Firms, Organizations, and States*, Cambridge, MA: Harvard University Press.

Iversen, T. and Soskice, D. (2013) 'A structural-institutional explanation of the Eurozone crisis', paper presented at the Political Economy Workshop, London, London School of Economics, 3 June.

Leontief, W. (1941) *The Structure of the American Economy*, New York: Oxford University Press.

Lipset, S. M. and Rokkan, S. (1967) *Party Systems and Voter Alignments: Cross-National Perspectives*, New York: The Free Press; London: Collier-Macmillan.

Majone, G. (2014) *Rethinking the Union of Europe Post-Crisis. Has Integration Gone Too Far?* Cambridge, Cambridge University Press.

McCormick, J. P. (2007). *Weber, Habermas and Transformations of the European State: Constitutional, Social, and Supranational Democracy*, Cambridge: Cambridge University Press.

Moravcsik, A. (2005) 'The European Constitutional Compromise and the Neofunctionalist Legacy', *Journal of European Public Policy*, 12 (2), pp. 349–86.

Neal, L. (2007) *The Economics of Europe and the European Union*, Cambridge: Cambridge University Press.

Neumann, J. von (1935–37) 'Uber ein Okonomisches Gleichungs-System und eine Verallgemeinerung des Brouwerschen Fixpunktsatzes', in *Ergebnisse eines Mathematischen Kolloquiums*, Vienna, VIII, pp. 73–83. (English translation: 'A Model of General Equilibrium'. *The Review of Economic Studies*, 9, pp. 1–9.)

North, D. C. and Weingast, B. R. (1989) 'Constitutions and Commitment: The Evolution of Institutions Governing Public Choice in Seventeenth Century England', *The Journal of Economic History*, 149, pp. 803–32.

Pasinetti, L. L. (1977) *Lectures on the Theory of Production*, London: Macmillan.

Quesnay, F. (1758) *Tableau économique*, Versailles.

Rae, D. W. and Taylor, M. (1970) *The Analysis of Political Cleavages*, New Haven, Yale University Press.

Rogowski, R. (1987) 'Political Cleavages and Changing Exposure to Trade', *The American Political Science Review*, 81 (4) (December), pp. 1121–37, doi: 10.2307/1962581.

Ross, E.A. (1938) *Principles of Sociology*, 3rd ed. New York: D. Appleton-Century Company.

Scharpf, F. W. (2010) 'The Asymmetry of European Integration, or Why the EU Cannot be a Social Market Economy', *Socio-Economic Review*, 8 (2), pp. 211–50.

Scharpf, F. W. (2012) *Legitimacy Intermediation in the Multilevel European Polity and Its Collapse in the Euro Crisis*, Cologne: Max Planck Institute for the Study of Societies.

Scicluna, N. (2012) 'EU Constitutionalism in Flux: Is the Eurozone Crisis Precipitating Centralisation or Diffusion?', *European Law Journal*, 18 (1), pp. 489–503.

Scitovsky, T. (1958) *Economic Theory and Western European Integration*, London: Allen and Unwin.

Soskice, D., Hope, D. and Iversen, T. (2016) 'The Eurozone and Political Economic Institutions', *Annual Review of Political Science*, 19, pp. 1545–77.

Truman, D. (1962) *The Governmental Process: Political Interests and Public Opinion*, New York: Knopf.

Tuori, K. and Tuori, K. K. (eds.) (2014) *The Eurozone Crisis: A Constitutional Analysis*, Cambridge: Cambridge University Press.

PART I

Comparative Historical and Institutional Perspectives

2 Fiscal States and Sovereign Debt Markets

A New Paradigm for Apprehending Historical Structural Change

D'MARIS COFFMAN

2.1 Introduction

Sovereign debt markets in their modern form have existed in Europe for nearly two centuries. While antecedents can be found in Britain, the Netherlands and the Italian city-states, the practice of borrowing from international capital markets in a currency other than a nation's own dates from the 1820s and the Rothschild's Prussian Loan. Two hundred years of sovereign borrowing have supplied historians, economists and market commentators alike with economic and market data, financial news and archival material with which to debate the historical determinants of sovereign borrowing. This chapter explores the theoretical defensibility of a variety of approaches, considers both the causal and symptomatic elements in the Schumpeterian tradition, explores the extent to which policymakers mobilise such research in defence of a variety of positions, and concludes with a plea for a revitalised 'fiscal sociology', which is characterised by a non-Marxist structuralism, and that is particularly attentive to sectoral interdependencies, social relations and economic dynamics. This 'New Fiscal Sociology' not only builds on Joseph Schumpeter's claim, echoing Rudolph Goldscheid, that 'the budget is the skeleton of the skate stripped of all misleading ideologies', but also extends that analytic framework (Schumpeter, 1954 [1918], p. 6). In the twenty-first century, a rounded fiscal sociology must include not just expenditure but also both taxation and public borrowing.

2.2 'History is not about the past; it is about arguments we have about the past'

In the first of three Nathan I. Huggins Lectures at Harvard University on the long decline of African slavery in the United States, Ira Berlin opened with the observation: 'History is not about the past; it is about arguments we have about the past' (Berlin 2015, p. 1). This *bon mot*, a variant of one coined by Bismarck biographer and Holocaust historian Jonathan Steinberg, goes to the heart of how policymakers should, but rarely do, make use of historians' research and historical experience. Too often, instead, we have reckless pronouncements, such as that of Tim Worstall, a regular contributor to *Forbes*, who, in an article headlined 'Greece Has Been in Default for 50% of Its Time as an Independent Country', sought to portray the Greeks as serial defaulters who should never had access to international capital markets in the first place, and whose national independence had, in fact, been built upon shirking its external debt (Worstall, 2015). For modern commentators, there is often a temptation to draw fatuous analogies or to mine historical events as a basis for elaborating unscientific claims, or for scoring political points.

While the worst offenders are easily dismissed as demagogues, more mainstream and presumably more responsible scholars have engaged in similar tactics under a thin guise of scientific enquiry. Carmen Reinhart and Ken Rogoff's widely successful *This Time Is Different: Eight Centuries of Financial Folly* (2009) attempts to discern secular trends, characterise periodic fluctuations and even derive economic laws that govern maximum debt-to-GDP ratios, optimal debt loads and even the frequency and magnitude of economic crises and financial crashes over more or less the past millennium. Such an intellectual project, which rests on a massive empirical exercise, echoes Jean Lescure's rather more sophisticated historical explorations in *Des crises generales et périodiques de surproduction* (*Of General and Periodic Industrial Crises*) first published in 1906 (Lescure, 1906), but without Lescure's emphasis on structural change and intermediate levels of analysis.

Although separated by more than a century, Reinhart and Rogoff's book, far more than Lescure's treatise, depends on the tenability of late nineteenth-century assumptions that the historical past represents a kind of vast laboratory, suitable for exploring transcendent natural laws, and that historians are essentially naturalists who seek to discover and describe historical truths. In other words, for Reinhart and Rogoff, the object of exploration is the past, in an effort to get it to reveal occult economic laws. Lescure, by contrast, understood that the proper focus of interest should be structural change. Few modern academic historians would see themselves in the nineteenth-century view of their profession, but political scientists and economists all too often look to the past for such purposes.

In the face of such frivolous exercises, such as that of Reinhart and Rogoff, policymakers justifiably wonder, in turn, if historians' findings can really be relevant to the present. Simply repeating George Santayana's famous mantra that 'those who cannot remember the past are condemned to repeat it' rarely convinces anyone who is not already sympathetic to the historical analogy thus advanced (Santayana, 1905). After all, crude heuristics, such as the 90 per cent rule promulgated by Reinhart and Rogoff (2009), which do not acknowledge the possibility of fundamental structural changes in the economy and, in fact, deny such possibilities, only serve to essentialise fiscal rules, which buttresses proponents of austerity and encourages inappropriate policy responses.[1]

There is, however, a place for properly drawn historical analogies, which depend instead on noticing specific structural similarities and inflection points, that in turn either precipitated the circumstances in which we find ourselves today or, alternatively, have enough parallels as to provide tightly controlled studies of specific economic mechanisms. With respect to the recent Eurobond crisis, one of the most useful ones for scholars and policymakers alike has been the tightly drawn comparison between the first period of financial globalisation in the nineteenth century (1873–1913) and the recent return of globalised finance in the post-1989 period, but especially, vis-à-vis the European Union, after the formation of the Eurozone in 1999. Mauro, Sussman and Yafeh (2002; 2006) inaugurated this strain of research, after noticing structural similarities while investigating emerging markets bond spreads in the 1990s.

Much of Section 2.2 is concerned with the elaboration of the historical experience of nineteenth-century bond markets, with an eye both to identifying the salient features that should concern economists and policymakers today and to understanding how the evolution and

---

[1] In an effort to counter this, Elroy Dimson and David Chambers organized a 'Financial History Workshop' in July 2015 at Judge Business School in collaboration with the CFA Foundation in which they encouraged participants to reflect on appropriate uses of financial history for practitioners and regulators; also, in a similar vein, Vincent Bignon and his colleagues at the Banque de France organized a conference entitled 'Economic History and Economic Policy' in December 2015 to reflect on the same issues.

development of these markets has contributed to the current institutional frameworks governing the Eurozone. Ali Coşkun Tunçer's exploration in Chapter 5 of the role of collective creditor action in this period represents an example of the former approach, while Duncan Needham's discussion in Chapter 6 of the institutional evolution of the European Monetary Union offers an example of the latter.

This distinction between 'symptomatic' and 'causal' significance of seismic shifts in state finance was first framed by Joseph Schumpeter in his proposal for a closely historicised 'fiscal sociology' in the wake of a debates about a putative crisis of the tax state after World War I (1918, pp. 4–7). Originally published in German, the article, entitled 'The Crisis of the Tax State', was only translated into English in 1954, to coincide with the publication of his *History of Economic Analysis*. Much as was intended in 1918, its English translation was offered as a contemporary intervention into Cold War debates about the growing 'tax state' in view of the step-changes in defence and social welfare spending in the post-war period. Since this is further described in Section 2.6, it sufficient now simply to note that Schumpeter was concerned with the consequences, occasionally intended but most often not, of the fiscal activities of the state.

As Jürgen Backhaus explained in 2004, fiscal sociology considers 'the ramifications of the fiscal activities of the state into areas which are not their primary target. These effects may occur in sectors not directly affected such as related markets, but they may also occur outside the economic sphere proper, such as in politics, culture, religion, or society at large' (Backhaus 2004, p. 1). Although Schumpeter's intellectual project has not received the attention it has deserved, in the early twenty-first century, there have been attempts to revive the sub-discipline, directly with a series of essays based on the Erfurt Conference on Fiscal Sociology (Backhaus, 2005) and with it the establishment of The Krupp Foundation Chair in Public Finance and Fiscal Sociology, and indirectly through its application to the cardinal case of excise taxation in the British Isles (Coffman, 2013), which was foundational to the advent of the Hobbesian Leviathan. In a limited sense, David Hume anticipated Schumpeter's intellectual project:

In every nation, there are always some methods of levying money more easy than others, agreeably to the way of living of the people, and the commodities they make use of. In Britain, the excises upon malt and beer afford a large revenue; because the operations of malting and brewing are tedious, and are impossible to be concealed; and at the same time, these commodities are not so absolutely necessary to life, as that the raising their price would very much affect poorer sort. These taxes being all mortgaged, what difficulty to find new ones! What vexation and ruin of the poor! (Hume, 'Of Public Credit,' 1753, p. 171)

Most of the analysis in this chapter, however, is concerned in the first instance with those causal significances: about the role of private finance, particularly private finance of infrastructure projects, in the growing demand for sovereign debt in nation-states where private capital markets were insufficient to finance such ventures, about the establishment of London as the pre-eminent financial centre, about the failure of Napoleon III's attempts to internationalise the franc and thus the limited but important remit of the Latin Monetary Union (discussed in more detail in Chapter 4) and about the demise of the bimetallic standard and the rise of the gold standard. For many scholars, these are key features of the 'rise of the liberal state' and the means used to pay for it (Cardoso and Lains, 2010). In effect, the following sections seek to elaborate the similarities and equally salient differences between that world so famously described by Keynes in *The Economic Consequences of the Peace* and our world of today:

The inhabitant of London could order by telephone, sipping his morning tea in bed, the various products of the whole earth, in such quantity as he might see fit, and reasonably expect their early delivery upon his doorstep; he could at the same moment and by the same means adventure his wealth in the natural resources and new enterprises of any quarter of the world, and share, without exertion or even trouble, in their prospective fruits and advantages; or he could decide to couple the security of his fortunes with the good faith of the townspeople of any substantial municipality in any continent that fancy or information might recommend. He could secure forthwith, if he wished it, cheap and comfortable means of transit to any country or climate without passport or other formality, could despatch his servant to the neighbouring office of a bank for such supply of the precious metals as might seem convenient, and could then proceed abroad to foreign quarters, without knowledge of their religion, language, or customs, bearing coined wealth upon his person, and would consider himself greatly aggrieved and much surprised at the least interference. But, most important of all, he regarded this state of affairs as normal, certain, and permanent, except in the direction of further improvement, and any deviation from it as aberrant, scandalous, and avoidable. The projects and politics of militarism and imperialism, of racial and cultural rivalries, of monopolies, restrictions, and exclusion, which were to play the serpent to this paradise, were little more than the amusements of his daily newspaper, and appeared to exercise almost no influence at all on the ordinary course of social and economic life, the internationalization of which was nearly complete in practice. (Keynes 1919, section ii.4)

None of these observations about the causal significance of these trends depends on an acceptance (or alternatively rejection) of the value of 'fiscal sociology', but this chapter closes with the vigorous suggestion that the symptomatic or consequential significances equally deserve consideration. They form the subject of Chapter 13 in this volume.

2.3 The Historical Experience of Sovereign Bond Markets

Sovereign bond markets in the modern sense date from the early nineteenth century. Large-scale, permanent, continuous markets for government debt had existed in Britain, France, the Netherlands and the Italian city-states for centuries, but these polities denominated their debt in their own currencies. Moreover, the debt securities issued by early modern sovereigns were usually marketed to their own subjects, in an explicit attempt to reduce reliance on traditional banking syndicates upon which European crowns had often depended (Coffman, Leonard and Neal, 2013; Neal, 1990). Modern financial economists for their part also observe a distinction between sovereign borrowing as such (countries borrowing in a currency other than their own, usually a reserve currency, from international capital markets) and government borrowing (countries borrowing in their own currencies, usually from their own citizens).

By the nineteenth century, few European states, with the noted exceptions of Britain and France, were able to mobilise large-scale resources with domestic borrowing, and instead, following the advent of Rothschild's Prussian Loan, borrowed from foreign creditors through loans denominated in sterling (Cardoso and Lains, 2010; Neal, 1998), which traded on the London Stock Exchange. Although some of these funds were raised for military purposes (most notably in the case of newly independent Latin American states), the relative European peace from 1815 to 1870 (and from 1815 to 1848 especially) greatly reduced military expenditures. Instead the majority of funds raised were to support public expenditure, especially the construction of infrastructure networks on the continent or industrial development (construction of mines, for instance, or steel works). In Britain, private capital markets were deep enough to finance such ventures, leading in turn to robust markets for corporate debt and equity securities there.

As Coffman and Neal (2014) argued in their introduction to their four-volume *History of Financial Crises* for the Routledge *Critical Concepts in Finance* set, the origins of modern infrastructure finance can be found in the Long Nineteenth Century (1789–1914), which witnessed a steady succession of asset-price bubbles, the foci of which were technological innovations that disrupted existing transportation networks: canals, steamships and railroads (v. II, p. 1). Each of these projects was characterised by the 'lemons problem' classically described by Akerlof (1970). New technologies and start-up firms, by their very nature, entail information asymmetries that make it difficult for investors to evaluate risks. As a consequence, many investors diversify their portfolios blindly, and in the process under-price the risk associated with the so-called lemons while over-pricing the risk associated with better prospects.

This process, described by venture capitalist and financial economist Bill Janeway (2012, pp. 135–56) as 'banal', has the theoretical consequence, when the bubble bursts, of clearing out the deadwood while protecting the stronger firms. In reality, however, generalized credit constriction, caused by financial contagion, can bankrupt otherwise viable ventures (Coffman and Neal, 2014, v. 2, pp. 1–2). Yet regardless of that dynamic, bubbles of any magnitude also have the effect of financing Schumpeterian waste (Janeway, 2012), or the process by which speculative finance is mobilized to support experimentation and the construction of new infrastructure networks, which otherwise would be prohibitively risky. Bubbles form when the availability of credit, coupled with poor returns from more mainstream investments, cause investors to change their risk appetites and embrace new opportunities that they might otherwise deem too risky. This finding has recently shown to be empirically robust (Bordo and Landon-Lane, 2013) and is consistent with the theoretical argument advanced by Roberto Scazzieri in Chapter 7 of this volume. In such market conditions, capital-intensive, infrastructure projects with transformative potential are excellent candidates for speculation.

The first of these modern speculative infrastructure bubbles was the Canal Mania of 1793, which occurred during a longer period of canal-building in England and Wales during the Revolutionary and Napoleonic Wars (1790–1815). Although this episode has many of the features of the later cases, it can be distinguished by the regulatory regime. The Bubble Act of 1720 had not yet been repealed, thus the public trading of shares on the London Exchange was restricted to joint-stock companies which had parliamentary charters (Harris, 1997). The consequence of this is that most of the Canal Mania shares were locally and relatively closely held. As Arnold and McCartney (2011) have argued, there are significant technical hurdles to estimating the rates of return from available dividend data.

After the Act's repeal in 1825, venture finance became far easier and much less expensive, as firms had access to national capital markets. The 'Steamship Mania' of 1824–25, which depended on the canals built just decades earlier, was part of a wider bubble (involving foreign stocks and country banks) that led to a spectacular crash in 1825 (Neal, 1998; Williams and Armstrong, 2008). As Williams and Armstrong (2008) observe, the new steamship lines were casualties of wider market conditions; only three of seventy lines promoted in 1824–25 were to be found in business in 1827 (p. 646). Yet despite the carnage, the number of steamships and the tonnage they carried rose steeply over the following decade. 'Steamship Mania' may have killed off most of its progeny, but it seemed to only encourage public enthusiasm for the new technology.

The term 'Railway Mania' refers to episodic railway speculation in Britain and North America in the mid-nineteenth century. In Britain, the first seeds of what was to come could be seen as early as 1824–25, when the very early railways debuted alongside steamships. This was followed by the 'Little Railway Mania' of 1835–37, though it paled in comparison to The Railway Mania of 1845–47. It remains unclear to what degree the bubble was driven by regulatory change, as the Joint Stock Companies Act of 1844 made it easier to incorporate new ventures. Limited liability would be introduced in 1855, but the earlier legislation cleared away many of the hurdles that had been hastily thrown up after the 1825 repeal.

Moreover, new financial instruments, including subscription shares (allowing investors to make instalment payments en route to a fully paid up share) re-appeared in the 1840s after falling into disuse in

England and Wales after the collapse of the South Sea Bubble. At the same time, the Bank of England had slashed interest rates in the early 1840s, leaving income-dependent retail investors to chase returns. The Bank changed course abruptly, however, amidst a bullion crisis that coincided with the Irish Famine, which is what caused the railway bubble to snap. While some contemporaries blamed accounting fraud (Bryer, 1991), others argue that the evidence for that is limited (MacCartney and Arnold, 2003). This was, however, the first time since the early 1720s when relatively ordinary investors were left holding the bag. The gains, in terms of increasing the size of the railway network, were unmistakable, but there have been few credible attempts to estimate either the contribution of speculative finance to the gains or the welfare losses to individual investors.

What we do know, however, is that continental observers were well aware of the vast resources mobilised to build these canals, steamship and railway networks. After the Crash of 1824–25, which saw a collapse in the foreign stock market, there was less enthusiasm for the bonds of both newly independent Latin American Republics and nations, such as Greece, which had shrugged off the Ottoman Empire. Mid-century foreign investors and domestic ones both generally preferred domestic British securities, though this began to change after the Revolutions of 1848, when continental European powers responded to the crises of 1848 with massive public expenditure programmes to build infrastructure that rivalled that of Britain (Cardoso and Lains, 2010). By 1860, the *Money Market Review* was publishing weekly price lists of 'foreign stocks' (sovereign bonds of foreign countries listed on the London Exchange), 'colonial stocks' and domestic securities (mostly railways and mines) along with market news and analysis. Printed in English, this periodical and the more widely circulated *Investors Monthly Manual* (1869–1929) provided prospective investors with reliable market information as well as evidence for the depth and variety of debt securities traded in London.

These securities bore some striking differences from those we see traded in sovereign credit markets today. First, they were generally of very long duration (twenty to eighty years), and were treated as perpetuities by contemporaries (Mauro, Sussman and Yafeh, 2006). We know this because scholars have access to the valuation tools used by contemporaries. Many 'emerging market' bonds contained lottery clauses, in which a sinking fund was used to retire a percentage (usually 5 per cent on twenty-year bonds) of the certificates outstanding. Almost all sovereign bonds, wherever issued, were denominated in sterling, and exceptions usually contained exchange-rate clauses (Flandreau and Sussman, 2004), even within the Latin Monetary Union. Following the British example of seventeenth- and eighteenth-century debt securities, which were collateralised by excise revenues, foreign and colonial bonds in the nineteenth century (except those issued by other core European sovereigns) often contained collateral clauses, specifying either specific tax revenues, customs duties or infrastructure projects as security. These provided viable mechanisms of creditor action, such as that described by Tunçer in Chapter 5. These bonds, including the 5 per cent Chinese Imperial Government bond reproduced in Figure 2.1, had very specific provisions that outlined payment schedules and the purposes to which the funds would be put.

The prospectuses of these and also of domestic British government and corporate securities were published in the financial press.

In the period from 1873 to 1914, Mauro, Sussman and Yafeh (2006) estimate that well over half the European and North American sovereign bonds issued were floated on the London Exchange. Paris, Berlin and eventually New York trailed behind (followed distantly by Vienna and a handful of other small exchanges), with Paris and Berlin representing the only significant volume. The Paris stock market, whose development had been arrested by French memories of the eighteenth-century collapse of the Mississippi Scheme, had traditionally been restricted to a limited number of securities, all of high denomination (i.e. usually a minimum of 500 francs), most notably the 3 per cent and 5 per cent *rentes*, which were the French equivalent of British consols. By mid-century, that started to change, and Paris, as well as a handful of French regional exchanges, began to list industrial concerns. Paris was elevated further by the establishment of the Latin Monetary Union in 1865, which represented Napoleon III's attempt to internationalise the franc and to rival the British pound sterling. The original treaty was signed by France, Belgium, Italy and Switzerland. The emperor hoped that the LMU, which used a bimetallic standard, would attract additional members (Greece was the first to join in 1867), which it did. Spain, Romania, Austria-Hungary, Peru, Colombia, Venezuela, Finland, Serbia, Bulgaria, the Danish West Indies, and the Papal States at varying times either used the franc system or entered into

Figure 2.1 Chinese Government Bond 1913

separate agreements with the French (Willis, 1901), which today would be described as 'bilateral swap' agreements between the respective treasuries.

As a currency union, the LMU was doomed by structural problems inherent in bimetallism. It coincided, however, with the growing the volume of franc-denominated sovereign debt floated on the Parisian exchange, though Russian sovereign debt, placed by Rothschild's and used to finance modernisation after 1863, represented the lion's share of the total. Peruvian, Columbian, Venezuelan, and Spanish sovereign debt traded primarily on the London Exchange, while Austrian securities traded mainly in Vienna and Berlin. As Mauro, Sussman and Yafeh (2006) observed, there was considerable path dependence in the institutional framework: the distribution of sovereign bond issuance in 1914 looked surprisingly like emerging market issuance in 2002. As Yuning Gao elaborates in Chapter 14, China (via off-shore RMB markets in Hong Kong) may well join London, New York, Tokyo and Berlin as a significant locus of emerging markets finance in the decades to follow, but the geographical persistence of international capital markets is surprising. It has survived decolonisation and the relative disappearance of these markets in the post-war period.

While the roots of financial globalisation in the nineteenth century can be found in the decade of nation-building that began with Italian Unification, included the American Civil War and the emancipation of the serfs in Russia, and culminated in German Unification in 1871, the period is conventionally dated as having begun in 1873. The French call it the Belle Époque (1873–1914). As Keynes noticed in the paragraph quoted earlier and as modern scholarship has confirmed, this period was marked by free movement of labour and capital (O'Rourke and Williamson, 1995; Clemens and Williamson, 2004) and a sophisticated and specialised financial press. But there were also salient differences. Compared to the fourth quarter of the nineteenth century, which was the heyday of European nation-states and their overseas empires, the early twenty-first century saw the advent of robust multinational organisations, especially the European Union. Moreover, between the Dubai Agreements of 2001 governing the Argentinian default and the Eurozone Debt Crisis, sovereigns were largely immune from creditor action, though that changed sharply with the Greek debt crisis.

Having provided a narrative account of how sovereign debt markets evolved in this period, it is now appropriate to consider the chief determinants of sovereign borrowing, which, while held distinct in econometric analysis, are in fact overlapping in practice (Mauro, Sussman and Yafeh 2006).

2.4 Sovereign Borrowing and Overlapping Causal Factors: The Credible Commitment Thesis in Context

The recent Eurozone Debt Crisis, coming on the heels of the financial crisis and Great Recession, has provoked a renewed interest in the determinants of public borrowing. One approach, labelled the World Bank Consensus and favouring sound macroeconomic policies and fundamentals, was essentially politically neutral (Sachs et al., 1995; Min, 2003). On the other hand, the Washington Consensus has emphasized neo-liberal institutions, especially the protection of property rights, particularly those of creditors, trade liberalization, and insistence on fiscal discipline (North and Weingast, 1989; Acemoglu et al., 2005). New approaches have focused on monetary institutions in a much narrower sense (pointing out the contradictions in the European Monetary Union and the tensions within the post–Bretton Woods monetary system), while yet others still have emphasized that political stability remains the key determinant of sovereign borrowing in emerging markets. The positions taken in these debates also roughly correspond to the policy recommendations for confronting sovereign defaults, though some international players, most notably the International Monetary Fund (IMF), have shifted their positions in recent years.

Perhaps unsurprisingly, advocates of the aforementioned positions look to the eighteenth-century British origins and nineteenth-century European experiences to buttress their arguments. For architects of the Washington Consensus, the seminal work was North and Weingast's (1989) analysis of the Glorious Revolution of 1688–89. This article, known conventionally as the 'Credible Commitment' thesis, has cast a twenty-five-year shadow over the institutional and constitutional pre-conditions of sovereign creditworthiness. They argued that the establishment of parliamentary supremacy over public finance created an environment in which investors could rely upon the state to meet its financial promises. This fundamental constitutional re-alignment provided the institutional pre-conditions for the Financial Revolution, which in turn secured Britain's rise to great power status. Explanations of Britain's presumptive economic and financial dominance of eighteenth- and nineteenth-century Europe have long rested on interpretations of these institutional changes. Just as accounts of the British Industrial Revolution have furnished models of industrialization and prescriptions for developmental economists (Rostow, 1960;

Gerschenkron, 1962), North and Weingast's thesis has furnished similar ammunition to those who wish to pair sovereign creditworthiness with economic performance (Demirguc-Kunt and Levine, 2001; Graff, 2003).

For nearly two decades, this stylised fact enjoyed widespread acceptance among historians, economists, political scientists and legal theorists. Recent revisionist scholarship has challenged key tenets of the 'credible commitment' thesis (Carruthers, 1996; O'Brien and Hunt, 1999; Mauro, Sussman, and Yafeh, 2006; Clark, 2007; Coffman, Leonard and Neal, 2013; Murphy, 2013), but the theory still has adherents amongst those who wish to emphasise the pernicious influence of rent-seeking elites on the credibility of constitutional and institutional arrangements in emerging markets (Acemoglu and Robinson, 2012). Those who have, however, accepted the revisionist position have shifted the focus from specific constitutional arrangements to the complex interplay of a multiplicity of commitment mechanisms and institutional arrangements, as well as the role played by robust secondary markets for government securities, that together created an environment in which eighteenth-century investors were willing to place their trust and capital in the hands of the British state over its foreign rivals (Coffman, Leonard and Neal, 2013). This is what Pabst and Scazzieri (2016) have described as the 'material constitution' of any polity, one that perhaps exercises a greater force in practice than the actual written documents.

Further attempts to refine this analysis will depend on intermediate levels of analysis, including an examination of a country's level of economic development, the regional distribution of its public expenditure coupled with the fiscal mix of direct and indirect taxation, the specific mix of primary, secondary and tertiary sectors and their geographical distribution, and related issues. (Cardinale and Coffman, 2014). All except the most recalcitrant supporters of the Washington Consensus have moved beyond crude formulations of predatory landed elites versus thrifty merchants and early industrialists who demand probity in public finance.

Moreover, there are scholars who continue to dispute the chronology. Patrick O'Brien and Philip Hunt (1999) and D'Maris Coffman (2013) have both argued vigorously that the institutions necessary for good governance of the public finances were put in place prior to the Glorious Revolution. On the other hand, Ron Harris (2004) has argued that it would take another 150 years for public creditors to acquire the tools they needed to monitor the probity of British public finances. Some who follow the critics who would argue institutional quality was really a feature of the nineteenth not eighteenth century have turned their attention to other nineteenth-century institutions that might have contributed to investor confidence, including acceptance of the gold standard (Bordo and Rockoff, 1996) and membership in the British Empire and its sterling bloc (Ferguson and Schularik, 2006).

A number of empirical studies have provided additional challenges to the 'credible commitment' thesis. In particular, interest rates did not decline substantially during the half-century following the Glorious Revolution period, thereby casting doubt on the idea that 1688 represented a turning point in the British state's borrowing capacities. These studies also show that political events (notably adverse war news, especially fears of invasion) rather than institutional reforms had the greatest influence over the willingness of investors to commit capital to the British state (Mauro, Sussman, and Yafeh, 2006). Others have argued that interest rates were never the main mechanism for transmission to markets of confidence in institutional frameworks (Levine and Zervos, 1998), which is echoed by Larry Neal's (Davis and Neal, 1998; Coffman, Leonard, and Neal 2013) repeated observation that the volume of British public debt issued in the eighteenth century increased markedly even as interest rates remained relatively high.

Debates about the historical experience of sovereign borrowing in nineteenth-century Europe thus have implications for those who debate the determinants of sovereign borrowing today, but there are important caveats. Regardless of the importance of institutional frameworks, whether constitutional, political or multinational agreements governing currency regimes, there remains the basic reality that levels of public borrowing remained relatively flat among the great powers from 1873 to 1913, even as some engaged in competitions in public expenditure such as the Anglo-German naval race. This can be shown empirically (Flaundreau and Zumer, 2004). But despite that fact, bond spreads did not converge towards market leaders, either between those countries on the gold standard or between those who were part of bimetallic currency blocs such as the Latin Monetary Union or the Scandinavian Monetary Union (Bae and Bailey, 2011). In other words, there was no equivalent of the post-1999 'lemons problem.' There might have been a currency union, but there was no central authority like the European

Central Bank to set interest rate policy, nor were there fiscal agreements in place via a mechanism like the Maastricht Treaty. So the parallels with the post-1999 European experience in that sense remain limited. Instead, it might be more profitable to enquire into the political economy of taxation and public borrowing in nineteenth-century Europe.

2.5 From 'State' to Social Interdependencies

Before the widespread acceptance of dynamic stochastic general equilibrium (DSGE) frameworks, with their assumption of rational expectations and minimal frictions associated with time-inconsistent policymaking (Barro and Gordon, 1983), there was widespread acceptance of the non-fiscal effects of taxation. In the early twentieth century, Seligman (1892, 1910) focused on the 'shifting incidence' of commodity taxation as a justification for preferring an income tax (Coffman, 2013, p. 110). To make sense of this discussion, some vocabulary may be useful to non-specialist audiences.

Economists classify taxes as 'direct' or 'indirect'. Direct taxes, such as income taxes or corporation taxes, are assessed upon individuals, firms and other legal entities. Indirect taxes, on the other hand, are levied on goods or services at the point of production, point of import/ export or point of sale. In Europe, direct taxes on land have existed since antiquity; commodity taxation arose in most states during the late medieval period and grew in variety, frequency and scale in the early modern period. Although today most indirect taxes are either value-added taxes or sales taxes, historically excise taxation (which still exists on some commodities like petroleum, alcohol, and tobacco) was preferred because levying taxes on manufacturers or importers tended to minimise the cost of collection over doing so on consumers.

On a theoretical level, direct taxation is borne by the legal entity on which it is imposed. While it can be avoided (and may even be evaded), that burden cannot be 'shifted' onto other legal entities. In the early modern period, some regimes, most notably France, permitted the purchase and sale of privileges that exempted legal entities from taxation (Matthews, 1958), but that practice was abolished in continental Europe with the French Revolution and never existed to any great extent in Britain. In effect, with direct taxation, the legal incidence (who is obliged to pay) and the economic incidence (who in fact bears the economic costs) are the same.

The economic burden of indirect taxation, however, is subject to being 'shifted', depending on the elasticity of prices, onto the consumer (forward-shifted), the producer of the raw materials (back-shifted) or, alternatively, it might be capitalised by rendering the production process more efficient and less laborious. For mainstream economists, the assumption was that in the absence of technological innovation, the burden of indirect taxation would always eventually result in higher wages. More recently, however, as such modes of analysis have come under sustained attack, there is an increased awareness that both back-shifting onto the producers of raw materials (especially the primary sector) and forward-shifting onto consumers (in the form of higher prices) can be viable strategies for a considerable period of time, whatever the eventual economic incidence. These debates rested on more or less robust empirical foundations, usually buttressed by data from grain markets (Coffman, 2015). As a result of wide-ranging influence of these economic writers, indirect taxation is ordinarily thought to be regressive, as the costs are most often borne by consumers (regardless of income) or by producers of raw materials without relative power in the marketplace.

Theoretically, this has been known in English economic literature since the seventeenth and eighteenth centuries. As Coffman (2013) observed, early twentieth-century tax theorists were well aware of a sophisticated body of polemical literature that debated the economic incidence of centuries' worth of excise taxation on bear and ale (Seligman, 1892, 1910; Kennedy, 1913; Turner, 1916). While most of these writers concluded that the real innovation of eighteenth-century English taxation was its compensatory nature (it had both progressive indirect taxation and regressive direct taxation), they were aware of the non-fiscal effects that various strategies might have on producers, merchants and consumers alike, and were equally concerned that consumers were almost always either landowners, merchants or labourers themselves.

William Petty's *Treatise on Taxes* (1769 [1662]) was the first attempt to grapple systematically with the question of how different fiscal regimes might shape society. He formulated a notion of value that pre-figured Adam Smith, synthesised many earlier writers' thoughts on the economic incidence of various types of taxation, theorised the circulation of money and considered the effects of various taxes on the probable balance of trade. But primarily he was interested in the social effects of taxation, the extent to which public expenditure might in turn mitigate the unintended consequences and the effects of both taxation and expenditure on what we would today recognise as sectoral interdependencies (Coffman, 2013, pp. 198–203). He thought the 'Hearth Tax', a tax on houses, was the optimal method of taxation (and the most just), but that the conclusion is ultimately less interesting than the method he used to arrive at it. In effect, he anticipated Schumpeter's fiscal sociology as well as Diamond and Mirrlees's theories of optimal taxation (Diamond and Mirrlees, 1971).

2.6 A Plea for Historical Fiscal Sociology

Thus far we have primarily considered the causal significance of the historical determinants of sovereign borrowing, with only limited analysis of the symptomatic significance of the different strategies employed by particular states. Although much more could be written about these topics, there is scarcely space in this current volume to explore the differential consequences of various fiscal regimes in nineteenth-century Europe for the countries in question. Those wishing to understand these topics in detail would do well to start with comparative studies of the fiscal regimes themselves, which elaborate, in a comparative framework, the structure of taxation, expenditure and public borrowing (Bonney, 1995; Cardoso and Lains, 2010). Instead, the much more urgent task for those wishing to understand the political economy of the Eurozone today is to understand the evolution of these fiscal regimes in the post-war period.

Such a project is the premise behind the work presented in Chapter 13. We urgently need more and better research into fiscal variation within the Eurozone, research that was actively discouraged by the fiscal rules envisioned by the Maastricht provisions. After all, to impose fiscal rules is to adopt a policy of indifference to how they are followed. Yet a given country's fiscal mix (the proportion of direct and indirect taxation), the economic incidence of indirect taxation (how successfully manufacturers are able to shift the economic burden), the strategies used by taxpayers to avoid (or in some cases, even evade) taxation, let alone the non-fiscal effects (from welfare effects to broader sociological phenomenon), and the extent to which public expenditure either mitigates or exacerbates these effects should all be urgent areas of study, areas which have been neglected for far too long by the European Commission and the European Council. Such work would contribute to studies like those in Chapters 8 and 11.

Yet it is possible and even urgently necessary to go further and consider the need to revive the discipline of 'fiscal sociology', but to do so in a strictly historicised manner. We must avoid the temptation simply to provide ammunition to pundits who would attribute to Greece a 'culture of tax evasion' or to Britain a 'corporate culture of tax avoidance', or simply to assume that Scandinavian income equality is straightforwardly the outcome of two post-war generations of high marginal tax rates. Such crude applications of 'fiscal sociology' are self-defeating, but a rigorous and robust enquiry into the variety of European fiscal regimes, broadly re-conceived to include taxation, expenditure and borrowing, will help us to understand the different political, religious, legal and social cultures of taxation, and how those cultures contribute to the evolution and maintenance of structural economic forms. In this way, a New Fiscal Sociology represents a fresh approach for apprehending historical structural change. In societies where the state represents between a fifth and a half of the economy, it would be naïve indeed to neglect the sociological ramifications of the strategies it uses to tax, borrow and spend.

References

Acemoglu, D. and Robinson, J.A. (2006) *Economic Origins of Dictatorship and Democracy*, Cambridge: Cambridge University Press.

Acemoglu, D. and Robinson, J.A. (2012) *Why Nations Fail: The Origins of Power, Prosperity and Poverty*, London: Profile.

Acemoglu, D., Johnson, S. and Robinson, J.A. (2005) 'Institutions as a Fundamental Cause of Long-Run Growth', in P. Aghion and S. Durlauf (eds), *Handbook of Economic Growth*, 1: 385–472.

Akerlof, G.A. (1970) 'The Market for "Lemons": Quality Uncertainty and the Market Mechanism', *The Quarterly Journal of Economics*, 84, no. 3 (August): 488–500.

Arnold, A.J. and McCartney, S.M. (2011) 'Veritable Gold Mines before the Arrival of Railway Competition: But Did Dividends Signal Rates of Return in the English Canal Industry?' *Economic History Review*, 64: 214–36.

Backhaus, J.G. (2004) 'Joseph A. Schumpeter's contributions in the area of fiscal sociology: a first approximation', *Journal of Evolutionary Economics*, 14: 143–51.

Backhaus, J.G. (ed.) (2005) *Essays on Fiscal Sociology*, Frankfurt: Peter Lang.

Bae, K.-H. and Bailey, W. (2011) 'The Latin Monetary Union: Some Evidence on Europe's Failed Common Currency', *Review of Development Finance*, 1 (April–June): 131–49.

Barro, R.J. and Gordon, D. B. (1983) 'Rules, Discretion, and Reputation in a Model of Monetary Policy', Journal of Monetary Economics, 12: 101–21.

Berlin, I. (2015) *The Long Emancipation: The Demise of Slavery in the United States*, Boston: Harvard University Press.

Bonney, R. (ed.) (1995.) *Economic Systems and State Finance*. Oxford: Clarendon Press.

Bordo, M. and Landon-Lane, J. (2013). 'Does Expansionary Monetary Policy CauseAsset Price Booms: Some Historical and Empirical Evidence', NBER Working Paper. No. 19585, October.

Bordo, M. and Rockoff, H. (1996) 'The Gold standard as a Good Housekeeping Seal of Approval', *Journal of Economic History*, 54: 389–428.

Bryer, R.A. (1991) 'Accounting for the 'Railway Mania' of 1845: A Great Railway Swindle?' *Accounting, Organizations and Society*, 16, no. 5/6: 439–86.

Cardinale, I. and Coffman, D. (2014) 'Economic Interdependencies and Political Conflict: The Political Economy of Taxation in Eighteenth-Century Britain', *Economia Politica: Journal of Analytical and Institutional Economics*, 31, no. 3: 277–300.

Cardoso, J.L. and Lains, P. (eds.) (2010) *Paying for the Liberal State: The Rise of Public Finance in Nineteenth-Century Europe*, Cambridge: Cambridge University Press.

Carruthers, B. (1996) *City of Capital: Politics and Markets in the English Financial Revolution*, Princeton: Princeton University Press.

Clark, G. (2007) 'What Made Britannia Great? How Much of the Rise of Britain to World Dominance by 1850 Does the Industrial Revolution Explain?' *The New Comparative Economic History: Essays in Honor of Jeffrey G. Williamson*: 33–57.

Clemens, M.A., and Williamson, J.G. (2004) 'Wealth Bias in the First Global Capital Market Boom, 1870–1913', *The Economic Journal*, 114, no. 495: 304–337.

Coffman, D.D. (2013) *Excise Taxation and the Origins of Public Debt.* Basingstoke: Palgrave Macmillan.

Coffman, D.D. (2015) 'The Political Economy of Grain Markets.' In M. Baranzini, C. Rotondi, and R. Scazzieri, (eds), *Resources, Production and Structural Dynamics*. Cambridge: Cambridge University Press, pp. 53–71.

Coffman, D., Leonard, A. and Neal, L.D. (2013) *Questioning Credible Commitment: New Perspectives on the Rise of Financial Capitalism*, Cambridge: Cambridge University Press.

Coffman, D.D. and Neal, L.D. (2014) *The History of Financial Crises*, 4 vols., Abingdon: Routledge.

Davis, L. and Neal, L. (1998) 'Micro Rules and Macro outcomes: The Impact of Micro Structure on the Efficiency of Security Exchanges, London, New York, and Paris, 1800–1914', *The American Economic Review*, 88, no. 2: 40–45.

Demirguc-Kunt, A. and Levine, R. (2001) *Financial Structure and Economic Growth: A Cross-Country Comparison of Banks, Markets, and Development*, Cambridge: MA, MIT Press.

Diamond, P.A. and Mirrlees, J.A. (1971) 'Optimal Taxation and Public Production I: Production Efficiency, II: Tax Rules', *American Economic Review*, 61: 8–27, 261–78.

Ferguson, N. and Schularick, M. (2006) 'The Empire Effect: The Determinants of Country Risk in the First age of Globalization, 1880–1913', *The Journal of Economic History*, 66 (June): 283–312.

Flandreau, M. and Sussman, N. (2004) 'Old Sins: Exchange Rate Clauses and European Foreign Lending in the 19th Century', CEPR Discussion Papers 4248.

Flandreau, M. and Zumer, F. (2004) *The Making of Global Finance, 1880–1913*, Paris: OECD Development Centre Studies.

Gerschenkron, A. (1962) *Economic Backwardness in Historical Perspective*. Cambridge, MA: Harvard University Press.

Graff, M. (2003) 'Financial Development and Economic Growth in Corporatist and Liberal Market Economies,' *Emerging Markets Finance and Trade*, M.E. Sharpe, Inc., vol. 39 (2, March): 47–69.

Harris, R. (1997) 'Political Economy, Interest Groups, Legal Institutions, and the Repeal of the Bubble Act in 1825', *The Economic History Review*, 50, no. 4: 675–696.

Harris, R. (2004) 'Government and the Economy, 1688–1850', in R. Floud and P. Johnson (eds.), *The Cambridge Economic History of Modern Britain*, Cambridge: Cambridge University Press, vol. I, pp. 204–37.

Janeway, W.H. (2012) *Doing Capitalism in the Innovation Economy: Markets, Speculation and the State*, Cambridge: Cambridge University Press.

Kennedy, W. (1913) *English Taxation 1640–1799: An Essay on Policy and Opinion*, London: Frank and Cass, Ltd.

Keynes, J.M. (1919) *The Economic Consequences of the Peace*. London: Macmillan.

Lescure, J. (1906) *General and Periodic Industrial Crises* (the first English Translation of Jean Lescure's *Des crises generales et périodiques de surproduction*). (co-eds. D.Coffman and A.Kabiri) (Forthcoming Anthem Books, *Ideas That Built Europe*, 2017).

Levine, R. and Zervos, S. (1998) 'Stock Markets, Banks, and Growth', *The American Economic Review*, 88, no. 3: 537–58.

Levine, R. (with A. Demirguc- Kunt) (2001) *Financial Structure and Economic Growth: A Cross-Country Comparison of Banks, Markets, and Development*, Cambridge, MA: MIT Press.

Levy, H. (1911) *Monopoly and Competition: A Study in English Industrial Organization*, London: Macmillan and Co.

Matthews, G.T. (1958) *The Royal General Farms in Eighteenth-Century France*, New York: Columbia University Press.

Mauro, P., Sussman, N. and Yafeh, Y. (2002) 'Emerging Market Spreads: Then versus Now', *The Quarterly Journal of Economics*, 117, no. 2: 695–733.

Mauro, P., Sussman, N. and Yafeh, Y. (2006) *Emerging Markets and Financial Globalization: Sovereign Bond Spreads in 1870–1913 and Today*, Oxford: Oxford University Press.

McCartney, S. and Arnold, A.J. (2003) 'The Railway Mania of 1845–1847: Market Irrationality or Collusive Swindle Based on Accounting Distortions?', *Accounting, Auditing & Accountability Journal*, 16, no. 5: 821–52.

Min, B.S. (2003) 'FDI and Trade: Links in the Case of Malaysia', *Journal of the Asia Pacific Economy*, 8, no. 2: 229–250.

Murphy, A.L. (2013) 'Demanding "Credible Commitment": Public Reactions to the Failures of the Early Financial Revolution', *The Economic History Review*, 66: 178–97.

Neal, L.D. (1990) *The Rise of Financial Capitalism: International Capital Markets in the Age of Reason.*, Cambridge: Cambridge University Press.

Neal, L.D. (1998) 'The Bank of England's First Return to Gold and the Stock Market Crash of 1825,' *Federal Reserve Bank of St. Louis Review*, 79 (May–June): 53–76.

North, D. and Weingast, B. (1989) 'Constitutions and Commitment: The Evolution of Institutional Governing Public Choice in Seventeenth-Century England', *Journal of Economic History* (December): 803–32.

O'Brien, P.K. and Hunt, P.A. (1999) 'England 1485–1815', in R. Bonney (ed.), *The Rise of the Fiscal State in Europe, C. 1200–1815*, Oxford, Oxford University Press, pp. 53–100.

O'Rourke, K. and Williamson, J.G. (1995) 'Open Economy Forces and Late 19th Century Swedish Catch-Up: A Quantitative Accounting', *Scandinavian Economic History Review*, 2: 171–203.

Pabst, A. and Scazzieri, R. (2016) 'The Political Economy of Constitution', *Oeconomia (History, Methodology, Philosophy)*, 6, no. 3: 337–362.

Petty, W. (1769 [1662]). *A Treatise of Taxes [and] Contributions*. In Petty, W. (1769) *Tracts, Chiefly Relating to Ireland: Containing: I. A Treatise of Taxes and Contributions: II. Essays in Political Arithmetic: III. The Political Anatomy of Ireland*. Dublin: Printed by Boulter Grierson.

Reinhart, C.M. and Rogoff, K.S. (2009) *This Time Is Different: Eight Centuries of Financial Folly*, Princeton: Princeton University Press.

Rostow, W.W. (1960) *The Stages of Economic Growth: A Non-Communist Manifesto*, Cambridge: Cambridge University Press.

Sachs, J.D., Warner, A. Åslund, A. and Fisher, S. (1995) 'Economic Reform and the Process of Global Integration', *Brookings Papers on Economic Activity*, no. 1: 1-118.

Santayana, G. (1905) *The Life of Reason: The Phases of Human Progress*, New York: Prometheus Books.

Schumpeter, J.A. (1954 [1918]) 'The Crisis of the Tax State', *International Economic Papers*, iv: 5–38.

Seligman, E.R.A. (1892) *On the Shifting and Incidence of Taxation*. [Baltimore]: American Economic Association.

Seligman, E.R.A. (1910) *The Shifting and Incidence of Taxation*, 3rd edn. New York: The University of Columbia Press.

Turner, E.R. (1916) 'Early Opinion about English Excise.' *The American Historical Review* 21, no. 2: 314–318.

Williams, D.M. and Armstrong, J. (2008) 'Promotion, Speculation and Their Outcome: The "Steamship Mania" of 1824–1825.' In S. A. Roberts (ed,), *Aslib Proceedings*, vol. 60, no. 6, pp. 642–660. Emerald Group Publishing Limited.

Willis, H. P. (1901) *The Genesis of the Latin Monetary Union*. Chicago: University of Chicago Press.

Worstall, T. (2015) 'Greece Has Been in Default for 50% of Its Time as an Independent Country', *Forbes Magazine* (online), 1 July, www.forbes.com/sites/timworstall/2015/07/01/greece-has-been-in-default-for-50-of-its-time-as-an-independent-country

3 | Creating Stable Systems of Public Finance in the United States and Germany

Lessons for the Eurozone

JAMES MACDONALD

3.1 Introduction

One of the commonly repeated criticisms of the European Monetary Union (EMU) is that it attempted to create monetary union without political union. To its early critics this doomed it to failure (Feldstein, 1997; Salvatore, 1997). Many of the proponents of the Euro were, in fact, federalists who saw monetary union as a step in the direction of a political union for which the population of Europe was not yet ready. However, they reasoned, this was not necessarily a cause for concern. The European project had always operated on a ratchet basis – moving step by step towards the 'ever closer union' envisaged by the Treaty of Rome. If one step created a problem, a solution would be proposed which moved the project another rung up the ladder. It would be the same with the Euro. It might be imperfect, but any problems that arose would be ironed out by further steps towards integration.

The problem with this strategy was that it was blindsided by the suspension of disbelief by financial markets which acted as if political union was already in place. Money was lent to the less competitive members of the Eurozone as if there was no longer any meaningful sovereign risk involved. The problem was compounded by banking regulations which classified all EMU member-state debt as 100 per cent risk free and therefore not subject to capital requirements. As a result, Greece was able to borrow at only ten basis points more than Germany. In other countries, such as Spain and Ireland, the debt build-up was in the private sector, but the same calculations applied. The local banks were implicitly backstopped by their governments, and those governments were in turn implicitly backstopped by the Eurozone as a whole. The result was that debts in a number of countries rose to levels that were inherently unsustainable even before the crisis broke. When the markets woke up to the scale of the problems in the wake of the Lehman crisis, the resulting rise in interest spreads not only made apparent but also exacerbated the unsustainability of these debts.

The Eurozone member states now faced a problem with no easy solution. The financial crisis was so great that it could not be solved by a modest move towards integration but by a great leap forward. Instead of one step up the ladder at a time, four of five steps had to be broached all at once. The crisis seemed to prove what the sceptics had said all along: that monetary union without political union was inherently unstable. The only way to re-establish a financially stable system was to either move forwards towards political union or backwards towards a Europe of monetarily independent states (although the short-term financial costs of the latter would be severe). Yet the populations of the member countries did not want either – their normal predisposition towards further union having been seriously dented, both by the costs imposed on them by the financial crisis and by their loss of confidence in the leaders who had so blithely led them into it.

Given the inherent difficulties in both paths, the only currently plausible solution is to undertake the minimum further political integration that is compatible with financial stability. It is here that the histories of the United States and Germany are relevant. Both these countries are federal systems which evolved out of independent (or nearly independent) states. In both cases, the political systems that were initially created were financially decentralized. And in both cases, the countries found themselves moving, slowly but ineluctably, towards greater levels of centralization in response to financial crises. The financially stable federal systems that the two countries eventually built, however, were based on different sets of underlying principles.

3.2 The American Experience

The United States started its existence, like the European Union, as a confederation of independent states. The Continental Congress, created in 1776, had no powers of taxation and depended entirely on contributions from its member states. The War of Independence led to the creation of levels of debt that the market was unwilling to fund – as was scarcely surprising when the Continental government had no reliable source of income. Yet, the amount of debt involved was not inherently unsustainable. It was politics that made it appear so. Most Americans were suspicious of strong government, and they were reluctant to surrender local sovereignty to a central state with the power to tax.

Nationalists and Federalists, however, believed that without political integration the confederation could not last. Without a central state that could raise taxes and borrow money, America would not be able to defend itself. The war of independence had led to hyperinflation, and in the end had only been won because of French intervention. Moreover, as an economic bloc, the confederation was even weaker than the European Union would later be. The individual American states not only issued their own currencies, they also followed their own trade policies. Increasingly they were in competition with each other.

The solution was a great leap forward whereby the loosely confederated states were transformed into truly United States. Political union was accompanied by fiscal, monetary and commercial union. The federal government was given the sole right to mint money and to levy customs duties. This not only prevented commercial rivalry between the states; it also gave the government a source of income that could be used to fund the outstanding debt.

The fiscal purpose of the new constitution was made clear in the statement that the federal government would enjoy the power of taxation 'to pay the debts and to provide for the common defence and general welfare of the United States'. At the time, it was debt and defence that were the main concerns. The provision for 'general welfare' was to become important only at a later date.

To further cement the fiscal union, the federal government took over the debts of the states. The assumption of state debts was highly controversial. The amounts outstanding were not evenly distributed. Some states had borrowed using paper money that had become worthless. Other states had already settled much of their debt at a discount. There were, therefore, winners and losers in the pooling of obligations. Massachusetts was the biggest winner, Virginia and Maryland among the major losers. In the end the assumption was only able to go through by a piece of behind-the-scenes horse-trading which moved the capital to a new city on the banks of the Potomac. However, the United States had one great advantage over the European Union: its debts had all been incurred in the common cause of fighting for independence. The consolidation of the public debt, although contentious, was part of a process that was already under way to equalize the financial costs of the war among the states.

The operation of consolidation and refunding was remarkable. Alexander Hamilton, the Secretary of the Treasury, managed to restructure a debt, much of it hitherto in default, at a lower cost than it had originally been contracted. He was not aided by 'collective action clauses' to force dissentients into acquiescence. His only carrot, other than his persuasive powers, was that only the restructured debt would benefit from the security of the new federal tax revenues. In the end, the new consolidated debt amounted to around 40 per cent of GDP, and was funded at an interest cost of around 1.5 per cent of GDP. This was not a heavy burden, even for objectors to a tax-levying central government.

Hamilton's conversion created three large issues of government debt out of a myriad of old claims. This helped to create a liquid market which contributed to keeping yields down. It also created a large body of public creditors with a financial attachment to the federal government. One of Hamilton's arguments for consolidating the debt was that it would help cement the union. His opponents disliked his scheme for the same reason.

The new constitution was far better designed than the old one. The defence of the nation could now be undertaken without financial meltdown. However, it did not resolve the question of the balance of fiscal responsibility between the states and the federal government. The states had lost the right to mint money and to collect customs, as well as the ability to conduct foreign policy, but they retained most of their other powers and still saw themselves as largely sovereign entities. They were still able to raise taxes and borrow money, and they managed to circumvent some of the limitations on their monetary powers by setting up state banks which could issue notes backed by state bonds.

In the 1830s, a wave of state borrowing raised the total level of state debt to close to $200 million, more than 10 per cent of GDP (Ratchford, 1941). At this point it was higher than the federal debt, which was rapidly falling towards zero as a result of growing customs revenues and minimal government responsibilities. The frontier states in particular took upon themselves the funding of infrastructure projects to develop the wilderness. In the 1840s, many states found themselves in serious financial straits (Wallis, Sylla and Grinath, 2004). Once again there was a movement for the federal government to take over the local debt, but this time it did not work. The biggest reason may have been that, unlike the debts of the 1780s, the state debts of the 1830s were not incurred in some national emergency, but for often ill-considered projects for purely local benefit. If financial discipline was to be maintained, the states would have to sort out their own affairs.

The upshot was that nine out of twenty-one states defaulted. And in the wake of this disastrous experience, most states realized that only self-imposed rules would avoid a repeat performance (Wallis, 2004). In the 1840s and 1850s, eighteen states imposed restrictions on borrowing, and their number has continued to grow. Currently forty-six states have debt limitations, and forty-two have balanced-budget requirements (Schutz, 1935; Conti-Brown and Skeel, 2012). The heyday of state borrowing passed in the 1840s, and state debts are now a small fraction of federal debts (Figure 3.1).

Yet that was not the end of the story. The states may have accepted that their fiscal reach was inherently limited, but their ambition was taken up by cities and towns. In the late nineteenth and early twentieth centuries, it was municipalities which were the largest borrowers in the Union. While the federal debt fell continuously from its Civil War peak to a mere 1 per cent of GDP by 1913, municipal debt rose from 1 per cent of GDP in 1840 to 13 per cent in 1913.

Much of this borrowing was for urban infrastructure and amenities. However, the municipalities also took responsibility for such welfare measures as existed prior to the New Deal. In the early years of the Great Depression from 1929 to 1931, while the Hoover government

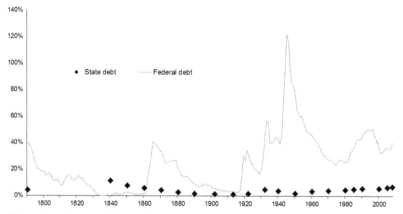

Figure 3.1. State and federal debt as a percentage of GDP, 1790–2008
Source: Historical Statistics of the United States of America

was running a surplus and paying down debt, the municipalities were borrowing heavily. By 1932, municipal debt had reached 28 per cent of GDP, a level that proved to be beyond their inherent fiscal capacity. By 1934, 37 out of 310 towns with population of more than 30,000 were in default. A total of 3,250 local governmental bodies of all kinds defaulted during the Depression (Hart, 1938).

Since the financial debacle of the War of Independence, it had been understood that the country needed a borrower of last resort to deal with national emergencies. The constitution had specified that the federal government's powers of taxation, inherently necessary to support a public debt, were there to 'provide for the common defence and the general welfare of the United States'. At the time, the first objective was all that counted. The provision for 'general welfare' was simply to allow space for unimagined eventualities. Now, in the 1930s, a new doctrine grew up that an economic crisis could be just as threatening as a military one, and that the government should respond, as in time of war, by acting as a borrower of last resort. The demonstration of the fiscal limits of state and municipal borrowing capacity showed that only the federal government could take on this role.

With the election of Franklin Roosevelt and the arrival of the New Deal in 1933, the new balance of fiscal responsibility became clear. Local borrowing stopped while federal borrowing rose sharply, with federal debt doubling between 1932 and 1940 (Figure 3.2).

After the unsustainable peak of the early 1930s, municipal debt fell back to the more modest levels at which it had been stable in the late nineteenth century (Figure 3.3).

The current American system of fiscal federalism is stable in terms of its balance of powers and responsibilities. This does not mean that the system is necessarily financially stable at the different levels of government taken individually (all levels of government have taken on liabilities, especially for pensions, that it is not clear that they can easily fulfil as the population ages), but rather that the division of power between the different levels is clear.

The federal government has unlimited borrowing power and is the only 'borrower of last resort' capable of dealing with emergencies. The states and cities have limited borrowing power and their debts are largely confined to capital investment. The states do take some responsibility for countercyclical spending in downturns through their role in food stamps and Medicaid, both of which rise in recessions and fall in

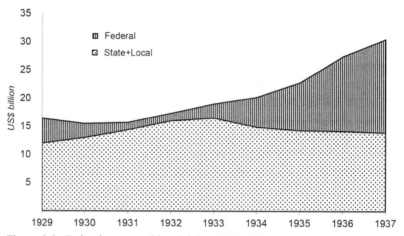

Figure 3.2. Federal, state and local debt, 1929–1937
Source: Hart (1938)

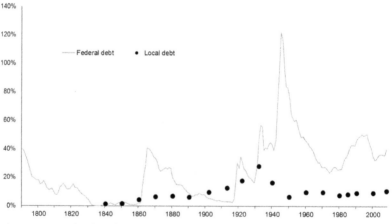

Figure 3.3. Federal and local debt as a percentage of GDP, 1790–2008
Source: Historical Statistics of the United States.

periods of growth. However, they receive substantial transfers from the federal government for this purpose, amounting to around 15 per cent of combined state and local budgets. They are not expected to undertake countercyclical deficit spending.

The issue of moral hazard, whereby the localities indulge in unsustainable borrowing on the assumption of a federal bailout, was answered by the refusal of the federal government to take over the debts of the states in the 1840s. It was also made clear by the reaction in Washington to the financial difficulties of New York City in the 1970s. An initial approach for support in October 1975 was rejected outright, giving rise to the famous 'FORD TO CITY: DROP DEAD' headline in the *New York Daily News* (October 30, 1975). One month later the federal government relented because of fears of the consequences if the country's financial centre was allowed to default, but imposed terms so harsh that no city would ever willingly contemplate asking for aid again (Dunstan, 1995).

3.3 The German Experience

In the 1860s and 1870s, two European countries were created by uniting a number of states with long histories of independence. Both countries established central governments with parliaments presided over by constitutional monarchs. However one, Italy, became a fiscally centralized state, while the other, Germany remained a fiscal federation. Why was this?

One partial answer may be that Italy became a united kingdom in March 1861, before the outbreak of the American Civil War. The lessons of that war about the cost of attempting to reassert independence from a unitary state made Bavaria, at least, insist on the retention of many privileges, among them the right of secession, when it joined the German Empire in 1871.

A more important answer lies in the financial cost of unification. In Italy, Piedmont incurred almost the entire cost of unifying the country. Its public debt grew by more than seven times between 1847 and 1861. By that time, its debt constituted 55 per cent of the Italian total, whereas its population was only 20 per cent (Plebano, 1899–1902). It therefore had a large incentive to create a fiscally centralized state which would consolidate the debt of all its constituent members. And as in the case of the United States, Piedmont could make a strong argument that the majority of its debt had in any case been assumed in the common cause of national liberation.

In Germany, by contrast, the cost of unification was paid for by the indemnity imposed on France at the end of the Franco-Prussian War in 1871. The total debt of all the German states in 1871 amounted to 3.7 billion marks, while the French indemnity came to 4 billion marks.

Moreover, Prussia, by far the most dominant state in the union, had a debt that, unlike Piedmont's, was lower than the national average. Consolidation of the debt would therefore have disadvantaged Prussia for the same reasons that it benefitted Piedmont.

Because it comprised more than 60 per cent of its land mass and population, Prussia dominated Germany without the need for a centralized state. Decentralization allowed it to maintain a number of privileges that it might otherwise have had to give up. As a result, the Reich had limited tax powers consisting largely of customs duties, certain tolls and excises, and the income from the postal system. The states were committed to making up budget shortfalls, but as a quid pro quo, the 'Frankenstein' clause of 1879 committed the Reich to returning any surplus customs and excise income over a certain threshold to the states.

By contrast, the states themselves had a privileged position within the union, enjoying considerable tax revenues and relatively few responsibilities. Among their sources of income were the state-owned railways which by this stage were profitable businesses. In Prussia's case, income from the state railway was higher than the interest on the state debt.

In 1913, Reich income represented no more than 30 per cent of total central and local government revenue (Schremmer, 1989). The system was stable only because the responsibilities of the government were still modest. It remained to be seen how it would cope in an emergency.

The World War I provided just such a test, and it stretched the system beyond its capabilities. The customs income of the state collapsed as a result of the Allied blockade, and while other sources of revenue rose, in real terms the Reich's overall income declined. The result was that the cost of the war was covered entirely through borrowing. The public debt of the central government rose to thirty-two times its pre-war level; whereas in 1913 it had represented only 17 per cent of the total public debt, it now constituted 80 per cent (Schremmer, 1989). This massive rise in debt, unsupported by adequate taxation, was one of the main causes of the post-war inflation.

The World War I, like the American War of Independence, demonstrated that large-scale wars required a properly funded central government which could act as borrower of last resort. The result, in Germany, was a centralization of fiscal powers under the

Weimar Republic. The Reich gained the power of direct taxation, and also took over the railways.

The next step in fiscal centralization came as a result of a process that in many ways mirrored events in the United States. During the late 1920s, the German states and towns went on a borrowing spree which weakened their financial position. The law of 1924, designed as part of the Dawes Plan to re-establish financial stability after the hyperinflation of the early post-war years, put strict limits on the ability of the central bank to finance the government. At the same time, a law of 1927 placed additional obligations on local governments to support the unemployed. After 1929, and particularly under the Brüning government from 1930–32, local governments were the only ones to undertake countercyclical borrowing. The central government was running an overall surplus after factoring in the Social Insurance fund (Figure 3.4).

By 1932, many states and cities had defaulted on their debts in order to continue funding welfare provision. The result was further central limits on the autonomy of local government. Under Hitler, almost all fiscal power was centralized, and under the radical new economic policies of Hjalmar Schacht, the state took over responsibility for countercyclical spending (Figure 3.5).

The Nazi period was the high water mark of government centralization in Germany. After the war a federal democracy was put in place in West Germany. Its level of fiscal centralization, although

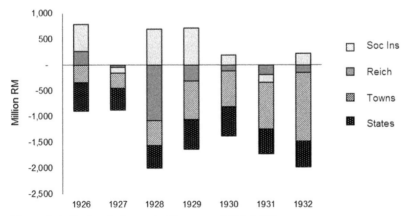

Figure 3.4. Budget balances in Germany, 1926–1932
Source: James (1986)

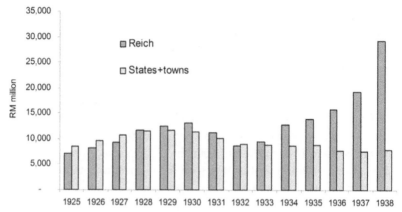

Figure 3.5. Central and local government spending, 1925–1938
Source: Andic and Ververka (1964)

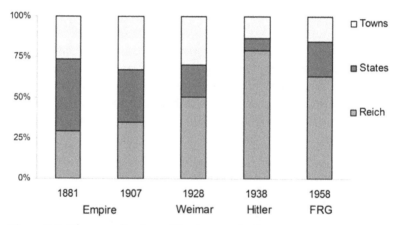

Figure 3.6. The centralization of fiscal power in Germany
Source: Andic and Ververka (1964)

reduced from Hitler's day, was still greater than that of the Weimar
Republic (Figure 3.6).

The German federal system operates on different principles from the
American one. Instead of relying on self-contained areas of responsibility enforced largely by market discipline, Germany has a highly

complex system of overlapping responsibilities kept in balance by rules. Most taxes are established at the federal level, and revenues are then redistributed both to the Länder and between the Länder (Seitz, 2000). The result is that the Länder have little tax autonomy but considerable spending power. The Länder receive around 40 per cent of total government revenues, but they are independently able to set less than 5 per cent of the total (Zipfel, 2011).

Unlike in the United States, where each level of government is 'on its own' in terms of solvency, the principle of 'solidarity' is incorporated into the German constitution. In order to offset the risk that states and cities would act irresponsibly in the expectation of a central bailout, strict limitations on borrowing power have been established. In 1969, the constitution was amended to allow greater fiscal freedom, with the inevitable result that borrowing increased at all levels of government. And given the considerable spending power available to the Länder, they were able to build up debts that were higher than those of the American states. Total state debt is around 25 per cent of GDP in Germany, compared to less than 10 per cent in the United States (Figure 3.7).

Even before the Great Recession hit in 2008, it was becoming clear that the system needed reforming. The federal government had almost no power to control the states' borrowing, and while many states had

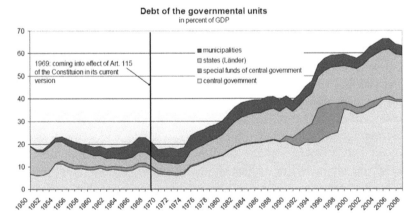

Figure 3.7. Public borrowing in the federal republic of Germany, 1950–2008
Source: Federal Ministry of Finance, Public Finance and Economic Affairs Directorate, *Reforming the Constitutional Budget Rules in Germany*, Berlin, 2009.

rules that limited their borrowing to 'investment purposes', these rules were often interpreted very loosely. By the 1990s, two states – Bremen and Saarland – had run up unsustainable debts and were able successfully to sue the federal government for support on the basis of the constitutional obligation of solidarity. The German Länder were the largest subnational borrowers in Europe, and it was clear that their ability to borrow on such a scale was based in large part on the assumption that they would be supported by the federal government. In the late 1990s, the American states had debts that were equal to 51 per cent of their total income (including federal transfers), or 66 per cent of their independent tax revenue. The German Länder had debts that were 175 per cent of their total income, or 1,926 per cent or their independent tax revenue. Yet the average S&P rating for the American states was AA, compared to AA+ for the German Länder (Rodden, 2006).

The Great Recession was a catalyst for reform. The financial crisis called into question the sustainability of government debts, and the Eurozone crisis highlighted the risks of implicit guarantees within federal systems. The result was the 2009 'debt brake' law which reinforced the role of rules within the system. Under these rules, after a lead-in period, the Länder governments have to balance their budgets under normal circumstances. The federal government may run a deficit of no more than 0.35 per cent of GDP under normal circumstances. In an economic emergency, as declared by the federal government, countercyclical borrowing is allowed. However it must be offset by subsequent surpluses.

Even with the debt brake law there remain some reasons to question the stability of the German system of fiscal federalism. The central government does not have a monopoly of borrowing for economic emergencies, and there remains an implicit bailout provision in the German constitution. Taken together, these could lead to the possibility of the 'tail wagging the dog'. However, there are a number of offsetting characteristics which should prevent this from happening.

In the first place, the federal government has a preponderant position in the system. It sets tax levels, and it determines the rules that govern borrowing at all levels of government. It is the central government that decides if there is an emergency that warrants overriding the normal operations of the debt brake law. The fiscal autonomy of the local governments is therefore inherently limited.

In practice, moreover, the federal government already has the preponderant role in countercyclical borrowing. In 2010, out of a total budget deficit of 4.1 per cent of GDP, only 0.7 per cent was attributable to the Länder.

Since the financial crisis hit, the spread between federal and Länder borrowing costs, although relatively modest, has doubled, as has the spread between the different Länder (Zipfel, 2012). This implies the existence of some market-based incentives to maintain fiscal discipline. However, the principle buttress of stability in the German system of fiscal federalism is the application of rules imposed from the centre.

3.4 Lessons for the Eurozone

History shows that fiscal systems need borrowers of last resort to deal with military and economic emergencies. It has also shown that this function cannot be carried out by subnational governments. In the first place, such governments have inbuilt financial limits. Their powers of taxation are usually limited to a greater or lesser extent, and more importantly they do not control all the levers of macroeconomic policy, in particular the power to control money. Markets are therefore less willing to lend large sums to them, all other things being equal, than to governments with unlimited powers of taxation and full control of macroeconomic levers. Moreover, while subnational governments have inbuilt fiscal limits, they also have an inherent tendency to over-borrow in the expectation of a central bailout. Therefore, their ability to run deficits needs to be held in check by some combination of market forces, self-limiting statutes, centrally imposed rules, and credible no-bailout provisions. Governments subject to this combination of internal and external constraints are never going to be good borrowers of last resort.

In the absence of a central government with borrowing powers, the EMU member states were (and still are) the theoretical borrowers of last resort within the Eurozone. The Stability and Growth Pact enshrined in European Monetary Union was supposed to ensure that their fiscal behaviour under normal economic conditions was sufficiently sound that they would not run out of borrowing power during an economic downturn even though they no longer had the support of domestic central banks that could act as lenders of last resort. The discipline was reinforced by explicit no-bailout provisions and a prohibition on the European Central Bank from financing government deficits.

However, the financial crisis exposed a number of flaws in this arrangement. First, a number of states started EMU from positions far weaker than were originally supposed to be acceptable. Second, some countries ignored the provisions of the Pact, and one, Greece, went so far as to present false accounts to hide its fiscal excesses. Third, in Ireland and Spain, fiscally responsible policies masked underlying private-sector credit booms which destroyed the appearance of public solvency when they burst, taking down domestic banking systems with them. The result was that these states started to find it impossible to borrow in the market, and they were therefore no longer able to act as borrowers of last resort to support their economies.

The response of the Eurozone member states was reluctantly to break the no-bailout provisions of EMU, first by setting up the European Financial Stability Facility (EFSF) and the European Financial Stabilization Mechanism (EFSM), and when that proved insufficient, by allowing the ECB to declare its willingness to act as a lender of last resort for member governments. The quid pro quo of these arrangements, however, was the imposition of a level of fiscal retrenchment that, while less severe than would have occurred in the face of a complete loss of credit, was sufficiently great to offset the automatic fiscal stabilizers that would normally have operated in a recession. The result was that the economies of these countries suffered greater economic downturns after they were 'bailed out' than before.

At the same time, all countries in the Eurozone were required to sign up to a reinforced program of fiscal discipline that would ensure that such a crisis never recur, and there would never again be the risk of national governments looking for central bailouts. As a result, countries whose credit was still sound, such as Germany, were obliged by the new EU provisions (and in Germany's case by its own 2009 debt brake law) to run a balanced budget (defined as a structural deficit no greater than 0.5 per cent of GDP) except in the face of a serious domestic economic downturn. They had no remit to respond to economic conditions in the Eurozone as a whole. Since economic conditions in Germany were good, with unemployment falling to 5.1 per cent, there was no way for the country to run a deficit within the rule book even had it wanted to.

The EMU member states are therefore treated, in terms of their relation with the Eurozone, as is they are subnational governments in need of strict fiscal discipline. Only in relation to their own economies do they have any, albeit limited, ability to pursue countercyclical deficit spending. The result for the Eurozone has been the de facto disappearance of any borrower of last resort, even though economic conditions in the EMU area as a whole would require one. Since the Eurozone crisis struck in 2010, unemployment in the member states has risen from 10 per cent to 11.5 per cent at the end of 2014. Yet at the same time, the combined budgetary deficit of the Eurozone countries has fallen from 6.2 per cent to 2.4 per cent of GDP (European Commission, Eurostat, 2015a; 2015b). In the United States, by contrast, budget deficits and unemployment have risen and fallen more or less in tandem, as would be expected if automatic fiscal stabilizers followed their normal course. The US budget deficit fell from 9 per cent of GDP in 2010 to 2.8 per cent in 2014, while unemployment fell from 9.1 per cent to 5.7 per cent (Federal Reserve Bank of St. Louis, FRED, 2015a; 2015b).

The outcome bears out concerns expressed as long ago as 1994 by Barry Eichengreen and Tamin Bayoumi:

If U.S. experience is any guide, the fiscal restraints of the Maastricht Treaty ... if vigorously enforced ... could significantly diminish the stabilization capacity of national budgets ... EC member states should no more assume principal responsibility for fiscal stabilization in Europe than do state governments in the United States. But ... while there is no question that fiscal stabilization is more appropriately handled at the EC level, the treaty makes no provision for expanding the Community's fiscal role ... [V]igorously applying the deficit excessive deficits procedures of the treaty to the national budgets of member states would leave post-Maastricht Europe with significantly less automatic stabilization than the U.S. economic and monetary union. (Eichengreen and Bayoumi, 1994, p. 791)

Events of the past five years have proved even worse than Eichengreen and Bayoumi had foreseen. The Eurozone has not only had less automatic stabilization than the United States; its system of fiscal federalism has resulted in policies that have been pro-cyclical rather than countercyclical.

The Eurozone faces a number of choices, none of them easy, all of which (other than the dissolution of the monetary union) require greater levels of fiscal integration than are currently considered politically acceptable. A partial solution might involve altering the Stability and Growth Pact to encourage, and possibly even require, governments to make budgetary decisions based on economic conditions within the Eurozone as a whole as well as within domestic economies individually. However, this would not get around the problem that the member states would remain inherently less-than-ideal borrowers of last resort for the reasons outlined previously. More plausibly, the Eurozone should move towards political union, establishing a central government with sufficient powers of taxation and borrowing to provide itself with a functioning borrower of last resort. Failing such moves towards integration, the Eurozone will continue to live with a system with an inbuilt tendency to fiscal crisis that can only be contained at the cost of high levels of unemployment.

References

Andic, S., and Ververka, J. (1964) 'The Growth of Government Expenditure in Germany', *Finanzarchiv*, 18 (23), pp. 169–277.

Conti-Brown, P. and Skeel, Jr., D. A. (eds.) (2012) *When States Go Broke: The Origins, Context, and Solutions for American States in Fiscal Crisis*, Cambridge: Cambridge University Press.

Dunstan, R. (1995) 'Overview of New York City's Fiscal Crisis', *CRB Note* 3.1, California Research Bureau: California State Library.

Eichengreen, B. and Bayoumi, T. (1994) 'The Political Economy of Political Restrictions: Implications for Europe from the United States', *European Economic Review*, 38 (3–4), pp. 783–91.

European Commission, Eurostat (2015a) *Unemployment rate by sex and age – quarterly average*. Available at: http://appso.eurostat.ec.europa.ue/nui/show.do. Accessed 20 June 2015.

European Commission, Eurostat (2015b) *Government deficit/surplus, debt and associated data*. Available at: http://appso.eurostat.ec.europa.ue/nui/show.do. Accessed 20 June 2015.

Federal Ministry of Finance, Public Finance and Economic Affairs Directorate (2009) *Reforming the Constitutional Budget Rules in Germany*, Berlin.

Federal Reserve Bank of St. Louis, FRED (2015a) *Civilian unemployment rate – seasonally adjusted*. Available at: https://research.stlouisfed.org/fred2/graph/?id=UNRATE. Accessed 20 June 2015.

Federal Reserve Bank of St. Louis, FRED (2015b) *Federal surplus or deficit [-] as percent of gross domestic product*. Available at: https://research.stlouisfed.org/fred2/graph/?id=FYFSDFYGDP. Accessed 20 June 2015.

Feldstein, M. (1997) 'The Political Economy of the European Monetary Union: Political Sources of an Economic Liability', *The Journal of Economic Perspectives*, 11 (4), pp. 23–42.

Hart, A. G. (1938) *Debts and Recovery: A Study of Changes in the Internal Debt Structure from 1929 to 1937 and a Program for the Future*, New York: Twentieth Century Fund.

James, H. (1986) *The German Slump: Politics and Economics 1924–1936*, Oxford: Oxford University Press.

Plebano, A. (1899–1902) *Storia della Finanza Italiana nei Primi Quarant'anni dell'Unificazione*, Torino: Roux e Varengo.

Ratchford, B. U. (1941) *American State Debts*, Durham, NC: Duke University Press.

Rodden, J. A. (2006) *Hamilton's Paradox: The Promise and Peril of Fiscal Federalism*, Cambridge: Cambridge University Press.

Salvatore, D. (1997) 'The Common Unresolved Problems with the EMS and EMU', *The American Economic Review*, 87 (May), pp. 224–26.

Schremmer, D. E. (1989) 'Taxation and Public Finance: Britain, France, and Germany', *The Cambridge Economic History of Europe*, vol. VIII: *The Industrial Economies: The Development of Economic and Social Policies*, Cambridge: Cambridge University Press, pp. 315–494.

Schutz, W. J. (1935) 'Limitations on State and Local Borrowing Powers', *The Annals of the American Academy of Political and Social Science*, 181 (September), pp. 118–24.

Seitz, H. (2000) 'Fiscal Policy, Deficits and Politics of Subnational Governments: The Case of the German Laender', *Public Choice*, 102 (3–4), pp. 183–218.

Wallis, J. J. (2004) *Constitutions, Corporations, and Corruption: American States and Constitutional Change, 1842–52*, NBER Working Paper 10541, Cambridge, MA: National Bureau of Economic Research.

Wallis, J. J., Sylla, R. E., and Grinath, A. (2004) *Sovereign Debt and Repudiation: The Emerging Market Crisis in the U.S. States, 1839–1843*, NBER Working Paper 10751, Cambridge, MA: National Bureau of Economic Research.

Zipfel, F. (2011) *German Finances: Federal Level Masks Importance of Länder*, Frankfurt: Deutsche Bank Research.

Zipfel, F. (2012) *Debt Structure of the Federal States*, Frankfurt: Deutsche Bank Research.

4 A Historical Perspective on the European Crisis

The Latin Monetary Union

LUCA EINAUDI

4.1 Introduction

The history of monetary unification in Europe has been a combination of national and supranational unions that is much longer than usually thought. Not only the Roman Empire and Carolingian Europe had created periods of extended monetary uniformity across large parts of the continent, but several more restricted transnational efforts had been pursued from the renaissance onwards, especially in the German-speaking world, awaiting political unification. The largest and most resilient precedent to EMU in Europe, however, is the Latin Monetary Union (LMU, 1865–1926). This episode is related to an economic and financial structure very different from the one we know today, with a dominant specie money (gold and silver rather than fiat money) and central banks having a more limited role. Continuous wars between European states played a relevant role in undoing or consolidating cooperation, especially by causing the suspension of the gold or silver convertibility of paper money but also by undermining the political basis for cooperation.

Despite these obvious differences, we can still find some interesting lessons in comparison with today's Euro by retracing how the LMU was formed, how its expansion was attempted, how it reacted to difficulties by redrawing the rules, even if it meant to adopt tighter monetary policies, and how it lasted over a long period with a narrower role and finally was disbanded without much regret when national priorities took over after the repeated major economic and political shocks of World War I and postwar reconstruction and monetary stabilization.

4.2 Origins of the LMU

The LMU has its origins in long-term historical heritage, with cross-border trade exchanges facilitating the use of a common (even if not a single) currency and geopolitical links and alliances. The empire created by Napoleon I across a large section of Europe included by 1812 an undeclared monetary union, based on the French monetary system, the franc Germinal of 1803. A franc was a silver coin of 5 grams of silver at 90 per cent fineness; another coin in general circulation was a 20 francs gold piece of 6,45 grams of 90 per cent fineness. This meant that a fixed 15.5-to-1 ratio was established at the mint between gold and silver, the system known as bimetallism. The territories involved included France, continental Italy and Belgium. Italy was divided between the Kingdom of Italy of Viceroy Eugène de Beauharnais (Italian lira), the Kingdom of the Two Sicilies of Gioachim Murat (Neapolitan lira), the Principality of Lucca and Piombino of Elisa Bonaparte (franc di Lucca) and the territories of Rome, Florence, Turin and Genoa annexed by France (French francs). It was one currency under four different names and separate rulers, symbols and images. In his memoirs written in St Helena, Napoleon recalled his unifying effort for Europe, which explicitly included trade, legislation, systems of measures and currency (Einaudi 2001). The penetration of French coinage had not been complete in the most peripheral parts of the Empire (such as Southern Italy) and the restoration of most pre-revolutionary rulers in 1815 after the Congress of Vienna shattered this monetary community.

The franc imposed itself again during the following decades, through the weight of cross-border transactions and the overwhelming circulation of French coinage, compared to the limited and confused circulation of small neighbouring states. The King of Sardinia was the first to give up on his attempts to restore pre-revolutionary monetary system and decided instead to reintroduce the franc in 1816, under the thin disguise of the 'New Piedmontese lira'. The Piedmontese monetary system was extended progressively to the whole of Italy in 1859–70, in parallel with the process of national political unification. The 1831 revolution gave Belgium its independence from the Netherlands, and the new State decided to introduce the Belgian franc, copied from the French model. After the civil war of 1847, Switzerland chose a less decentralized political system, and unified its monetary system as well, replacing in 1850 the separate coinage of each canton with the Swiss franc, based on the French model.

Some uniformity had been achieved among the countries mentioned, informally and without any international agreement, under the typical pressure of the period towards modernization, unification, simplification and economic development and international trade. The oscillations of bimetallism, however, started to break this uniformity in the late 1850s and early 1860s, requiring an intergovernmental agreement to prevent new obstacles to trade. From 1848 onwards, new inflows of gold into Europe, as a consequence of the California gold rush, had caused a decline of the price of gold relative to silver. A central element of bimetallism was the right for individuals to bring freely silver and gold metal to the mints and to have it transformed into legal currency at the official price (minus a small mint fee). Therefore, in the 1850s, gold was minted in unprecedented quantities, increasing monetary supply, while silver coins tended to be hoarded and/or melted because of their higher value as a good in comparison to their legal value as a currency. The disappearance of small change in silver coins led to petitions by commercial interests for a solution, to various official enquiries and to the adoption of diverging policies in the various countries concerned, particularly France, Italy, Belgium and Switzerland. Ultimately all agreed that the silver content of small silver coins had to be reduced, transforming them into tokens with a higher legal value than their silver content at market price, in order to neutralize speculators. Switzerland acted first, in 1860, deciding on a strong reduction of the silver fineness of its coins from 90 per cent to 80 per cent, followed by Italy which adopted in 1862 the 83.5 per cent fineness, suggested by a French commission. The French government instead reduced the silver content of only the smallest silver coins, keeping the others at 90 per cent. The growing divergence in small divisionary silver coinage led the Bank of France to start refusing Swiss coins of reduced value in 1864.

4.3 Creation of the LMU

This chaotic situation triggered official reactions, which in turn provoked a Belgian proposal to conclude an agreement between governments to solve the differences. After a lengthy exchange of diplomatic correspondence, official negotiations began, and a Monetary Conference was called in Paris and concluded with the creation of the Monetary Convention of 23 December 1865.

France, Italy, Belgium and Switzerland were parties to the agreement meant to resolve problems of monetary circulation of silver coinage between neighbouring countries to facilitate trade. The agreement was not defined formally as a monetary union. The name 'Latin Monetary Union' was imposed by a hostile British press, to highlight its alien nature to the United Kingdom. The Convention mandated that state cashiers of member states would accept each other's gold and silver coinage at a par, even if some coins were called francs and others lire and the images impressed on them represented exclusively national rulers and symbols.

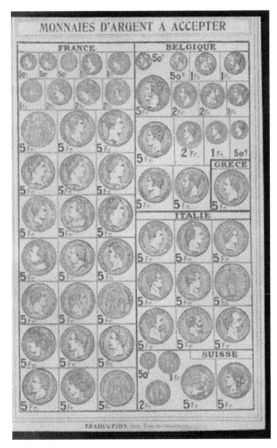

Figure 4.1 French notice indicating which silver coins of the Latin Monetary Union should be accepted on the eve of World War I
Source: Collection of the Author

There was a 1-to-1 fixed exchange rate, based on the intrinsic gold and silver content of the coins. All coins not in line with the new common system were to be re-coined. This measure concerned essentially silver divisionary pieces of 1 and 2 francs and of 50 and 20 cents, all reduced to tokens with only 83.5 per cent silver content. The 5 francs silver coin (popularly known as écu) remained as the only silver piece of full value at 90 per cent silver (Einaudi 2001). As a safeguard against overissue of the depreciated silver divisionary coins, the agreement included a limit of 6 francs per inhabitant for the production of such coins in each member state. The agreement was limited in time and could be renewed.

In fact, it was a limited coinage union rather than a full monetary union, given that outside the scope of the agreement were left both copper coins and banknotes, and national banks of issue were not involved in the negotiations. It was an incomplete agreement, as it would quickly become clear at the implementation stage, with a complex system of multiple and partially common currencies but not a single currency, created without being fully aware of it.

In fact, multiple exchange rates developed:

1. The exchange rate between the gold coinage of member states: such exchange rate remained a fixed 1-to-1 at all times for the state cashiers of all member states, without ever encountering any limitations despite wars, inconvertibility and financial crises.
2. The exchange rate for 5 francs silver écus with 90 per cent silver content: it remained fixed at 1-to-1, but new issues were limited through national quotas from 1874 onwards by a new Monetary convention, and prohibited altogether from 1879. From the 1880s France threatened to return to other members' their silver écus circulating in France or held in the vaults of the bank of France, asking for gold in exchange, an operation which would have been very expensive for the issuers (mainly Italy and Belgium) because of the strong fall of the price of silver relative to gold.
3. The exchange rate between silver divisionary coins at the reduced rate of 83.5 per cent: it remained fixed at 1-to-1 but a ceiling to total issues was set from the beginning of the LMU in 1865 to 6 francs per inhabitant, prohibiting any new issue above this ceiling. Exchange of information on annual monetary issue was decided, in order to control the respect of limits. Stocks which had migrated

in other countries were periodically returned to the issuer. Italy renationalized them in 1893 and Greece in 1908.

4. The exchange rate between banknotes and gold coins: it was aligned to that of gold coins in ordinary times but fluctuated widely when countries adopted temporary inconvertibility of their paper currencies in gold or silver (Italy and the Papal State reached a depreciation of paper up to 20 per cent and Greece up to 40 per cent in the 1870s, and even France was to adopt inconvertible paper currency for a short time as a consequence of the Franco-Prussian War).

The clash between supporters of the gold standard and bimetallism was another factor which hampered the LMU, together with the fluctuation of the relative price of gold and silver, wars and national financial instability.

4.4 Enlarging the Latin Monetary Union

In 1866–67 those problems were not yet visible to the general public, and the LMU entered a phase of expansion. During the negotiations a more ambitious view of the agreement than the finance ministries' point of view emerged. It was not just an issue of facilitating transactions across borders; it also became an attempt to create a European or universal currency through the development of federalist ideas. These views were developed chiefly by Felix Esquirou de Parieu, Vice President of the Council of State of Napoleon III, lawyer and economist, and they were embraced by the French Ministry of foreign affairs to promote French political ambition. Parieu headed the early monetary conferences of the LMU, and began writing articles for an international audience from a theoretical and practical in point of view, coming to form between 1866 and 1870 a much larger project for a 'Europa' currency, a European federation, a European commission and a European parliament, with the possibility of enlarging it further if the United States was willing to participate (Parieu 1870; see also Einaudi 2001, 46–54).

The French government, under the joint intellectual leadership of Parieu and the political-diplomatic network of the Quay d'Orsay (French Ministry of foreign affairs), attempted to enlarge the Monetary Union by inviting all European countries and the main world powers to the 1867 International Monetary Conference in Paris. Twenty countries were invited, including LMU members, German States, Scandinavian states, the Austro-Hungarian Empire, the United Kingdom, Spain, the United States, and the Russian and Ottoman empires (Einaudi 2000). The conference produced a surprising consensus for an international gold standard and the LMU coinage system. The creation of a central representative coin was planned as a pivot of the system. It was a gold piece of 25 francs-lire-pesetas, equal to 1 new British pound (whose weight would have to be reduced by less than 1 per cent), to 5 US dollars (whose weight would also have to change by a little more than 1 per cent) and to 10 Austria-German florins.

The post-conference developments were not as positive in terms of reaction by the key governments, whose delegates often had only a very limited mandate, purely as observers in the case of Britain.

In the United Kingdom the Disraeli government indeed rejected the proposal, as did the popular press of the time. Things changed when the Conservatives were defeated and a Liberal government took over in 1868, headed by Gladstone. His new Chancellor of the Exchequer, Robert Lowe, was convinced that the project on the continent was successful and that joining it was essential for the United Kingdom. Lowe also considered that the British gold coinage was worn down by a long circulation and had lost so much of its weight through wear and tear that it was now in fact below legal tender requirements so that a complete re-coinage was needed anyway, as the economist William Stanley Jevons had argued. In 1869, Lowe proposed to the British parliament to proceed to equalize the pound to 25 gold francs and to keep the difference in value (approximately 0.8 per cent, as the pound was worth 25.22 francs in gold weight) as a mint tax to cover for the cost of re-coinage. The proposal caused a storm of opposition, and even Gladstone declared privately to be astonished by it. Only free traders, some economists, mint officials and chambers of commerce supported Lowe, while the City, the Bank of England and the press opposed it. Ultimately the refusal of the French treasury and of the Bank of France and private bankers to abandon bimetallism in favour of the gold standard destroyed the opportunity to involve the United Kingdom.

Sweden and Austria-Hungary adopted a gold coinage according to the rules set at the Paris Conference (a 10 francs Carolin coin in Sweden from 1868 and a 20 francs (8 florins) coin in Austria-Hungary from 1870). Those coins were accepted at par by French state cashiers, by decision of the French finance ministry. A similar move was made by Russia in the 1880s (5 gold rubles for 20 francs) when it started accessing the French capital market for government loans, associated to a military alliance. Spain and Romania adopted the full LMU monetary system, under the name of peseta and lei, in the late 1860s, followed by a number of Latin American countries and later by Serbia and Bulgaria, while even the Finnish government (under Russian rule) enquired about joining.

Southern German states supported international monetary union as a part of a strategy to resist Prussian expansionism, but Bismarck temporized, waiting for the opportunity to crush Napoleon III on the field. The Franco-Prussian war of 1870–71 provided such opportunity and led to the creation of the German Empire and the German mark, based on a third of the Prussian thaler rather than on any international agreement. British and German refusal of the plan for international unification led to the collapse of possible enlargements of the Latin Monetary Union.

4.5 Decline and Stabilization

The political and military problems encountered by France in Northern Europe were not the only obstacles. A different type of difficulty emerged even faster with southern Europe. Enthusiastic candidates appeared very rapidly, from Greece to the Papal State, from Spain to Austria-Hungary and Romania, attracted by the opportunity to import and adopt a credible and stable international currency and also to access the French capital market. However, these countries were very fragile from the point of view of public finances and the capacity to maintain a fixed exchange rate.

The first problems in the practical management of the LMU were linked to the rapidly growing Italian government debt, due to the construction of a national infrastructure in a country that was completing its unification between 1859 and 1870. War with Austria in 1866 led to the inconvertibility of Italian banknotes into gold and silver coins. Paper money issue was increased to finance government deficit and the war, leading to depreciation of paper money and migration of coinage to France and Switzerland. Forms of monetary issue not covered by the Monetary Convention were expanded in Italy (paper money of ordinary denominations as well as very small denominations, together with copper coinage), reinforcing the flight of Italian currency to France and Switzerland, preventing those countries from minting their full share of coinage. This situation generated tension in the LMU, but was ultimately resolved reinforcing the rules on new issues and with the Italians agreeing to withdraw small-size banknotes (but this solution did not hold).

The Papal State also contributed to discrediting the confidence that France and Switzerland could have in managing an orderly membership of smaller states with problematic public finances. The Papal State applied immediately to join the LMU in 1866. It obtained a temporary authorization to issue coinage accepted in France while the negotiations for membership dragged on but then took advantage of French tolerance to overissue by 10 to 1 its silver divisionary coinage with reduced silver content. Most of it migrated to France, because of inconvertible paper money, and to pay for French troops defending the Pope from the Kingdom of Italy and Garibaldi. When formal negotiation to join the LMU were completed, after more than two years of delays, artfully created by the Papal Secretary of State Antonelli, the latter ultimately declared his inability to join the monetary union unless exempted from most of its rules. In particular the Pope could not submit to limits of issue and the obligation to repatriate silver divisionary coinage on demand from other members of the Union, revealing that it had already minted large quantities of divisionary silver. The French government, taken by surprise, prohibited the circulation of Papal coins in its territory. Private French citizens holding Papal coinage faced losses when selling it to private banks, creating a major scandal. The Papal State was pushed out of the LMU system in 1870, but within a few months it was invaded by Italy and annexed except for the Vatican.

Greece was another problematic case, although it created more confusion than real disruption in monetary circulation. Greece was the first and only state to complete accession to the LMU after the four founding members. It joined in 1868 and, in order to reassure its monetary allies, asked to have its new coinage minted in Paris through French private bankers. Greek wars for national unification and financial weaknesses, however, led to inconvertibility of its paper currency in 1869 and again from 1877 to 1910, with large exchange rates depreciations of the paper currency, and to a debt default in 1893.

These events, together with the sale of a small amount of Greek coins at a discount in Paris by private bankers acting without authorization from the Greek government, determined foreign control of part of Greek monetary issue from 1869, and to limitations to Greek membership of LMU.

Greece accumulated substantial foreign debt in the 1880s to pay for military spending and to modernize the country. The 1890s brought an international economic depression, and Greek exports faded because of weak international demand and also because of French protectionist policies. Greece suspended payment on its foreign debt in 1893, when it consumed 33 per cent of its budgetary receipts and had reached more than 160 per cent of GDP (Levandis, 1944). A depreciation of the paper drachma by 60 per cent in early 1893 also made the payment of interests prohibitive. Initially a new international loan was been floated at 5 per cent, to help the Greek government to overtake what seemed a temporary problem. After a few months, however, the adverse effect of declining exchange rates proved to be the final element for bankruptcy. The Greeks announced a 70 per cent reduction on the interest of all gold loans on a temporary basis. Negotiation with foreign bondholders started with Germany taking a hard line and France and Britain a more lenient one, but did not produce results for several years. In 1897, Greece was defeated in a new war against the Ottoman Empire, and the European powers stopped the invasion in exchange for foreign control of Greek finances. To satisfy bondholders, an International Committee for the Management of Greek Debt was created. Greek debt was jointly guaranteed by France, Great Britain and Russia in 1898. In the end Greece paid back all its debt at par in gold until the 1940s, with interest rates below the original level.

The problems encountered in managing the LMU convinced the strongest members of the Union to block further enlargements (refusing all other applications for membership, coming mainly from southern or central Europe and the Balkans and from Latin America) and to restrict the field of action of the LMU for the future, not extending it to paper money. The Scandinavian Monetary Union, created in 1873, had instead extended the union to paper money.

After the adoption of the gold standard by Germany and the United States in 1873, the price of gold started declining worldwide, and the LMU suspended its new silver issues to prevent speculation and to avoid receiving demonetized German silver. New rules had to be set within the monetary union to manage the exit from pure bimetallism, initially on a provisional basis (because a large part of the French establishment was still attached to the old system) and then permanently. A diminished LMU moved towards a gold standard.

The French defeat at Sedan caused the fall of the Second Empire and ended the political cooperation necessary for monetary unification. However, the internal difficulties of the LMU had already weakened the willingness to accept 'Southern', 'Balkanic', or 'Latin' members, financially weak and unstable.

4.6 The Long Persistence of the LMU after the End of its European Ambitions

In the 1880s the LMU appeared in difficulty: 'les jours de l'Union Latine sont comptés' argued Cernuschi (1884), a bimetallist pamphleteer and French delegate at some of the monetary conferences to reestablish the monetary role of silver. Bimetallists accused the LMU of preventing an international agreement for a more abundant monetary supply needed for growth. Three international monetary conferences, called by the United States in 1878, 1881 and 1892, failed to reestablish silver along with gold as the international standard (Russell 1898). The US objective was to expand the monetary base, adding silver to it, and to re-energize the world economy, hampered by the scarcity of gold, declining prices and repeated large financial crises and recessions between 1873 and 1896. Most countries were willing to agree that some form of re-monetisation of silver would be helpful, but hoped that others would take up the burden and risks of adopting a depreciated and discredited silver coinage. Each country wished to reserve for itself the precious and prestigious gold standard, considered a guarantee of the sanctity of contracts and interests of bondholders and other creditors. Fortunately the failings of cooperation between policymakers were compensated by the natural expansion of gold supply at the end of the century. The demand for gold was accommodated by large inflows of gold bullion due to discoveries in Alaska, Klondike and South Africa (Vilar 1974, 407). This eased the scarcity of gold reserves and created a moderate inflation, lightening the burden on debtors, without the need for silver money.

The LMU instead managed progressively to renegotiate and tighten its internal rules, through a series of conferences concluded with several new Monetary Conventions. Some rules were adjusted, making it an essential part of the international gold standard, but at the cost of a more limited monetary issue and of a reduced role and meaning of the Union itself. It survived despite a trade war between Italy and France in the late 1880s and diverging military alliances (France entered into an alliance with Britain; Italy instead turned to an alliance with Germany and Austria-Hungary). The French were at the time tempted to use their holdings of Italian silver écus as a weapon against Italy, but the cost of dissolution remained too high and trade advantages persisted (Chausserie-Laprée 1911).

In 1889, Italy considered its position but decided not to leave the LMU because the cost of it would be too high: it would have to redeem in gold the large amounts of its silver currency held abroad by other members of the union (the Italian economist and Finance Minister Magliani expected this operation to cost 50 million lire), and Italy would not derive much advantage from withdrawal (Willis 1901, 242). In 1893, Italy asked for the renationalization of its subsidiary coinage, buying it back from the other LMU members: it was finding it harder and harder to satisfy the needs of ordinary transactions. Trade imbalances and monetary speculation meant that only about 30 per cent of its silver divisionary coinage was in the country and the rest was abroad or lost. Greece followed the Italian example and chose to renationalize its divisionary silver coinage in 1908. Paradoxically, after 1896, the problem for Switzerland and the other northern members of the union was reversed; the departure of Italian small change coinage created a scarcity, also because economic growth was picking up. Successive arrangements were made to expand the limits of issue of divisionary silver. By 1908, the overall 1878 limit had tripled in size, from 471.5 million francs to 1.386 billion francs.

While in the LMU, Italy faced high public debt and periods of fear of contagion from other countries' sovereign defaults. After the Argentinian default of 1890, on the basis of high ratios of interest payments over tax revenues, financial analysts identified as the next possible casualties: Greece, Portugal, Italy and Brazil (Flandreau and Zumer 2004). Of those countries, only Italy avoided default during the last decade of the nineteenth century, despite its debt/GDP ratio being close to 120 per cent. Italy resisted mainly thanks to the large remittances it was receiving from Italian workers who were massively emigrating abroad at the time (De Cecco 1990). This episode shows that contagion is far from inevitable in case of default of a single country.

4.7 The End of the Latin Monetary Union

Once most of the serious discussions about the problems of the LMU stopped, its demise paradoxically became closer. The solution to the question of how to neutralize old silver stocks, as well as the temptations of inflationary paper issues, had been solved thanks to a period of high economic growth and trade expansion that benefitted all LMU countries. Per capita income increased substantially between 1898 and 1914. The LMU persisted but declined in relevance because of the growth of other forms of monetary issue (banknotes, bank deposits). Furthermore, the financialisation of the economy during that phase of globalization further marginalized metallic money. By 1914, only 5 per cent of the monetary base in Italy was in gold and silver LMU coins. Part of the outstanding stocks of silver écus was melted and quietly reminted by member states with the enlarged quotas of silver divisionary coins allocated in 1908. 'Chaque jour l'Union se liquide d'elle même' (Chausserie-Laprée 1911, p. 215) concluded an appraisal of the LMU in 1911.

In 1914, the favourable economic and monetary conditions of 1898–1914 suddenly disappeared. World War I ended the substance of intercirculation, and the whole system collapsed because it had lost much of its importance. Each country reacted to the financial shock of World War I in a different manner, without coordinating with its monetary partners and choosing different levels of monetary financing of the war effort. Switzerland remained non-belligerent. Belgium and France were drawn into the war already in 1914; the former was mostly invaded and occupied by Germany, while the latter faced war on its territory and financed the war mainly through loans and some monetary expansion. The French franc depreciated in relation to the Swiss franc and to the lira, because Italy maintained its neutrality for the first year of war. Gold convertibility was immediately suspended while military mobilization started.

Italy entered the war in 1915 and then met a faster depreciation of its currency than France did. The Greek drachma faced a meltdown despite entering the war only much later. The rules of the Union were not formally eliminated, but each country faced public and private hoarding of gold and silver coinage through uncoordinated issue of substitute emergency currency, from paper to tokens (in metal or using post stamps, issued by local authorities, chambers of commerce or banks), effectively suspending the monetary intercirculation of the Union, given that such forms of money were not accepted outside the issuing country or even outside more limited geographical areas.

When the war and immediate postwar period ended, it was time to proceed to monetary stabilization and to return to metallic convertibility (gold standard or gold exchange standard). Each LMU member state stabilized at a different level and date, according to its situation and political choices, making the pursuit of the monetary union impossible. Switzerland had kept its prewar gold convertibility without any change, deciding alone to leave the Union early in 1920. The others waited longer. In Italy, Mussolini had opted in 1926 for 'quota 90,' an exchange rate of 90 lire per pound (before the war it was 25.22 lire per pound). This policy choice required a re-valuation of the lira in comparison to its market exchange rate. Belgium re-valued its currency even more, at 34.85 Belgian francs to the pound. France chose instead to support economic activity and employment with a depreciated currency and stabilized in 1928 at a much lower rate, 125 francs to the pound (Ministero delle finanze 1927). The desire to exit the franc zone in favour of the dollar also counted in the Italian decision to end the monetary 'sympathy' between French, Italian and Belgian exchange rates, which had continued in the early 1920s despite all the swings and crises of the period.

The LMU was formally disbanded at the end of 1926 with an exchange of diplomatic communications, which simply acknowledged a fait accompli, a divergence in the face of a major economic trauma which caused a wide divergence in economic conditions and a choice in favour of national priorities. By then the liquidation did not cause significant costs.

4.8 Conclusion: EMU and LMU

The LMU experience suggests that rules can be changed and monetary unions can be more resilient than many think, but that difficulties persist through time between countries with different levels of economic and financial strength. A monetary union seems to be a never-ending construction site of reforms in order to create effective

mechanisms of governance, fill gaps, add rules and negotiate institutional expansion (a truly unified monetary system, a unified central
bank system, unified banking supervision and regulation). The LMU
used a series of additional monetary conventions and agreements
between 1874 and 1893 to tighten the rules, and then member states
sought more autonomy within the Union, thanks to forms of monetary issue outside the limitations of the LMU. Despite having closed
the monetary gaps of LMU, today the EMU is adding new elements
to tighten rules on deficits, debt and inflation, together with controls
and sanctions, starting under the name of Stability pact (1997),
continuing with its first reform to weaken it (2005) and then
reinforce it after the discovery of Greek fraud in 2009, through a
series of measures between 2010 and 2013 ('European semester',
'Euro Plus pact', 'SixPack') (for the history of European Monetary
Union, see James 2012). LMU has also entered a phase of new
creative mechanisms to enlarge monetary supply in new, creative
and unconventional manners (quantitative easing) in order to escape
the deflationary effects of rules applied in an excessively rigid
manner.

The efforts to prevent the spillover of budgetary and inflationary
problems from one country to the other, by imposing tight monetary
and fiscal rules can become counterproductive. Continuous tightening
of rules ends up producing excessively narrow rules that damage
economic growth and can destabilize the economic and financial
system in the opposite direction, provoking deflation. The LMU
struggled to block excessive silver issue in the 1860s and 1870s,
resenting its inflationary and distributional effects, but then found itself
with excessively restrictive monetary policy.The gold standard in the
1880s and 1890s caused deflation. International cooperation to
increase monetary supply by distributing the cost between all the main
actors failed. Only the chance of new gold discoveries on a global scale
at the turn of the nineteenth and twentieth centuries eased the supply of
gold and made the gold standard a sufficiently expansionary monetary
system. The problem reappeared after World War I, to be solved only
with the adoption of fiat currencies after the disasters of the Great
Depression. It is not necessary, however, to have a monetary system
based on gold to run the risk of focusing on excessively tight fiscal and
monetary policies.

Forms of flexibility remain essential to prevent monetary union from exploding. The incompleteness of LMU's monetary arrangement paradoxically afforded its weakest members to resort to periods of holiday from the rules through temporary devaluations. No such possibility exists today, so that flexibility from the effects of prolonged austerity on the internal demand requires an accommodating monetary policy (including ultralow interest rates, European Central Bank's Securities Markets Program and the Long Term Refinancing Operation). More flexibility on fiscal rules would also be necessary, instead of the rigidity of the mandated cyclically adjusted balanced budget and the reduction of debt to GDP ratio at the mandated rate of 1/20 of the amount exceeding 60 per cent of GDP. Economic growth must be one of the main targets of both economic and monetary policy, because declining per capita incomes corrode the fabric of European societies and threaten the credibility of whole European construction towards its citizens.

The weight of readjustment of disequilibria must not be left entirely to deficit countries, but must be shared at least in part by surplus countries whose prosperity is also due to such disequilibria. Keynes had tried in vain to press this point during the negotiations for the creation of an international financial order at the end of World War II. Adjustment by countries with low economic growth is much more difficult if Germany refuses to adopt a more expansionary stance internally. Wage competition with very low inflation leads to deflation. Austerity and slow growth end up increasing further the real burden of government debt.

Without the possibility of devaluation, the issue of competitiveness within a monetary union persists, and more expansionary policies are needed in surplus countries in order not to force a readjustment on productivity, unemployment and wages.

Despite all these difficulties, abandoning the monetary union is not an easy solution for weaker countries. Italy has shifted between fixed and flexible exchange rate fifteen times in the last 160 years, before, during and after the LMU, yet it has achieved a higher average GDP growth under fixed exchange regimes than under flexible ones (2.8 per cent versus 1.6 per cent). Once in a monetary union, the disadvantages of leaving it can be sufficiently strong to extend membership in the long term, no matter the cost.

Table 4.1 *A comparison of LMU and EMU*

	LMU	EMU
Period	1865–1926	1999–ongoing
Initial members	France, Italy, Belgium, Switzerland	Eleven countries
Enlargements	Greece (1868), several other candidates were rejected (Spain, Austria-Hungary, Romania, Bulgaria, Serbia, Finland, the Papal State)	Greece, Slovenia, Slovakia, Malta, Cyprus, Estonia, Latvia
Currency	Multiple gold and silver currencies with 1-to-1 exchange rate and bimetallism	Single currency, the Euro, fiat money
Incomplete institutions	Lacked common central bank (informal central role of the Bank of France), monetary control over paper money and copper coinage	Lacked crisis lender to governments, fiscal and banking union, common banking supervision and regulation, adequate growth policies
Renegotiation process	Unanimity to achieve new monetary conventions, but strongest governments (France and Switzerland) forced partial rule changes	Strongest governments (Germany, the Netherlands, Finland) force rules and policy changes in exchange for financial support
Sovereign default or restructuring	Greece (1893), not followed by other LMU members	Greece (2012)
Feared costs of dissolution of the monetary union	Disruption of trade, liquidation of silver coinage at a loss for governments	Disruption of trade and finance, devaluations, sovereign debt risks, divergence in interest rates

References

Cernuschi, H. (1884) *Le grand procès de l'Union Latine*, Paris: Guillaumin.

Chausserie-Laprée, P. (1911) *L'Union Monétaire Latine, son passé, sa situation actuelle, ses chances d'avenir, et sa liquidation éventuelle*, Paris: Rousseau éditeur.

De Cecco, M. (1990) *L'Italia e il sistema finanziario internazionale 1861–1914*, Bari: Laterza.

Einaudi, L. (2000) 'From the Franc to the "Europe": Great Britain, Germany and the Attempted Transformation of the Latin Monetary Union into a European Monetary Union (1865–73)', *The Economic History Review*, 53.2 (May), pp. 284–308.

Einaudi, L. (2001) *Money and Politics: European Monetary Unification and the International Gold Standard (1865–1873)*, Oxford: Oxford University Press.

Flandreau, M. and Zumer, F. (2004) *Les origines de la mondialisation financière, 1880–1913*, Paris: Etudes du Centre de Développement OCDE.

James, H. (2012) *Making the European Monetary Union*, Cambridge, MA: Belknap Press of Harvard University Press.

Levandis, J. A. (1944) *The Greek Foreign Debt and the Great Powers 1821–98*, New York: Columbia University Press.

Ministero delle finanze (1927) *Le esperienze monetarie prima e dopo la guerra, vol.II, La tecnica delle stabilizzazioni*, Rome: Provveditorato generale dello Stato.

Parieu, F. E. de (1870) *Principes de la science politique*, Paris: Sauton Libraire Editeur.

Russell, H. B. (1898) *International Monetary Conferences*, New York: Harper & Brothers Publishers.

Vilar, P. (1974) *Or et monnaie dans l'histoire*, Paris: Flammarion.

Willis, H. P. (1901) *A History of the Latin Monetary Union, A Study of International Monetary Action*, Chicago: Chicago University Press.

5 | Conditionality, Fiscal Rules and International Financial Control in the European Periphery before 1914

ALI COŞKUN TUNÇER

5.1 Introduction

Following the recent European sovereign debt crisis, introducing and enforcing effective fiscal rules have increasingly been put forward as a remedy for ensuring fiscal discipline among the members of the Eurozone. The implications of different policy instruments, especially in regards to political feasibility and credibility, have been extensively debated amongst the economists and policymakers. Strict policy conditionality, mostly in the form of adopting a credible austerity package, has been put forward as a major requirement for financial assistance through European Stability Mechanism and Economic Adjustment Programme. At the extreme end, several proposals include establishment of independent fiscal agencies or fiscal councils in debtor states as a solution to the deficit bias of Eurozone countries (Castellani and Debrun, 2005; Grauwe, 2011; Hagemann, 2011; Kaplanoglou and Rapanos, 2013; Featherstone, 2015; Ioannidis, 2015).

This chapter explores how European financial markets dealt with similar problems and solutions in the past, and discusses the functioning and evolution of lending conditionality and fiscal rules during 1870–1914, when global capital flows were at their peak. One of the consequences of the global expansion of capital markets during this period was the rapid increase in sovereign from surplus to deficit countries, which eventually led to defaults on foreign obligations in many debtor states (Suter, 1990).[1] As a response to defaults, foreign bondholders and their respective governments adopted several coercive tools, which included seizing the assets of debtor countries through military intervention, imposing trade restrictions and preventing access

---

[1] Including Tunisia (1868), Ottoman Empire (1876), Egypt (1876), Spain (1877), Argentina (1890), Portugal (1892), Greece (1893), Serbia (1895) and Brazil (1898).

to future credit. More refined solutions sought to reduce default risk through issue of loans, which were contracted on strict conditions. These different enforcement mechanisms, repayment incentives and lending strategies constituted the pillars of global governing of sovereign debt before 1914.

The focus of this essay is on the effectiveness of lending conditionality via international financial control (IFC), which was introduced following defaults in a number of heavily indebted countries in the European periphery from 1860s to the World War I. IFC meant a partial or full loss of fiscal sovereignty for debtor countries, as it would assume the right of administering certain revenues of defaulting states on behalf of creditors. The first known example was established in Tunisia in 1869. Several others in the region, including Egypt, the Ottoman Empire, Serbia, Greece and Bulgaria, followed suit.[2] In the case of Egypt, the establishment of IFC led to a direct takeover of the state finances and complete loss of political sovereignty, whereas in the Ottoman Empire, IFC took charge of several revenue sources and administered them on behalf of foreign creditors. These more direct methods of control that emerged during 1875–76 had some key differences from the later episode of IFC, which appeared in Serbia and Greece during 1895–98. In these two cases the administrative structure of IFC became more refined, the extent of its control was more limited, and it mainly focused on measures concerning fiscal and monetary discipline. Having been administered by the representatives of foreign creditors and their respective governments, these multilateral enforcement bodies introduced a different set of fiscal and monetary rules in each country in return for reinstating credibility and restoring access to the international financial markets.

In this context, the chapter is structured as follows. In the next section, I document the evolution of IFC in the European periphery and present the most prominent cases in the region: Ottoman Empire, Egypt, Greece and Serbia. Section 5.3 provides comparative evidence on the performance of IFC in administering the revenues of debtor states, and its impact on the credibility of the defaulting sovereigns. Section 5.4 elaborates on the issue of 'ownership' of policy advice in

[2] For a comparative history of sovereign debt and international financial control in the Ottoman Empire, Egypt, Greece, and Serbia, see Tunçer (2015). For Bulgaria, see Avramov (2003) and Tooze and Ivanov (2011). For Tunisia, see Zourai (1998).

pre-1914 context. I suggest that political resistance to IFC and its operations can be interpreted as a sign of lack of ownership, and I explore the relationship between political regime types of debtor governments and lack of ownership in search of some explanations. In conclusion, I highlight that the success of lending conditionality in the form of IFC was mainly determined by the willingness and ability of the debtor governments to comply with the advice of their foreign creditors. I conclude that this cooperative attitude with foreign advice and control was mainly driven by the absence of political representation of taxpayers.

5.2 Conditionality and International Financial Control before 1914: A Review

Sovereign debt contracts are unique as they are concluded between parties that do not enjoy the same degree of legal immunity. Despite the lack of legal enforcement by a third party in the case of a default, debtor countries still repay their debts because of the costs of default, which are positively correlated with the ability of creditors to impose effective sanctions (Bulow and Rogoff, 1988; Kelly, 1998). Historically, in the context of the pre-1914 sovereign debt market, creditors employed a combination of direct and indirect forms of enforcement ranging from military interventions to preventing access to future credit.[3] Creditors also sought ways to strengthen the terms of sovereign debt contracts to claim their debts on legal grounds. Arbitration, renegotiation, sinking fund and collective action clauses were incorporated into agreements in order to reduce the risk of default and create incentives for repayment (Wynne, 1951; Choi, Gulati and Posner, 2012: 140–148). Moreover, bondholder protective organisations, such as British Corporation of Foreign Bondholders (1868), were established to provide market-based solutions to the debt renegotiations and collective action of bondholders (Mauro and Yafeh, 2003;

---

[3] For the use of military intervention until the Second Hague conference in 1907, see Adams (1890), Borchard (1925: 314) and Finnemore (2003). For trade sanctions, see Rose (2005). For preventing access to future credit, see Eaton and Gersovitz (1981), Bulow and Rogoff (1989) and Panizza, Sturzenegger and Zettelmeyer (2009). For a general discussion on sanctions and costs of default, see Borchard (1951), Kaletsky (1985), Mitchener and Weidenmier (2010) and Waibel (2011).

Esteves, 2013).[4] Although the term 'conditionality' has frequently been used in the context of IMF lending, it can be interpreted as yet another mechanism to reduce the risk of future default, since it implies that if a country takes certain specified actions, continued financing will be provided (Drazen, 2002; Dreher, 2009; James, 2003). In this broad sense of the term, IFC or foreign control over the revenues of the defaulting states was a direct form of conditionality as it increased the likelihood of future repayment of debts for creditors, and it implied a set of conditions for borrower countries to access international financial markets in the long term.

IFC in the European periphery was organised as revenue-collecting agents because of a particular feature of sovereign debt contracts. In pre-1914 sovereign debt market, most of the bond issues of peripheral countries were implemented on the basis of a security, which could be placed beyond the reach of the borrowing country and be used only for the service of the relevant loan. These pledges could be very general and suggest that the bond repayment was secured 'upon the entire revenue and assets and domains of the borrower', or they could be as specific as particular real estates of a sovereign or some other tangible assets (Wynne, 1951: 82). More frequently, bonds before 1914 were secured with *future revenues* from certain resources of the borrower sovereign. Depositing assets or assigning securities meant that, in theory, in the case of a default it would be relatively easy to seize these assets or demand hypothecated revenues in order to compensate the loss of creditors.

These future revenues could come from governmental monopolies or other public services, commercial enterprises such as mines, or other future tax revenues. In majority of cases, indirect taxes and custom revenues from specified ports or products of the borrower were the most popular choice, as they constituted a stable source of revenue (Hyde, 1922: 534–35; Wynne, 1951: 82–91). Although most of these pledges were quite valuable, creditors were aware that securing future revenues for the payment of a loan did not mean that sovereign borrower would in fact utilize them for this purpose or manage them in a way that would prove beneficial to the lender. In order to address

---

[4] More recent contributions point out that CFB's significance in the pre-1914 sovereign debt is overrated; instead it was the leading investment banks and intermediaries who would give the right signals to the creditors (Flandreau and Flores, 2009; Flandreau, 2013).

this problem, in certain cases lending would be linked to the condition of establishing 'creditor committees', which were responsible for monitoring how the funds would be spent. An earlier example of this was the guaranteed Ottoman loan of 1855, which was granted by the Great Powers to support the Ottoman Empire against Russia during the Crimean War of 1854. One condition of the guarantee was to use the proceeds entirely for war purposes, and British and French representatives were assigned to monitor the spending of funds. The role of these commissioners, who were sent to Istanbul despite the opposition of the Ottoman government, was to verify the treasury accounts and ensure the funds were in fact spent in support of the army. A problem with these types of arrangements was the lack of enforcement if the debtor state did not comply with the lending conditions. In fact, in this specific example, due to the opposition of the Ottoman government to the arrangement, the work of the foreign commission started only in January 1856, after several army contracts had already been signed in order to evade its control. By September 1856, all funds were spent and the commission finished its work.[5] Similar problems emerged especially in the case of a default, as there was no automatic mechanism to transfer the hypothecated revenues of defaulted governments to the creditors. As early as the 1860s, well before any of the defaults took place in the European periphery, in an article published in the *Economist*, contemporary observers highlighted the potential limitations of the existing system of sovereign lending on the basis of guarantees:

Loans made on specific securities to a foreign state are never the most satisfactory sort of loans and this for a single plain reason: the property which is pledged is almost wholly under the control of the indebted state, and if that state is inclined to repudiate, there is a necessary difficulty in getting at the security. Such is especially the case if the security consists, as is ordinarily the case, of a certain part of the state revenue. First it depends on the state itself whether that revenue is ever collected; and secondly, it depends on the state itself whether that revenue shall be paid to creditor ... It is quite true that the creditors may apply to their own government for protection. If the English, for example, lend their money to Turkey upon certain specific securities, they may apply more or less successfully to their own government

---

[5] For a detailed discussion of pre-1914 guaranteed bonds including the Ottoman loan of 1855, see Esteves and Tunçer (2016a, 2016b).

to obtain for them the annual income of those securities. But if the government consent to give its aid, the probably result will be a political complication of which no one can foresee the end: and this is the best event, for if the government decline to aid by force the claims of its subject, we may be sure they will receive nothing from their repudiating debtor.[6]

This article, written in fact with reference to a new bond issue of the Ottoman Empire, predicted almost exactly the sequence of potential pitfalls when the bonds were secured with specific revenues. To put it in other words, the pledged revenue could become a security in the hands of creditors if it could indeed be removed from the defaulting sovereign and transferred to the creditors. However, in practice this was not possible due to the nature of these revenue sources. Therefore, the proposed solution was to use an organisation independent from the defaulting sovereign to administer and control the pledged revenues on behalf of bondholders, and to transfer the receipts from these sources to all creditors for the unpaid debt (Hyde, 1922: 535; Borchard 1951: 91). I name these ad hoc foreign revenue administration agents, which appeared in Egypt (1876), the Ottoman Empire (1881), Serbia (1895) and Greece (1898), collectively as IFC.

The historical literature on IFC is limited to a few documentary studies published by contemporaries to outline their major functions and administrative structure (Deville, 1912; Andreades, 1925; Borchard, 1951; Wynne, 1951). One line of literature treats IFC on legal grounds and discusses them in the context of international law (Borchard, 1951: 93; Waibel, 2011: 42). Recent contributions in economic history literature argue that IFC was a form of 'supersanction' which helped to enforce sovereign debt contracts, and that they were effective tools to reduce the cost of borrowing for the defaulting countries (Mitchener and Weidenmier, 2010). As opposed to economic and legal literature on the IFC, historiographies of the defaulting countries usually approach them in the context of imperialism debate, since a direct consequence of foreign control was the partial loss of fiscal and/or political sovereignty of the debtor states. In this view, foreign control of government revenues is seen as an extension of imperialist rivalry over the Middle East and the Balkans before 1914 (Crouchley, 1938; Levandis, 1944; Blaisdell, 1966; Zourai, 1998).

---

[6] 'The New Turkish Loan', *Economist* [London, England], 22 December 1860: 1417.

In this essay, I focus on the mechanism through which IFC functioned and reinforced the credibility of the defaulting sovereigns in comparative perspective. Unlike previous lines of research, I avoid labelling and discussing IFC as 'sanctions', or 'punishment', or direct instruments of imperialism. Instead, I highlight the fiscal dimension of IFC as revenue-collecting foreign agents and the lending conditionality it implied. In order to provide the historical context to the discussion, the next section focuses on the mechanism through which IFC operated in the region and the particular characteristics of each case. I then elaborate on the questions of ownership and success record of IFC.

5.3 Evolution of International Financial Control in the European Periphery

For the period 1870–1913, it is possible to identify two distinct waves of sovereign defaults taking place during 1875–1882 and 1890–1900. Response to these defaults not only varied from case to case, but there were also differences between the two episodes due to the evolution of institutions governing international sovereign debt market and more particularly of IFC. As mentioned briefly in the introduction, the earlier period witnessed more direct forms of IFC, whereby the creditors got more extensively involved in the financial affairs of defaulting countries. After 1890, the involvement of IFC into financial affairs remained relatively limited and supervisory. In the following subsections I first focus on the initial era of IFC, namely political and fiscal control in Egypt and the Ottoman Empire, respectively. I then turn my attention to the experience of Serbia and Greece, which was characterized by lesser degrees of infringement into the sovereignty of debtor states.

5.3.1 From Military Takeover to Fiscal Control: Egypt and the Ottoman Empire

The first IFC in the European periphery during the 1870–1914 period appeared in Egypt in 1875. Despite being a semi-autonomous country, Egypt was de jure part of the Ottoman Empire until 1914 and ruled by hereditary pashas called the Khedives. In 1862, for the first time in Egypt's history, the Khedive negotiated a state loan with the permission of the Ottoman Sultan. This loan was followed by several others, and during the 1862–75 period the Egyptian government issued ten

Table 5.1 *Summary of foreign loans, 1854–1913*

	Number of foreign loans contracted	Total nominal value of foreign loans (m£)	Debt per capita (£)	Average effective interest rate (%)	Average yield (%)
BEFORE IFC					
Egypt	9	69	7.2	8.5	8
Ottoman Empire	18	219	8.9	8.6	8.6
Serbia	17	16	6.2	6.7	6.2
Greece	9	26	6.5	6.3	7.1
AFTER IFC					
Egypt	10	55	7.5	4.5	5.4
Ottoman Empire	23	90	6.2	4.7	4.7
Serbia	7	25	9.1	5.1	5.4
Greece	8	29	7.8	5	10.7

Source: Tunçer (2015). *Notes:* The periods before IFC are 1862–76 for Egypt, 1854–76 for the Ottoman Empire, 1879–1893 for Greece and 1881–94 for Serbia. The period after IFC is 1881–1913 for the Ottoman Empire, 1876–1913 for Egypt, 1898–1913 for Greece and 1895–1913 for Serbia. To eliminate double counting I only account for new issues and exclude bond conversions. Population estimates are from Maddison averages of same periods. Bond yields are average values before and after IFC, starting with the first date of borrowing, excluding episodes of defaults and ending in December 1913.

bonds with the support of several British and French banking houses (see Table 5.1). The main lending conditionality for these bonds was the requirement to assign some of the tax revenues to the repayment of these loans. These included the land taxes of the several provinces, general revenues of the Egyptian state and personal estates of the Khedive. Taken together, the overall guarantees corresponded to almost the entire revenues of the Egyptian government in 1875, hence it was not possible to contract further loans in international markets with a similar guarantee (Wynne, 1951: 582; Crouchley, 1938: 122; Tunçer, 2015: 29–34).

Meanwhile, the default of the Ottoman Empire in late 1875 had a direct impact on Egyptian credit abroad; it was no longer possible to obtain new loans from the international financial markets, and in April 1876, the payment of Egypt's treasury bonds was suspended. This failure led to the foundation of IFC under the official name of *Caisse de la Dette Publique Égyptienne* on 2 May 1876. Directed by foreign commissioners nominated by their respective governments the *Caisse* was authorized to receive the revenues intended to service the debt directly from the local authorities. Taxes from several Egyptian provinces, the salt and tobacco taxes along with custom revenues, which corresponded to almost three-quarters of total government revenues in 1876, were assigned to the *Caisse*. The Egyptian government committed itself not to modify these revenues or to contract any new loans without the consent of the *Caisse*. In November 1876, in addition to the *Caisse*, a special administration of the railways and of the port of Alexandria was established and placed under the direct control of a commission of foreign creditors. Moreover, two controllers-general (one British and one French) would be appointed, who would supervise the entire fiscal administration of the country, one mainly responsible for expenditures and the other for revenues. The budget was still to be framed by the Khedive and his ministers, though with the assistance of controllers-general. Finally, a special administration of Khedive's personal lands would also be placed under a separate international control.

The political consequence of all these new regulations was the exclusion of the Khedive from the administration of Egyptian finances and transition from the personal government of the Khedive to a government by an executive council whose leading members were foreigners. This radical change first led to the burst of violent riots that later gained an anti-European character. It eventually resulted in military intervention of Britain in 1882. Within a few months after the British took charge, the Anglo-French dual control was abolished. The British Consul-General was given authority over all the English advisors that were placed in the Egyptian ministries. However, the British consuls did not have the power to modify the previous agreement with the bondholders. French government and bondholder representatives refused to permit any reduction in the authority of the *Caisse*. Moreover, the separate administrations of railways and estates of the Khedive, on all of which France was represented, were maintained (Wynne, 1951: 621–22).

From 1885 onwards, Egyptian finances started to improve, and by 1890 the budget yielded a surplus. In the meantime, the *Caisse* kept servicing the debt and accumulating extensive amount of reserve funds and refused the give authorisation to the Egyptian government to use any balance for the purposes of additional expenditure. The commissioners were content to maintain the *Caisse* as an agent managing the servicing of the debt; however, its extensive privileges had started to become too restrictive. This led to a new agreement between Britain and France in April 1904, the *Entente Cordiale*, which introduced a change in the constitution of the *Caisse*. After the agreement, the Egyptian government obtained full control of the reserve funds, leaving the *Caisse* a small reserve plus a working balance. The rigid model of balance was abandoned and the Egyptian government regained more control over fiscal matters. In theory, the *Caisse* still possessed considerable powers of control, retaining its position in Egypt until the complete repayment of the debt. However, its functions were now limited to receiving certain assigned revenues on behalf of the bondholders and ensuring the payments due (Crouchley, 1938: 169–79; Feis, 1974: 393; Tunçer, 2015: 48–52). The *Caisse*'s emergence out of a combination of political, economic and legal factors meant a direct form of conditionality, as it transferred the entire fiscal policymaking into the hands of foreign creditors in return for future access to international financial markets.

A similar process led to a different form of IFC in the Ottoman Empire, which faced default almost at the same time as Egypt did. Starting with the Crimean War in 1854, issuing bonds in international markets became the most important way of dealing with budgetary difficulties for the Ottoman Empire. From 1854 to 1876, the Ottoman government contracted eighteen loans with a total face value of £219 million. In general, these loans had similar lending conditionality arrangements and were secured by a wide range of direct and indirect tax revenues, custom duties and Egyptian tribute. Financial markets were aware of the unsustainability of this rapid increase in debt, especially after the crisis of 1873 when overseas lending came to an end and it became almost impossible for the Ottoman government to contract a new loan. In October 1875, the Ottoman government first suspended part of the interest payments, and in January 1876 defaulted on all of its outstanding debt, which then stood at around £191 million (Pamuk, 1978; Kiray, 1988; Eldem, 2005). This was a 'long-predicted catastrophe',[7] but what made it exceptional was the scale of it, as it was the biggest sovereign default to date.[8]

European press referred the event as 'financial barbarism',[9] which also meant that the international financial markets were closed to the Ottoman Empire after 1876 until the government and bondholders could reach a reasonable deal. The successful settlement of the debt would not be achieved until 1881. According to the agreement, the outstanding debt of the empire was reduced from about £191 million to £96 million, and unpaid interest payments, which amounted £62 million, were reduced to approximately £10 million. In return, the Council of the Administration for the Ottoman Public Debt (thereafter the Council) was established to represent the bondholders and act in their interest. The government agreed to transfer the revenues from the tobacco and salt monopolies, several custom duties and the silk tithe of several provinces to the foreign creditors, who would have complete freedom to decide on the way of collection and production (Tunçer, 2015: 58–63).

Starting from 1883, the Council established more than twenty offices in the various provinces of the Empire extending from Yemen to Salonika, which were administered from the central office in Istanbul. This was an extensive tax collection network employing around 4,500–5,000 officers (including inspectors, collectors, security guards etc.). The lessons derived from the Egyptian experience, and the fear of resistance from the local population, made the representatives of the bondholders choose the gradual method of replacing the existing local staff, introducing new techniques of production and reforming the existing collection system for the ceded revenues. One of the biggest obstacles the Council faced during this period was the widespread 'armed banditry' and opposition to the administration of foreign creditors. However, the opposition to the presence of the Council remained limited to popular resistance, since there were no conflicts between the Ottoman government and the Council (Quataert, 1983; Tunçer, 2015: 64–76).

---

[7] 'The Turkish Repudiation', *Economist* [London, England] 9 Oct. 1875: 1190.
[8] The other two significant cases were Spain, which defaulted on an outstanding debt of £170 million, and Egypt on around £100 million as discussed earlier (Suter, 1990: 67–69).
[9] 'The Turkish Default', *Economist* [London, England] 6 Nov. 1875: 1310.

Despite the popular armed resistance to the Council, it turned out to work efficiently in its management of the resources for which it was responsible. The revenues from both direct contributions (silk, salt, spirits, stamps and fisheries) and *Tobacco Régie* increased significantly. In fact, after 1889, the Ottoman government decided to extend the rights of the Council to collect revenues for its own account. According to the agreement, the Council would be responsible of collecting the revenues especially for those loans concerning the railways, together with tithes of several provinces. The Council, after collecting and reducing the collection expenses, would transfer the entire net revenue to the government. Therefore, the expenses of administration and collection of these revenues were borne by the revenues themselves, and did not fall upon the revenues ceded to the bondholders. From the perspective of the Ottoman Empire this arrangement was preferable for two reasons. First, it showed the government's willingness to do everything in its power to reinstate its credibility in the eyes of the creditors. Second, it reflected the fact that creditors have proven to be more successful at collecting and administering the revenues than the Empire's own agents. The creditors, on the other hand, saw the transfer of fiscal sovereignty as a sign of trust between them and the government, which in return secured the position of the Council in the overall fiscal system of the Empire (Tunçer, 2015: 64–78).

This brief historical presentation of sovereign debt in Egypt and the Ottoman Empire highlights some important aspects of pre-1914 lending conditionality. In both cases, international political considerations played an important role in the way IFC was established and organised. However, the legal justification of such control was based on the lending conditionality clauses included into the bond contracts – that is, hypothecation of future revenues to the repayment of bonds. Once in operation, IFC transformed into direct form of conditionality as it secured access of Egypt and the Ottoman Empire to international financial markets by imposing a set of changes in fiscal policy. In Egypt, although IFC was originally planned to play a similar role as in the Ottoman Empire, it eventually became a prelude to the British military takeover and it was reinforced by other means of political and economic control. The Egyptian government did not have any choice but to 'cooperate', hence the weight of the *Caisse* in overall tax collection remained significant until 1904. The IFC in the Ottoman Empire, on the contrary, operated without the intermediation of the political representatives of the creditor states involved, hence its success would still depend on the 'ownership' of the Ottoman government. Bond-holder representatives, having autonomy on the way they managed hypothecated revenues, implemented both short- and long-term solutions in an attempt to compensate for their losses and to increase the ceded revenues, and eventually started managing revenues on behalf of the Ottoman government as well.

5.3.2 From Fiscal Control to Financial Supervision: Serbia and Greece

IFC established in 1875–76 in Egypt and the Ottoman Empire was economically and politically costly for creditors and their respective governments, since such an infringement upon the sovereignty resulted in popular armed resistance in both cases. Therefore, when the new wave of sovereign debt crisis hit the small Balkan economies during 1890s, creditors and their respective governments were aware of the need to introduce more indirect and less costly forms of managing and transferring revenues.

Although IFC came into existence in Serbia three years earlier than Greece in 1895, the history of Serbia's sovereign debt did not begin until it was recognised as an independent state at the Berlin Congress of 1878.[10] From its independence to 1893, the Serbian government contracted seventeen loans in the financial markets of London, Paris and Vienna with a face value of around £16 million and an average effective interest rate of 6.7 per cent (see Table 5.1). The repayments of these loans were secured on future revenues of the state, including import duties, revenues from railways, land taxes of several provinces and monopolies of tobacco and salt. However, these loans were not enough to meet increasing state expenditures driven mostly by railway building, debt service and military spending.

By 1893, the outstanding debt of the country had reached around £13 million and the annual charges on the debt stock were consuming more than one-third of state revenues. In the meantime, with the default of Greece in the same year, there were further increasing

---

[10] The only exceptions to this were the loans granted in support of independence wars against the Ottoman Empire during the 1860s and 1870s with the help of Russia (Feis, 1974: 262; Gnjatovic, 2009: 5; Hinic et al., 2014; Sundhaussen, 1989: 500).

concerns regarding the financial condition of Serbia. In late 1894, the Serbian monarch Milan started lobbying for a financial arrangement. A loan contract was signed on December 26, 1894, payments of which were secured by the state monopolies of petroleum, cigarette paper, matches, salt and overall revenues. The proposed scheme also envisaged the establishment of a special administration consisting of four delegates – two nominated by the Serbian government and two by contracting banks – to collect and administer the receipts from monopolies on a monthly basis. The Serbian National Assembly rejected this scheme, as the arrangement was seen as very similar to what was offered to Greece at the time and implied a loss of financial control and an empowerment of a foreign financial group to supervise the conversion of foreign debt.

The decision to reject a debt conversion meant that by mid-1895 the government was unable to meet the amount due in interest and principal on the floating debt. In June 1895, negotiations to discuss a solution started between the syndicate of underwriting banks from London, Paris, Vienna and Berlin, the Russian government and the Serbian officials in a conference at Karlsbad. Eventually a new loan with a face value of around £14 millions at 4 per cent interest rate was agreed upon to convert the outstanding debt. This was secured on the net profits of certain railways, stamp duty, customs duties, profits from the salt monopoly and the revenue from the monopoly on mineral oils, matches and cigarette paper. More importantly, the Autonomous Administration of Monopolies at Belgrade (hereafter the Administration) would control these revenues for the purposes of servicing the debt (Tunçer, 2015: 79–99).

The managing council of the Administration was appointed by a royal decree from the Ministry of Finance, but the freedom of action of the Serbian government was still limited: two out of six members were representatives of the foreign creditors. Other members included the governor and the vice-governor of the National Bank of Serbia and two Serbian nationals appointed with the recommendation of the Administration. Overall, from 1895 to 1913, the Serbian government managed to contract a new series of loans with a face value of £39 million and an average effective interest rate of 5 per cent (see Table 5.1). Despite the initial discontent, once in operation, the government and the Administration worked more or less in harmony, and the net yield of the monopolies and other pledged revenues steadily grew to an extent that it not only covered the interest payments on the outstanding debt but also yielded a surplus. Although the Administration remained autonomous, it was bound by the technical and legal decision of the Ministry of Finance; therefore, it did not enjoy the greater flexibility and freedom of the Ottoman Council or the Egyptian *Caisse* (Lampe and Jackson, 1982: 156–95; Tunçer, 2015: 79–99).

Unlike Serbia, the history of sovereign debt in Greece can be traced back to 1820s when Greece contracted three loans amounting to £6.8 million to finance its independence war against the Ottoman Empire. These issues were secured with the future tax revenues of the Greek state, including custom duties, the salt mines and fisheries and ultimately all public revenues. However, it was not easy to raise tax revenues in the newly founded state, and in 1843 the Greek government defaulted on all three loans (Wynne, 1951: 283–87; Kofas, 1981). That year marked the beginning of a long isolation from international financial markets. Despite repeated attempts of bondholder representatives, it was not until the 1860s that the parties formally began discussing proposals for a settlement, and a mutually satisfactory agreement had not been reached until September 1878.

From 1879 to 1893, the Greek government contracted nine loans with a face value of approximately £25 million and an average effective interest rate of 6.7 per cent. Similar to other cases, payments of these bonds were secured through the special assignment of revenues. Among the loans contracted during this period, the Monopoly Loan of 1887 had a special place because it came with a particular lending conditionality, which later became the foundation on which the IFC was built. According to the agreement, besides the hypothecation of monopoly revenues, the creditors were given the right to establish a Monopoly Society (*Société de Régie des Revenues de Gréce*). This company was put under the control of the Greek government and granted the right to administer, collect and supervise the assigned revenues. The company was subject to Greek laws and was to be terminated upon the settlement of the loan. At the same time, the government was required to make up the difference from the treasury if the proceeds of the assigned monopolies were insufficient to meet the annual charges of the loan. In return for these concessions, the Greek government managed to contract the largest loan with the lowest effective interest rate in this period. However, the Monopoly Loan was not enough to stop the deterioration of the Greek finances.

In 1893, because of worsening economic conditions, the government defaulted on its foreign obligations. Moreover, the revenues, which were under the administration of the Monopoly Society, were handed directly to the public treasury, thus violating the earlier agreement with the creditors (Levandis, 1944: 55–69; Lazaretou, 2005).

From the outset, one of the main concerns of the bondholders was the Greek government's unilateral modification of the Monopoly Society's rights, and the earlier agreement on the way in which these hypothecated revenues were collected. The revenues specially assigned as guarantees for the service of different loans consisted of the customs receipts from several major ports, tobacco tax, stamp dues, receipts of the monopolies of salt, petroleum, playing cards, matches, cigarette paper and emery and the revenues of several railways. The committee was keen to combine these revenues to create a surplus for the servicing of the debt. Furthermore, unlike other cases of sovereign debt settlement, creditors were concerned about the state of the money market, in particular the instability of the exchange rates and excessive amount of notes in circulation. As the Greek government opposed to several proposals of creditors and demanded significant reduction in the outstanding debt, the negotiations almost came to a dead end. Meanwhile, in 1897, Greece found herself in conflict with the Ottoman Empire over the Cretan Question, which led to the Greek-Turkish War of 1897 and the defeat of Greece. According to the peace terms, determined through the mediation of six powers (Austria-Hungary, France, Germany, Great Britain, Italy and Russia), Greece was to pay a war indemnity, which made the financial position of the country even worse. Under these circumstances, Greece no longer had any bargaining power with its creditors.

In 1898, the Greek government agreed to sign the Law of Control with the representatives of foreign powers. IFC was to be operated by a commission established in Athens and composed of diplomatic representatives of the mediating powers. The gross proceeds of the monopolies (salt, petroleum, matches, playing cards and cigarette paper), tobacco, stamp and import dues collected by the customs house of Piraeus were assigned to service the debt. Finally, the collection of these revenues was placed in the hands of the Society registered in Greece, which would be under the absolute control of the Commission. Immediately after the delegation of the Commission, the representatives of the powers started to investigate ways to improve and extract the highest sum from the revenues under their control. Therefore, in order to introduce a change in the production methods, the Commission could ask the government to modify the relevant laws and regulations regarding certain revenues, but did not enjoy the same right of direct management of revenues as in Egypt, the Ottoman Empire and Serbia. In order to increase the revenues under its control, the Commission urged the government to pass certain laws to modify production and taxation of revenues under its control. However, these bills were either not passed by the Greek Chamber or, when they were passed and became law, were not enforced by the government. Part of the problem was the unwilling-ness of the Greek government to cooperate with the foreign creditors. As a result, the Commission also showed reluctance to act as a trustee for future loans in international financial markets (Tunçer, 2015: 100–22).

The Greek and Serbian cases show significant differences com-pared to the direct forms of control exercised over the Ottoman and Egyptian finances. The degree of cooperation of Greek and Serbian governments was not as extensive as the previous two cases, and IFC operated in a politically more challenging environment, hence the problem of ownership of IFC policies became even more important. Moreover, the tax collection was organised with the intermediation of semi-independent companies, which increased the scope of free-dom for the governments. In the next section I compare the varying degrees of success of IFC in a more systematic way. I then explore the issue of ownership or the willingness and ability of governments to cooperate with IFC.

5.4 Success and Extent of International Financial Control

In this section I aim to establish the degree of control exercised by IFC in a comparative way and relate it to the success in restoring access of debtor states to international financial markets. As a measure of cred-ibility and sovereign risk, it is possible to rely on monthly bond spreads to judge the degree of recovery following defaults.[11]

---

[11] Bond spreads are calculated as the difference between current yield of representative bonds of each country minus the British consol and French rentes yields. See the notes for Figure 5.1 for details.

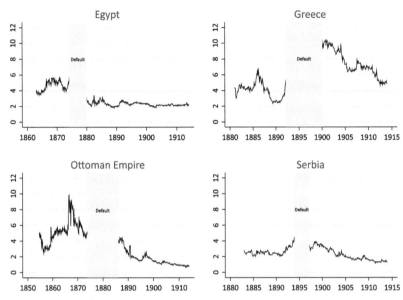

Figure 5.1 Bond spreads, 1850s–1913

Source: Tunçer (2015). The bonds used in calculations are as follows. Greece: 5% Independence Loans of 1879 (Old Greek loans converted), 5% Loan of 1881. Turkey: 6% Loan of 1852 and 1854, 6% Loan of 1858, 6% Loan of 1863–1864; 6% Loan of 1862, 5% Priority Bonds, 4% Priority Loan (new issues in 1890), 4% Loan of 1891. Egypt: 5% preferred Loan of 1877, 7% Loan of 1862, 3.5% preferred Loan of 1890. Serbia: 5% Loan of 1881, 5% Loan of 1890, 4% Loan of 1895. The spread expressed as percentage points is the difference between the current yield of bonds and British consols. In the case of Serbia, as the price quotes are from Paris, I used French rentes to calculate bond spreads.

As seen from Figure 5.1, the impact of IFC following debt settlement was a steady decline in bond spreads in all four cases. However, in the longer term, the Ottoman Empire and Egypt benefitted from a much more significant decline: compared to pre-IFC period of borrowing, the bond spreads declined on average 96 per cent and 80 per cent, respectively. At the end of 1913, bond spreads of Egypt were around 2.1 per cent whereas the Ottoman bond spreads were as low as 0.78 per cent. For Serbia and Greece, the decline in bond yields was not as fast: in 1913, compared to pre-IFC period, bond spreads declined around 70 per cent in Serbian case and almost 55 per cent in the case of Greece. By the end of 1913, Serbian bond spreads stood at 1.2 per cent whereas Greek spreads were still at a relatively high level of 7.7 per cent. Overall, the evidence suggests that IFC was not

always successful in reinstating creditworthiness, and there was
no uniform response of markets towards the lending conditionality
introduced by IFC.

A possible venue to seek an explanation for this difference is the
degree of control exercised by bondholder representatives over host
countries, which can be considered in administrative and fiscal terms
(see Table 5.2). In terms of administration, in Egypt the IFC had the
most extensive privileges; foreign control over Egyptian politics and
finance was reinforced by additional means and organisations, and the
Caisse transformed into the *imperium in imperio*. In the case of the
Ottoman Empire, the Council also enjoyed the freedom of directly
collecting the revenues assigned for the repayment of the outstanding
debt. In doing so, it established an extensive network and worked in
harmony with the Ottoman government, which was willing to extend
the privileges of the IFC. On the other hand, in Serbia and Greece, the
IFC operated via relatively more independent organisations and
did not penetrate into the finances of these economies as much as in
Egypt or in the Ottoman Empire. In the case of Greece, diplomatic
representatives, who had supervisory power over tax collection, found
themselves in conflict with the parliament, and it proved to be difficult
to implement most of the fiscal reforms. In Serbia, the administration
and the government worked in relative harmony. However, unlike
in the other cases, the majority of the managing council of the Administration consisted of Serbian nationals, including the president and
vice-president of the National Bank and two government officials,
who contributed positively to the political justification of the
Administration.

In fiscal terms, as seen from Figure 5.2, the revenues under the
control of IFC steadily increased in most of the cases. The most
significant loss of fiscal sovereignty took place in Egypt, where the
IFC revenues constituted on average 40 per cent of total revenues of
the government. In its early years, the revenues under the control of the
Caisse reached more than 70 per cent, creating unrest among the
taxpayers. In the case of the Ottoman Empire, the revenues controlled
by the Council on behalf of the creditors was on average 13 per cent;
however, after taking into account the revenues controlled on behalf of
the Ottoman government, the assets under the control of the Council
reached up to 35 per cent of all revenues of the state. For Greece
and Serbia, the shares were, respectively, on average 29 per cent and

Table 5.2 IFCs in comparison: *The administrative structure and reforms*

	Egypt (Caisse)	Ottoman Empire (Council)	Serbia (Administration)	Greece (Commission)
Period	1876–1914	1882–1914	1895–1914	1898–1914
Managing council	Bondholder	Bondholder	Bondholder/government	Diplomatic
Composition of the management	Germany, Great Britain, Austria-Hungary, Russia, France and Italy	Britain, France, Netherlands, Germany, Italy and Austria-Hungary bondholders, and a representative of the Ottoman government.	France and Germany bondholders, director and four representatives of Serbian government.	Diplomatic representatives of Austria-Hungary, France, Germany, Great Britain, Italy and Russia
Revenue administration	Direct collection and legislative power	Direct collection	Supervision and direct collection	Supervision
Acting as a trustee	Yes	Yes	Yes	No
Monetary reform	Extensive	Limited	Limited	Extensive
Resistance	Contraband/armed	Contraband/armed	Political	Political

Source: Tunçer (2015)

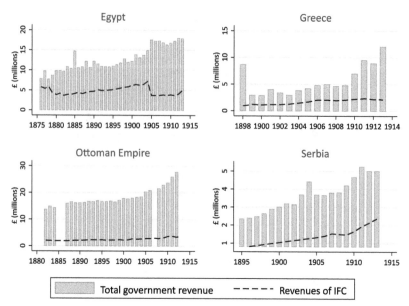

Figure 5.2. Revenues collected by IFCs (in millions of £), 1876–1913
Source: Tunçer (2015)

35 per cent for the period IFC was in operation. In all cases the
revenues of IFC at least doubled from the first year of exercising
control to the onset of World War I. In absolute terms, the Ottoman
Council was the biggest of all – at least after the Entente Cordiale,
which changed the constitution of the *Caisse* and significantly reduced
its influence in the overall Egyptian finances. Despite high level of
revenues under control, in terms of growth performance, the Ottoman
Council and the Egyptian *Caisse* managed an average annual growth
rate of around 2 per cent and 0.7 per cent, respectively. On the other
hand, the Greek Commission and the Serbian Administration enjoyed
an average annual growth rate of around 6 per cent. In other words,
despite the political resistance, IFC in the Balkans performed relatively
more efficiently in increasing its revenues. This was partly due to the
low costs of collection in Serbia and Greece mostly conditioned
by the type of revenue each IFC controlled and the monetisation level
of each economy.

To summarise, the enforcement and conditionality introduced by
IFC was effective in improving the credibility of the defaulting sovereigns. They achieved this by regularly transferring the surplus from

assigned revenues to the bondholders in order to compensate for their losses. On the other hand, local resistance to/cooperation with IFC took place in changing degrees. After the initial discontent was over, IFC in Egypt and the Ottoman Empire worked with relatively little political challenge to their control and had extensive freedom over fiscal matters. In Serbia, thanks to the administrative structure of the IFC and strong representation of Serbian government in the Administration, the role of IFC was mostly confined to a supervisory level. Finally, in the case of Greece, the political resistance to IFC remained strong throughout the period, and the influence of the Commission was limited to monetary affairs. In the next section I explore the issue of resistance towards IFC and propose a framework to interpret the different degrees of political compliance with foreign creditors.

5.5 Political Regimes and Resistance to International Financial Control

Based on the historical presentation so far, it can be suggested that the success of IFC in reinstating the credibility of debtor states was considerably influenced by its political environment, and more specifically the degree of political representation of taxpayers. This view is in line with the recent studies in fiscal sociology, which highlight that two important characteristics of the state-building process are the emergence of a social contract based on negotiation and bargaining around tax and the institution-building incentive provided by the revenue drive. Combined, these two characteristics increase the legitimacy of the state and accountability between the state and its citizens. Studies on long-term history of fiscal states echo these views and emphasize that negotiation and trust in functioning of fiscal systems were common elements in emergence of modern fiscal states (Tilly, 1990; Brautigam, Fjeltstad and Moore, 2008; Martin, Mehrotra and Prasad, 2009 Yun-Casalilla and O'Brien, 2012: 12–13). This perspective provides a useful framework to consider the relationship between taxation, the public debt and the conditionality in the form of international financial control in the European periphery. Unlike many other debtor countries, the Ottoman Empire, Serbia, Greece and Egypt were not faced with the trade-off between taxation and borrowing, as their ability to borrow was restored by IFC. Moreover, the degree of development of the liberal fiscal state and evolution of representative institutions were different in each case, which had an impact on the incentives of the governments. An implication of the representative institutions for these dominantly agrarian economies of the region would be strong influence of the countryside in decisions over taxation of the rural sector given there existed a competitive election system, which resulted in rural representation.

In terms of political regime, for the most of the nineteenth century, the Ottoman Empire remained an authoritarian monarchy despite several reforms aimed at modernising the state apparatus and significant political transformations (Karpat, 1972). An Ottoman parliament and the constitution emerged for the first time in 1876, with an aim of introducing accountability over fiscal matters and regularising the authority of the Sultan. In practice, however, this development did not empower any group other than the existing Ottoman political elite and bureaucracy. That is why when Abdulhamid II decided to suspend the constitution and the parliament just two years later, his decision met with no resistance. A representative assembly was successfully established only after the Young Turk Revolution of 1908. From that year onwards, the assembly had the power to pass legislation over Sultan's authority, and the dominant political force was the nationalist Committee of Union and Progress, which eventually led the Empire into World War I (Brown, 2002: 23–26). As for the tax revenues, they mostly relied on the traditional tithe collected almost exclusively with the help of tax farmers. In order to finance the costly reforms and shift the tax burden from the countryside to the urban centres, the government repeatedly but ultimately unsuccessfully attempted to replace tax farming with salaried tax collectors. Moreover, the taxation system remained heavily reliant on land tax. Custom duties had the potential to be a significant revenue source; however, due to the capitulations and bilateral trade treaties, the Ottoman government was not able to modify the rates unilaterally. Only in 1905, the powers agreed for a minor increase in the import taxes. Finally, the personal tax, a symbol of transition to the modern tax state, was only introduced in 1903 (Shaw, 1975; Quataert 1994: 764–855; Karaman and Pamuk, 2010: 598; Özbek, 2010; Aytekin, 2013). To summarise, unlike many European countries during the same period, in evolution of fiscal institutions in the Ottoman Empire, representation and negotiation with local elite played a very minor role. Throughout the period the Ottoman

Empire struggled to introduce a centralized tax collection system and had to share most of the tax revenues with other intermediaries such as local notables and tax farmers. Moreover, most of the revenues were based on direct taxes levied mainly upon the land. To put it crudely, at the time the Ottoman Empire defaulted on its foreign debt, it was a state that was unable to tax. Given its lack of monopoly over taxation, the Ottoman government was more willing to cooperate with the foreign creditors.

Egypt went through a completely different political transformation; nonetheless, the negotiation with local elites and limited government were not the determinants of increases in fiscal capacity before 1914. As early as 1841, Egypt managed to move away from tax farming thanks to the centralisation policies of Muhammad Ali. From Muhammad Ali's death in 1848 to the establishment of the European control in 1876, the country was dominated by the dynastic state of the Khedives. Although there was a 'Consultative Chamber of Delegates' since 1866 consisting of provincial notables and landowners, it did not have any significant power over taxation. In 1882, the new Khedive introduced the first constitution, which gave more authority to the Chamber; however, the constitution was never fully implemented, and when Britain took control of Egypt the same year, it was suspended. Under the British rule, two representative assemblies were founded in Egypt, but they had very limited power over fiscal matters. The Legislative Council consisted of representatives of provincial assemblies, but it could not pass any law and only had a consultancy role over the budget. The General Assembly, on the other hand, consisted of mostly provincial notables. Although it could not propose any legislation, it had veto power on taxation and no new tax could be imposed without its approval. However, the influence of these institutions remained limited under the British rule, as on the side of the expenditure the *Caisse* was almost the sole authority. Moreover, Khedive's British financial advisor served as the key political figure, since he had veto power over all financial legislation. As regards the type of taxes, the land tax constituted a significant part of total revenue and was collected with the help of accountants established in several villages. Although there were efforts to reduce the burden on the peasantry, the land tax was still considered as the most oppressive form of taxation in Egypt even under the British rule. As for indirect taxes, government officials also collected custom duties and it had the rate of 1 per cent on exports and 8 per cent on imports, while the collection cost was as low as 4 per cent of collected duties. However, Egypt was also bound by free trade treaties and capitulations of the Ottoman Empire (Crouchley, 1938: 42–57; Shaw, 1962; Fahmy, 2002; Aharoni, 2007; Ezzel-Arab, 2009; Tunçer, 2015: 174–75). Overall, in Egypt the British controllers were the main deciding actors over fiscal matters, and the role of parliament remained very limited until 1904 when the power of the *Caisse* over spending was reduced and its funds were partly returned under the control of the Egyptian government.

The relationship between fiscal and political institutions in the Balkans was rather different. Following the Greek independence, the three powers, which guaranteed Greek independence in the Protocols of 1832, implemented a monarchy without any constitutional restrictions. The first Greek constitution and representative assembly emerged in 1844 as a result of a coup d'état against King Otto. Despite the liberal nature of the constitution, there was no significant change in the existing political picture, as the king maintained his influence over the parliament until he was overthrown by another coup in 1862. According to the new constitution of 1864, the representative assembly elected by universal direct suffrage held the whole legislative power. From 1875 to the 1890s, C. Trikoupis emerged as the main political leader and a proponent of economic and political westernization. He supported the settlement of foreign debt and striking a deal with creditors. The implication of this plan in fiscal terms was more taxation, which was not a popular remedy. After 1895, he was followed by T. Deliyannis, who represented a more traditionalist and populist view which was in favour of the idea of Greater Greece and a more adventurous foreign policy. Competition between these two political parties shaped the attitudes towards IFC.[12] In terms of a tax collection system, starting from the 1860s the tithe was collected in cash, and in the 1870s the fiscal policy constantly aimed at lowering the tax burden on the peasants via replacing direct taxation by indirect consumption taxes. As a final step, in 1880, the tithe was abandoned, tax farming

---

[12] The picture only slightly changed following another coup d'état in 1909 – similar in spirit to the Young Turk revolution of 1908 – and a new constitution in 1911, which introduced a second chamber, called the Council of State, with supervisory function over legislation (Clogg, 1997; Spyropoulos and Fortsakis, 2009).

was abolished and a new agricultural fiscal system was introduced reducing the burden on landowners. After the 1860s, Greece's fiscal policy rested on the principles of deficit financing and the low taxation of the higher classes and the peasantry. Greece was amongst the last countries in Europe to implement income and inheritance taxes, respectively, in 1910 and in 1898. And to compensate for the under-taxation of the peasantry, which constituted the largest voting group in Greece, the fiscal burden of both direct and indirect taxation fell on the middle class and the urban sector. Peasants effectively escaped the burden of indirect taxes as they operated mostly with subsistence farming (Palamas, 1930; Dertilis, 1986; Minoglou, 1995; Tunçer, 2015: 176–77).

Finally, in Serbia, there were significant similarities to Greece in terms of evolution of the taxation system and political institutions. From the early years of the autonomy until the late 1860s, the Serbian state continued to modernize the administrative structure and its army. Prince Milan Obrenović, who remained in power from 1868 to 1889, carried Serbia to independence and introduced a new constitution with significant provisions for parliamentary rule. The dominant party in the assembly until 1880s was the Liberal Party, which was supportive of restricting the powers of the king and of improving representative and parliamentary institutions. From 1887 to the onset of World War I, the Radical Party, which ideologically relied on peasant populism, remained in power. In 1889, a new constitution voted by the National Assembly gave the executive power to the king in conjunction with the National Assembly, which exercised the legislative authority. The State Council, consisting of members appointed partly by the king and partly by the Assembly, had the power to decide on the provincial taxes and loans, the expropriation of private property for public purposes and the final settlement of debts. In terms of evolution of fiscal institutions, from 1815 onwards, when Serbian principality was granted independence in tax collection by the Ottoman government, the revolutionary leader Prince Miloš treated local tax farmers as salaried officials, holding them responsible for collecting the head-tax without letting them getting a share of the proceeds. With low taxation and mass peasant freehold landownership, the situation remained favourable for the peasantry. During the 1880s and 1890s, the budget was permanently in deficit, which only changed after the fiscal consolidation in 1903. As for different type of taxes, from the early years of independence, the major indirect tax revenue was the custom duties imposed on the border trade with Austria-Hungary. In the later years, as Serbia turned into a land of monopolies, the receipts from these constituted an important indirect tax category. Despite the importance of indirect taxes, direct tax on land income also remained considerable until 1914. In 1884, a new reform introduced a progressive tax rate in land, which favoured large producers and wealthy peasants. The opposition from this group prevented the introduction of heavy taxes at the top of the scale. In 1889, due to peasant pressure, a new reduction in land tax was introduced. For the remaining period, the Serbian budget increasingly relied on the taxation of urban sector and merchants, and the importance of direct taxes from the rural sector gradually diminished in the overall revenues of the state (Lampe, 1971; Palairet, 1979; Gnjatovic, 2009; Hinić et al., 2014; Tunçer, 2015: 177–78).

The success of IFC in transferring funds from revenues under its management was heavily influenced by the underlying source of these revenues. In the cases of Egypt and the Ottoman Empire, the dominance of direct taxes from land meant a relatively small rate of growth in total revenues transferred to the creditors. Nonetheless, these countries enjoyed a greater recovery in their borrowing costs due to their political compliance with foreign creditors. On the contrary, in the small Balkan economies of Serbia and Greece, the underlying revenue source of IFC was mostly indirect taxes, which were relatively easier to manage and had significantly higher growth rates and better performance. However, this did not necessarily lead to a corresponding recovery in spreads, as IFC in these two cases faced constraints and resistance to its policies.

5.6 Conclusion

This chapter demonstrates the multidimensional character of a pre-1914 enforcement and conditionality mechanism implemented by the foreign creditors following sovereign defaults. IFC resulted in a partial loss of fiscal sovereignty, the extent of which was different in each case depending on the international political considerations and local institutions. As a direct form of conditionality, fiscal rules introduced by IFC were effective in improving the credibility of the defaulting sovereigns; however, the speed and extent of recovery largely depended on the degree of cooperation of debtor governments with the policies of IFC. In explaining the lack of ownership in the context of IFC, the essay mainly highlighted the role of the political regime type, more specifically political representation of taxpayers. The limited fiscal capacity of the Ottoman Empire and Egypt created an incentive for the central governments to cooperate with foreign creditors and be fully compliant with the conditionality. This cooperation helped to gain access to cheap foreign capital until the onset of World War I. In the absence of representative political institutions, these two countries did not face with the political costs of conforming to fiscally oppressive policies of IFC. On the other hand, young democracies of the Balkans, as in Serbia and Greece, where the centralisation of fiscal systems was already under way, were less willing to share the tax revenues with foreign creditors, and for that they were penalised (or not rewarded as much as the others) in the international financial markets. The broader conclusion to be drawn from this comparison is the importance of policy environment predefined by the political and fiscal institutions of the debtor governments. In the context of pre-1914 sovereign debt market, these institutions not only determined the success of conditionality and fiscal rules in reinforcing the credibility of debtor governments but also acted as constraints or stimuli in terms of country ownership of an IFC programme.

In this chapter it was not possible to analyse the impact of lending conditionality in the form of IFC on the long-term development of fiscal capacity of debtor governments. Although the Ottoman Empire and Egypt were able to borrow during this period on a long-term basis with very low costs, there was limited accompanying transformation of political institutions and fiscal centralisation. It can be argued that reinforced credibility combined with lack of developed political institutions slowed down the fiscal centralisation even further, as the governments were more willing to choose the less costly path of borrowing. On the other hand, in Serbia and Greece, IFC operated in a relatively more developed fiscal and political institutional framework; hence the governments were less willing to cooperate with foreign creditors, which resulted in more costly borrowing. The high cost of borrowing, especially in the case of Greece, acted as a catalyst to reform the monetary and fiscal institutions even further and accelerated its move towards fiscal centralisation. Testing these arguments would require going beyond the cases of this chapter.

References

Adams, H. C. (1890) *Public Debts – An Essay in the Science of Finance*, New York: D. Appleton and Company.

Aharoni, R. (2007) *The Pasha's Bedouin: Tribes and States in the Egypt of Mehmet Ali, 1805–1848*, Routledge: New York.

Andreades, A. (1925) *Les contrôles financiers internationaux*, Athens.

Avramov, R. (2003) 'Advising, Conditionality, Culture: Money Doctors in Bulgaria, 1900–2000' in M. Flandreau, *Money Doctors: The Experience of International Financial Advising 1850–2000*, Routledge: New York.

Aytekin E. A. (2013) 'Tax Revolts during the Tanzimat Period (1839–1876) and before the Young Turk Revolution (1904–1908): Popular Protest and State Formation in the Late Ottoman Empire', *Journal of Policy History*, 25, pp. 308–33.

Blaisdell, D. C. (1966) *European Financial Control in the Ottoman Empire*, AMS Press, Inc.: New York.

Borchard, E. (1925) *The Diplomatic Protection of Citizens Abroad or the Law of International Claims*. The Banks Law Publishing: New York.

Borchard, E. (1951) *State Insolvency and Foreign Bondholders – Volume I – General Principles*, Yale University Press: New Haven.

Brautigam, D., Fjeldstad, O.-H. and Moore, M. (2008). *Taxation and State-Building in Developing Countries: Capacity and Consent*, Cambridge University Press: Cambridge.

Brown, N. J. (2002) *Constitutions in a Nonconstitutionalist World*, State University of New York Press: Albany.

Bulow, J. and Rogoff, K. S. (1988) 'A Constant Recontracting Model of Sovereign Debt', *Journal of Political Economy*, 95.6, pp. 155–78.

Bulow, J. and Rogoff, K. S. (1989) 'Sovereign Debt: Is to Forgive to Forget?', *American Economic Review*, 79.1, pp. 43–50.

Castellani, F. and Debrun, X. (2005) 'Designing Macroeconomic Frameworks: A Positive Analysis of Monetary and Fiscal Delegation', *International Finance*, 8, pp. 87–117.

Choi, S. J., Gulati, M. and Posner, E. A. (2012) 'The Evolution of Contractual Terms in Sovereign Bonds', *Journal of Legal Analysis*. Open access.

Clogg, R. (1997) *A Concise History of Greece*, Cambridge University Press: Cambridge.

Crouchley, A. E. (1938) *The Economic Development of Modern Egypt*, Longmans, Green and Co.: London.

Dertilis G. (1986) *Banquiers, usuriers et paysans. Réseaux de crédit et stratégies du capital en Grèce (1780–1930)*, Fondation des Treilles Editions La Découverte: Paris.

Deville, F. (1912) *Les contrôles financiers internationaux et la souveraineté de l'état*, Paris, Limoges.

Drazen, A. (2002) 'Conditionality and Ownership in IMF Lending: A Political Economy Approach', IMF Working Paper.

Dreher, A. (2009) 'IMF Conditionality: Theory and Evidence', *Public Choice*, 141, pp. 233–67.

Eaton, J. and Gersovitz, M. (1981) 'Debt with Potential Repudiation: Theoretical and Empirical Analysis', *Review of Economic Studies*, 48.2, pp. 289–309.

Eldem, E. (2005) 'Ottoman Financial Integration with Europe: Foreign Loans, the Ottoman Bank and the Ottoman public debt', *European Review*, 13.3, pp. 431–45.

Esteves, R. P. (2013) 'The Bondholder, the Sovereign, and the Banker: Sovereign Debt and Bondholders' Protection before 1914', *European Review of Economic History*, 17.4, pp. 389–407.

Esteves, R. and Tunçer, A. C. (2016a) 'Feeling the Blues: Moral Hazard and Debt Dilution in Eurobonds before 1914', *Journal of International Money and Finance*, 65, pp. 46–68.

Esteves, R. and Tunçer, A. C. (2016b) 'Eurobonds Past and Present: A Comparative Review on Debt Mutualization in Europe', *Review of Law and Economics*, 12.3, pp. 659–88.

Ezzel-Arab, A. (2009) 'The Fiscal and Constitutional Program of Egypt's Traditional Elites in 1879: A Documentary and Contextual Analysis of 'al-Lā'iha al-Wataniyya'('The National Program')', *Journal of the Economic and Social History of the Orient*, 52, pp. 301–24.

Fahmy, K. (2002) *All the Pasha's Men – Mehmed Ali, His Army and the Making of Modern Egypt*, The American University in Cairo Press: Cairo.

Featherstone, K. (2015) 'External Conditionality and the Debt Crisis: The 'Troika' and Public Administration Reform in Greece', *Journal of European Public Policy*, 22.3, pp. 295–314.

Feis, H. (1974) *Europe, the World's Banker 1870–1914*, Kelley: New York.

Finnemore, M. (2003). *The Purpose of Intervention: Changing Beliefs about the Use of Force*. Cornell University Press: Ithaca.

Flandreau, M. (2013) 'Sovereign States, Bondholders Committees, and the London Stock Exchange in the Nineteenth Century (1827–68): New Facts and Old Fictions', *Oxford Review of Economic Policy*, 29.4, pp. 668–96.

Flandreau, M. and Flores, J. (2009) 'Bonds and Brands: Foundations of Sovereign Debt Markets, 1820–1830', *The Journal of Economic History*, 69.3, pp. 646–84.

Gnjatovic, D. (2009) 'Foreign Long Term Government Loans of Serbia 1862–1914', Bank of Serbia Working Paper. 2009–03.

Grauwe, P. D. (2011) 'A Less Punishing, More Forgiving Approach to the Debt Crisis in the Eurozone', CEPS Policy Brief, No. 230.

Hagemann, R. (2011) 'How Can Fiscal Councils Strengthen Fiscal Performance?' *OECD Journal: Economic Studies*, 2011.1, pp. 75–98.

Hinić, B., Đurđević, L. and Šojić, M. (2014) 'Serbia/Yugoslavia: from 1884 to 1940', in *South-Eastern European Monetary and Economic Statistics from the Nineteenth Century to World War II*, Bank of Greece, Bulgarian National Bank, National Bank of Romania, Oesterreichische Nationalbank.

Hyde, C. C. (1922) 'The Negotiation of External Loans with Foreign Governments', *The American Journal of International Law*, 16.4, pp. 523–41.

Ioannidis, M. (2015) 'How strict is 'strict conditionality'? The new Eurozone agreement on Greece', *European Law Blog*, http://europeanlawblog .eu/?p=2716#sthash.GZ1ZLCgz.dpuf, accessed 23 March 2015.

James H. (2003) 'Who Owns "Ownership"? The IMF and Policy Advice' in M. Flandreau (ed.), *Money Doctors: The Experience of International Financial Advising 1850–2000*, Routledge: New York.

Kaletsky, A. (1985) *The Costs of Default*, Priority Press Publications: New York.

Kaplanoglou, G. and Rapanos, V. T. (2013) 'Fiscal Deficits and the Role of Fiscal Governance: The Case of Greece', *Economic Analysis and Policy*, 43.1, pp. 5–27.

Karaman, K. and Pamuk, S. (2010) 'Ottoman State Finances in European Perspective, 1500–1914', *The Journal of Economic History*, 70, pp. 593–629.

Karpat, K. (1972) 'The Transformation of the Ottoman State, 1789–1908', *International Journal of Middle East Studies*, 3, pp. 243–81.

Kelly, T. (1998) 'Ability and Willingness to Pay in the Age of Pax Britannica, 1890–1914', *Explorations in Economic History*, 35.1, pp. 31–58.

Kiray, E. Z. (1988) *Foreign Debt and Structural Change in 'the Sick Man of Europe' – The Ottoman Empire – 1850–1875*, unpublished PhD thesis, MIT.

Kofas, J. V. (1981) *Financial Relations of Greece and the Great Powers 1832–1862*, East European Monographs: New York.

Lampe, J. R. (1971) 'Financial structure and the economic development of Serbia, 1878–1912', PhD, University of Wisconsin.

Lampe, J. R. and Jackson, M. R. (1982). *Balkan Economic History, 1550–1950: From Imperial Borderlands to Developing Nations*, Indiana University Press: Bloomington.

Lazaretou, S. (2005) 'The Drachma, Foreign Creditors, and the International Monetary System: Tales of a Currency during the 19th and the Early 20th Centuries', *Explorations in Economic History*, 42.2, pp. 202–36.

Levandis, J. A. (1944) *Greek Foreign Debt and the Great Powers 1821–1898*, Columbia University Press: New York.

Martin, I. W., Mehrotra, A. K. and Prasad, M. (2009) *The New Fiscal Sociology: Taxation in Comparative and Historical Perspective*, Cambridge University Press Cambridge.

Mauro, P. and Yafeh, Y. (2003) 'The Corporation of Foreign Bondholders', IMF Working Paper, No. 03107.

Minoglou, I. (1995) 'Political Factors Shaping the Role of Foreign Finance: The Case of Greece (1832–1932)', in J. Harriss, J. Hunter and C. M. Lewis (eds.), *The New Institutional Economics and Third World Development*. Routledge: London.

Mitchener, K. J. and Weidenmier, M. D. (2010) 'Supersanctions and Sovereign Debt Repayment', *Journal of International Money and Finance*, 29.1, pp. 19–36.

Özbek, N. (2010) 'Osmanlı İmparatorluğu'nda Gelir Vergisi: 1903–1907 Tarihli *Vergi-i Şahsi* Uygulaması.' *Tarih ve Toplum Yeni Yaklaşımlar*, 10, pp. 43–80.

Palairet, M. (1979) 'Fiscal Pressure and Peasant Impoverishment in Serbia before World War I', *The Journal of Economic History*, 39, pp. 719–40.

Pamuk, Ş. (1978) Foreign Trade, Foreign Capital and the Peripheralization of the Ottoman Empire 1830–1913, PhD thesis, University of California, Berkeley.

Palamas, L. K. (1930) *History of Monetary Enactments in Greece, 1828–1885*, Hestia: Athens.

Panizza, U., Sturzenegger, F. and Zettelmeyer, J. (2009) 'The Economics and Law of Sovereign Debt and Default', *Journal of Economic Literature*, 47.3, pp. 651–98.

Quataert, D. (1983). *Social Disintegration and Popular Resistance in the Ottoman Empire, 1881–1908: Reactions to European Economic Penetration*, New York University Press: New York.

Quataert, D. (1994) 'The Age of Reforms', Part 4 of H. Inalcik et al. (eds.), *An Economic and Social History of the Ottoman Empire 1600–1914*, vol. 2, Cambridge University Press: Cambridge.

Rose, A. K. (2005) 'One Reason Countries Pay Their Debts: Renegotiation and International Trade', *Journal of Development Economics*, 77, pp. 189–206.

Shaw, S. J. (1962) *The Financial and Administrative Organization and Development of Ottoman Egypt, 1517–1798*, Princeton University Press: Princeton.

Shaw, S. J. (1975) 'The Nineteenth-Century Ottoman Tax Reforms and Revenue System 1517–1798', *International Journal of Middle East Studies*, 6.4, pp. 421–59.

Spyropoulos, P. K. and Fortsakis, T. (2009) *Constitutional Law in Greece*, Kluwer Law International: The Netherlands.

Sundhaussen, H. (1989). *Historische Statistik Serbiens, 1834–1914: mit europäischen Vergleichsdaten*, R. Oldenbourg: München.

Suter, C. (1990) *Debt Cycles in the World Economy: Foreign Loans, Financial Crises and Debt Settlements, 1820–1990*, Westview Press: Boulder.

Tilly, C. (1990) *Coercion, Capital and European States, AD 990–1990*. Blackwell: Cambridge, MA.

Tooze, A. and Ivanov, M. (2011) 'Disciplining the "Black Sheep of the Balkans": Financial Supervision and Sovereignty in Bulgaria, 1902–38', *The Economic History Review*, 64, pp. 30–51.

Tunçer, A. C. (2015) *Sovereign Debt and International Financial Control: the Middle East and the Balkans, 1870–1913*. Palgrave Macmillan: Houndmills, Basingstoke.

Waibel, M. (2011) *Sovereign Defaults before International Courts and Tribunals*, Cambridge University Press: Cambridge.

Wynne, W. (1951) *State Insolvency and Foreign Bondholders: Volume II: Selected Case Histories of Governmental Foreign Defaults and Debt Readjustments*, Yale University Press: New Haven.

Yun Casalilla, B. and O'Brien, P. (2012) *The Rise of Fiscal States: A Global History, 1500–1914*. Cambridge University Press: New York.

Zourai, A. J. (1998) 'European Capitalist Penetration of Tunisia, 1860–1881', Unpublished PhD Thesis, University of Washington.

6 | *Snakes and Ladders*

Navigating European Monetary Union

DUNCAN NEEDHAM

6.1 Introduction

On 1 January 2002, the citizens of the Eurozone forsook 'the coins for Cortez' men looking out on to Darien; the money of Mozart for his music and Molière for his manuscripts; of Tiberius for his treasure and Krupp for his cannon' (Marsh 2009: 206). European statesmen had long contemplated monetary union, unafraid to evoke the memory of Charlemagne to soothe deep-seated national hostilities.[1] But while the major European currencies had been pegged for most of the previous century, the Euro was a different proposition.[2] Why, three years after locking their exchange rates, did the 315 million citizens of nations as geographically and culturally distinct as Finland, Greece and Luxembourg awake to find themselves using the same notes and coin? The Eurozone is not an Optimal Currency Area – labour is insufficiently mobile, the region absorbs economic shocks asymmetrically and fiscal policy is not harmonised.[3] As Martin Feldstein predicted in 1997, the costs of European monetary union (lower growth and higher unemployment) have outweighed the gains from increased trade and the creation of an independent European Central Bank (Feldstein 1997).

This chapter explains the genesis of the Euro within the strategic concerns of the two principal players, France and Germany. Others were involved, but with these two countries comprising more than half

---

[1] Speech by President François Mitterrand at Aachen City Hall, 20 October 1987, quoted in Dyson and Featherstone 1999: 73.

[2] For the Latin Monetary Union formed by France, Switzerland, Italy and Belgium in 1865, see Redish 1993: 68–85. For the Scandinavian Currency Union formed by Sweden and Denmark in 1873 (and joined formally by Norway in 1875), see Bergman, Gerlach and Jonung 1993: 507–17.

[3] Frankel and Rose argued in 1998 that the Eurozone might *become* an Optimal Currency Area following the establishment of the monetary union (Frankel and Rose 1998: 1009–25).

the Eurozone's economic output, Franco-German policy was paramount. As Charles de Gaulle pointed out in the early 1960s, 'l'Europe, c'est la France et l'Allemagne. Les autres, c'est les légumes' (quoted in Giesbert 1993: 280). It stresses the importance of monetary union to the wider project of European political union, driven by the German post-war policy of 'exaggerated multilateralism' – regaining national sovereignty through international integration – and by the French desire, particularly after the 1956 Suez debacle, to project diminished power on the global stage.[4] The economics of European monetary union have never completely added up.[5] But the political and geopolitical arguments have always made a great deal of sense. Indeed, it is only when we peer through the lens of the Cold War that the picture comes into focus. As befits a process that was shaped by the intrigues of international diplomacy, the journey towards the Euro resembles a game of 'snakes and ladders' – the snakes lying in wait for whenever monetary storms exposed the economic contradictions of European monetary union; the ladders hoisted to facilitate ever-closer Franco-German cooperation within the ebb and flow of the Cold War.

6.2 Square One: The Early Moves

An aversion to floating exchange rates has permeated post-war European economic policy. At Bretton Woods in 1944, the European delegates scarcely needed the US Secretary of the Treasury to remind them that

---

[4] The goal of a reunified Germany 'integrated in the European community' was enshrined in the 1955 Paris Treaties that ended the Allied occupation of West Germany. In November 1978, Chancellor Schmidt commented to the Bundesbank central council: 'The more successful we are in the areas of foreign policy, socioeconomic matters, and military matters, the longer it will be until Auschwitz sinks into history ... it is all the more necessary for us to clothe ourselves in this European mantle', quoted in Mourlon-Druol 2012: 240; Dyson and Featherstone 1999: 308; Anderson 1997: 80–107.

[5] Harold James points out that monetary union was 'a response to genuine (and still existing) problems of currency instability and misalignment at the international level' and 'not simply ... a fundamentally political project'. This chapter agrees with James's analysis, while stressing that political and geopolitical concerns provided critical momentum at the key junctures (James 2012).

All of us have seen the great economic tragedy of our time. We saw the worldwide depression of the 1930s. We saw currency disorders develop and spread from land to land, destroying the basis for international trade and international investment and even international faith. In their wake, we saw unemployment and wretchedness – idle tools, wasted wealth. We saw their victims fall prey, in places, to demagogues and dictators. We saw bewilderment and bitterness become the breeders of fascism and, finally, of war. (United Nations Monetary and Financial Conference 1948: 81)

After nearly six years of war, and with international monetary relations fixed by the Bretton Woods agreements, military considerations remained uppermost. Launching the European Coal and Steel Community in May 1950, French Foreign Minister Robert Schuman explained that binding the two industries most necessary for war at the supranational level 'will make it plain that any war between France and Germany becomes not only unthinkable, but materially impossible' (The Schuman Declaration, quoted in Szász 1999: 1). This was especially important given the need for German rearmament to counter the threat of Soviet expansion. Hence French Prime Minister René Pleven's proposal for a European Defence Community, agreed with West German Chancellor Konrad Adenauer, but voted down by nationalists in the French parliament in August 1954.

Military considerations also breathed life into the proposals for economic integration considered by the foreign ministers of the European Coal and Steel Community at Messina in June 1955. In November 1956, American pressure forced the French and British to withdraw their troops from the Suez Canal, nationalised by President Nasser four months earlier.[6] It was clear that France and Britain no longer enjoyed great power autonomy. As Adenauer remarked to the French foreign minister on the day the decision was taken to withdraw,

France and England will never be powers comparable to the United States and the Soviet Union. Nor Germany, either. There remains to them only one way of playing a decisive role in the world; that is to unite to make Europe. England is not ripe for it but the affair of Suez will help to prepare her spirits for it. We have no time to waste: Europe will be your revenge. (Quoted in Feldstein 1997: 27)

---

[6] The Americans were upset at both the lack of consultation and the impact the Anglo-French action would have on their attempts to draw Egypt into an anti-Soviet alliance.

'Unripe' England chose ever-closer ties to the American superpower. France turned to her neighbours, building on the foundations of the European Coal and Steel Community to establish the European Economic Community (EEC) with the 1957 Treaty of Rome, and signing the bilateral 1963 Elysée Treaty which pledged friendship and collaboration with West Germany on foreign policy, cultural and youth affairs.[7]

The Treaty of Rome established a Monetary Committee, charged with promoting 'the co-ordination of the policies of Member States in monetary matters to the full extent necessary for the functioning of the Common Market'.[8] With the major European currencies pegged to the dollar and linked to gold under the Bretton Woods arrangements, there appeared to be little need for elaboration.[9] As Harold James points out, 'so long as capital markets were not connected with each other and exchange rate policies were not problematical, the case for greater monetary cooperation was pretty weak' (James 2012: 44). The Treaty of Rome was primarily concerned with trade – what Jacques Delors would later call the 'marriage contract' (Cockfield 1994: 133–34). France would open its markets to West German goods and the Germans would subsidise French agriculture through the Common Agricultural Policy (CAP), regarded by the French as their major achievement at the Rome summit. The CAP sought to stabilise food prices throughout the EEC. An appreciating D-mark (revalued by 4.75 per cent in March 1961) threatened to undermine that stability by increasing German purchasing power. This would generate food price inflation in France as her farmers exported more of their produce. As a consequence, the European Commission recommended in

[7] Adenauer regarded the Elysée Treaty as both 'a political dam against the advance of Eastern Communism' and 'an alternative to American hegemony' (Dyson and Featherstone 1999: 272).

[8] Member states were also enjoined 'to maintain confidence' in their currencies, *Treaty Establishing the European Economic Community*, 25 March 1957, articles 104, 105 and 107 (European Economic Community 1962). Fluctuation margins between European currencies versus the dollar were narrowed from 1 per cent to 0.75 per cent with convertibility in 1958.

[9] The Treaty of Rome's articles on exchange rate policy echo the IMF's Articles of Agreement. Kaplan and Schleiminger note that the Europeans were 'careful not to tread on the toes of the IMF about exchange rates'. Indeed, in 1961 the D-mark and Dutch guilder were revalued by 4.75 per cent with very little consultation in Europe, but a great deal of consultation in Washington (James 2012: 45; Kaplan and Scheiminger 1989: 219).

October 1962 that members' exchange rates be irrevocably fixed.[10] This proposal gained little traction, partly because the Bretton Woods system was still functioning, but also because of the divide between the 'monetarists', who believed that monetary union could *drive* economic and political union, and the 'economists' who believed that monetary union should *crown* economic union.[11]

This was the fault line that ran through the European monetary debate. Should monetary union be the instrument or the goal of economic and political union? There was little theoretical support for the notion that monetary union would drive economic convergence. There was even less practical support from the 'strong currency' nations, principally West Germany and Holland, for whom monetary union would mean a greater share of the cost of defending the fixed parities. At Bretton Woods, Keynes had lost the argument with the Americans over a more equal response to current account imbalances. Surplus nations could continue accumulating currency reserves while deficit nations were invariably forced to deflate. Monetary union implied a pooling of reserves, or at least a greater symmetry of policy adjustment. But as the Dutch central banker Marius Holtrop pointed out, why should the thrifty ant share its resources with the profligate cricket? (Szász 1999: 13).

By the late 1960s the cracks in the Bretton Woods system, magnified by Robert Triffin in 1959, had become fissures as the United States pursued its policy of guns (in Vietnam) and butter (the Great Society) without raising taxes sufficient to pay for either.[12] The resulting balance of payments deficits would have forced devaluation and/or deflation on any other country. But the Americans did not have to defend the dollar against other currencies; they had to convert dollars into

---

[10] The European Commission's October 1962 'Action Plan' also set in train the process that produced the Committee of Central Bank Governors which met from July 1964. In January 1965, European Commissioner Robert Marjolin referred to monetary union as an 'inevitable obligation' (Szász 1999: 8).

[11] The term 'monetarist' here must not be confused with the monetary theory that emanated from the University of Chicago and was briefly in vogue in the early 1980s.

[12] In 1959 Triffin explained to the Joint Economic Committee of the US Congress that global economic growth required the United States to supply dollar reserves through continued balance-of-payments deficits, and that these continued deficits would themselves undermine confidence in the dollar (Triffin 1960: 1–20).

gold at $35 per ounce. For President de Gaulle, irritated at the 'exorbitant privilege' that allowed the issuer of the world's reserve currency to run 'deficit[s] without tears', requests to convert French dollar reserves into gold were intended to discipline American policy (Chivvis 2006: 708). If the Europeans had presented a united front, this might have worked. But strategic considerations continued to drive international monetary policy. With West Germany reliant on American military resources, particularly in West Berlin, Bundesbank President Karl Blessing assured Federal Reserve Chairman William McChesney Martin in March 1967 that the Germans would not join the French in demanding American gold for their dollar reserves (Marsh 2009: 44).

French attacks on the dollar's privileged position included a series of 'unhelpful' interventions on sterling, the first line of defence for the Bretton Woods system.[13] These contributed to the 14.3 per cent devaluation announced by the British government in November 1967. But with sterling no longer overvalued and the dollar protected by the de facto American refusal to convert central bank reserves into gold, speculators turned their attention to the franc as the French government struggled to cope with higher production costs and *les événements de mai 1968*. The outcome was an ill-tempered 'Group of Ten' summit at Bonn in November 1968.[14] Despite Chancellorial and Bundesbank support for a D-Mark revaluation, West German Economics Minister Karl Schiller refused. He feared for the nascent economic recovery and implemented a package of fiscal measures to lower import prices and raise export prices instead. If the Germans would not revalue the D-Mark, then de Gaulle would not devalue the franc.[15] But with the General out of office after April 1969, the European Commission could proceed with its strategy of

---

[13] In July 1967, French foreign minister Maurice Couve de Murville 'acquainted the press' with his view that British membership of the EEC would first require a sterling devaluation (Callaghan 1987: 196).

[14] UK Chancellor Roy Jenkins advised Prime Minister Harold Wilson that 'German obstinacy, and Schiller's tactics and personality, have made it an extremely trying experience for all of us' (Owen 1976).

[15] French Finance Minister François-Xavier Ortoli discussed a 10 per cent franc devaluation in November 1968 but was overruled by de Gaulle. The franc was eventually devalued by 12.5 per cent in August 1969, and the D-Mark revalued by 8.5 per cent in October 1969 (Szász 1999: 24–25).

'widening' (admitting Britain, Denmark and Ireland) and 'deepening' (closer economic and monetary union).[16]

'Deepening' gathered momentum with the incoming West German Chancellor Willy Brandt's desire to build a 'western flank' for his *Ostpolitik* – establishing relations with East Germany, and 'normalising' relations with the Soviet Union, towards the ultimate goal of German reunification (Dyson and Featherstone 1999: 272). Despite possessing 'neither expertise nor enthusiasm for monetary issues', Brandt latched on to the European Commissioner for Economic and Financial Affairs' proposals for economic and monetary union (the 'Barre Plan') launched in February 1969.[17] This was part of Brandt's grand strategy of *Westbindung*, embedding West Germany within the EEC and NATO to assuage Western fears of a reunited Germany while strengthening his negotiating hand with the Soviet Union. All this to avoid the nightmare of German isolation – ending up on the wrong side of the balance of power equation that had proved so disastrous between 1914 and 1945.[18] As Brandt later explained, he was interested in European monetary union primarily for the free hand it gave him in the East (Szász 1999: 29). So while French Finance Minister Valery Giscard d'Estaing could promote monetary union at the meeting of heads of state and government at The Hague in December 1969 in pursuit of greater symmetry against the dollar, Brandt was laying down a path to German reunification.

6.3 The Werner Report and the European Currency 'Snake'

As a consequence of Brandt and Giscard's initiative, the heads of state and government commissioned a report from a committee chaired by

[16] Britain, Ireland and Denmark acceded to the EEC on 1 January 1973. Norway decided not to join after a referendum voted against it in September 1972.

[17] The 'Barre Plan' was a watered-down version of European Commissioner for Economic and Financial Affairs Raymond Barre's February 1968 'Monetary Plan of Action' which had called for the elimination of fluctuation margins between member currencies, a system of mutual financial assistance, adjustment only after mutual consent and the introduction of a single European unit of account.

[18] Pompidou noted that by signing the 'Eastern Treaties' in September 1970, a resurgent West Germany was acting 'without asking for permission', as it had done two years earlier at the Bonn summit in the monetary field. Pompidou's efforts to 'rebalance' the EEC help to explain his support for British membership (Szász 1999: 28).

the Prime Minister of Luxembourg, Pierre Werner, 'to identify the basic issues for a realization by stages of economic and monetary union' ('Werner Report' 1970: 35). The Werner Report was published in October 1970 and adopted in diluted form by the heads of state and government in March 1971. It recommended economic and monetary union to be achieved in three stages. Economic union would mean that 'the principal decisions of economic policy will be taken at Community level and therefore that the necessary powers be transferred from the national plane to the Community plane' ('Werner Report' 1970: 26). Monetary union would require 'an area with a single currency and a centralised monetary policy', albeit the report made clear that this 'may be accompanied by the maintenance of national monetary symbols' ('Werner Report 1970: 10). But monetary union was just a staging post – a 'leaven for the development of political union which in the long run it will be unable to do without' ('Werner Report' 1970: 26).

Stage One would run for three years from 1 January 1971 and involve a narrowing of the fluctuation margins between member currencies. By 30 June 1972 there would be an outline for a European Monetary Cooperation Fund (a 'potential Federal Reserve System for Europe') to finance currency intervention.[19] Stage Two was to involve financial market integration, the abolition of capital controls, the further narrowing of currency fluctuation margins and increased short-term economic coordination. During Stage Three exchange rates would be 'irrevocably' fixed, there would be full economic convergence and the institution of a Community-level system of central banks.[20]

Stage One was delayed by the onset of Bretton Woods' dying convulsions, themselves brought on by Richard Nixon's attempts to boost domestic growth ahead of the 1972 US presidential election. Lower interest rates generated an outflow of capital from the United States that saw the Bundesbank take in the equivalent of 1 per cent of West German GDP over the foreign exchanges in just 40 minutes of trading on 5 May 1971 (Owen 1976). Four days later, having closed the foreign exchange markets and failed to coordinate a joint float of

---

[19] The proposed Fund would technically be under the European Commission's control (James 2012: 63).

[20] The Werner Report was approved, slightly watered down, by a resolution of the Council and the Representatives of the Governments of the Member States on 22 March 1972. This was the first formal adoption of a plan to deepen monetary, financial and fiscal integration.

Community currencies against the dollar, the Germans floated the D-Mark.[21] On 15 August, fearing for US gold reserves, Nixon ended the convertibility of the dollar into gold at $35 per ounce. As André Szász points out, a floating dollar made European currency coordination both more necessary and more difficult (Szász 1999: 38). More necessary, since each country's competitive position would be affected by wider currency fluctuations; more difficult because policy differences would be reflected in very visible currency moves rather than opaque central bank reserve statistics.

Stage One finally began with the birth of the European currency 'snake' in April 1972. Fluctuations between member currencies were limited to 4.5 per cent (versus a potential 9 per cent agreed at the Smithsonian realignment of the broader Bretton Woods currencies in December 1971), with the burden of adjustment resting on the weak rather than the strong.[22] Although nurtured by the European Commission, the snake assumed a somewhat 'non-EEC' character from the outset. The parity grids were administered at the Bank for International Settlements in Switzerland, that is, at an institution outside the EEC.[23] Members included the United Kingdom and Ireland (briefly, and before their accession to the EEC in January 1973), Denmark and Sweden (before Denmark joined the EEC in January 1973 and more than two decades before Sweden joined in 1995) and Norway (which has never joined the EC). Switzerland also considered joining in 1975, only to be rebuffed by France which feared the consequent 'hardening' of the snake.[24] Of the founder members of the EEC, France left in January 1974, rejoined in July 1975 and left definitively in March 1976 after expending at least $4 billion of reserves in a failed

---

[21] The Dutch guilder floated alongside the D-Mark.

[22] The Smithsonian agreement permitted individual currencies to fluctuate by 2.25 per cent either side of a central rate against the dollar, i.e. by 4.5 per cent. If one currency fell from the top of its 4.5 per cent range to the bottom at the same time as another currency rose from the bottom of its range to the top, then these currencies would move by 9 per cent against each other. Graphically, the group of European currencies moving together within the broader band resembled a 'snake in a tunnel'.

[23] The 'director' of the European Monetary Cooperation Fund was a BIS staff member (James 2012: 14).

[24] Switzerland, along with Austria and Spain, maintained a de facto relationship with the snake while outside the EEC (Mourlon-Druol 2012: 23; Szász 1999: 40).

defence of the franc.[25] Italy left in February 1973. By 1977, with a membership of Germany, Holland, Belgium, Luxembourg and Denmark, the 'mini-snake' increasingly resembled the asymmetric D-Mark zone that France and the European Commission had sought to avoid. It certainly did little to protect the French economy from either D-Mark strength or dollar weakness.

6.4 The European Monetary System

In 1977, with France outside the snake and progress on closer European integration stalled, 'Euro-sclerosis' had set in. Notwithstanding European Commission President Roy Jenkins's efforts to exhort European union through 'monetary proselytising', it would take another geopolitical spur to quicken monetary integration.[26] The initiative came from Willy Brandt's successor Helmut Schmidt's frustration with the waywardness of President Carter's economic and foreign policy. Schmidt regarded the US President as 'a dangerous nitwit' with 'no notion of strategy' (Szász, quoted in Marsh 2009: 78; Schmidt, quoted in Szász 1999: 52). Carter's expansionary economic policies stimulated renewed capital flight, lowering the dollar against the D-Mark and threatening both the Bundesbank's successful battle against inflation and the competitiveness of German exports. Carter's unpredictably on defence further convinced Schmidt of the importance of the Franco-German alliance.[27] As with Brandt's *Ostpolitik* a decade earlier, a strategic challenge generated a monetary response. Germany could insulate herself against American unpredictability on defence by sharing French military capability; France could insulate herself against American unpredictability on economic policy by sharing German monetary credibility.[28]

---

[25] The French were annoyed at the British for allowing sterling to fall below $2 for the first time on 5 March 1976 (Needham 2014: 97).

[26] Jenkins used the first Jean Monnet Lecture in October 1977 to argue for monetary union as a catalyst for political union (Mourlon-Druol 2012: 139; Jenkins 1991: 474).

[27] In April 1978, President Carter abandoned the neutron bomb without consulting his European allies. As Mourlon-Druol points out, Schmidt's monetary initiative preceded Carter's announcement by at least two months. But having convinced his government 'with difficulty' that American neutron bombs should be deployed on German soil, the episode reinforced Schmidt's frustration with the Carter administration (Mourlon-Druol 2012: 185; James 2012: 153).

[28] The prospect of further EEC enlargement provided a third catalyst.

France had left the snake because depleted foreign exchange reserves were insufficient to protect the franc from higher French inflation. To satisfy *amour propre*, any new monetary arrangement she might join had at least to appear more symmetrical.[29] In 1978, Schmidt and Giscard, in concert with Jenkins, oversaw the design of an Exchange Rate Mechanism (ERM) which included a 'divergence indicator' based on the European Currency Unit (ECU) comprised of a weighted average of member currencies.[30] The intention was that the D-Mark (most likely) could approach at its upper intervention point without any other currency necessarily approaching its lower intervention point. This would, in theory, make the ERM more symmetrical than the snake, since intervention on behalf of the weaker currencies would be less frequent. Also, if the D-Mark approached its upper intervention point, the Bundesbank could sell D-Marks and buy dollars (rather than the weaker European currencies), push down the ECU, and thus improve the competitiveness of *all* member currencies against the dollar. But shifting more of the burden of adjustment on to the Bundesbank could mean increased creation of D-Marks to buy dollars. This might threaten published targets for the growth of the domestic money supply. On 30 November 1978, Schmidt agreed with Bundesbank President Otmar Emminger that West German money supply targets would take precedence over the creation of D-Marks to buy foreign currency within the ERM, an agreement made public in March 1979 (Marsh 2009: 83–85). This was an immediate breach of the new 'rules of the game'. Coupled with the shelving of plans for a European Monetary Fund (empowered to issue conditional loans drawn from pooled member resources) in favour of modestly increased responsibilities for the European Monetary Cooperation Fund, it produced little more than a snake with a new skin. This 'new' system certainly worked to West Germany's advantage. As Finance Ministry Secretary of State Manfred Lahnstein explained to British Chancellor Denis

[29] Giscard had staked his prestige when announcing in May 1975 that the franc would rejoin the snake; ejection in 1976 was a personal defeat. Schmidt described the EMS as 'swimming trunks, make-up, since the French are entering for the third time into a European monetary alliance that they have already left twice', quoted in Mourlon-Druol 2012: 238.

[30] The ad hoc committee appointed to flesh out Schmidt's proposals was Franco-German-British, comprising Bernard Clappier (Governor of the Banque de France), Horst Schulman (Schmidt's senior economic adviser) and Kenneth Couzens (Second Permanent Secretary at HM Treasury).

Healey just before launch, 'the key principle of German economic policy was to persuade the French and Italians to pay to lower the value of the D-Mark so as to make Germany more competitive' (Healey, quoted in Marsh 2009: 80; Healey 1989: 438–39). This aim was shared at the highest level with Schmidt telling Prime Minister James Callaghan that 'one effect' of his monetary plan 'would certainly be to weaken the German mark' (quoted in Mourlon-Druol 2012: 165).

The ERM commenced operation in March 1979. Its first four years coincided with the second oil shock, a global economic downturn and, perhaps equally significantly, a defining moment in the presidency of François Mitterrand. Elected in May 1981 and faced with rising unemployment, Mitterrand had initially boosted demand, nationalised the banks and several large companies, lowered working hours and the retirement age and increased welfare benefits. This produced two franc devaluations within a year.[31] But in 1982, facing a large current account deficit and a possible approach to the IMF, Mitterrand began executing an economic U-turn (Dyson and Featherstone 1999: 142). Having declared that the budget deficit would be limited to 3 per cent of GDP, he announced in March 1983 that his government would embark upon a policy of economic *rigueur*, partly in order that the franc could remain in the ERM, albeit after a further devaluation.[32] David Marsh identifies this decision, taken with the advice of Finance Minister and future European Commissioner Jacques Delors, as 'a turning point in the chronicle of European money' (Marsh 2009: 100). It was made in consultation with Bonn, which agreed to share the cost of the currency adjustment by revaluing the D-Mark by 5.5 per cent versus a franc devaluation of just 2.5 per cent. This came shortly after Mitterrand marked the twentieth anniversary of the Elysée Treaty by supporting recently elected Chancellor Helmut Kohl's decision to allow nuclear missiles on West German soil (Marsh 2009: 97–99). Once again, strategic considerations were shortening the path to monetary union.

---

[31] There were also two D-Mark revaluations, three Dutch guilder revaluations, four Italian lira devaluations, three Danish krone devaluations (and one revaluation), one Belgian franc devaluation (and one revaluation), and an Irish punt devaluation (Padoa-Schioppa 2000: 223).

[32] A budget deficit limit of 3 per cent of GDP would later form part of the Euro convergence criteria.

Economic *rigueur* and remaining in the ERM meant aligning the French economy more closely with West Germany rather than continuing with expansionary policies behind the capital controls that had remained in place since 1968 (in breach of France's treaty obligations). The *franc stable* would remain pegged to the D-Mark in the ERM until 1986. Without Mitterrand's *tournant*, it is likely that the ERM would have reverted to being a D-Mark hard currency zone *sans* the franc.

6.5 The Single European Market and the 'Trilemma'

Mitterrand's 1983 *tournant* was a defining moment. It may not have been *the* defining moment. A claim may also be made for Jacques Delors' presiding over the creation of the Single European Market as President of the European Commission from January 1985.[33] In this he was aided by Margaret Thatcher's former treasury minister, Lord Cockfield, appointed European Commissioner for Internal Market, Tax Law and Customs in 1985. Cockfield was the principal architect of the Single European Act which, crucially for monetary union, provided for the free movement of capital throughout the EEC after July 1990. This cut through the arguments of the 'economists' – that monetary union must *follow* economic convergence. Once capital controls were removed, member states were subject to the remorseless logic of the 'trilemma'; in the absence of a large stock of foreign exchange reserves, a country may only fix its currency if it accepts the monetary policy of the most powerful economy, in this case West Germany. Without capital controls and a large stock of reserves, countries wishing to exercise monetary policy autonomy must allow their currencies to float.[34] Unregulated capital flows undermine most attempts to run an independent monetary policy alongside a fixed exchange rate. Having chosen to stay in the ERM in 1983, the French were agreeing to closer monetary union by signing the Single European Act. As Harold James points out, '[I]n 1985, Delors had reached the conclusion that free capital movement was essential to the realization of the 1992 program, and that it was equally apparent that

---

[33] The Single European Act was the first revision to the 1957 Treaty of Rome.

[34] The 'trilemma' may be extended to the 'inconsistent quartet' with the addition of a free trade objective. We can take the free trade aspiration of the Single European Market as a given.

the free circulation of capital would require a new approach to monetary policy' (James 2012: 213).

Why did France agree to the free movement of capital? Part of the answer lies in the French Treasury's long-standing efforts to modernise French industry by exposing it to international competition. This process gained momentum after Mitterrand's 1983 *tournant* with the deregulation of French capital markets, a process that was taking place across Europe.[35] Free movement of capital requires the freedom for banks to operate across borders, which itself implies some harmonisation of monetary policy. But there was another, older reason for the Single European Act to contain a monetary dimension. The *Financial Times* explained that Jacques Delors' call for the ECU to become a reserve currency grew out of the traditional French view that 'the burden placed on the dollar is too great: a Community currency would enable central banks to diversify their resources' (Cheeseright 1985). A single European currency would help to 'persuade the US to introduce the internal discipline which would make for relative stability on the foreign exchanges' (Cheeseright 1985). The former French Finance Minister was using the same argument that de Gaulle, Pompidou and Giscard had used in the 1960s and 1970s. The Americans, who had allowed the dollar to rise from less than four francs in 1980 to more than ten francs in 1985, must be subjected to the same discipline as everyone else. This would not happen while they enjoyed a virtual monopoly on issuing the world's currency reserves.

If France was once again in the position of *demandeur* of closer monetary union, why did the Germans agree? After all, viewed from Bonn, the ERM was working rather well. As Dorothee Heisenberg points out,

German businesses were in the internationally unique position of having their cake and eating it too – with the Bundesbank setting interest rates according to the exigencies of the German economy and the EMS limiting exchange rate fluctuations with their trading partners. The cost of occasional revaluations of the DM under the EMS regime was far less than the potential costs of monetary union with France, let alone Italy or Spain. (Heisenberg 2005: 97)

Opening up other member states' markets to German capital to drive convergence was a long-standing aim of the ordo-liberals in the

---

[35] West Germany removed its capital controls in 1974. The United Kingdom dismantled its controls between 1977 and 1979.

Bundesbank and the German Finance Ministry. If capital outflows could hold the D-Mark down and maintain the competitiveness of German industry at the same time, then so much the better. But this did not require monetary union, even less a single currency. As late as 1988, the Bundesbank was arguing that 'the EMS in its present form would ... provide sound underlying conditions for the internal market to function smoothly' (quoted in Chang 2003: 228). Szász explains that 'the Germans had their own misgivings about a monetary dimension in the Treaty, but once it was clear that some countries made this a condition for accepting the completion of the internal market, it was obvious to Chancellor Kohl that he had to find a compromise' (Szász 1999: 93–94).

There was another reason why monetary union gained traction after 1985. The election of Mikhail Gorbachev as General Secretary of the Communist Party of the Soviet Union offered the prospect of a new *Ostpolitik*, and the ultimate prize of German reunification. But to secure support for reunification, Kohl needed to show renewed commitment to the twin pillars of the Western alliance – NATO and the EEC.[36] This was especially important when in 1986 President Reagan offered to eliminate all ballistic nuclear missiles, without consulting his NATO allies, at the Reykjavík summit. Soviet entreaties and American unpredictability pushed the Germans closer to the French. In 1988, Mitterrand and Kohl marked the twenty-fifth anniversary of the Elysée Treaty by creating the Franco-German Defence Council. During the negotiations, Mitterrand adviser Jacques Attali made the link between defence and monetary policy explicit by suggesting 'so that we can have a balance, let us now talk about the German atom bomb' – the D-Mark (Marsh 2009: 114). This produced the Franco-German Economic and Finance Council, a largely consultative body that nonetheless marked a new stage in Franco-German monetary cooperation.

6.6 The Train Leaves the Station: Towards the Single Currency

Despite the promise of capital market liberalisation under the terms of the Single European Act and the linking of monetary policy to defence policy, two franc devaluations in quick succession following the

---

[36] Mitterrand conceded that he could not prevent German reunification, but he could affect its timing.

appointment of the expansionist Prime Minister Jacques Chirac in 1986 confirmed West German scepticism about the merits of closer monetary union. As Mitterrand's adviser Elisabeth Guigou warned in 1987, the EMS could be 'blown away on the next monetary storm' just as the Werner Plan had been fifteen years earlier. Certainly, Chirac did little to promote monetary harmony with his criticisms of the Bundesbank's 'egotistical' monetary policy and his specious claim that the January 1987 ERM realignment was 'a crisis of the D-Mark, not the French Franc' (Marsh 2009: 112). In reality, this 'rancorous' realignment was as much to do with the precipitous decline of the dollar that ended with the Louvre Accord signed by the Group of Seven nations in February 1987 (Marsh 2009: 102–03). This prompted Gaullist ministers to place EMS reform back on the agenda during 1987. If France were to accept the monetary policy of a hegemon, in accordance with the 'trilemma', better that the hegemon be a European Community institution operating under French influence than the Bundesbank or, worse, the US Federal Reserve.

A further step was taken with French Minister of Finance Édouard Balladur's January 1988 proposal for 'the construction in the longer term of a zone with a single currency' (Szász 1999: 102). This marked the culmination of a series of coordinated speeches in favour of monetary union by senior French politicians, which would likely have had as little impact as previous initiatives had they not coincided with the 'policy entrepreneurialism' of West German Foreign Minister Hans-Dietrich Genscher, as concerned as Willy Brandt had been to build a 'western flank' to his own *Ostpolitik*. To the chagrin of the Bundesbank and the Ministry of Finance, Genscher responded in February 1988 with his 'Memorandum for the creation of a European monetary space and a European Central Bank', which stressed the need for monetary union to accompany the completion of the single European market by 1992. Helmut Kohl followed this with a speech in which he stated that 'we shall only achieve the political unification of Europe if we also create a common currency for Europe', agreeing with Genscher that the Germans should use the opportunity presented by their six-month Presidency of the European Council in 1988 to provide a 'signal for the creation of a European monetary space and a European Central Bank' at the forthcoming Hanover summit (Szász 1999: 105–06).

Momentum gathered with Mitterrand's second presidential election victory in May 1988. Having defeated his Gaullist Prime Minister,

Jacques Chirac, Mitterrand confirmed on the eve of the Hanover summit in June that France would finally meet her treaty obligations by removing capital controls (Marsh 2009: 118). He further agreed with Chancellor Kohl that the committee of EEC central bankers (and other independent figures) to be appointed on Genscher's initiative to enquire further into monetary union would be headed by the newly reappointed head of the European Commission, Jacques Delors.[37]

The Delors Committee produced its final report in April 1989. The significance lay less in its content than in the unanimity of the 'epistemic community' of central bankers and independent experts that authored it. This was achieved partly with the promise that the proposed European System of Central Banks Council would be committed to price stability and 'independent of instructions from national governments and Community authorities'.[38] A future European Central Bank would be modelled on the Bundesbank. But it was also because some of the signatories doubted that their recommendations would ever be implemented. Bank of England Governor Robin Leigh-Pemberton later admitted that 'most of us, when we signed the Report in May 1989, thought that we would not hear much about it. It would be rather like the Werner Report' (Blair 1999: 151).

As with the Werner Report, there would be three stages. The first, commencing on 1 July 1990, would entail 'a greater convergence of economic performance through the strengthening of economic and monetary policy coordination within the existing institutional framework' (Blair 1999: 30). There would be no new institutions, but capital flows would drive monetary convergence. Stage Two would involve the creation of the 'the basic organs and structure of the economic and monetary union' – a European Monetary Institute (to replace the European Monetary Cooperation Fund), and then a European Central Bank (Blair 1999: 33). This would require an amendment to the Treaty of Rome, and therefore an intergovernmental conference. Stage Three, the irrevocable fixing of currencies, would take place in January

---

[37] The import of having the EMU enthusiast heading the committee was not lost on the British Chancellor Nigel Lawson, who referred to Delors' appointment as a 'disaster' for his and Mrs Thatcher's attempts to undermine EMU (Lawson 1992: 903).

[38] This nuance perhaps escaped Margaret Thatcher, who was furious that both the Governor of the Bank of England and the President of the Bundesbank, who she had expected to veto the proposals, signed the report (Delors Report 1989: 22).

1999 at the latest. A single currency, while not essential for monetary union, would be 'a natural and desirable further development ... [and] clearly demonstrate the irreversibility of the move to monetary union' (Delors Report 1989: 15).

The EEC heads of government gathered in Madrid in June 1989 to adopt the Delors Report and agree to the intergovernmental conference without fixing a precise date. Once again, international relations opened up a shortcut. On 9 November 1989, the East German authorities opened the gates through the Berlin Wall. A week later, having delayed setting a date for the intergovernmental conference for electoral reasons, Helmut Kohl agreed that the conference should start before the end of 1990.[39] More than ever the West Germans needed a 'western flank' for reunification.[40] At the Dublin European Council in June 1990, the heads of government confirmed that the inter-governmental conferences on political and monetary union would commence on 14 December 1990 (Szász 1999: 131). Four months later at an extraordinary Council in Rome, they agreed that Stage Two would begin on 1 January 1994. The timetable for Stage Three was set at the Maastricht Council in December 1991, where the convergence criteria were also laid down. In order to proceed from Stage Two to Stage Three, a member state had to have:

1. inflation of no more than 1.5 percentage points above the average rate of the three EU member states with the lowest inflation over the previous year;
2. a national budget deficit at or below 3 per cent of GDP;
3. national public debt not exceeding 60 per cent of GDP[41];
4. long-term interest rates no more than two percentage points above the rate in the three EU countries with the lowest inflation over the previous year;
5. no currency devaluations within the previous two years.

Monetary union could commence in 1997 if the majority of member states had achieved the convergence criteria. Otherwise the start date would default to 1 January 1999.

---

[39] West German parliamentary elections were scheduled for December 1990.
[40] There is a suggestion that Kohl preferred to give up some of the Bundesbank's power, rather than his own, to secure German reunification.
[41] A country with a higher level of debt could still adopt the Euro provided its debt level was falling steadily.

In the interim, of course, were the monetary storms of 1992–93 that saw sterling withdraw from the ERM on 16 September 1992 ('Black Wednesday'), the Italian lira depart the next day, and the 'battle of the franc' commence with the *petit oui* in the French referendum on the Maastricht Treaty.[42] The battle ended, after the expenditure of much French reserves, with the widening of the ERM intervention bands from 0.75 per cent to 15 per cent in July 1993. Nonetheless, a victorious France emerged even more committed to EMU, little swayed by the sight of a low inflation, export-led recovery outside the ERM across the English Channel. As the French European Commissioner for monetary affairs commented in 1995, 'If the single currency does not arrive, the very existence of the single market would be threatened' (Marsh 2009: 184). The Bundesbank's Otmar Issing agreed: 'The decisive moment came with the currency crises of 1992–93 ... I and others came to the conclusion that the Common Market would not survive another crisis of this dimension' (Marsh 2009: 185). More to the point, an ERM collapse would have seen an appreciating D-Mark decreasing the competitiveness of German exports with negative consequences for both growth and unemployment. As Richard Portes points out, 'the only way to go was back to floating or capital controls, or forward to full monetary union ... [and] going back would endanger the very integrity of the Union' (Portes 2001).

Given that EMU was conceived partly to protect Europe from the vicissitudes of US economic policy, it is ironic that the project was given a fair wind by the 'Clinton boom' of the mid-1990s. A stronger US economy and an appreciating dollar boosted European growth which had dipped, partly as a consequence of German reunification, but also because of the deflationary measures taken by member states to meet the Maastricht criteria. This provided a contrast with the early years of both the snake and the ERM when US policy had been less conducive. But the key was the compromise brokered by Jacques Delors in 1989 over central bank independence. A European Central Bank free from political interference looks very different to the proposals that emerged from the Werner Committee in 1970 and the Bonn summit in 1978. Without an independent European Central Bank,

---

[42] On 20 September 1992, a French referendum approved the Maastricht Treaty by 51 per cent to 49 per cent. For a lively account of the 'battle of the franc', see Marsh 2009: 162–75.

there would have been little German support for monetary union; without German support, there would be no monetary union. With this support, some judicious fudging of the convergence criteria, and a little creative fiscal accounting, the monetary aspirations of the founders of the European Economic Community, the drafters of the Werner Plan, the architects of the European Monetary System and the members of the Delors Committee were realised as eleven European nations devolved monetary policy to the European Central Bank in July 1998 and locked their currencies on 1 January 1999.[43]

6.7 Conclusions

This chapter has focused on the journey towards monetary union from the perspective of France and Germany. Why were (most) other member states keen to participate? For the periphery nations, membership offered the benefits of imported monetary discipline and a seat at the European 'high table'.[44] There is also Richard Baldwin's 'domino theory of regionalism' – 'an event that triggers closer integration within an existing bloc harms the profits of non-member exporters, thus stimulating them to boost their pro-membership political activity' (Baldwin 1993). This explains why Italians accepted the 'Europe tax' imposed to help to meet the Maastricht criteria. Italy was an enthusiastic founding member of the EEC, and has been prepared to accept some domestic deflation justified in terms of 'Euro-discipline'.[45] By contrast, as Nigel Lawson explained to Mrs Thatcher at the launch of the ERM in 1978 (just three years after the referendum on continued UK membership of the EEC), any such deflation would be 'political suicide' for a British government (Lawson 1978).[46] This was most apparent after Black Wednesday in 1992.

---

[43] In October 1996, three days before the convergence criteria forecast deadline, Eurostat approved an 'exceptional' transfer of 37.5 billion francs (0.45 per cent of GDP) of pension funds from France Telecom to the French government (European Commission and World Bank 1999: 93–94).

[44] The prospect of budgetary savings with lower interest rates was not lost on the periphery nations (James 2012: 257).

[45] There is also the suggestion that policymakers from Southern Europe supported monetary union because it would take power away from their national institutions which they felt were incapable of modernizing their own countries.

[46] Underlining in the original.

Dyson and Featherstone suggest that the French have been playing a 'three-level game' with monetary union. The French state could use monetary integration and the discipline of increasingly mobile capital to drive the modernisation of French industry. Also, EMU was a means of 'binding down' the German leviathan by 'Europeanizing' monetary policy. Finally, EMU was intended to protect the French economy, and especially the CAP, from the volatility that flowed from the US monetary hegemon. All three levels of this game pointed to monetary union preceding economic or political union. This put the French 'monetarists' at odds with German 'economists' who insisted that monetary union should 'crown' economic and political union.

As with any negotiation, the process involved compromise. The Germans have not yet reached the 'top square' on the snakes-and-ladders board – European political union.[47] But they have achieved German reunification, the free movement of capital and an independent ECB. The French have not achieved political control over European monetary policy. But they have reduced European dependence on the dollar and insulated their economy somewhat from the vagaries of US policy, the recent global financial crisis notwithstanding. In this light, the Germans appear to have done rather better, and this is borne out by the recent performance of the respective economies. Nonetheless, the French were starting from a weaker negotiating position, economically if not militarily. Indeed, the story told here is one of the French skilfully using the ebb and flow of the Cold War to persuade the Germans that monetary union could precede both economic and political union. To this extent, discussion of how far the Eurozone constitutes an Optimal Currency Area may be relevant for how policymakers deal with the manifest challenges thrown up by the Great Recession. It is less relevant to explaining how we got here.

References

Anderson, J. J. (1997) 'Hard interests, soft power, and Germany's changing role in Europe' in Katzenstein, P. J. (ed.), *Tamed power: Germany in Europe*. Ithaca: Cornell University Press, pp. 80–107.

Baldwin, R. E. (1993) 'A domino theory of regionalism', *National Bureau of Economic Research Working Paper No. 4465*.

---

[47] German attempts to impose fiscal discipline on member states backfired when they breached the terms of their own 1997 Stability and Growth Pact.

Bergman, M., Gerlach, S. and Jonung, L. (1993) 'The rise and fall of the Scandinavian Currency Union 1873–1920', *European Economic Review* 37: 507–17.

Blair, A. (1999) *Dealing with Europe: Britain and the negotiation of the Maastricht Treaty*. Aldershot: Ashgate.

Callaghan, L. J. (1987) *Time and chance*. London: Collins

Chang, M. (2003) 'Franco-German interests in European monetary integration', in Kirshner, J. (ed.), *Monetary orders: ambiguous economics, ubiquitous politics*. London: Cornell University Press, pp. 218–35.

Cheeseright, P. (1985) 'Reserve currency role for Ecu urged by EEC President', *Financial Times*, 15 January.

Chivvis, C. S. (2006) 'Charles de Gaulle, Jacques Rueff and French international monetary policy under Bretton Woods', *Journal of Contemporary History* 41: 701–20.

Cockfield, F. A. (1994) *European Union: creating the single market*. London: Wiley.

'Delors Report' (1989) Committee for the Study of Economic and Monetary Union *Report on economic and monetary union in the European Community ['Delors Report']*. Luxembourg: Office for Official Publications of the European Communities.

Dyson, K. H. F. and Featherstone, K. (1999) *The road to Maastricht: negotiating economic and monetary union*. Oxford: Oxford University Press.

European Commission and World Bank (1999) *European Union accession: the challenges for public liability management in Central Europe*. Washington, DC: World Bank.

European Economic Community (1962) *Treaty establishing the European Economic Community*. London: Her Majesty's Stationery Office.

Feldstein, M. (1997) 'The political economy of the European Economic and Monetary Union: political sources of an economic liability', *Journal of Economic Perspectives* 11: 23–42.

Frankel, J. A. and Rose, A. K. (1998) 'The endogeneity of the Optimum Currency Area criteria', *Economic Journal* 108: 1009–25.

Giesbert, F.-O. 1993. *La fin d'une époque*. Paris: Fayard Seuil.

Healey, D. W. (1989) *The time of my life*. London: Michael Joseph.

Heisenberg, D. (2005) 'Taking a second look at Germany's motivation to establish economic and monetary union: A critique of 'economic interests' claims', *German Politics* 14: 95–109.

James, H. (2012) *Making the European Monetary Union: the role of the Committee of Central Bank Governors and the origins of the European Central Bank*. London: Belknap Press.

Jenkins, R. H. (1991) *A life at the centre*. London: Macmillan.

Kaplan, J. J. and Schleiminger, G. (1989) *The European Payments Union: financial diplomacy in the 1950s*. Oxford: Clarendon.

Lawson, N. (1978) 'The European Monetary System', in *The Churchill Archives, THCR 2/1/2/12A*. Cambridge: The Churchill Archives.

Lawson, N. (1992) *The view from No. 11: memoirs of a Tory radical*. London: Bantam.

Marsh, D. (2009) *The Euro: the politics of the new global currency*. London: Yale University Press.

Mourlon-Druol, E. (2012) *A Europe made of money: the emergence of the European Monetary System*. London: Cornell University Press.

Needham, D. J. (2014) *UK monetary policy from devaluation to Thatcher, 1967–82*. Basingstoke: Palgrave Macmillan.

Owen, J. G. (1976) 'The collapse of the Bretton Woods system, 1968–1973', Treasury Historical Memorandum no. 3, The National Archives, T267/36. London: The National Archives.

Padoa-Schioppa, T. (2000) *The road to monetary union in Europe: the emperor, the kings, and the genies*. Oxford: Oxford University Press.

Portes, R. (2001) 'A monetary union in motion: the European experience', *CEPR Discussion Paper No. 2954*.

Redish, A. (1993) 'The Latin Monetary Union and the emergence of the international gold standard', in Bordo, M. D. and Capie, F. H. (eds.) *Monetary regimes in transition*. Cambridge: Cambridge University Press, pp. 68–85.

Szász, A. (1999) *The road to European monetary union*. Basingstoke: Macmillan.

Triffin, R. (1960) *Gold and the dollar crisis: the future of convertibility*. New Haven: Yale University Press.

United Nations Monetary and Financial Conference (1948) *Proceedings and Documents, vol. 1*. Washington, DC: United States Government Printing Office.

'Werner Report' (1970) Commission of the European Communities *Report to the Council and the Commission on the realisation by stages of economic and monetary union in the Community ['Werner Report']*. Luxembourg: Commission of the European Communities.

PART II

Multi-Level Interdependencies

7 | Liquidity Architectures and Production Arrangements
A Conceptual Scheme

ROBERTO SCAZZIERI

7.1 Introduction: Political Economy of Liquidity

The Eurozone is a nexus of monetary, credit and fiscal arrangements. Its constitution straddles two distinct, and often contrasting, views of the economy. One approach looks at the economy as a system of exchanges and 'constructs a "vision" of economic life out of the theory of exchange' (Hicks, 1976, p. 212). The other approach describes the economy as a macro-system generating a 'flow of wealth, which is so far homogeneous that it can be greater or less' (Hicks, 1976, p. 210).[1]

Important features and objectives of European Monetary Union reflect the exchange-oriented conception of the economy. Reduction of transaction costs due to uncertainty in the value of units of account and means of payment features prominently among the objectives of the Euro system. Robert Mundell's classic paper on the project of a European currency is a clear instance of this: 'The expectations of exchange rate changes greatly unsettle the money markets, make planning difficult, and in the long run weaken the control a government has over economic policy' (Mundell, 1969, p. 4). Other features of the Eurozone and of the European Union, such as the Stability and Growth Pact (1997) and the Fiscal Compact (2012), are closer to the systemic view (as described earlier) for their focus on macroeconomic objectives (growth and employment) and aggregate requirements (public finance constraints). These objectives and requirements, more than market coordination features per se, have brought to light increasing asymmetries between member states (see, e.g., Basevi and D'Adda, 2014) as well as discrepancy between integration processes in the economic and the social domains (see, e.g., Rodrick, 2011).

---

[1] John Hicks calls the two approaches, respectively, *catallactics* (theory of exchange) and *plutology* (theory of wealth) (Hicks, 1976).

Both views of European Monetary Union overlook the nexus between liquidity arrangements and the debt-credit relationships constitutive of any complex system of interdependent productive activities. This situation must be assessed against the condition that liquidity loans provide the essential buffer bridging time asymmetries between productive activities and making an integrated system of productive activities feasible (Cardinale and Scazzieri, 2016).

This chapter outlines a conceptual framework addressing the political economy of liquidity in a *credit production economy* organized as a system of interdependent debt-credit relationships in the production sphere.[2] This framework is then applied to discussing the political economy of liquidity in the Eurozone. The Eurozone's architecture entails macro-objectives (such as the aggregate price level, or member states' debt to gross domestic product ratio) with no immediate consideration of liquidity requirements at intermediate levels of aggregation. As a result, provision of liquidity is detached from the liquidity requirements arising at the sectoral and inter-sectoral level, and macroeconomic policies target aggregate variables without directly addressing the disaggregate structure of debt-credit relationships. As we shall see, this cleavage is central to the existing Eurozone architecture, and is partly responsible for its internal tensions. Section 7.2 outlines a theory of liquidity as coordinating mechanism in a system of interdependent activities arranged along the time dimension. Section 7.3 investigates the alternative liquidity requirements that one may identify by decomposing the aggregate economy into vertically integrated sectors *or* into horizontally integrated industries. Sections 7.4 and 7.5 examine, respectively, liquidity crises and structural dynamics as conditions generating specific strains and stresses (and requiring specific responses) in the debt-credit configuration of a credit production economy. Section 7.6 concludes the chapter by discussing alternative liquidity policy scenarios that might be associated with different approaches to the decomposition and aggregation of economic activities in the Eurozone.

---

[2] In a credit economy, 'the payment of a debt is an exchange of debts' (Hicks, 1982, p. 266). A *credit production economy* is a credit economy whose debt-credit configuration reflects the asymmetric positions (and responses) of processes on the 'debt side' and processes on the 'credit side' within a production system consisting of interdependent processes of different durations (see Cardinale and Scazzieri, 2016; see also Keynes, (1973 [1933] for a discussion of the related concept of a *monetary production economy*).

7.2 Complementarities over Time and Debt-Credit Relationships: The Liquidity Nexus

Liquidity conditions are a principal feature of economic systems characterized by division of labour and interdependence between separate production units (such as industries, vertically integrated sectors or whole sub-economies). This is increasingly so as activities carried out within individual units become increasingly differentiated from one another in terms of their respective durations and time profiles. The political economy of the Eurozone reflects multiple patterns of interdependence between member states, regions and productive sectors whose interaction entails a complex web of liquidity arrangements. These arrangements have relatively persistent features (*liquidity architectures*) that may be distinguished from contingent modes of liquidity provision. Liquidity architectures connect micro-processes with overall outcomes while avoiding reference to unique causal paths. In this way, those architectures overcome indeterminacy while preserving contingency.

The fundamental liquidity architecture of any given system derives from a limited set of component units. Symmetrical or asymmetrical dependencies between those units determine the liquidity configuration of the system. For example, any two productive sectors may be related to one another symmetrically if the output of each sector is necessary to the activity of the other sector, or asymmetrically if the output of one sector is necessary to the activity of the other sector, but not vice versa. Sectors may also be related across time when the activity of one sector at time t makes the activity of another sector at time $t+k$ feasible (or, respectively, unfeasible). This may be seen if we consider sectors as fabrication stages in a vertically integrated process. In this case, the output of a sector undertaking fabrication stage $f(t)$ may be necessary to the activity of another sector undertaking fabrication stage $f'(t+k)$. This means that there is *complementarity over time* between the two sectors and that lack of intertemporal co-ordination could make the over-all vertically integrated process unfeasible. Sectoral relationships can be addressed by considering the way in which sectors are related to one another within any given period *or* across different periods. In the former case, the analytical tools of the Quesnay-Leontief tradition (multi-sectoral modelling) (Quesnay, 1758; Leontief, 1941; Leontief, 1991 [1928]) highlight inter-sectoral relationships by identifying the relative positions of different sectors or groups of sectors. In the latter case, the analytical tools of the Hicksian and Swedish traditions (complementarities over time and sequential causality) (Myrdal, 1939; Hicks, 1973) highlight patterns of synchronisation across time, thus allowing identification of gaps and loopholes between the time profiles of different sectors. The conceptual tools of both analytical traditions are necessary to visualize the internal structure of liquidity architectures, the multiple causal mechanisms inherent to them and the policy trade-offs deriving from the co-existence of those mechanisms.[3]

Debt-credit relationships arise even in the simplest economic systems once we allow for asymmetries between the time profiles of different activities. They become even more central to the working of the economic system in the case of complex production arrangements. The more a system of interconnected production activities allows for intermediate stages (goods needed in the production of themselves or of other goods), the more liquidity formation and liquidity utilization become an issue to be addressed at almost every step of production. This has a twofold impact on liquidity. Long-lasting processes *need* liquid funds as credit to production; short-lasting processes make liquid funds *available* due to their shorter capital turnovers. As the complexity of production interdependences increases, it is more and more likely that asymmetries between time profiles will also increase. This makes more liquid funds available in certain sectors of the economy as well as increasing the need for liquidity in other sectors. These processes can result in either virtuous or vicious circles, which are related in a fundamental way to the institutional set up determining how demand for credit is met in the system. The relationship between sectoral interdependencies, liquidity crises, and financial instability is a classical theme of the structural theories of industrial fluctuations. The vantage point of these theories is a combination of the multi-sectoral perspective with the sequential causality point of view. This approach is distinctive of the investigation of medium-term economic dynamics carried out by Albert Aftalion (1908–1909, 1909, 1913), Dennis Holme Robertson (1914, 1915) and Marco Fanno (1993 [1931]) at the beginning of the twentieth century and later pursued by Friedrich

---

[3] The relationship between the 'horizontal causality' of the Quesnay-Leontief tradition and the 'vertical causality' of the Hicksian and Swedish tradition is discussed in Landesmann and Scazzieri (1990).

August von Hayek (1941) and John Hicks (1973; 1977). It is worth to look back at this analytical tradition by paying attention to liquidity crises considered *both* as disturbances of existing complementarities and as triggers of structural transformation (see also Scazzieri, 2015).

Debt-credit relations may be generated by asymmetries between the time profiles of interdependent production processes, but may also be independent of production relationships. In the case of debt-credit relationships generated within the production sphere, a disruption of credit arrangements makes producers engaged in long-lasting processes unable to return loans from producers engaged in short-lasting processes. On the other hand, in the case of debt-credit relationships generated within the exchange sphere, a disruption of credit arrangements makes traders engaged in long-term trading unable to return loans from traders engaged in short-term trading. The interface between debt-credit arrangements in the production sphere and those in the exchange sphere becomes an important issue when dealing with the way in which financial institutions could match the liquidity needs arising in the production sphere. In fact, there is a two-way relationship between liquidity needs and debt-credit arrangements. Liquidity needs may or may not be met depending on the availability and cost of liquidity provision from the financial sphere. At the same time, structural transformations within the production sphere may offer investment opportunities unavailable in the financial sphere. This is the situation described by John Hicks in his account of the prerequisites of the First Industrial Revolution and of the large-scale fixed-capital investment associated with it:

Circulating capital is continuously *turned over*; it is continually coming back for reinvestment. But fixed capital is *sunk*, it is embodied in a particular form, from which it can only gradually, at the best, be released. In order that people should be willing, in an uncertain world, to *sink* large amounts of capital, they must either themselves be in possession of other resources, which they hold in a more liquid form, so that they can be quickly realized to meet emergencies; or they must be confident of being able to borrow – and that means borrowing from someone else (it may be a bank) who is able to borrow, or who has liquid funds. In the end, it is the availability of liquid funds which is crucial. (Hicks, 1969, pp. 144–45)

Hicks's argument is interesting for its intertwining of developments relating to technology, state of uncertainty, and availability of liquid funds. His analysis suggests the working of mutually reinforcing conditions: uncertainty reduction combined with technological innovations and institutional changes in the financial sphere (growth of financial markets) made it possible to sink large amounts of funds into fixed capital assets, thereby allowing a transformation of productive structures that would have been otherwise unfeasible. More recently, Larry Neal interpreted this development as a major trigger of the First Industrial Revolution in England: national and international capital markets made large liquidity injections possible, thereby allowing the transition to production techniques associated with a high proportion of fixed to circulating capital (Neal, 1990).[4] Debt-credit relationships that had previously been to a large extent circumscribed within the financial or the production sphere without much spillover from one sphere to the other came to be associated with flows of funds between the two spheres. As a result, institutional arrangements characterizing financial transactions (*financial architectures*) became major channels of transmission of change stemming from either domain. This could boost liquidity provision to industry, while making industry itself dependent on the specific features of the existing financial institutions.[5]

---

[4] According to Larry Neal, 'the changes in the patterns of international capital movements that occurred under the impact of wars and revolutions two centuries ago [that is, at the time of the First Industrial Revolution] had a larger significance ... in order to unravel the history of the industrial revolution in Great Britain ... The argument depends ... on assigning a much larger role to the international capital markets of the time than had previously been reported' (Neal, 1990, p. 218). In particular, these liquidity injections into the production system are a major factor explaining 'how resources were shifted from traditional manufacturing into the new leading sectors that were emerging in heavy industry. Investment in heavy industry clearly got a major boost from wartime demands, and its existence after the war provided the basis for even cheaper capital goods. Those, in turn, facilitated the spread of modern manufacturing techniques throughout the British manufacturing sector, and to an increasing extent those techniques were reaching the American and Continental manufacturing sectors as well' (Neal, 1990, p. 220; see also Neal, 2000).

[5] This may be seen in terms of Hicks's representation of the financial system as a 'hierarchy of financiers, who may be arranged in rings': '[e]ach ring lends to the ring outside it and borrows from the ring inside it; at the centre of all the rings is the Central Bank. Industry can raise funds *at various points of the rings*; but in order that *its needs should be fully met*, each of the rings must play its part. In equilibrium, each of the financiers, wherever situated, has to make a profit and each has his problem of liquidity ... Even if the rate of interest, as it appears at the centre of the system ... is reduced to zero, or almost to zero, the marginal cost of capital to industry will not be reduced to zero. It is in this sense that there can be a

For example, the institutional sphere generated a shift from fundamental uncertainty to risk (as in the case of the maritime insurance industry in the seventeenth century, discussed in Leonard, 2015) or from risk to fundamental uncertainty (as with the collapse of the computable risk framework in credit markets as a result of the financial crisis of the early 2000s). These shifts may be independent of structural changes in production systems but may have a decisive influence on the latter by favouring existing patterns of coordination through insurability, or disrupting existing coordination by lack thereof.

The intertwining of financial and production spheres entails that liquidity shortages or gluts arising in either sphere can spread across the whole system of interconnected activities. For example, lack of credit at any given stage of production may trigger a liquidity shortage limited to that stage or bring about a general liquidity shortage spreading from the production to the exchange sphere. On the other hand, the accumulation of liquid reserves at some stage of production may trigger a liquidity glut that may either be limited to that stage or bring about a general liquidity glut spreading from that stage to the rest of the economy through channels provided by interdependencies between production processes. Similarly, shortage of credit to traders in some financial markets may trigger a liquidity shortage limited to those markets or it may bring about a general liquidity shortage spreading from the financial to the production sphere through channels provided by market interdependencies. On the other hand, accumulation of

"floor to the rate of interest" (the effective rate of interest) even in long-period equilibrium' (Hicks, 1967, p. 58; emphasis added). This hierarchical configuration of liquidity provision highlights the relative autonomy of the debt-credit relationships that link one layer of the hierarchy to another (conditions making a debt-credit relationship feasible between two adjacent layers of the financial hierarchy may not be as effective if other points of that hierarchy are considered). This configuration highlights the complexity of the relationship between the production system and the financial system once the complementarity between the two systems is established, for liquidity provision able to meet the liquidity needs of productive activities would require appropriate conditions at each layer of the financial hierarchy (it is noteworthy that conditions making liquidity provision feasible at one point of the hierarchy do not necessarily facilitate liquidity provision at another point). We may conjecture that the particular form taken by the hierarchical arrangement of the financial system in any given context can be an important influence on the conditions of liquidity provision, and in particular on the relationship between the structure of interest rates and the liquidity needs of the production system (see also Hicks, 1989, chapter 13).

liquid reserves in some financial markets may trigger a liquidity glut that may either be limited to those markets or bring about a general glut across the system.

7.3 Vertical Integration, Sectoral Disintegration and Liquidity Provision

The arrangement of production processes relative to one another is an important factor determining the way in which liquidity needs arise and may be satisfied within the economic system (see Section 7.2). This suggests that effective liquidity provision will have different characteristics depending on which configuration of interdependencies defines the architecture of the system. Constraints and opportunities of the macroeconomic type prevail in a system in which the most important linkages are provided by connections within each vertically integrated sector (that is, within each bundle of processes leading to a particular final consumption good, or set of such goods). Final demand changes are likely to differently affect liquidity needs in each vertically integrated sector. This is because a macroeconomic expansion or contraction is likely to differently affect the different vertically integrated sectors, so that liquidity reserves may accumulate or decumulate *at different speeds* across the whole spectrum of vertically integrated sectors. At the same time, an economic system in which production linkages are primarily between stages of production within each vertically integrated sector (rather than between different sectors) is unlikely to generate 'endogenous' debt-credit relationships within the production sphere. Liquidity shortages or gluts arising across the spectrum of vertically integrated sectors are unlikely to compensate each other via the temporal asymmetries (the 'stops and go') inherent to systems of interdependent production activities. For this reason, economic systems of the 'vertical' type tend to produce liquidity needs they are by themselves unable to satisfy, or liquidity opportunities they are by themselves unable to absorb. This means that the liquidity required (or generated) within the system translates more or less directly into macroeconomic bottlenecks (or opportunities). In general, bottlenecks can be overcome (and, respectively, opportunities used) depending on macroeconomic policy responses. Liquidity adjustment would be external to the structure of interdependencies within the production sphere, and may reflect institutional arrangements independent of inter-sectoral relationships.[6] On the other hand, an economic system whose fundamental architecture is provided by horizontal linkages *between sectors* delivering intermediate goods to one another is associated with liquidity bottlenecks and opportunities of a different type. This is because, in this case, the most important linkages are provided by intermediate goods whose position within the system *can* make them independent of specific configurations of final demand (see Hicks, 1985; Hagemann and Scazzieri, 2009; Scazzieri, 2009). In particular, intermediate goods used in a plurality of heterogeneous production processes (versatile intermediate goods) make the economic system move from a vertical to a horizontal configuration of interdependence (Baranzini and Scazzieri, 1990; Cardinale and Scazzieri, 2011). Interchangeable parts manufacturing and general purpose technologies are historically important instances of process specialization along the construction/utilization divide (see, respectively, Rosenberg, 1963, 1969; Helpman, 1998). Process specialization of this type generates a core of productive activities that may be functional to the production of a variety of final consumption goods (Rosenberg and Trajtenberg, 2001; Carter and Leontief, 2005). For this reason, economic systems of the horizontal type generate liquidity needs they may be able to satisfy independently of external sources of funding. This inherent flexibility is a distinctive feature of horizontal systems relative to vertical systems, and can be explained by the 'sectoral disintegration' characterizing a horizontal system of interdependent production activities.[7] In fact, we may expect sectoral disintegration

---

[6] The principle of effective demand, which was originally introduced in Malthus's *Principles of Political Economy*, is a way to express the need for external liquidity in a viable (self-sustaining) vertical economy (Malthus, 1820). In fact, Malthus held the view that 'a process of investment is likely to generate a level of productive employment that cannot sustain itself unless there is a source of additional effective demand external to the production system' (Baranzini and Scazzieri, 1990, p. 286). At the root of Malthus' s emphasis on external sources of demand (and, correspondingly, of 'liquid' purchasing power) is the idea that 'the labour commanded by commodities entering necessary consumption is generally less than the labour commanded by the total output produced by any given quantity of labour (Baranzini and Scazzieri, 1990, p. 286). See also Amendola, Froeschle and Gaffard (1993) for an extension of this property to a dynamic economy under conditions of structural change.

[7] The 'Method of Sectoral Disintegration' is discussed by Hicks in his analysis of different approaches to the treatment of capital goods in a production economy (Hicks, 1973, p. 5).

to proceed hand in hand with increasing division of labour and specialization of processes. As long as disintegration leads to introduction of
an increasing number of intermediate goods, the structural flexibility
of the economic system is likely to increase. This is because the versatility of intermediate goods is also likely to increase as the system moves
to higher stages of sectoral disintegration. For example, interchangeable
parts manufacturing and general-purpose technologies would make
intermediate goods to enter *multiple* processes of different types. This
allows any given production structure to 'recede' from specific configurations of final demand, and to shift liquidity from one configuration of
production to another in times of economic and/or technological
change. A change in the composition of final demand may lead to
liquidity gluts affecting the construction stages of commodities whose
demand is falling. At the same time, there will be liquidity shortages at
the construction stages of commodities whose demand is rising. Under
conditions of intermediate goods versatility, 'local' shortages and gluts
may compensate each other, and the idle liquidity reserves accumulating at the construction stages of commodities in falling demand may be
directed to the construction stages of commodities whose demand is
expanding, thus facilitating the funding of overall structural change.

To sum up, vertical integration and sectoral disintegration call
attention to alternative routes along which liquidity needs arise and
can be satisfied. Vertical integration highlights the need for exogenous
generation of liquidity. Funding needs may arise within the system
due to lack of effective aggregate demand.[8] These funding needs
become increasingly important when increasing process specialization
increases the distance of a significant number of production processes
from final demand.[9]

Lending and borrowing are essential components of interdependence between production processes. However, lending and borrowing

---

[8] For example, in a 'vertical' corn-steel economy, steel workers require foodstuff
produced by agricultural workers, and agricultural workers require tools produced
by steel workers, but their respective needs and deliveries cannot be synchronised
within the production system. This highlights the need for macroeconomic
coordination as a means to meet the needs arising within each vertical sector.

[9] A production system in which division of labour maps the difference between
final consumption goods is likely to consist of processes running in parallel and
requiring little or no time coordination. Any significant increase in division of
labour through sectoral disintegration and intermediate production is likely to
enhance the need for coordination over time.

take different forms depending on whether vertical integration or sectoral disintegration defines the structural configuration of the economic system (see Hicks, 1990). With vertical integration, liquidity needs reflect the distance of production processes from final consumption. In this case, liquidity provision takes a *macroeconomic character*, as time coordination presupposes the availability of liquid funds generated *outside* the production system. Sectoral disintegration brings a different picture. In this case, liquidity needs reflect the distances between different specialized processes from each another. As a result, liquidity provision takes a *structural character*, as it may be achieved through funds generated *within* the system of interdependent processes. The two approaches to liquidity provision (macroeconomic versus structural) entail different attitudes to liquidity policy and have different implications for the working of any given system of debt-credit relationships. These implications are discussed in the following section.

7.4 Liquidity Crises: Constraints and Opportunities

Liquidity is important to the working of any economic system primarily as a means to overcome the asymmetries inherent to a nexus of interdependent activities by transforming lack of coordination into a pattern of complementarities over time. This can be seen as follows. Consider a set of interdependent processes of production and consumption such that each process delivers a particular commodity while requiring other commodities produced within the system as its inputs. It is generally the case that different commodities are associated with production periods of different lengths. As a result, *lack of synchronisation* is the normal state of affairs whenever products of different processes are required in each other's production.

Any system of interconnected activities shows two fundamentally different patterns of interdependence. On the one hand, activities may be complementary to one another within the same time period so that, say, activity i cannot take place at t unless also activity j is carried out at the same time. This *complementarity in time* calls attention to synchronisation requirements that may be necessary for certain activities to be operated at all. For example, there are activities that may require a large infrastructure that will not be built unless a minimum degree of infrastructure utilization is attained. In this case, complementarity in time takes the form of joint utilization of the same infrastructure by a variety of different activities. This pattern of interdependence gives immediate expression to minimum scale requirements and is not necessarily associated with introduction of a specific specialization pattern between activities (Scazzieri, 2014). A different pattern of interdependence may be observed when specialized activities are coordinated with one another across several time periods. In this case, activity i cannot take place at time $t+1$ unless activity j has already taken place at time t. This condition of *complementarity over time* calls attention to precedence patterns between activities, and to the need of coordinating activities across time. For example, short-lasting activities (such as the finishing tasks in a manufacturing process) may require intermediate inputs delivered by long-lasting activities (such as the construction tasks in the fabrication of machine tools). Here a twofold coordination problem arises: (1) activity j may require an intermediate input delivered by activity i and; (2) activity i must deliver the required intermediate input to activity j *before* activity j is completed. Condition (1) points to the existence of *technological complementarity* across activities; condition (2) highlights the potential for *debt-credit relationships* across time-periods. Both complementarity in time and complementarity over time entail liquidity conditions for the economic system to work. With complementarity in time, liquidity is needed to provide the initial advance for the set of synchronised activities to start. After the initial liquidity advance has started the process, liquidity would again be available at the end of each turnover period (as with Quesnay's agricultural cycle). With complementarities over time, liquidity is needed in order to smooth out the differences between the time profiles of different activities. Here, liquidity allows coordination between interdependent but not fully synchronised activities, and gets generated at the end of the turnover period of any given activity. In the former case, liquidity is provided and absorbed at regular intervals coinciding with the time length of each period (say, each agricultural cycle); in the latter case, when activities are complementary across several time periods, liquidity is generated and absorbed by multiple activities *at different points of time*.

Any system of interdependent activities rests upon liquidity conditions of either type, or of both types. François Quesnay's *Tableau Économique* (Quesnay, 1758) provides a picture of interdependence in which the initial liquidity provision (*avances primitives*) allows both generation of liquidity at discrete points of time within the agricultural sector (these points are determined by the length of the agricultural production cycle) and a virtually continuous generation of liquidity within the manufacturing sector (this is made possible by the shorter turnover periods in this sector[10]). Liquidity arrangements for the single period tend to prevail when interdependence between activities within each period is more important than interdependence between activities across different periods. Liquidity requirements are relatively predictable when liquidity needs and provision may be scheduled at regular time intervals; a more complex picture emerges when interdependent activities of different lengths infuence the overall turnover of liquidity. In the latter case, liquidity requirements reflect the fine structure of interdependencies between activities of different lengths, and liquidity provision may take the form of a continuous process made possible by coordination between the different turnover periods of distinct activities. Lack of funds needed for overall reproduction generates a *macroeconomic lacking*, which may in turn be associated with generalized unemployment and/or inflationary pressure due to contraction in the overall availability of goods. On the other hand, the lack of funds that would be needed for coordination over time of sequentially related activities generates a *structural lacking*, which may bring about bottlenecks for certain activities and accumulation of reserves for other activities.[11]

---

[10] The latter condition is explicitly discussed in Cesare Beccaria's *Elementi di economia pubblica* (ms. *circa* 1769, first published 1804). This work emphasizes the relationship between the rate of growth of the overall social product and the *frequency* at which new liquidity can be generated within the manufacturing subsystem of the economy (Beccaria, 1971 [ms. *circa* 1769], p. 390).

[11] The distinction between macroeconomic lacking and structural lacking suggests one important reason why, in assessing the effectiveness of monetary policy, 'in addition to the relation between money stock and income, it would also be worth examining the relation between credit flow and income, particularly if the financial surpluses and deficits of the various sectors of the economy open up' (Masera, 1984, p. 199). In fact, structural lacking emphasizes the need of intersectoral financial flows that are not necessarily consistent with credit targets of macroeconomic type (see also Modigliani and Papademos, 1987, for a discussion of the relationship between bank and non-bank credit that is relevant in this context). Differently from macroeconomic lacking, structural lacking calls attention to the relationship between the timing of flows and the accumulation of stocks (reserves of liquidity) (Hicks, 1974; Scazzieri, 1994).

A *liquidity crisis* is brought about when liquidity provision is disrupted due to either macroeconomic lacking or structural lacking, or both. In either case, lack of liquidity entails disruption of the existing pattern of coordination between production processes. In general, a liquidity crisis is also associated with the decoupling of financial architecture from the internal structure of the production system (see also Section 7.3). This decoupling may lead to liquidity shifts across different sectors of the economy. Depending on prevailing historical conditions, these shifts may lead to economic decline or trigger innovation and structural change.

7.5 Division of Labour, Liquidity and Structural Dynamics

As we have seen, different patterns of interdependence are associated with different liquidity requirements. They are also associated with different routes along which liquidity provision may be made. There is a fundamental distinction between (1) the interdependence of activities carried out within the same time period and (2) the interdependence of activities carried out at different time periods. Either type of interdependence requires the provision of liquidity, since in either case a mismatch is possible between what is materially required at any given time and what is materially available to activities taking place at that time. In case (1), funds are required at discrete time intervals to allow the system to reproduce the material conditions for its existence; in case (2), funds are needed to allow the economic system to 'fill in' waiting times when the material requirements due to patterns of precedence between activities cannot be immediately satisfied. Bottlenecks due to liquidity shortage may affect the working of the economic system along either route. Macroeconomic lacking and structural lacking are respectively associated with the two types of bottlenecks and entail different approaches to liquidity provision.

Macroeconomic lacking presupposes a liquidity bottleneck at the level of the production system as a whole. This means that new liquidity cannot be generated *within* the system once lacking sets in, and opens the way to liquidity provision through monetary and credit policies of the macroeconomic type. Structural lacking presents a completely different picture. In this case, lacking presupposes coordination mismatches between different activities. This entails that additional liquidity may be generated either by introducing new linkages within the existing boundaries or by linking up with activities external to those boundaries.[12] Structural lacking calls attention to both bottlenecks and opportunities. Mismatches due to lack of coordination over time may be associated with *both* liquidity shortages for certain activities and accumulation of liquidity reserves in other activities. This can be seen by considering that, in general, activities associated with short turnover periods (*short activities*) have to be coordinated with activities associated with long turnover periods (*long activities*). For example, short activities delivering a final consumption good (say, rice) have to be coordinated with long activities delivering a certain instrument of production (say, a properly irrigated rice field). Field preparation and rice production belong to the same vertically integrated process, which includes a 'construction phase' (field preparation) and a 'utilization phase' (rice production) (for this distinction, see Hicks, 1973). Liquid funds are needed for starting the construction phase of the process before completion of the utilization phase of the same process; they are also needed when carrying out the utilization phase by operating capital equipment before the proceeds from selling final products are available. Indeed, liquidity needs increase with the time distance between start of the construction phase and completion of the utilization phase.

Splitting any vertically integrated process into separate components may be a way to release liquid funds from within the vertically integrated process and make them available (in 'concentrated amounts') to some of its specialized components. For example, activating the construction phase separately from the utilization phase introduces two distinct activities that are both shorter than the original process. This means that less liquid funds would be needed provided the completion date of the new construction process coincides with the start date of the new utilization process. But this is no longer the case if the two dates

---

[12] In the case of macroeconomic lacking, liquidity requirements presuppose an economic system with clearly identified boundaries, and it is possible to immediately recognize the overall scale of activity for which liquidity is needed. In its most common form, the relevant economic unit would be the national economic system, even if the same argument would apply to other economic units as well. In the case of structural lacking, the focus of attention shifts to the relationship *between* different activities, and the identification of boundaries is no longer a primary concern. Indeed, in some cases it is possible to overcome structural lacking by introducing linkages between activities that cut across traditional boundaries between different economic systems or subsystems.

do not coincide. For in this case liquidity *may or may not* be released depending on whether the time distance from beginning to end of either process (including waiting times due to lack of time coordination) is shorter than the overall duration of the original vertically integrated process. Division of labour and specialization of processes may be conducive to a liquidity advantage in the sense that, in a system of fully coordinated activities, less liquid funds are needed to complete any given process (see also Leijhonhufvud, 1986). Indeed, any mismatch between completion and start dates of sequentially related processes makes liquidity shortages or liquidity gluts to appear either in long or in short processes depending on which point of time is considered. A developed division of labour may allow the endogenous formation of liquid funds if the splitting of processes takes place along the construction/utilization divide rather than along the dividing lines between different final consumption goods. In this case, time mismatches between construction and utilization processes can become an independent source of liquidity, for the economic system may generate a *liquidity shift* (from long to short activities), and this in turn may release funds previously locked in reinvestment cycles (Einarsen, 1938) making those funds available to investment in new productive facilities.[13] To sum up, increasing the division of labour and specialization of processes may increase *both* the vulnerability of the economic system to liquidity shortages and its ability to undertake liquidity shifts and withstand liquidity shocks. The final balance depends on the way in which increasing specialization modifies the structural configuration of the economic system. If specialization leads to an increase in the number of vertically integrated sectors delivering final consumption goods, it is likely that the vulnerability of the economic system to final demand fluctuations will also increase. (For example, a demand contraction would trigger a generalized liquidity need that the economic system would be unable to meet.) On the other

---

[13] Johann Einarsen defines reinvestment cycles as 'those cycles which may manifest themselves in the reinvestment because the number of capital instruments produced in different years varies in magnitude and because the capital goods produced in the same year will need replacement rather simultaneously ... We call these cycles *pure (or generating) reinvestment cycles* ... In capital production just as in populations large generations will be followed by echos. The pure reinvestment cycles are, therefore, due to the uneven age distribution within the stock of capital instruments in society' (Einarsen, 1938, pp. 38–39).

hand, specialization leading to an increase in the number of 'division points' between production stages for a sufficient number of commodities is likely to increase the system's ability to withstand liquidity shocks. This is because increasing specialization influences the construction/utilization divide by increasing the number of production stages carried out as *independent* specialized processes. As a result of increasing process specialization, mismatches between 'long' and 'short' activities are likely to become more common, and this is likely to increase the ability of the system to *withstand* fluctuations through liquidity shifts (see argument earlier in the chapter). Historical experience shows remarkable differences in economic systems' vulnerability to liquidity shortages and suggests that alternative patterns of division of labour may be at the root of these differences. John Hicks called attention to the drawbacks of extensive specialization between vertically integrated processes in the manufacturing economies of late medieval and early modern Italy and Flanders:

The best documentary instances of more or less industrialized countries being pushed right back into the pre-industrial condition, are those of Italy and Flanders in the sixteenth and seventeenth centuries. No doubt, there were political causes which had much to do with their economic decline; but it is surely no accident that their early industrialisms, as compared with those of our day, were very narrowly based. They did indeed have other industries besides textiles; but the concentration upon textiles – the necessary concentration, in the technical conditions of that day – was such that when their advantage in textiles was gone, there was nothing else to which they could turn. (Hicks, 1959, p. 174*n*)

The experiences of Britain and the United States after the First Industrial Revolution were strikingly different from the Italian and Flemish cases considered by Hicks. For in their case final demand, upheavals could ultimately be buffered by taking advantage of manifold separations between construction and utilization processes, and of the multiple cross-process linkages that this separation allowed (Rosenberg, 1963, 1969; Yan and Ames, 1965). In this case, mismatches between 'long' and 'short' activities could trigger liquidity shifts from one activity to another, thereby increasing the overall industrial resilience of the economic system and initiating waves of structural innovation (Janeway, 2012).

However, liquidity crises may or may not trigger inter-sectoral liquidity shifts. In a production system of vertically integrated processes separated from each another along dividing lines coinciding with the distinction between different final consumption goods, liquidity crises are unlikely to lead to liquidity shifts between construction and utilization phases. This can be seen as follows. Consider a system made of two vertically integrated sectors S_i and S_j delivering final consumption goods x_i and x_j respectively and operating alongside each other at any given time. Both S_i and S_j include a construction phase (C_i and C_j respectively) and a utilization phase (U_i and U_j respectively). Demand contraction for the final commodity produced by either sector (say, S_i) would not directly translate into availability of additional liquidity for the other sector (S_j), for in this case demand contraction would initially involve lengthening of utilization phase U_i (via the lengthening of utilization time of existing – already constructed – capital equipment) and accumulation of idle reserves at construction phase C_i (no further construction of capital equipment will be carried out at this phase). This is the well-known process by which demand contraction generates accumulation of idle reserves that in turn induce further contraction along the sequence of connected production stages (Aftalion, 1908–1909, 1913; Robertson, 1915, 1926; Fanno, 1993 [1931]). Given the vertical configuration of the system, idle reserves within sector S_i are unlikely to generate additional liquidity for sector S_j (the accumulation of reserves within construction stage C_i does not entail that additional funds could be channelled from C_i to C_j). The situation is different with an economic system in which 'sectoral disintegration' has taken place (Hicks, 1973, p. 5). In this case, it is as if there were 'two kinds of "firms"': those which make capital goods, now identified as "machines", and those which use them. The accounting distinction between Consumption and Investment is converted into an industrial division' (Hicks, 1973, p. 5). In the latter case, construction and utilization processes operate *alongside each other*, and there will not be a time synchronisation constraint to shifting liquidity reserves accumulated at construction stage C_i to construction stage C_j.

This means that a 'local' demand contraction for one particular final consumption good might simultaneously lead to: (1) liquidity withdrawal from processes delivering intermediate goods to the finishing process for that commodity and (2) increased liquidity supply to processes delivering intermediate goods for other final consumption goods. In our example, demand contraction affecting only final commodity x_i can lead to the withdrawal of liquidity from the construction processes delivering capital equipment to x_i and to increased liquidity supply for the construction processes delivering capital equipment to x_j.

To sum up, demand contraction is likely to have different outcomes depending on which set of interdependencies is most relevant. An economic system organized as a set of vertically integrated sectors with few or no linkages across sectors is subject to liquidity crises that may originate in one or few sectors and may propagate to most or all sectors due to liquidity bottlenecks arising in sequence across sectors. The reason for this is that demand contraction in a particular sector is likely to lead to withdrawal of liquidity from the utilization phase of that sector and to accumulation of idle reserves at the construction phase of the same sector. This process may in turn evolve into liquidity gluts for other sectors and eventually for the economic system as a whole, while idle reserves accumulate in the system.[14] The response to demand contraction may be very different in the case of an economic system organized in a sectorally disintegrated way. Here the structural configuration of the system consists of processes separated from each another according to the construction/utilization divide. Processes delivering intermediate goods needed to produce final commodity i would be operated alongside with the processes delivering commodity i itself. As this condition generalizes to multiple commodities, the economic system takes the form of a multi-tier structure in which short and long processes are activated side by side. In a depression, the utilization sectors are unable to secure short-term liquidity from

---

[14] The idea of a system-wise generation of 'free capital' (liquidity glut) in the course of economic depressions derives from concentration of attention on the vertical configuration of the economic system, and on the macroeconomic repercussions of the imbalances internal to its productive structure. This type of structure makes macroeconomic adjustment a necessary *prerequisite* of liquidity adjustment and brings to light the role of liquidity dynamics external to the production system. In this connection, Mentor Bouniatian had argued that the liquidity shortages characterizing the last phase of an economic expansion are a type of investment carried out through an increase of 'monetary reserve', that is, an increase of 'potential purchasing power' (Bouniatian, 1922, p. 297; see also Bouniatian, 1908; Aftalion, 1909). This is considered to be the monetary counterpart of the 'reserve of industrial capital' that is also being accumulated during crises (Bouniatian, 1922, p. 297). Bouniatian also pointed out that economic depression and price deflation entails a *decrease* in the degree of concentration of capital funds (Bouniatian, 1933, pp. 138–40). This unlocking of funds may in turn become a source of macroeconomic liquidity provision once recovery has begun.

construction sectors thereby facing short-term liquidity shortages that could bring the turnover of circulating capital to a halt. At the same time, equipment renewals in construction sectors are reduced or completely discontinued, and amortisation funds are shifted into monetary reserves that might eventually be a source of liquidity provision when the depression is over. Conversely, demand expansion for one or more final commodities results in increased speed of turnover for circulating capital goods in the utilization sectors delivering those commodities, and generates accumulation of liquidity in those sectors. At the same time, construction sectors may face liquidity shortages due to the increasing capital equipment needs in those sectors. These shifts of liquidity opportunities and constraints between utilization and construction sectors explain the coexistence of liquidity shortages and gluts during economic expansions and contractions.[15] To sum up, inter-sectoral liquidity shifts are essential to allow the transformation of productive structures without significant recourse to external funding. However, a necessary condition for the viability of this process is that the direction of liquidity shifts be consistent with the requirements of liquidity adjustment for construction and utilization sectors in the upswings and downswings of economic activity.[16]

7.6 Liquidity Policy under Structural Change: Alternatives for Europe

Liquidity needs are inherent to any economic system based on division of labour. Such needs are bound to increase as division of labour increases the distance between production of intermediate goods and

---

[15] The preceding argument entails that an economic system organized as a set of vertically integrated sectors – with few or no inter-sectoral linkages – is more likely to face a liquidity lacking (or, alternatively, a liquidity glut) of the macroeconomic type. On the other hand, an economic system organized as a set of sectorally disintegrated and interdependent industries is more likely to meet liquidity shortages and gluts that are sectorally specific in origin and may or may not develop into a systemic condition depending on the direction of financial flows under given behavioural and institutional arrangements.

[16] We may conjecture that this condition is more likely fulfilled when intermediate goods are produced in specialized sectors. In this case construction sectors would not be constrained to the provision of capital equipment for specific final commodities, so that 'direct' liquidity shifts between construction and utilization sectors would be possible. In a sectorally disintegrated economy, the existence of a 'general purpose' intermediate goods sector (or subsystem) is a major condition helping liquidity compensation within the system.

final consumption, as well as the distance between the lengths of production processes. Different system configurations are associated with different liquidity needs (see Section 7.5). In particular, alternative patterns of division of labour require different approaches to liquidity provision. When division of labour follows the pattern of distinction between vertically integrated sectors, liquidity needs are predominantly of the macroeconomic type. In this case, liquidity is either brought into the system or taken out of it, and liquidity formation by means of changes in the sectoral composition of output is to a large extent irrelevant. On the other hand, when division of labour follows the sectoral disintegration pattern, liquidity needs are predominantly of the structural type. In this case, liquidity absorption and liquidity formation derive from complementarities over time between processes of different durations. Liquidity provision suitable to a vertically integrated structure (i.e. suitable to an economic system in which division of labour follows the vertical pattern) may not be suitable to an economic system in which sectoral disintegration has established itself to a significant extent. For macroeconomic provision (or withholding) of liquidity affects the set of production processes *as a whole* and may thus be ineffective in taking advantage of opportunities arising from specific time arrangements of processes relative to each other. For example, macroeconomic liquidity provision could make structural changes more difficult if it allows obsolete processes to continue while at the same time not affording enough liquidity to processes of a new type. This may be a serious drawback if sectoral disintegration has proceeded to a sufficient degree, because in this case liquidity bottlenecks and opportunities are primarily associated with differences between the durations of production processes. Liquidity transfers along specific routes would be needed to take advantage of liquidity reserves accumulated within the system. As we have seen, liquidity shortages affecting the utilization stage of contracting activities are likely to be associated with the formation of liquidity reserves at the construction stage of the same activities. Under sectoral disintegration, liquidity should be channelled to construction processes further removed from the utilization stage until this additional liquidity may be used in starting processes of a new type. At this point, we may expect a phase of accelerated structural change as more and more processes of the new type are substituted for processes of the old type. Adequate and targeted liquidity provision is a fundamental component of this dynamics. Without sufficient liquidity transfers from old to new construction processes, structural change cannot take place and the economy is likely to be stuck in a condition of structural standstill. In short, liquidity provision may or may not trigger structural change depending on where liquidity is generated and where it is absorbed. In this type of economy, liquidity provision through purely aggregate (macroeconomic) policy measures may not be effective in triggering structural change due to the 'unqualified' character of the economic expansion thereby generated (see Cardinale and Scazzieri, 2016).[17] In short, macroeconomic policy of the purely aggregative type may be effective in a vertical economy requiring external injections (or withdrawals) of liquidity. On the other hand, a purely aggregative policy is likely to be ineffective in a sectorally disintegrated system, as that system requires a type of liquidity governance consistent with its cross-sectoral bottlenecks and opportunities.

The structural approach to liquidity calls attention to the fact that *different liquidity policies* may be needed depending on which type of structural interdependencies is prevailing (see also Hicks, 1967). A low degree of sectoral disintegration entails vertically integrated sectors coordinated with one another via the macroeconomic effective demand condition (Pasinetti, 1981, 1993). On the other hand, a high degree of sectoral disintegration entails that specialized sectors would run in parallel but would be coordinated with each other via complementarities both within any given period and across different periods (Hicks, 1973; Quadrio Curzio, 1986, 1996). Both liquidity needs and liquidity provision can be significantly different depending on the underlying type of economic structure.[18] For example, macroeconomic liquidity expansion may induce aggregate growth in a vertical economy without inducing significant changes in the underlying division of labour; however, the same liquidity policy may block the internal formation of liquidity in a sectorally disintegrated economy thereby slowing structural change and even thwarting economic expansion.

[17] The effectiveness of a growth-enhancing liquidity policy presupposes the effective targeting of liquidity provision so as to foster liquidity transfers between different categories of long processes (see discussion earlier in the chapter).
[18] The relationship between production structure and the liquidity needs associated with that structure is a fundamental condition influencing the *effectiveness* of monetary policy (see del Vecchio, 1930, 1932).

Macroeconomic liquidity contraction may have similarly divergent outcomes in the two types of economy. In a vertically integrated economy, contraction could make it impossible to overcome liquidity bottlenecks and is likely to set the economy on a declining or negative growth path. On the other hand, in a sectorally disintegrated economy, contraction may trigger structural changes by drawing liquid funds away from old processes and triggering internal liquidity shifts from old to new processes. As we consider liquidity policy at the Eurozone level, it is therefore essential to identify which production linkages are strongest, and to evaluate which linkages liquidity policy is expected to trigger.[19] In particular, no assessment of liquidity policy can overlook the fact that liquidity provision can take alternative routes (macroeconomic versus structural), that a macroeconomic *or* a structural liquidity policy may alternatively be the most effective one depending on which type of linkages is most important, and that different policy responses may be appropriate depending on whether the system in view is the Eurozone as a whole or a collection of its component subsystems.[20] The 'expansion versus austerity' debate entails concentration of attention on vertical linkages and avoids consideration of inter-sectoral linkages. This makes it difficult to disentangle the manifold structural implications that alternative policy options may have for different subsystems (countries) and for the whole Eurozone economy. In fact, either policy may trigger or thwart structural change depending on the prevailing type of economic structure. An expansionary liquidity policy may trigger economic expansion at the macroeconomic level in a vertically integrated economy. On the other hand, expansionary policy applied to a sectorally disintegrated structure may lead to macroeconomic contraction if the additional liquidity going to old processes makes liquidity transfers towards new processes more difficult. The structural configuration of the system also affects the

[19] This interdependence between the weight of different linkages and the effectiveness of different types of policy entails that the appropriate policy in a liquidity crisis cannot be 'predetermined on an a priori basis', but depends 'on the severity of the crisis and on its structural and topical characteristics' (Masera, 2015).

[20] It is also important to acknowledge that different structural architectures may be relevant depending on the time horizon one is considering, and that appropriate policy responses may vary accordingly (Ornaghi, 1990, Scazzieri, 2012).

outcome of austerity policy, for this policy is likely to trigger depression in a fully vertically integrated structure. However, the same policy may be compatible with macroeconomic expansion if sectoral disintegration allows sufficient formation of endogenous liquidity. To conclude, different economic structures (or different components of the same structure) would respond differently to any given liquidity measure. Structural liquidity analysis is needed to assess alternative outcomes and is essential to informed policy choice in the Eurozone.

References

Aftalion, A. (1908–1909) 'La réalité des surproductions générales: essai d'une théorie des crises générales et périodiques', *Revue d'économie politique*, 22 (1908), pp. 696–706; 23 (1909), pp. 81–117, 201–29, 241–59.

Aftalion, A. (1909) 'La théorie de l'épargne en matière de crises périodiques de surproduction', *Revue d'histoire des doctrines économiques et sociales*, pp. 229–62.

Aftalion, A. (1913) *Les crises périodiques de surproduction*, 2 volumes, Paris: Rivière.

Amendola, M., Froeschle, C. and Gaffard, J. L. (1993) 'Sustaining Structural Change: Malthus's Heritage', *Structural Change and Economic Dynamics*, 4 (1, June), pp. 65–79.

Baranzini, M. and Scazzieri, R. (1990) 'Economic Structure: Analytical Perspectives', in M. Baranzini and R. Scazzieri (eds.), *The Economic Theory of Structure and Change*, Cambridge and New York: Cambridge University Press, pp. 227–333.

Basevi, G. and D'Adda, C. (2014) 'Overview: Analytics of the Eurozone Crisis', in D. Daianu, G. Basevi, C. D'Adda and R. Kumar (eds), *The Eurozone and the Future of Europe. The Political Economy of Further Integration and Governance*, Houndmills, Basingstoke: Palgrave Macmillan, pp. 9–22.

Beccaria, C. (1971, ms. *circa* 1769) *Elementi di economia pubblica*, in C. Beccaria, *Opere*, ed. S. Romagnoli, Firenze, Sansoni, vol. I, pp. 383–649.

Bouniatian, M. (1908) *Wirtschaftskrisen und Ueberkapitalisation. Eine Untersuchung über die Erscheinungsformen und Ursachen der periodischen Wirtschaftskrisen*, München: Ernst Reinhardt.

Bouniatian, M. (1922) *Les crises économiques. Essai de morphologie et théorie des crises économiques périodiques et de théorie de la conjoncture économique*, Paris: Giard.

Bouniatian, M. (1933) *Crédit et conjuncture*, Paris: Giard.

Cardinale, I. and Scazzieri, R. (2011) 'Tasks, Functions and Structural Change: Towards a Dynamic Theory of Production', paper presented at the conference *Innovation, Economic Change and Policies: An Out-of-Equilibrium Perspective*, Rome, University of Rome La Sapienza, mimeo, 17–19 November.

Cardinale, I. and Scazzieri, R. (2016) 'Structural Liquidity: The Money-Industry Nexus', *Structural Change and Economic Dynamics*, 39 (December), pp. 46–53.

Carter, A.P. and Leontief, W.W. (2005) 'The Position of Metalworking Industries in the Structure of an Industrializing Economy/Situación estructural de las industrias metal-mecánicas en las economías industrializadas', *Estudios de Economía Aplicada*, 23 (August), pp. 249–86.

del Vecchio, G. (1930) *Grundlinien der geldtheorie*, Tübingen, Mohr.

del Vecchio, G. (1932) *Ricerche sopra la teoria generale della moneta*, Milano, Università Bocconi.

Einarsen, J. (1938) *Reinvestment Cycles and their Manifestation in the Norwegian Shipping Industry*, Publication n. 14 from the University Institute of Economics Oslo, Oslo, J. Chr. Gundersen Boktrykkeri.

Fanno, M. (1993 [1931]) 'Production Cycles, Credit Cycles and Industrial Fluctuations', *Structural Change and Economic Dynamics*, 4, pp. 403–37.

Hagemann, H. and Scazzieri, R. (2009) 'Capital Structure and Economic Transitions: An Introductory Essay', in H. Hagemann, and R. Scazzieri, (eds.) *Capital, Time and Transitional Dynamics*, Abingdon and New York: Routledge, pp. 1–39.

Hayek, F. A. (1941) *The Pure Theory of Capital*, London: Macmillan and Co.

Helpman, E. (ed.) (1998) *General Purpose Technologies and Economic Growth*, Cambridge, MA and London, MIT Press.

Hicks, J. (1959) *Essays in World Economics*, Oxford: Clarendon Press.

Hicks, J. (1967) *Critical Essays in Monetary Theory*, Oxford: Clarendon Press.

Hicks, J. (1969) *A Theory of Economic History*, Oxford: Clarendon Press.

Hicks, J. (1973) *Capital and Time. A Neo-Austrian Theory*, Oxford: Clarendon Press.

Hicks, J (1974) *The Crisis in Keynesian Economics*, Oxford: Basil Blackwell.

Hicks, J. (1976) '"Revolutions" in Economics', in S. Latsis, ed., *Method and Appraisal in Economics*, Cambridge: Cambridge University Press, pp. 207–18.

Hicks, J. (1977) *Economic Perspectives: Further Essays on Money and Growth*, Oxford, Clarendon Press.

Hicks, J. (1982) 'The Foundations of Monetary Theory', in J. Hicks, *Money, Interest and Wages*, vol. II of J. Hicks, *Collected Essays on Economic Theory*, Oxford: Basil Blackwell, pp. 236–75.

Hicks, J. (1985) *Methods of Economic Dynamics*, Oxford, Clarendon Press.

Hicks, J. (1989) *A Market Theory of Money*, Oxford, Clarendon Press.

Hicks, J. (1990) 'The Unification of Macro-Economics', *The Economic Journal*, vol. 100 (401), pp. 528–38.

Keynes, J. M. (1973 [1933]) 'A Monetary Theory of Production', in D. Moggridge (ed.), *The Collected Writings of John Maynard Keynes*, vol. xiii ('The General Theory and After. Part I. Preparations'), London and Basingstoke: Macmillan and St. Martin's Press for the Royal Economic Society, pp. 408–11.

Janeway, B. (2012) *Doing Capitalism in the Innovation Economy. Markets, Speculation and the State*, Cambridge: Cambridge University Press.

Landesmann, M.A. and Scazzieri, R. (1990) 'Specification of Structure and Economic Dynamics', in M. Baranzini and R. Scazzieri (eds.), *The Economic Theory of Structure and Change*, Cambridge: Cambridge University Press, pp. 95–121.

Leijhonhufvud, A. (1986) 'Capitalism and the Factory System', in R.N. Langlois (ed.), *Economics as a Process. Essays in the New Institutional Economics.* New York: Cambridge University Press, pp. 203–23.

Leonard, A. (2015) *Marine Insurance: International Development and Evolution*, Basingstoke: Palgrave Macmillan.

Leontief, W. (1941) *The Structure of the American Economy*, New York, Oxford University Press.

Leontief, W. (1991 [1928]) 'The Economy as a Circular Flow', *Structural Change and Economic Dynamics*, 2(1), pp. 181–212.

Malthus, T.R. (1820) *Principles of Political Economy*, London, Murray.

Masera, R. (1984) 'Monetary Policy and Budget Policy: Blend or Dichotomy?' in R.S. Masera and R. Triffin (eds.), *Europe's Money. Problems of European Monetary Co-ordination and Integration*, Oxford: Clarendon Press, pp. 196–223.

Masera, R. (2015) 'Macro Prudential Policy as a Reference for Economic Policies: A Hicksian Perspective', Workshop 'Between Theory and Policy: Political Economy of Crisis', National Lincei Academy, Interdisciplinary Research Centre 'Beniamino Segre', Rome, 27 October.

Modigliani, F. and Papademos, L. (1987) 'Money, Credit and the Monetary Mechanism', in M. de Cecco and J.P. Fitoussi (eds.), *Monetary Theory and Economic Institutions*, London, Macmillan, pp. 121–60.

Mundell, R.A. (1969) 'A Plan for a European Currency', paper prepared for discussion at the American Management Association Conference on Future of the International Monetary System, mimeo, New York, 10–12 December.

Myrdal, G. (1939) *Monetary Equilibrium*, London, Edinburgh and Glasgow: William Hodge and Company.

Neal, L. (1990) *The Rise of Financial Capitalism: International Capital Markets in the Age of Reason*, Cambridge, Cambridge University Press.

Neal, L. (2000) 'How It All Began, the Monetary and Financial Architecture of Europe during the First Global Capital Markets, 1648–1815', *Financial History Review*, 7 (2, October), pp. 117–40.

Ornaghi, L. (1990) 'Economic Structure and Political Institutions: a Theoretical Framework', in M. Baranzini and R. Scazzieri (eds.), *The Economic Theory of Structure and Change*, Cambridge, Cambridge University Press, pp. 23–44.

Pasinetti, L.L. (1981) *Structural Change and Economic Growth: A Theoretical Essay on the Dynamics of the Wealth of Nations*, Cambridge: Cambridge University Press.

Pasinetti, L.L. (1993) *Structural Economic Dynamics: A Theory of the Economic Consequences of Human Learning*, Cambridge: Cambridge University Press.

Pasinetti, L.L. (2007) *Keynes and the Cambridge Keynesians A 'Revolution in Economics' to be Accomplished*, Cambridge, Cambridge University Press.

Quadrio Curzio, A. (1986) 'Technological Scarcity: An Essay on Production and Structural Change', in M. Baranzini and R. Scazzieri (eds.), *Foundations of Economics. Structures of Inquiry and Economic Theory*, Oxford and New York, Basil Blackwell, pp. 311–38.

Quadrio Curzio, A. (1996) 'Production and Efficiency with Global Technologies', in M. Landesmann and R. Scazzieri (eds.), *Production and Economic Dynamics*, Cambridge: Cambridge University Press, pp. 105–39.

Quesnay, F. (1758) *Tableau économique*, Versailles.

Robertson, D.H. (1914) 'Some Material for a Study of Trade Fluctuations', *Journal of the Royal Statistical Society*, 77 (Part II, January), pp. 159–68.

Robertson, D.H. (1915) *A Study of Industrial Fluctuation; an Enquiry into the Character and Causes of the So-Called Cyclical Movements of Trade,* London: P.S. King.

Robertson, D.H. (1926) *Banking Policy and the Price Level: An Essay in the Theory of the Trade Cycle*, London: P. S. King & Son.

Rodrick, D. (2011) *The Globalization Paradox*, Oxford: Oxford University Press.

Rosenberg, N. (1963) 'Technological Change in the Machine Tool Industry, 1840–1910', *The Journal of Economic History*, 23 (4, December), pp. 414–43.

Rosenberg, N. (1969) 'Introduction', in *The American System of Manufactures: The Report of the Committee on the Machinery of the United*

States, 1855, and the special reports of George Wallis and Joseph Whitworth, 1854, edited with an introduction, by N. Rosenberg, Edinburgh, Edinburgh University Press, pp. 414–43.

Rosenberg, N. and Trajtenberg, M. (2001) *A General Purpose Technology at Work: The Corliss Steam Engine in the Late 19th Century*, Centre for Economic Policy Research, Discussion paper series, n. 3008.

Scazzieri, R. (1994) 'Economic Theory and Economic History', in H. Hagemann and O. Hamouda (eds.), *The Legacy of Hicks: His Contributions to Economic Analysis*, London: Routledge, pp. 225–40.

Scazzieri, R. (2009) 'Traverse Analysis and Methods of Economic Dynamics', in H. Hagemann and R. Scazzieri (eds.), *Capital, Time and Transitional Dynamics*, Abingdon, UK and New York, Routledge, pp. 96–132.

Scazzieri, R. (2012) 'Structural Economic Dynamics. Decisions. Methods and Theories', in H.M. Kramer, H.D. Kurz and H.-M. Trautwein (eds.), *Macroeconomics and the History of Economic Thought. Festschrift in Honour of Harald Hagemann*, London: Routledge, p. 314–28.

Scazzieri, R. (2014) 'A Structural Theory of Increasing Returns', *Structural Change and Economic Dynamics*, 29 (June), pp. 75–88.

Scazzieri, R. (2015) 'The Medium-Term Approach to Economic Crises: A Framework', Workshop 'Between Theory and Policy: Political Economy of Crisis', National Lincei Academy, Interdisciplinary Research Centre 'Beniamino Segre', Rome, 27 October.

Yan, W.P. and Ames, E. (1965) 'Economic Interrelatedness', *The Review of Economic Studies*, 32 (4, October), pp. 299–310.

8 Political Economy and the Constitution of Europe's Polity

Pathways for the Common Currency beyond Neo-Functional and Ordo-Liberal Models

ADRIAN PABST

8.1 Introduction

The Eurozone crisis has been variously described in financial or in fiscal terms, caused either by an over-leveraged banking system or by unsustainable budget deficits and national debt, or indeed both at once. But perhaps with the exception of Greece, neither holds true for individual euro-members or for the common currency area as a whole (Wolf 2014; Wallace 2016). The combined banking and sovereign debt crisis is symptomatic of a more fundamental set of structural problems such as trade imbalances, productivity differentials and the disconnection between financial flows and investment in productive activities that require a systemic analysis. By contrast with much of modern economics and political science that rest on rational choice and methodological individualism, this chapter seeks to develop an alternative political economy that can conceptualise the *constitution* of Europe's polity – the complex economic, political and social space in which the Eurozone is inscribed.

From this political economy perspective, I argue that the euro-area in its current configuration is characterised by the primacy of harmonisation over mutualisation. This is a legacy of the neo-functional model of integration and the ordo-liberal model of coordination, which privilege joint procedures and common rules rather than the sharing of risks, rewards and resources. Mutualisation – the search for reciprocal arrangements based on a balance of interests – offers a plausible and constructive alternative to transform the Eurozone in line with the constitution of Europe's polity. The chapter charts a path beyond the current debate that portrays the European Monetary Union (EMU) either as a misconceived experiment which should be abandoned in favour of national currencies (e.g. Pissarides 2013; Flassbeck and Lapavitsas 2015a, 2015b), or as a project beset by failures which require centralisation (e.g. Marsh 2013; Sinn 2014), or as an arrangement which can work better with a different institutional and policy mix (e.g. Sandbu 2015; Stiglitz 2016). A constructive alternative is important because, as Paul Wallace (2016: 54) has suggested, 'the flawed design of the monetary union occurred as politicians ignored the lessons not just of economic history but of economic theory'.

My chapter runs as follows. First of all, the current crisis of the Eurozone can only be understood as part of a particular economic, political and social domain in which EMU is embedded. The domain in question is not limited to a set of institutions and rules within which markets, states and individuals interact (Buchanan 1990) but extends to political and social structures that encompass both cooperation and conflict at – as well as across – different levels (Ornaghi 1990; Pabst and Scazzieri 2012). As an analytical framework, the approach to the political economy of constitution followed in this essay explores the multi-level dependencies that characterise economic integration within and between national states and transnational markets (Pabst 2014; Pabst and Scazzieri 2016; cf. Polanyi 2001).

Second, ordo-liberalism shares with the proposed 'political economy of constitution' the idea that the economic field is not self-standing, but rather part of an overarching social field that encompasses society and the state. However, ordo-liberal thinkers view the social domain as grounded in the constitutional-legal order, which subordinates social ties to state laws and market contract. By bracketing social relationships out of the picture, the effect of ordo-liberal policies – creating the 'framework conditions' (*Rahmenbedingungen*) for perfect competition – is to dis-embed the economy from society and to re-embed political and social ties in predominantly contractual relations, which ignores the Eurozone's structural problems.

Third, the dominant logic of European integration since the 1957 Rome Treaties has been neo-functionalism, which posits spill-over effects from economic interdependence to political unity (e.g. Haas 1961; Sandholtz and Stone Sweet 1997, 1998). Analogous to the concept of path dependency, neo-functionalism explains why European integration has privileged monetary integration over both a fiscal and a political union. Combined with the influence of ordo-liberalism, this has constrained EMU crisis management and official proposals for reform.

Fourth, the European polity within which EMU is inscribed is neither a federal super-state nor a free-trade area, but rather a political system *sui generis* (e.g. Hix 2005; Zielonka 2006, 2008). This system consists of hybrid institutions, overlapping jurisdictions, multiple membership, polycentric authority and multi-level governance. As a unique polity, Europe contains a certain set of opportunities and constraints for political and economic cooperation. These opportunities and constrains provide the resources for a different exit from the Eurozone crisis and they can embed EMU in the political and social relations which provide the trust and cooperation on which a viable common currency depends.

Section 8.2 provides a brief outline of the wider causes of the Eurozone crisis. Section 8.3 develops a political economy of constitution as an analytical architecture to describe and explain the wider domain in which the Eurozone is inscribed. Section 8.4 examines ordo-liberal principles and policy prescriptions that underpin the creation of EMU and the Eurozone crisis management since early 2010. Section 8.5 provides an account of the (neo-)functional logic that has shaped the process of integration and the building of the European polity. Section 8.6 suggests a number of alternative pathways for the Eurozone. The final section provides some concluding reflections.

8.2 On the Nature of the Eurozone Crisis

At the root of the Eurozone crisis is a balance-of-payments disequilibrium that is connected with a mismatch between savings and investment. Globally, emerging markets in Asia, Latin America and the Gulf built up about US$10 trillion of foreign reserves from 1997 to 2007, which they invested largely in US and European sovereign and corporate bonds (Wolf 2014). That, in turn, fuelled financial flows between banks between the euro-area and the United States and within the Eurozone (Borio and Disyatat 2011), providing cheap money and an influx of capital that was reinforced by low interest rates across the whole euro-area and facilitated substantially higher borrowing by both households and states (Sandbu 2015; Wallace 2016).

In conjunction with a specific incentive structure that favoured certain sectors such as finance, insurance and real estate over other sectors such as high-tech manufacturing and industry, the ensuing monetary expansion contributed to the build-up of credit and property bubbles in the United States and Europe (Roubini and Mihm 2011; cf. Brenner 2006). When these bubbles burst in 2008–09 amidst the global 'credit crunch', the result was a pan-European banking crisis that involved state bailouts and was followed from early 2010 onwards by a sovereign debt crisis (Blyth 2013; Hall 2013). The mutual dependence of banks and sovereigns that had developed for a decade brought countries to the brink of bankruptcy and the common currency to breakup point. With banks holding a significant share of total sovereign bonds, governments had little choice but to bail out all those banking conglomerates that were considered 'too big to fail'. In turn, that led to ballooning budget deficits, which the recession exacerbated through a combination of lower tax revenues and higher expenditure as a result of the automatic stabilisers (in particular higher welfare payments).

Moreover, the Eurozone's banking and sovereign debt crisis has shed light on an unsustainable balance-of-payments disequilibrium among members of the euro-area that is associated with long-standing trade imbalances between surplus countries at the core and deficit countries in the periphery (Wolf 2014: 45–88; Sandbu 2015: 25–47; Wallace 2016: 58–87). For example, Germany's persistent current account surplus, which is sustained by domestic under-consumption (due to stagnating real wages and a lack of investment), amounts to about €250 billion per year or has averaged more than 6 per cent of GDP between 2007 and 2013. It neither benefits German workers, nor is it re-invested in the peripheral countries or even at home. Before the 2008 financial crash, this surplus helped to drive the high levels of lending by German banks to Ireland and the southern Eurozone members, above all Greece. Since then, Germany's low domestic demand (through excessive wage restraint) has hindered the rebalancing of these disequilibria between creditors and debtors, which are also linked to significant differences in competitiveness and productivity. Competitiveness and productivity differentials rest on a series of fundamental structural dynamics within and across Eurozone countries, notably the evolution of wages and investment (both public and private) in capital equipment, R&D and training (both academic and vocational skills).

There are substantial and growing divergences among Eurozone members in relation to job protection and product-market regulation that reduce the ability of the common currency area to absorb internal and external shocks such as financial crises or economic recessions. In addition, the flexibility of the Euro is hampered by professional and trading cartels as well as other monopolistic practices that reduce job creation, which are key to boosting growth in order to reduce the significant debt overhang in countries such as Spain, Italy and France. To this must be added insufficient levels of education and skills that limit productivity and innovation, reducing the competitiveness of the Eurozone and the EU economy as a whole.

These processes highlight a number of overlapping structural issues, *inter alia* (a) the connections between production and consumption activities; (b) the relative weight and interaction of different economic sectors; (c) the financial architecture and its relations to the rest of the economy; (d) debt-credit relationships and the evolution of both liquidity formation and utilisation (Scazzieri, Chapter 7 in this volume); (e) the institutional and political framework within which fiscal and monetary policy is decided and implemented and how it affects the wider economy; and (f) the impact of European Economic and Monetary Union (EMU) on these (and other) factors, notably capital mobility and investment (dis)incentives.

More fundamentally, these and other interdependencies tend to influence existing and new interests at the sectoral, national and European levels. Here it is instructive briefly to reflect on the relationship between interest and money. As Wolfgang Streeck (2015) has argued, the tradition of economic and social theory, which builds on Max Weber, is right that money is not merely a universal symbol for the value of goods and services or a neutral medium of exchange. Rather, a monetary system is *also* the product of a ruling organisation that privileges the interests of certain dominant groups over the competing and conflicting interests of other groups. It therefore has asymmetric distributive effects engendering contention and contestation. So if money is a politico-economic institution, then it follows that the economy is not a technical subsystem of modern society which functions according to the principle of instrumental rationality: 'The fundamental insight of political economy is forgotten: that the natural laws of the economy, which appear to exist by virtue of their own efficiency, are in reality nothing but projections of social-power relations which present themselves ideologically as technical necessities' (Streeck, 2015: 10).

In the case of EMU that was designed largely based on the Deutsch-mark and the Bundesbank, a single monetary system tends to enforce the interests of one 'variety of capitalism' – the more supply-based northern model – over against the interests of other 'varieties' – the more demand-based southern model. Especially in the wake of the 2008 financial crash which hit the South of the Eurozone harder than the North (in terms of the collapse of credit), the undervaluation of the euro enhanced Germany's competitiveness and exacerbated the bal-ance-of-payments crisis. Crucially, neither domestic deflation in the Southern members nor long-term substantial fiscal transfers from Northern members (amounting to 5–10 per cent of GDP) are politic-ally realistic or socially sustainable. For this reason, the Eurozone is now associated with growing economic divergence and it is stuck in an impasse – caught between a technocratic indifference to democracy and a populist dereliction of duty.

Therefore, the Eurozone requires a different political economy if it is to avert stagnation and the erosion of democratic rule. Options for a more flexible currency regime that reduces the Eurozone's imbalances and thereby mitigates the structural disparities 'range from a return to national currencies, via the temporary or permanent introduction of parallel currencies, together with capital controls, right through to a Keynesian two-tier currency system' (Streeck 2015: 24–25). This would require a new global monetary and financial regime capable of combining a social market economy with a functioning democracy. However, one potential problem with this approach is that it may end up replacing the dominant logic of harmonisation and the concomitant imposition of one set of interests with the logic of coordination, which views competing interests as rival and ultimately incompatible.

By contrast, this chapter argues that the alternative logic of mutua-lisation highlights shared interests. Key to this is the notion that money is a good and not merely a commodity (Polanyi 2001). As a supra-national currency regime that can foster trade, financial integration and economic growth, the euro is in principle a public good that has the potential to offer advantages to different groups and even society as a whole. However, it requires its members to accept not just discipline based on common rules (including deficits and debt) but also reciprocal obligations to address structural problems as outlined above, and also trade imbalances, productivity differentials, as well as a lack of incen-tives for investment in production, R&D and skills to boost growth (in particular in low-skill, low-innovation regions of the euro-area). These and other problems can only be resolved by taking into account the political and social ties that constitute the polity in which the euro is inscribed. The following sections provide some conceptual and policy ideas of how to transform the Eurozone in line with the constitution of Europe's polity.

8.3 Political Economy and Europe's Polity: An Analytical Architecture

8.3.1 Economics, Political Science and Political Economy

The partitioning of social reality into the foundational categories of individual, state and market correlates with the strict separation of academic disciplines that characterises the relationship between economics and political science. This disciplinary divide deepened after the Marginalist revolution of the 1870s insofar as both were no longer seen as branches of political economy but instead as new sciences in their own right (Screpanti and Zamagni 2005: 380–450). In economics the split occurred in the wake of Marshall (Marshall 1890) and in politics it arose as part of the influence of Comte (see Collini, Winch and Burrow 1983; Manent 2010). Connected with this was a growing accentuation on theories of rational choice, instrumental reason and methodological individualism at the expense of the classical analysis of system-wide opportunities and constraints, including bounded rationality, uncertainty and the shaping of individual agency by shared norms reflected in institutions. Since systemic opportunities and constraints are associated with different institutional and organisational patterns that affect the division of labour and exchange, each system encompasses alternative *political economies*. Seen from this perspective, the rational-choice framework stemming from the Marginalist Revolution has reduced the range of possibilities to a *single* political economy that can merely accommodate a limited array of policy options. Applied to the Eurozone, it has restricted the focus on binary opposites (austerity vs. anti-austerity, creditor vs. debtor, core vs. periphery), which neglect the underlying structural problems and different alternatives to the prevailing model.

In part this is the outcome of a long process in the history of economic thought. Since the end of the nineteenth century, the body of social sciences (notably economics, politics and social theory) has become increasingly fragmented under the pressure of increasing autonomy and ever-greater specialisation, both in terms of fields of inquiry and analytical tools. At the same time, the respective 'objects of study' (such as the economy, the political system or society) are increasingly intertwined with one another. Political institutions are key in defining the boundaries of the economic system and its different institutional and organisation patterns that affect the division of labour and exchange. Crucially, as Lorenzo Ornaghi remarks,

the integrating role of political institutions appears to increase with the degree of complexity and organization of economic action. The relation of political institutions with economic structure then becomes essential for two distinct reasons. First, it provides a better analytical-historical perspective on the links between political economy and 'political order' (the latter is not coincident with the type of 'order' that is associated with the existence of the State). Secondly, it contributes to a 'dynamic' interpretation of the contemporary relations between State institutions and economic order. In turn, this is the only route to an analysis emphasizing the link between order and transformation in a theory of the intersections between economic and political cycle. (Ornaghi 1990: 25)

Thus, the modern separation of economics from political science coincides with a split between economic structures and political institutions, which has reduced the scope of political economy and separated the analysis of both markets and states from the social connections in which they are inscribed.

By contrast, political economy explores the complex links between the economy and the polity with a particular emphasis on different forms of sociability that constitute the domain within which markets, states and individuals interact. In this perspective, the domain of political economy rejects not only the strict separation of economics from politics and other similarly antagonistic binary opposites such as state vs. market, the national vs. the supranational level or individual vs. collective interest. It also views social relations as more primary than either state-administrative or market-commercial arrangements – a constitutive domain that embeds the economic-political domain (Polanyi 2001). Thus, political economy seeks to theorise the overarching constitution of the domain within which markets, states and individuals interact and the social structures in which both cooperative and conflictual relationships are grounded (Pabst and Scazzieri 2012; Pabst 2014). Contrary to the rational-choice, market-exchange framework, the political economy approach followed in this essay focuses on the ordering of different functions and an arranging of different positions, which embed both the economic and the political field in the complex structures of social interdependencies that help to constitute society. The 'political economy of constitution' is thus a sphere of partially realised social connections that represents a certain 'constitution of interests' (Pabst and Scazzieri 2016).

Other scholars in the field have conceptualised the constitutional dimension of political economy, for example James Buchanan (1990). According to him, the domain of constitutional political economy is concerned with

the working properties of rules and institutions within which individuals interact, and the processes through which these rules and institutions are chosen or come into being. The emphasis on the choice of constraints distinguishes this research program from conventional economics, while the emphasis on cooperative rather than conflictual interaction distinguishes the program from much of conventional political science. (Buchanan 1990: 1)

Buchanan is right to argue that constitutional political economy differs from neo-classical economics and modern political science to the extent that it goes beyond purely contractual arrangements and conceptualises the wider constitution of the domain within which institutions, rules and policy choices occur – including the conditions for a cooperative framework of reciprocal exchange in the pursuit of mutual benefit. However, Buchanan assumes that conflict is more primary than cooperation and he fails to account for the social ties that pre-exist both. Moreover, conflict and cooperation rest on 'methodological individualism and rational choice' (Buchanan 1990: 1), which presupposes that the 'primary units' of society are rationally driven, utility-maximizing individuals who are bound together by contractual arrangements after all.

This approach has important implications for the political economy of the Eurozone. In the case of EMU, the exclusive focus on formal, juridical arrangements tends to neglect at least two dimensions: first, the hybrid, multi-level system of economic and monetary governance that has shaped the single currency both before and since the crisis (e.g. Scharpf 2010); second, the complex and multi-layered social relations both within and across localities, regions and states. These dimensions create specific path dependencies that are fundamentally ambivalent (see Mény 2014). They can act either as factors of inertia and even failure by slowing down crisis management or by hindering crisis resolution, or they can point to alternative possibilities in relation to both the overarching institutional structure and specific policy ideas.

For these reasons, the problem with Buchanan's conception of constitutional political economy is that it ends up subordinating social relationships to the formal functioning of markets and states. Patterns of social interaction at various levels are subsumed either under political relations within or between states or under economic transactions in the national or global marketplace. In this manner, his approach ignores more fundamental social connections that occur at, as well as across, different levels. The approach of this essay is different insofar as the main focus is on the political and the social bonds that underpin both conflict and cooperation. Such connections are more complex than the rather homogeneous, contractual links associated with either state sovereignty or global commerce. To theorise social connections, it is necessary to rethink the fundamental conceptual building blocks, including the nature of interests and institutions that involve both cooperation and conflict as well as the overarching constitutional framework.

8.3.2 *Interests, Institutions and Constitution*

Contrary to standard rational choice theories in economics and political science, interests are relational in two ways. First, the interests of individuals, groups and larger social 'units' such as sectors or entire states are not simply the sum of their individual parts but extend to 'clusters' that reflect the relative positioning (Cardinale, Chapter 9 in this volume). Second, individual, group and larger relational interests are embedded within a set of relationships that are irreducible to purely contractual arrangements because the relative *initial* positions are not a matter of choice. As Ornaghi has argued, the very etymology of the term 'interest' (*inter-esse*) emphasises the 'in-betweenness' of social actors (Ornaghi 1990). This conception relates 'interest' to the reciprocal constraints and opportunities that characterise participation in a specific social space. Whereas rational-choice based economics and politics tend to focus on individual private interests or collective public interests, the political economy to which this essay adheres is concerned with the relational structure of general interests and the multilayered positioning of specific interests that are partially convergent and divergent at different levels.

In addition to relational interests, political economy theorises institution in more associative ways. Any given political-economic model presupposes the design of a specific institutional and organisational structure, insofar as it requires the arrangement of human actions in view of a particular set of objectives. Max Weber's distinction between organisation and association is useful in clarifying this concept: '[a]n 'organisation' (*Betrieb*) is a system of continuous purposive activity of a specified kind', whereas an association (*Verein*) is 'a corporate group originating in a voluntary agreement and in which the established order claims authority over the members only by virtue of a personal act of adherence' (Weber 1947 [1922]: 28). In view of this discussion, a political economy consistent with the hybrid character of society can be a specific organisation (*Betrieb*) embedded in a wider space of social connections (*Verein*).

Here one can go further than Weber to make the point that contractualist and voluntarist theories of institution ignore the pre-existing social ties into which individuals are born and which are not a matter of personal choice at each point in time (Pabst 2014). These ties provide both constraints and opportunities in relation to conflict and cooperation. Crucially, a focus on pre-existing social ties can overcome a series of dualisms that characterise modern political economy, including instrumental vs. non-instrumental action, hierarchical vs. vertical interaction, intended vs. non-intended outcome and homogeneous vs. heterogeneous interdependence. By conceptualising the economic and political fields as ultimately embedded in the social domain, the alternative political economy which this essay proposes can offer a richer conceptualisation than those approaches that focus exclusively on the contractualist and voluntarist arrangements underpinning the institutions of states and markets.

The focus on social ties and bonds that *pre-exist* the emergence of conflict and cooperation links institutions to constitution. Such connections are characterised by more hybrid relationships rather than the more homogeneous links associated with state sovereignty and global commerce (as indicated above). Therefore, different rules and institutions are grounded in different types of sociability that point to the

existence of a more fundamental social domain that can be conceptualised in terms of *civil society* (Pabst and Scazzieri 2012). Accordingly, a
broader account of 'constitution' presupposes a multiplicity of partially overlapping connections at different levels. This is to say that
constitution allows individuals and social groups to relate to other
individuals and social groups at a certain level while relating to yet
other individuals and social group at another level. Here the *proximity
model* of civil society provides a relevant interpretive framework insofar as in this model 'individuals or groups derive their identity from a
variety of attributes' such that 'some of those attributes are central in a
given relational domain but secondary in another domain' (Pabst and
Scazzieri 2012: 345; see also Scazzieri 1999). In a social domain whose
structuring follows the above pattern, sociability is linked to multiple
forms of connectivity in two different ways. First, the distance between
individuals or social groups is characterised by a significant variety
across society. Second, the notion of distance is a function of the nature
of interdependence in question, for example, profession, location or
cultural affinity. Therefore, the notion of proximity shifts the emphasis
away from a single set of standards towards a more plural, inclusive
space of dispositions and connections.

Linking together interests, institutions and constitution is the notion of
association that reflects the complex sociability constituting the domain
of political economy. For the purposes of this essay, I define 'association'
as diverse forms of social interactions that have potential for *both*
conflict and cooperation and that are not reducible to any of the above
dualisms or to the binary logic that underpins them. My approach draws
upon a view of sociability and association as plural and hybrid. One
possible objection to the argument of this essay is to say that the internal
structure of society is so diverse as to produce 'parallel societies' within a
given territory and its people, not to mention diversity across countries
and cultures. Indeed, there has been much discussion about the growing
pluralism of late modern societies, including the pervasiveness of fundamental disagreements (political, economic, social and ethical) and the
inability to resolve such disagreements rationally (e.g. Hirschman 1977;
MacIntyre 2000 [1981]). This has led thinkers as diverse as Isaiah Berlin
and John Rawls to argue that key substantive values are incommensurable and that therefore it is only possible to 'agree to disagree' and to
settle for certain procedural mechanisms such as contractual arrangements backed by the rule of law (Berlin 1969; Rawls 1971).

This is relevant for the political economy of the eurozone. According to a number of economists such as Jürgen Stark (a former ECB board member), the Eurozone crisis reveals the incompatible values and cultures between different members of the euro-area: '[I]n contrast to many Eurozone countries, Germany has reliably pursued a prudent economic policy. While others were living beyond their means, Germany avoided excess. These are deep cultural differences and the currency union brings them to light once again' (Stark 2015: 11). However, I contend that such and similar oppositions between commensurable and incommensurable values rest on an unwarranted dualism. The notions of sociability and association (as defined above) can help to overcome this opposition in the direction of a multi-layered social space in which there can be both disagreement on some substantive choices and also agreement on other substantive choices. Therefore, diversity and pluralism are not *inherently* antagonistic, and the notion of constitution is key to understanding that there are certain pre-existing social arrangements and patterns of sociability on which both conflict and cooperation rest.

In short, the domain of *political economy* cannot be defined as a space of freely choosing individuals; rather, it presupposes conditions of sociability that are compatible with a number of different patterns of social congruence. Within that domain, *constitution* refers to the architectural structure that provides relative persistence to potential social arrangements. And within that constitutional framework, the relations and associations between individuals or social groups mark the partial actualisation of the existing potential for cooperation or conflict. This suggests that neither action nor interest is independent of the conditions of sociability. On the contrary, performing an action is always embedded in social practices that involve specific goals and interests, which arise from the existing patterns of interdependence. Therefore interests are defined within a complex social structure in which human practice overcomes the dualism between instrumental and non-instrumental actions, intended and unintended outcomes, and individual and collective levels.

8.3.3 Political Economy and the Eurozone

The interplay of interests, institutions and the constitution highlights alternative conceptions of political economy that provide a more complex understanding of the Eurozone than standard models in economics or political science. The euro-area tends to be analysed from the perspective of either economics or political science. Both disciplines differ on the respective role of markets and states or the relative importance of individuals and groups in the allocation and distribution of resources (see Section 8.3.2). These differences notwithstanding, the two disciplines view the common currency in binary terms, separating the economic logic of supranational integration from the political logic of national legitimacy and intergovernmental cooperation. Such binary terms lead to the absorption of politics into economics (e.g. North, Wallis and Weingast 2010) or vice versa (e.g. Blyth 2013). The former emphasises the need for austerity to deal with the sovereign debt crisis, while the latter accentuates the case for financial reform to address the banking crisis. Despite these important policy differences, both fields rest on instrumental rationality, the maximisation of utility and a trade-off between rival interests – a zero-sum game of winners and losers in which conflict is more fundamental than cooperation (e.g. creditors vs. debtors or banks vs. taxpayers). This represents a rather narrow conception of political economy that cannot theorise the complex constellation of interests across the Eurozone (see Hall 2014: 1233–34).

In principle, political economy differs from both economics and political science, notably by rejecting the separation between the two fields and also the bracketing of the social relations in which both are embedded. However, the dominant accounts of political economy – including Keynesian and neo-classical approaches – seem to share the same logic of antagonistic binary opposites that characterises economics and political science, including the opposition between the national political and supranational economic levels. In the case of EMU, Keynesianism and neo-classical thinking share the argument that the imbalance between a centralised monetary policy and nationally determined economic policy is unsustainable (see McNamara 1998). That is why both Keynesian and neo-classical economists support the creation of a Eurozone-wide banking union, followed by a fiscal union and finally by a political union (e.g. Howarth and Quaglia 2013). Even though these two conceptions of political economy diverge on other specific policy prescriptions (most of all, austerity or stimulus and supply-side reforms or demand-managed growth), their agreement on the solution to the Eurozone crisis reflects a wider conceptual convergence.

In fact, the prevailing approaches to political economy view markets, states and individuals as foundational categories that constitute the economic-political domain. However, what remains unexplained is why these categories are – or should be – seen as given and on what type of social relations they depend (Pabst 2014). Compared with certain strands in economics and political science, Keynesian and neo-classical political economy rejects the assumption that states, markets and individuals pertain to strictly separate, self-contained fields. Yet the economic-political domain is conceptualised independently from the domain of social relations, that is, the manifold and complex social ties that underpin both the interdependence and the interactions between individuals and groups. For this reason, the dominant theories of political economy focus on the purely contractual arrangements of market and state at the expense of social bonds on which both trust and cooperation ultimately rely (Hall and Soskice 2001). By expanding the economic-political field, they end up subsuming the social domain under the logic of exchange or the logic of power (or indeed both at once).

For all these reasons, this essay outlines a political economy of the Eurozone that focuses on the constitution of the European polity in terms of substantive political and social ties. Such a political economy is rooted in the view of the social sphere as a multi-layered set of relations that involve both convergent and divergent interests between individuals or social groups. This account of the social as more primary than the economic or the political is a useful tool to analyse potential patterns of cooperation within and across different societies, and to explore possible ways in which a mutually beneficial organisation of diverse interests may be established. The social denotes a continuum of interests and institutions that cannot be partitioned into self-contained fields such as the economic or the political. Rather than being founded purely on formal theories and concepts that abstract from social relations (as in much of economics and political science), political economy reflects the specific fabric of given societies (Pabst 2014; Pabst and Scazzieri 2016). Thus political economy shifts the emphasis away from constitutively separate interests to the 'co-constitution of interests' – a structured space of social relations that is prior to decisions about the allocation and distribution of resources.

This alternative account of political economy is key to a better account of EMU, as the Eurozone economy and the European polity are characterised by hybrid institutions, overlapping jurisdictions, polycentric authority and multi-level governance (cf. Hix 2005; Zielonka 2006; Scharpf 2010). In other words, different rules and institutions are grounded in different types of sociability, and the ultimate source of social interactions is civil society – defined as 'the primary constitution of connectivity in which markets and states operate [. . . and which] *embeds* the causal structures determining the relationship between intended and unintended outcomes in any given social domain' (Pabst and Scazzieri 2012: 337–38). Applied to the euro-area, this means that the numerous social ties that constitute the political-economic domain are not simply a given reality that economics and political science either ignore or subsume under the logic of exchange or the logic of power. On the contrary, these ties point to partially realised connections that could give rise to different settlements (as explored in Section 8.6).

8.4 Ordo-Liberalism and the European Monetary Union

From the perspective of political economy as defined in the previous section, ordo-liberalism is central to the debate about the principles and possible policy pathways for the Eurozone. Ordo-liberal ideas have shaped the genesis of the common currency and also the responses to the current crisis (Allen 2005; Bulmer 2014). Unlike certain strands in modern economics and political science, the ordo-liberal tradition – in the work of Walter Eucken, Wilhelm Röpke, Franz Böhm, Hans Großmann Doerh, Alexander Rüstow and Alfred Müller-Armack – does not regard the economic field as an autonomous, self-contained system. Instead, it shares with political economy the idea that the various fields are interdependent (Megay 1970; Nicholls 1994). Indeed, the economic order is seen as a part of the overarching social order, which encompasses society and the state.

However, the fundamental difference compared with the conception of political economy which this essay develops is the nature of the social order. For ordo-liberal thinkers, the social domain rests on a fundamental dichotomy (Kolev 2010): 'rules of the game' (order) and 'moves of the game' (process). This distinction underpins the notion of 'social market economy' that denotes the specifically German 'variety of capitalism' (Nicholls 1994; Hall and Soskice 2001 [esp. Casper 2001]; Ptak 2009) and is enshrined in the 2009 Lisbon Treaty – with the state defining the order (via laws and regulations) and the market driving the process (via free competition). The interaction between 'order' and 'process' also translates into policy principles: the states ensures the right 'framework conditions' (*Rahmenbedingungen*) to generate a market order that is both competitive and stable (in terms of prices and liquidity).

Applied to the Eurozone, this helps to explain the stance of core, creditor countries such as Germany, the Netherlands, Austria and (previously) Finland on issues such as austerity, the refusal (partially or fully) to mutualise debt and supranational common rules – most notably the 2011 fiscal pact with the automatic 'debt brake'. Crucially, the ordo-liberal conception of political economy, which shapes German-led policy on the euro (see Körner and Trautwein, Chapter 10 in this volume), presupposes that the social, economic and political fields rest on a legal-regulatory order that is more primary than social ties or political association. Jürgen Stark's analysis encapsulates this foundational premise:

German thinking is founded on 'ordoliberalism', an approach arising from the recognition that markets need rules to be set and enforced by government. From this perspective the most important principles are the primacy of price stability; the promotion of competition in all markets; the protection of property rights; freedom of contract; and the idea that individuals should bear the risks of their own decisions and the losses of banks should not be borne by the whole of society. (Stark 2015: 11)

Arguably, the ordo-liberal way of thinking is largely shared by both neo-classical and Keynesian economists. Consider the following two quotes from F.A. Hayek:

We can 'plan' a system of general rules, equally applicable to all people and intended to be permanent (even if subject to revision with the growth of knowledge), which provides an institutional framework within which the decisions as to what to do and how to earn a living are left to the individuals. (Hayek 1939: 198–90)

The functioning of competition not only requires adequate organization of certain institutions like money, markets, and channels of information – some of which can never be adequately provided by private enterprise – but it depends, above all, on the existence of an appropriate legal system, a legal system designed both to preserve competition and to make it operate has beneficially as possible. (Hayek 1944: 43)

By contrast with Hayek, Keynes supported a greater degree of state intervention to correct market disequilibria. However, it is equally true that both believed that markets could only work based on general rules upheld by states: mirroring the rule of law, economic rules need to be both *a priori*, fixed and *a posteriori*, discretionary in order to combine predictability with the ability to respond to changing circumstances. This broad approach to economics shared by Hayek and Keynes emerged from a tradition of political liberalism and the moral theory of utilitarianism (Skidelsky 2006, 2009). In short, it is possible to suggest that neo-classical economics and Keynesianism share with ordo-liberalism a commitment to the primacy of the constitutional-legal order that foregrounds the economic, political and social fields.

The reference to ordo-liberalism is not merely of conceptual or historical interest. On the contrary, the ordo-liberal understanding of what it sees as the policy errors in the 1920s and 1930s shapes contemporary critiques of the global economy in general and the euro area in particular. In each case, ordo-liberalism views the failure properly to regulate bank lending and the concomitant excess of cheap credit as a major cause of the financial and euro crises. Linked to this is the set of distinctly ordo-liberal policy prescriptions, including austerity and automatic 'debt brakes' in order to bring about balanced budgets and competitive market equilibria (Bonefeld 2012; Bulmer 2014). In fact, ordo-liberalism regards any other type of government intervention (such as a fiscal stimulus or the restructuring of debt) as a misallocation of resources that generates either bubbles (credit and property bubbles) or unsustainable aggregate demand (budget deficits) – or again both at once. From an ordo-liberal perspective, this applies not just to Eurozone members such as Greece, Ireland, Portugal, Spain and Cyprus but also to other economies like the United States, the United Kingdom and Iceland.

Moreover, ordo-liberal economists insist on strict versions of moral hazard and the validity of Ricardo's equivalence theorem. In the context of EMU, the former implies that bailouts of private or public sector debtors induce ever-greater systemic risk-taking. The latter suggests that the artificial expansion of either aggregate demand (through activist fiscal policy such as deficit spending) or the money supply (through activist monetary policy such as 'quantitative easing') ends up producing the opposite outcome to the one intended. For rationally driven economic actors supposedly include in their calculation future hikes in tax and in price inflation, thereby depressing both spending and borrowing.

For these reasons, ordo-liberalism advocates a rules-based management of state spending and market liquidity in order to attain price stability and a competitive economic equilibrium (Casper 2001; Stark 2015).

From this discussion, it is clear that there are fundamental differences with both neo-classical and Keynesian policy ideas. Neo-classical economists tend to believe that all markets, including financial markets, are ultimately self-correcting, while Keynesian economists usually assume that government intervention such as fiscal stimulus can prevent a sub-optimal market equilibrium (e.g. insufficient aggregate demand and/or a liquidity trap as a result of the paradox of thrift). However, both share with ordo-liberalism the conception that the economic and political fields need to be firmly embedded in a constitutional-legal order in which the purpose of states is to remove obstacles to market competition and price movements. So like neo-classical economics and Keynesian thinking, ordo-liberalism tends to bracket social relationships out of the picture. Indeed, all three approaches to political economy view the economy and the polity as dis-embedded from society and social ties as embedded in the predominantly contractual relations that govern markets and states (Polanyi 2001). The priority of the economic and the political over the social rests on the primacy of the constitutional-legal order, that is, a set of principles, rules and regulations that subsume social ties under abstract, general categories of private profit or public utility.

As a result, the logic that underpins both the overarching 'order' and the 'process' favours those social relations which are compatible with the requirements of markets and states, that is, relations that privilege instrumental rationality and utility maximisation over other forms of reason and the pursuit of shared, substantive ends. In short, the various approaches such as ordo-liberalism, neo-classical economics and Keynesianism restrict the domain of political economy at the expense of complex, hybrid social ties on which trust and cooperation depend. The next section shows how this logic has shaped European integration and EMU from the outset.

8.5 (Neo-)Functionalism and the Building of the European Polity

Historically, the origins of the European Union go back to the interwar years and the early post-1945 period. Initially, the experience of two world wars and the Great Depression of 1929–32 convinced national leaders to create an ambitious supranational project, namely the European Defence Community (EDC) and the European Political Community (EPC) in 1952. The EDC sought to establish a pan-European defence force, while the EPC envisioned a supranational political system: a bicameral system composed of a directly elected parliament ('the Peoples' Chamber') and a senate appointed by national assemblies, coupled with a supranational executive accountable to the parliament (Kaiser 2007). Following the rejection of the EDC and the EPC by the French National Assembly in 1954, Germany, France, Italy and the Benelux countries settled for the more limited European Economic Community (EEC) that was built on the cooperation of the 1951 European Coal and Steel Community. The 1957 Rome Treaty, which established the EEC, enshrined a specific logic that views political union largely as the result of spill-over effects from economic integration (Wallace 1990) – also known as functionalism and later neo-functionalism. This (neo-)functional logic underpins the key milestones of economic integration: the 1970 Werner Report that laid the founda-tions for the European Exchange Rate Mechanism (ERM); the European single market created in 1985; European Monetary Union that was enshrined in the 1992 Maastricht Treaty and launched in 1999 (e.g. Dyson and Featherstone 1999; cf. Eichengreen 2012).

Conceptually, functionalism and neo-functionalism are not syn-onymous (see, *inter alia*, Mitrany 1933, 1948, 1965, 1966, 1976; Haas 1961, 1964; Sewell 1966; Wolf 1973; Groom and Taylor 1975), but their differences do not alter my argument that both are compatible with the main precepts of ordo-liberalism. The crucial point is that the dominant model of European integration rests on the (neo-) functionalist logic, which views closer regional and national ties in terms of three closely connected factors: first, positive spill-over effects from growing economic interdependence to greater political union; second, shared institutions to resolve disputes and build a common legal framework for states and markets; third, supranational market rules that replace national regulatory regimes (*inter alia*, Haas 1961; Sandholtz and Stone Sweet 1997, 1998; Sandholtz, Stone Sweet and Fligstein 2001). Thus, the (neo-)functionalist logic assumes that enhanced economic exchange and legal harmonisation will over time produce closer political cooperation and unification – a logic that is compatible with the ordo-liberal argument that the economic and political fields are grounded in the constitutional-legal order.

According to Ernst Haas, David Mitrany and other theorists of functionalism, there are three main mechanisms through which multi-level economic interdependence would produce political integration (Mitrany 1933, 1948, 1965, 1966, 1976; Haas 1961, 1964; Sewell 1966). First of all, positive spill-over effects. Such effects can be either functional or political or both at once. Functional spill-over effects denote the interconnection of various *economic* sectors or issue-areas, and the integration in one policy-area spilling over into others because integration in one economic sector creates incentives and dynamics for integration in other sectors. Political spill-over effects refer to the creation of supranational governance models such as the EEC, the EC or later the EU – with supranational institutions like the Commission and the ECJ that create an integrative movement, which has been called 'competence creep'. The combination of functional and political spill-over effects takes the form of an increased number of transactions and negotiations among member-states, which leads to the creation of supranational institutions that are increasingly disembedded from social connections at the local, regional and national levels.

The second mechanism is a transfer in domestic allegiances to the supranational level, especially on the part of interest groups and associations that can better advance their own material interests at the supranational than the national level. Given the growing regulatory complexity and the lack of information at lower stations, both policy- and decision-making as well as implementation and oversight require supranational institutions – so the (neo-)functional argument goes. Third, the dynamic of integration is such that functional spill-over effects, coupled with supranational institutions, produce an ever-greater process of technocratic automaticity. In this manner, supranational structures gain increasing agency, as their power and autonomy is self-reinforcing. Taken together, these three mechanisms imply that political union is an inevitable side effect of increasing integration in economic sectors within and across different states.

Jean Monnet's Community method encapsulates the logic of (neo-)functionalism: unlike the other founding fathers of European integration such as Alcide de Gasperi, Robert Schuman or Konrad Adenauer (Kaiser 2007), he tended to eschew politics in favour of central administration and technical solutions. Monnet and other influential figures like Belgium's leader Paul-Henri Spaak were primarily concerned with post-war reconstruction and economic growth through supranational rules. As such, Monnet's method consisted in imposing centrally determined, abstract standards and formal mechanisms that had the effect of weakening the locally diverse, embodied and informal social connections that underpin both markets and states. In this manner, the Community method favoured by Monnet and Spaak ultimately drove a wedge between Europe's supranational technocratic institutions and economic exchange, on the one hand, and local, regional and national political institutions and civic ties, on the other hand (see Siedentop 2001).

Since the 1950s and 1960s, Monnet's Community method has been supplemented by other mechanisms and instruments of closer integration, above all intergovernmental cooperation (see, *inter alia*, Keohane and Hoffmann 1991; Moravcsik 1998), the so-called open method of coordination (Zeitlin, Pochet and Magnusson 2005) and multinational governance and elements of a political system that is *sui generis* (e.g. Hix 2005). However, the (neo-)functionalist logic remains central to the process of European unification. All the main supranational institutions such as the European Commission or the European Court of Justice are technocratic in design. The Commission in particular combines bureaucratic regulation with a managerialist approach to policy design and implementation. In principle, both the European Parliament and the Council of Ministers are more political in nature, but their pursuit of the common public good is severely restricted by ideological divisions and sectional interests. (Neo-)Functionalism is so pervasive that it continues to structure the EU's entire ethos, developing 'procedure as a substitute for policy' (Allen and Wallace 1977) – a characterisation that applies not only to the failed 1999 Lisbon Agenda but also to the Eurozone crisis management since early 2010 (cf. Marsh 2013; Bulmer 2014; Wallace 2016).

At the same time, the EU's *modus operandi* has led to an ever-growing degree of centralisation of decision- and policy-making and the concomitant transfer of competencies from localities, regions and nations to Brussels. For example, the imperative of common product standards as part of the single market entails a unitary, centralised system of bureaucratic regulation (e.g. Majone 1994, 1995; Keleman 2002). That system is enforced by the Commission and policed by the Court of Justice. What this has done is to reduce the diversity of distinct goods and services based on specific skills in different parts of Europe. It also has had the effect of undermining self-regulation and mutual control within the framework of guilds or other voluntary professional associations. Moreover, the (neo-)functionalist approach championed by Monnet and his political heirs has favoured a concentration of wealth and productive assets. The single market has tended to put a premium on economies of scale and thereby favoured large producers over small and medium-sized enterprise. This is true for sectors as diverse as agriculture, manufacturing, industry, retail or financial services. Neither EU competition policy aimed at avoiding cartels and monopolistic practices nor EU subsidies have achieved a proper balance between small and large businesses and a diversified economy that reflects the diverse capabilities of the European society as a whole.

Thus, there is a gulf between Monnet's neo-functionalist method to deliver an overarching political project, on the one hand, and the scale of the common economic challenges, on the other hand. Cross-border financial ties, economic exchange and legal harmonisation – so the neo-functionalist argument goes – are primary precisely because they are the most appropriate foundations for a supranational polity. But with political integration lagging behind, neo-functionalism has over time reinforced the modern 'disembedding' of the economic field from the social field and a re-embedding of social relations in economic transactions (see, once more, Polanyi 2001). In the case of Europe, this is exemplified by the single, bureaucratically regulated market that has taken precedence over a shared political culture, social solidarity and environmental sustainability.

Linked to this priority is a tendency to privilege the convergence of national states and transnational markets over an 'ever closer union among the peoples of Europe' – the original ambition of the 1957 Rome Treaty as enshrined in its preamble. In this manner, the predominance of the functionalist logic, which has governed European integration since the failure of the EDC and the EPC in 1954, helps to explain why the single currency lacks a robust political project that can correct the design faults of the euro such as the lack of a proper banking union – a commitment that requires much greater coordination and authority than the EMU's current governance structure allows (Mény 2014).

Therefore, one alternative to (neo-)functionalism is not to create a federal super-state that lacks popular consent, but rather to promote the associative ties that bind together countries and peoples. This would include the social practices, customs and traditions that provide the fabric for European (and international) society. As a matter of observation, the EU is neither a Franco-German federalist super-state nor a purely Anglo-Saxon glorified 'free-trade' area. Rather, the Union – despite its many imperfections – is perhaps best described as a polity with a political system *sui generis*. Indeed, Europe's polity is characterised by hybrid institutions, overlapping jurisdictions, multiple membership, polycentric authority and multi-level governance (Hix 2005; Zielonka 2006, 2008). Within this polity, social relations are hybrid, not monolithic, that is, not just vertical and instrumental but also horizontal and non-instrumental. Connected with this is the fusion of intended with non-intended outcomes and of homogeneous with heterogeneous interdependence. The question is whether ordo-liberal and (neo-)functionalist approaches are compatible with the diversity of the social domain on which the economic and political fields ultimately depend for trust and cooperation that are necessary for the functioning of EMU.

8.6 Alternative Pathways for the Eurozone

Since the start of the Eurozone crisis in early 2010, four different scenarios have been discussed both in academic research and public policy making (see, *inter alia*, Eichengreen 2010; Marsh 2013; Sandbu 2015; Stiglitz 2016; Wallace 2016). First, a full break-up and a return to national currencies. Second, a partial break-up that could take three forms: either a core euro area without the peripheral countries, or Germany's exit, or a northern and a southern Eurozone with different exchange rates and different interest rates. Third, an increasing centralisation of decision-making based on a combination of intergovernmental and supranational elements (e.g. creating a banking, fiscal and political union). Fourth, a full federalisation of the entire Eurozone with a joint finance ministry, centralised taxation and other key features of a single state.

Arguably, ordo-liberalism supports the second and the third scenario while neo-functionalism champions the fourth scenario. By limiting the options to a (partial or full) break-up or to a variant of supranational centralisation, both the ordo-liberal and the neo-functional approach to the political economy of the Eurozone restrict the range of possible pathways for the common currency (Mény 2014). All these pathways fail to resolve the crisis because they neither work on their own terms nor address the structural issues as outlined earlier. Ordo-liberalism advocates three objectives that are mutually incompatible: first, maintaining a stable euro internally and externally (no more than 2 per cent price inflation and limited fluctuations vis-à-vis major global currencies); second, securing the viability of the European banking system, in particular large and systemically important banks; and third, preserving the fiscal sovereignty of the core, creditor countries by ruling out debt mutualisation and a 'transfer union' of cross-national fiscal support for the peripheral, debtor states.

In the case of EMU, it is possible to pursue any two of these three objectives but impossible to achieve all three simultaneously and in full. The reasons is that without either a measure of debt mutualisation or fiscal transfers (in the form of debt restructuring), the debtor states risk defaulting. In turn, this would increase inflationary pressures and over time force the ECB to raise interest rates, thereby reducing economic growth and increasing both public deficits and national debt. The threat of sovereign defaults might also bring about another banking crisis, as Europe's banks are the single largest holders of sovereign bonds. According to some estimates, German banks alone hold about €350 billion worth of sovereign bonds denominated in euros, which represents 15 per cent of German national output. Moreover, the deleveraging of Europe's largest banks, coupled with the new capital requirements of the Basel III agreement, is accelerating and amplifying capital flight from the periphery to the core, which is exacerbating the balance of payments disequilibrium. The mutual dependence of overleveraged banks and highly indebted states creates a vicious circle of bailouts, rising debt, deleveraging, illiquidity, insolvency and further bailouts (Bibow 2003; Wallace 2016).

To break out of this vicious circle that could bring down the entire euro area, different pathways compared with the ordo-liberal and neofunctional approaches are needed. In this context, an alternative approach that focuses on the constitution of Europe's polity can help to devise alternative political economies. The mark of this approach is to embed the complex process of production and exchange in a set of political and social ties that are characterised by partially realised connections and multiple dimensions of interaction. Thus, both formal institutions and market arrangements take shape within a wider social domain that avoids the choice between the largely vertical relationships within the political field and the predominantly horizontal relationships within the economic field (Pabst 2014; Pabst and Scazzieri 2016). By focusing on the complex, hybrid social ties, different political economies favour alternative pathways that combine the endurance of general social connectivity (over time and across space) with the flexibility of arrangements, which are specific to particular periods and places.

In policy terms, such an approach would seek to resolve the Eurozone crisis and transform the common currency in the following ways. First of all, it would tie the recapitalisation of Europe's over-indebted and under-capitalised (including the highly indebted regional banks such as the Spanish *cajas* and the German *Landesbanken*) to increased lending to the large number of small and medium-size enterprise that are starved of capital and have much greater needs than large businesses (see below). Such a recapitalisation could be done out of an expanded European Stability Mechanism in which both Eurozone members and the ECB have stakes.

Second, the perspective to which this chapter adheres can help to reconfigure fiscal policy. It would abandon pro-cyclical fiscal policy (as a result of the 2011 fiscal pact and the 'debt brake') in favour of some measure of debt restructuring (both public and private) and a shift in government spending from consumption to investment in productive activities (including sectors with a higher multiplier such as high-tech manufacturing). This could include two concrete reforms: (1) new fiscal rules that distinguish government spending on consumption from government spending on investment, with constraints on consumption expenditure and incentives for investment expenditure where returns exceed the costs of capital and (2) the partial mutualisation of debt and the creation of ECB-issued Eurobonds with limits on the overall amount of debt taken out by Eurozone members and restrictions to spend the funds coming in from new debt issues on investment in education, infrastructure or housing.

Third, a political economy of constitution offers possible pathways for a renewed growth strategy based on several components: (1) a credit policy that channels bank lending into small and medium-sized enterprise and other businesses currently starved of capital (including a new lending facility akin to the US Small Business Administration that provides loans or partial guarantees, which could either be a separate institution or linked to the European Investment Bank); (2) a European strategy for boosting investment in transport, energy, information and communication networks as well as in education and R&D by creating Eurozone (or even EU-wide) project bonds and using instruments such as risk-sharing finance facilities or loan guarantees (project bonds could attract institutional investors such as pension funds, insurance companies and perhaps even sovereign wealth funds); (3) promoting innovation to raise both labour and capital productivity in the periphery countries by focusing on high-tech manufacturing and industry (this could, for example, include German businesses setting up more subsidiaries in the southern part of the Eurozone); and (4) a novel strategy to harness the benefits of technology to serve people's needs and wants while also supporting labour in areas where human care and craft are indispensable – including [a] design and innovation, [b] education, health and social care and [c] maintenance of buildings and cultural inheritance.

8.7 Concluding Reflections

The political economy that this chapter outlines has far-reaching implications for the Eurozone. It offers an overarching analysis that describes and explains the multi-level dependencies of the political and the social domain, which is irreducible to the economic and monetary field. Instead, the focus is on the social ties that underpin both state laws and market contracts. This political economy also transcends the separation of micro processes from macro outcomes that characterises conventional approaches, including most neo-classical, monetarist and Keynesian theories. Thus, it rejects the sole emphasis on the impersonal links of laws and contracts in favour of interpersonal social ties, which pre-date patterns of conflict and cooperation. Moreover, the 'political economy of constitution' views systems and structures in non-deterministic ways without ignoring path dependencies that provide constraints on crisis management/resolution and fundamental reforms. In this manner, it offers alternative pathways that centre on the primacy of political and social ties over formal institutions and economic exchange.

   Finally, the political economy that this chapter has outlined can offer conceptual resources for transforming the Eurozone in line with the constitution of Europe's polity. By contrast with the prevailing model of top-down neo-functional harmonisation or *ad hoc* ordo-liberal coordination, the alternative is the mutualisation of risks, rewards and resources. This involves a shift in emphasis from formal rules and joint procedures towards substantive common ends such as shared interests at the sectoral and regional levels with the involvement of diverse professional bodies and social groups alongside state institutions. Such an approach can transform the *status quo* while avoiding either the breakup or the centralisation of the Eurozone. One model is a multi-national association of member states that not only pool sovereignty but also devolve power to the most appropriate level in line with the principles of solidarity and subsidiarity. If the Eurozone is to be a public good for the citizens of its members and for the global economy, then it needs to reflect the interdependencies and relational interests of Europe's polity.

Acknowledgement

Support from the James Madison Charitable Trust for this research is gratefully acknowledged.

References

Allen, C.S. (2005) '"Ordo-Liberalism" Trumps Keynesianism: Economic Policy in the Federal Republic of Germany and the EU', in B. Moss (ed.). *Monetary Union in Crisis: The European Union as a Neo-Liberal Construction*. London: Palgrave Macmillan, pp. 199–221.

Allen, D. and Wallace, W. (1977) 'Political Cooperation: Procedure as a Substitute for Policy', in H. Wallace et al. (ed.), *Policy-Making in the European Communities*, London: Wiley, pp. 227–46.

Berlin, I. (1969) 'Two Concepts of Liberty', in idem, *Four Essays on Liberty*. Oxford: Oxford University Press, pp. 118–72.

Bibow, J. (2003) 'Is Europe Doomed to Stagnation? An Analysis of the Current Crisis and Recommendations for Reforming Macroeconomic Policymaking in Euroland', The Levy Economics Institute Working Paper No. 379 (May), online at http://papers.ssrn.com/sol3/papers .cfm?abstract_id=414400 (accessed 13 September 2013).

Blyth, M. (2013) *Austerity: The History of a Dangerous Idea*. Oxford: Oxford University Press.

Bonefeld, W. (2012) 'Freedom and the Strong State: On German Ordoliberalism', *New Political Economy*, Vo. 17, no. 5 (October): 633–56.

Borio, C. and Disyatat, P. (2011) 'Global imbalances and the financial crisis: link or no link', Working Paper 346 (Basel: Bank for International Settlements), available online at www.bis.org/publ/work346.pdf

Brenner, R. (2006) *The Economics of Global Turbulence: The Advanced Capitalist Economies from Long Boom to Long Downturn, 1945–2005*. London: Verso.

Buchanan, J.M. (1990) 'The Domain of Constitutional Political Economy', *Constitutional Political Economy*, vol. 1, no. 1: 1–18.

Bulmer, S. (2014) 'Germany and the Eurozone Crisis: Between Hegemony and Domestic Politics', *West European Politics*, vol. 37, no. 6 (November): 1244–63.

Casper, S. (2001) 'The Legal Framework for Corporate Governance: The Influence of Contract Law on Company Strategies in Germany and the United States', in P.A. Hall, and D. Soskice, (eds.), *Varieties of Capitalism* (Oxford: Oxford University Press), pp. 337–60.

Collini, S., Winch, D. and Burrow, J. (1983) *That Noble Science of Politics: A Study in Nineteenth-Century Intellectual History*. Cambridge: Cambridge University Press.

Dyson, K.H.F. and Featherstone, K. (1999) *The Road to Maastricht: Negotiating Economic and Monetary Union*. Oxford: Oxford University Press.

Eichengreen, B. (2010) 'The Breakup of the Euro Area', in A. Alesina and F. Giavazzi (eds.), *Europe and the Euro*. Chicago: The University of Chicago Press, pp. 11–51.

Eichengreen, B. (2012) 'European Monetary Integration with Benefit of Hindsight', *Journal of Common Market Studies*, vol. 50, no. 1: 123–36.

Flassbeck, H. and Lapavitsas, C. (2015a) *Nur Deutschland kann den Euro retten: Der letzte Akt beginnt*. Frankfurt am Main: Westend.

Flassbeck, H. and Lapavitsas, C. (2015b) *Against the Troika: Crisis and Austerity in the Eurozone*. London: Verso.

Groom, J.R. and Taylor, P. (1975) *Functionalism: Theory and Practice in International Relations*. London: University of London Press.

Haas, E.B. (1961) 'International Integration: The European and the Universal Process', *International Organization*, vol. 15: 366–92.

Haas, E.B. (1964) *Beyond the Nation-State: Functionalism and International Organization*. Stanford, CA: Stanford University Press.

Hall, P.A. (2013) 'The Political Origins of our Economic Discontents: Contemporary Adjustment Problems in Historical Perspective', in M. Kahler and D. Lake (eds.), *Politics in New Hard Times*. Ithaca, NY: Cornell University Press, pp. 129–49.

Hall, P.A. (2014) 'Varieties of Capitalism and the Euro Crisis', *West European Politics*, vol. 37, no. 6 (November): 1223–43.

Hall, P.A. and Soskice, D. (eds.) (2001) *Varieties of Capitalism*. Oxford: Oxford University Press.

Hayek, F.A. (1939) 'Freedom and the Economic System', reprinted in *Socialism and War*. Chicago: The University of Chicago Press, pp. 189–212.

Hayek, F.A. (1944) *The Road to Serfdom*. Chicago: The University of Chicago Press.

Hirschman, A.O. (1977) *The Passions and the Interests: Political Arguments for Capitalism before Its Triumph*. Princeton, NJ: Princeton University Press.

Hix, S. (2005) *The Political System of the European Union*, 2nd rev. ed. London: Palgrave Macmillan.

Howarth, D. and Quaglia, L. (2013) 'Banking Union as Holy Grail: Rebuilding the Single Market in Financial Services, Stabilizing Europe's Banks and 'Completing' Economic and Monetary Union', *Journal of Common Market Studies*, vol. 51, no. 1: 103–23.

Kaiser, W. (2007) *Christian Democracy and the Origins of European Union*. Cambridge: Cambridge University Press.

Keleman, R.D. (2002) 'The Politics of "Eurocratic" Structure and the new European agencies', *West European Politics*, vol. 25, no. 4 (September): 93–118.

Keohane, R.O. and Hoffmann, S. (1991) *The New European Community: Decision-making and Institutional Change*. Boulder, CO: Westview Press.

Kolev, S. (2010) 'F.A. Hayek as an Ordo-Liberal', *Hamburg Institute of International Economics* Research Paper, August.

MacIntyre, A. (2000 [1981]) *After Virtue: A Study in Moral Theory*, 3rd ed. (London: Duckworth).

Majone, G. (1994) 'The Rise of the Regulatory State in Europe', *West European Politics*, vol. 14, no. 3 (June): 77–101.

Majone, G. (1995) *The European Community as a Regulatory State*. Leiden: Nijhoff.

Manent, P. (2010) *Les métamorphoses de la cité: Essai sur la dynamique de l'Occident*. Paris: Flammarion; English trans. *Metamorphoses of the City: On the Western Dynamic*. Cambridge, MA: Harvard University Press.

Marsh, D. (2013) *Europe's Deadlock: How the Euro Crisis Could Be Solved: and Why It Won't Happen*. New Haven, CT and London: Yale University Press.

Marshall, A. (1890) *Principles of Economics*. London: Macmillan.

McNamara, K.R. (1998) *The Currency of Ideas: Monetary Politics in the European Union*. Ithaca, NY: Cornell University Press.

Megay, E. N. (1970) 'Anti-Pluralist Liberalism: The German Neoliberals', *Political Science Quarterly*, vol. 85, no. 3: 422–42.

Mény, Y. (2014) 'Managing the EU Crises: Another Way of Integration by Stealth?', *West European Politics*, vol. 37, no. 6 (November): 1336–53.

Mitrany, D. (1933) *The Progress of International Government*. New Haven, CT: Yale University Press.

Mitrany, D. (1948) 'Functional Approach to World Organization', *International Affairs*, vol. 23: 350–63.

Mitrany, D. (1965) 'The Prospect of European Integration: Federal or Functional', *Journal of Common Market Studies*, vol. 4, no. 2: 119–49.

Mitrany, D. (1966) *A Working Peace System*. Chicago: Quadrangle Books.

Mitrany, D. (1976) *The Functional Theory of Politics*. New York: St. Martin's Press.

Moravcsik, A. (1998) *The Choice for Europe: Social Purpose and State Power from Messina to Maastricht*. London: Routledge.

Nicholls, A.J. (1994) *Freedom with Responsibility: The Social Market Economy 1918–1963*. Oxford: Oxford University Press.

North, D.C., Wallis, J.J. and Weingast, B.R. (2010) *Violence and Social Orders: A Conceptual Framework for Interpreting Recorded Human History*. Cambridge: Cambridge University Press.

Ornaghi, L. (1990) 'Economic Structure and Political Institutions: A Theoretical Framework', in M. Baranzini and R. Scazzieri (eds.), *The Economic Theory of Structure and Change*. Cambridge: Cambridge University Press, pp. 23–44.

Pabst, A. (2014) 'The Constitutional vs. the Contractualist Tradition: A Foundational Divide in Political Economy'. Paper presented at the Cambridge Research Seminar in Political Economy, Emmanuel College, Cambridge, 6 February.

Pabst, A. and Scazzieri, R. (2012) 'The Political Economy of Civil Society', *Constitutional Political Economy*, vol. 23, no. 4 (October): 337–56.

Pabst, A. and Scazzieri, R. (2016) 'The Political Economy of Constitution', *Œconomia – History, Methodology, Philosophy*, vol. 6, no. 3 (December): 337–62.

Pissarides, C. (2013) 'Is Europe Working?', LSE Regius Professorship Inaugural Lecture, 12 December, available online at www.lse.ac.uk/public Events/events/2013/12/20131212t1830vOT.aspx

Polanyi, K. (2001 [1944]) *The Great Transformation: The Political and Economic Origins of Our Time*. Boston: Beacon Press.

Ptak, R. (2009) 'Neoliberalism in Germany: Revisiting the Ordoliberal Foundations of the Social Market Economy', in Mirowski, P. and Plehwe, D. (eds.), *The Road From Mont Pèlerin: The Making of The Neoliberal Thought Collective*. Cambridge, MA: Harvard University Press, pp. 103–25.

Rawls, J. (1971) *A Theory of Justice*. Cambridge, MA: Harvard University Press.

Roubini, N. and Mihm, S. (2011) *Crisis Economics: A Crash Course in the Future of Finance*. London: Penguin.

Sandbu, M. (2015) *Europe's Orphan: The Future of the Euro and the Politics of Debt*. Princeton, NJ: Princeton University Press.

Sandholtz, W. and Stone Sweet, A. (1997) 'European Integration and Supranational Governance', *Journal of European Public Policy*, vol. 4: 297–317.

Sandholtz, W. and Stone Sweet, A. (eds.) (1998) *European Integration and Supranational Governance*. Oxford: Oxford University Press.

Sandholtz, W., Stone Sweet, A. and Fligstein, N. (2001) *The Institutionalization of Europe*. Oxford: Oxford University Press.

Scazzieri, R. (1999) 'Modelli di società civile', *Filosofia politica*, 13 (3, December): 363–78.

Scharpf, F.W. (2010) *Community and Autonomy: Institutions, Policies and Legitimacy in Multilevel Europe*. Frankfurt: Campus Verlag.

Screpanti, E. and Zamagni, S. (2005) *An Outline of the History of Economic Thought*. Oxford: Oxford University Press.

Sewell, J.P. (1966) *Functionalism and World Politics*. Princeton, NJ: Princeton University Press.

Siedentop, L. (2001) *Democracy in Europe*, new ed. London: Penguin.

Sinn, H.-W. (2014) *The Euro Trap: On Bursting Bubbles, Budgets, and Beliefs*. Oxford: Oxford University Press.

Skidelsky, R. (2006) 'Hayek versus Keynes: The Road to Reconciliation', in E. Feser (ed.), *The Cambridge Companion to Hayek*. Cambridge: Cambridge University Press, pp. 82–110.

Skidelsky, R. (2009) *Keynes: The Return of the Master*. London: Allen Lane.

Stark, J. (2015) 'The historical and cultural differences that divide Europe's union', *Financial Times*, 12 February, p. 11.

Stiglitz, J. (2016) *The Euro: How a Common Currency Threatens the Future of Europe*. New York: W.W. Norton & Co.

Streeck, W. (2015), 'Why the Euro Divides Europe', *New Left Review*, no. 95 (September–October): 5–26.

Wallace, P. (2016) *The Euro Experiment*. Cambridge: Cambridge University Press.

Wallace, W. (ed.) (1990) *The Dynamics of European Integration*. London: Pinter Publishers.

Weber, M. (1947 [1922]) *Wirtschaft und Gesellschaft*. Tübingen: Mohr [Paul Siebeck], trans. *The Theory of Social and Economic Organization*. New York: The Free Press of Glencoe.

Wolf, M. (2014) *The Shifts and the Shocks: What We've Learned – and Have Still to Learn – from the Financial Crisis*. London: Allen Lane.

Wolf, P. (1973) 'International Organization and Attitude Change: A Re-examination of the Functionalist Approach', *International Organization*, vol. 27 (July): 347–71.

Zeitlin, J., Pochet, P. and Magnusson, L. (2005) *The Open Method of Coordination in Action*. Brussels: Peter Lang.

Zielonka, J. (2006) *Europe as Empire: The Nature of the Enlarged European Union*. Oxford: Oxford University Press.

Zielonka, J. (2008) 'Europe as a Global Actor: Empire by Example?' *International Affairs*, vol. 84, no. 3: 471–84.

9 Sectoral Interests and 'Systemic Interest'

Towards a Structural Political Economy of the Eurozone

IVANO CARDINALE

The Eurozone is not just a currency area. It is also a supranational level of decision-making and hence a political arena, based on a dense fabric of interdependencies that span multiple levels of aggregations (countries, regions, industrial sectors) and have both economic and political nature.

The standard tools of micro- and macro-economic analysis, which have largely been used to think about the Eurozone, are not well suited to represent those interdependencies and make sense of their implications for analysis and policy. In fact, neither micro nor macro approaches represent the internal structure of the Eurozone, that is, the constituent units and their interdependencies.

In this chapter, I argue that in order to understand the political economy of the Eurozone, we need to add an intermediate level of analysis – that of industrial sectors (see also the final chapter in this volume). This level of analysis i.s particularly important, because industrial sectors have historically been a crucial factor underlying a country's political configuration (see Ferguson, 1995) and are a major source of influence on EU-level decision-making (Coen, 2007, 2009). The focus on sectors as socio-political aggregations was also particularly strong in the formative phases of political economy, as I discuss in this chapter.

For our purposes, sectors can be seen as potential interest groups: they have interests in particular policies, although they do not necessarily organise themselves to influence policy-making. The structure of sectoral interdependencies can thus provide a heuristic for the configuration of political interests at the sectoral level. In particular, in this chapter I reinterpret two central results of structural economic analysis to throw light on fundamental yet largely unexplored aspects of the political economy of the Eurozone, as well as of political economy more generally.

216

The first is that representations based on circular interdependencies (i.e. input-output tables) provide a model to assess the compatibility and trade-offs between the particular interests of sectors and the need to preserve the viability of the economic system as a whole. Specifically, I refer to the Hawkins-Simon conditions for the viability of an economic system (Hawkins and Simon, 1949; Duchin and Steenge, 2007; Steenge, 2011; Nikaido, 2014), which show that any given economy can be viable and grow with different sectoral weights. In political economy terms, this means that it is possible to shift value added from one sector to another (thus benefitting some sectors over others) whilst keeping systemic coherence. I then introduce the concept of 'systemic interest', which I define as an interest in preserving the viability of the economic system as a whole. Systemic interest is a generalisation of the traditional category of national interest, and can be operationalised through the Hawkins-Simon conditions. The foregoing analysis leads to asking whether the Eurozone has features that make relevant actors consider its viability as part of their systemic interest.

The analysis of sectoral and systemic interests leads to developing a political economy interpretation of another central result in structural economic analysis. Pasinetti (1973) has shown that any given system of interdependencies can be represented equivalently through a circular representation that explicitly shows inter-industry relationships and intermediate goods (as in input-output tables), or through a vertically integrated representation that emphasises final goods, each of which is produced through a series of production phases performed across multiple industrial sectors. This formal equivalence is an important result for this chapter's political economy analysis. In fact, I argue that it makes it possible to overcome the dichotomy (Blyth, 2003) between, on the one hand, the view that the interests of groups are determined by economic structure, and, on the other hand, the view that interests are 'ideationally constructed' in a way that is autonomous from economic structure. In fact, this chapter's approach suggests that, since a given economic structure can be represented in analytically alternative ways, which lead to different configurations of interests, interests cannot be seen as being univocally 'determined' by economic structure. At the same time, interests cannot be seen as being merely 'constructed' in ways that are independent by structure, because there exist 'objective' interdependencies between sectors. I thus introduce the concept of 'structurally grounded' interests, that is, interests that are compatible with existing economic structure but are not univocally defined by the latter.

The preceding analysis leads to envisioning *political economy maps* of the Eurozone, based on coalitions of interest groups within and across countries, which can try to influence decision-making at the national and supranational levels. Moreover, it suggests that the different possible coalitions also depend on how the groups involved visualise interdependencies.

Besides offering categories for analysing the political economy of the Eurozone, this approach contributes to two traditions in economic and political analysis. One is the aforementioned political science tradition on the political representation of economic interests (Lipset and Rokkan, 1967; Hirschman, 1968; Rae and Taylor, 1970; Rogowski, 1987). This tradition considers the economic interests of sectors but not their interdependencies, thereby struggling to capture the existence of systemic interest.

The other tradition to which this chapter contributes is that of structural economic analysis. In fact, in Quesnay's (1972 [1759]) seminal conceptualisation of interdependencies, sectors were seen as economic activities but also as socio-political aggregations. Subsequent work left this dimension on the background (see Cardinale, 2012); most notably for our purposes, twentieth-century models of sectoral interdependencies (Leontief, 1941; von Neumann, 1945; Sraffa, 1960) only focussed on the economic dimension of industrial sectors as productive activities, not considering their potential socio-political dimension. This chapter suggests that those models can provide important heuristics for understanding the socio-political dimension of industrial sectors. In a sense, the aim is of the chapter to 'complete' the rediscovery of sectoral interdependencies that started in the mid-twentieth century. This is indeed the idea underlying the 'Structural Political Economy' (SPE) approach: using representations of the economy at intermediate levels of aggregation not only to study economic phenomena but also as heuristic tools for political economy analysis (Cardinale 2012, 2015; Cardinale and Coffman, 2014; Cardinale and Landesmann, Chapter 11 in this volume; Cardinale and Scazzieri, 2017; Chapter 17 in this volume).

The Eurozone is a complex and multidimensional nexus of interdependencies. We cannot take for granted that the relevant political actors (in this case, sectors) will visualise the full range of relevant configurations of particular and systemic interests. The SPE approach proposed here aims to provide categories for exploring the range of interests, interdependencies and coalitions, and hence understand the political economy paths open to the Eurozone. Or, more specifically, the paths that the political economy of the Eurozone makes it possible to envision and pursue.

9.1 Sectoral Models of the Economy

Much of the debate on the Eurozone has adopted a macro or micro level of analysis (see Chapter 17 in this volume for a detailed discussion). For our purposes, the problem is that both aggregate (macro) and microeconomic representations do not show the internal structure of the economy. For example, representations based on the production function, such as Solow's (1956) model of economic growth, portray an economy as a black box in which inputs of aggregate labour L and aggregate capital K are used to produce aggregate output Y:

$$Y = F(K, L)$$

Because of the aggregate level of analysis, this formulation does not allow us to see the internal structure of the economy. For example, it is not clear which sectors produce national output and in what proportions. Two countries might have a similar GDP, but one might specialise in agriculture and the other in manufacturing. An aggregate representation does not allow us to see this difference.

This is also true for microfounded macroeconomic models. In fact, those models show the aggregate economy as the sum of individual actors (households and firms). In models in which actors are homogeneous (e.g. Kydland and Prescott, 1982), the macroeconomy behaves as if it was an agent (indeed, the 'representative agent'). In models in which agents are heterogeneous (see Krusell and Smith, 2006), it is possible to model different proportions between groups. However, because interdependencies are not considered, the dynamics of the aggregate are simply the sum of individual behaviours (see Pasinetti, 2012; Solow, 2012).

In order to appreciate the internal structure of an economic system and its implications for political economy, we need to resort to representations that break down the macroeconomy into constituent parts at intermediate levels of aggregation (in this case, industrial sectors) and show their interdependencies.

The first formalised representation of the internal structure of the economy was arguably François Quesnay's (1972 [1759]) *Tableau économique*, which describes 'the circulation of money and commodities in relation to both the expenditure of revenue and the technical and social relationships between the two main sectors of the economy' (Vaggi, 2008; see also Eltis, 1984, Pasinetti 1977). However, the idea of interdependencies among aggregations that are both economic activities and socio-political groups was already present in the 'political arithmetik' tradition (e.g. Petty, 1662; Davenant, 1698; King, 1936 [1696, 1697]; see Cardinale and Coffman, 2014).

Quesnay's insight was more recently built upon by von Neumann (1945), Sraffa (1960) and Leontief (1941). The latter explicitly presented his *Structure of the American Economy* as an attempt to construct a modern *Tableau* (see also Leontief, 1991 [1928]). The structure of interdependencies is also the basis of multi-sectoral models of structural economic dynamics (Quadrio Curzio 1967, 1975; Lowe, 1976; Pasinetti 1981, 1993; Baranzini and Scazzieri, 1990; Landesmann and Scazzieri, 1996; Hagemann, Landesmann and Scazzieri, 2003; Scazzieri, 2012; Scazzieri, Baranzini and Rotondi, 2015). Moreover, Quesnay's idea has provided the conceptual basis of statistical models of multi-sectoral growth (Stone and Brown, 1962) and is to this day the foundation of input-output tables regularly produced by statistical offices worldwide (Wixted, Yamano and Webb, 2006).

An input-output table of the Quesnay-Leontief type, in Pasinetti's (1977, chapter III) formulation, is presented in Table 9.1. The table is to be read as follows. Aggregate output is broken down into the output of n-1 industrial sectors (x_1 to x_{n-1}) and a final sector.

Table 9.1 *An input-output table of the Quesnay-Leontief type.*

Inputs	Outputs			
	Industry 1	Industry 2	Industry j	Final sector (consumption)
Commodity 1	$q_{11}p_1$	$q_{12}p_1$	$\cdots\ q_{1j}p_1$	$\cdots\ q_{1n}p_1$
Commodity 2	$q_{21}p_2$	$q_{22}p_2$	$\cdots\ q_{2j}p_2$	$\cdots\ q_{2n}p_2$
	$\vdots$	$\vdots$	$\vdots$	$\vdots$
Commodity i	$q_{i1}p_i$	$q_{i2}p_i$	$\cdots\ q_{ij}p_i$	$\cdots\ q_{in}p_i$
	$\vdots$	$\vdots$	$\vdots$	$\vdots$
Final sector (value added)	$q_{n1}p_n$	$q_{n2}p_n$	$\cdots\ q_{nj}p_n$	$\cdots\ q_{nn}p_n$

Each row shows the output of a sector (e.g. good 1) as an input into the other sectors (the input of good 1 into processes 1, 2, 3, ..., n-1) and a final demand of good 1 (d_1). Each column shows how production of a good (e.g. good 1) uses the output of other sectors as inputs; it also shows the value added over the value of such inputs.

This representation allows us to visualise the sectors that make up the macroeconomy. In addition – crucially for our purposes – it shows the interdependencies among those sectors. For instance, sector 2 depends on sector 1 because its output is an input to sector 1; it also uses the output of sector 1 as an input. Of course not all sectors depend on all other sectors, so that some coefficients may be 0 (or very small).

By unveiling relevant aggregations and their interdependencies, this representation makes it possible to conceptualise and observe the structure of an economic system. From the empirical viewpoint, input-output tables can be constructed for any system (such as regions, groups of regions, groups of countries, etc.), although they are primarily developed for national economies. For the purposes of studying the sectoral structure of the Eurozone, the World Input-Output Database (WIOD) is particularly useful, as it shows, for over forty countries including all EU member states, interdependencies between each sector in a given country and all sectors in all other countries.

9.2 Sectoral Interests and 'Systemic Interest'

The aforementioned structural models have wide-ranging implications for political economy analysis, and more specifically for how we think about the Eurozone. In particular, they make it possible to add a level of economic and political interests: that of industrial sectors. But in order to do so, we need to make a conceptual shift from purely economic analysis to one that is also political.

In particular, we should go back to the insight, central to Physiocracy and the 'political arithmetik' tradition, that economic sectors are also 'social classes'.[1] In more modern terms, the insight is that economic sectors potentially correspond to interest groups. Economic

---

[1] Elsewhere (Cardinale, 2012) I analyse how this conception of 'classes' differs from that based on types of income (wage, profit, rent). The latter was largely adopted by classical political economists and Marx, although Marx (1894) himself recognises the possibility of interest groups different from social classes in Book III of *Capital*.

sectors have interests, for instance in obtaining economic policies that favour them, and there is the possibility that they will seek some form of political influence to protect those interests. Economic sectors can be either potential or manifest groups in Truman's (1962) sense. Truman distinguishes between potential interest groups, which are latent and could organise themselves under certain conditions, for instance if threatened, and manifest interest groups, which are already organised and exert active pressure on decision-making. What matters for our purposes is the *possibility* that economic sectors seek some form of political influence. In fact, the purpose of this analysis is to explore the possibilities for conflict and cooperation that a given economic structure makes possible, independently of realised outcomes.

Studying economic interests on the basis of structural models, which highlight sectoral interdependencies, can lead to very different insights as compared to existing perspectives. In fact, the political representation of economic interests is a classic theme in political science and is also at the core of the political economics approach (Truman, 1962; Buchanan and Tullock, 1962; Olson, 1965; Becker, 1983; Rogowski, 1987; Ferguson, 1995; Persson and Tabellini, 2002). However, those approaches do not consider economic interdependencies. Hence, they overlook that the pursuit of particular interests must take into account the interests of other actors, as I discuss later in the chapter. Furthermore, approaches in economics that do take into account interdependencies – for example those that are explicitly inspired by Quesnay – have focussed on material and technological interdependencies, leaving aside the political aspect (Cardinale, 2012). The structural political economy approach can be seen as using the tools offered by the latter set of approaches (structural economic models) to understand the problem addressed by the former set of approaches, i.e. the political representation of economic interests.

The first result of structural economic analysis that I want to discuss is the so-called Hawkins-Simon conditions for the viability of an economic system (Hawkins and Simon, 1949; see also Nikaido, 2014; Duchin and Steenge, 2007; Steenge, 2011). An economic system satisfies the Hawkins-Simon conditions if 'the state of technology expressed by [the technology matrix] is such as to allow a net production, that is an excess production of goods produced relative to goods used as means of production' (Quadrio Curzio, 1967, pp. 56–57). In other words, the economy is viable (it is able to reintegrate the means of production utilised at the beginning of the production process) and produces a surplus. It has been shown that the ability of the system to reproduce itself and produce a surplus – that is, its ability to grow – is compatible with different sectoral proportions. In other words, the system could be preserved and grow with different relative weights of sectors.

From the political economy point of view, this means that there is potential for conflict between sectors: a sector might want to grow relative to others and, within limits, this would not compromise the viability of the system. This is important, because if there was only one proportion among sectors that made the system viable, any attempt to modify that proportion would not be sustainable, hence conflict would not be compatible with the preservation of the system.

Cardinale and Landesmann (Chapter 11 in this volume) explore such sectoral conflicts of interests in the context of the Eurozone (see also Chapter 17 in this volume). For example, take the conflict between tradable and non-tradable sectors with respect to policies leading to real exchange rate devaluation (see also Körner and Trautwein, Chapter 10 in this volume). In general, tradable sectors' interest lies in competitiveness vis-à-vis foreign competitors, which depends on relative cost considerations. Non-tradable sectors, on the other hand, are interested in domestic demand. Therefore, non-tradable sectors would oppose fiscal austerity measures leading to real exchange rate devaluation, as such measures are likely to reduce real incomes and therefore domestic demand. Tradable sectors, instead, would favour such measures: they would not be highly affected by lower domestic demand, whilst being made more competitive by real exchange rate devaluation.

In principle, the system could be viable under a range of sectoral proportions; hence, there is room for conflict over policies that influence the real exchange rate. However, beyond certain proportions, the crisis of some sectors can affect other sectors through interdependencies, so that the latter may be damaged too. In fact, non-tradable sectors must take into account that tradable sectors need to be competitive enough to guarantee the long-run sustainability of the external accounts of the country, which is central for the long-term viability of an open economy. Moreover, tradable sectors contribute to domestic demand through their export earnings. Conversely, tradable sectors depend on non-tradable sectors for a significant proportion of their inputs, and therefore their interest in real exchange rate devaluation is tempered by the need to secure the continuity (and quality) of the supply of these inputs.

The foregoing argument refers to conflicts within each country. When applied to the Eurozone level, it suggests that tradable sectors of advanced countries are against real exchange rate appreciation relative to catching-up countries, for this would lead to a deterioration of their competitive positions. Yet their interests need to take into account the systemic implications of a lack of real exchange rate adjustments.

The representation of the economy based on sectoral interdependencies thus highlights the *possibility of conflict* as well as the *necessity to keep conflict within a systemically sustainable level* – one that guarantees that the system as a whole is not jeopardised. Therefore, each sector has a particular interest in its own survival and expansion, as well as a 'systemic' interest in the preservation of the system to which it belongs, which is itself necessary for its survival. Systemic interest derives from interdependencies, and expresses the fact that a structural view does not simply disaggregate output by sector, but shows the interdependencies among them: on this view, the economy is a *system* in the strong sense of the term.

The concept of systemic interest generalises and operationalises the traditional category of national interest, which has central importance both in political science (e.g. Morgenthau, 1954; Finnemore, 1996) and economics (e.g. List, 1885 [1841]; Kuznets, 1971). It is a generalisation because it makes it possible to study whether an interest in the preservation of the system is present not only at the national level but at any other level under consideration, such as the supranational or regional ones.

The concept of systemic interest can also operationalise 'national interest' because it provides a criterion to judge the compatibility and trade-offs between particular (in this case, sectoral) interests and systemic interest. For example, List (1996 [1827], letter 6, p. 87) observes that '[canals] and railroads may do great good to a nation, but all waggoners will complain of this improvement. Every new invention has some inconvenience for a number of individuals, and is nevertheless a public blessing'. In a similar vein, for Kuznets (1971), two fundamental requirements for economic development are the role of the state as an agency for resolution of conflicts among group interests and the presence of a 'feeling of community', that is, the idea of a national interest that goes beyond the interests of groups and subgroups. In both cases, whilst the intuition of a trade-off between particular interests and national interest is central to the analysis, it is less clear how to study it.

Systemic interest can help to operationalise the analysis of such trade-offs. Specifically, the Hawkins-Simon conditions can be seen as an operational tool to investigate the trade-off between particular interests and systemic interest. This operationalisation has interesting properties. One is that systemic interest is a condition concerning sectoral proportions (i.e. basically *a constraint*), which is satisfied by a plurality of proportions. Therefore, systemic interest is not to be understood as corresponding to only one (optimal) policy, which may or may not be pursued because of conflicts of interest. The upshot is that, unlike in analyses such as those typical of the political economics approach (see Persson and Tabellini, 2002), in which there is one optimal economic policy that is often not implemented because of conflicts of interests, an SPE approach suggests that a plurality of sectoral proportions is compatible with viability of the system. Therefore, a plurality of policies satisfies the constraints imposed by systemic interest.

It is important to emphasise that systemic interest derives from interdependencies. In models that do not theorise interdependencies, connections between groups cannot be specified, so that it is not clear if the decline of a group has any effects on other groups (see Rogowski, 1987; Persson and Tabellini, 2002). Therefore, it becomes difficult to specify why a sector should have an interest that others sectors are not excessively penalised by the policies it favours.

The foregoing reasoning leads to another implication of the operationalisation of systemic interest. In fact, it makes it possible to overcome the assumption that political action that takes into account 'national interest' is based on a normative commitment. Rather, action on the basis of an interest in the preservation of the system is often a necessary condition for the pursuit of particular interests in the presence of interdependencies (Cardinale and Coffman, 2014 explore this point in the context of taxation in eighteenth-century Britain).

9.3 Beyond Structural Determination and 'Ideational Construction': Sectors' Interests as 'Structurally Grounded'

Analyses of how political actors form their interests, and hence their stance within the political arena, have traditionally been characterised by a dualism (see Blyth, 2003). At one extreme, interests are seen as structurally determined, that is, univocally determined by the economic structures within which actors are located. At the other extreme, actors construct their interests on the basis of 'ideas' that are autonomous from economic structures. Several attempts have been made to devise approaches that can reconcile objective economic structure with 'ideas'. This problem is important for the understanding the political economy of the Eurozone, for it leads to problematising how relevant actors (in this case, sectors) understand their own interests, and therefore how they articulate their stance in the political arena.

An SPE perspective offers a route to overcome the aforementioned dualism. In fact, in the view presented here, interests are neither structurally determined nor simply 'ideationally constructed' They are not structurally determined because a given structure of sectoral interdependencies can be represented in different yet equivalent ways. A key result of structural economic analysis is particularly useful here. Pasinetti (1973) shows that a given economy can be represented equivalently (1) as a set of interdependencies between industrial sectors that exchange intermediate goods (a 'horizontal' representation – the one we have followed in this chapter) or (2) as a set of final goods, each of which is produced through a series of interactions between several sectors (a 'vertical' representation).[2] I have shown elsewhere (Cardinale, 2012) that if a given group adopts a 'horizontal' representation of the system to which it belongs, the 'particular' interest becomes salient, because such representation highlights the different sectors and the possibility to shift value added from one to another. In contrast, a 'vertical' representation highlights systemic interest, as it shows that every final good is produced by the system as a whole, though stages of fabrication that involve several industries.

As analytically equivalent representations of the same economic structure highlight different interests, several representations are equally grounded in existing interdependencies. Hence, sectoral interests cannot be seen as being univocally determined by objective conditions. But interests are not simply 'ideationally constructed'. Structural models suggest that there exist objective, if multiple, configurations of interdependencies, so that *not everything goes*. Therefore, the

---

[2] The final chapter of this volume, Scazzieri (Chapter 7 in this volume) and Cardinale and Scazzieri (2016) explore the implications of horizontal and vertical representations for a range of political economy problems.

distinction becomes one between interests that are structurally grounded and interests that are not, in the sense that they misrepresent structural interdependencies. In the above example, constructions of interest based on vertical or horizontal representations of interdependencies are both structurally grounded. On the other hand, if tradable sectors favour austerity policies that damage non-tradable sectors beyond the limits of systemic viability, it is likely that they are misrepresenting (or ignoring) existing interdependencies.

9.4 Political Economy Maps of the Eurozone

The foregoing analysis suggests a considerable shift in how we conceive of the political economy of the Eurozone. So far, coalitions of interests have mostly been thought about in terms of macroeconomies and nation states, as shown by analyses in terms of Southern vs. Northern or core vs. peripheral countries. That level of analysis is no doubt relevant, because crucial decision-making powers reside at the level of nation states. However, the intermediate level of aggregation discussed here adds a further dimension to the picture – the level of sectoral interdependencies *within* and *across* countries.

Models of sectoral interdependencies have traditionally been interpreted with reference to national economic systems. Whilst some interdependencies are between sectors within a country, others are with sectors in other countries, especially in tightly integrated areas such as the Eurozone. When a given policy choice is to be made at the supranational level, we can envision the formation of two types of potential coalitions.

For decisions based on negotiations among states (e.g. in the European Council), we can envision that, within each country, potential coalitions are formed among sectors that favour a certain policy and those which favour a different one. Such coalitions would try to secure their government's support for the preferred policies at the supranational level.

For decisions taken directly at the supranational level (e.g. by the European Commission), we can expect that coalitions will be created within each country and across countries, based on interdependencies between sectors, in an attempt to influence supranational policymaking directly.

The foregoing argument suggests that the possibility of influencing decision-making at the supranational level potentially entails the formation of coalitions of interests based on sectoral interdependencies within and across countries. It is important to note the multiplicity of such *political economy maps*. For each decision, different potential coalitions are generated, within and across nations. So sector A may be aligned with sector B against sector C with regard to some policies, but with sector C against sector B with regard to other policies. This multiplicity has important implications. First, it is likely that coalitions change depending on the issue at stake (although some coalitions might hold across a range of issues). Second, we know from the literature on overlapping cleavages (see, e.g., Lipset and Rokkan, 1967; Hirschman, 1968; Rae and Taylor, 1970; Rogowski, 1987) that overlaps tend to prevent excessive polarisation of conflict. At the same time, overlaps might make the 'return' on sectors' 'political investment' less clear. This could explain the policy stalemates that often characterise decision-making in the EU.

The multiplicity of 'structurally grounded' configurations of interests, discussed earlier, provides an important additional insight for political economy maps in the Eurozone. In fact, in this view coalitions are not univocally determined by existing interdependencies; they depend on the representations of interdependencies that sectors adopt. In the language used in this chapter, they are not structurally determined but structurally grounded. Because multiple representations of interdependencies are grounded in the objective economic structure at any given time, the specific way a sector represents its interest is one of the many that are possible (and potentially grounded). This implies that, if sectors visualise interdependencies differently, they might form different coalitions. Furthermore, different representations of interdependencies imply a different visualisation not only of sectoral interests, but also of systemic interest (see Cardinale and Landesmann, Chapter 11 in this volume, for a discussion of national and EU-level representations of systemic interest.

It is important to note that, whilst the foregoing analysis might suggest a potentially endless variety of configurations of interests, it is likely that there be significant path dependence in the representation of interests, which restricts the visualisation of the full spectrum of potential interdependencies and orients sectors towards considering some constructions of interests over others.

One reason for path dependence may have to do with the 'cognitive' difficulty to consider the whole spectrum of potential interdependencies; in this case, the status quo can offer a satisficing solution and the starting point for 'local' explorations (Simon, 1997; Gavetti and Levinthal, 2000).

Another reason may be that economic interdependencies sometimes change faster than representations thereof, so that some sectors do not realise quickly enough that interdependencies have changed. In this sense, the persistence in how sectors represent their own interests may have to do with the fact that the mutual shaping of structures and interests is not instantaneous, but occurs over time (Bourdieu, 1979; Sewell, 1992; Cardinale, 2017). As a result, there is no guarantee that interdependencies and interests will match at any given moment. This suggests that an interesting approach could be to study continuity and change in both economic structures and the representations of interests on the part of sectors, and to consider their matches and mismatches.

The manifold interests involved in the intricate fabric of political economy interdependencies of the Eurozone arguably exert considerable centrifugal forces. Under what conditions can we envision the presence of a centripetal balance to those forces?

9.5 Is There a 'Systemic Interest' in the Eurozone?

An SPE approach suggests that, because of sectoral interdependencies, a sector or coalition will not push conflict beyond the level at which the whole system is damaged, because at that point the sector itself would be affected. In Section 9.2 I have defined such interest as 'systemic interest', that is, an interest in the preservation of the system. Specifically, interdependencies require that sectoral proportions are kept within a range compatible with the viability of the whole economic system.

A corollary of this analysis is that systemic interest is present in any economy integrated enough that changes in proportions affect viability. If that were not the case, sectors would not need to take into account systemic interest in the pursuit of their particular interests. Therefore, whether a certain system (e.g. a country, a supranational area, a region or a group of sectors) is self-contained enough to have a systemic interest is not something we can posit a priori; it is an empirical question. For example, systemic interest could be present within a group of regions but not within a country, because those regions are much more integrated with each other, or perhaps with regions abroad, than with the rest of their own country. Moreover, systemic interest could be present at different levels at the same time, such as in the case of national and EU-level systemic interests (Cardinale and Landesmann, Chapter 11 in this volume).

In order to determine in what political economy aggregations there can be a systemic interest, we need to define which aggregation displays interdependencies that allow us to define it as a system. So our question becomes: Is the Eurozone a system integrated enough that its preservation is in the interest of sufficiently relevant coalitions?

In order to establish the relevant system, that is, the level at which a systemic interest could be identified – whether or not it is actually recognised as such by the relevant political actors – we can use Herbert Simon's (1962) criterion of 'near decomposability.' For Simon, 'in a nearly decomposable system, the short-run behavior of each of the component subsystems is approximately independent of the short-run behavior of the other components' (Simon, 1962, p. 474). Hence, in our case the relevant system of analysis will be one that has the characteristics of the subsystems described by Simon.

In our context, the criterion of near-decomposability can be operationalised by assessing the relative strength of internal and external interdependencies. If *internal* interdependencies are relatively stronger, we can expect the existence of a systemic interest in the Eurozone, which constrains internal conflicts. Political actors will (or should, in principle) realise that policies that affect some sectors beyond a certain extent will damage the whole system, thereby penalising them too.

If *external* interdependencies are relatively stronger, our heuristic suggests that some sectors might seek integration outside the Eurozone, thereby being less interested in its viability. As a result, they would be less concerned about the sectors they are geographically proximate to, but not integrated with. Hence, there would be no systemic interest to counteract centrifugal forces. Interestingly, export-oriented sectors may assume that they are not integrated in the national system because their final demand is largely foreign; however, interdependencies on the side of inputs imply that disruption of some sectors might damage export-led ones too.

The foregoing approach makes it possible to take into consideration centrifugal forces, which derive from the variety of different objectives and are reflected in the multiple overlapping political economy maps of the Eurozone, as well as centripetal forces, i.e. systemic interest; and whether the latter is sufficient to counterbalance the former. In short, a heuristic to think whether there can be a systemic interest at the Eurozone level is to ask: How strong are internal interdependencies as compared to external interdependencies?

This approach aims to ground the interest in the Eurozone's viability in sectors' interest to preserve the system to which they belong. Of course, this is an analysis of whether a given political economy affords a systemic interest *in principle*. In practice, however, interests can be visualised differently according to the representation adopted. Hence, even if objective structures entail the existence of a systemic interest, sectors may not be aware of it, let alone act accordingly at the political level.

In closing, it is important to note that, whilst the analysis of this chapter is based on a specific structural model (i.e. circular interdependencies expressed by input-output tables), its approach can be developed also with respect to other models, which will yield additional insights. For example, the input-output models considered here are concerned with flows of commodities across industries. However, the constitution of stocks – both material such as infrastructure, and non-material such as supranational legal systems – can be just as important a component of systemic interest (Quadrio Curzio, 1967, 1975; Cardinale, 2015). Moreover, the Hawkins-Simon conditions have been reinterpreted in this chapter to operationalise systemic interest in a way that emphasises the need to preserve the economic system's capacity to reproduce itself. However, systemic interest is no less important for political choices that lead to structural change. For example, it may be a useful category for analysing the fiscal sociology of sovereign debt (Coffman, Chapter 2 in this volume; Coffman, 2013). It can also help to shed light on the political economy structures that allow the type of public investment that is often a pre-condition of structural change (Janeway, 2012), and the political economy conditions under which sectors are willing to support economic transitions ('traverses') whose outcome in terms of sectoral distribution is uncertain (Cardinale, 2015). When structural change is the focus of the analysis, definitions of systemic interest based on maximum potential growth could be particularly useful.

9.6 Conclusion

As a *sui generis* polity and political system (Chapter 17 in this volume; Pabst, Chapter 8 in this volume; White, Chapter 16 in this volume), the analysis of the Eurozone does not lend itself to an unproblematic use of received categories. The structural political economy approach proposed in this chapter aims to provide heuristics for studying the structure of political economy interests in the Eurozone.

This analysis suggests that the space of interdependencies in the Eurozone is complex and multifaceted, and so is the potential for configurations of particular and systemic interests. We cannot take for granted that sectors visualise all the relevant interdependencies, or that the construction of interests takes into account all the relevant possibilities. The SPE approach proposed here aims to provide categories for academic analysis of the Eurozone, but also for public debate, opening up to a variety of visualisations of interests, interdependencies and coalitions. This analysis thus aims to provide a route for grounding the process of European integration in the structure of economic and political interdependencies, and potentially to make relevant political actors aware of the existence of such interdependencies.

This chapter has focussed on economic (or, more specifically, productive) interdependencies between sectors. However, analytical categories such as the structural grounding of interests, the interplay of conflict and cooperation, and systemic interest can also be used to describe other types of interdependencies, notably of political, cultural or social nature. By doing so, and by comparing the different schemes of interdependencies thus obtained, one could find different structural representations of the Eurozone, and hence different readings of the fundamental combinations of particular and systemic interests.

The ultimate question that this chapter poses has to do with the extent to which the Eurozone is a political economy field integrated enough that its preservation and development are in the interest of a sufficiently relevant coalition of political economy actors. Or if it can *become* integrated enough.

References

Baranzini, M. and Scazzieri, R. (1990) 'Economic Structure: Analytical Perspectives', in M. Baranzini, and R. Scazzieri, (eds), *The Economic Theory of Structure and Change*. Cambridge: Cambridge University Press, pp. 227–333.

Becker, G. S. (1983) 'A Theory of Competition among Pressure Groups for Political Influence', *The Quarterly Journal of Economics* 98 (3) (August): 371.

Blyth, M. (2003) 'Structures Do Not Come with an Instruction Sheet: Interests, Ideas, and Progress in Political Science', *Perspectives on Politics* 1 (4): 695–706.

Bourdieu, P. (1979) *Algeria 1960: The Disenchantment of the World, the Sense of Honour, the Kabyle House or the World Reversed*. Cambridge: New York: Cambridge University Press.

Buchanan, J. M. and Tullock, G. (1962) *The Calculus of Consent, Logical Foundations of Constitutional Democracy*. Ann Arbor: University of Michigan Press.

Candela, G. (1975) 'Il Modello Economico di François Quesnay', *Giornale degli Economisti ed Annali di Economia*, 34: 69–94.

Cardinale, I. (2012) 'The Political Economy of Circular Interdependencies and Vertical Integration: Opening the Black Box of "National Interest". SSRN Scholarly Paper ID 2357981. Rochester, NY: Social Science Research Network. http://papers.ssrn.com/abstract=2357981.

Cardinale, I. (2015) 'Towards a Structural Political Economy of Resources', in M. Baranzini et al. (eds), *Resources, Production and Structural Dynamics*. Cambridge: Cambridge University Press, pp. 198–210.

Cardinale, I. (2017) 'Beyond Constraining and Enabling: Towards New Microfoundations for Institutional Theory'. *Academy of Management Review*, forthcoming.

Cardinale, I. and Coffman, D. (2014) 'Economic Interdependencies and Political Conflict: The Political Economy of Taxation in Eighteenth-Century Britain', *Economia Politica: Journal of Analytical and Institutional Economics*, 31 (3): 277–300.

Cardinale, I. and Scazzieri, R. (2016) 'Structural Liquidity: The Money-Industry Nexus', *Structural Change and Economic Dynamics*, 39 (December), pp. 46–53.

Cardinale, I. and Scazzieri, R. (2017) *The Palgrave Handbook of Political Economy*. London: Palgrave Macmillan.

Coen, D. (2007) 'Empirical and Theoretical Studies in EU Lobbying', *Journal of European Public Policy*, 14(3): 333–45.

Coen, D. (2009) *Lobbying the European Union: Institutions, Actors and Policy*. Oxford: Oxford University Press.

Coffman, D. (2013) *Excise Taxation and the Origins of Public Debt*. Basingstoke: Palgrave Macmillan.

Davenant, C. (1698) *Discourses on the publick revenues, and on the trade of England: in two parts, viz. I. Of the use of political arithmetick, in all considerations about the revenues and trade. II. On credit, and the means and methods by which it may be restored. III. On the management of the King's revenues. IV. Whither to farm the revenues, may not, in this juncture, be most for the publick service? V. On the public debts and engagements*, London, printed for J. Knapton

Duchin, F. and Steenge, A. E. (2007) 'Mathematical Models in Input-Output Economics', Rensselaer Working Papers in Economics, n. 0703.

Eltis, W. (1984) *The Classical Theory of Economic Growth*. London: Macmillan.

Ferguson, T. (1995) *Golden Rule: The Investment Theory of Party Competition and the Logic of Money-Driven Political Systems*. Chicago: University of Chicago Press.

Finnemore, M. (1996) *National Interests in International Society*. Ithaca, NY: Cornell University Press.

Gavetti, G. and Levinthal, D. (2000) 'Looking Forward and Looking Backward: Cognitive and Experiential Search', *Administrative Science Quarterly*, 45: 113–37.

Hagemann, H., Landesmann, M. A. and Scazzieri, R. (2003) *The Economics of Structural Change*. Cheltenham, UK and Northhampton, MA: Edward Elgar Pub.

Hawkins, D. and Simon, H. A. (1949) 'Note: Some Conditions of Macroeconomic Stability', *Econometrica*, 17: 245–48.

Hirschman, A. (1968) 'The Political Economy of Import-Substituting Industrialization in Latin America', *The Quarterly Journal of Economics*, 82 (1, February): 1–32.

Hishiyama, I. (1960) 'The Tableau Economique of Quesnay', *Kyoto University Economic Review*, 30 (1): 1–46.

Janeway, W. H. (2012) *Doing Capitalism in the Innovation Economy: Markets, Speculation and the State*. Cambridge: Cambridge University Press.

King, G. (1936) *Two Tracts by Gregory King (a) Natural and Political Observations and Conclusions upon the State and Condition of England* [1696]. *(b) Of the Naval Trade of England Ao. 1688 and the National Profit then arising thereby* [1697], edited with an introduction by George E. Barnett. Baltimore: Johns Hopkins Press.

Krusell, P. and Smith, A. A. (2006) 'Quantitative Macroeconomic Models with Heterogeneous Agents', *Econometric Society Monographs*, 41: 298.

Kuznets, S. (1971) *Economic Growth of Nations: Total Output and Production Structure*. Cambridge, MA: Belknap Press of Harvard University Press.

Kydland, F. E. and Prescott, E. C. (1982) 'Time to Build and Aggregate Fluctuations', *Econometrica*, 50 (6): 1345–70.

Landesmann, M. A. and Scazzieri, R. (eds) (1996) *Production and Economic Dynamics*. Cambridge and New York: Cambridge University Press.

Leontief, W. W. (1941) *The Structure of the American Economy, 1919–1929*. Cambridge, MA: Harvard University Press.

Leontief, W. W. (1991 [1928]). 'The Economy as a Circular Flow', *Structural Change and Economic Dynamics*, 2 (1): 181–212.

Lipset, S. M. and Rokkan, S. (1967) *Party Systems and Voter Alignments: Cross-National Perspectives*. New York and London: The Free Press and Collier-Macmillan.

List, F. (1996 [1827]) *Outlines of American Political Economy in Twelve Letters to Charles J. Ingersoll*, Wiesbaden: Böttinger.

List, F. (1885 [1841]) *The National System of Political Economy*. London: Longmans, Green.

Lowe, A. (1976) *The Path of Economic Growth*. Cambridge: Cambridge University Press.

Morgenthau, H. J. (1954) *Politics among Nations: The Struggle for Power and Peace*. New York: Knopf.

Nikaido, H. (2014) 'Hawkins-Simon Conditions', in S. N. Durlauf and L. E. Blume (eds), *The New Palgrave Dictionary of Economics*. Second Edition. Basingstoke: Palgrave Macmillan, 2008. The New Palgrave Dictionary of Economics Online. Palgrave Macmillan. 15 June 2014 www.dictionaryofeconomics.com/article?id=pde2008_H000027, doi: 10.1057/9780230226203.0708

Olson, M. (1965) *The Logic of Collective Action*. Cambridge, MA: Harvard University Press.

Pasinetti, L. L. (1973) 'The Notion of Vertical Integration in Economic Theory', *Metroeconomica*, 25 (1): 1–29.

Pasinetti, L. L. (1977) *Lectures on the Theory of Production*. London, Macmillan.

Pasinetti, L. L. (1981) *Structural Change and Economic Growth: A Theoretical Essay on the Dynamics of the Wealth of Nations*. Cambridge and New York: Cambridge University Press.

Pasinetti, L. L. (1993) *Structural Economic Dynamics: A Theory of the Economic Consequences of Human Learning*. Cambridge and New York: Cambridge University Press.

Pasinetti, L. L. (2009) 'Il Tableau Économique e le economie moderne', in G. de Vivo (ed), *Il Tableau Économique di François Quesnay*, Milano, Fondazione Raffaele Mattioli, pp. 109–24.

Pasinetti L. L. (2012) 'Second Afterword', in R. Arena and P. L. Porta (eds), *Structural Dynamics and Economic Growth*. Cambridge: Cambridge University Press.

Persson, T. and Tabellini, G. E. (2002) *Political Economics: Explaining Economic Policy*. Cambridge, MA: MIT Press.

Petty, W. (1662) *A treatise of taxes and contributions: shewing the nature and measures of crown-lands, assessements, customs, poll-moneys ...; with several intersperst discourses and digressions concerning warres, the church, universities, rents & purchases ...: the same being frequently applied to the present state and affairs of Ireland*. London: printed for N. Brooke.

Phillips, A. (1955) 'The Tableau Économique as a Simple Leontief Model', *The Quarterly Journal of Economics*, 69 (1): 137–44.

Quadrio Curzio, A. (1967) *Rendita e distribuzione in un modello economico plurisettoriale*. Milan: Giuffrè.

Quadrio Curzio, A. (1975) *Accumulazione del capitale e rendita*. Bologna: Il Mulino.

Quesnay, F. (1972 [1759]). *Quesnay's Tableau Économique*. Eds. Marguerite Kuczynski and Ronald L Meek. London; New York: Macmillan; A.M. Kelley for the Royal Economic Society and the American Economic Association.

Rae, D. W. and Taylor, M. (1970) *The Analysis of Political Cleavages*. New Haven CT: Yale University Press.

Rogowski, R. (1987) 'Political Cleavages and Changing Exposure to Trade', *The American Political Science Review*, 81 (4, December): 1121–37.

Scazzieri, R. (2012) 'Structural Economic Dynamics: Methods, Theories and Decisions', in H. M. Krämer, H. D. Kurz and H.-M. Trautwein (eds), *Macroeconomics and the History of Economic Thought*. Abingdon, Oxfordshire: Routledge, pp. 314–28.

Scazzieri, R., Baranzini, M. and Rotondi, C. (2015) 'Resources, Scarcities and Rents: Technological Interdependence and the Dynamics of Socio-economic Structures' in M. Baranzini et al. (eds), *Resources, Production and Structural Dynamics*. Cambridge: Cambridge University Press, pp. 427–84.

Sewell Jr., W. H. (1992) 'A Theory of Structure: Duality, Agency, and Transformation', *American Journal of Sociology*, 98: 1–29.

Simon, H. A. (1962) 'The Architecture of Complexity', *Proceedings of the American Philosophical Society*, 106 (6) (12 December): 467–82.

Simon, H. A. (1997) *Administrative Behavior: A Study of Decision-Making Processes in Administrative Organizations*, 4th ed. New York: Free Press.

Solow, R. M. (1956) 'A Contribution to the Theory of Economic Growth', *The Quarterly Journal of Economics*, 70 (1) (February): 65.

Solow R. M. (2012) 'First Afterword', in Arena R. and Porta P. L. (eds), *Structural Dynamics and Economic Growth*. Cambridge: Cambridge University Press.

Sraffa, P. (1960) *Production of Commodities by Means of Commodities; Prelude to a Critique of Economic Theory*. Cambridge: Cambridge University Press.

Steenge, A. E. (2011) 'On the Evolution of Multi-Sectoral Models; Optimality and Beyond', in M. Ciaschini and G. C. Romagnoli (eds), *L'economia italiana: metodi di analisi, misurazione e nodi strutturali; Saggi per Guido M. Rey*. Milan: Franco Angeli, pp. 92–114.

Stone, R. and Brown, A. (1962) *A Computable Model of Economic Growth*. London: Chapman and Hall.

Truman, D. B. (1962) *The Governmental Process: Political Interests and Public Opinion*. New York: Knopf.

Vaggi, G. (2008) 'Quesnay, François (1694–1774)', in S. N. Durlauf and L. E. Blume, (eds), *The New Palgrave Dictionary of Economics*, 2nd ed. Basingstoke: Nature Publishing Group, pp. 816–26.

von Neumann, J. (1945) 'A Model of General Economic Equilibrium', *The Review of Economic Studies*, 13 (1, January): 1–9.

Wixted, B., Yamano, N. and Webb, C. (2006) 'Input-Output Analysis in an Increasingly Globalised World', *OECD Science, Technology and Industry Working Papers*. Paris: Organisation for Economic Co-operation and Development. www.oecd-ilibrary.org/content/workingpaper/303252313764.

PART III

Political Economy of Structural Governance

10 German Economic Models, Transnationalization and European Imbalances

FINN MARTEN KÖRNER
AND HANS-MICHAEL TRAUTWEIN

10.1 Introduction

The blame game over the causes of the Eurozone debt crisis has an asymmetric side and a symmetric one. The asymmetric position is mostly taken by Germans and other "Northerners" who put the blame for the financial problems in the South and the Far West of the Eurozone primarily on the governments and peoples of the respective countries. It is not denied that the booms and busts in those regions were reinforced by the activities of banks from Germany and other countries in the EU core. Yet, the crisis is essentially interpreted as a moral hazard problem. As Hans-Werner Sinn, an opinion leader among German economists, likes to put it provokingly, "the Club Med was having a party" instead of making its member economies more competitive under the favourable financial conditions gained with access to European Monetary Union (EMU) in its initial phase. It is asserted that when the financial crisis ended the party, the "Club Med" wielded its political power, in some complicity with the banks' lobbies, to make Northern taxpayers pick up the bill.[1] In this asymmetric view, the only cure of the crisis is a reversal of the spending excesses, either by austerity and internal devaluation or, if that fails, by exit from EMU and external devaluation.

The more symmetric position was expressed as "it takes two to tango" by Christine Lagarde, then French finance minister, in a series of interviews in 2010.[2] Lagarde argued that wage restraint and fiscal consolidation in Germany prior to the global financial crisis had contributed to getting EMU out of balance. In her view, Germany should take

---

[1] See, e.g., Sinn (2012) and "Hans-Werner Sinn: 'Euro ist in Explosion begriffen'", *Die Presse*, 19 April 2012.
[2] The series started with an interview in the *Financial Times*, 15 March 2010.

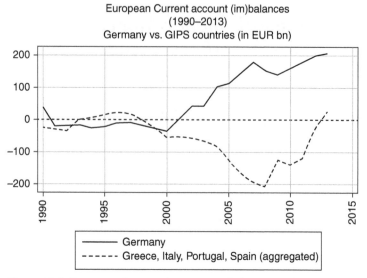

Figure 10.1 European Current Account (im)balances, 1990–2013
Source: own computation; data: OECD

responsibility for fighting the Eurozone debt crisis by boosting internal demand so as to allow the countries in crisis to re-converge. Even after moving to the position of the IMF managing director, Lagarde has called for "allowing somewhat higher inflation and wage growth in countries like Germany" as "an aspect of pan-European solidarity" in balancing lower inflation and wage cuts in Southern Europe (*Wall Street Journal*, 8 March 2013). The symmetric view on the Eurozone crisis is aptly illustrated by scissor diagrams of diverging current account balances, most prominently put forward by Paul Krugman, another opinion-leading economist (see, e.g., Krugman 2011) but also by many others. In this vein, Figure 10.1 demonstrates that the evolution of the current account deficits of Greece, Italy, Portugal and Spain since the start of EMU in 1999 is almost exactly mirrored by the development of current account surpluses in Germany's balance of payments.

There is actually no direct correspondence in the sense that the net exports of Germany would have gone to the GIPS countries;[3] the

---

[3] In the context of the crisis the notion of the "I" in the GIPS acronym changes with contexts, sometimes referring to Italy, sometimes to Ireland. If both are implied, GIIPS will be used in the following.

surpluses were largely run up in trade with partners outside the Eurozone. Yet, both sides in the crisis debate tend to explain the diagram in terms of a divergence in international competitiveness. Barely a decade after having been regarded as the "sick man of Europe", with sluggish growth and high unemployment, and shortly after the deepest recession since the Great Depression, Germany has made a comeback as an "economic model" with strong exports and low unemployment.[4]

It is not the first time that the German economy is considered as a comeback model. The "economic miracle" in the 1950s and 1960s, by which West Germany recovered relatively quickly from the destruction from the World War II, was also based on a strong export orientation of the manufacturing sectors. The same was the case with "Modell Deutschland", the constellation by which the West German economy in the late 1970s and 1980s overcame stagflation. Nor is it the first time that contemporaneous observers have argued that German trade surpluses contribute to bringing the international monetary order out of balance. Current account imbalances and speculations on a revaluation of the Deutsche Mark (DM) featured prominently in the breakdown of the Bretton Woods system in the early 1970s. Twenty years later, when the EMS crisis of 1992–93 accelerated the forward escape into monetary union, a major cause was seen in the restrictive monetary policy of the Bundesbank, whose power to set interest rates in the European Monetary System (EMS) was largely derived from Germany's strong trading and net lending position.

Thus there appears to be continuity in the export orientation of the German economy – a continuity that, on the other hand, seems to be conducive to disruptions of the international monetary order time and again. The purpose of this chapter is to examine this critical relationship. We argue that there is indeed a persistent base configuration of industrial production, macroeconomic policies and socio-political governance since the 1950s that permits the stylization of economic development in Germany (West Germany before 1990) in terms of a model. Yet, there is not just one German economic model. As we will show, the different stages of development can be described as three distinct

---

[4] The sickness talk lingered on until 2007; cf. Sinn (2007). For representative media coverage, compare *The Economist* of June 5, 1999 ('The sick man of the euro') and April 14, 2012 ('Germany's economic model').

varieties of a base configuration in which some of the macroeconomic components and mechanisms at work have changed over time. There are, however, two different mindsets of model thinking in Germany that have been remarkably stable in their interaction with the formal institutions of the German economy. We refer to these two mindsets as *ordo-liberalism* and *neo-mercantilism*, while labelling the three stage varieties as *model D – mark I, II* and *III*, in correspondence with the macroeconomic environments of the Bretton Woods, EMS and EMU regimes. The present stage, *model D – mark III*, is characterized by the transnationalization of German industries and finance in conjunction with the supranationalization of monetary policy. "Transnationalization" describes the process of building supply chains, often within the firm or corporate network, across national borders. In the manufacturing sector, a large portion of it is "near-shoring", that is, the relocation of tasks and stages of production to neighbouring countries, with the primary aim of reducing unit costs. In the financial sector, a large portion of transnationalization activities relate to transfers of risks and to regulatory arbitrage. Near-shoring and financial integration are facilitated by the "supranationalization" of monetary policy which is constituted by the introduction of the euro as common currency and the European Central Bank (ECB) as monetary authority of the Eurozone. Both trans- and supranationalization can, to a certain extent, be explained as logical and historical consequences of the export orientation of the German economy. Since these developments reduce the national government's autonomy in controlling macroeconomic conditions, we argue that they tend to render the traditional mindsets of ordo-liberalism and neo-mercantilism obsolete. Moreover, those mindsets may become obstructive to coping with the fact that Germany is no longer a "small open economy", but a core region of the larger and more diverse EU economy.

The remainder of the essay is structured as follows. In Section 10.2 we provide a brief account of the political economy literature in which German post-war economic development has been described in terms of a model variety of capitalism. In this light, we compare the two dominant approaches of German model thinking: ordo-liberalism as the normative mindset of policy speakers and economists; and neo-mercantilism as the practical mindset of policymakers and business leaders. In Sections 10.3–10.5 we describe the three main stages, in which the German economy has evolved along with the exchange rate regimes that define the model varieties. Our three-stage history is strongly stylized in terms of three analogous settings that describe the different working conditions of the model varieties under their respective exchange-rate regime. Each stage story follows a chronology of success, dynamic instability and transformation. In Section 10.3, *model D – mark I* refers to the "German economic miracle" in the years between 1951 and 1972, comprising the golden age and decline of the Bretton Woods regime. In Section 10.4, *model D – mark II* (or "Germany Inc.") captures the main factors underlying the Bundesbank hegemony between 1975 and 1995, an era largely congruent with the effective lifetime of the EMS. In Section 10.5, *model D – mark III* (or "Germany Going Global") features the transnationalization of the German economy in synchrony with the emergence and convulsions of the Eurozone. Section 10.6 concludes with a discussion of the performance of the different model varieties and some reflections on the pitfalls in the model thinking of the two mindsets that currently prevail in Germany.

10.2 Policy and Business Models

Looking back on the past six decades might make it hard to detect any model design in Germany's economic development. For most of that period the general course of business and economic policy may give the impression of a muddling through, or pragmatic adjustments to pressures, rather than the pursuit of well-crafted strategies in a coherent institutional framework. And yet, there are some characteristics of economic life in Germany that have led economists and other social scientists to describe it as a "socio-economic model", "enterprise-coordinated economy", "German production regime", "Rhenanian" variety of capitalism or "social market economy".[5]

10.2.1 The German Variety of Capitalism

All the labels mentioned in the previous section refer to a core set of interdependent institutions that began to receive attention in the eras of

---

[5] An authoritative account of German economic history since 1945 is provided by Abelshauser (2011); an English version of some of its core chapters is found in Abelshauser (2005). On the economists' side of the literature on the evolution of the German variety of capitalism, see, e.g., Giersch et al. (1992), Carlin (1996), Lindlar (1996), Carlin and Soskice (2009), and Bonatti and Fracasso (2013).

the "economic miracle" and "Modell Deutschland", when Bonn still was the capital of the Federal Republic (hence the label "Rhenanian"). The typical list of institutions in the political economy literature comprises:[6]

- universal banking with long-term engagement in industries;
- regulated competition and corporatist coordination of firms in regional and sectoral clusters;
- applied research and knowledge transfer from higher education institutions and research institutes to industries;
- vocational training in a dual system of intra-firm apprenticeship and public education;
- co-determination by works councils and participation in company supervisory boards;
- coordinated sectoral wage bargaining;
- social insurance (health, old-age and unemployment);
- fiscal federalism;
- central bank independence and rule-based monetary policy;
- openness to international trade.

It is argued in the literature that this combination has created a comparative institutional advantage for German exports of diversified quality products – especially in the manufacturing of machinery, vehicles or pharmaceuticals, the champions among the export industries since the 1950s. The origins of the German production regime can even be traced back to the era of the first globalization, the four decades between the German "founding epoch crisis" (*Gründerkrise*) in 1873 and the outbreak of the World War I (Abelshauser 2011: 28–44). Despite many changes and structural breaks,[7] there is indeed remarkable continuity in its basic composition and functioning.

The comparative institutional advantage of the German economy is largely traced back to industrial patterns of specialization on diversified quality production which is knowledge-intensive and requires

---

[6] The following is a synthetic account of the economic and historical literature on "the German model", largely based on the references in footnote 5. We accept some, but not all of the responsibility for oversimplifying.

[7] In this longer perspective, the breaks were the World War I and ensuing hyperinflation (1914–23), the Nazi regime and the World War II (1933–45), the oil price shocks in the 1970s (1973–79) and German reunification (1990).

large and specific long-term investments in capital and skills. These investments carry great risks, but many of them also have the potential to generate positive externalities. In the German model set of institutions, risk-sharing and the exploitation of agglomeration and network effects is not entirely left to market forces, but jointly coordinated by private sector agents and the state at different levels of aggregation. The universal banking system provides relatively stable long-term finance to industry (as compared to market-based systems). Interlocking share-holding gives banks' representatives on the supervisory boards of big companies (and vice versa) a role in the coordination of business strategies within and across various industries. The close relationship between banks and industries has led to talk about "Germany Inc." (*Deutschland AG*). However, competition is relatively strictly regulated by anti-cartel legislation and efforts to avert or control monopoly. Small and medium-sized enterprises are fostered as backbones of regional economies and supplier networks of key industries. Coordination through chambers and federations allows firms of all sizes to cooperate in sectoral and regional clusters. Their cooperation is supported by the states (*Länder*) which are regional sovereigns in the provision of education at all levels and technology transfer from research institutes.

German corporate governance also includes coordination of management decisions with the employee side on the supervisory boards and through works councils at plant and company level. Wage setting, however, is done by industrial unions and employer federations that coordinate the bargaining process on a sectoral basis. Since companies strongly rely on firm- and sector-specific skills, which give their "insider" staff hold-up power, employers have an interest in setting sectoral standard wages outside the firm. The standard provides, in turn, the base for setting efficiency wages inside the leading companies, to enhance productivity and product quality.

To make it feasible for employees to invest in the required skills and to reduce their lock-in risks, vocational training provides them with certified and marketable qualification. Social insurance, which is mainly organized in comprehensive Bismarckian (earnings-related) pay-as-you-go schemes, protects them against firm-specific unemployment, health and pension risks.

German macroeconomic policies are generally characterized by a conservative fiscal and monetary policy stance with a pronounced anti-inflation bias. Keynesian-style demand management is anathema, at least officially. Long before EMU, the central bank (Bundesbank) enjoyed operative independence and followed a rule-based policy to keep inflation down. The Bundesbank took the lead in the wage-setting game of the trade unions, whenever it suspected them of striving for wage increases (absolute and relative) that could set off a wage-price spiral. Higher interest rates and ensuing cutbacks in jobs would be punishment for excessive wage settlements. When the unions came to understand this mechanism, wage bargaining usually produced the desired wage restraint. The introduction of the euro ceded monetary sovereignty to the supranational ECB, and it is argued that non-accommodating fiscal policy now plays the role of creating incentives for wage moderation (Carlin and Soskice 2009). The underlying system of fiscal federalism is both restrictive and redistributive: tax revenue sharing between the states and the federal government works as a restraint on public spending, especially at the local level, and fiscal equalization between the states provides for interregional risk-sharing. Compared to other, more centralized countries, Germany is thereby less prone to boom-and-bust cycles from property bubbles in the core regions.

The anti-inflation bias in German macroeconomic policies is closely connected to the long-standing export orientation of German industries, which dates back to the industrialization process before the World War I and reconstruction after the Second World War (Giersch et al. 1992: 12–15, Lindlar 1996: 152–55, Abelshauser 2011: 32–36, 256–62, Körner 2014: ch. 2). As domestic demand was weak in those periods, diversified quality production in German industries could realize economies of scale and scope only by expanding their sales beyond the confines of the domestic markets. While virtuous circles of diversification, quality advantages and increasing returns to scale have repeatedly generated monopolistic quasi-rents for German exporters, cost competitiveness of German wages vis-à-vis other industrializing and industrialized countries remains a permanent concern in public debates: wage rises should be restrained in order to keep inflation down, and vice versa, lest the German economy loses jobs in its export industries. There is a consensus, even on the unions' side, that economic growth in Germany relies heavily on exports. This common understanding has, from early on in the 1950s, contributed to a general openness to international trade and European integration.

Given all these interlocking relationships between finance, corporate governance, industrial relations and macroeconomic policies, the literature on the German variety of capitalism stresses the importance of complementarities and path dependence in the institutional framework of the German economy. Despite many structural breaks, adjustment pressures and recurring talk about sclerosis and other sickness symptoms (e.g., Giersch et al. 1992, Siebert 2005, Sinn 2007), the framework is generally considered as rather resilient to crises and adaptive to structural change in the world economy (e.g., Carlin 1996, Abelshauser 2005, 2011, Carlin and Soskice 2009).

10.2.2 Ordo-Liberal and Neo-Mercantilist Mindsets

Thinking about the German economy in terms of a model is not, of course, confined to a specific literature in the social sciences. Inside Germany it is actually part of the institutional framework itself, considering that prevalent belief systems and normative theories are informal institutions that have an influence on the formal structures (North 1990: ch. 5). Two varieties of normative model thinking are widely spread in German business, economics and politics. The first is *ordo-liberalism*, which functions as a policy model in the sense of a theoretical mindset for political discourse in official and academic contexts. The second is *neo-mercantilism*, a business model in the sense of a practical mindset of policymakers, business executives and other stakeholders in German industries.

Ordo-liberalism as an economic doctrine has its origins in the works of Walter Eucken (1940, 1952) and the Freiburg School. It is based on the idea that economic growth and social welfare are best promoted if the state regulates the economy in such a way that its functioning comes as close as possible to the purely theoretical norm of perfectly competitive markets. In contrast with *laissez faire* liberalism, this requires a strong state, to create a market order that prevents private enterprises from attaining and abusing market power. Yet, ordo-liberalism is opposed to state control of the economy, Keynesian stabilization policies and other concepts of political management of market processes. The emphasis is on *Ordnungspolitik*, a notion that does not have any close equivalent in the English-speaking world. It signifies that state governance should be confined to regulatory policy, that is, to the setting and enforcement of rules for competition *and* cooperation in the markets and the civil society. A related tenet of ordo-liberalism is the "interdependence of orders", demanding that the political and social subsystems of society be compatible with the economic order. To avoid any abusive concentration of power, the political order should be a democracy with proper checks and balances, and the social order should provide for equal opportunity. This is at the back of the political self-image of Germany as a "social market economy", a concept propagated by Alfred Müller-Armack and Ludwig Erhard in the founding years of the Federal Republic. It stresses the importance of social insurance and consensus-oriented industrial relations as a complement of competition policy.[8]

Ordo-liberalism is no longer considered as the cutting-edge in teaching and research at German universities.[9] Yet, the political thinking of academic economists is still framed in ordo-liberal terms. Among the politically most influential economists in Germany, a large number is affiliated to ordo-liberal think tanks and/or pledges allegiance to ordo-liberal principles.[10] The latter have been invoked like mantras in inner-German debates about policy options in the Eurozone debt crisis. Not all economists are fundamentally opposed to the preservation of the euro by way of joint action and fiscal transfers, but a large number of economics professors among the activists engaged in campaigns against the rescue policies of the ECB and Eurozone governments is conspicuous.[11] The modern ordo-liberal mindset revolves largely

---

[8] See Stützel et al. (1982) for an English-language collection of standard texts on ordo-liberalism and the social market economy. It is noteworthy that some of the elements now considered as specifically German post-war ingredients – such as co-determination, anti-cartel legislation, and central bank independence – were imposed on the West German polity by the military governments in the US and British zones of West Germany, partly against Erhard's will; see Buchheim (1999) and Hentschel (1999).

[9] In 2009, when the University of Cologne planned a re-orientation of its economics department from an institution with a strong ordo-liberal heritage to more international-style quantitative macroeconomics, German economics actually saw a redux edition of the *Methodenstreit*, almost exactly 100 years after the earlier rounds; for a collection of essays in controversy, see Caspari and Schefold (2011).

[10] See the rankings of economists with greatest standing in politics, media and research, run by the *Frankfurter Allgemeine Zeitung*; see, e.g., FAZ (2013). Economists in favour of Keynesian macroeconomic policies are a relatively small minority compared with other European countries (not to speak of the United States).

[11] Most prominently, a group of (retired) professors filed complaints against EMU and rescue actions at the German constitutional court in 2011; three out of the four were economists. The euro-sceptic party AfD (*Alternative for Germany*) is

around warnings of moral hazard. There is, of course, nothing specifically ordo-liberal, or German, about concerns with the transnational socialization of private losses that occurs whenever banks and states considered too big to fail are bailed out by taxpayers in the Eurozone. The ordo-liberal perspective, however, is peculiar in that it tends to reduce the explanation of the Eurozone debt crisis to a lack of order. It is argued that if only the rules of "sound finance" at different levels of regulatory, monetary and fiscal policies had been sufficiently enforced and complied with, such a thing as the Eurozone debt crisis would never have happened. Other explanations that, for example, refer to current account imbalances and systemic risks in corresponding capital flows are generally dismissed or belittled.[12]

This is a point at which the ordo-liberal mindset is fully congruent with neo-mercantilism, the other species. The latter is based not so much on theoretical constructs, other than perhaps Michael Porter's *Competitive Advantage of Nations* (Porter 1990) as on mixes of pragmatic business thinking and nationalist sentiment. Neo-mercantilism is not a school, but rather an attitude widespread in the worlds of business, industrial policy, industrial relations and the media – though most of those who take it would not even know, or care about, its name. The signature tune of neo-mercantilism is the belief in the crucial importance of the "competitiveness of the nation". In this perspective, a primary task of economic policy is seen in fostering the domestic industries' success in international markets. The state is correspondingly regarded as a representative agent of the business interests that domestic firms have in the rest of the world. The quality of state governance is measured in terms of net exports to GDP ratios and the gains and losses of global market shares. Again, this is not a specifically German idea. But it is cultivated with special fervour in the self-image of Germany as an "export nation" that traditionally celebrates its top-three positions in global exports statistics like victories in world championships.

---

headed by an economics professor, and hundreds of academic economists have signed appeals to stop rescue actions in the Eurozone.

[12] Sinn (2007) actually drew attention to the problems of large surpluses in the German current account before the onslaught of the great financial crisis. Yet, his explanation too ran along ordo-liberal lines, interpreting the trade surpluses as the flipside of an alleged capital flight from Germany, which in his view was caused by trade unions' abuse of market power and excessively high wage levels.

Table 10.1 *Ordo-liberal and neo-mercantilist positions on economic and social policy*

	Ordo-Liberalism	Neo-Mercantilism
Competition	Full	Strategic
State intervention in markets	None, in principle	Selective supply-side support
Monetary policy stance	Stable value of money	Competitive disinflation
Fiscal policy stance	Balanced budgets	Functional export finance
Industrial relations	Consensus orientation	Corporatist wage setting
Social insurance	Security and subsidiarity	Buffer for structural change
International trade	Free	Free exports

Table 10.1 may help to understand the similarities and differences between ordo-liberal and neo-mercantilist views on elements of the German model described in Section 10.2.1. In the area of competition policy, ordo-liberals argue for control of market power and support for small and medium-sized enterprises under aspects of "approximating" full competition. Neo-mercantilists tend to tolerate local market power, if it helps to turn domestic firms into global players; they are also in favour of industrial policies or other selective supply-side measures to back up German firms in their competition with foreign companies. Ordo-liberals, on the other hand, reject (in principle) selective measures, in particular if they aim at protecting big companies, and are strongly opposed to global demand management. In their view, the sole objective of monetary policy is to keep the internal and external value of money stable, as they deem this to be essential for preserving the allocative efficiency of the price mechanism. Neo-mercantilists are largely content with inflation rates lower than those in the export markets. Disinflation campaigns of monetary policy are accepted insofar as their recessionary effects on the labour market tend to produce wage restraint in the short term. They are all the more welcome if their liquidity premium effects on the currency lead, in the medium term, to the "competitive advantage" of lower costs of finance. The same applies to the fiscal policy stance, as long as the subsidies that are considered essential for the competitiveness for German industries remain untouched. Ordo-liberals, on the other hand, plead for

balanced budgets and debt brakes, as they dispute any fundamental difference between public debt and private household debt. They defend the system of collective wage bargaining and co-determination as a fair way of avoiding industrial conflicts – and tend to ignore that consensus is strongly backed up by legal obligations to negotiate for agreements before any industrial action may be taken. Neo-mercantilists are more outspoken in this regard and point out that collective wage bargaining is to serve the objective of keeping German unit labour costs at competitive levels. They also have a functional understanding of social insurance as a fund for handling the social costs of rationalization and other adaptation to structural change in the export industries; they demand, nevertheless, that the fund be trimmed continuously so as to minimize the payroll tax effect on labour costs. Ordo-liberals defend social insurance as a system for basic protection of equal opportunity, but they too are constantly concerned about its fiscal sustainability. They tend to worry even more about moral hazard, that is, potential abuse of the system, and insist on the principle of subsidiarity, according to which basic responsibility remains with the individual and the family. Finally, ordo-liberals plead for free trade, whereas neo-mercantilists do the same with the reservation that foreign "dumping" must be sanctioned and that German industries should be supported by more strategic trade policy.

This comparison of ordo-liberals and neo-mercantilists may look like a caricaturing juxtaposition of lofty principles and their opportunistic application in real life, but it is not far from reality. Leading politicians, and in particular the prime ministers of the states (Länder), can be seen giving ordo-liberal speeches on Sundays and travelling in a mercantilist spirit with business delegations to export destinations on Mondays. Academic economists, too, may shift between the mindsets, or even blending them, depending on the contexts in which they are arguing. All this may, again, not be considered as specifically German. The ordo-liberal mindset is not too far off the international mainstream in economics, and neo-mercantilists operate almost everywhere in the world. Again, however, it would be difficult to find many examples of countries of the economic size of Germany, where such mindsets are so widespread, deeply ingrained and connected to model thinking in a peculiarly cyclical fashion. Whenever the German economy is in a crisis, appeals abound to return to the ordo-liberal policy model, or to retrieve the spirit of competitiveness and reinvent the business model of export-driven growth. Whenever other countries are in crisis, often out of step with Germany, the institutional framework and thrifty orderliness of the competitive export nation are presented as a model for them.

Thus, both mindsets work in a certain division of labour and continuity, despite various conflicts between them. The snag is that they equate the requirements of economic and social policies in a large economy with the individually rational behaviour of private households and firms. The representative agent in the ordo-liberal policy model is the Swabian housewife – a thrifty, orderly character that is obsessed with reminding others of their duty to play by the rules.[13] And the representative counterpart in the neo-mercantilist business model is the Swabian tinkerer – the resourceful engineer from the same area, one of the core regions of German export industries. *Caveat debtor* is their categorical imperative, but they need borrowing customers in order to make their economy thrive. Hence, there is a microeconomic fallacy in both mindsets, as it is ignored that, in a large export-driven economy, success at the level of firms and households may breed failure at the macroeconomic level if there are no offsetting imports. In the long run, moreover, the expansionary dynamics of the German economy make the fiction of the nation state as the collective agent of its industries less tenable. In the following sections we describe those dynamics in terms of three stages in which the German model of export-oriented growth has evolved.

10.3 Model D – Mark I: Bretton Woods

The post-war economic history of West Germany is a story of export-driven growth. Prior to reunification there was only one year (1980) in which net exports were not positive, and growth in net exports led to rises in GDP growth in almost all business cycles (see Figure 10.2). Increases in net exports and their igniting effects on GDP growth also coincided roughly with the introduction of new exchange rate regimes: West Germany's accession to the Bretton Woods system in the early 1950s, the formation of the European "currency snake" in the 1970s,

---

[13] "The *schwäbische Hausfrau* – southern Germany's thrifty Swabian housewife – is frequently invoked by Angela Merkel. The German chancellor argues that Europe has been living beyond its means and can learn from these women's frugal housekeeping and balanced budgeting" (Kollewe 2012; in *The Guardian*, 17 September 2012).

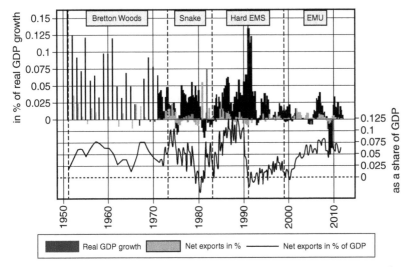

Figure 10.2 The contribution of net exports to German GDP growth, 1951–2012

Source: own computation; data: Deutsche Bundesbank, destatis, Statista

and the "hard re-launch" (competitive disinflation) of the European Monetary System (EMS) in 1983. Reunification did not change this pattern. After an initial swing in the German balance of payments, trade surpluses bounced back, and shortly after the introduction of the euro net exports began to rise strongly even in reunited Germany.

The conjunction of German net exports with shifts in the international monetary order is not a coincidence. The success of the German economic model in terms of trade surpluses and GDP growth is closely connected with the rise of fixed exchange rate regimes, and the model had to transform itself each time when the regimes dissolved due to imbalances to which German trade and finance had contributed significantly. As mentioned in the introduction, three varieties of the German model can be discerned in the consecutive stages of the "economic miracle" of the 1950s and 1960s (*model D – mark I*), the "Germany Inc." of the 1980s *(mark II)*, and the present variety of "Germany Going Global" *(mark III)*. Our three-stage history in the following sections is strongly stylized, as we describe the driving forces and working conditions of all model varieties in analogous settings, in order to facilitate comparison between them. Each episode follows a chronology of success, dynamic instability and transformation.

10.3.1 The Working Conditions of the Post-War Economic Miracle

At the end of the World War II Germany lay in ruins, divided into several zones by the victorious Allies and later, in the Cold War, deeply separated into an Eastern and a Western part. The economy was paralyzed in the post-war years, while millions of refugees, displaced persons, and other migrants from the Eastern parts of the former German Empire crowded into the West, where large parts of the living quarters in the cities had been destroyed. Money had lost its value, and public opinion had it that the only markets that worked until 1948 were the black markets.

A quarter of a century later, at the time of the breakdown of the Bretton Woods system, West Germany could look back on decades of unprecedented economic growth, (over)full employment, low inflation and the rise of the deutsche mark (henceforth: D-mark, as in colloquial German) to the status of an international reserve currency, which had been earned by a strong net exports position (see Figure 10.2). All this was considered an economic miracle. It belongs to the founding myths of the Federal Republic that the miracle was accomplished by the Marshall Plan, the currency reform of 1948 and political designing of a social market economy. This triad certainly contributed to the economic recovery and political stabilization in the late 1940s, but its influence on later developments has often been overrated. It has been argued in the literature that German growth was part of a normal catching-up process in a reconstruction period also seen in other countries with different economic policy regimes at the time (in particular Italy, France, and Japan; see Buchheim 1999). It has been pointed out that post-war West Germany was particularly well positioned to catch up.[14] The forced formation of physical capital and technical skills during the World War II had led to high levels of productivity. Much of the capital stock was of most recent vintage and still intact after the war, despite the bombings. Furthermore, a large, highly skilled and disciplined labour force was available at comparatively low real costs, because wages had been frozen at their 1935 levels and domestic migration created further pressure on wages.

---

[14] Detailed evidence is provided by Abelshauser (2011: chs. II–VI) and, in shorter English articles, by Krengel (1963), Dornbusch (1993) and Carlin (1996).

So when the internal monetary disorder and external isolation were overcome between 1948 and 1953, the starting conditions for the economic miracle were extraordinarily favourable.

The re-entry of (West) German industries onto international markets was facilitated by the combination of the 1948 currency reform, the Marshall Plan of the same year, the Korean War boom of 1950–51, IMF membership in 1952 and the 1953 London Debt Agreement (Körner 2014: 32–34). The currency reform, which was largely of US design,[15] restored monetary order. The Marshall Plan (European Recovery Program) did not bring much financial relief for West Germany, but it gave a first signal of support for European integration. The Korean War boom created additional external demand for German industrial products, thereby helping to turn around Germany's negative balance of payments. Finally, the London Debt Agreement reduced the external debt of the Federal Republic substantially and helped West Germany to regain access to international capital markets. Another step in that process was the accession to the International Monetary Fund (IMF) in 1952 and integration into the Bretton Woods system of fixed exchange rates in 1953. Based on a relatively high (4.20:1) exchange rate of the D-mark to the US dollar, the economic miracle was set on track.

The macroeconomic driving forces of the miracle were a combination of restrictive monetary and fiscal policies under the exchange rate target and a "productivity illusion" in the wage policies of the trade unions: real wages were increasing, but lagging productivity growth. In the following, we illustrate these and other working conditions of *model D – mark I* by a system of equations and inequalities, to facilitate comparison with the working conditions of the *mark II* and *III* varieties. The system is not derived from an optimization model or fully articulated functional relationships. It is a simple stylization of the essential elements of export-led growth under the Bretton Woods regime. The model ingredients are grouped in three blocks: labour

---

[15] Ludwig Erhard got most of the credit for the reform, but the planning for it had essentially been done by Gerhard Colm, Joseph Morrell Dodge and Raymond Goldsmith on behalf of the US military government. Colm and Goldsmith (originally Goldschmidt) were actually two of the many German economists forced into emigration by the Nazis in and after 1933; see Hagemann (1999, 2005).

market conditions, the macroeconomic policy regime and trade and growth.

The labour market in model D – mark I

$$w_D < w_{RoW} \qquad (I.1)$$

$$a_D = a_{RoW} \qquad (I.2)$$

$$0 < (\widehat{w}_D - \widehat{p}_D) < \widehat{a}_D \qquad (I.3)$$

The variables w and a denote nominal wage rates (levels) and labour productivity (parameter) in Germany *(D)* and the rest of the world *(RoW)*, respectively. While nominal wages in Germany ranged below average *(I.1)*, productivity was, at least, at average levels *(I.2)*. Inequality *(I.3)* describes the productivity illusion, with $\widehat{w}$, $\widehat{p}$, $\widehat{a}$ as the rates of change in wage, price and productivity levels: real wage increases, while positively, were consistently below increases in productivity in those years.

The macroeconomic policy regime

$$i_D > i_{RoW} \qquad (I.4)$$

$$G_D \leq T_D \qquad (I.5)$$

$$\widehat{e}_{DM/U\$} = 0 \qquad (I.6)$$

$$\widehat{p}_D < \widehat{p}_{RoW} \qquad (I.7)$$

$$\left(\frac{w/p}{a}\right)_D < \left(\frac{w/p}{a}\right)_{RoW} \qquad (I.8)$$

Inequality *(I.4)*, where i_i denotes nominal interest rate levels, signifies a relatively restrictive stance of monetary policy. *G*, *T* in *(I.5)* are government expenditures and tax revenues under a regime of balanced budgets and fiscal restraint.[16] Equation *(I.6)* describes the monetary policy target of keeping the nominal dollar exchange rate, *e*, unchanged. Since, at the same time (as in *I.7*), inflation rates were kept lower compared to the rest of the world (by virtue of *1.4*), nominal wage rises became compatible with "productivity illusion" *(I.3)*, producing a labour cost advantage for German industries *(I.8)*.

---

[16] In the strict sense, German governments ran a budget surplus only until 1957, yet the deficits incurred until the end of the Bretton Woods system were significantly lower than in most other OECD countries.

Trade & Growth

$$NX_D = EX - IM = S - I > 0 \tag{I.9}$$

$$\widehat{ORA}_D > 0 \tag{I.10}$$

$$\hat{y}_D = b\widehat{NX}_D \tag{I.11}$$

Equation (I.9) describes German net exports (EX-IM) as dual gap, with net capital exports written in terms of "excess aggregate savings" (S larger than aggregate investment, I). During the Bretton Woods Regime foreign capital markets were largely restricted and outward foreign direct investment from Germany was still at very modest levels. Net capital exports were therefore largely accomplished by the accumulation of dollar reserves (official reserve assets, ORA in *I.10*). The final equation describes German GDP growth, $\hat{y}$, as a function of changes in the net export position, which contributed to 44.9 per cent of real growth in the Bretton Woods era (Körner 2014: 63).

10.3.2 Dynamic Instability of the Bretton Woods System

The Bretton Woods system of fixed exchange rates was dynamically instable because of its inflation bias. The underlying gold-dollar standard was "a half-way house between an asset-backed system and a paper money standard" (Spahn 2001: 128).[17] Given that all other central banks in the system oriented their interest rate policies towards stabilizing the dollar exchange rates of their domestic currencies, the Fed as the central bank of the dollar-providing country was free to follow other targets – the well-known *(n-1)* implication of fixed exchange rate regimes under fiat money standards. The explicit target of stabilizing the dollar price of gold was soon exposed as a constructional flaw in terms of the Triffin dilemma. Under the capital account restrictions and exchange controls of the post-war decades, other countries in the system ran up current account surpluses in order to accumulate the US dollars needed as international liquidity and official reserve assets, if they wanted to avoid overly restrictive interest rate policies. The system's functioning thus implied the willingness of the United States to incur current account deficits. The growth of world GDP through world trade led inherently to a supply of dollars in excess

---

[17] For a historical account, see also Eichengreen (1996: ch. 4).

of their backing by US gold reserves. There was no point at which the system would be automatically stopped from turning from a dollar hunger to a dollar glut. The leading players, that is, the Fed and in particular the US government, had no (sufficiently strong) incentives to abstain from making use of the exorbitant privilege of paying net imports by printing dollars (Eichengreen 2011). While the Korea War boom (1950–53) helped to still the dollar hunger and to produce self-sustained growth in the Bretton Woods system, the financing of the Vietnam War (1965–73) contributed to its destabilization and subsequent stagflation in the world economy.

During the 1950s and 1960s the Bretton Woods regime of fixed exchange rates permitted a systematic undervaluation of the D-mark, helping West Germany to enjoy export-led growth. Towards the end of the 1960s, the dollar glut was increasingly perceived as a dilemma of "imported inflation".[18] When the Bundesbank accommodated the dollar inflows from net exports in pursuit of the exchange rate target, monetary stability was under threat, and with it the unit labour cost advantage of German industries. Realignments with D-mark revaluation were discussed since 1968 and favoured by the Bundesbank and the Social Democrats, but the conservatives under leadership of chancellor Kiesinger and finance minister Strauß refused, for fear of losses in the export industries (see, e.g., James 1996, ch. 8). Nevertheless, market expectations of D-mark revaluation led to speculative capital flows to Germany that reinforced the problem of imported inflation. The Bundesbank attempted to sterilize the dollar inflows with high interest rates, but this invited only further speculative attacks on the dollar by a flight into the D-mark. A realignment with a 9 per cent revaluation of the latter in 1969 did not eliminate the problem, and when the Bundesbank could no longer sterilize dollar inflows without attracting more of them, it let the D-mark float in May 1971. Various attempts were made to reform the Bretton Woods system by further revaluations of the German currency, but the faltering fixed exchange rate regime broke finally down in the spring of 1973. Within the ten years between 1969 and 1979, the D-mark/US dollar exchange rate fell from 4.00:1 to 1.70:1, with severe consequences for the German economy.

---

[18] For a discussion of the Bundesbank's view on imported inflation, see von Hagen (1998: 457 f) and the internal view in the Bundesbank's "Geschäftsbericht"(1964: 23) and their then-vice president Emminger (1986: 34).

10.4 Model D – Mark II: European Monetary System

Even though the revaluation of the D-mark mitigated the first OPEC oil price shock of 1973–74, it put German industries under strong cost pressures. Various sectors in the "old heavy industries", such as coal mining, steel production and shipbuilding, began to shrink, while other industries were cutting jobs to stay competitive despite the surge of the external value of the D-mark. After years of "overemployment" and imports of immigrant workers from Southern Europe in the 1960s, unemployment began to rise in a stepwise fashion after 1972 (see Figure 10.3). This was the start of an upward trend which was broken only recently, roughly a decade after the introduction of the euro.

Figure 10.3 appears to indicate a stable Phillips curve trade-off between employment and price level stability in Germany between the 1980s and the early 2000s, for a period when its existence was most vehemently denied in mainstream macroeconomics. In the 1970s, the picture was less clear, but that was the time when monetary policy in Germany began to mark the priority of price level stabilization. The member countries of the European Economic Community had agreed in 1972 to keep their exchange rates pegged within wider bands in the "European currency snake." The snake was a rather loose regime, with EEC and non-EEC countries entering and leaving at a rather high frequency. The upward pressure on the D-mark vis-à-vis other European currencies rose when the Bundesbank introduced monetary

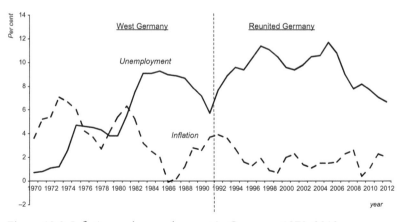

Figure 10.3 Inflation and unemployment in Germany, 1970–2012
Source: own computation; data: destatis; Deutsche Bundesbank

targets in late 1974 in order to bring down inflation. This forced other countries to choose between following suit by restrictive interest rate policies, devaluating within the snake or letting their currencies depreciate outside that arrangement. Exchange rate volatility and inflation differentials remained high throughout the 1970s and threatened to undermine European integration. Thus, towards the end of the decade, the French and German governments took the initiative for further cooperation in the European Monetary System (EMS).

10.4.1 The Working Conditions of Germany Inc.

Once the EMS was established in 1979, the Bundesbank took the lead again. The D-mark carried a liquidity premium for three reasons. The first was a thick market externality, with Germany being the largest economy in the system, making up more than 30 per cent of EMS GDP and internal trade. The second reason was the status of the D-mark as an international reserve currency, and this interacted with the third, the anti-inflationary stance of the Bundesbank's policy which in turn created expectations of further revaluation. As was pointed out in Section 10.2.1, the Bundesbank had enjoyed operative independence since the 1950s; starting from 1975, it followed a rule-based policy to keep inflation at levels around 2.5 per cent.[19] Its monetary target was intended to set a clear signal for the wage-setting game of the trade unions, in order to curb expectations of wage-price spirals. The Bundesbank did not shy away from generating recessions through higher interest rates whenever it deemed wage settlements to be excessive. The sacrifice ratios of Germany (in terms of the unemployment costs of disinflation) were relatively high during the EMS era (Trautwein 2010: 57–61).

By the 1980s, the unions had come to play by the rules of the game, aiming primarily at wage rises in line with productivity growth and the Bundesbank's target rate of inflation. Instead of attempting to run wage policies that would compensate for past losses from unexpected inflation and provide for similar shocks in the future, they negotiated with the employers in a cooperative climate about working hour

[19] The monetary policy rule was set out as a dynamic version of quantity-theoretical equation of exchange in which first M0, the monetary base, and later M3, a broad money aggregate, were used as intermediate targets; see Deutsche Bundesbank (1995: ch. 4).

reductions, training programmes and other work conditions. The spirit of international competitiveness that had been cultivated as an element of national pride in the era of the economic miracle was recreated in a modernized form. Together with the bank-based coordination of industries (see Section 10.2.1) the cooperation of trade unions and employers produced the self-image of *Germany Inc. (Deutschland AG)*, an export nation that functions like a well-diversified enterprise in the world market (Abelshauser 2011: 480–509).

The liquidity premium on the D-mark manifested itself in relatively low interest rates vis-à-vis the other EMS economies. In combination with wage moderation the premium gave German firms a cost advantage over their international competitors. The fixed exchange rates restored a regional undervaluation of the German currency and induced a strong upward trend of net exports in the 1980s.[20] As these tended to create imbalances within the EMS, numerous realignments with devaluations of other EMS countries took place until 1983, when France and other countries began to turn to a strategy of "competitive inflation". The rationalization pressure through realignments and EMS-external appreciation of the D-mark in the early 1980s kept German industries competitive, but it led to massive losses of jobs (see Figure 10.3), despite wage moderation in terms of D-mark unit labour costs. Unemployment became as persistent as the interest rate differentials and net exports which indicated undervaluation of the German currency even during the period of competitive disinflation. The continued rise in trade volumes and net exports was nevertheless interpreted as proof that the creative destruction inherent in the export orientation of *Germany Inc.* generated more job opportunities than it eliminated.

The working conditions of the *Germany Inc.* model can be written in analogy with *Model D – mark I* (Section 10.3.1). The shades on variables and signs in the following system of equations and inequalities mark the differences in comparison to the *mark I* model.

---

[20] It should be noted though that the surge of German trade surpluses in the early 1980s was only partly an intra-European affair. It was also favoured by a strong appreciation of the US dollar in the Volcker era. The D-mark/US dollar exchange rate rose from 1.70 in 1980 to 3.46 at the time of the Plaza accord of the G-5 in 1985, but dropped back to 1.56 in 1987, stopped only by the Louvre accord.

The labour market in model D – mark II

$$w_D > w_{RoEMS} \tag{II.1}$$

$$a_D > a_{RoEMS} \tag{II.2}$$

$$(\widehat{w}_D - \widehat{p}_D) = \widehat{a}_D \tag{II.3}$$

Under the EMS regime, Germany was ahead of the rest of the EMS countries *(RoEMS)* – or at least far above the average – in terms of nominal wages and labour productivity. The trade unions followed essentially a strategy of real wage increases in line with productivity growth *(II.3)*.

The macroeconomic policy regime

$$i_D < i_{RoEMS} \tag{II.4}$$

$$G_D > T_D \tag{II.5}$$

$$\widehat{e}_{DM/ECU} = 0 \tag{II.6}$$

$$\widehat{p}_D < \widehat{p}_{RoEMS} \tag{II.7}$$

$$\left(\frac{w/p}{a}\right)_D < \left(\frac{w/p}{a}\right)_{RoEMS} \tag{II.8}$$

Equation *(II.4)* reflects the liquidity premium in German finance through the interest rate differentials between the D-mark and other EMS currencies. Fiscal policies were less restrictive than under the Bretton Woods regime; after reunification, the German government borrowed heavily – at home and in the international capital markets – in order to finance the reconstruction and development of Eastern infrastructure *(II.5)*. Equation *(II.6)* describes the exchange rate target with the ECU, but it should be noted that in the first years of the EMS, between 1979 and 1983, many member currencies were devalued by frequent realignments, so that the D-mark rose in value. Strict exchange rate stability occurred only after 1987, until the EMS crisis led to floating and devaluation of various EMS currencies in 1992–93. Apart from a brief period after reunification when domestic demand and the reorganization of social insurance drove German inflation rates and wage costs above the levels in other countries (of which many were in a slump), inflation was mostly lower in Germany than in the rest of the EMS, and so were unit labour costs *(II.7 and II.8)*.

Trade & Growth

$$NX_D = EX - IM = S - I + (T - G) > 0 \qquad (II.9)$$

$$\widehat{KEX}_D > 0 \qquad (II.10)$$

$$\hat{y}_D = b\widehat{NX}_D \qquad (II.11)$$

Equation *(II.9)* describes German net exports in terms of a three-gap analysis, taking into account that the "excess savings" reflected in the net exports now also were to cover the public deficits that had become a regular feature of fiscal policies in Germany. Due to financial market liberalization in the rest of the EMS and other parts of the world, trade surpluses could now largely be offset by capital exports rather than the accumulation of dollar reserves; these exports were mainly carried out in terms of international bank lending and foreign portfolio investment. In *(II.10)* the hat on top of *KEX* symbolizes a growth of foreign asset holdings (stocks), and hence a structural net lender position, rather than capital flows alone. As can be seen from Figure 10.2, net exports still functioned as a growth engine in the mid-1975, when the introduction of monetary targetry by the Bundesbank bedded for the EMS, and in the early 1980s, at the end of the second OPEC recession *(II.11)*. The picture changed, however, with German reunification: the redirection of supplies of West German industrial goods from external demand to internal demand in the new Eastern Länder, as well as increased imports, created a swing in the German balance of payments. During the 1990s, exports were less important for economic growth in Germany.

10.4.2 Dynamic Instability of the European Monetary System

The EMS was originally created as a regime with symmetric duties of intervention. A parity grid related to the synthetic European Currency Unit (ECU) defined the intra-EMS exchange rates which were to be stabilized by all of the involved central banks. However, as mentioned earlier, market forces quickly transformed the "European paper money standard" into a "DM club" (Spahn 2001: ch. 7). This reproduced the *n-1* problem that had destabilized the Bretton Woods system, but now it carried a reversed sign, that is, a disinflation bias instead of an inflation bias. While all other central banks in the EMS attempted to preserve external stability by stabilizing their D-mark exchange rates, the Bundesbank gave priority to internal stability in terms of low inflation. The German price level played the role of a nominal anchor for the EMS. Due to the liquidity premium on the D-mark, the Bundesbank set the levels of short-term interest rates for all EMS economies. The central banks and governments in the other countries faced the problematic choice between devaluation and the propagation of interest rate shocks. Realignments led to further softening of their currencies, with further increases in inflation and interest rate differentials, whereas externally induced disinflation tended to lead to losses of output, income and jobs; only rarely was it achieved by a boost in productivity growth. Eventually none of the two options could be politically sustained.

After its "hard relaunch" in the competitive disinflation of the later 1980s, the EMS was nevertheless believed to be self-stabilizing. It was argued that, as the long-term costs of realignments appeared to outweigh their benefits, all member countries would have incentives to "import stability" by reducing their inflation rates to German levels. Yet, the EMS was dynamically unstable, as the selection of the key currency was based not only on its stable value but also on success in export competition. The unit cost advantage of German industries led to persistent trade deficits in other member economies, which had to be compensated with interest premia in order to attract (or retain) capital. As pointed out earlier, this amounted to an asymmetry of adjustment burdens in the system. Whenever German inflation was on the rise and the Bundesbank reacted by raising interest rates, other countries ran overproportional risks of recession. The asymmetry of adjustment burdens showed itself drastically in 1990–91, when the reunification boom got Germany out of step with the cyclical downturn in the rest of the world. The subsequent swing in the German balance of payments did not indicate any willingness on the German side to shift from a net lending to a net borrowing position in the longer term. This would have been a prerequisite for stabilizing the EMS, yet market expectations stayed anchored in the belief that a reunited Germany would remain a net lender. The dynamic instability of the EMS became fully obvious in the system's crisis in 1992–93, which forced several members to let their currencies float and depreciate strongly. For those who refused to do this (such as France) or did it late, succumbing to speculative attacks (such as Italy and Sweden), sacrifice ratios soared to levels even higher than those of Germany (Trautwein 2010: 60). However, when all this happened, the EU was already set on the track towards EMU.

10.5 Model D – *Mark III:* European Monetary Union

After the reunification boom came the hangover. Unemployment was strongly on the rise in the early 1990s, not only in the newly associated East, where the centralized economy of the former GDR underwent a disruptive transformation, but also in the West, where the revaluation of the D-mark in the wake of the EMS crisis hit export industries hard (see Figure 10.3). Apart from the brief interlude of the dot-com bubble around the year 2000, GDP growth was anemic, at an average rate of less than 1.3 per cent for the years between 1995, when the final decision to start EMU was taken, and 2005, the last year before the export engine finally got German GDP growth up and going again (see Figure 10.2).

10.5.1 The Working Conditions of Germany Going Global

What in the context of the Eurozone debt crisis has been praised as the latest version of "Germany's economic model" (*The Economist* April 14, 2012) was not at all considered as model-like in the early years of European Monetary Union. There was much complaint about Germany having taken the role of the "sick man of the euro" (*The Economist* June 5, 1999; see also Siebert 2005, Sinn 2007). In comparison with *Models D, mark I* and *II*, a number of key features in the macroeconomic regime had indeed changed considerably. An evident and intended consequence of EMU was, of course, that German monetary policy was no longer run autonomously, as the Bundesbank had now become subordinate to the European Central Bank (ECB). To mark some continuity with Bundesbank policy, the ECB took its headquarters to Frankfurt and officially announced a two-pillar strategy of monetary aggregate and inflation targeting. However, in practice, the conduct of ECB policy came to be oriented towards Anglo-American-style inflation targeting rather than German-style M3 targeting.[21]

---

[21] Prior to EMU there was some debate in which Bernanke and Mihov (1997), Clarida and Gertler (1997) and others argued that the reaction function of the

Another, even more apparent break with German policy traditions was the dynamic inconsistency of German fiscal policy under the rules of the EMU "Stability and Growth Pact". When the membership conditions for EMU were negotiated in the 1990s, German government officials had insisted – often with high moral overtones on the evils of profligate public spending in the south of Europe – on strict and continuous compliance with ceilings on public deficits (3 per cent of GDP) and public debt (60 per cent of GDP). However, Germany violated this very deficit criterion from 2001 until 2005. To add insult to injury, Germany used its political clout to avert the sanctions stipulated by the pact, and pressed for a reform of the pact that relaxed the conditions of compliance. It may have been macroeconomically sensible to ignore the (rather arbitrarily chosen) deficit limits in a situation when German fiscal austerity tended to turn weak Eurozone growth into recession. Yet those who break the rules they had proposed (and imposed on others) can hardly claim to be acting as a model.

German industries had also lost their premium finance advantage with the introduction of the euro. The interest rate differentials between EMU member countries shrank to almost nil between 1998 and 2008. Together with the reunification hangover and the bursting of the dot-com bubble, which hit Germany especially hard, this reduced investment and employment in Germany, where the lowering of interest rates induced property booms and (what was believed to be) catch-up growth in the EMU periphery, together with a faster rise in price levels. Unlike before, relatively lower inflation in Germany no longer translated into relatively lower costs of finance. On the contrary, it implied higher real interest rates and reinforced domestic stagnation as well as capital exports to Ireland, Spain and other destinations with better growth prospects.

The weakness of the German economy was most obvious in the labour market. In 2005, unemployment reached new peak levels, with more than five million people on the dole and an unemployment rate near 12 per cent (see Figure 10.3). Eastern enlargement of the EU and

Bundesbank never differed substantially from inflation targeting under the standard Taylor rule. Dornbusch (1997), Schmid (1999) and Gerberding et al. (2004) countered that M3 mattered for the Bundesbank's decision-making on the base of real-time data and for the public's formation of inflation expectations.

the opening-up of the Chinese economy offered new options of off-shoring labour-intensive parts of industrial production. Apart from actual relocation, the mere threat of outsourcing and offshoring contributed to wage moderation and downward wage adjustments through structural shifts in the composition of the workforce. Regular long-term employment was increasingly replaced by temporary and fixed-term contracts, subcontracting and other types of precarious employment, often also in cross-border constructions. Collective wage bargaining was hardly effective in East Germany, and the trade unions began to lose ground in the West. Another hard blow to the labour market consensus of Germany Inc. came with the "Hartz IV" set of laws, introduced by the red-green coalition government (Social Democrats and Green Party) in 2005. These "activating" labour market reforms were similar to the "workfare" policies introduced in the United States in the 1990s, aiming at lowering reservation wages by cutting unemployment benefits and reducing the qualification gaps between insiders and outsiders in the labour market. However, the latter (and a greater part of the social democratic constituency) perceived the Hartz IV reforms largely as widening the gaps, since the risks of falling amongst the "working poor" and "simply poor" were increased considerably.

Despite all these perceived weaknesses, German exports were strong and net exports surging, even in the years before 2005 (see Figure 10.2). There was much talk of a "split cycle", with the export industries booming, domestic demand weakening and unemployment high and rising. Aroused by some provocative statements by Sinn about Germany suffering from a "pathological export boom" and turning into a "bazaar economy", a debate started about the observable transnationalization of German industry production. Sinn (2006, 2007) argued that the coexistence of an export boom with rising unemployment was not a paradox, as both had their common cause in excessively high and downward rigid wages for low skilled workers. This was, in his view, the explanation for the offshoring of labour intensive stages of production and an excessive, and hence "pathological" specialization on capital-intensive production of export goods. According to Sinn, the concentration towards customization and marketing activities at the downstream ends of the supply chains – "bazaar activities" in his terminology – is accompanied by a rapid decline of the value added share in German exports per unit of output. Sinn interpreted the current account surpluses of the time essentially as a capital flight from

Germany, for lack of profitable investment opportunities. His diagnosis was heavily disputed, not only because it went against the neo-mercantilist pride of industrial success held in much of the public opinion. It was criticized for being an overly simplistic application of the factor price equalization theorem of neoclassical trade theory, disregarding the positive net employment effects of outward foreign direct investment (FDI) and intermediate goods imports.[22] Other critics agreed with Sinn in regard of an excessive reliance on exports for growth and employment, but argued that he got the therapy all wrong; in their view the real problem was weak domestic demand, following from the decline in net real wage incomes and from excessive public and private saving.[23]

Sinn's interpretation of structural change in German exports as excessive specialization has been confronted with the "great reorganization view" (Snower et al. 2009) which emphasizes a trend towards geographic decomposition of value chains and increasing heterogeneity and flexibility of work.[24] This view is theoretically and empirically harder to grasp, but ultimately more plausible – not least in view of the relative performance of the German economy just before, during and after the great financial crisis. With some advantage of geography, German industries took to near-shoring labour-intensive activities in their value chains to lower-cost destinations in nearby Eastern EU countries (mainly Poland, Czech Republic, Slovakia, and Hungary). Outward FDI, even to destinations further away (such as China), went hand in hand with increases in intermediate goods imports, but also in final goods exports. Production processes of German firms became in short time much more transnational than, for example, their

---

[22] See, e.g., Sachverständigenrat (2004: 459–510), Pflüger (2006), Snower et al. (2009). For a brief summary of the debate and further references see also Koske and Wörgötter (2010: 9, box 1).

[23] See, in an *ex post* survey, Horn et al. (2010). Among the critics were Peter Bofinger, member of the German council of economic advisors *(Sachverständigenrat)*, and Paul Krugman, who has untiringly blogged against the "Sinners" and German beggar-thy-neighbour policies for a long time (summarizingly: Krugman 2013). More recently, in connection with the Eurozone debt crisis, the same views have been shared by the United States Department of Treasury (2013) and leading officials of the International Monetary Fund.

[24] The reorganization view refers to a booming literature on "heterogenous firms", "fragmentation", "trade in tasks" etc.; for surveys, see Baldwin (2006) and Milberg and Winkler (2013).

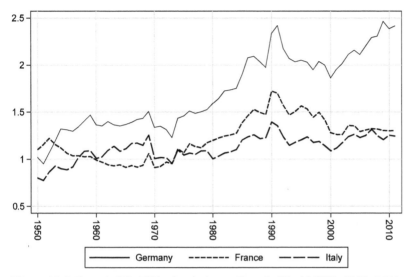

Figure 10.4 Share in World Trade relative to Share in World GDP, 1950–2011
Source: own computation; data: Penn World Table 8.0 (2013)

counterparts in the other two big Eurozone economies, France and Italy. An indirect but clear indication for this is share of the respective country in world trade (arithmetic mean of exports and imports) relative to its share in world GDP, as illustrated by Figure 10.4.

Figure 10.4 shows a parallel rise in the trade/GDP ratios in all three economies in the 1980s, largely due to the increase of intra-industry trade and intermediate goods trade inside the European Union. After 1990, China and other emerging market economies expanded their trade in the world markets at rates much higher than their GDP growth; this is the main explanation behind the dip in the trade/GDP ratios of Germany, France and Italy in the 1990s. While the "China effect" lingered on in the latter two economies, the German trade/GDP ratio climbed back to earlier levels in the 2000s, due to strong growth of exports of final goods and imports of intermediate goods. The transnationalization of production by German firms appears also to have slowed down the relative decline in the share of manufacturing value added in German GDP as compared to France and Italy.[25]

---

[25] The share of manufacturing value added in German GDP decreased from 29.7% in 1980 to 22.6% in 1995 and 20.7% in 2010. The corresponding figures for France are 23.6% (1980), 16.6% (1995) and 10.7% (2009; 2010 not reported).

Going by the evidence of Figures 10.2, 10.3 and 10.4, the German economy proved to be quite resilient to the global financial crisis and its follow-up, the Eurozone debt crisis. This is why it has recently acquired model status again. Despite the deep dips that GDP growth (−5 per cent) and exports (−25 per cent) took in the year after the Lehman Brothers panic of Autumn 2008, growth and exports bounced back quickly, and unemployment continued to fall to levels not seen since the early 1990s. Whatever the effects of labour market reforms, wage moderation and/or efficient transnationalization of production, the recovery and resilience of the German economy would hardly have been possible without two other factors. The first was the enormous rise in the specific demand for German products (primarily vehicles, machine tools, other machinery, and chemical products) from catching-up growth in China, Eastern Europe, and other emerging markets. Exports to China, in particular, rose from 7 billion Euros in 1999 to almost 75 billion Euros in 2014, and China jumped from rank 15 among Germany's trading partners to rank 3 over the same period. The other factor, strongly augmenting the effects of the first, was the protection from revaluation and appreciation afforded by the Eurozone. The export boom of the 2000s would have been hardly sustainable if Germany had still had a national currency. The flight back to safe havens and the deleveraging in the banking business seen after 2008 would have led to a surge in the value of that currency, as in the early 1970s, 1980s, and 1990s. The EMU countries that first ran large trade deficits and then into debt crises worked like a protective belt for the German economy. They prevented the euro exchange rate from rising, and hence implicitly re-established Germany's old undervaluation advantage of Bretton Woods and the EMS.[26]

The working conditions of the *Germany Going Global* model can thus be written in analogy with *Models D – mark I* and *II* (Sections 10.3.1 and 10.4.1). The shades on variables and signs in the following system of equations and inequalities mark the differences in comparison to the *mark II* model.

26 The Eurozone countries' divergent current account balances led to unsustainable paths of foreign debt within EMU, which proved irreversible by internal real exchange rate changes alone (Körner and Zemanek 2013).

The labour market in model D – mark III

$$\hat{w}_D < \hat{w}_{RoEMU} \qquad (III.1)$$

$$a_D > a_{RoEMU} \qquad (III.2)$$

$$(\hat{w}_D - \hat{p}_D) < \hat{a}_D \qquad (III.3)$$

Until 2011, nominal wage growth in Germany was lower than in the EMU average *(III.1)*. The majority opinion in the German council of economic advisors had long since demanded that real wage growth stay behind labour productivity growth in order to reduce unemployment *(III.3)*. This was indeed the case for the total economy, as real wages increased by 0.3 per cent per year on average between 2001 and 2011, whereas labour productivity (real GDP per hours worked) grew by 1.2 per cent per year (OECD.Stat).

The macroeconomic policy regime

$$i_D \leq i_{RoEMU} \qquad (III.4)$$

$$G_D \leq T_D \qquad (III.5)$$

$$\hat{e}_{DM/\text{€}} \equiv 0 \qquad (III.6)$$

$$\hat{p}_D < \hat{p}_{RoEMU} \qquad (III.7)$$

$$\left(\frac{w/p}{a}\right)_D < \left(\frac{w/p}{a}\right)_{RoEMU} \qquad (III.8)$$

Inequality *(III.4)* reflects the liquidity premium on German assets in and after 2010, when large spreads between German sovereign bond yields and those of other EMU currencies re-emerged (see also Figure 10.6). In the first years of EMU, when Germany was not considered a model, the intra-EMU differentials between nominal interest rates and bond yields had shrunk to a minimum; for those years, *(III.4)* would rather be written with an equals sign. Inequality *(III.5)* represents the balanced-budget amendment, or "debt brake", which was written into the German constitution in 2009. Despite countercyclical spending in the Great Recession of 2009–10, the fiscal policy stance can be characterized as restrictive. Equation *(III.6)* is another expression for European Monetary Union; the D-mark/euro exchange rate was "irrevocably" fixed with the transition from the national to the supranational currency. Working conditions *(III.7)* and *(III.8)* read as in the earlier *D models*, but contain a crucial difference

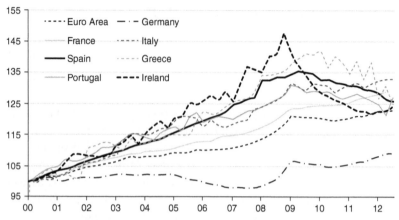

Figure 10.5 Unit labour costs in the Eurozone (2000 = 100)
Source: own computation; data: Eurostat

in the underlying mechanism: the unit labour cost advantage is now mainly caused by a stagnation of real wages, not by lags in their rise (*mark I* "productivity illusion") or a surge in labour productivity (*mark II* rationalization). The gap between unit labour costs in Germany and the EMU average, and in particular the GIIPS countries, widened spectacularly until 2008 and has not substantially narrowed from below ever since (see Figure 10.5).

Trade & Growth

$$NX_D = EX - IM = S - I > 0 \qquad (III.9)$$

$$\widehat{KEX}_D > 0 \qquad (III.10)$$

$$\hat{y}_D = b\widehat{NX}_D \qquad (III.11)$$

Equation *(III.9)* returns to a dual gap expression for describing German net exports, since the absorption of private savings by public deficits is less important than in the *mark II* model, while the GDP shares of gross fixed investment (private and public) are conspicuously low. As capital exports *(KEX)* continued to finance the trade surpluses *(III.10)*, their structure shifted further towards foreign direct investment and cross-border bank loans, reflecting the ongoing transnationalization of production and finance. As can be seen from Figure 10.2, net exports functioned again as a growth engine after 2005 and after the dip in the Great Recession of 2008–09 *(III.11)*.

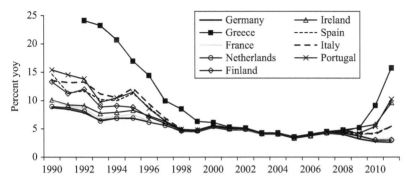

Figure 10.6 Eurozone sovereign spreads vs. 10-year German bunds, 1990–2011
Source: Körner and Zemanek (2013); data: Eurostat

10.5.2 Dynamic Instability of the European Monetary Union

In January 2009, at the tenth anniversary of EMU, the euro looked like a success story – at least in terms of internal and external monetary stability. Inflation rates in the Eurozone had been on average lower than German inflation rates under the Bundesbank's rule in prior decades, and in Germany they were far lower than in either *mark I* or *mark II* periods. Part of the explanation was certainly the global Great Moderation, but – contrary to the fears of many a German professor – there was no evidence of an inflation bias in the monetary union. The external value of the euro had come to be 12 per cent higher (effective exchange rates) than at the start. The euro share in the world's official foreign exchange reserves had risen from 17.9 per cent to 26.0 per cent.

Yet, when the European part of the global banking crisis transmuted into the GIIPS sovereign debt crisis in late 2009, speculation about a dynamic instability of EMU began to proliferate. A combination of Figures 10.5 and 10.6 shows why Germany is generally seen at the fulcrum points of European imbalances. The compression of interest rate levels after the establishment of the ECB in June 2008 ("euro birth" in Figure 10.6) induced booms in the GIPS periphery (except in Italy), which were financed by a strong expansion of private-sector debt. These booms were interpreted – by many investors, for quite some time – as parts of a natural catching-up growth process that would contribute to real convergence in the monetary union. After the intra-EMS exchange rate risks had vanished in the late 1990s, the markets apparently did not price in any sovereign default risks. This could be interpreted as the general expectation – contrary to the stipulations of the Maastricht treaty – that member countries in trouble would be bailed out by the union.

When the Lehman Brothers shock hit European money markets and banks had to be bailed out by their home countries, German insistence on the subsidiarity principle ("each country should look after its own banks") made investors worry that sovereigns overburdened with socialized bank debts (such as Ireland and Spain) would not be bailed out by the union. The (largely unrelated) case of upward corrections of Greek public deficit figures in October 2009 – a context in which German officials repeatedly insisted on sticking to the "no bail-out" clause of the Maastricht treaty – sparked fears of contagion and set the Eurozone debt crisis going in 2010. Once the crisis was under way, the gaps in unit labour cost developments (Figure 10.5) between Germany and the GIIPS countries received increased attention. It was argued that the GIIPS would have to increase the competitiveness of their industries (i.e. lower their unit labour costs) to the levels of Germany's. It is, however, extremely difficult to increase productivity *(a in III.8)* in times of fiscal austerity, which is the strategy the GIIPS countries were obliged to follow by request of their lenders (represented by the "troika" of the EU commission, the ECB and the IMF). It is equally difficult to lower real wages *(w/p)* in austerity, as disinflation and sector-wise falling prices require an overproportional reduction in nominal wages. The easier way out would be a narrowing of the cost gap achieved by wage rises in Germany, but in a monetary union (with irreversibly fixed exchange rates) there is no way to force a surplus country in a net lender position to engineer such a move. Even if GDP growth in Germany is strong enough to pull up real wages, there is the "risk" that it also increases productivity (Verdoorn's law), as in the *mark II* model.

Another option is to try to bring down the interest rate spreads again. This is what the ECB has been trying to achieve. It is extremely difficult, however, for a common monetary policy to deal with asynchronous business cycles in the union (akin to the asymmetric shocks of Optimum Currency Area theory). The situation in the EMU after the start of the sovereign debt crisis in 2010 bears some resemblance to the situation in the EMS after the exchange rate crises of 1992–93. Again, the German economy is out of step with the economies of other member economies. This time the shock is different. It is not the positive shock of German reunification, but the negative shock of the global financial crisis that has led to a boom-bust reversal outside Germany and an upswing within Germany, generated by the combination of extra-EMU demand in a state of implicit undervaluation and a mix of capital inflows and reflows from the EMU periphery.

Here we will not speculate whether the monetary union is bound to break up, or how it can be saved. Shocks of the size of German reunification or the Lehman Brother panic do not happen very frequently, and the oscillations of the first EMU decades may give way to greater convergence. For the latter, however, institutional change at EMU level is required to make the system more resilient. The decision and opinion makers in Germany have their own ideas about the nature of that change.

10.6 Conclusions

Our analogous structuring of the working conditions of *Models D – mark I–III* helps to identify the core in what may be described as the German economic model. The changes in response to the environments under the different exchange rate regimes of the past six decades are mainly contained in conditions *(1)–(5)*, which concern wage and interest rate levels relative to those of other countries, as well as the fiscal policy stance. Continuity is embodied in conditions *(6)–(11)*. Exchange rate stability *(6)* in combination with relatively low inflation *(7)* and unit labour costs *(8)* has been conducive to an undervaluation of German products that has favoured exports and reduced imports. Net exports *(9)* have almost always been positive, even at times when public deficits absorbed greater shares of domestic output. Capital exports *(10)* have changed their character in the course of transnationalization of finance and production, from official reserve accumulation to increasing volumes of private-sector activities in cross-border bank lending, portfolio investment and direct investment. The concomitant increase in the degree of control of industries in foreign countries may well be considered as the "maturing" of a permanent net lender. All this has led to a strong and continuous reliance of GDP growth in Germany on impulses from the export industries.

Different neo-mercantilist positions towards the rest of Europe may be discerned at the three stages of this undervaluation-based model of export-led growth. In the Bretton Woods era, other European countries were essentially seen as competitors for international liquidity (US dollars). In the EMS era, the focus was set on the common internal market of the EU as an outlet. In the EMU era, the focus has shifted to global competition (even with low-wage countries such as China), in which monetary union provides the "competitive advantage" of a belt of "underperforming countries" that protect German industries from exchange rate appreciation.

The global competition perspective implies a return of *mark III* to some characteristics of the *mark I* model. As many German companies have outgrown their domestic markets, they treat the country like a small open economy in global competition, using the euro as a vehicle for undervaluation. German governments (of whichever colour) treat the euro like a foreign currency (in some analogy with the gold-dollar standard), reacting to the loss of monetary policy autonomy with balanced-budget amendments of the constitution.

Both approaches conform to the mindsets of ordo-liberalism and neo-mercantilism. Yet their old recipes can hardly work for the whole of a monetary union. "Competitiveness" campaigns in neo-mercantilist spirit are inadequate insofar as not all countries can have persistent surpluses in the current account; some have to persistently import more than they export, or there have to be temporary swings in the current account balances of most members to allow for offsetting changes. In a monetary union, there is no way to produce such swings by realignments. The painful and risky alternative is internal devaluation by reductions of income and expenditures; the sacrifice ratios in terms of losses of GDP growth over the changes in the current account tend to be rather large. A less painful alternative may be fiscal expansion in the net lending economies at the core of the union. Instead, however, ordo-liberals have pleaded for "fiscal consolidation" in the core regardless of what happens in the periphery. As it has been mentioned before, this is because both ordo-liberals and neo-mercantilists follow the categorical imperative of *caveat debtor*. This may be rational at the individual level, but net exporters need borrowing customers in order to make their economy thrive. Hence, there is a microeconomic fallacy in both mindsets, as it is ignored that in a large, export-driven economy such as Germany, success at the level of firms and households may breed failure at the macroeconomic level if there are no offsetting imports. It is not well understood in Germany that the cherished "competitiveness" of the national industries is partly based on the crisis in other EMU countries, insofar as the letter prevents the appreciation of the euro; it is thus based on instability and divergence in the union rather than the opposite.

In the long run, moreover, the expansionary dynamics of the German economy undermine the plausibility of the neo-mercantilist fiction of the nation state being the collective agent of its industries and their employees. The export orientation of the economy has delivered far less income growth hitherto in the EMU era than it did in the Bretton Woods and EMS eras. With monetary union, the risks of unemployment following from realignments and exchange rate crises are lower than before. Yet this has come along with the stagnation of average incomes, a rising share of precarious employment and a more unequal distribution of income and wealth. The latter two phenomena are more attributable to global changes in labour market conditions than to EMU, but European integration has also contributed to making companies more footloose. This has increased the asymmetry of adjustment burdens when counterparty risks in exports materialize. It is largely the wage-earning taxpayers and savers that have to foot the bill – either in terms of socialized losses incurred by too-big-to-fail banks and other financial institutions, or by direct losses on foreign assets and indirect losses through financial repression.

The export orientation of the German economy has been a driving force of European monetary union and the transnationalization of industrial production and finance. The long-run net effects of both developments on the German economy and other involved economies are likely to be positive. It is not monetary integration or industrial and financial transnationalization as such that confront German politicians and voters with the unpopular choices between having to make transfers to overindebted banks and/or to overindebted EMU member states – or, if EMU were to break up, to unemployed domestic residents and industries in need of restructuring. These choices follow from the "net exports" orientation of what may be considered the German economic model. They illustrate that neo-mercantilism is not compatible with a stable and well-performing monetary union. It is not impossible to make (some) ordo-liberal ideas compatible with the realities of European integration and other transnational activities of private-sector agents that dissolve the traditional boundaries and orders of nation states. Yet, with due respect for the Swabian housewife, the prevalent fallacies of composition would have to go.

Acknowledgment

Both authors gratefully acknowledge financial support from the Volkswagen Foundation.

References

Abelshauser, W. (2005) *The Dynamics of German Industry: Germany's Path Towards the New Economy and the American Challenge*. New York: Oxford: Berghahn Books.

Abelshauser, W. (2011) *Deutsche Wirtschaftsgeschichte. Von 1945 bis zur Gegenwart*, 2nd ed. München: Beck.

Baldwin, R. (2006) Globalisation: The Great Unbundling(s). Chapter 1, in *Globalisation challenges for Europe*, ed. by the Secretariat of the Economic Council. Helsinki: Finnish Prime Minister's Office. URL: http://vnk.fi/hankkeet/talousneuvosto/tyo-kokoukset/globalisaatioselvitys-9-2006/artikkelit/Baldwin_06-09-20.pdf

Bernanke, B. and Mihov, I. (1997) What Does the Bundesbank Target? *European Economic Review* 41: 1025–53.

Bonatti, L. and Fracasso, A. (2013) The German Model and the European Crisis, *Journal of Common Market Studies* 51 (6): 1023–1039.

Buchheim, C. (1999) The Establishment of the Bank deutscher Länder and the West German Currency Reform, in: Deutsche Bundesbank (ed.), *Fifty Years of the Deutsche Mark. Central Bank and the Currency since 1948*, Oxford: 55–100.

Carlin, W. (1996) West German Growth and Institutions, 1945–90. Ch. 15 (pp. 545–79) in *Economic Growth in Europe since 1945*, ed. by Nicholas Crafts and Gianni Toniolo. London: CEPR.

Carlin, W. and Soskice, D. (2009) German Economic Performance: Disentangling the Role of Supply-Side Reforms, Macroeconomic Policy and Coordinated Economy Institutions, *Socio-Economic Review* 7 (1): 67–99.

Caspari, V. and B. Schefold (2011) *Wohin steuert die ökonomische Wissenschaft? Ein Methodenstreit in der Volkswirtschaftslehre*. Frankfurt, New York: Campus Verlag.

Clarida, R. and Gertler, M. (1997) How the Bundesbank Conducts Monetary Policy. Ch. 10 (pp. 363–406) in *Reducing Inflation: Motivation and Strategy*, ed. by Christina Romer and David Romer. Chicago: Chicago University Press.

Deutsche Bundesbank (1995) *The Monetary Policy of the Bundesbank.* Frankfurt: Deutsche Bundesbank.

Dornbusch, R. (1993) The End of the German Miracle, *Journal of Economic Literature* 31: 881–85.

Dornbusch, R. (1997) Comment on Clarida and Gertler. Ch. 10 (pp. 407–12) in *Reducing Inflation: Motivation and Strategy*, ed. by Christina Romer and David Romer. Chicago: Chicago University Press.

Eichengreen, B. (1996) *Globalizing Capital: A History of the International Monetary System.* Princeton: Princeton University Press.

Eichengreen, B. (2011) *Exorbitant Privilege: The Rise and Fall of the Dollar and the Future of the International Monetary System.* Oxford: Oxford University Press.

Emminger, O. (1986) *D-Mark, Dollar, Währungskrisen.* Stuttgart: Deutsche Verlags-Anstalt.

Eucken, W. (1940) *Grundlagen der Nationalökonomie.* Jena: Gustav Fischer. English translation: *The Foundations of Economics. History and Theory in the Analysis of Economic Reality.* London: William Hodge.

Eucken, W. (1952) *Grundsätze der Wirtschaftspolitik.* Bern/Tübingen: Francke / J.C.B. Mohr.

FAZ (2013) F.A.Z. Ökonomenranking: Auf diese Forscher hört das Land. *Frankfurter Allgemeine Zeitung*, 4 September.

Gerberding, C., Worms, A. and Seitz, F. (2004) *How the Bundesbank Really Conducted Monetary Policy: An Analysis Based on Real-Time Data*, Deutsche Bundesbank Discussion Paper Series 1: Economic Studies 25. Frankfurt: Deutsche Bundesbank, Research Centre.

Giersch, H., Paqué, K.-H. and Schmieding, H. (1992) *The Fading Miracle: Four Decades of Market Economy in Germany.* Cambridge: Cambridge University Press.

Hagemann, H. (1999) Gerhard Colm. In *Biographisches Handbuch der deutschsprachigen wirtschaftswissenschaftlichen Emigration nach 1933* (vol. 1: 104–12), ed. by Harald Hagemann and Claus-Dieter Krohn. Munich: K.G. Saur.

Hagemann, H. (2005) Dismissal, Expulsion and Emigration of German-Speaking Economists after 1933, *Journal of the History of Economic Thought* 27 (4): 405–20.

von Hagen, J. (1998) Geldpolitik auf neuen Wegen (1971–1978), in Deutsche Bundesbank (ed.), *Fünfzig Jahre Deutsche Mark – Notenbank und Wlihrung in Deutschland seit 1948*, München: C.H. Beck: 439–73.

Hentschel, V. (1999) Ludwig Erhard - Vater der Sozialen Marktwirtschaft: Legende oder Wirklichkeit?, in *Peter Hampe (1999) 50 Jahre Soziale Mark(t)wirtschaft: eine Erfolgsstory vor dem Ende?* München: Olzog, 17–33.

Horn, G., Sturn, S. and van Treeck, T. (2010) Die Debatte um die deutsche Exportorientierung, *Wirtschaftsdienst* (1): 22–28.

James, H. (1996) *International Monetary Cooperation since Bretton Woods.* New York: Oxford University Press.

Körner, F.M. (2014) *Wechselkurse und globale Ungleichgewichte: Wirtschaftsentwicklung und Stabilität in Bretton Woods I und II.* Wiesbaden: Springer Fachmedien.

Körner, F.M. and Zemanek, H. (2013) On the Brink? Intra Euro-area Imbalances and the Sustainability of Foreign Debt, *Review of International Economics* 21 (1): 18–34.

Kollewe, J. (2012) Angela Merkel's Austerity Postergirl, the Thrifty Swabian Housewife. *The Guardian,* 17 September.

Koske, I. and Wörgötter, A. (2010) *Germany's Growth Potential, Structural Reforms and Global Imbalances.* OECD Economics Department Working Papers 780. Paris: OECD.

Krengel, R. (1963) Some Reasons for the Rapid Growth of the German Federal Republic, *Banca Nazionale del Lavoro Quarterly Review* 64: 121–44.

Krugman, P. (2011) Wishful Thinking and the Road to Eurogeddon, *New York Times,* 7 November 7.

Krugman, P. (2013) Those Depressing Germans, *New York Times,* 3 November.

Lindlar, L. (1996) *Das mißverstandene Wirtschaftswunder: Westdeutschland und die westeuropäische Nachkriegsprosperität.* Tübingen: Mohr Siebeck.

Milberg, W. and Winkler, D. (2013) *Outsourcing Economics: Global Value Chains in Capitalist Development.* Cambridge: Cambridge University Press.

North, D. (1990) *Institutions, Institutional Change and Economic Performance.* Cambridge: Cambridge University Press.

Pflüger, M. (2006) Die These vom "pathologischen Exportboom" – Einige kritische Anmerkungen, *Ifo-Schnelldienst* 59 (1): 19–22.

Porter, M. (1990) *The Competitive Advantage of Nations.* New York: The Free Press.

Sachverständigenrat [für die Begutachtung der gesamtwirtschaftlichen Entwicklung] (2004) *Erfolge im Ausland – Herausforderungen im Inland. Jahresgutachten 2004/05.* Wiesbaden: Sachverständigenrat.

Schmid, P. (1999) *Monetary Targeting in Practice: The German Experience.* Center for Financial Studies Working Paper, 3. Frankfurt: Center for Financial Studies.

Siebert, H. (2005) *The German Economy: Beyond the Social Market.* Princeton: Princeton University Press.

Sinn, H.-W. (2006) The Pathological Export Boom and the Bazaar Effect: How to Solve the German Puzzle, *The World Economy* 29: 1157–75.

Sinn, H.-W. (2007) *Can Germany Be Saved? The Malaise of the World's First Welfare State*. Cambridge, MA: MIT Press.

Sinn, H.-W. (2012) The ECB's Action Will Not Have a Good Ending, *The International Economy* 26 (Spring): 21.

Snower, D., Brown, A. and Merkl, C. (2009) Globalization and the Welfare State: A Review of Hans-Werner Sinn's 'Can Germany Be saved?', *Journal of Economic Literature* 47: 136–58.

Spahn, H.-P. (2001) *From Gold to Euro: On Monetary Theory and the History of Currency Systems*. Berlin, Heidelberg, New York: Springer.

Stützel, W., C. Watrin, H. Willgerodt and Hohmann, K. (eds.) (1982) *Standard Texts on the Social Market Economy: Two Centuries of Discussion*. Stuttgart, New York: Gustav Fischer.

Trautwein, H.-M. (2010) European Macroeconomic Policy: A Return to Active Stabilization?, ch. 3 (pp. 51–72) in *The Return to Keynes*, ed. by Bradley Bateman, Toshiaki Hirai and Maria Cristina Marcuzzo. Cambridge, MA: Harvard University Press.

United States Department of the Treasury (2013) *Report to Congress on International Economic and Exchange Rate Policies (Oct 31, 2013)*. Washington, DC: U.S. Department of the Treasury

11 Exploring Sectoral Conflicts of Interest in the Eurozone

A Structural Political Economy Approach

IVANO CARDINALE AND MICHAEL
LANDESMANN

11.1 Introduction

The recent Eurozone crisis has made clear that the build-up of external imbalances and foreign debt positions are amongst the major unresolved problems in the European Monetary Union construction. The real exchange rate[1] is a crucial variable in both issues, and developments in current accounts and in the real exchange rate between Europe's 'Northern' and 'Southern' economies were indeed a major focus of attention in the build-up to the recent crisis and following the outbreak of the crisis.

The possibility to influence the real exchange rate through policies can generate conflicts of interests. However, whilst such conflicts are usually framed in terms of Eurozone-level or national-level interests, in this chapter we highlight the important sectoral component of conflicts of interest, which can lead to rethink, qualify or question received dichotomies such as 'North versus South'.

As a first approximation, each of the two issues is associated with a fundamental sectoral cleavage: there is a conflict of interest between *tradable and non-tradable sectors* for what concerns developments in the real exchange rate, and between *financial and real sectors* with respect to the accumulation of foreign debt positions and their possible write-offs. We shall discuss these issues in the context of the European 'North-South problem' which is associated with systematic external accounts weaknesses of the 'Southern' economies (the lower- and

---

[1] The real exchange rate is an indicator of price competitiveness, which takes into account both nominal exchange rates and relative price levels (or relative unit cost developments).

medium-income European economies[2]). The latter are generally seen as 'potential catching-up economies', that is, economies which move on a (potentially) higher income and productivity growth path than the more advanced ('Northern') economies. We shall, in the course of this chapter, explore the reasons for these external accounts weaknesses and how these materialised before the beginning of the recent crisis and since its outbreak. The build-up of external accounts disequilibria cumulates in foreign debt positions and these can become a major concern in the context of a regime change in international financial markets. The processes of winding down such debt positions (both of the private and the public sectors) are a major concern to the banking sectors with repercussions for the real economy. It is these issues which we discuss from the point of view of 'sectoral interests' in the course of the crisis, but also in the period prior to the crisis.

The analysis of how 'sectoral interests' articulate themselves in relation to particular economic variables (such as the real exchange rate or external debt positions) can lead to interesting insights into the political-economy dynamics (at national and European levels) when adopting different sectoral decompositions of an economy (in this case: tradable versus non-tradable sectors and financial versus real sectors).

But the emphasis on conflicts of interests should not obscure the fact that the aforementioned sectors are to some degree interdependent, within each country and at the Eurozone level. For example, within each economy the non-tradable sector's aversion to real exchange rate devaluation (which might reduce real incomes and thus domestic demand through accompanying austerity measures) could be tempered by the need that the tradable sector be competitive enough to guarantee the long-run sustainability of the external accounts of the country,

---

[2] The analysis in this essay is not going to be limited to Eurozone countries. For countries within the Eurozone, the developments of the real exchange rate will be the relevant variable. For countries outside the EMU, adjustments in the nominal exchange rate (in addition to the real exchange rate) and the choice of exchange rate regime remain an issue in the context of European 'North-South' relationships. As the recent dramatic developments with respect to Greece have shown, even Eurozone member countries are not immune to speculations regarding radical changes in exchange rate settings (namely 'Grexit'). Thus, although we often use the term 'Eurozone' in this chapter, we in fact refer to the wider range of 'Southern (European) economies' that face situations not dissimilar to those faced by countries which are already members of the EMU. Where differences between these groups of economies exist, they will be pointed out.

which is central for the long-term viability of an open economy. At the Eurozone level, the interest of tradable sectors of advanced countries (the 'North') to avoid real exchange rate appreciation (relative to the 'South'), which would lead to a loss in their competitive positions, may be tempered by the risk of a considerable fall in demand in the 'Southern economies' if that real exchange rate adjustment were not to take place.

This form of interest in the viability of the system, which can be called 'systemic interest' (Cardinale, Chapter 9 in this volume; Cardinale and Coffman, 2014; Cardinale, 2015), may lead sectors to support policies that are beneficial to them only indirectly, that is, because they favour the viability of the system as a whole. Whilst perception of systemic interest is by no means always present, we show that the crisis has in many respects acted as a catalyst, making systemic interest apparent (at the national or Eurozone levels) irrespective of whether it was then acted upon.

In this chapter we explore the interplay of particular and systemic interests surrounding adjustments in the real exchange rate, in its implications for external imbalances and debt write-off. We adopt both of the aforementioned sectoral classifications – tradable versus non-tradable and financial versus real – to characterise the political-economic dynamic in the EU both before and during the crisis. We show how this level of analysis complements, and sometimes contradicts, the results of analyses based on standard divides, such as 'North-South'.

We proceed as follows. In Section 11.2, we first discuss the rationale for using interdependencies between economic sectors as heuristics for political interdependencies, and how this analytical representation affords visualization of the interplay of particular and systemic interests. We then specify the operationalization of our key analytical tools – sectors and interdependencies – as developed in various strands of theoretical and empirical economic analysis. In Section 11.3 we provide the background for the build-up of external imbalances and foreign debt positions in the Eurozone, by following the trajectories of advanced and catching-up countries before and during the crisis. In Section 11.4 we focus on external imbalances and the conflict between tradable and non-tradable sectors. We reconstruct conflicts of interest before the crisis and show that the crisis has arguably made systemic interest apparent. In particular, we argue that systemic interests might derive from interdependencies among sectors as well as macroeconomic conditions to which all sectors in an economy are subject. In Section 11.5 we move to the other policy issue, that is, the problem of foreign debt positions, and the associated conflict between financial and real sectors. In this case too we reconstruct sectoral conflicts of interests and the forms of systemic interests made apparent by the crisis. Moreover, we show that the interplay of sectoral interests may also interact with another political dimension, which has to do with government's consideration of the tax burden on the national economy. In Section 11.6 we further refine the analysis by considering the heterogeneity of firms with sectors. We suggest that the crisis can modify interests within a given sector, thus affecting the stance of that sector as a whole with respect to the policy issues at stake. In Section 11.7 we discuss how the overlap of interests at multiple levels (within sectors, and across sectors and countries) and across multiple policy issues can lead to a relatively unclear articulation of interests, which may be responsible for prolonged periods of 'muddling through' in policy-making. We also discuss whether the attempts at crisis resolution are likely to have a 'nationalist' or an 'integrationist' bias. Section 11.8 brings the chapter to a close.

11.2 On Political and Economic Interdependencies

11.2.1 The Economic and the Political

This chapter is based on a conceptualization of conflicts of interests within the Eurozone[3] in terms of the interplay of economic interdependencies between sectors. 'Sectors' will in this analysis be defined in ways that seem particularly relevant given the features of the Eurozone. Conflicts of interest between those sectors (but also confluence of such interests in periods of crisis) are then analysed with regard to particular policies.

This analytical approach has roots in the history of economic thought where, in early representations of the internal structure of an economy, there was great awareness that productive sectors carried economic interests that could seek political representation (Cardinale and Coffman, 2014). A notable example is that of writings in the

---

[3] For a clarification on the use of the term 'Eurozone' here, see footnote 2 to this chapter.

tradition of Political Arithmetic in England (see, e.g., Petty, 1662; Davenant, 1698; King, 1936 [1696, 1697]; see Coffman, 2013) as well as Physiocracy in France (especially Quesnay, 1972 [1759]), which discussed aggregations of economic activities in such a way that they corresponded to socio-political interests.

Quesnay's (1972 [1759] *Tableau Economique,* which arguably presents the first formalized model of interdependencies between sectors (see Phillips, 1955; Hishiyama, 1960; Candela, 1975; Vaggi, 2008; Pasinetti, 2009), represents a very interesting starting point for our analysis because it presents a conceptual prototype for considering the interests between interdependent sectors.

Our analysis can take advantage of the much more sophisticated techniques of structural analysis that have been inspired by Quesnay and classical political economy. For example, in the first half of the twentieth century, multi-sectoral models have been developed by von Neumann (1945), Leontief (1941) and Sraffa (1960), and have in turn provided the foundations for multi-sectoral models of economic dynamics (Quadrio Curzio 1967, 1975; Pasinetti 1981, 1993; Baranzini and Scazzieri 1990; Landesmann and Scazzieri 1996; Hagemann, Landesmann and Scazzieri, 2003).

Leontief connected his work directly to Quesnay, and saw his *Structure of the American Economy* (1941) as an attempt to construct a modern *Tableau.* But Leontief developed input-output techniques to focus on the study of material and technological interdependencies, thus not pursuing their socio-political dimension. In a sense, this chapter aims to initiate a line of empirical work that could 'complete' Leontief's rediscovery of Quesnay, by revisiting Quesnay's insights about the coupling of economic and political analysis.

It is important to note, however, that we do not assume the relevant aggregations of interests at the outset. We will rather see what coalitions may emerge on the basis of the policy issues we want to discuss. So the basic idea is to take economic interdependencies as a 'model' (or even a heuristic) of the structure of economic interests in society, thereby operationalizing what Truman (1962) calls 'potential' interest groups.

In attributing political interests to economic sectors we depart from classical political economy, which took 'classes', defined on the basis of types of income (rent, profit, wage), as the relevant forms of aggregation. A proxy for the interest of a sector could be its value added, irrespective of how it is distributed among types of income within that sector (see Cardinale, 2012). In other words, different 'classes' (workers, managers, shareholders) associated with the same sector might have an interest in their sector expanding at the expense of others. This does not exclude conflicts between types of income receivers within each sector, or indeed across the economy, but suggests that in some historical contexts, it can be more relevant to define interests on the basis of sectors rather than classes.

This analytical approach is not meant to be normative but mostly explanatory, although at times it might highlight possibilities for cross-sector alliances that are not otherwise evident, or the presence of systemic interests that are not recognised. More specifically, our analysis points to the existence, in a given configuration of sectoral interdependencies, of the potential for conflicts of interest as well as coordination among them. This structural point of view is compatible with at least two forms of coordination of sectoral interests. One is that in which sectoral actors coordinate themselves, either through a non-coordinated bargaining process or through institutionalised agencies. The other possibility is that central institutions, notably governments, act to coordinate industrial interests in view of some 'general' objective. Each of these possibilities holds at both the national and cross-country levels. At the national level, both forms of coordination are well documented. At the cross-country level, a form of coordinating function is carried out by cross-country sectoral lobbies, which have been influential in articulating the interests of cross-country sectors and in having them represented at the supranational level of decision-making, as is shown by the literature on EU-level lobbying (see Coen 2007, 2009 for a review). The other form of coordination is carried out by supra-national institutions such as the European Commission, or organizations such as the WTO at the global level. It must be noted that, among the various influences on public policy, our approach highlights those that are due to sectoral interests, but their relative weight may vary considerably from case to case. For example, in what follows we argue that the *electoral dimension* might play a much stronger role than sectoral interests in policy decisions concerning debt write-off.

Our analysis points to the structure of economic interests, which obviously does not exhaust the range of political interests and cleavages. There are many more (cultural, linguistic, ideological), which may overlap with, or cut through, cleavages based on economic interests.

Yet economic interests are often highly relevant, if only because they tend to have much political clout, as has been shown empirically in the literature on EU interest groups. Of course the reverse could be true: political motives may be prior, and lead to economic alliances that make sense economically only ex post, or that are simply 'satisficing' from an economic point of view, and are rather based on political motives. More generally, this begs the question of whether the economic and the political can really be separated a priori. Whilst we provide heuristics to think about the interplay between economic and political interests, a general discussion of the distinction is beyond the scope of this chapter (but see the concluding chapter of the volume).

Another caveat, which is especially relevant at the empirical stage, is that observed interdependencies – and the inferences we make about their validity as heuristics for political groups – may reflect the status quo but do not necessarily imply an impossibility to change; hence, their constraining effects may be less stringent than observed interdependencies suggest. In fact, interest formation at the sector level and sectoral interdependencies evolve in a dynamic context, as we attempt to show in our analysis of the crisis of the Eurozone.

11.2.2 Particular and Systemic Interests

A crucial property for our purposes is that structural representations of the economic system allow us to visualize possible conflicts of interests, but also the conditions whereby the system as a whole is viable.

For example, if we take input-output interdependencies, the system can reproduce itself and grow with different sectoral proportions, that is, with different relative weights of sectors. Such different sectoral compositions will have an impact on the growth potential of the economic system as a whole and also on whether sectoral output potentials are fully exploited, but the system could be viable with different sectoral configurations in the sense of yielding an overall positive growth rate. If we interpret this analytical result from the point of view of economic and political interests, we can infer that there is room for conflict between sectors, as some sectors may expand relative to others without compromising the viability of the system.

At the same time, such conflicts are systemically sustainable so long as the system remains within sectoral proportions that are compatible with its capacity to reproduce itself. Beyond those limits, the crisis of some sectors can affect other sectors through interdependencies, so the latter may be damaged too.

This suggests that, in pursuing its own interests, each sector may need to balance the particular interests in its own preservation and expansion, and the 'systemic' interest in keeping the system to which it belongs viable. An important implication is that in this scheme, the 'public interest' (or 'public good') is not something abstract, but is grounded in systems of interdependencies, and in sectors' awareness thereof (Cardinale and Coffman, 2014).

Each structural representation is based on different conditions for systemic coherence. In the case of systems represented through input-output interdependencies, we need to consider conditions of viability such as reproducibility with a non-negative growth rate. But if we extend the representation, as we do in this chapter, to include interdependent sectors within and across interdependent countries, we need to define at least two types of viability. One is sectoral, and has to do with reproducibility along the lines described earlier; it might entail different constraints if we consider interdependencies within and across countries (e.g. the consideration of the possibility to import necessary inputs and to export excess product). The other type of viability has a macroeconomic character, and – in the context of the topics discussed in this chapter – has to do with the sustainability of external accounts and debt sustainability issues of national economies in or linked to the Eurozone. These macroeconomic conditions are necessary for the long-term viability of an open economy, and again may impose additional constraints when we consider macroeconomic interdependencies with other countries.

Moreover, if we adopt a dynamic representation of the system, which allows for structural change, we need to account for the possibility that disrupting existing patterns of interdependencies may be necessary for structural change itself. But in such cases, which include attempts to rebalance national economies through policies, there may be fundamental uncertainty concerning the trajectory of the traverse, which could make it difficult for sectors to ascertain ex ante whether certain policies (e.g. industrial policy) are in their interest (Cardinale, 2015).[4]

---

[4] We do not want to assume, however, that in the presence of structural change the political weight of sectors always varies proportionally with their economic weight. Among the reasons why this may not be the case, we could mention that incumbent sectors may depend more heavily on political support, as well as have

The consideration of structural change also leads to a 'dynamic' view of systemic interest, which is not to be equated with a standard condition of reproducibility. In this case, systemic interest needs to be perceived in the necessity of structural change, which can provide the basis for a higher growth trajectory or the emergence from a situation of 'non-viability'. A realignment of sectoral interests might take place in such a context.

In other words, in a dynamic representation there could be low- and high-growth paths that are viable and sustainable. As a result, different configurations of systemic interest could be pursued, each of which leads to a different growth trajectory.

Furthermore, the viability conditions of different trajectories depend to an important extent on the investment in and maintenance of certain 'stocks', both material (e.g. infrastructure) and immaterial (legal frameworks, coordination devices, etc.). The Eurozone crisis and its possible resolution may be seen as contributing to switches between high- and low-growth paths because of its effects on such material and immaterial stocks. It may also introduce new coordination devices, for example through deeper integration, which help the articulation of systemic interests connected to a high-growth trajectory. Or it could deplete existing material stocks, for example, by slowing down investment in infrastructural projects.

Whilst the case of systemic interest under structural change is clearly relevant for the Eurozone, in this work we concentrate on the sectoral and macroeconomic types of viability conditions mentioned earlier, which are particularly relevant for a system such as the Eurozone, with its tight multi-level interdependencies between countries, as well as between sectors within and across countries.

In the presence of sectors that are highly interdependent across countries, a crucial issue is to consider the cleavages that are generated in response to the main policy issues at stake. In particular, in this chapter we consider real exchange rate adjustments and debt write-off as the key policy issues, and look at what the sectoral cleavages are likely to be (tradable versus non-tradable and financial versus real, respectively).

established political connections. Moreover, emerging sectors might often make smaller claims on the national rather than the international arena (e.g. the WTO).

The political science literature on cleavages (Lipset and Rokkan, 1967; Hirschman, 1968; Rae and Taylor, 1970; Rogowski, 1987) has shown that it is important to establish whether cleavages reinforce or overlap with each other. In the former case, the interests of sectors A and B are aligned against the interests of sectors C and D across the main policy issues. In the latter case, sectors A and B have similar interests (and different from C and D) with respect to one policy issue, but A's and C's interests are aligned (against B and D) with respect to another policy issue. It is usually found that overlapping cleavages may be an element of cohesion because they avoid polarization of conflicts (Coser, 1956). In the following analysis, we argue that the overlap of cleavages may render the payoffs of each policy unclear. Given the perception of greater uncertainty of interest formation at the cross-country level, established configurations of systemic interest, such as the national ones, may be more salient than supranational ones, although they may lead to lower-growth trajectories.

11.2.3 Analytical Representations

Analytical representations of economic interdependencies always imply an initial decision about aggregation to define the unit of analysis.[5] There are, moreover, two ways to proceed with aggregation: (1) assume that the units subsumed under the aggregate are homogenous or (2) allow for some degree of heterogeneity also within the aggregate.

While we shall opt for various types of 'sector' definitions in our analysis (a relevant form of 'intermediate level of aggregation'), we shall nonetheless also point to heterogeneity within our 'sector' aggregates (e.g. enterprises of different size classes or different degrees of export exposure). In fact, there might be tensions within a sector (because of its internal heterogeneity) on how to define the 'sector's interest' and hold a certain coalition together, especially when circumstances change, as in the passage from the pre-crisis to the crisis situation.

Another point is that individual entities might belong to different aggregates. In fact, sectors can be defined in different ways, for

---

[5] We shall focus on definitions of sectors and interdependencies starting from a production theoretical angle, leaving other definitions for future work.

example, by 'product' (which in statistical reality is always a basket of products) or by 'process', the latter referring to similarity of technologies used across enterprises (e.g. energy-intensive processes and less-energy-intensive processes).

These different forms of sector aggregations are not just an analytical matter but will articulate themselves in the political arena depending on the subject matter (e.g. trade negotiations taking place by product lines versus the impact of energy price hikes that are more relevant in relation to processes). Moreover, a choice for one or the other definition of sector implies a focus on the situation (and dynamics) in different markets: a product definition will focus on the output market while the process definition on the market for inputs. The 'process' definition based on 'technological similarity' might also direct one towards an interest in 'process innovation', while the product definition leads to a focus on 'product innovation' and all that this entails in terms of interests in favourable conditions (but also competitive outcomes) for such innovations.

In our analysis we use a definition of sectors by product. Moreover, among the many possible techniques of analysis of interdependencies, we use input-output interdependencies but also the differentiated dependence of sectors on different components of demand (such as domestic versus external demand) to characterise sector interdependencies. However, it is well known that input-output analysis focuses on sales and purchases of products and services within an accounting year ('flows') rather than the utilisation of 'stocks'. And whilst from the political-economic point of view the individual or joint use of 'stocks' (such as pieces of infrastructure or pools of skilled labour) might be as important a constitutive element in the formation of 'interests' as flow input-output relationships,[6] we leave such analysis to future work.

---

[6] Just as certain representations (e.g. Pasinetti's (1973) use of vertically integrated sectors) investigate the links of sector activities (directly and indirectly) to final products, there are also other analytical representations which emphasise the (direct and indirect) links to the use of specific primary inputs; these could refer to the uses of primary natural resources such as lands of different quality, of other natural resources, but also of skills of particular segments of the labour force. The dependence on a common input can, of course, be of great relevance for the formation of common interests. This goes in both directions: from the point of view of dependence of production activity on the availability and supply (at a certain price) of a particular primary input and also from the perspective of the

11.3 Two Issues and Two Cleavages

We shall now embark on the substantive application of the more general analytical approach discussed in the preceding sections on a central issue of European integration: that of 'North-South' cleavages and, more specifically, the issue of persistent 'external imbalances'. These lead to the build-up of external debt which characterises relationships between a significant set of low-/medium-income countries in the European economy (we use the term 'the South' for these economies) and some of the more advanced economies ('the North').

We shall focus on the real exchange rate as the crucial concept as, in the build-up to the recent financial (and Eurozone) crisis, real exchange rate movements and – linked to this – current account imbalances were a major focus of attention in the Eurozone. The build-up of external imbalances and of foreign debt positions is now generally considered to be one of the major unresolved problems in the construction of the European Economic and Monetary Union (EMU) (see Giavazzi and Spaventa, 2010; Jaumotte and Sodsriwiboom, 2010; Darvas, 2012; European Commission, 2012). Although the relationships between 'Southern' and 'Northern' economies within the EMU will be the core of the following analysis, the 'North-South' problem in Europe is not restricted to the set of member countries of the EMU. Also other low-/medium-income countries in Europe (such as those in Southeast Europe; see Landesmann, 2015a) suffer from what we shall call 'structural current account imbalances', and many of them are also linked to the Eurozone with some form of a fixed exchange rate regime.

As we shall apply a 'structural political economy' approach (Cardinale, Chapter 9 in this volume; Cardinale, 2015) it is necessary to go beyond country differentiation ('Northern' and 'Southern' economies) and also specify interest formations on the basis of 'sectors' that identify economic activities in relation the overall productive system and their interrelationships (see the discussion in Section 11.2).

---

input itself e.g. particular skill segments of the labour force being interested where the demand – directly and indirectly – for their skills will come from.

The notion of 'primary input' can also be extended to the direct and indirect dependence on the availability of a *particular type of infrastructure* or *legal/ institutional settings* on which different (forwardly linked) sectors depend to different degrees. Again this is of political relevance for 'interest formation' vis-à-vis the provision of such infrastructure and legal/institutional settings.

In this respect we employ two different types of 'sectoral classifications' in the following: first, that between 'tradable' versus 'non-tradable' sectors; and second, 'real' versus 'financial' sectors or interests. The use of both these sectoral schemes to characterise the pre-crisis and crisis political-economic dynamic in the EU also serves the purpose to show that multiple sectoral classifications can be employed to analyse a specific historical situation.

We argue that the analysis of the pattern of real exchange rate developments is a good testing ground for a political-economic analysis of interest articulation across sectors within and across countries and their implications for 'systemic' issues at the EU level.

The fact that there are periods of widely diverging real exchange rates and ensuing current account and debt developments across EU member states shows that the interests between tradable and non-tradable sectors get (at least over certain time periods) quite differently resolved in different EU economies (See Figures 11.1 and 11.2). Why is this the case?

One reason could simply be the *size* of the country: a priori one would think that big economies can rely more on the domestic market and hence overall policy should be biased in favour of the non-tradable sector. However Germany is a counterexample (see the discussion that follows).

Another reason could be the *level of development*: lower income/lower productivity countries are prone to current account deficits (see

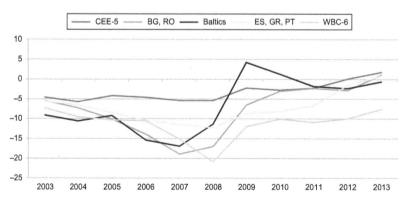

Figure 11.1 Current account in % of GDP.
ĊEE-5 refers to Czech Republic, Hungary, Poland, Slovakia and Slovenia; WBC-6 comprises Albania, Bosnia and Herzegovina, Macedonia, Montenegro, Serbia and Kosovo.

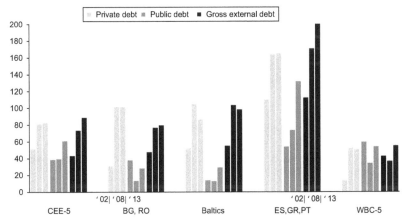

Figure 11.2 Debt in % of GDP, 2002, 2008, 2013 – private, public, external. CEE-5 refers to Czech Republic, Hungary, Poland, Slovakia and Slovenia; WBC-5 comprise Albania, Bosnia and Herzegovina, Macedonia, Montenegro and Serbia.

Landesmann, 2015a, 2015b). There are a number of reasons why that is so. Catching-up economies can offer higher rates of return as they move along a higher productivity growth trajectory compared to more advanced economies. This leads to attracting net capital imports and thus to current account deficits. Other reasons could come from the trade accounts and underlying expenditure patterns in a catching-up economy: both upgrading and high-income growth require or imply importing superior capital goods and consumer goods produced so far only in advanced economies. More problematic aspects can arise from the fact that capital inflows themselves fuel an expectation of currency appreciation, which attracts further speculative inflows. Similarly, the fast urbanisation and agglomeration that accompany catching-up put strain on urban land rents, which in turn attracts speculative capital and 'distorts' price structures in favour of non-tradable sectors.

Thus it is likely that a 'Union' (defined here simply as a set of countries with highly integrated product and capital markets) which encompasses advanced economies and catching-up economies will be prone to showing 'structural'[7] current account imbalances (see also

---

[7] We use the notion 'structural' here to point to the systematic explanation of these imbalances from the nature of the relationship between advanced and catching-up economies and not derived from random 'external shocks'.

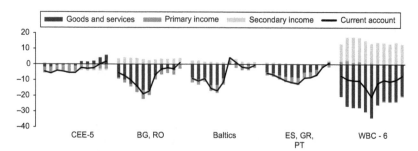

Figure 11.3 Composition of the current account of the balance of payments, 2003–2013, in % of GDP

Landesmann and Hanzl, 2016). Before looking at the implications of such imbalances for 'systemic' viability at the level of the EU as a whole, we return briefly to the articulation of sectoral interest groups in advanced ('Northern') and catching-up ('Southern') economies.

Can we establish that there is a systematic bias in the 'South' towards a stronger position of non-tradable sector interests and a bias in the opposite direction in the 'North'? If this is the case, it is an important ingredient in the political economy of the EU and has implications for its governance structure. In fact, we argue that there is a dynamic *bifurcation in Southern economies* towards two quite different trajectories: on one trajectory there is indeed an evolving bias towards the non-tradable sector, while on the other trajectory there is a more balanced development in which the tradable sector's capacities are strengthened along with growth in the non-tradable sector. In the first case, there could be serious instability along this trajectory, while in the second case, a more balanced development will not violate the longer-term external accounts constraint.

Figures 11.1–11.4 provide empirical evidence that such a bifurcation indeed exists. (See CEE-5 developments compared to the developments in the other groups of European catching-up economies.)

What are the arguments for such possible biases? As previously mentioned, a catching-up process is characterised by two issues: (1) productivity catching-up which – following Balassa and Samuelson – proceeds more strongly in the tradable sector; and (2) a tendency to have a deficit on the trade account which results simply from the fact that the GDP growth rates in catching-up economies are higher than in the main trading partners, and thus – in a situation with constant real exchange rates – even with equal import and export (income) elasticities

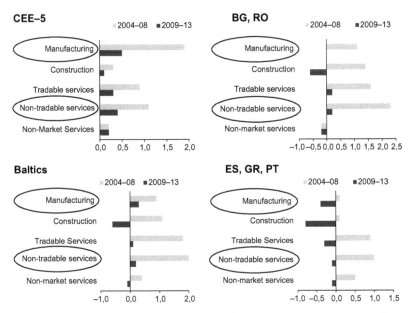

Figure 11.4 Contributions to GDP growth by sectors, percentage points 2004–2008 and 2009–2013 (from constant prices)

compared with advanced economies, trade balances would be negative (see the literature on balance-of-payments constrained growth, e.g. Thirlwall, 1979; McCombie and Thirlwall, 2004; Setterfield, 2011). Moreover, there are good arguments in favour of import elasticities being higher in catching-up economies as there is a need to import capital goods and consumer goods of high quality and covering a greater 'variety range' from technologically more advanced economies.

From this situation one can argue that there are *two possible trajectories* open to deal with the situation of high initial trade deficits in which catching-up economies typically find themselves: one is to make a major attempt to close the trade deficit over time, the other is to allow the trade deficit to linger on and accept the debt burden which builds up as a consequence.

For both scenarios there can be cumulative causation processes at work which enforce one or the other trajectory. First is the *'lingering on' scenario*, which was already described earlier: the cumulative processes are the result of net capital imports putting pressure on the real exchange rate, which makes investment into the non-tradable sector more attractive and imposes a strain on the tradable sector. Follow-up consequences of investment into the non-tradable sector are relative price (including asset price) developments which encourage speculative flows into the non-tradable sector. Second, cumulative processes supporting a *trajectory of a Balassa-Samuelson variety* result from the scope for strong productivity catching-up in the tradable sector making this sector attractive for investment (and also attracting a qualitatively good labour force which can be offered higher relative wage growth compared to the non-tradable sector). Foreign investment adds to the knowledge/technology transfer and hence to the dynamic of productivity catching-up. This leads to technology and product quality upgrading and, consequently, to a 'climbing up the ladder' in comparative advantage and a shift of trade specialisation, moving towards higher-income-elastic products and higher-value-added components of the production chain (see Landesmann and Stehrer, 2001, 2006, who demonstrated this type of trajectory in a number of models).

Empirical evidence that such a bifurcation into two trajectories exists is provided in Figure 11.5, where we show real effective exchange rate (REER) developments of the range of lower-/medium-income EU economies over the 2000–2008 period on one axis and changes in global market shares of these economies over the same period on the other axis. We can clearly see that a group of lagging EU economies showed moderate real exchange rate appreciation over that period (this set of countries includes all the Southern EU economies plus Croatia and Slovenia) with no or very small increases in global (export) market shares, while another group of economies

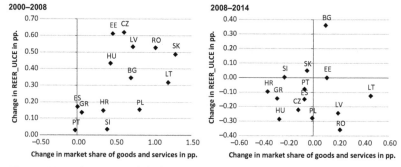

Figure 11.5 Change in global export market shares and change in REER, 2000–2008 and 2008–2014

reveal the 'virtuous circle' of strong increases in real exchange rates combined with strong increases in their global (export) market shares (this group comprises all the Central European New Member States and the Baltics).

Thus we have established both a theoretical basis and empirical evidence in favour of these two trajectories for catching-up economies. We now want to establish *possible biases* (in the tradable versus non-tradable sector trade-off) *amongst advanced economies*. A parsimonious argument is that once a bias has been established in one trading partner in an interdependent trading situation, there has to be a symmetric bias in the other trading partner. But let us go beyond this and consider whether a 'mercantilist bias' exists in the case of some of the 'Northern' economies; not all of them have such a bias as we can observe from the very different situations of, for example, Germany and the United States. Let us start with the behavioural analysis of the 'Savings-Investment' balance. From long-term empirical trends, the US situation is the more typical one; as countries get richer, their savings rates fall. If they remain attractive for investment, therefore, they will have a negative savings-investment balance and hence a deficit on the current account. On the other hand, we also have the example of Germany, which shows a bias towards the tradable sector. How do we explain that? We can postulate *two possible trajectories amongst advanced economies*.

The *US trajectory* is based on its attractiveness for international capital flows even if it shows a chronic current account deficit. Why is this the case? One argument is the global reserve currency argument: because of the sheer size and depth of US financial markets and the importance of the Fed as 'the' global monetary authority which can back up with its issuance power the US private and public debt positions, the United States is seen as a 'safe haven' even when – over extended periods of time – the current accounts remain negative. Expectations regarding US currency developments are therefore highly uncertain even when there are sustained current account deficits (which in other countries' situations would move markets to expect depreciation). The cumulative causation argument also works here: trust in the power of the Fed leads to capital inflows, thus stabilising or even appreciating the US dollar in spite of current account deficits, which makes investors feel safe in investing in non-tradable and tradable sectors (more in the former if there are real appreciation pressures; more in the latter if the various components driving the real exchange rate – wages, productivity, nominal exchange rate – suggest a moderate depreciation), which in turn sustains a longer-term current account deficit position of the US economy and a sustained national investment-savings gap.[8]

The *'German' trajectory* also applies to Japan and – in due course – to other Southeast Asian economies. Empirical evidence suggests that the export sector in an economy is the sector with the highest productivity growth. Hence, a strategy that tends to support exports (and thus expand the weight of this sector in the overall economy) would also drive productivity growth in the economy as a whole. This motivation lies behind a 'mercantilist strategy' in catching-up economies, but also applies to advanced economies. There might be an ingrained Listian tradition in Germany which continues to motivate this strategy – possibly a leftover of the catching-up phase in the second half of the nineteenth century – which might also have transferred to Japan (and from there to other East Asian economies).

Hence also amongst advanced economies, different possible trajectories with regard to 'structural current account' positions can persist, and with this a difference in the policy emphasis with respect to the tradable and non-tradable sector.

We now return to the issues which might be generated by the problem of 'structural external imbalances' in the European context. Given the previous argument, there are potentially four groups of economies: (1) advanced economies with sustained current account surpluses; (2) advanced economies with sustained current account deficits; (3) low-/medium-income economies with sustained current account deficits; and (4) low-/medium-income economies with moves towards balanced or sustainable current accounts.[9] What does the

---

[8] Although we have concentrated here on the United States as an example of an advanced economy with a 'structural current account deficit', many of the arguments can also be applied to other advanced economies such as e.g. the United Kingdom. Although the global reserve currency argument does not apply (or not to the same extent as to the US dollar), the arguments regarding depth of capital markets, the relative trust in the competence of monetary authorities and also the backing of debt positions with an underlying valuable asset and capital structure (including human capital) which has been built up over centuries can be applied also in this case.

[9] We leave out the case of low-/medium-income countries with sustained current account surpluses – although they exist at the global level – because they do not feature in the European context. Strong currency manipulation, capital controls and protectionist measures are required to sustain such a position for a catching-up

presence and interaction of these four groups mean, first, for the functioning of the EU and the European economy more widely and, second, for political economy issues by which we mean the articulation of interest groups at the national and EU levels and its impact on policy-making and policy reforms?

Before we come to that, let us summarise the factors which lead a 'Southern' country to move towards trajectory (3) above (i.e. unsustainable external imbalances). Among the external factors, financial integration leads to cheap access to external finance and allows protracted periods of external disequilibrium in catching-up economies. Moreover, EMU membership or fixed exchange rate regimes seemingly make exchange rate risk disappear. The result is high indebtedness, often denominated in foreign exchange. Furthermore, external creditors from the EU can rely on a likely bailout if external debt becomes unsustainable. This generates a moral hazard issue in the EMU/EU because of contagion fears in the financially highly integrated region.

Among the internal factors, catching-up economies have initially undervalued land prices and high expectations of land price appreciation (also because of rural-urban migration). This makes real estate investment attractive. On top of that – especially relevant in transition economies in Eastern Europe – there is catching-up not only in productivity but also in expenditure structures which favour the distributive sector (wholesale/retail etc.) and other services sectors. Many of these are part of the non-tradable sector that mostly require urban or suburban locations and thus add to the pressure on land prices.

Similarly, we can summarise the internal and external factors which lead an advanced economy towards the choice of trajectory (1) (favouring the tradable sector) above. Among the external factors, there is high demand for investment goods and high-quality, high-income-elastic products by the South, which favours a positive trade balance of advanced economies trading with catching-up economies. Further, the aforementioned attractiveness of higher capital returns in catching-up economies favours net capital flows into these economies. This results in positive capital accounts in advanced economies and negative ones in

economy (which does not have the advantage of deep capital markets, international trust in its monetary authorities, etc.). However, this is not an option for countries that are either members of the EU or in various types of association agreements or aspire to such, as any such arrangements do not allow such type of policy interventions.

the catching-up economies ('capital flowing down-hill'), which is complementary to the current account developments where negative trade balances in the catching-up economies need to be financed by net capital inflows from the advanced economies.

The internal factors, instead, could refer to a relatively stagnant domestic market in advanced economies, for example because of ageing, rising inequality, and a satiation of good investment opportunities in mature economies. Once we have established the factors that move an advanced economy towards trajectory (1) and a catching-up economy towards trajectory (3), we can concentrate on the bilateral relationship between *'Northern' surplus country and 'Southern' deficit country* and later on introduce other relationships including countries which follow trajectories (2) and (4). Giving priority to this bilateral relationship reflects of course the interest in this paper in analysing a 'North-South' relationship at the European level characterised by *structural external imbalances*.

The political-economic question we shall attempt to address now is why (1) unsustainable current account imbalances between the 'North' and the 'South' developed in Europe prior to the crisis and (2) what were the differentiated patterns of adjustment which took place post-crisis. In this respect we discuss the political-economic processes which lie behind these developments using the framework of sectoral interests introduced earlier.

In Section 11.5 we then expand the analysis employing an alternative sectoral decomposition into 'real' and 'financial' sectors or interests and discuss their respective positions with respect to debt build-up prior to the crisis and possible debt relief or debt restructuring post-crisis.

11.4 Conflicts over Imbalances: Tradable versus Non-Tradable

In most countries there is potentially a conflict of interest between 'tradable' and 'non-tradable' sectors: tradable sectors are predominantly interested in staying competitive in relation to foreign competitors (hence, in relative cost conditions), as well as maximising their access to foreign markets. Non-tradable sectors, on the other hand, are dependent on sales on the domestic market and thus interested in factors that strengthen domestic demand.

There are, of course, interdependencies between non-tradable and tradable sectors: input-output relationships show that non-tradable sectors provide (directly and indirectly) a sizable share of the required inputs of the tradable sectors, and hence quality and cost of these supplies matter for the competitiveness of the tradable sector. Similarly, tradable sectors make, through their export earnings, contributions to domestic demand on which the non-tradable sector depends. Further, there are interrelated learning processes and technological spillovers that are of mutual interest to both of these sectors. Moreover, the tradable sector is responsible for an important macroeconomic constraint that is, the trade balance, which is of great importance for the longer-run viability of an economy in an open international context. We shall return to this important 'systemic interest' later in the chapter.

Despite these various interdependencies, there still remains a certain amount of 'conflict of interest' between the two types of sectors, as an economy might be viable (at least over a certain time horizon) with different weights and evolutions of these sectors.[10] Let us briefly discuss the implications of such a conflict of interest between tradable and non-tradable sectors, first in a national context and then at the EU level.

In a national context, tradable sectors would – as mentioned earlier – emphasise the importance of 'competitiveness'; this would allow such sectors to expand and raise incomes (and employment) in that sector. There are, of course, various ways to increase 'competitiveness': one route is through low unit costs (at current exchange rates); the other would be through the supply of high-quality products. In the following we talk about relative unit costs always in a way which adjusts unit costs for quality levels. In this way we define a 'real exchange rate', which is the central concept we use in the discussion that follows.

Let us now explore potential conflicts of interest between tradable and non-tradable sectors in relation to the real exchange rate. Tradable sectors will expand sales and incomes through a favourable real exchange rate (i.e. depreciation) as long as the Marshall-Lerner conditions are satisfied.[11] However, a depreciated real exchange rate

---

[10] If there were only a unique balance of the two types of sectors to attain 'viability' of an economy, there would be little ground to analyse 'conflicts of interest', as any articulation of such interests would tend to make the economy as a whole non-viable.

[11] The Marshall-Lerner conditions specify the conditions under which the relative demand (quantity) effects from an exchange rate depreciation outweigh the terms-of-trade (i.e. relative price) effects on the overall (nominal) balance of trade.

also means that imports will be relatively expensive, and hence non-tradable sectors (and final consumers), which depend on such imports, will be negatively affected. Further, if increased cost competitiveness is achieved by driving down wage rates (or rationalising on employment, which also lowers unit costs in the tradable sector), this could negatively affect domestic demand on which the non-tradable sector depends. Furthermore, achieving real exchange rate depreciation through nominal devaluation will entail a pressure on domestic inflation through the exchange rate pass-through. This in turn depresses domestic real incomes.

What about the conflict of interest the other way around, from the behaviour of the non-tradable sector on the tradable sector? The non-tradable sector by definition is less affected by rising costs.[12] Its sales are only indirectly dependent on foreign markets and its interest lies in the purchasing power on the domestic market. It is thus interested in positive domestic income developments and high spending out of these incomes. The attitudes towards wage policy, public spending policy, exchange rate policy (effect on import prices and thus domestic real incomes) and even monetary policy[13] are therefore likely to differ between non-tradable and tradable sectors.

Of course, there is also plenty of common 'systemic' interest between the tradable and non-tradable sectors at the national level: both must be interested in the viability of the domestic economy in the long run and hence in observing the constraints on external imbalances which in turn depend on external financing conditions. But even there, the

---

[12] We say here 'less' because the non-tradable sector is not immune to rising unit costs, since there are still substitution effects between domestically supplied tradables and non-tradables affecting the shares of the two types of sectors in domestic demand.

[13] Shortly on monetary policy: both sectors in principle are interested in low inflation; the tradable sector because it keeps the sector competitive and the non-tradable sector because it keeps real incomes *ceteris paribus* high. However, the two sectors can disagree on how low inflation is to be achieved. In fact, if domestic inflation is contained through high interest rates, this could affect the two sectors differently. Relatively high domestic interest rates would invite capital inflows which exert pressure on the exchange rate to appreciate; this is detrimental to the cost competitiveness of the tradable sector but beneficial in terms of lower import prices for the non-tradable sectors. Similarly, a general fall in domestic demand because of high interest rates would be particularly detrimental for the non-tradable sector but might have beneficial implications on reducing wage rates and costs for the tradable sector.

burden of adjustment might fall to different degrees on the two types of sectors if the external imbalances constraint is violated. An external debt shock might imply a long-term requirement for the domestic economy to be in a depressed state (in order to suppress domestic demand, thus affecting particularly the non-tradable sector) and might, furthermore, induce a strong adjustment in the real exchange rate in the direction which is beneficial for the competitiveness of the tradable sector.

Let us now explore the articulation of sectoral interests (tradable versus non-tradable sectors) in their historical contexts in Europe, and especially during the 2000–2014 period, in which the 'North-South' relationship went through a number of phases. Furthermore, this relationship took place in different economic and institutional contexts depending on whether countries were within the Eurozone, within the EU but not in the EMU, or whether one includes countries outside the EU but integrated in the wider European economic space.[14] Let us briefly sketch the developments over two phases: pre-crisis (2000–2008) and crisis (2009–2014).

The *pre-crisis phase* saw the development of – at times explosive – current account deficits in 'Southern' European economies (see Figure 11.3). The reasons are – by now – well known: there was an interest rate convergence within the Eurozone and also a compression of interest rates in associated 'Southern' economies which were not EMU members but had opted for one or the other type of a pegged or fixed exchange rate regime. Interest rate compression, combined with a belief (and a documented record) of higher growth rates of catching-up economies, led to a strong incentive for high capital inflows into these countries. Whether these capital injections were mainly invested into the tradable or the non-tradable sectors depended on other factors (see earlier discussion).

What about *real exchange rate adjustment*, which is the crucial variable in the case of sustained 'North-South' external imbalances? Obviously, tradable groups in advanced and catching-up economies are competitors; any movement in the real exchange rate in favour of one group will thus reduce the competitive position of the other group.

---

[14] As mentioned in footnote 2, we consciously extend the analysis beyond the EU as the 'North-South' issues are also relevant for the 'wider European integrated economic space'.

Hence from a 'sectoral interest' perspective there is a conflict of interest there. What about *tradable versus non-tradable sector interest groups* in relation to the real exchange rate? Here it is obvious that real appreciation favours the non-tradable groups in both advanced and catching-up economies (always seen from the angle of the respective economy).

Thus we can think of a matrix of 'sectoral interests' in relation to real exchange rate movements (we look at the situation always from the point of view of a particular country appreciating its real exchange rate).

Matrix 1. *Conflict/Complementarity Matrix in the case of real exchange rate appreciation*

		Catching-Up	
		Tradable	Non-tradable
Advanced	Tradable	$(-,+)$	$(-,-)$
	Non-tradable	$(+,+)$	$(+,-)$

Note: a minus $(-)$ sign means a particular sector in a country disapproves of real exchange rate appreciation; a $(+)$ sign means a particular sector approves of real exchange rate appreciation. The first entry in the bracket always refers to the country – depicted in the horizontal dimension – which undergoes the exchange rate appreciation; the second entry in the bracket shows the approval or disapproval by the respective interest group of the other country – depicted in the vertical dimension. Hence, a bracket containing the same signs indicates a convergence of interests, whereas different signs indicate a conflict. Thus we can interpret the entries in the matrix in the following way: a $(-,+)$ sign in the top-left quadrant means that the tradable sector in each country disapproves of real exchange rate appreciation, always seen from the respective country's angle. The $(+,+)$ sign in the bottom-left quadrant means that the non-tradable sectors in each country have an interest in real exchange rate appreciation which is also approved by the tradable sector in the other country.

What emerges from this matrix is interesting in that, in relation to the real exchange rate developments, there are conflicts of interests between the same sectors in the two types of economies, and joint interests across the complementary sectors in the two economies. Thus real exchange rate appreciation is approved by the non-tradable sectors in the country where this real appreciation occurs and approved by the tradable sector of the other country (bottom left-hand entry). On the other hand, real exchange rate appreciation is disapproved by the tradable sector where this real appreciation occurs, but is approved by the tradable sector of the other country (top left-hand entry) and disapproved by the non-tradable sector of the other country (top right-hand entry).

The crisis made the unsustainability of the previously built-up current account positions of a range of 'Southern' economies apparent. As the crisis erupted in quite a few of the Southern economies, the situation moved towards a so-called 'sudden stop'. This means that financial markets reacted to the increase in uncertainty with an unwillingness to allow any further net capital flows to come into these countries and in quite a few of these there were net capital outflows (see again Figure 11.3 where a turnaround from negative to positive current accounts implies a move towards net capital outflows).

The developments of 'North-South' relationships in Europe during the crisis have put a lot of strain on the policy framework that underlies European integration (see Giavazzi and Spaventa, 2010; Jaumotte and Sodsiwiboon, 2010; Darvas, 2012; European Commission, 2012; Landesmann, 2015b). The crisis revealed that North-South relationships within the EMU and also in relation to countries closely linked to the EMU were not organised in a policy context that assured sustainability. Furthermore, if not addressed, it would lead to serious adjustment processes or – in a worse outcome – to protracted 'crises' in countries' developments and also for the European integration process itself. What was this policy context?

The pre-crisis period showed serious deficits in capital market arrangements within the EU and in relation to countries which are strongly economically linked with the EU. From today's perspective it seems an almost incomprehensible negligence in the set-up of the Single Market not to have immediately moved towards a pan-European monitoring and supervision system of financial institutions. It was clear from the very beginning that the financial market would be the most integrated amongst the three markets (goods and services, capital, labour) as capital is historically the most mobile factor. Hence the neglect of pan-EU supervision mechanisms can arguably be explained by political-economic considerations such as the resistance of national supervisory bodies (acting in conformity with the interests of national financial institutions that benefit from close links to these national supervisory bodies) to give up competences. The implications of this deficiency in the EU/EMU policy framework are discussed further in Section 11.5.

Two other factors played a role in allowing the 'external imbalances' in the European economy to move towards unsustainable paths: one was the mistaken belief – in the context of a very incomplete integration context of the EU – that 'external imbalances' within a Union do not matter. The other was the exclusive focus of policy constraints imposed on fiscal developments and the public debt (entrenched in the Growth and Stability Pact, the GSP) but a neglect of private-sector debt developments. In any case, the build-up of unsustainable external imbalances between 'North' and 'South' in Europe went along without any check at the pan-European (or EU) level.

This deficiency became very apparent during the crisis and the urgency with which – although with some delay – policy-makers moved towards the setting up of joint supervisory mechanisms at the EU (or Eurozone) level as one pillar of the 'Banking Union' is a reflection of this. Furthermore, attention has been given to developing a 'Macroeconomic Imbalance Procedure' (MIP) in the wake of the crisis, although it still has many unsatisfactory aspects (for a discussion of MIP, see, e.g., Gros and Giovannini, 2014; de Grauwe, 2012; Belke and Dreger, 2013).

In this sense, we consider the crisis as an instance which made 'systemic interest' apparent. Making 'systemic interest' apparent does not, however, mean that this automatically leads to political-economic constellations which initiate actions in the direction of 'systemic interest'.

Let us now discuss what causes sectoral interests to move towards recognising 'systemic constraints' which could either take the form of a macroeconomic constraint (such as unsustainable external imbalances or debt sustainability) or a recognition of the importance of inter-sectoral interdependencies.

A crisis situation such as the one which arose for a number of 'Southern economies' in 2008–09 with a shift of the current account regime towards a 'sudden stop' (see Figure 11.3) meant that both the North and the South faced regime changes with regard to these two types of constraints (of inter-sectoral relationships and macroeconomic constraints); furthermore, these articulated themselves at the national level and the inter-country level (i.e. in North-South relationships).

An overview of the different types of constraints can be obtained from the following matrix depicting the situation with the outbreak of the crisis in 2008–09.

Matrix 2: *The nature of national and cross-country constraints in the wake of the financial crisis*

	Sectoral interdependencies		Macroeconomic constraints	
	National	International	National	International
North	Weak banks hitting other economic activities	Sales constraint hits tradable sector	Growth slowdown	Export weakness hits domestic economy
South	Financing crisis	External finance dries up	Severe recession	Current account closure; sudden stop

Exploring the different entries in this matrix, we see that the financial crisis hit the pattern of sectoral interdependencies through the worsening of the services provided by the financial sector to the other sectors of the economy. This was more severe in the 'South' than in the 'North', as the debt sustainability issue of the (private-sector) borrowers was much more apparent in the South (due to the 'credit bubble') than in the North. On the issue of sectoral interdependencies, we can also see an international dimension (second column), as the tradable sectors in the 'Northern surplus economies' faced a constraint in their exporting possibilities in the South and Southern (sectoral) economic activities faced the additional constraint on borrowing from abroad.

As regards macroeconomic constraints, the North suffered from a general growth slowdown induced partly from a less well-functioning domestic credit system and from the international transmission of the growth slowdown in its export markets. The South experienced a much more severe impact on growth through the dysfunctional domestic banking system and the dramatic shift in the current account constraints due to the 'sudden stop' of further net capital inflows.

Do these regime changes also change the nature of sectors' strategies as depicted in the earlier Matrix 1, which showed the pattern of congruence or conflict of sectoral interests? We would argue that in times of crisis, it is possible that sectoral interests can indeed shift in the light of the more binding constraints experienced during the crisis which have been depicted in Matrix 2.

First of all, there is an interest by the economy at large to deal with the weak banking system; this is an issue we examine in Section 11.5. Further, still in this context, there has to be an interest by the 'South' to recover access to external finance on which many activities, and in particular importers, depend. Third, there might be a shift in the attitude of the non-tradable sector in the South to switch its strategy and support a real depreciation of the currency, which reduces domestic demand (in the short run, real devaluation is achieved through wage restraint) but might allow the export and the import competing sector to recover. Through the induced macroeconomic effects (lifting somewhat the balance-of-payments constraint) and spill-over effects on the non-tradable sector supplying inputs to the tradable sector, this might induce a shift in strategy of the non-tradable sector.

Let us move to inter-country sector strategies. In the pre-crisis period the tradable sector in the Northern country was not interested in a real depreciation of its trading partners, as this would erode its competitive position. Once the crisis results in a severe recession in the Southern economy – which prior to the crisis soaked up the net exports from the North – this hits the tradable sector in the North. As a real depreciation of the Southern economy leads to a relaxation of its external accounts constraint and thus allows a recovery, this would favourably affect the exporting potential for the Northern exporters. This output effect of a real depreciation of the South might outweigh the negative effect derived from a deteriorating (relative price) competitive situation of the North. The Northern tradable sector interests might thus realign behind a real depreciation of the South.

We can also examine economies that do have the option of nominal devaluations as a path towards real devaluation. This refers to 'Southern' economies not being part of the Eurozone which could switch from a pegged regime towards a more flexible regime or, taking the more extreme case such as envisaged with Greece during the crisis, to the possibility of an EMU member leaving the Eurozone. There the domestic and international situation with respect to devaluation will be seen quite differently in countries which have built up a large stock of Euro-denominated debt and other countries where the levels of Euro-denominated debt is much smaller. In the former a nominal devaluation would lead to a near *pari passu* increase in that country's foreign debt ratios, while in the latter the impact of nominal devaluation will be less severe. Hence we would expect different behaviour in the realignment of sectoral interests behind a nominal devaluation between these two sets of economies depending on the respective levels of foreign-exchange-denominated debt levels.

The preceding analysis has shown that either a change in external environment (e.g. international financial crisis) or national economic developments (e.g. external imbalances transcending certain threshold levels) can change 'sectoral interests'.[15] Furthermore, developments in the internal or external context can lead to a change in whether a constraint (be it of the macroeconomic variety or one expressing inter-sectoral interdependencies) becomes binding and thus influences a country's economic trajectory overall and the formulation of sectors' interests.[16] Lastly, the weights of different constraints can change depending on external and internal developments, thus influencing overall economic trajectories and having a differentiated impact on sectoral interests and the conflictual or congruence stances amongst these. This includes conflicts and congruence constellations at national and international levels.

The preceding analysis thus suggests an interplay of particular and systemic interests. Furthermore, in order to make conjectures about which ones prevail in a given country, it is important to consider *how relevant domestic interdependencies are, compared to external interdependencies.*

The general point that seems to emerge from the analysis is that systemic interest could indeed align previously conflicting sectoral interests, but perhaps for different reasons and/or through different policies. For example, if the systemic interest considerations of the tradable sector of the advanced economy do indeed have to do with ensuring sufficient demand from catching-up economies, then this result could be achieved through domestic demand policies in the latter economies, without

---

[15] It would be interesting to empirically test for 'switchover points' when the sectoral interests change as a result of the aforementioned 'thresholds' being crossed with respect to variables characterising the external environment (e.g. downturn in export demand resulting from a move of trading partners into recession) or the national macroeconomic situation.

[16] In Section 11.7, we come back to analysing situations in which internationally oriented sectoral interests switch towards a 'nationalist stance'. Historical examples show such a switch of industrial interests, e.g. Germany in the 1930s. An example in the other direction, i.e. towards a more international definition of industrial interests, would be the production relocation moves by Japanese industrial groupings over the 1990s and 2000s.

necessarily requiring real exchange rate adjustments, at least in the short run. On the other hand, the non-tradable sector of the catching-up country's interest in the sustainability of the current account would necessarily require real exchange rate adjustments. If this is the case, it could happen that even in the presence of strong systemic interest, there could still be a conflict as to the policies to be adopted, which could further delay measures that are of interest to many sectors.

The recent Eurozone crisis has shown how conflicts of interest across sectors (within an economy) and those across economies (the 'North' and the 'South') which arise from unsustainable external imbalances might get resolved in one way or the other in the course of a crisis. Furthermore, such resolution of sectoral and country interests might encounter complicated political-economic resistances, which can lead to outcomes with very unequal burden-sharing of costs of adjustment and to sub-optimal outcomes for the Eurozone as a whole.

Thus the resolution or non-resolution of inter-sectoral and inter-country cleavages can result in different outcomes, that is, stagnation-ary versus growth trajectories, more or less unbalanced growth between Northern and Southern economies, and balanced versus unbalanced growth across sectors within domestic economies. The outcome also depends on inter-country policy agreements (or non-cooperative bargaining outcomes) and on changing policy framework conditions. The latter case is explored further in Section 11.7.

11.5 Conflicts over Debt: Financial versus Real

External imbalances are a flow problem, which is associated with the stock problem of the build-up of foreign debt positions. This adds another sectoral divide, between real and financial sectors, over pol-icies to be adopted with respect to potential debt write-off.

In the longer run there is an underlying conflict of interest between the real and the financial sector: the financial sector can reap gains from a 'bubble-bust' pattern while the real sector does not have an interest in it and has to bear the costs of the moral hazard/bail-out situation in a 'closed economy' setting. In an 'open economy' setting the issue is more complicated as the 'moral hazard' issue becomes internationalised. In this situation two types of asymmetries can emerge: the responsibility for a bail-out might be shifted away from the governments under which international banks' subsidiaries operate and to the governments where the headquarters of the mother banks reside, as it is in these countries that the banks are seen as 'systemically relevant'. The second asymmetry emerges from the relative distribution of real economy adjustments in conditions when 'sudden stops' of capital flows occur. In this case the governments and international institutions which provide emergency finance to a country that is subject to such sudden stops can *de facto* dictate the pattern of adjustment in the affected country, as the latter cannot raise finance to continue operating vital services without such support. An example of such a situation emerged in the case of the Greek 'crisis agreements'. The interests of French and German banks and worries about bail-outs clearly affected the French and German governments' stance over the Greek 'rescue' package and the pattern of adjustment of the Greek economy in the wake of these rescue packages.

However, in the pre-crisis period there was no striking conflict between 'real' and 'financial' interests. The pre-crisis period saw a strong emphasis on financial markets integration. Banks and other financial institutions could gain a lot from arbitrage processes as precursors of full market integration in the EU:[17] thus, there were gains from low levels of financial intermediation in catching-up economies, from undervalued land prices, from catering to segments of the population which did not have access to the credit market so far, and so on. Hence financial institutions represented a strong lobby in favour of financial markets integration, discouraging too strong supervision and regulation (which would increase their costs) and in favour of widening credit activity towards segments of the population which did not have access to credits in the past. Furthermore, big banks had advantages in risk pooling, would be the main beneficiaries of the moral hazard issue mentioned earlier (i.e. likelihood of a bail-out in case things go wrong) and were thus prime movers in the financial integration and debt build-up in Europe's South prior to the crisis.

Another group that benefitted from financial markets integration were international speculators, which are faster than others in moving in and out of investments across borders. Their activities added to the volume of capital movements in and out of emerging

---

[17] In fact, a potential for gains from arbitrage reflects incomplete market integration. If all barriers of market integration had disappeared (i.e. if the world – or the EU – were really 'flat'), so would any gains from arbitrage.

economies; in the case of flexible exchange rate regimes, this applies to speculators in foreign-exchange transactions as well, thus contributing to exchange rate volatility.

What about the interest groups representing the 'real economy'? These would not stand in the way of financial markets integration in the period before the crisis as international liquidity 'fuels' their own activities: providing finance for multinationals' investments, and credit to households and SMEs that require finance to purchase goods and services and undertake investments, and others. Hence there is *no striking conflict of interest between 'real' and 'financial' interests in the pre-crisis 'boom/bubble' period*[18].

The crisis can be seen as enforcing the transversality condition, that is, making unsustainable debt positions of the private and public sectors (particularly in economies lacking their own central banks) apparent. The crisis hits both the financial sector and the real sector in catching-up economies and through debt write-offs and the decline in import demand also the financial and real sectors in the advanced economies.

We now attempt a similar analysis regarding *complementarity/conflict of interest between real and financial sectors* in the aftermath of the financial crisis, as we did in Section 11.4 with regard to real exchange rate adjustments, but this time with respect to *debt write-off*.[19] As we shall see, the situation becomes more complicated than the one analysed in Section 11.3, as the issue of debt write-off adds another dimension than simply analysing the relationship between the two (private) sectors because it involves the tax payers (at national or international levels) which are likely to be burdened by such debt write-offs.

Let us first analyse the case of a bank debt write-off in the 'Southern' country, in a situation in which the burden of this debt write-off is carried by the tax-payers of the same country.

---

[18] Of course, this is not completely the case, as the real sector would, for example, not be interested in undue exchange rate volatility which results from speculative behaviour on foreign-exchange markets.

[19] A similar analysis regarding conflicts of interest using the real versus financial sector decomposition could be undertaken with respect to 'financial sector reforms' and the EMU 'banking union'. Both are issues hotly debated in the wake of the recent crisis, and policy steps were taken in this direction. This topic would also lend itself to an application of a *structural political economy* analysis, but we shall not cover it in this chapter.

Matrix 3. *Conflict/Complementarity Matrix in the case where debt write-off in the South is borne by the tax-payers of the domestic economy*

		Catching-Up	
		Real	Financial
Advanced	Real	(~, −)	(~, +)
	Financial	(+, −)	(+, +)

Note: ~ means 'indifference'

In this situation we can see that a 'debt write-off' (if enforced by the government) is welcomed by the financial sector of the respective country and also by the financial sector of the other country (bottom right-hand entry), as reduction of bad debt items in the balance sheets of banks also contributes to the health of the banking system in the integrated financial system in the EU as a whole. On the other hand, a bank debt write-off is not welcomed by the 'real' sector in the respective country, as it would have to carry the costs of such a debt write-off in this case; the 'real' sector in the other country is not affected by this in the short term – hence the ~ (i.e. indifference) sign (top left-hand quadrant).

The constellation in this case is different from the previous matrix where we had a strict complementarity: tradable sector interests in one country were aligned with non-tradable sector interests in the other country. In this case the financial sectors in both countries are interested in debt write-offs in the South because of the strong interdependence of financial institutions across the EU and hence an interest that the banks' balance sheet situation improves in all countries. On the other hand, there is a conflict of interest between the 'real' and 'financial' sectors within a country as – in the situation where the costs of the debt write-off is borne by the tax payers of the respective countries – the real sectors of each country do not welcome a debt write-off, at least in the short run.[20]

---

[20] In the short term, bank rescue operations within a country by the government add to the fiscal constraint and hence induce additional austerity pressures in the South. In the longer run, the improved balance sheets of the banks should support the operation of the credit system, thus making it beneficial to both sectors.

However, as we have argued, the crisis makes apparent the need to obey the transversality condition (i.e. bringing the debt situation back on a sustainable path). A recognition of this 'systemic interest' means a shift in sectoral interest constellations that would make the matrix look like Matrix 4 below:

Matrix 4. *Conflict/Complementarity Matrix in the case where debt write-off in the South is borne by the tax-payers of the domestic economy – the case to ensure viability of the domestic financial system.*

		Catching-Up	
		Real	Financial
Advanced	Real	(~ , +)	(~ , +)
	Financial	(+, +)	(+, +)

Note: ~ means 'indifference'

Which systemic interest considerations could make the real sector of the catching-up economy approve of debt write-off? At issue in a crisis situation is the survivability of the banking system with its implications for credit provision to businesses (especially SMEs) and to households for facilitating purchases of goods and services. In an environment in which the existence of the financial system as the provider of essential services for the economy as a whole (and thus the 'real sector') is threatened, the cost-benefit calculations of the real sector – on the one hand having to bear the costs of bank bail-out, on the other hand being vitally dependent on 'liquidity' and credit provision in its operation – might lead to a switch from perceiving a net cost of a bail-out to a net benefit. Such a situation is depicted in Matrix 4 (See change of sign in bottom-left corner entry). Hence, a crisis situation might lead to a convergence of interests between the two sectors. It is also interesting that in this case, the two types of constraints – the macroeconomic constraint to restore debt sustainability and the inter-sectoral interdependence constraint of the financial sector providing essential services to the real sector – are involved to lead to a recognition of a 'systemic interest'.

Let us now discuss the situation in which bank debt write-off involves other countries' holders of debt titles. In this case, the debt write-off of private sector debt in one country might directly negatively affect the financial interests in the other country – and then also further negatively affect the 'real' sector in the other countries (as their tax payers might have to step in). Hence in this situation the conflictual situation does move to the international arena, and we get the following matrix:

Matrix 5. *Conflict/Complementarity Matrix in the case where debt write-off in the South is borne by the banks (and the tax payers) in the advanced (Northern) economy.*

		Catching-Up	
		Real	Financial
Advanced	Real	(+ or -, +)	(+ or -, +)
	Financial	(-, +)	(-, +)

When the costs of the debt write-off are borne by the debt holders of other countries, there will be a congruence of interests in the South in that a debt write-off is good both for the real and the financial sectors within the country but not necessarily welcomed by the financial sector in the other country. Whether it is welcomed by the real sector in the other country depends on the (balance-sheet) situation of the financial sector there: if it is relatively strong, then the real sector in the other country will be able to reap a net benefit from the debt write-off, because export prospects to the previously debt-constrained Southern economy will improve. On the other hand, if the banking system in the advanced economy is in a bad state, then the tax payers in that country might have to step in to rescue the banks over there. This is indicated by the (+ or −) signs in the entries of Matrix 5, and it also serves as an explanation of the drawn-out process of the 'troika' in deciding on the debt write-off in the case of the Greek banks. In this case the long waiting period served to allow the banks in the French and German economies to recover somewhat from the initial impact of the financial crisis so that an additional shock from a debt write-off in Greece would not require any rescue operations by the French and German governments of their own banks.

However, the situation with regard to debt write-off in this case involves not only the consideration of private sector interests in the two economies but also the interests of the tax-payers in these economies. We thus deal with a more complicated interest constellation (and thus bargaining situation) than is depicted in Matrices 4 and 5: on the one hand, there is the direct effect of a debt write-off in the South affecting the financial and real sectors in the North as depicted in Matrix 5. On the other hand, there is an involvement of the tax-payers' interest in the North, as the interdependence of financial sectors in the two economies (the 'contagion fear') recedes into the background when private holders of 'bad debt' get substituted by public holding of bad debt. This is exactly what happened in the second phase of the Greek crisis.

The government in the North is thus likely to make its own cost-benefit calculation on whether the tax burden on its own population, which a debt write-off in the South would involve, is outweighed by other considerations of interdependencies. On the one hand, as the fear of financial contagion across the banking sectors recedes into the background, the Northern government shifts its sectoral concerns from its financial sector to the impact a debt-trap situation in the South might have on the real sector of its economy (its export possibilities). On the other hand, there are also other, more far-reaching 'systemic concerns' that may drive the Northern government's behaviour in its relation to the South, which concern the long-term viability of the EMU framework as a whole.

We can thus see, in the case of the debt write-off, that the political economy setting involves not only sectoral interests but also government actions. Such actions may themselves be driven by (at times changing) weights of sectoral interests, but also reflect the governments' own evaluation of particular or systemic (domestic or Eurozone) interests.

11.6 Within-Sector Heterogeneity and the Dynamics of Sectoral Interest Formation

In this section we discuss the implications of 'within-sector heterogeneity' and also deal in more detail with the tax-payers versus private-sector interests issue. Whilst we cannot discuss these issues comprehensively here, we need to consider such issues in order to obtain a full picture of the formation of 'sectoral interests' and the behaviour of governments as representing sectoral interests but also acting on behalf of 'national systemic interests'. Furthermore, both governments and sectoral interests situate themselves in an international arena which may have both cooperative and non-cooperative bargaining features. The 'systemic interest' also goes beyond the national level and has a EU/EMU/European or global dimension.

Let us start by considering 'within-sector heterogeneity'. How does within-sector heterogeneity, for example, that the tradable sector is composed of companies which are more domestic market–oriented and thus compete with imports and other companies which are highly export-oriented, affect our analysis? We shall see that this can have far-reaching consequences for the formation of the 'sector's interest'. Furthermore, in the course of changing circumstances, such as the move from a pre-crisis to a crisis situation or from a regime with low levels of international integration to one with a high level of international integration, 'sector interests' which reflect within-sector composition will change as well.

Because of the above-described heterogeneity, the extent to which different companies within the same 'sector' will be affected by national versus international inter-sectoral relationships and by specific macro-economic constraints will differ. As the weights and relevance of these constraints are changing – for example, affected by a general slowdown of international trade or an international financial crisis – firms within that sector will be differently affected, and this differentiated impact will feed into the formation of 'sector interests', at times leading to a dramatic shift in orientation.

Let us give some concrete examples in the context of our previous analysis. Tradable sectors are characterised by both import-competing and export activities. Allowing for a distribution of firms along an axis according to whether they are more domestic market– or more export-oriented, we can say that the import-competing firms differ from mostly export-market oriented firms in that the former are interested in the level of domestic demand for their output, while the latter are largely unaffected by it. In contrast, both sets of companies have an interest in 'price competitiveness', and hence would be interested in real exchange rate devaluation. However, the domestic market–oriented, import-competing firms also have to consider in which way real exchange rate devaluation is achieved. For example, a fall in wage incomes – either through a fall in wage rates or an employment shake-out – would improve productivity levels, but would also affect the levels of domestic demand, which is of particular concern to domestic market–oriented companies.

Let us now analyse the impact of a regime change from pre-crisis to crisis, on the composition of the tradable sector and hence on the formation of 'sector interest': an unfolding economic crisis does lead to a depressed domestic economy, and hence there could be more pressure towards real exchange rate depreciation. This could lead to 'beggar-thy-neighbour' policies in the form of competitive (real) devaluations, that is, everybody trying to get a bigger slice of a shrinking pie. To turn this into a positive sum situation, awareness and 'coordination devices' have to be employed to follow 'systemic interest' at the Eurozone level and coordinate the relative expansion of domestic markets with surplus countries taking a lead. This push towards coordinated action would coincide with the interests of the 'Northern' export-oriented firms which are interested to overcome the growth blockages in the 'Southern' economies, part of which would be to accept a relative (real) depreciation in the South.

Domestic market–oriented firms in the North, in contrast, would be the drivers towards domestic market expansion in the North (and less interested in real exchange rate appreciation as this would reduce their competitiveness in the domestic market vis-à-vis imports). We can thus see that the different components of a tradable sector would articulate their interests differently during the crisis period.[21]

The 'interest formation' of a sector thus depends at any point of time on the composition in that sector (e.g. weights of predominantly import-competing firms versus export-oriented firms). However, there is also another relevant issue here: the degree to which the particular interests of constituent groups within a sector get 'political voice'. On the one hand, this will depend on the resources such groups have at their disposal and their willingness to use them for that purpose. On the other hand, it will also depend on the extent to which the issues with which they are mostly concerned might be picked up by other interest groups in other sectors. Thus there could be cross-sectoral alliances of similarly interested component groups in other sectors. Furthermore, there will be differences in the extent to which such interests would be supported by the 'general public'.

---

[21] Similarly, we could analyse how the heterogeneity of the financial industry in a country (e.g. between those that are mainly operating in the domestic market and those which are heavily involved in international operations) articulate different interests with respect to debt write-off in a period of crisis.

For example, there might be two groups of banks within a 'Northern' financial industry: one group has become heavily exposed in having issued credit to a Southern economy, whilst the other has been mainly involved in credit operations towards Northern domestic borrowers. In 'normal times' these two groups of banks will articulate their respective interests on a range of issues: on the one hand, on policies which support credit activity on the domestic market, such as public subsidies to SMEs; on the other hand, on policies which support credit activity abroad, such as support for credit-finance of exporting firms including those which are strongly involved in such activities in 'Southern' economies. None of their activities, however, touches 'systemic interest' in the North in 'normal times'. The situation can, however, change dramatically in a serious 'Southern debt crisis'. In such a situation, the financial groups heavily involved in having issued large volumes of credit in the South would get worried about a possible jump in non-performing loans and, if this reaches a certain level, the worsening position of these banks might reach 'systemic risk' levels. In this situation, the position of the financial industry as a whole (at national or Eurozone levels) might be at risk, and it is at this point that the particular interest of this segment of the banking industry can acquire systemic importance.

This example shows that, in changing circumstances, what was a particular interest of one segment of an industry starts to dominate the 'sector interest' as a whole and, in a further sequence, touches upon 'systemic interest' leading to that sector position getting a stronger, possibly decisive 'public voice' at the national or international level. This process, by which the interests of a sector's segment obtain a prominent position in the formation of sector interest and, in consequence, affect policy interventions (at the national or EU levels), played an important role in the recent Eurozone crisis. This can furthermore show up in cross-country alliances of similarly affected segments of either the same (e.g. German and French banks) or other industries (such as exporting firms which have been supplying Southern customers which – in the crisis situation – become cut off from access to any further credit).

A final issue that we want to address in this section refers to multi-membership of individual actors in different sectoral classifications. We saw in Sections 11.4 and 11.5 that external imbalances and foreign debt positions are deeply connected, yet the cleavages they generate are distinct but overlapping, in that individual actors in general do not belong just to single sector classifications, but rather to a number of such classifications – for example, firms might be 'real' and in the 'tradable sector' or 'financial' and in the 'tradable' sector. Hence we have to deal with the *multi-classification membership of individual actors*.

Does this multi-sector/multi-classification membership of individual actors lead to better or worse outcomes in terms of crisis resolution dynamics of the European Union? One hypothesis could be that such multi-classification memberships leads to an alleviation of conflict situations (see, e.g., Lipset and Rokkan, 1967; Hirschman, 1968; Rae and Taylor, 1970; Rogowski, 1987) because (1) individual actors do not invest all their 'interest capital' into the membership in a single sector, but participate in a number of sectors. Interest capital thus gets diversified. On the other hand – and this could be hypothesis (2) – this interest capital diversification also leads to a less clear-cut articulation of interests (which also gets reflected in their organisational representation) and thus might make bargaining structures less clear-cut. This could have drawbacks in arriving at a bargaining solution and the enforcement of such a bargaining solution.

The two hypotheses may well be verified at the same time, and lead to situations where there are no sharp, dichotomous conflicts, yet there is the risk of a stalemate and prolonged periods of "muddling through".

11.7 Overlapping Sectoral Conflicts and the Political Economy of the Eurozone

We now move further in the discussion of crisis resolution and address more widely the question of 'forces of cohesion' and 'forces of disintegration' in the European Union.

A key issue in this respect is whether a crisis situation generates a tendency towards a *'nationalist bias'* through a re-positioning of sectoral interests and of interests within each sector. A crisis could, of course, also generate the opposite, that is, an *'international integrationist bias'* of sectoral interests. We shall analyse reasons for both of these biases to occur in pre-crisis and crisis situations (or even in different phases as the crisis evolves).

In general terms, when individual actors attempt to position themselves in terms of interest constellations, we have to consider the uncertainty context regarding the 'pay-off matrix', the time discount factors used by the different agents and the knowledge about the other players' coherence of (domestic) interest constellations. Furthermore, in the European context, we are in a situation of many players with very complicated coalition politics. This uncertainty issue might lead to a bias towards a more nationalist stance, for example because the knowledge about the own country's sectoral interests and their interdependencies is higher than that of the other players. Moreover, the firmer institutional anchorage of national bargaining and coordination mechanisms might make convergence upon 'systemic interest' at the national level more likely than at the European or global level. In addition, in a multi-player bargaining situation at the European level, a country's weight will be greater if national coordination or bundling of interests takes place prior to the international bargaining.

The nationalist bias might be reinforced by the additional process that unfolds in the course of the crisis, namely the shift from issues of conflict and congruence of private-sector interests to the involvement of government interest related to the burden on the tax-payers. This involves distinct patterns of political representation of interests, electoral politics, etc. It is thus no longer just an issue of checking 'viability of an interdependent economic system', but requires the recognition of the additional dimension of political and electoral dynamics. Furthermore, it is likely that for some issues, the electoral dimension could end up having much more weight than the complex balance of interests across different sectoral cleavages.[22]

The nationalist bias might be particularly relevant because of the current stage of EU integration, in which the electoral dimension is still predominantly a national one. In fact, the intermediate (i.e. incomplete) level of (political and institutional) integration has a number of implications (1) for policy formation at the national and the EU/EMU levels and (2) for the growth and development trajectories which the EU and parts thereof are likely to move along. We shall turn to these issues now within the context of our 'sector interest'– based analytical framework.

---

[22] This is more likely to be the case in, e.g. debt write-offs, as these involve discrete interventions in stock adjustments as compared to the external imbalances issue where policy interventions (in the form of wage policies, industrial policies, etc.) only have a gradual impact.

We shall also attempt to show that changes or reforms in some of the aspects of the EU/EMU policy framework might in turn affect sectoral interest constellations and thus growth and development trajectories.[23]

The Eurozone displays the typical persistent asymmetries that are a pervasive characteristic of monetary unions (e.g. structural external imbalances), but it does not have the necessary mechanism to deal with them (e.g. debt pooling, fiscal centralization, banking union). Hence, it can be conjectured that the coupling of the structure of a highly integrated European economy and the institutional structure of the EU/Eurozone is affecting the viability conditions of the European economy, forcing it upon a lower than 'potential growth' trajectory. Let us see why.

Monetary unions tend to display *persistent asymmetries*, three of which are *external imbalances, disproportional (i.e. uneven) growth across countries and regions*, and *uneven inflation rates* across an otherwise integrated economic region. Why do such persistent asymmetries arise and why do they constitute a special problem for monetary unions, especially an incompletely developed one such as the European Monetary Union?

In a nutshell, whilst asymmetries are typical of any set of integrated economies, a monetary union puts in place an institutional setup in which the resolution of problems requires coordinating interests at different levels (e.g. sectoral, regional, national). These are often conflicting, and even when they converge upon a systemic interest in conflict resolution, some actors might have a much more urgent need than others in such a resolution. Let us explore this conjecture in more detail.

In principle, the asymmetries mentioned in the preceding paragraph are 'natural' across any set of economically integrated economies: there is no a priori reason why countries or regions should have balanced production and expenditure patterns which would not give rise to external imbalances, or why they should all grow at the same growth rates (given that the sources of growth – labour force and its utilisation, capital accumulation and technical progress – might develop quite

---

[23] As we have suggested at various points in this essay, 'viability' conditions can be established in quite diverse 'equilibria', some of them leading to long-term stagnation others allowing sustainable growth. These viability conditions are furthermore conditioned on the policy and (international) institutional frameworks in place.

unevenly across countries or regions). Finally, given that there are significant segments of goods and services sold in markets which are either not at all or only partly tradable or have significant transport, transactions and information costs attached to them, the arbitrage processes enforcing similar price levels and thus inflation rates can only work partially. Hence there is room for differential inflation rates, reflecting different cost-push, demand-pull and expectations-driven processes even in otherwise highly integrated economies.

We would expect such 'asymmetries' to occur across any set of integrated economies and regions. But what is special about monetary unions, and why do we emphasise the problem of 'persistence' of such asymmetries? Here we come to the core of the problem the Eurozone faces: in any other set of integrated economies or regions, there are reaction mechanisms to the development of such asymmetries, which do not threaten the institutional set-up as the ones on which a monetary union is built.

External imbalances get reflected in the build-up of external credit and debt positions, and if financial markets consider such positions at any time unsustainable or unprofitable, this will induce a change in credit behaviour, mechanisms of de-leveraging, withdrawal of banks from certain regions, etc. But no cross-country institutional framework is involved in such developments. Similarly, if there are uneven growth processes which lead to differential real income developments, possible employment consequences emanate from these, as well as impacts on the development of social security supports for the population. Again this will not lead to political-institutional consequences at a cross-country level, but rather to certain responses by private actors such as migration, relocations of firms, etc. Finally, differential inflation rates, if these threaten external imbalances by making some countries and regions uncompetitive and others more competitive, will in turn lead to mobility decisions of private actors, wage responses to induced labour market impacts and adjustments in the willingness to lend across regions. Furthermore, if countries do not form a currency union, different inflation rates will lead to exchange rate responses or a switch from one exchange rate regime to another (e.g. from pegged to floating).

As already stated, 'asymmetries' occur across any set of integrated economies and regions. However, monetary unions face specific problems. In fact, they build a rather complex cross-country institutional and policy framework which goes well beyond the market integration processes described above. It is this cross-country institutional and policy framework that comes under strain once 'persistent asymmetries' develop across countries and regions within a monetary union.

Let us examine these strains with our model of sectoral interests. Sectoral interests are some of the main movers behind integration processes in general and monetary integration specifically. Single Market integration and then monetary integration was very much in the interest of internationally operating companies to allow easier access to a widening market, reduce transaction costs, eliminate exchange rate risks and allow the much freer expansion of financial activities across the European economy (from which also non-Eurozone financial institutions, such as those located in the City of London, benefitted). As companies operating in different sectors and countries are differently affected by such acts of integration (reducing, on the one hand, their market power in the home market and losing discriminatory access to domestic policy makers, but gaining freer access to other countries' markets, on the other hand) the political economy behind such integration steps is complex. It will reflect both within-sector heterogeneity (which – as we argued earlier – are constitutive for the formation of 'sector interests') as well as the differentiation of such interests across sectors and countries.

The articulation of sector interests and their influence on country-specific political processes are a crucial source of the specific institutional structure and policy framework associated with the EMU. It is interesting for our purposes to analyse how these policy frameworks are holding up to the strains of 'persistent asymmetries' and the impact of the recent financial crisis, and how sectoral interests react and get reformulated as a result. In other words, we want to understand how the reactions of sectoral interests to crises, that is, when it becomes evident that some of the 'asymmetries' are no longer viable to persist in the same way, can act as 'forces of cohesion' or as 'forces of disintegration' of the Eurozone.

Let us start with 'external imbalances'. In Section 11.5 we discussed the formation of 'sector interests' in the context of the emergence of external imbalances and also considered a possible switch of such interests when 'external imbalances' are deemed to be unsustainable. This could, for example, be the result of a change in the external environment in the form of asymmetric shocks strongly affecting a particular country's export prospects or a financial markets crisis that might affect the perception of sustainability of external imbalances of particular members in a Monetary Union (MU[24]). We also discussed that such realignment of 'sector interests' across interdependent economies might lead to sector interests taking either a more 'nationalist' or a more 'integrationist' view of 'systemic interest'. The bias towards a 'nationalist view' can result from higher coordination costs of cross-country constellations supporting an integrationist approach towards systemic interest as compared to the well-tested ground of national political processes to come to a realignment of sector interests in view of national viability issues. *There is thus rivalry between the conceptions of 'viability' or 'sustainability' of development trajectories at the national and the cross-country levels.*

An additional asymmetry might derive from the fact that some countries might be more dependent on the resolution of their specific country-level 'viability' problem (e.g. unsustainable external imbalances) by also tackling cross-country coordination aimed at achieving a high-growth scenario for the MU as a whole. Other countries, in contrast, might well be able to pursue a high-growth trajectory for their country without resolving coordination issues for the MU as a whole. This cleavage might coincide with whether the country is a structural 'surplus' or a 'deficit' country; it would also depend on other issues, such as the degree of openness of the country, the degree of its inter-connections with other MU countries as against connections with economies outside the MU, and so forth.

To be more concrete: a country of the EU's 'Southern periphery' (e.g. Greece, Portugal, Bulgaria), which is also a 'structural deficit' country, might be heavily dependent on export markets in the EU, while a set of 'Northern' EU member countries (Germany, Netherlands) might have strong trade exposure outside the EU. In this case the Southern EU member countries have a stronger interest (once domestic sectoral interests have converged to a joint position with regard to moving their own economy towards a viable trajectory) in

---

[24] We speak here more generally of MUs instead of EMUs, as these features pertain to monetary unions in general, where the disappearance of exchange rate risks and the externality effects of central monetary institutions gives a certain degree of credibility to weaker member states which their own monetary authorities would not possess.

a cross-country resolution of the external imbalances problem in the EU as a whole (e.g. through a differentiated reflationary process or coordinated wage agreements which lead to a 'real devaluation' of the Southern member countries relative to the Northern ones) than would the Northern EU member countries. The latter might lose out in their relationships with non-EU economies (e.g. relative loss of competitiveness) if they agreed to an EU-coordinated solution, and this loss might – from their perspective, and particularly from the perspective of the tradable sector in these economies – be greater than the gain they make from resolving the 'EU systemic viability' problem. Hence a coordinated agreement – Northern and Southern economies – towards the viability of a higher growth trajectory of the EU as a whole might not come about.

A similar type of analysis can be conducted with respect to the issue discussed in Section 11.6, that is, the issue of debt relief for (unsustainably) indebted countries in the EU South. In fact, debtor countries (and the dysfunctional banking sectors in particular) would be much more dependent on a cross-country agreement on debt relief than are creditor countries. Nonetheless, creditor countries also can gain from a well-executed programme of debt relief. In fact, such a programme would help not only the banks with a high share of non-performing loans on their balance sheets but also a wider range of sectors that suffer from slow or negative growth in export markets that are important to them. But we can see that (1) within-sector heterogeneity plays a role, as banks in the creditor countries are differentially exposed to the problem countries and (2) the range of sectors affected by the stagnation or contraction effect of the non-viable debt situation in the 'Southern economies' might not be that wide, so that the impact might not be an existential threat to many, if not all, of them. This is very different in the debtor country, where the debt crisis has led to the 'non-viability' of a continued growth trajectory and a collapse of certain sectors with significant multiplier effects. We can thus see that also in a situation in which the resolution of a debt crisis in a set of 'Southern economies' might require cross-country agreements, such agreements might be hindered by the issues of *asymmetry of urgency of 'Northern' versus 'Southern' interests at sectoral and national levels*, as well as the more diffused nature of forming 'sector interests' in the Northern countries.

Finally, we come to another instance of 'asymmetry' linked to conducting a joint monetary policy when there are uneven pressures with regard to inflationary processes in the Eurozone. A number of observers (see, e.g., Mongelli and Wyplosz, 2009) have remarked that the monetary policy rule of the ECB reflects the weight of the German and other 'Northern' economies over-proportionately (i.e. beyond their weights in the Eurozone's GDP). To analyse the reasons for this, we come back to the issue of resolving external imbalances in the Eurozone through real depreciations (in the deficit countries) and appreciations (in the surplus countries). It is well-known that due to nominal wage rigidities, it is much easier to achieve a real exchange rate adjustment in a chronic 'deficit country' in the context of an overall positive inflation rate, as in this case real depreciation can be achieved without cutting nominal wage rates. In such a situation a monetary policy rule, which reflects more strongly 'Northern' rather than 'Southern' inflation rates, results in the ECB not pursuing a policy that would facilitate real exchange rate adjustment of 'Southern economies'. Hence their adjustment is likely to become much more drawn out, and the achieved growth trajectory of these economies as well as the EU as whole might be much lower than the one which could be achieved if these asymmetries were not reflected in the conduct of monetary policy at the Eurozone level.

The foregoing analysis suggests that the cross-country institutional and policy frameworks of monetary unions (MUs) impose crisis resolution mechanisms that require coordinating different interests. This may be a crucial component of why 'asymmetries' (such as external imbalances) persist for longer amongst member countries than these would without MU. This also means that the 'stocks' resulting from such asymmetries (e.g. debt positions) can reach very high levels within an MU – as shown by the levels of private-sector debt to GDP ratios in Southern Eurozone member countries before the crisis (see Figure 11.2). Consequently, the strain caused by such stocks as evidence of 'persistent asymmetries' can also be higher in a MU than in a set of countries linked through pure market integration. And this might explain a paradoxical situation: whilst a monetary union could be associated with a higher growth path, a union with an incomplete state of integration might actually be forcing a lower growth path on the union as a whole, or at least on some of its members, as compared to a weaker system of coordination without monetary union.

11.8 Conclusions

In this chapter we have put forward a new way to understand the major unresolved problems of the European Economic and Monetary Union (EMU). In particular, we have studied conflicts between tradable and non-tradable sectors for what concerns external imbalances, and between financial and real sectors with respect to foreign debt positions. We have shown that this lens suggests a reading of the political economy of the Eurozone that cuts across, complements and often questions received dichotomies typical of country-level analysis, such as North versus South.

We started by reconstructing the particular interest that each sector has for each policy issue at stake, and how the crisis has made systemic interest apparent by highlighting interdependencies across sectors and macroeconomic constraints that affect all sectors within each country and within the Eurozone.

We then showed that, in the case of potential debt write-offs, the aforementioned analysis of sectoral interests needs to be complemented by a different dimension, which has to do with government's interest to consider the tax burden on its national economy. To further refine the analysis, we considered the heterogeneity of firms within sectors, showing how the crisis can change their interests, thus reconfiguring the positioning of the sector as a whole within the political economy arena.

The result of the overlap of conflicting interests within sectors and across sectors and countries is likely to be two-fold. On the one hand, coalitions of interests are unlikely to be the same across all policy issues, and this should prevent over-polarization of conflict. On the other hand, overlaps might make the payoffs of political action less clear, with the result that interest groups might invest less in having their stances represented. The combination of these effects can explain the policy stalemates that often characterize decision-making in the EU, and it suggests that extended periods of "muddling through" may be inherent in the interface between the political economy of the EU and its institutional setup.

The difficulty of coordinating interests at multiple levels may also be at the root of the interplay between forces of integration and disintegration in the EMU. In fact, the last part of the chapter reconstructed how sectoral and country-level interests are at play within the institutional set-up of a monetary union, and how this can lead to stances in favour of further integration or disintegration. We have suggested that a monetary union potentially makes possible a higher-growth trajectory than 'mere' trade integration does, but its institutional setup requires a complex coordination of interests at multiple levels. The EMU is currently in what could be defined an 'intermediate level of integration', which lacks elements such as debt pooling, fiscal centralization and a full-fledged banking union. Coordinating interests in such an institutional setup is particularly difficult, and this is arguably leading to a paradoxical result: a monetary union at an intermediate level of integration could be imposing (especially for some economies) a growth trajectory that is not only lower than that of a fully integrated union but even lower than that of simple trade integration outside a monetary union. This analysis suggests the need to open the discussion – in academic analysis, policy circles and the public debate at large – on possible forms of integration that avoid this paradoxical result but are compatible with the complex configurations of sectoral and systemic interests discussed in this chapter.

References

Baranzini, M. and Scazzieri, R. (1990) 'Economic Structure: Analytical Perspectives', in M. Baranzini and R. Scazzieri (eds), *The Economic Theory of Structure and Change*, Cambridge: Cambridge University Press, pp. 227–333.

Belke, A. and Dreger, C. (2013) 'Current Account Imbalances in the Euro area: Does Catching Up Explain the Development?', *Review of International Economics*, 21 (1, February), pp. 6–17.

Candela, G. (1975) 'Il Modello Economico di François Quesnay', *Giornale degli Economisti ed Annali di Economia*, 34, pp. 69–94.

Cardinale, I. (2012). 'The Political Economy of Circular Interdependencies and Vertical Integration: Opening the Black Box of "National Interest"'. SSRN Scholarly Paper ID 2357981. Rochester, NY: Social Science Research Network. http://papers.ssrn.com/abstract=2357981.

Cardinale, I. (2015) 'Towards a Structural Political Economy of Resources', in M. Baranzini et al. (eds), *Resources, Production and Structural Dynamics*, Cambridge: Cambridge University Press, pp. 198–210.

Cardinale, I. and Coffman, D. (2014) 'Economic Interdependencies and Political Conflict: The Political Economy of Taxation in Eeighteenth-Century Britain', *Economia Politica. Journal of Analytical and Institutional Economics*, 31(3), pp. 277–300.

Coen, D. (2007) 'Empirical and Theoretical Studies in EU Lobbying', *Journal of European Public Policy*, 14(3), pp. 333–45.

Coen, D. (2009) *Lobbying the European Union: Institutions, Actors and Policy*, Oxford: Oxford University Press.

Coffman, D. (2013) *Excise Taxation and the Origins of Public Debt*. Basingstoke: Palgrave Macmillan.

Coser, L. (1956) *The Functions of Social Conflict*, London: Routledge and Kegan Paul Ltd.

Darvas, Z. (2012) 'Intra-Euro Rebalancing Is Inevitable, but Insufficient', *Bruegel Policy Contribution* Issue 2012/15, August.

Davenant, C. (1698) *Discourses on the publick revenues, and on the trade of England: in two parts, viz. I. Of the use of political arithmetick, in all considerations about the revenues and trade. II. On credit, and the means and methods by which it may be restored. III. On the management of the King's revenues. IV. Whither to farm the revenues, may not, in this juncture, be most for the publick service? V. On the public debts and engagements*, London: printed for J. Knapton.

De Grauwe, P. (2012) 'In Search of Symmetry in the Eurozone', CEPS Policy Brief, No. 268 (May).

European Commission (2012), 'Current Account Surpluses in the EU', European Commission DG ECFIN, *European Economy 9/2012*.

Giavazzi, F. and Spaventa, L. (2010) 'Why the Current Account May Matter in a Monetary Union: Lessons from the Financial Crisis in the Euro Area', *CEPR Discussion Papers* No. 8008.

Gros, D. amd Giovannini, A. (2014) 'The "Relative" Importance of EMU Macroeconomic Imbalances in the Macroeconomic Imbalance Procedure'; Instituto Affari Internazionali (IAI).

Hagemann, H., Landesmann, M.A. and Scazzieri, R. (eds.) (2003) *The Economics of Structural Change*. Cheltenham, UK; Northhampton, MA: Edward Elgar.

Hirschman, A. (1968) 'The Political Economy of Import-Substituting Industrialization in Latin America', *The Quarterly Journal of Economics*, 82, (1, February), pp. 1–32.

Hishiyama, I. (1960) 'The Tableau Economique of Quesnay', *Kyoto University Economic Review*, 30 (1), pp. 1–46.

Jaumotte, F. and Sodsriwiboon, P. (2010) 'Current Account Imbalances in the Southern Euro Area', *IMF Working Paper* WP/10/139, June.

King, G. (1936) Two Tracts by Gregory King (a) Natural and Political Observations and Conclusions upon the State and Condition of England *[1696]*. (b) Of the Naval Trade of England Ao. 1688 and the National Profit then arising thereby [1697], edited with an introduction by G. E. Barnett, Baltimore: Johns Hopkins University Press.

Landesmann, M. A. (2015a), 'Structural Dynamics of Europe's Periphery – Which Are the Main Issues?', *Journal of Economic Policy Reform*, Special Issue, 2015.

Landesmann, M. (2015b) 'The New North-South Divide in Europe: Can the European Convergence Model Be Resuscitated?', in J. Fagerberg, S. Laestadius and B. R. Martin (eds), *The Triple Challenge for Europe: Economic Development, Climate Change, and Governance*, Oxford: Oxford University Press, pp. 60–87.

Landesmann, M. A. and Hanzl, D. (2016) 'Correcting External Imbalances in the European Economy', in M. Belka, E. Nowotny, P. Samecki and D. Ritzberger-Grünwald (eds), *Boosting European Competitiveness*, Cheltenham: Edward Elgar Publishing, pp. 14–36.

Landesmann, M. A, and Scazzieri. R. (eds) (1996) *Production and Economic Dynamics*, Cambridge and New York: Cambridge University Press.

Landesmann, M. A. and Stehrer, R. (2001) 'Convergence Patterns and Switchovers in Comparative Advantage', *Structural Change and Economic Dynamics*, 12 (4, December), pp. 399–423.

Landesmann, M. A. and Stehrer, R. (2006) 'Modelling International Economic Integration: Patterns of Catching-Up and Foreign Direct Investment', *Economia Politica: Journal of Analytical and Institutional Economics*, 23, (3), pp. 335–62.

Leontief, W. W. (1941) *The Structure of the American Economy, 1919–1929*, Cambridge, MA: Harvard University Press.

Lipset, S. M. and Rokkan, S. (1967) *Party Systems and Voter Alignments: Cross-National Perspectives*, New York: The Free Press; London, Collier-Macmillan.

McCombie, J. S. L. and Thirlwall, A. P. (2004) *Essays on Balance of Payments Constrained Growth: Theory and Evidence*, London: Routledge.

Mongelli, F. P. and Wyplosz, C. (2009) 'The Euro at Ten: Unfulfilled Threats and Unexpected Challenges', in B. Mackowiak, F. P. Mongelli, G. Noblet and F. Smets (eds), *The Euro at Ten: Lessons and Challenges*, Frankfurt Am Main, European Central Bank, pp. 24–57.

Pasinetti, L. L. (1973) 'The Notion of Vertical Integration in Economic Theory', *Metroeconomica*, 25 (1), pp. 1–29; reprinted in L. L. Pasinetti (ed.), *Essays on the Theory of Joint Production*, London: Macmillan; New York: Columbia University Press, 1980, pp. 16–43.

Pasinetti, L. L. (1981) *Structural Change and Economic Growth: A Theoretical Essay on the Dynamics of the Wealth of Nations*, Cambridge and New York: Cambridge University Press.

Pasinetti, L. L. (1993) *Structural Economic Dynamics: A Theory of the Economic Consequences of Human Learning*, Cambridge and New York: Cambridge University Press.

Pasinetti, L. L. (2009) 'Il Tableau Économique e le economie moderne', in G. de Vivo (ed), *Il Tableau Économique di François Quesnay*, Milano, Fondazione Raffaele Mattioli, pp. 109–24.

Petty, W. (1662) *A treatise of taxes and contributions: shewing the nature and measures of crown-lands, assessements, customs, poll-moneys . . .; with several intersperst discourses and digressions concerning warres, the church, universities, rents & purchases . . .: the same being frequently applied to the present state and affairs of Ireland*, London: printed for N. Brooke.

Phillips, A. (1955) 'The Tableau Économique as a Simple Leontief Model', *The Quarterly Journal of Economics*, 69 (1), pp. 137–44.

Quadrio Curzio, A. (1967) *Rendita e distribuzione in un modello economico plurisettoriale*, Milan, Giuffrè.

Quadrio Curzio, A. (1975) *Accumulazione del capitale e rendita*, Bologna, Il Mulino.

Quesnay, F. (1972 [1759]). *Quesnay's Tableau Économique*. Eds. M.. Kuczynski and R. L. Meek. London; New York: Macmillan; A.M. Kelley for the Royal Economic Society and the American Economic Association.

Rae, D. W. and Taylor, M. (1970) *The Analysis of Political Cleavages*, New Haven, CT: Yale University Press.

Rogowski, R. (1987) 'Political Cleavages and Changing Exposure to Trade', *The American Political Science Review*, 81 (4, December), pp. 1121–37.

Setterfield, M. (2011) 'The Remarkable Durability of Thirlwall's Law', *PSL Quarterly Review*, 64 (December), pp. 393–427.

Sraffa, P. (1960). *Production of Commodities by Means of Commodities; Prelude to a Critique of Economic Theory*, Cambridge: Cambridge University Press.

Thirlwall, A. P. (1979) 'The Balance of Payments Constraint as an Explanation of International Growth Rate Differences', *Banca Nazionale del Lavoro Quarterly Review*, 32 (March), p. 45–53.

Truman, D. B. (1962) *The Governmental Process: Political Interests and Public Opinion*. New York: Knopf.

Vaggi, G. (2008) 'Quesnay, François (1694–1774)', in S. N. Durlauf and L. E. Blume (eds), *The New Palgrave Dictionary of Economics*, 2nd ed., Basingstoke: Nature Publishing Group, pp. 816–826.

von Neumann, J. (1945) 'A Model of General Economic Equilibrium', *The Review of Economic Studies*, 13 (1, January 1), pp. 1–9.

12 | *The Impact of the Economic Crisis on European Manufacturing*

MARCO FORTIS

12.1 Introduction

The new European Commission reasserted the strategic target of bringing the manufacturing industry's share of EU's GDP back up to 20 per cent by 2020, from the current share of less than 16 per cent. However, is this target realistic? The risk today is that it will remain a dream unless there is a change of EU's current economic policy and a strong European domestic market is restored. In fact, the real problem of EU's industry is not, as many would think, its external competitiveness, but the dramatic fall in EU's domestic demand from 2009 onwards.

In the euro area (EA) in particular, private consumption, investment and jobs have declined, but not exports. The EA certainly needs reforms and investment in research and innovation to become more competitive worldwide. However, the EU and the EA are already competitive enough on international markets, especially in the manufacturing sector. By contrast, European households and consumers, along with a large part of service sector (wholesale and retail sales distributing manufactured products on domestic markets) are 'losing competitiveness', not the European industrial systems themselves. In the EA excluding Germany, the other three largest countries are losing too much purchasing power and investment because of an excess of austerity.

According to World Bank data, in 2011 the EU was the most important player in manufacturing production worldwide, with value added of 2.4 trillion dollars, followed by China with 2.3 trillion dollars and the United States with 1.9 trillion dollars. Actually, China, which has gained ground in the last three years, and the EU are roughly equivalent: these are the two giants of world manufacturing.

According to the Trade Performance Index compiled by ITC (International Trade Centre) for UNCTAD (the United Nations Conference on Trade and Development) and WTO (World Trade Organization), EU countries are by far the most competitive in world trade. Considering the three most competitive countries in world trade in twelve different manufacturing sectors, in 2013 EU countries occupied twenty-seven of the thirty-six best positions: Germany had the top nine positions, Italy eight, while France, Sweden, Finland, the Netherlands and Belgium had the remaining ten best positions. Two countries alone in the EA, Germany and Italy, together held the seventeen top positions.

According to Eurostat data, in 2013 the EU recorded a trade surplus with the rest of the world[1] for non-food manufactured products of about 392 billion euros. This is the second-best performance worldwide after China, well ahead of Japan and South Korea, while the United States is in deficit.

In 2013, twenty-one EU countries recorded an extra-EU manufacturing trade surplus of 465 billion euros. Germany generated 229 billion euros of this total manufacturing trade surplus, but the other twenty countries with a positive balance generated an additional 236 billion euros: Italy contributed with 70 billion euros, France with 44 billion euros, Sweden and Ireland both with 22 billion euros, Spain and Austria both with 16 billion euros, and so on.

In 2013, only seven EU countries recorded a manufacturing trade deficit totalling a negative balance of 73 billion euros. One of these countries had a large deficit of about 56 billion euros: the Netherlands, which acts as a 'port of Europe' for extra-EU imports of many primary commodities and much merchandise.

From 2002 to 2013, the EU's trade balance for non-food manufactured products increased by 274 billion euros, going from 118 billion euros to the new historic record of 392 billion euros in 2013. About half of this astonishing improvement was generated by Germany, but the rest of the EU also contributed with an additional increase of more than 135 billion euros, mainly from Italy, the United Kingdom, Spain, France, Ireland, Austria, the Czech Republic, Hungary and Poland.

From these data, it is clear that the EU is a strong and competitive global player in the manufacturing sector, with excellent performance on international markets. However, many European manufacturers are suffering a long and deep production crisis, mainly because of the

---

[1] Excluding intra-European Union trade.

dramatic decline of the European domestic market. The same has occurred in the construction sector. From 2008 to 2013, at constant values, investment declined in the EU by about 400 billion euros, two-thirds of which was in construction and another third in machinery and transport equipment. Moreover, private consumption in the EU as a whole, excluding Germany, declined by about 120 billion euros.

The manufacturing industry is a strategic pillar for Europe in the global context. If we want to defend and develop a stronger European manufacturing sector, we need to not only enhance our competitiveness on international markets but also quickly rebuild a strong and dynamic European domestic market.

For these reasons, in the second half of 2014, the Italian Presidency of the European Union Council raised the crucial problem of a more balanced economic policy in the EU, with less austerity and more growth, with a strong commitment to investment and the creation of new jobs.

At the end of 2014, the EU introduced the Juncker Plan for Europe with 300 billion euros of new investment. Now this plan's financing appears to be very weak, and its presumed financial advantage is probably too optimistic. A more ambitious economic and industrial plan is necessary to re-launch the Eurozone's economy. This plan should combine a reform of the excessively rigid Fiscal Compact within the Stability and Growth Pact, with investment in crucial areas (such as infrastructure, energy, technology-science, modernization of industrial machinery, and schools) and national deficit targets supported by the issue of EuroUnionbonds.

12.2. Hara-kiri in the Eurozone's Domestic Market and Intra-EMU Trade

The economic crisis in Europe and particularly in the Eurozone was made worse throughout 2011–14 by economic policies marked by excessive fiscal rigour. This rigour was to some extent necessary in order to correct and stabilize serious imbalances in countries' public finances and balance of payments, but its implementation has been too massive and mechanical. There was lack of adequate solidarity among Europeans, and not enough attention for growth, investment and socio-economic equilibrium. Indeed, economic policies did not pay enough attention to the importance of maintaining the integrity of the EMU market, a historic goal that today is seriously at risk (Fortis and Quadrio Curzio 2013, 2014, 2016).

From 2008 to 2013, the GDP of the EU-28 decreased in volume by 144 billion euros at 2010 prices; the EMU's GDP dropped by 215 billion euros and the EMU's GDP excluding Germany declined by 274 billion. In the latter case, it is as if the economies of three countries like Portugal, Slovakia and Slovenia had disappeared from the European map.

In the same period the United States' GDP – where the global crisis began but where economic policy decisions did not compromise economic growth – increased in volume by 672 billion euros at 2010 prices: it is almost as if two new countries of economic size similar to that of Austria and Poland had been created from scratch. In contrast, in the Eurozone Germany's almost isolated growth from 2008 to 2013, spurred by exceptionally low interest rates and a significant increase in public spending (not allowed in the other EU countries), was still rather modest and equivalent to just slightly more than the creation of a new Lithuania and Latvia.

In the Eurozone minus Germany, 172 billion euros of private consumption and 378 billion euros of investment were lost in six years. This deep recession had a dramatic impact on employment: in the Eurozone, excluding Germany, 7 million jobs were lost from 2008 to 2013. This contrasts with the number of jobs in the United States, which has now surpassed pre-crisis levels.

ECB President Mario Draghi pointed out in the speech 'Unemployment in the Euro area', delivered on 22 August 2014 at the Annual central bank symposium in Jackson Hole, that

the euro area has suffered a large and particularly sustained negative shock to GDP, with serious consequences for employment. ... Whereas the United States experienced a sharp and immediate rise in unemployment in the aftermath of the Great Recession, the euro area has endured two rises in unemployment associated with two sequential recessions. From the start of 2008 to early 2011, the picture in both regions is similar: unemployment rates increase steeply, level off and then begin to gradually fall. This reflects the common sources of the shock: the synchronisation of the financial cycle across advanced economies, the contraction in global trade following the Lehman failure, coupled with a strong correction of asset prices – notably houses – in certain jurisdictions. From 2011 onwards, however, developments in the two regions diverge. Unemployment in the United States continues to fall at more or less the same rate. In the euro area, on the other hand, it begins a second rise that does not peak until April 2013. This divergence reflects a second, euroarea-specific shock emanating from the sovereign debt crisis, which resulted in a six-quarter recession for the euro area economy. Unlike the post-Lehman shock, however, which affected all euro area economies, virtually all of the job losses observed in this second period were concentrated in countries that were adversely affected by government bond market tensions. (Draghi, 2014)

The Eurozone's inability to find a right balance between financial rigour, re-launching growth and reducing unemployment have been stressed by Alberto Quadrio Curzio (2014a, 2014b, 2015a, 2015b), who has also underlined the weakness of the so-called Juncker Plan (Quadrio Curzio 2014c, 2014d).

The European economic crisis, made worse by austerity policies, caused a significant decrease in intra-EU trade and is creating a dangerous regression of the large single market that has emerged with the introduction of the euro. This is also to the disadvantage of such countries as Germany itself, which did not suffer a serious domestic economic crisis.

Europeans are squandering the progress of the euro's single market they had constructed over the years. This in spite of the extraordinary and far-reaching results obtained up until the beginning of the crisis. Indeed, in terms of imports, from 1999 to 2008 the intra-EMU trade of the seventeen countries had increased at current values from 877 billion to 1,545 billion euros, an increase of 668 billion, of which an additional 191 billion euros had benefitted Germany, 61 billion in favour of France, 58 billion to Italy and 47 billion to Spain.

On the other hand, if we compare 2013 data with that of 2008, we can see that intra-Eurozone trade has remained stationary. The contraction of domestic demand in the euro area due to excessive austerity above all affected the foreign trade of the biggest exporting countries, such as Germany and Italy. Compared to 2008, in 2013 the Eurozone's imports from Germany were about 30 billion euros less (as if Germany had lost the equivalent of 60 per cent of its entire current Italian market), whereas the Eurozone's imports from Italy declined by 13 billion euros (more or less as if Italy had lost the equivalent of 80 per cent of its entire Spanish market). (See Table 12.1)

If Europe does not put something more substantial on the table than the current (modest) Juncker Plan to support growth, with adequate

Table 12.1 *Imports of euro area from individual EMU countries: 1999–2008–2013 (in billions of euros)*

	1999	2008	2013	1999–2008 change	2008–2013 change
Austria	32.7	62.3	69.9	29.6	7.6
Belgium	93.1	190.8	191.3	97.6	0.5
Cyprus	0.3	1.5	1.2	1.1	−0.3
Germany	234.4	425.1	395.4	190.7	−29.7
Estonia	1.1	2.5	3.3	1.4	0.9
Spain	62.7	109.2	111.6	46.5	2.4
Finland	14.4	23.2	18.4	8.7	−4.8
France	145.6	206.9	201.5	61.3	−5.4
Greece	4.9	7.7	8.3	2.8	0.7
Ireland	28.6	39.1	38.1	10.5	−1.0
Italy	101.2	158.8	145.6	57.6	−13.2
Luxembourg	4.9	14.8	11.3	9.9	−3.5
Malta	0.7	1.6	1.3	1.0	-0.3
Netherlands	126.5	249.4	288.7	122.9	39.3
Portugal	15.0	22.6	26.2	7.7	3.6
Slovenia	5.1	10.1	12.3	5.0	2.2
Slovakia	5.8	19.7	26.6	13.9	7.0
TOTAL 17 COUNTRIES	*877.0*	*1,545.2*	*1,551.0*	*668.2*	*5.8*

Source: Compiled by the author on data from Eurostat

volumes of investment and domestic demand which would also automatically re-launch intra-EU trade, the European project risks a dramatic setback. First, German policy makers appear not to be sufficiently aware of this. It would be a shame if they became aware of this when it was too late. Too late for all of Europe but also for Germany, which has been living under the illusion that it can do without the EU, instead focusing its exports on Russia, China, the Middle East and South America (i.e. on economies that have been stagnating or growing less in recent years).

12.3 Europe Is More Competitive Than One Would Think, but It Excessively Sacrificed Its Own Domestic Demand

The big conceptual error at the core of the failure of the European economic policy inspired by Germany and the northern European countries is the false myth of lost competitiveness. If Europe is not growing – this is the dogma – it is not because it is masochistically destroying its own domestic market with an exasperated policy of fiscal rigour without growth, as reality has demonstrated in the difficult four-year period of 2011–14. According to the advocates of austerity, low economic growth rather stems mainly from European countries', and particularly southern European countries' inexorable loss of competitiveness on international markets. In their opinion, the erosion of market share of many EU countries' exports, including Italy, should be the most obvious proof of this. This view ignores a fundamental fact: since China emerged on the global scene, all developed countries' market shares have shrunk. However, the EU's market share (including Italy's and Spain's) has declined less than those of the United States, Canada and Japan. This has been particularly true for exports of manufactured goods, since the euro's introduction and up until 2013.

The European Commission and the dogmatic advocates of rigour and competitiveness (but not of growth, the 'forgotten clause' in the implementation of the Stability and Growth Pact) do not seem to be sufficiently aware of three other fundamental aspects. The first is that historically, the dynamics of EU countries' GDP over the past twenty years, for better or worse, has been almost totally determined by domestic demand and not by exports, with the exception of Germany. Therefore, what is important for restarting GDP growth is boosting investment and consumption in the Eurozone, rather than the belief that if Portugal, Spain, Greece, France or Italy export just a little more, the Eurozone will magically return to growth.

The second point is that extra-EU trade should provide the measure of the international competitiveness of European economies. One would then discover that in 2013, twenty-one out of twenty-eight EU countries had a trade surplus in manufactured goods with extra-EU countries. Indeed, in 2013 Germany had a positive trade balance in manufactured goods with extra-EU countries of 229 billion euros, Italy had a surplus of 70 billion, and France had one of 44 billion. Even Spain and Portugal had non-EU trade surpluses in manufactured goods of 16 and 5 billion euros, respectively. Actually, southern Europe's existing trade deficits are intra-EU and almost all with Germany. This is actually the result of the euro's single market, a market associated with a single currently introduced specifically to encourage intra-EU trade. The German economy has benefitted the most from the intro-duction of the euro, moving away from the previous over-valued

Deutsche Mark. Making France or Greece into improbable exporters of Mercedes and BMWs will not solve the problems of the euro and its governance.

The third point is that the European Commission should update its competitiveness indicators. Its rather scholastic tables in the *Macroeconomic Imbalances Procedure* on market share no longer adequately explain whether countries are competitive or not (these data regularly and unjustly downgrade Italy, for example). Nor are these indicators adequate for designing a prudent strategy for European industrial policy, as they constantly refer to essentially qualitative competitiveness indices based on interviews, such as those of the World Economic Forum (WEF) and of the Lausanne-based IMD. These indices run the risk of providing misleading images of the competitiveness of our continent and its nations. But most of all these indices refer mainly to efficiency factors of national economic systems, which in the economies of southern Europe are undoubtedly lacking (thus the importance of reforms), but in some countries, and particularly in Italy, these are nearly always reversed in reality by the competitiveness of companies operating concretely on the markets.

There are actually much more sophisticated, authoritative and realistic competitiveness indicators for industrial systems that the EU should be using. One example is UNIDO's Competitive Industrial Performance Index, which, compared to the WEF, places Germany first, not fifth, Italy ninth, not forty-ninth (!), and France eleventh, not twenty-third (Andreoni 2015; www.unido.org, Statistical Country Briefs).

Most importantly, the International Trade Centre, an agency of UNCTAD's and the WTO, for several years has compiled a detailed range of competitiveness indicators in global trade for 189 countries in 14 sectors: this is the Trade Performance Index (TPI), recently cited also by other authors (Tiffin 2014). Below we provide some of the latest data for 2013 that the readers can find also at http://legacy .intracen.org/appli1/tradecom/TPIC.aspx.

These data contradict any misleading or self-evaluating idea of Europe as being non-competitive on international markets (see also Said 2015). Indeed, in the collection of first, second and third places for international competitiveness in the fourteen sectors considered, the TPI gives thirty out of the total forty-two positions to various EU-28

Table 12.2 *Trade Performance Index 2013, UNCTAD-WTO. The most competitive countries/areas in the world trade*

(Number of top placings in the rankings of 14 different sectors of the world trade)

	Number of first placings	Number of second placings	Number of third placings	Total number of top placings
Countries of EU28	12	11	7	30
of which: Germany	*8*	*1*	*0*	*9*
Italy	*3*	*5*	*0*	*8*
China	0	2	1	3
South Korea	0	0	1	1
Japan	0	0	0	0
United States	0	0	0	0
Other Countries	2	1	5	8

Source: Compiled by the author on data from International Trade Centre.

countries. The EU's major competitors come up with relatively poor results, with China holding just three positions, South Korea one, and the United States and Japan none. Russia and Algeria excel only in minerals, and Malaysia in consumer electronics (Table 12.2).

Germany was the clear leader in 2013 in terms of competitiveness in international trade, winning first place in eight sectors and taking second place in another one. But Italy comes right after the Germans with first places in three sectors (textiles, leather-shoes and clothing) and five second places (basic manufactures including metals and ceramics, non-electronic machinery, electronic components, transport equipment and miscellaneous manufacturing including plastic articles and eye-glasses). Moreover, Italy took seventh place in the important sector of processed food. No other nation in the world aside from Germany can boast such a series of leading positions as Italy can in the International Trade Centre's competitiveness line-up (Table 12.3). In 2013 'Made in Italy's' nine premium sectors exported goods worth 376 billion dollars, creating a significant foreign trade surplus of 152 billion dollars.

Other countries in the EU-28 also place importantly in TPI's line-up. Besides the Netherlands' good performance, which mainly hides

Table 12.3 Position of G-6 countries, China and South Korea in the ranking of competitiveness of the Trade Performance Index UNCTAD-WTO Year 2013

(ranking in each sector worldwide; in bold the placements among the top 10 most competitive countries)

	Germany	Italy	China	South Korea	Japan	France	United Kingdom	United States
Fresh food	27	37	50	79	89	6	42	8
Processed food	1	7	24	71	88	3	42	38
Wood and paper	1	25	36	50	53	28	35	31
Textiles	2	1	3	8	35	19	22	35
Leather products	15	1	2	38	74	16	21	40
Clothing	15	1	2	47	79	12	19	41
Chemicals	1	28	24	9	8	4	21	6
Basic manufactures	1	2	6	4	7	27	32	47
Non-electronic machinery	1	2	5	11	12	10	14	25
Electronic components	1	2	40	17	5	20	26	30
IT & Consumer electronics	12	22	8	7	40	18	15	23
Transport equipment	1	2	18	3	12	14	34	35
Miscellaneous manufacturing	1	2	8	41	9	23	27	25
Minerals	31	46	75	66	85	28	23	21

Source: Compiled by the author on data from International Trade Centre UNCTAD/WTO

re-exports of goods that are simply transiting its ports, Spain's first place in fresh food stands out, Finland's second place in wood and paper, France's third place in processed food, and Sweden's third places in non-electronic machinery and wood and paper.

In sum, this classification shows that the EU and many of its member countries are undeniably competitive on world markets. The case of Italy is especially instructive. Economic crisis in Italy is not due to a loss of competitiveness, but to the decline in domestic consumption and investment. This is clearly shown by the dynamics of industrial turn-over. Indeed, during the first stages of the crisis, that is, the second half of 2008 and the first part of 2009, Italian industry's total turnover declined more or less in line with German and French industry. Then, from the second half of 2009 until the first half of 2011, it recovered similarly to Germany and France. From 2011 on, however, the trend in Italy's turnover completely diverges from that of Germany and France. The latter follow a not particularly brilliant but more or less flat trend, whereas Italy undergoes a devastating drop (Figure 12.1). This extra-ordinary decline is wholly due to the collapse of domestic sales due to austerity (Figure 12.2), since the turnover of Italian industry on non-domestic markets continues with a dynamic that is actually better than Germany's (Figure 12.3).

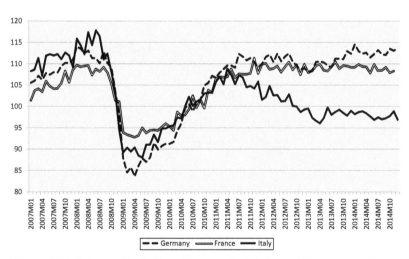

Figure 12.1 Industry Excluding Construction. Index of Turnover – Total (Index 2010 = 100. Seasonally adjusted and adjusted data by working days)
Source: Compiled by the author on data from Eurostat

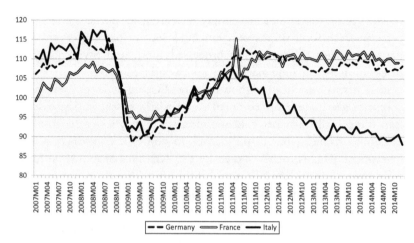

Figure 12.2 Industry Excluding Construction. Index of Turnover – Domestic Market (Index 2010 = 100. Seasonally adjusted and adjusted data by working days)

Source: Compiled by the author on data from Eurostat

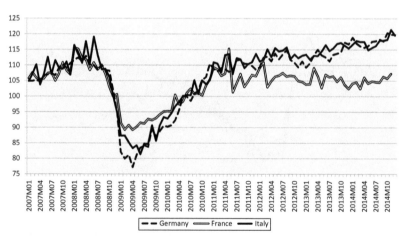

Figure 12.3 Industry Excluding Construction. Index of Turnover – Non-Domestic Market (Index 2010 = 100. Seasonally adjusted and adjusted data by working days)

Source: Compiled by the author on data from Eurostat

The collapse of industrial production due to the austerity measures introduced in 2011–12, in large part disproportionate in view of Italy's actual public finances, was particularly dire in Italy and especially affected manufacturers of consumer goods and goods linked to construction. From 2007 to 2014 Italy's total value added for all economic activity at 2010 prices dropped by 8 per cent. The most severe decline occurred in manufacturing (−16.7 per cent) and construction (−31.3 per cent). Within manufacturing, the hardest-hit sectors in terms of decline in value added were the textile, apparel and shoes industries (−14.9 per cent), furniture and other goods (−29.6 per cent) and transport equipment (−27.5 per cent). Furthermore, from 2007 to 2014 Italy experienced a decline in employment of approximately 952,000 in all sectors of the economy. Most of this decline occurred in manufacturing, with a loss of 678,000 workplaces, and in construction, which lost 405,000 jobs. At the same time, there were 215,000 new jobs in the service sector.

The implementation of excessively heavy fiscal measures in a strong manufacturing country such as Italy had a dramatic effect on the real economy in the form of a decline in manufacturing and construction, with relative declines in employment in both sectors. Only excessive austerity can explain these negative data, since, as we have seen from an earlier discussion, Italy's industrial turnover destined for export actually grew slightly during the crisis.

12.4 Austerity and the Real Economy: the Case of Italy

Italy's case is emblematic of the enormous fiscal efforts made by a country that did not have particularly negative fundamentals. In spite of this, rating agencies and markets severely punished it in 2011, and Italy subsequently had to adopt drastic financial manoeuvres to prove the sustainability of its public finances.

International public opinion did fully acknowledged Italy's fiscal efforts. Therefore, it is worth to call attention to the following points (see Ministero dell'Economia e delle Finanze 2014; Banca d'Italia 2015; IMF 2015):

1. *Italy had the lowest percentage growth of public debt in monetary terms during the crisis.* From 2008 (the beginning of the global crisis) to 2014, due to extremely rigorous fiscal policies, Italy had the lowest percentage growth of public debt in monetary terms of

all countries in the Eurozone, and in comparison to the United
Kingdom and the United States. (Greece is excluded from this
comparison because its debt was subject to an international bailout,
so the comparison is not homogeneous) (Table 12.4). Italy's public
debt increased from 2008 to 2015 by 464 billion euros, or by
27.8 per cent, while Germany's public debt over the same period
grew by 495 billion euros – that is, by 29.8 per cent. In contrast,
from 2008 to 2014, the public debt of other major European
countries of comparable dimensions grew in monetary terms much
more than Italy's and Germany's, both in absolute value and
percentage-wise. Some examples include Spain (+599 billion euros,
or +136.2 per cent); the United Kingdom (+811 billion pounds,

Table 12.4 *The dynamics of public debt in EMU countries, United
Kingdom and United States, 2008–2014 (in billions of national
currencies)*

Countries	2008	2014	Absolute changes	% changes
Slovenia	8.2	30.6	22.4	272.3%
Estonia	0.7	1.9	1.2	160.5%
Ireland	79.6	203.6	124.0	155.8%
Spain	439.8	1,039.0	599.2	136.2%
Cyprus	8.5	18.6	10.1	119.2%
Latvia	4.5	9.7	5.2	114.9%
Croatia	125.3	267.1	141.8	113.2%
Slovakia	19.2	40.4	21.2	110.0%
United Kingdom	783.0	1,593.5	810.5	103.5%
Luxembourg	5.4	10.7	5.3	98.2%
Finland	63.3	119.9	56.6	89.4%
Portugal	128.2	225.2	97.0	75.7%
United States	10,721.2	18,285.9	7,564.7	70.6%
France	1,354.2	2,036.7	682.5	50.4%
Austria	200.0	286.0	86.0	43.0%
Malta	3.8	5.4	1.6	41.1%
Belgium	327.5	427.8	100.3	30.6%
Netherlands	348.1	452.0	103.9	29.8%
Germany	1,660.2	2,155.1	494.9	29.8%
Italy	**1,671.2**	**2,135.0**	**463.8**	**27.8%**

Source: Compiled by the author on data from AMECO database

or +103.5 per cent); and France (+683 billion euros, or +50.4 per cent). Likewise, from 2008 to 2014, the US public debt grew by 7,565 billion dollars, or 70.6 per cent.

2. *Italy's debt/GDP ratio grew moderately during the crisis.* Even when we consider public debt not in value terms but as a percentage of GDP, Italy's debt grew relatively moderately from 2008 to 2014 in spite of the drastic decrease in Italy's GDP, and despite the burden of substantial funding that Italy, like other countries, had to provide to the European Financial Stability Facility. From 2008 to 2014, Italy's debt/GDP ratio increased by 28.9 per cent. In contrast, Germany (a virtuous country whose GDP, unlike Italy's, did not shrink but grew over this period, thus helping to contain the debt) had a debt/GDP ratio that grew less (+14.4 per cent) than Italy's. In the same period other major countries' debt/GDP ratios increased much more than Italy's, even though their GDPs did not fall nearly as much over this time span. Some examples include France +40.4 per cent; the United States +44 per cent; and the United Kingdom +72 per cent. These differences are even more marked if we compare the moderate rise in Italy's debt/GDP ratio in 2008–14 with the strong rise in debt/GDP ratios of those countries in difficulty which, in spite of the recession it was experiencing, Italy contributed to helping, thus also worsening its own debt/GDP ratio. The aforementioned countries in difficulty include Portugal with a +79.9 per cent rise in debt/GDP; Cyprus with +137.5 per cent; Spain with +149.5 per cent; and Ireland with +160 per cent (Table 12.5).

3. *Italy is the third-largest contributor in the euro area of aid to countries in difficulty and to the European financial instruments created during the economic crisis (the European Financial Stability Facility (EFSF) and the European Stability Mechanism (ESM)), to provide financial assistance to Cyprus, Greece, Portugal and Ireland.* In the period 2011–14, in spite of austerity and the difficult economic phase it was experiencing, Italy contributed more than 60 billion euros of growth of its own public debt to the EFSF and in bilateral loans to the countries in difficulty.

4. *The primary surplus of Italy's public finances is one of the highest in the world and over the past twenty years the most stable of all the member states of the EU.* It is well known that the primary balance is a government's budget balance before interest is paid. For this

Table 12.5 *The dynamics of public debt/GDP ratio in EMU countries,*
United Kingdom, United States and Japan, 2008–2014

Countries	2008	2014	% changes
Slovenia	21.6	82.2	279.6%
Ireland	42.6	110.8	160.0%
Spain	39.4	98.3	149.5%
Cyprus	45.3	107.5	137.5%
Croatia	36.0	81.4	126.1%
Estonia	4.5	9.8	120.0%
Latvia	18.6	40.4	117.6%
Slovakia	28.2	53.6	90.0%
Finland	32.7	58.9	80.3%
Portugal	71.7	128.9	79.9%
United Kingdom	51.6	88.7	72.0%
Greece	109.3	176.3	61.3%
Luxembourg	14.4	22.7	57.1%
United States	72.8	104.9	44.0%
France	67.8	95.3	40.4%
Italy	**102.3**	**131.9**	**28.9%**
Netherlands	54.8	69.5	26.9%
Austria	68.5	86.8	26.6%
Belgium	92.2	106.4	15.4%
Germany	64.9	74.2	14.4%
Malta	62.7	68.6	9.3%

Source: Compiled by the author on data from AMECO database

indicator, which highlights an economy's fiscal efforts, Italy stands
out as having presented an uninterrupted positive primary balance
from 1992 to 2014, with the sole exception of 2009, the peak of the
worst global economic crisis since World War II. If we take the EU,
the United States and Japan as a frame of reference and consider the
new ESA 2010 historical series which covers the period 1995–2014,
we can see that Italy was in primary surplus for nineteen of the last
twenty years. No other country has been able to do this. To compare, Germany, one of the most virtuous economies, had a primary
surplus for just twelve out of the last twenty years. In the same
period Spain had a primary surplus for just eleven years and since

2008 has been uninterruptedly in deficit; the United States has been in primary surplus for only nine years and has had a deficit since 2008; France had a primary surplus for just six years and has been in deficit since 2008; and the United Kingdom was in surplus for only five years and has been in deficit since 2002. Throughout the current crisis there were only two countries in the entire EU – but we can also extend our comparison to the United States and Japan – with a constantly positive primary budget balance from 2011 to 2014. Those two countries were Italy (which was already in surplus in 2010) and Germany. From 2011 to 2014 Italy and Germany had cumulative primary budget surpluses of 7 per cent and 8.4 per cent of GDP, respectively, proving to be the two most virtuous economies overall. For 2015, the European Commission is forecasting that both Italy and Germany will have a primary budget surplus of 1.8 per cent of GDP (Table 12.6).

5. *Italy's government deficit has been below 3 per cent of GDP for the period 2012–14.* Due to its sizeable primary surplus, Italy stopped infringement proceedings and maintained a budget deficit of less than 3 per cent of GDP, as required by the EU.

6. *Italy's public debt has the lowest long-term financial risk of all the countries in the EU.* Italy has already decisively dealt with the impact of its aging population on its public finances, still an important challenge for many European economies, with pension reforms introduced over the past twenty years and tight control of spending on health care and social assistance. As a result, the long-term sustainability indicator S2 calculated by the European Commission shows that Italy's public debt is the most sustainable over the long term of all European countries (European Commission 2014).

7. *Italy has a low level of aggregate debt (of households, non-financial companies and government) in relation to GDP.* The solid financial situation of the private sector is one of the strong points of the Italian economy. At the end of 2013, although it had grown moderately during the crisis, Italian household debt was about 43 per cent of GDP, one of the lowest levels in the world, 18 percentage points lower than the euro area average. As concerns Italian non-financial companies, their debt/GDP ratio of 111 per cent is considerably lower than the euro area's average of 128.5 per cent. Consequently, Italy's total debt – public and private included – is in line with the euro area average and below that of many other European economies.

Table 12.6 *General government primary balance, 1995–2016 (billions of euros; GBP for United Kingdom)*

	Germany		Spain		France		Italy		United Kingdom	
	Surplus	Deficit	Surplus	Deficit	Surplus	Deficit	Surplus	Deficit	Surplus	Deficit
1995		-116.8		-9.8		-22.8	34.8			-17.7
1996	0.5			-1.7		-6.4	45.7			-6.0
1997	10.0		3.2			-3.3	67.3		10.8	
1998	17.7		6.1		11.1		54.8		28.6	
1999	31.0		12.5		18.9		53.8		34.1	
2000	87.1		13.8		22.1		59.6		38.7	
2001		-1.0	16.9		22.4		35.0		28.5	
2002		-20.7	16.6			-3.6	32.1			-1.4
2003		-25.4	15.5			-18.4	21.7			-17.9
2004		-19.5	16.7			-13.9	15.1			-21.0
2005		-11.3	27.4			-9.6	5.0			-19.8
2006	28.2		38.2		3.4		13.3			-11.9
2007	74.9		38.5		1.5		52.1			-11.0
2008	68.0			-32.1		-7.4	36.5			-42.9
2009		-9.7		-99.9		-92.4		-13.4		-132.1
2010		-41.5		-81.2		-88.1	0.7			-104.8
2011	43.9			-75.0		-51.3	19.2			-70.6
2012	65.8			-78.0		-48.3	35.5			-89.0
2013	60.5			-37.1		-39.4	32.2			-49.7
2014 F	61.0			-24.2		-48.6	27.2			-49.4
2015 F	53.5			-13.6		-48.5	29.5			-34.2
2016 F	58.2			-6.0		-51.4	39.7			-16.7

Source: European Commission AMECO Database

8. *During the crisis, Italy made many sacrifices to keep its public finances in order,* sacrifices that perhaps many are not aware of, and that affected the public sector as well as households, which experienced a significant rise in taxes. Two examples are noteworthy: from 2008 to 2014 spending on public employees in Italy dropped from 170.3 billion to 162.7 billion euros (−4.5 per cent). In contrast, in Germany in the same period this spending increased from 189.1 billion to 223.7 billion euros (+18.3 per cent). At the end of 2008 Italian households' net wealth was the highest in the Eurozone, 2,941 billion euros, significantly higher than that of German households, at 2,684 billion euros. Since then, due to the crisis and austerity, Italian household wealth has remained practically stagnant in nominal terms and at the end of 2013 was 2,968 billion euros. In contrast, German household wealth has grown by 757 billion euros reaching 3,341 billion at the end of 2013 (the latest available Eurostat data).

Despite the decline in GDP and industrial production due to austerity and the collapse of domestic demand, Italy is still the second most important manufacturing country in the EU. Eurostat data from 2014 reaffirm that despite the deep domestic recession, Italy is still the second-largest EU country in terms of value added manufacturing (225 billion euros) after Germany (581 billion). In 2013, Italy had 4 million workers employed in manufacturing, compared to Germany's 7.4 million, France's 2.7 million and United Kingdom's 2.5 million. Germany's and Italy's manufacturing workers combined make up more than half of that number for the entire Eurozone.

Other noteworthy points: Italy is the only country in the EU with value added in industry (excluding construction) higher than that of Bavaria and Baden-Württemberg put together (the two federal states that are the pillars of German industry). Northwest and Northeast Italy combined are respectively the fourth and fifth most important European macro-regions in terms of industrial value added, after North Rhine-Westphalia, Bavaria and Baden-Württemberg. Central Italy is Europe's tenth biggest industrial macro-region (Table 12.7).

In spite of the severe domestic economic crisis, Italy is still a strong exporter and improved its foreign trade balance by 72.9 billion euros from 2010 to 2014 – Italy's trade balance was negative by 30 billion euros in 2010. In 2014, however, it closed with a surplus of 42.9 billion

Table 12.7 Germany and Italy lead the European industry: national and regional rankings by value added in the industry sector (except construction), 2011

(Value added in millions of euro; value added per capita in euro)

Top 15 Countries	Industry value added	Industry value added per capita	Top 15 EU NUTS1 Regions	Industry value added	Industry value added per capita	Top 15 EU NUTS2 Regions	Industry value added	Industry value added per capita
Germany	607,440	7,430	DEA - Nordrhein-Westfalen	131,887	7,391	ITC4 - Lombardia	75,791	7,843
Italy	266,918	4,496	DE2 - Bayern	120,065	9,576	DE11 - Stuttgart	51,261	12,807
United Kingdom	236,443	3,752	DE1 - Baden-Württemberg	118,669	11,035	DE21 - Oberbayern	44,278	10,054
France	227,576	3,502	ITC - Nord-Ovest	106,347	6,761	DEA1 - Düsseldorf	41,077	7,958
Spain	164,519	3,525	ITH - Nord-Est	79,358	6,944	ES51 - Cataluña	36,262	4,839
Netherlands	102,596	6,160	ES5 - Este (ES)	54,735	4,029	ITH3 - Veneto	35,196	7,254
Poland	83,300	2,188	DE9 - Niedersachsen	53,914	6,809	ITH5 - Emilia-Romagna	32,376	7,475
Sweden	70,547	7,493	FR2 - Bassin Parisien	43,393	4,030	IE02 - Southern and Eastern	31,998	9,600

Austria	59,918	7,154	DE7 - Hessen	42,280	6,969	DEA5 - Arnsberg	30,209	8,258
Belgium	54,094	4,917	ITI - Centro (IT)	42,255	3,650	FR71 - Rhône-Alpes	30,147	4,798
Czech Rep.	42,709	4,073	FR1 - Île de France	42,151	3,556	DE12 - Karlsruhe	26,714	9,735
Ireland	39,245	8,586	BE2 - Vlaams Gewest	36,625	5,790	DE71 - Darmstadt	26,359	6,927
Romania	37,896	1,770	FR7 - Centre-Est (FR)	35,137	4,603	DEA2 - Köln	26,195	5,963
Denmark	35,932	6,462	NL3 - West-Nederland	33,601	4,291	ITC1 - Piemonte	25,569	5,859
Finland	32,993	6,138	DEB - Rheinland-Pfalz	30,563	7,634	DE13 - Freiburg	20,599	9,367

Source: Compiled by the Edison Foundation on data from Eurostat

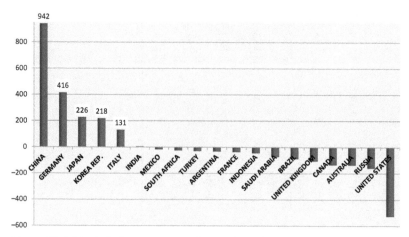

Figure 12.4 Trade Balances in Manufactured Products: G-20 Countries, 2013
(billions of US dollars)
Source: WTO

euros. Thus, there was an extraordinary improvement in the Italian
trade balance of 72.9 billion, the largest in absolute value in the EU,
considering that in the same period Germany's trade balance improved
by 62 billion euros. From 2010 to 2014 Italy's exports grew in absolute value by 60.6 billion euros, while imports decreased by 12.3
billion euros.

Italy is one of only five countries in the world, along with China,
Germany, Japan and South Korea, with a foreign trade balance of more
than 100 billion dollars for industrial manufactured products
(Figure 12.4). In 2014 Italy's exports of manufactured goods were worth
381.9 billion euros, an increase of 59.2 billion on 2010. Italy's manufacturing trade balance in 2014 set a new record, reaching 99.5 billion
euros. Italy is the second country in the EU and the world after Germany
in terms of its foreign trade surplus in manufactured goods. From
2010 to 2014 Italy's manufacturing trade balance rose from 37.8 billion
to 99.5 billion euros, an increase of 61.6 billion euros in four years.

12.5 Conclusions

During the crisis, Germany benefitted enormously from the industrial
point of view compared to the other major Eurozone countries. Indeed,

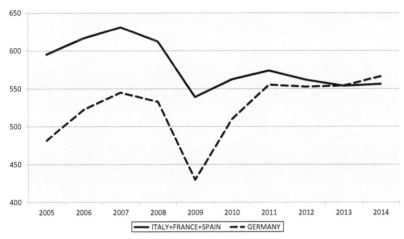

Figure 12.5 Manufacturing Gross Value Added Chain-Linked Volumes (2010) (billions of euro)

Source: Compiled by the author on data from Eurostat

Germany did not apply any particular austerity measures to its domestic economy. This allowed it to maintain domestic demand for consumption and investment but also a relatively robust level of public spending. This, combined with strong exports, prevented depressive effects on German industrial production. In contrast, Italy and Spain had to apply very restrictive fiscal policies, especially after the explosion of the sovereign debt crisis in the 'periphery' countries in 2011. Even France, in order to contain its budget deficit, was not able to implement particularly expansive economic policies (Fortis 2009, 2011a, 2011b, 2012, 2014).

The result of this was a real revolution in Europe in terms of the balance of power between the various manufacturing industries. In 2007, based on Eurostat data at 2010 prices, the value added of Germany's manufacturing industry was 86 billion euros lower than the total value added of the manufacturing industries of Italy, Spain and France put together. In 2014, on the other hand, German manufacturing in terms of value added exceeded that of Italian, Spanish and French industries combined. Once again, and not only in the area of public finance, the Eurozone crisis 'reinforced' Germany to the disadvantage of the other major Eurozone countries (Figure 12.5).

References

Andreoni, A. (2015) *The industrial competitiveness of Italian manufacturing: A comparison between the UNIDO's Competitive Industrial Performance Index, the WEF and the IMD rankings*. Presentation at the International Conference 'Where do we stand? Global perspectives on the industrial competitiveness of Italian manufacturing'. Milan, Catholic University, 27 January.

Banca d'Italia (2015) *Financial Stability Report*, No. 2/2015.

Draghi, M. (2014) *Unemployment in the Euro Area*, Annual central bank symposium, Jackson Hole, 22 August 2014.

European Commission (2014), Economic and Financial Affairs, *Report on Public Finances in EMU*, European Economy, 9/2014.

Fortis, M. (2009) *La crisi mondiale e l'Italia*, Fondazione Edison Series, Il Mulino, Bologna

Fortis, M. (2011a) *Dentro la crisi: 2009–2011. America, Europa, Italia*, Fondazione Edison Series, Il Mulino, Bologna

Fortis, M. (2011b) 'Growth to Become Poorer', *Economia politica – Journal of Analytical and Institutional Economics*, n. 1/2011, pp. 5–14.

Fortis, M. (2012) 'A Different Tale on Eurozone Debts', *Economia politica – Journal of Analytical and Institutional Economics*, n. 2/2012, pp. 161–71.

Fortis, M. (2014) 'Is Germany Stronger, Smarter or Slyer?', *Economia politica – Journal of Analytical and Institutional Economics*, n. 1/2014, pp. 3–9.

Fortis, M. and Quadrio Curzio, A. (2013) *Debito e crescita; L'equazione della crisi*, Fondazione Edison Series, Il Mulino, Bologna

Fortis, M. and Quadrio Curzio, A. (2014) *L'Europa tra ripresa e squilibri. Eurozona, Germania e Italia*, Fondazione Edison Series, Il Mulino, Bologna

Fortis M. and Quadrio Curzio A. (2016) *Riforme, ripresa, rilancio: Europa e Italia*, Fondazione Edison Series, Il Mulino, Bologna.

IMF (2015) *Fiscal Monitor. Now is the Time: Fiscal Policies for Sustainable Growth*, World Economic and Financial Surveys, April 2015

Ministero dell'Economia e delle Finanze (2014) *Pride and Prejudice; Something That No One Is Saying about Italy*, www.mef.gov.it

Quadrio Curzio, A. (2014a) 'L'illusione del rigore sostenibile', *Il Sole 24 Ore*, 14 August 2014, published in M. Fortis and A. Quadrio Curzio (2016), pp. 143–46.

Quadrio Curzio, A. (2014b) 'Più opere e meno squilibri per rilanciare l'Europa', *Il Sole 24 Ore*, 12 October 2014, published in M. Fortis and A. Quadrio Curzio (2016), pp. 261–64.

Quadrio Curzio, A. (2014c) 'Al piano Juncker serve un "motore" finanziario', *Il Sole 24 Ore*, 23 November 2014, published in: Fortis M. and Quadrio Curzio A. (2016), pp. 265–68.

Quadrio Curzio, A. (2014d) 'Juncker non basta, usiamo l'oro', *Il Sole 24 Ore*, 9 December 2014, published M. Fortis and A. Quadrio Curzio (2016), pp. 87–90.

Quadrio Curzio, A. (2015a) 'Il bazooka può creare l'embrione degli eurobond', *Il Sole 24 Ore*, 24 January 2015, published M. Fortis and A. Quadrio Curzio.

Quadrio Curzio, A. (2015b) 'La golden rule necessaria e il bonus per la ricerca', *Il Sole 24 Ore*, 21 Aprile 2015, published M. Fortis and A. Quadrio Curzio (2016), pp. 289–92.

Said, A.J. (2015) *The competitiveness of Italian Manufacturing: Outlook and strategic considerations*. Paper presented at the International Conference 'Where do we stand? Global perspectives on the industrial competitiveness of Italian manufacturing'. Milan, Catholic University, 27 January.

Tiffin, A. (2014) *European productivity, innovation and competitiveness: the case of Italy*, IMF Working Paper, May.

13 Fiscal Systems and Fiscal Union

Historical Variety and Policy Challenges

D'MARIS COFFMAN AND ALI KABIRI

13.1 Introduction: Fiscal Variety and the Need for the New Fiscal Sociology

In addition to the theoretical case advanced in Chapter 2 of this volume for a New Fiscal Sociology, there are pressing macroeconomic policy questions that such an approach could help answer. The sluggishness of the global recovery from the Great Recession of 2007–09, compounded in the Eurozone by the continuing sovereign debt crisis, has recently sparked criticism that over-reliance on monetary policy, particularly non-conventional monetary policy such as Quantitative Easing, at the expense of fiscal policy responses, has adverse consequences. The Bank of International Settlements issued such a warning in July 2015, namely that 'monetary policy has been overburdened for far too long . . . it must be part of the answer, but cannot be the whole answer' and others have followed (Blackstone, 2015). Those who share this critique come from a number of different methodological orientations. In this volume, Roberto Scazzieri's analysis in Chapter 7 of this volume is consistent with this finding, but even those who do not share a commitment to structural analysis have reached similar conclusions.

Using agent-based modelling, Giovanni Dosi and his colleagues have concluded that 'policy mixes associating unconstrained, counter-cyclical fiscal policy and monetary policy targeting employment is required to stabilise the economy. We also show that "discipline-guided" fiscal rules can be self-defeating, as they depress the economy without improving public finances' (Dosi et al., 2015, p. 166). In a similar vein and in a manner consistent with the analysis offered by Cardinale and Landesmann in Chapter 11, Olivier Blanchard, then chief economist of the International Monetary Fund, argued in July 2015:

[A] fiscal expansion by the core economies of the euro area would have a large and positive impact on periphery GDP assuming that policy rates remain low for a prolonged period. Under our preferred model specification, an expansion of core government spending equal to one percent of euro area GDP would boost periphery GDP around 1 percent in a liquidity trap lasting three years, about half as large as the effect on core GDP. (Blanchard, Erceg and Lindé, 2016, p. 1)

Brendon and Corsetti (2015) attack the pre-crisis consensus, known as 'The Great Moderation,' that 'monetary policy should play a primary role in economic stabilization', should concentrate solely on inflation-targeting, and that 'active fiscal policy is of limited additional usefulness' (p. 4; see also Blanchard, Dell'Ariccia and Mauro, 2010).

Although the reasons for this vary from location to location, and are more or less explicitly ideological in the United States, United Kingdom and those who follow their political logics, in the Eurozone, the constraint is partially constitutional. The European Central Bank sets interest rates for the Eurozone as a whole, while the absence of a fiscal union and the presence of fiscal rules under the Maastricht Treaty make coordination of fiscal policy extremely difficult. Moreover, while the ECB is taken as neutral and above the political process, fiscal policy is determined by the sensibilities of the national median voter, who has been forced to accept austerity. Yet as Fatás and Summers (2015) have also argued, the result of these 'fiscal consolidations' has been a 'negative impact on growth rates' and 'higher debt to GDP ratios'. Worse still, Brendon and Corsetti (2015) have concluded that contractionary fiscal policies in surplus countries have only served to magnify the balances elucidated by Cardinale and Landesmann in their Chapter 11 of this volume.

All of this sharpens the need to revisit fiscal policy, and especially to consider the non-fiscal effects of taxation and public expenditure. Although the approach we suggest is strongly rooted in a commitment to fiscal sociology and structural analysis, others have considered this question in recent months, usually with the aim of understanding wealth effects, welfare effects and consumption for the IMF, which under Blanchard's influence moved away from recommending austerity (Jaramillo and Chailloux, 2015). After all, fiscal stabilisers are notoriously difficult to get right, even in controlled circumstances (Corsetti and Muller, 2015). Gordon Brown's use of the VAT reduction in Britain in 2008 as economic stimulus worked, but not for the reasons the Treasury imagined; they expected marginal households to accelerate consumption of necessities, whereas in reality non-marginal households accelerated consumption of luxuries in an inter-temporal consumption shift (Crossley, Low and Wakefield, 2008).

In short, fiscal coordination and cohesion are under consideration again, but for different reasons that in the 2009–13 period, when some market commentators believed that a fiscal union was the only way to resolve the Eurozone Debt Crisis (Soros, 2013). Without a doubt, both the Great Recession and the sovereign debt crisis that followed have slowed institutional development within the Eurozone (Brendon and Corsetti, 2015, p. 2), but fiscal stabilisation is back on the agenda in 2016 because of fears of deflation, high unemployment, or 'secular stagnation' in the Eurozone. The stakes could not be higher, as Alexander Field noted in a recent study of the Great Depression: properly managed, fiscal policy can stimulate deep structural change during the recovery phase of prolonged recession, with pronounced welfare benefits (Field, 2011).

In examining the degree of variation in the fiscal systems of Eurozone states, this chapter has three goals. First is to use the data from Eurostat to analyse the configuration of regional, national and, insofar as is possible, sectoral interests. Particular attention is paid to the balance of direct and indirect taxation because of the relevance to the challenges identified by Cardinale and Landesmann in Chapter 11 of this volume. These differences in their turn reveal differing commitments to income redistribution, industrial policy, pricing of externalities (especially pollution) and fiscal incentives (discouraging home ownership, education or philanthropy and discouraging consumption, for instance, of tobacco or alcohol). The history of these differing solutions, particularly the postwar moment in the 1940s, but even more remote historical forces as well, can help to illuminate why reform is so elusive in many cases.

Second, the chapter argues that the variety in European fiscal systems presents a significant structural challenge to fiscal union, even if the terms of the fiscal union are meant to preserve national autonomy in this regard and focus instead on outcomes. Such variation has created and will continue to create opportunities for legal and tax arbitrage, of which some are predictable and some are the unexpected consequences of ad hoc solutions in moments of crisis. The current controversy about 'tax avoidance' strategies of transnational corporations should be understood in this context, rather than simply as a populist movement or as the expression of moral anxieties.

Third, the chapter aims to elaborate the political economy of taxation within the Eurozone, with special attention to the ideological contexts for the different fiscal mixes. Consensus, while not impossible, is much harder to achieve when these contexts are persistently ignored, and, even more alarmingly, when the politics of comprehensive austerity across the Eurozone does violence to the specificity of particular tax systems.

13.2 Fiscal Mixes and Social Structures

The relationship between fiscal mixes and social structures was theorised in detail in eighteenth-century Britain and France, which have assumed the status of paradigmatic cases. In the French context, Quesnay's work, as discussed by Cardinale and Landesmann in Chapter 11, has given rise to an entire tradition of input-output modelling (Quesnay, 1972 [1759]). In the British case, as discussed in Chapter 2, these debates have contributed to the theoretical distinction between the legal and real incidence of taxation, which in turn is critical to understanding the political economy of taxation in historical context and to economic theory more widely (Coffman, 2013; O'Brien, 1985, 1988).

In eighteenth-century Britain, building on earlier polemics from the mid-seventeenth century, the debates were primarily preoccupied with the economic incidence of excise taxation, particularly that on beer and ale, which represented the majority of the total excise revenue initially and the plurality later on, and the respective merits of excise taxation versus direct taxation of landed wealth (Braddick, 1996; Boyer, 1964; Beckett, 1985; Coffman, 2013; Cardinale and Coffman, 2014; Stasavage, 2003, 2007).

In brief, depending on the price elasticity of demand for a given commodity, the burden (or 'economic incidence') of an indirect tax may be shifted 'forward' onto the consumer in the form of higher retail prices or 'backwards' onto the wholesaler, manufacturer or producer of raw materials in the form of lower prices paid for the goods (Seligman, 1969a, 1969b). 'Over-shifting' is also possible, especially when the producers manage improvements in quality or enjoy monopoly power (Spoerer, 2008).

In the case of the English excise, the initial effect, in the 1640s, was for producers to shift the tax forward onto the consumers, which resulted in an ill-fated attempt on the part of Parliament to effect price controls via the old assizes on beer and bread (Coffman, 2013). Subsequently, both landowners and grain merchants argued that the more common strategy was to back-shift the duty onto the primary sector, via a reduction in prices paid for grain (Cardinale and Coffman, 2014) and subsequently in agricultural rents (Cofffman and Ormrod, 2014). The effect was so persistent, or at least believed to be, that many of the gentry preferred direct land taxes in lieu of an excise. There is also limited evidence that in some cases the brewing industry capitalised the costs, sparking consolidation, industrialisation and the adoption of innovation in this sector (Coffman and Gao, 2011; Mathias, 1959). More importantly, however, the system of compensatory taxation advanced by William Petty, which asked for a mix of direct and indirect taxation, was particularly helpful in maintaining systemic interests (Cardinale and Coffman, 2014; Petty, 1662).

Contemporary commentators were aware of all of these positions, and even anticipated the DSGE-approach when they asserted that in the long run this would be fed through the system into wages (Seligman, 1969a). This was, in part, because, as Coffman and Ormrod (2014) have recently noted, contemporary investigations in the British case were greatly abetted by the availability of grain price data and public accounts (see also Beveridge et al., 1965; Granger and Elliott, 1967; Mitchell, 1988).

The beauty of the eighteenth-century case for today's theorists is the relative simplicity of the economy and tax mix and of the evident mapping of the primary and secondary sectors onto political alignments and ultimately political parties. Today, as Ivano Cardinale explains in Chapter 9, the political-economic map of the Eurozone is far more complex. But fiscal sociology can help to elucidate it.

Finally, debates about tax evasion and tax avoidance depend to an extent on the fiscal mix. The rhetoric of populist outrage about tax avoidance usually falls on corporations or high-net-worth individuals who avoid, using legal or quasi-legal means, the burden of direct taxation. With indirect taxation, evasion, particularly in the form of smuggling or participation in the grey market, is more obviously criminal, and is attributed less to wealthy individuals and multinational corporations and more to the 'tax cultures' of particular countries, most often in the Mediterranean basin. As we see in the discussion that follows, this is perhaps less surprising when we consider the tax mix.

13.3 Fiscal Variety in the Eurozone: Taxation and Public Borrowing

Any attempt to understand fiscal variety in the Eurozone must begin with the data supplied by Eurostat, which is a Directorate-General of the European Commission. Eurostat has a formal constitutional role in the provision of statistical information to EU institutions, in promoting uniformity and harmonisation of statistical standards and in monitoring the reporting not only of member states but also of candidates for accession. During the Eurozone debt crisis, Eurostat was heavily criticised for having allowed Greece to falsify economic data at the time of inclusion, though most commentators have tended to put the blame more squarely with those that helped them to do so (Balzli, 2010). In any case, recent research by Savage and Verdun (2016) has shown that very significant improvements in statistical monitoring, statistical competence and in coordination between the various directorates.

More to the point, should the movement towards fiscal coordination in the Eurozone ever gain sufficient momentum to make a fiscal compact a likely outcome, Eurostat will play a pivotal role in monitoring and surveillance. Thus while external data sources on European fiscal variety might be helpful, at a policy level, the focus must be on further improving Eurostat's capabilities, which is most easily done by influencing the content of the respective five-year plans.

So what does Eurostat data tell us about fiscal variety within the Eurozone? At the most basic level, as Figure 13.1 illustrates, total government revenue as a percentage of GDP is unsurprising.

What is known now, but was not well understood before the Eurozone debt crisis, is how much disparity there is in the proportions of central, provincial and local taxation across the Eurozone, as well as considerable variation in the roles played by social security funds (Figures 13.2–13.5).

These differences were essentially ignored until it became clear during the Eurozone debt crisis that Spanish government borrowing at the provincial level was fuelling the crisis in Spain, whereas in Greece and Portugal the problematic debt had been issued by the central governments. Nevertheless, those borrowing patterns align neatly with the revenue generating capacities of these states. So even a top-level sketch such as this should suggest that any proposal for a fiscal compact must take into account the different federated structures within constituent member states.

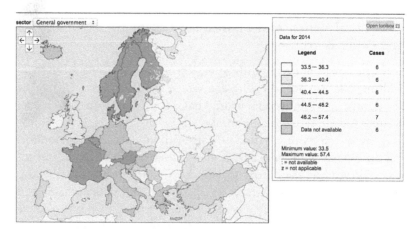

Figure 13.1 Total Government Revenue as a Share of GDP

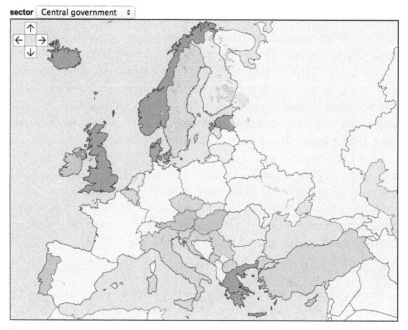

Figure 13.2 Central Government Revenue as a Share of GDP

Clearly these patterns do not tell the whole story, as Spain and Switzerland (to draw an example from outside the European Union) both have comparatively high levels of provincial and local taxation and low levels of central government borrowing, for

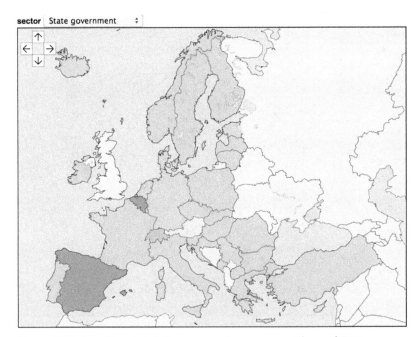

Figure 13.3 State/Provincial Government Revenue as a Share of GDP

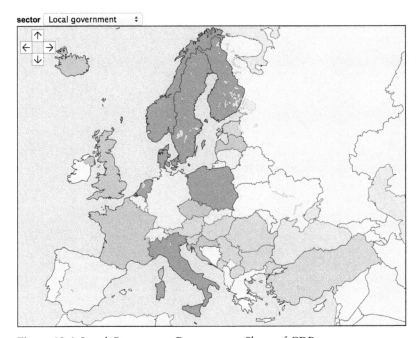

Figure 13.4 Local Government Revenue as a Share of GDP

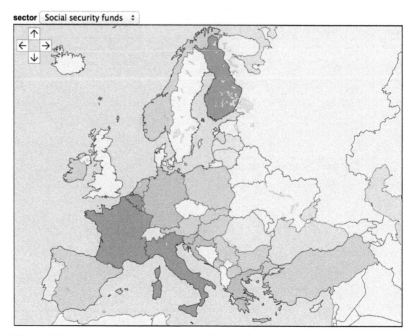

Figure 13.5 Social Security Funds as a Share of GDP

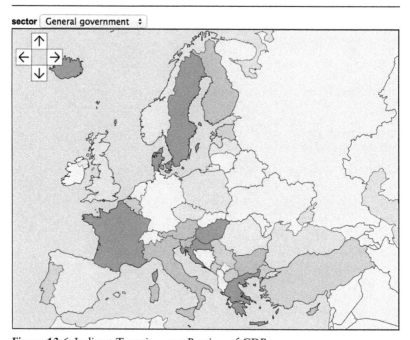

Figure 13.6 Indirect Taxation as a Portion of GDP

admittedly radically different reasons, but neither Spain nor Switzerland looks anything like Italy or France, which also have strong regional identities. Any solution which considers a fiscal compact from the top down will do violence to the provision of public goods, infrastructure investment and maintenance, and the non-tradable sectors of nations where the bulk of revenue collection is at the local level.

By a similar token, Figures 13.7–13.9 show the differences in indirect and direct taxation as a share of GDP, and also show the percentage of the economy represented by government output. In general, direct taxation is more highly correlated with government share of total output, which is not unexpected based on the analysis by Cardinale and Landesmann in Chapter 11. In effect, direct taxation in much of northern Europe is subsidizing and in some cases directly financing the non-tradable sector. Beyond that, high levels of indirect taxation in southern Europe partially explain the concerns about tax evasion in

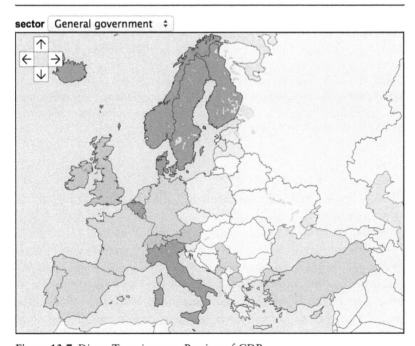

Figure 13.7 Direct Taxation as a Portion of GDP

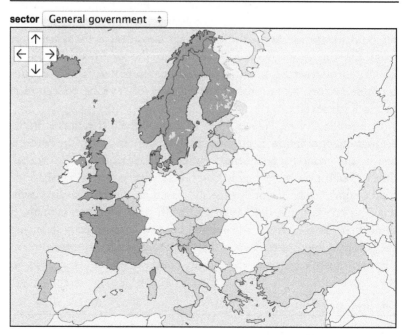

Figure 13.8 Government Output as Share of Economy

Moreover, as Figure 13.9 illustrates, the gap in 2009 between nominal and effective tax rates on corporations was very large in many core Eurozone states. Although it has closed somewhat in recent years, this suggests significant opportunities for tax arbitrage by individual member states. That, as much as evasion of indirect taxes, will have to be confronted and resolved if a fiscal union is to be possible (Lyons, 2011).

those countries, which do not themselves have particularly high levels of direct taxation.

Similar patterns exist for public expenditure within the Eurozone. Proposals for Eurobonds must acknowledge the extent to which much public borrowing in Europe is not at the central government level, not just in Spain (Neal and García-Iglesias, 2013). Otherwise, the problems now plaguing state and local government in the United States in a period where there are constitutional amendments embedding fiscal rules in state constitutions will plague the Eurozone as well (Liu, Tian and Wallis, 2013).

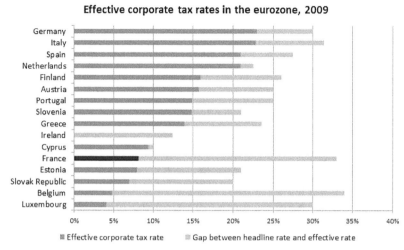

Figure 13.9 Gap between Nominal and Effective Direct Tax Rates on Corporations

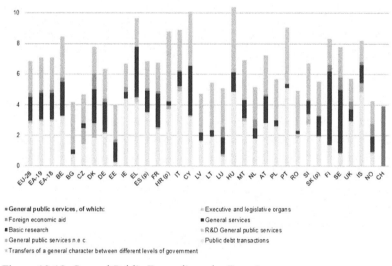

Figure 13.10 General Public Expenditure by Function

13.4 Fiscal Variety in the Eurozone: Public Expenditure

As Figure 13.8 suggests, government output is a substantial share of the economy in core Eurozone states and in the United Kingdom.

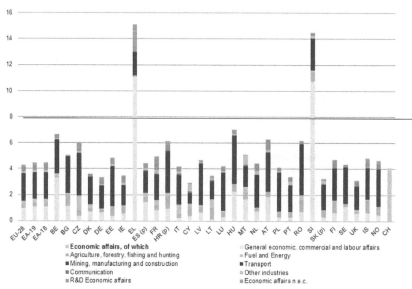

Figure 13.11 Public Expenditure on Economic Affairs

Ironically, this is least true for those countries most directly affected by the Eurozone debt crisis. Because Eurostat makes it possible to track 'government expenditure by function', a detailed examination of public sector balance sheets is possible.

A New Fiscal Sociology of the Eurozone has to be based on a detailed examination of this newly available data. Whether fiscal policy has to be coordinated as a step towards fiscal union or merely to ensure that fiscal stabilisers are neither at cross purposes nor a threat to systemic interests, what is needed is a much better understanding of why there is such variation in patterns of public expenditure. A top-level survey such as this can only really acknowledge the variations.

13.5 Challenges to Fiscal Union

Throughout the Eurozone debt crisis there have been repeated calls for a closer fiscal union. George Soros (2013) has been one of the most vocal proponents, but he is by no means alone in thinking that greater fiscal union would have helped to stabilise and protect the monetary union. More broadly, institution-building at the European Commission level was expected to accompany the adoption of a single currency, and most commentators lament the extent to which the Great Recession helped to arrest that process (Brendon and Corsetti, 2015).

Essentially, there are three key challenges to fiscal union, which are apparent at a structural level or as a product of structural analysis. The first is simply that in many countries, the majority of taxation, borrowing and expenditure occurs at a subnational level. Any fiscal union that does violence to that fact will invariably damage not only systemic interests within countries, but will also threaten the sorts of cross-border interests that Cardinale identified in Chapter 9. Second, the mix of direct and indirect taxation is highly particular and even idiosyncratic, even within regions like Scandinavia where this might otherwise be unexpected. These differences in turn correspond to systemic and particular interests within states and regions and are disrupted at great peril (Cardinale 2015; Cardinale and Coffman, 2014).Third, the fiscal cohesion might help the imbalances addressed by Cardinale and Landesmann, but can also serve to exacerbate them. Any commitment to a greater fiscal union must acknowledge that.

Finally, fiscal stabilisers function differently from monetary stabilisers. While greater monetary union and the establishment of the European Central Bank led to a preference for monetary stabilisers within the Eurozone and fiscal rules served to all but make fiscal stabilisers impossible, it does not necessarily follow that greater fiscal union will make fiscal stabilisers easier for states to deploy. Given the highly variegated fiscal mixes we have seen above, the reverse is entirely possible. Perhaps a commitment to the use of fiscal stabilisers may help to structure the development of fiscal union, but again that can do violence to underlying systemic interests.

13.6 Towards a Political Economy of Taxation for the Eurozone

Given the highly variegated nature of the Eurozone experience of taxation, borrowing and public expenditure within its constituent nations, both at the central and subnational levels, it seems unlikely that there is a single political economy of taxation in the Eurozone. There are political economies of taxation, which must be mapped through the insights employed from a new commitment to fiscal sociology and through adoption of the methodological approach identified by Cardinale in Chapter 9 and employed by Cardinale and Landesmann in Chapter 11.

But it would be an error to assume that top-down approaches to alter the fiscal mix on a national level, let alone an adoption of policies that would curtail or even limit outright local or provincial borrowing or public expenditure, could succeed. What the American experience outlined by James Macdonald in Chapter 3 should teach us is that in the absence of rigid fiscal rules, fiscal union need not accompany monetary union. The flexibility of different fiscal systems is not necessarily a drawback; rather, the welfare benefits and losses associated with the current system represent an empirical question. Like most such empirical questions, it takes resources to answer them. One very clear recommendation from this chapter is that the European Commission continue to expand the data collecting capacities of Eurostat.

13.7 Concluding Remarks

This has been a very brief overview of the degree of fiscal variation in the Eurozone and the problems attendant to it. There is a great deal more work to do in this area, but hopefully the pay-off, both in terms of theoretical moves towards a greater fiscal union and responsible and flexible adoption of fiscal stabilisers, is obvious. Just as Eurostat has made great strides in furnishing the data for such exercises, so too have economists in recognising the pre-crisis consensus ignored fiscal policy at its peril. While it is too early to call for a 'fiscal turn,' it is not too early to insist that a New Fiscal Sociology would go a long way to replenishing fiscal policy toolkits.

References

Balzli, B. (2010) '*Greek Debt Crisis: How Goldman Sachs Helped Greece to Mask Its True Debt*', *Spiegel online*.

Beckett, J.V. (1985) 'Land Tax or Excise: The Levying of Taxation in Seventeenth- and Eighteenth-Century England', *English Historical Review*, pp. 285–308.

Beveridge, W.H. et al. (eds.) (1965) *Prices & Wages in England from the Twelfth to the Nineteenth Centuries*, 2nd ed., 2 vols. London: Frank Cass.

Blackstone, B. (2015) 'BIS Warns of Overreliance on Monetary Policy', *Wall Street Journal*, 28 June.

Blanchard, O., Dell'Ariccia, G. and Mauro, P. (2010) 'Rethinking Macro-economic Policy', *Journal of Money, Credit and Banking*, 42, pp. 199–215.

Blanchard, O.J., Erceg, C. and Lindé, J. (2016) 'DP10716 Jump-Starting the Euro Area Recovery: Would a Rise in Core Fiscal Spending Help the Periphery?' *NBER Macroeconomics Annual 2016*, Volume 31. Chicago: University of Chicago Press.

Boyer, P.S. (1964) 'Borrowed Rhetoric: The Massachusetts Excise Contro-versy of 1754', *The William and Mary Quarterly*, 21(3), pp. 328–51.

Braddick, M.J. (1996) *The Nerves of State: Taxation and the Financing of the English State, 1558–1714*. Manchester: Manchester University Press.

Brendon, C. and Corsetti, G. (2015) 'COEURE Survey: Fiscal and Monetary Policies after the Crises', *CEPR Discussion Paper No. DP11088*.

Cardinale, I. (2015) 'Towards a Structural Political Economy of Resources', in M. Baranzini et al. (eds.), *Resources, Production and Structural Dynamics*. Cambridge: Cambridge University Press, pp. 198–210.

Cardinale, I. and Coffman, D. (2014) 'Economic Interdependencies and Political Conflict: The Political Economy of Taxation in Eighteenth-Century Britain', *Economia Politica: Journal of Analytical and Institutional Economics*, 31(3), pp. 277–300.

Coffman, D.D. (2013) *Excise Taxation and the Origins of Public Debt*. Basingstoke: Palgrave Macmillan.

Coffman, D.D. and Gao, Y. (2011) 'Capitalising Costs: Excise Taxation and Industrialisation, a Case Study of the Brewing Industry." Unpublished working paper.

Coffman, D.D. and Ormrod, D.J. (2014) 'Corn Prices, Corn Models, and Corn Rents: What Can We Learn from the English Corn Returns?' in M.A. Allen and D.D. Coffman (eds.), *Money, Prices, Wages: Essays in Honour of Nicholas Mayhew*. Basingstoke: Palgrave Macmillan, pp. 196–210.

Corsetti, G. and Müller, G.J. (2015) 'Fiscal Multipliers: Lessons from the Great Recession for Small Open Economies'. *Report to the Swedish Fiscal Policy Council*, 2. Stockholm: Finanspolitiska rådet.

Crossley, T., Low, H. and M. Wakefield. (2008) 'The Economics of a Temporary VAT Cut', *Fiscal Studies*, 30(1), pp. 3–16.

Dosi, G., Fagiolo, G., Napoletano, M., Roventini, A. and Treibich T. (2015) 'Fiscal and monetary policies in complex evolving economies', *Journal of Economic Dynamics and Control* 52, pp. 166–89.

Fatás, A. and Summers, L.H. (2015) 'The Permanent Effects of Fiscal Con-solidations'. SSRN Working Paper.

Field, A. (2011) *A Great Leap Forward: 1930s Depression and U.S. Economic Growth* (Yale Series in Economic and Financial History). New Haven: Yale University Press.

Granger, C.W.J. and Elliott, C.M. (1967) 'A Fresh Look at Wheat Prices and Markets in the Eighteenth Century', *Economic History Review*, 20(2), pp. 257–62.

Jaramillo, L. and Chailloux, A. (2015) *It's Not All Fiscal: Effects of Income, Fiscal Policy, and Wealth on Private Consumption*. No. 15–112. International Monetary Fund.

Liu, L., Tian, X. and Wallis, J.J. (2013) 'Caveat Creditor: State Systems of Local Government Borrowing in the United States', in O. Canuto Dos Santos Filho and L. Liu (eds.), *Until Debt do us Part: Subnational Debt, Insolvency, and Markets*. Washington, DC: The World Bank, pp. 539–90. Available at: http://documents.worldbank.org/curated/en/2013/01/17406420/untildebt-part-subnational-debt-insolvency-markets

Lyons, R. (2011) 'Just Say Non: The Facts on Corporate Tax Rates in Europe', www.ronanlyons.com/2011/05/17/just-say-non-the-facts-on-corporate-tax-rates-in-europe/

Mathias, P. (1959) *The Brewing Industry in England, 1700–1830*. Cambridge: Cambridge University Press.

Mitchell, B.R. (ed.). (1988) *British Historical Statistics*. Cambridge: Cambridge University Press.

Neal, L. and García-Iglesias, M.C. (2013) 'The Economy of Spain in the Eurozone before and after the Crisis of 2008', *The Quarterly Review of Economics and Finance*, 53(4), pp. 336–44.

O'Brien, P.K. (1985) 'Agriculture and the Home Market for English Industry, 1660–1820', *English Historical Review*, 100(397), pp. 773–800.

O'Brien, P. (1988) 'The Political Economy of British Taxation, 1660–1815', *Economic History Review*, 41(1), pp. 1–32.

Petty, W. (1662) *A Treatise of Taxes and Contributions: Shewing the Nature and Measures of Crown-Lands, Assessements, Customs, Poll-Moneys . . .; with Several Intersperst Discourses and Digressions Concerning Warres, the Church, Universities, Rents & Purchases . . .: The Same Being Frequently Applied to the Present State and Affairs of Ireland*, London, printed for N. Brooke.

Quesnay, F. (1972 [1759]) *Quesnay's Tableau économique*, edited, with new material, translations and notes by M. Kuczynski and R. L. Meek, London: Macmillan; New York: A.M. Kelley for the Royal Economic Society and the American Economic Association.

Savage, J.D. and A. Verdun (2016) 'Strengthening the European Commission's budgetary and economic surveillance capacity since Greece and the euro area crisis: A study of five Directorates-General', *Journal of European Public Policy* 23(1), pp. 101–18.

Seligman, E.R.A. (1969a [1931]) *Essays in Taxation*. New York: Augustus M. Kelley Publishers.

Seligman, E.R.A. (1969b [1899]) *The Shifting Incidence of Taxation*. New York: Augustus M. Kelley.

Soros, G. (2013) "How to Save the European Union from the Euro Crisis." *Speech delivered at the Center for Financial Studies, Goethe University in Frankfurt, Germany.*

Spoerer, M. (2008) 'The Laspeyres-Paradox: Tax Overshifting in Nineteenth Century Prussia', *Cliometrica*, 2, pp. 173–93.

Stasavage, D. (2003) *Public Debt and the Birth of the Democratic State: France and Great Britain, 1688–1789*. New York: Cambridge University Press.

Stasavage, D. (2007) 'Cities, Constitutions, and Sovereign Borrowing in Europe, 1274–1785', *International Organization,* 61(Summer), pp. 489–525.

14 | *China's Investment in the Eurozone*

Structure, Route and Performance

YUNING GAO

14.1 Introduction

After China joined the WTO in 2001, the Chinese government has begun to think about encouraging its national champions to 'go out', which means to invest more overseas for both international resource and international market. Considering the advantage of China's own firms and the process of capital account opening, outward direct investment (ODI) should be the best option for this strategy. Besides, with the booming of China's economy during the following decade, resource seeking, market exploration and technology transfer through merger and acquisition became more and more important. China's ODI to Eurozone economies was highlighted by the large proportion of mergers and acquisition other than green field investment.

The other side of the story is that the momentary accumulation of China's foreign exchange reserves provides the possibility of overseas investment both in ODI and portfolio investment. The US treasury and Eurozone government bond serve as safe assets of China's foreign exchange reserves but deliver quite low returns. This is also why this contribution not only provides the details of the regional and sectoral distribution of China's ODI to Eurozone but also discusses China's portfolio investment from the central bank and its sovereign wealth fund. Separate statistics of China's ODI provide details on its final destinations and help to understand the source of return.

14.2 China as the Rising Investor of the World

Before 2005, as an investor, China only played a very minor role around the world. By the end of 2004, China only contributed 0.6 per cent of world's ODI and was not able to be listed in the top twenty investors. In 2005, China's ODI for the first time represented more than 1 per cent of the world's total and ranked as the nineteenth largest investors that year. From then on, China's direct investment outflow has increased sevenfold, from USD12.3 billion to USD84.2 billion in 2012, when China contributed 6 per cent of the world's aggregate outflow and was listed as the third-largest direct investor globally after the United States and Japan. This is a new record after being No. 6 for three years after the financial crisis. However, measured by the stock of ODI, China's was still just the thirteenth-largest and its USD500 billion stock amounted to just 2.2 per cent of the world's total in 2012.

The basic problem of China's direct investment statistics is that the Ministry of Finance only counted the new projects as inflow for a year, but did not include follow-up investment or withdrawal from previous projects. Therefore, the direct investment inflow in China's balance of payments typically differs from these statistics. From 2005, the difference was USD18.8 billion, nearly one-third of the new FDI net inflow reported by the Ministry of Commerce. The total FDI inflow rose to USD147.8 billion in 2008, close to double as much as the new FDI net inflow. However, the total amount then dropped to USD11.8 billion in 2009. The convergence of the two measures suggests a decline in follow-up investment in existing projects.

For outgoing direct investment from China, there is also a difference in the two statistics. For instance, in 2012 new outgoings were USD 14.9 billion higher than total outgoings up to that point.

The total figure dropped from USD 53.5 billion in 2007 to USD 43.9 billion in 2008. By contrast, new outflows rose from USD 55.9 billion to USD 56.5 billion. After that, the total ODI rose to USD 62.4 billion in 2012 while the new ODI for 2013 had already reached USD 87.8 billion. The gap between them remained at 26 billion from 2011 and most of it can be explained by the fact that the retreat of overseas investment was much larger than retained profit (if any).

Unlike export, China's outward direct investment was overwhelmingly concentrated in Hong Kong, whose share almost doubled from 27.9 per cent in 2005 to 69 per cent in 2008, and then dropped to 58.4 per cent in 2012. The importance of Hong Kong was virtually the same in both the incoming and outgoing sides. In 2012, inflows from Hong Kong reached USD 71.3 billion (63.8 per cent of China's total) and outflows to Hong Kong represented about USD 51.2 billion (58.4 per cent of China's total).

The second-largest group of economies relevant to China's FDI and ODI are tax havens. The British Virgin Islands were the largest source of FDI to China, and the Cayman Islands were the second-largest

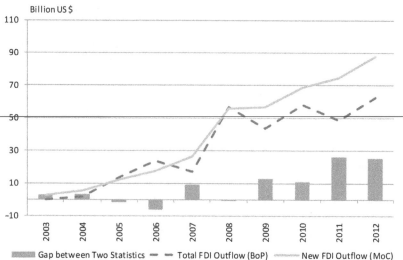

Figure 14.1 China's Outward Direct Investment and Its Projection
Source: Author's calculation based on MoC, NBS and SAFE (2013)

destination for many years. Hong Kong gradually replaced the tax havens after 2007 but the latter still obtained 15 per cent of China's ODI by 2011. In contrast, the proportion of Chiang Mai Zone in China's ODI, including Japan, Korea and ASEAN economies, expanded from 2.3 per cent in 2003 to 8.3 per cent in 2012. Besides, the European Union also expanded as the third-largest destination and was the destination of more than 10 per cent of China's ODI in 2011.

However, the official statistics of China's direct investment, both inward and outward, were seriously distorted by investments to and from Hong Kong. The problem of the dominance of Hong Kong in China's inflow has already been pointed out by many other researchers (UNCTAD, 1995; World Bank, 2002): a large proportion of direct investment via Hong Kong was 'round-tripping capital' seeking tax avoidance and other subsidiary benefits. The estimate from Xiao (2004) pointed out that around 40 per cent of China's incoming direct investment was this type of capital, and Hong Kong is no doubt its hub. However, details of the sources of these investments are still secret, meaning that nearly a quarter of total direct investment into China is unidentifiable.

For China's ODI, Hong Kong is also the by-pass destination (Liao and Tsui, 2012). Global Heritage Foundation set up a new China

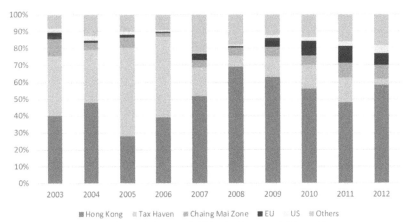

Figure 14.2 Regional Breakdown of China's Outward Direct Investment
Note: 'Tax Havens' refers to Bermuda, British Virgin Islands and Cayman Islands.
Source: Author's calculation based on MoC, NBS and SAFE (2013)

Investment Tracker database to record the final destination and sector of each deal. Hereby we can clarify the distribution of the ultimate destination of China's ODI. The total ODI of China in this database is quite close to the official statistics, which guaranteed its coverage ratio and did not miss any main investment deals.

Under this alternative statistics, resource suppliers, particularly Australia, Canada, Norway, Iran, Iraq, Qatar, Saudi Arabia, Kazakhstan and Russia, are the group of economies that obtained most ODI from China. China's ODI in these countries combined reached USD 21.6 billion in 2008 and increased to USD 31.8 billion in 2012 (especially significant was the USD 15.1 billion acquisition of Nexen by CNOOC), which amounts to nearly two-fifths of China's total ODI. Three investment projects from China's three oil national champions (USD 3.1 billion from CNOOC to Bridas [Argentina], USD 3.1 billion from Sinochem to Statoil [Brazil] and USD 7.1 billion from Sinopec to Repsol [Brazil]) made Latin America the top destination of China's ODI in 2010.

The EU emerged to be the third-largest investment destination of China in 2011 mainly because of two giant investment projects in the Eurozone, the USD 3.2 billion from CIC to GDF Suez (France) and the USD 3.5 billion from Three Gorges to Energias de Portugal. Rising direct investment from China to the United Kingdom then made the EU the second-largest destination by 2012. Interestingly, Hong Kong and

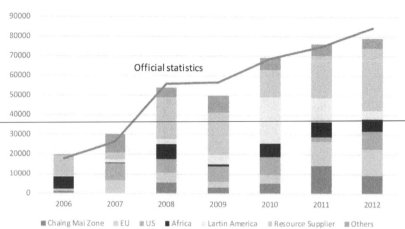

Figure 14.3 Regional Distribution of China's Outward Direct Investment
Source: Author's calculation based on Heritage Foundation (2013)

tax havens had no role in this ultimate destination statistics. This indicates they are purely by-pass of China's ODI to its real ultimate destination. This new statistics is an effective tool to understanding that China's main objective is no doubt resource seeking. Therefore, official statistics based on first destination are actually greatly misrepresenting the sectoral structure of China's ODI. Indeed, the reason why leasing and business services represent more than one-third (as high as 44 per cent in 2010) of China's ODI is because a large part of investments using Hong Kong and tax havens as their investment hub was recorded under business services investment rather than under their final targeting sectors.

According to official statistics, the mining sector, including energy resources (but excluded utilities), accounts for less than one-fifth of China's total ODI. In contrast, if we look at ultimate destination statistics, most outward direct investment from China between 2006 and 2012 concentrated on energy and metals sectors, which represented about three-quarters of total investment outflow (except 2007). A large share of investment in these sectors used the 'business services' in Hong Kong and some tax havens to reach their ultimate destinations. Interestingly, the dominance of the financial sector, including the USD 3 billion and USD 5 billion investments from CIC in Blackstone and Morgan Stanley in 2007, was also completely missed by official statistics.

Table 14.1 *Sectoral structure of China's ODI*

	2006	2007	2008	2009	2010	2011	2012
	Official statistics						
Mining	40.35	15.33	10.42	23.60	8.31	19.35	15.42
Manufacture	4.28	8.02	3.16	3.96	6.78	9.43	9.87
Wholesale and retailing	5.26	24.92	11.65	10.85	9.78	13.83	14.86
Leasing and business service	21.36	21.15	38.85	36.22	44.01	34.29	30.46
Finance	16.68	6.29	25.13	15.45	12.54	8.13	11.47
Others	12.06	24.29	10.80	9.91	18.59	14.97	17.92
	Real destination statistics						
Energy	48.13	7.97	42.26	52.81	55.16	53.00	57.71
Metals	36.88	21.59	43.13	25.54	14.47	20.79	14.52
Finance and real estate	7.06	65.21	12.69	15.94	15.63	8.67	13.11
Others	7.92	5.22	1.91	5.72	14.73	17.54	14.66

Source: Author's calculation based on MoC, NBS and SAFE (2013); Heritage Foundation (2013).

14.3 Direct Investment in the Eurozone

According to official statistics, the direct investment from China to the EU economies reached USD 7.56 billion in 2011 (Luxembourg receiving USD 1.86 billion), accounting for 10 per cent of China's total ODI (74.65 billion dollars), but dropped to USD 6.12 billion in 2012. However, investment having the EU as final destination contributed 17.1 per cent of China's total ODI in 2012, which rose to USD 13.5 billion in 2012 from USD 12.4 billion in 2011. Among all EU economies, the Eurozone played a very important role, with a peak of 80 per cent in 2011 but dropping to 40 per cent in 2012 because of the rise of the United Kingdom as another principal destination within the EU.

In the official statistics of China's ODI to Eurozone, the USD 3.2 billion investment from CIC to GDF Suez made France account for nearly 60 per cent of China's ODI in the Eurozone. Luxembourg played a similar role of Hong Kong. In 2009 and 2010, it was the first destination for 83 per cent of China's ODI to this region. This means that the role of Luxembourg was greatly overestimated during this period of time compared with the ultimate destination statistics. On the contrary, the missing record of USD 3.5 billion investment from

Table 14.2 *China's ODI in the Eurozone*

	2006	2007	2008	2009	2010	2011	2012
Luxembourg		4.2	42.1	2,270.5	3,207.2	1,265.0	1,133.0
		(1.11)	(10.52)	(83.27)	(83.35)	(21.54)	(39.02)
Germany	76.7	238.7	183.4	179.2	412.4	512.4	799.3
	(59.88)	(63.04)	(45.82)	(6.57)	(10.72)	(8.72)	(27.53)
France	5.6	9.6	31.1	45.2	26.4	3,482.3	153.9
	(4.37)	(2.54)	(7.76)	(1.66)	(0.69)	(59.29)	(5.30)
Netherland	5.31	106.75	91.97	101.45	64.53	167.86	442.45
	(4.14)	(28.20)	(22.98)	(3.72)	(1.68)	(2.86)	(15.24)
Other	40.5	19.4	51.7	130.2	137.4	445.8	375.2
	(31.60)	(5.11)	(12.93)	(4.77)	(3.57)	(7.59)	(12.92)

Source: Author's calculation based on MoC, NBS and SAFE (2013).

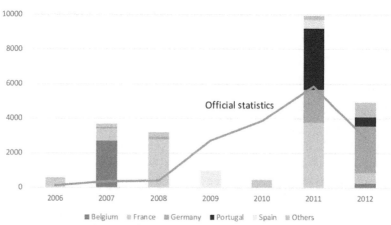

Figure 14.4 Distribution of China's ODI to the Eurozone
Source: Author's calculation based on Heritage Foundation (2013)

Three Gorges to Energias de Portugal greatly underestimated the total ODI from China to the Eurozone in 2011.

Under official statistics, leasing and business service is the main sector for China's ODI to the EU, especially between 2009 and 2010. This is no doubt because of investment services through Luxembourg. China's purchase of 21.35 per cent of GDF Suez resulted in the mining and utility sector representing 45 per cent of China's ODI in EU in 2011.

Table 14.3 *Sector distribution of China's ODI in the Eurozone*

	2007	2008	2009	2010	2011	2012
China's ODI to the European Union (official statistics)						
Mining and utility	7.9	−1.2	0.7	2.5	44.8	0.7
Manufacture	9.5	35.2	7.4	33.9	8.6	29.5
Wholesale and retailing	11.5	7.2	1.2	1.9	1.3	7.0
Leasing and business service	10.6	27.4	78.0	53.6	30.0	20.6
Finance	39.4	18.2	7.1	5.4	6.9	17.1
Others	21.1	13.2	5.6	2.7	8.4	25.1
China's ODI to the European Union (real destination statistics)						
Energy and metal		87.8		42.6	72.9	35.1
Manufacture	19.1	12.2		57.4	6.7	40.2
Finance	73.6				7.2	
Others	7.4		100.0		13.2	24.7

Source: Author's calculation based on MoC, NBS and SAFE (2013); Heritage Foundation (2013).

This was the largest direct investment project of China in the Eurozone and also one of the largest direct investment projects all around the world. Manufactures contributed 34 per cent of China's ODI to the EU in 2010 and 30 per cent in 2012, mostly due to the USD 2.7 billion acquisition of Volvo by Geely[1] followed by the USD 1.7 billion purchase of three German manufacturing firms, Putzmeister, Schwing and Kion.[2] Table 14.3 details the sectoral distribution of China's ODI in the EU.[3]

The typical route of direct investment from China to the Eurozone was through merger and acquisition. Contracted merger and acquisition investment (USD 37.8 billion) accounted for 43 per cent of China's total ODI in 2012. On the other hand, the EU economies represent one-third of total merger and acquisition investment, which

[1] Including the USD 900 million injection for operation.
[2] Including the purchasing of 70% of its subsidiary, Linde Hydraulics, for USD 340 million.
[3] Similar to the sectoral distribution of China's total ODI, the energy and metal sector is also the focal field of investment in China in 2008 and 2011. The investment in manufacturing sector was correctly recorded as the largest one in 2010 and 2012 in both statistics. However, as the sectoral structure of ODI to a specific region is more case-sensitive, the only contract of USD 1 billion investment from China Unicom to Telefonica (Spain) in 2009 made 'other sectors' the only option for that year.

means most ODI from China to the EU economies were merger and acquisition investment. Many of these mergers and acquisitions relied on the business service through Hong Kong and Luxembourg for tax avoidance on dividend, capital gains and profits.

For example, Sany Heavy Industry Group acquired a 90 per cent stake of the German concrete machinery firm Putzmeister through CITIC PE Advisors (China's leading private equity) for about 500 million euros. As Hong Kong would provide tax-free service on capital inflows, the Chinese investors would be able to use them as channels for overseas investment and retain their gains and profits there for reinvestment. Luxembourg provides similar services to capital inflows back from Eurozone economies and at least avoidance of double taxation from other economies. Combining them together, China's ODI followed a route to maximize return, but which distorts statistical evidence.Another way of China's ODI in the Eurozone was through leasing and financing. In 2009, the Chinese shipping giant COSCO concluded the thirty-five-year lease deal of the main dock at the Greek port Piraeus. In return, they have pledged to spend USD 700 million to construct a new pier and upgrade existing docks. By January 2013, they have invested 1 billion euros (USD 1.29 billion) for a 60 per cent stake in Piraeus port. In addition, in early 2012 Chinese banks (China Development Bank, Export Import Bank of China, Bank of China and China Construction Bank) established a USD 8–10 billion fund to finance the Greek merchant shipping industry in order to back Greek orders at Chinese shipyards.

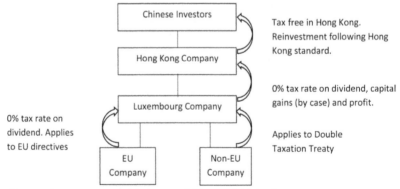

Figure 14.5 Investment Structure of China's ODI in the Eurozone
Source: Author's formulation

14.4 Portfolio Investment in the Eurozone

Although China has already successfully accumulated the second-largest foreign exchange reserves since 1996, nobody considered China as a potential portfolio investor. This is because those reserves were held by the People's Bank of China (PBoC) under the mandatory foreign exchange settlement policy, and the conservative strategy of PBoC relied only on US treasury to keep its level of return. This policy was gradually abandoned with the founding on 29 September 2007 of China's primary sovereign wealth fund, the China Investment Corporation.

The currency structure of China's foreign exchange reserves was quite comparable to the world average, where the proportion of the US dollar dropped from 70 per cent in 2001 to a little above 60 per cent in mid-2011. Meanwhile, the euro's share rose from 17 per cent in 2001 to 27 per cent in the second quarter of 2011 (about 595.3 billion euros, or USD 863.3 billion equivalent).

This level of euro reserves amounts to a considerable stock, even if it is still rather limited considering the huge amount of portfolio investment opportunities available in the Eurozone. China may be able to play a more important role in supra-national platforms such as the European Financial Stability Facility (EFSF) or the European

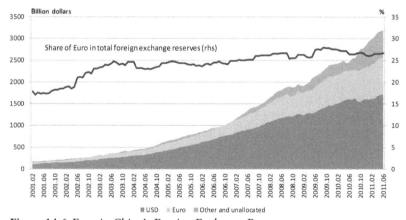

Figure 14.6 Euro in China's Foreign Exchange Reserves

Source: Author's calculation based on Bertaut and Tryon (2007); US Department of Treasury (2012)

Stability Mechanism (ESM) and increase its participation in solving the European sovereign debt crisis. For instance, in the 5 billion euro inaugural issuance of EFSF (January 2012), the Asian 14 per cent investment (excluding Japan), amounting to 700 million euros, mainly comes from China. China's Prime Minister Wen Jiabao stated that 'China ... will, as always, follow the practice of diversified investments ... Europe is one of the main investment markets for China's foreign exchange reserves, and China will continue to help settle the region's debt crisis through appropriate means' (Xinhuanet, 2012).

European sovereign bonds are no doubt a valuable opportunity for the People's Bank of China, and especially for the State Administration of Foreign Exchange, to diversify its foreign exchange reserves. However, China's Sovereign Wealth Fund, the CIC, held a different position, as they usually focused on long-term equity investment. The board director of CIC, Jiwei Lou, pointed out that their investment opportunities were in areas such as infrastructure and industrial projects (see CIC's purchase of about 30 per cent of GDF Suez for USD 3.15 billion in August 2011), and these projects can help the economic recovery of the Eurozone. Of the CIC's USD 135.1 billion global portfolio investment in 2010, USD 22.3 billion was in Europe (21.7 per cent of the total diversified investment).

Under China's current capital control, the portfolio investment to overseas market other than the central bank and the sovereign wealth fund is still quite limited. Before the birth of Qualified Domestic Institutional Investors (QDII) in April 2006, the portfolios of overseas wealth management business were not allowed to include any equities. Even after that, the overall amount of investment through QDIIs is limited. By the mid-2013, 113 QDIIs were awarded an overall investment quota of USD 88.3 billion. The market value of the portfolio of all QDII funds was just 65.754 billion Yuan, of which 3.2 per cent was distributed at the UK market while the Eurozone received less than 1 per cent by mid-2012.

14.5 Performance of China's Outward Investment

By the end of 2012, more than 16,000 Chinese investors had built up more than 22,000 affiliations overseas with foreign assets of slightly less than USD 2.3 trillion, which made for a sharp increase from USD

1.5 trillion in 2010 (MoC , NBS and SAFE, 2013). The key indicator of these investments is their return rate, which is generally given as the nominal rate of return on the stock of ODI, or increasingly the rate of return on the equity portion. Return data for an economy can be found under the current account of the balance-of-payments statistics, while the stock of ODI was collected by UNCTAD (2013), FDI statistics in a historical cost method, and IMF (2013) International Investment Position statistics in current cost methods.

Although more detailed work, such as adjustment for retained profit, needs to be done to calculate accurate returns, this streamlined method can provide at least a rough measure of investment returns. Xie and Jiang (2012) compared the return on equity (stock) of ODI of China and the United States by applying this method. If we apply their method, the return rate of China's ODI is just comparable with that of the United States between 2006 and 2008, being only 2–3 per cent lower. However, the return rate dropped considerably from 7.8 per cent in 2008 to just 4.5 per cent in 2009, being 4 per cent lower than that of the United States. Although the return rate recovered to 5.3 per cent in 2010, it again fell to 4.7 per cent in 2011 (author's estimation).

Furthermore, the estimation of return of China's ODI relies not only on income flows but also on the value adjustment of the stock of ODI. In balance-of-payments statistics, the magnitude and position change of direct investment usually does not coincide with the yearly investment flow, and the gap is usually interpreted as value adjustment. Interestingly, the value adjustment of China's ODI kept positive after 2001, which means that the overall loss was compensated by asset price appreciation. For instance, in 2012, if we consider the value adjustment of China's ODI, the return rate of China's ODI in 2012 would have been about 7 per cent.

This should be the most optimistic estimation, as usually mergers and acquisitions faced much larger potential loss compared with 'green field' investment while the former dominates China's ODI to Europe.

In contrast, the report by the Ministry of Commerce of China highlighted that only 30 per cent of China's overseas investment projects have become profitable. This reflects the total return rate of Chinese investments overseas, but also highlights the challenges facing China's overseas investment. One major issue for China's investors is the lack of international business experience. The story of the 'going out' of Chinese firms became a brand new reality only a decade ago.

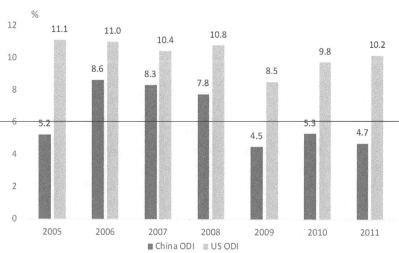

Figure 14.7 Return on Equity of the ODI of China and the United States
Source: Author's estimation based on SAFE (2013)

Compared with multinational companies from developed economies, the experiences of these Chinese newcomers mainly come from domestic markets with a rather short history. Other problems are the inefficiency in the operation of state owned enterprises, which currently dominate China's ODI, especially in the field of resource exploration and development. Large resource projects no doubt entailed much higher risks than other conventional and small projects. Furthermore, the strategic target of these large resource investors is mainly focussed on the amount of resources taken out rather than on profit gained from business activity. Therefore, losses are sometimes not counted in the performance measurement system of their supervisor, although more and more attention has been brought to this field.

Apart from lacking experience in international business operations, the knowledge of legal, cultural and other risks of the host economies is also very scarce among managers of overseas Chinese firms. Conflicts between corporate cultures and different approaches to business-government relations and to corporate social responsibility lead to serious challenges to the success of China's direct investment overseas.

In spite of this, the missing piece of the story is that many overseas projects or firms have not become profitable because of the 'last dollar effect' of infrastructural projects, which contribute a large proportion of China's ODI in Africa and Latin America. This effect indicates that most construction projects will not bring any profit before final completion, while many other projects can be put into operation piece by piece and generate an income flow from a very early stage of project life.

14.6 Conclusion

The rise of China as one of the main investors around the world is an event that cannot be neglected by any observer of the past decade. By applying non-official final destination statistics, we can identify that China's ODI mainly went to energy and metals sectors through all its principal resource suppliers globally. China's investment in the Eurozone was one of the key components of its overseas investment, taking second position among world destinations in 2012. As the largest source of merger and acquisition investment, Chinese investment in the Eurozone was seeking technology and infrastructure rather than primary resources, unlike Chinese investment in Africa and Latin America. In addition, the huge amount of euro reserves China accumulated in the past has been invested into Eurozone sovereign bonds or into the supranational bonds of EFSF and ESM. These investments would bring a much lower return than direct investment. However, the return rate of China's ODI was not that satisfactory for the reasons discussed earlier in the chapter. We would expect more experienced investors and rising investment from China in the Eurozone in the future, which should bring more and more opportunities than challenges to this region.

References

Bertaut, C. C. and Tryon, Ralph W. (2007) 'Monthly Estimates of U.S. Cross-border Securities Positions', Board of Governors of the Federal Reserve System International Finance Discussion Papers Number 910, November.

European Financial Stability Facility (EFSF) (2012) 'European Financial Stability Facility', www.efsf.europa.eu/attachments/efsf_presentation_en.pdf.

Heritage Foundation (2013) 'China Global Investment Tracker Database', http://thf_media.s3.amazonaws.com/2013/xls/China-Global-Investment-Tracker2013.xls.

International Monetary Fund (IMF) (2013) *Balance of Payment Database*, University of Manchester, ESDS International.

Liao, W. and Tsui, K. K. (2012) 'China's Outward Direct Investment: Evidence from a New Micro Dataset', HKIMR Working Paper No. 17/2012.

Ministry of Commerce (MoC) (2013) National Bureau of Statistics (NBS) and State Administration of Foreign Exchange (SAFE), *2012 Statistical Bulletin of China's Outward Foreign Direct Investment*, Beijing: China Statistics Press.

State Administration of Foreign Exchange (SAFE) (2013) 'The time-series data of Balance of Payments of China', www.safe.gov.cn/wps/portal/!ut/p/c5/04_SB8K8xLLM9MSSzPy8xBz9CP0os3gPZxdnX293QwP30FAn A8_AEBc3C1NjIxMjU6B8JG75YGMKdLubGRDQHQ5yLX7b8ciDz QfJG-AAjgb6fh75uan6BbmhEQaZAekAc9mgLQ!!/dl3/d3/ L2dJQSEv UUt3QS9ZQnZ3LzZfSENEQ01LRzEwT085RTBJNkE1U1NDRzNM TDQ!/?WCM_GLOBAL_CONTEXT=/wps/wcm/connect/safe_web_ store/state+administration+of+foreign+exchange/data+and+statistics/ balance+of+payments/03119b804c296bc0a405af4393d9cc2e.

UNCTAD (1995) *World Investment Report 1995*, New York: United Nations.

UNCTAD (2013) *UNCTAD STAT – Foreign Direct Investment Database*, http://unctadstat.unctad.org/ReportFolders/reportFolders.aspx?sRF_ ActivePath=p,5&sRF_Expanded=,p,5.

US Department of Treasury (2012) 'Holdings of U.S. Long-term Securities by Foreign Residents (monthly)', *Treasury International Capital (TIC) System Website*, www.treasury.gov/resource-center/data-chart-center/ tic/Pages/ticsec2.aspx#ussecs.

World Bank (2002) *Global Development Finance 2002*, Washington, DC: World Bank.

Xiao, G. (2004) 'Round-tripping Foreign Direct Investment and the People's Republic of China', ADB Institute Research Paper Series No. 58, July.

Xie, D. and Jiang. B. (2012) 'Performance of China's Outward Direct Investment (中国对外直接投资表现)', Shui On Center for China Business & Management, HKUST Business School, 20120130.

Xinhuanet (2012) 'Yearender: China, EU seeking opportunities for better partnership amid debt crisis', http://news.xinhuanet.com/english/china/ 2012-12/19/c_132050486.htm.

15 | Eurobonds for EMU Stability and Structural Growth

ALBERTO QUADRIO CURZIO

15.1 Introduction

The crisis within the Eurozone, which began in 2009, had (and still has) at least two main aspects. One is the problem of sovereign bonds issued by 'peripheral' member states. The other is the fall in the rate of growth of the Eurozone. Among the many proposals and political choices made to overcome the twin crisis, one concerned the so-called Eurobonds, which in fact cover a wide range of bonds.

The proposal to issue some kind of Eurobond has a long history that goes back at least to 1993 when Jacques Delors, at that time President of the European Commission, first made such a suggestion. Over the past twenty years the number of similar proposals has steadily increased.

The aim of this essay is to present in a systematic and comprehensive framework concrete proposals about Eurobonds, including those that I have made since 2004, and focussing on those I consider to be more institutionally important.

There has been reluctance to accept these proposals, and to date only a number of 'Rescuebonds' have been issued (since 2010) by what might be called the European Rescue Funds (officially EFSF and ESM). My interest in the subject of Eurobonds has many roots, which may be traced back to the two following lines of research.

The first line of research concerns gold as a quasi-money commodity (which in the past was also a standard of value or a *numéraire*) and as a real asset capable of functioning as the ultimate guarantee of value across centuries. This line of investigation connects with my interest in the problem of sovereign wealth funds. These are built on surpluses of trade balances in primary commodities and goods, often with remarkable consequences for financial markets where they operate as safe investments. This inquiry concerns the intersection of real and monetary phenomena under conditions of structural change in the world economy.

The second line of research refers to my studies on the institutional and economic aspects of the European Union (EU) and Economic and Monetary Union (EMU). I maintain that a true Union cannot rely exclusively on the euro and on rules for budget equilibrium and market competition. It also needs a structurally integrated economic system with appropriate economic policies and a strategy of investment in industry, infrastructure, techno-sciences and human resources across the EU[1]. Political union and cultural identity are very important but are not enough without a real structural integration of national economies, which might precede a possible political union.

Since 2004 (and also in the most recent years) I have dealt many times with proposals to introduce Eurobonds and establish some kind of European Fund in the EMU.[2]

In this essay, I examine five types of Eurobonds, which have been proposed in different occasions and by different people, including myself: the Unionbond, the Goldeurobond, the Stabilitybond, the Rescuebond and the EuroUnionBond. I focus on these five types from a point of view combining a political-institutional perspective with a political economy approach of a rather pragmatic type. This means that none of these proposals will be approached from a strictly analytical point of view. This choice is because both the Eurobond proposals and their critiques have been and still are strongly influenced by political considerations.

15.2 Unionbonds: Investment for Growth

Jacques Delors, as President of the European Commission in 1993, in the white paper, *Growth, Employment and Competitiveness,* which was both inspired and endorsed by him, made a proposal concerning the issuance of 'new facilities': Unionbonds (with the EU budget as collateral) and Convertibles (guaranteed by the European investment Fund-EIF). These new facilities were intended to be a means of

---

[1] In the past I wrote extensively on European Union and on European Monetary Union especially with an approach of institutional political economy. This is also the framework of this essay, which expands and clarifies the Working Paper 'Eurobond for EMU Stability, Convergence, Growth' (CRANEC, V.P., Catholic University, Milan, 2014)

[2] See especially: Quadrio Curzio (2004; 2008a; 2008b; 2008c; 2008d; 2008e; 2011a; 2011b); Prodi and Quadrio Curzio (2011; 2012a; 2012b).

financing investment in large infrastructural projects (Trans-European Networks) in fields such as energy, transport, telecommunications and the environment. A further assumption was made that the promoters of the projects themselves (public- and private-sector institutions) would be the beneficiaries of expected returns. These promoters would consequently also be responsible for contributing the capital and paying interest, while the EU would act as a guarantor for the bonds. In this scenario the EIB (European Investment Bank) was intended to fulfill the role of an 'adviser', but also to act as an agent on behalf of the European Commission for the issuing of bonds.

Nothing came out of this proposal, and all bond issues of an institutional European character remained the already existing ones of the EIB (European Investment Bank) and EIF (European Investment Fund).

In regard of Delors's proposal, there has been much commentary over the years, but more recently the focus of discussion has shifted towards Stabilitybonds (see Section 15.4) and Rescuebonds (see Section 15.5), which have nothing to do with Delors's proposal.

Delors himself, in an interview (Montefiori, 2010), confirmed his strong belief that Unionbonds would have an important role to play in financing large infrastructure, research, growth and employment projects. He also added that Tommaso Padoa Schioppa, who had collaborated with him over many years, shared this point of view. Delors maintained that Unionbonds should be accepted by Germany, as they are not financial instruments intended 'to cover the deficits of the past'.

15.3 GoldEurobonds: Debt Safety and Investment Push

This type of Eurobond proposal, which I made in 2008 (but first alluded to in 2004), has its roots in two long-standing interests of mine. First, I have been interested in the relationships between real and value-related (financial and monetary) economic phenomena, which made me analyze the role of gold (Quadrio Curzio, 1982b),[3]

---

[3] This volume (Chinese ed. 1988; Italian ed. 1989) has a preface by Romano Prodi and essays of outstanding experts on gold at that time (among them Aliber R.Z., Boyer De La Giroday F., Du Boulay L., Fells P., Languetin P., Larre R., Schwartz A. and Wittich G.), whose contributions deserve to be listed in the References section, even though I don't directly cite any of them throughout the rest of the chapter.

and later that of sovereign wealth funds (Quadrio Curzio and Miceli, 2010). Second, I have been interested in economic institutions such as the EU and the EMU (to which gold and Sovereign Funds also might be connected).

On this basis of idle European gold (Section 15.3.1), I proposed a Gold Development Fund issuing Eurobonds in order to finance Eurozone countries' debt from one side and investment/infrastructure from the other (Section 15.3.2).

15.3.1 Gold after Bretton Wood's Collapse

Looking at gold, I was dissatisfied with economic policy and institutional decisions since the events of 1968–71 (Quadrio Curzio, 1982b). My dissatisfaction derived more from economic history and economic institution than from principles of economic theory on gold. Focusing on the United States and the European Community, I came to the following conclusions.

The United States (in spite of the Gold Commission studies set up by President Ronald Reagan in 1981) acted, since the collapse of the Bretton Woods Agreements, to put an end to any role that gold might have as quasi-money. Europe, by contrast, has been completely inactive in spite of maintaining the highest official reserves to the European Monetary Cooperation Fund (EMCF) members and ECU countries: they amounted to 37.26 per cent of the world total – that is, 428 million ounces, against 264 million ounces of the United States.[4] As I argued,

Europe should have sought to defend flexibly, the price of gold. A coordinated plan of purchases – not of large quantities – put into effect when the price of gold was around $500 an ounce would have probably interrupted the decline in price. The effects might have been three [fold]: to maintain [the] competitiveness of gold with respect to the dollar and to avoid therefore liquid capital abandoning the former for the latter; to maintain consequently the value in dollars of European gold reserves; to take a step forward towards forms of gold 'coverage' of European currencies.' (Quadrio Curzio, 1982b, p. 16)

I further argued, '[t]he conclusion is therefore that if there is an area which at present should concern itself with elaborating a gradual

---

[4] The data in the essay are those available in January (and in some cases in the first quarter of) 2014 (*see* par. 7.3) when this essay was written. This fact has no consequences on the substance of the essay.

policy for the use of gold in international relations, this is Europe, whose reserves are such as to permit a freedom of movement which is unsurpassed by any other country, including the United States' (Quadrio Curzio, 1982b, p. 16). Thus, '[w]ithout imagining, then, a return to outdated forms of the gold standard, if gold can in part fulfil a stabilizing role, let us not be ashamed to use it' (Quadrio Curzio, 1982b, p. 16). And looking ahead, '[t]his will not, then, be a conclusion, but a starting point' (Quadrio Curzio, 1982b, p. 17). The course of the future, however, cannot be traced looking only at gold or at the international monetary system, as we must consider also – and perhaps above all – that during the 1970s, structural changes in the world economy had determined a crisis of the international monetary system. The backwash of this crisis on structural changes themselves had produced a tangle of consequences in which it is extremely difficult to separate causes from effects. The result had been that of calling attention once again to a reserve-value function of gold, which would provide a link between 'real factors' and 'monetary factors' (Quadrio Curzio, 1982b, p. 17; Quadrio Curzio, 1985).

These statements appear quite simple taking into consideration what happened in the past thirty years, and not out of place, given that gold remained a crucial reserve of the central banks.

After the establishment of the EU and EMU, I came back to my original idea that gold could have a role in dealing with the European economic policies beyond remaining an official reserve of ECB and national central banks. My idea was also highlighted by the successful experience of Sovereign Wealth Funds, which since the 1990s had developed at the intersection of real and financial activities (Quadrio Curzio and Miceli, 2009, 2010).

15.3.2 Euro-Gold-Development Fund and Gold-Eurobonds

In light of the situation described in the preceding section, I proposed creating a Euro-Gold-Development Fund (henceforth identified as EGDF) (Quadrio Curzio, 2008a, 2008b, 2009), in order to issue debt securities that would become the EMU's 'sovereign' bonds. The proposal I envisaged was more a draft than a project. The EGDF's assets should be constituted of the gold reserves of EMU countries, to be held as collateral to issue public debt securities. The contribution of each country to the EGDF must be equal to its quota of the EMU's GDP.

Once the capital stock and the paid-in-capital is fixed, those countries which do not have enough gold reserves to cover their quota must complete their commitment with other assets.

The statute of the EGDF should take into account many conditions planned specially in order, on one hand, to help the countries with high debt-to-GDP ratio to raise financing at interest rates lower than the ones available on the open market, and on the other hand to push these debtor nations to reduce their debt burden.

The main use of Euro-Gold-Development bonds would be the partial financing of national sovereign debt of EMU states. The interest rate should be higher than that EGDF would have to pay to its subscribers, but still lower than the market rates that individual states currently have to pay, given that all Eurozone countries are subject to a risk premium. The easiest solution would be to issue Gold-bonds at the interest rates of Germany's bund, which has the lowest interest rates.

Another use of the resources raised selling Gold-bonds might be the financing of merger operations within the EMU banking and industrial system. The purpose of such merger operations would be to facilitate the restructuring of such enterprises and to strengthen their position in the global economy. In a similar way the Gold-bond sales might be the financing investment in infrastructures within EMU.

Admittedly, the proposals outlined above were only a multifaceted starting point with numerous potential developments connected to gold reserves. This aspect could see Italy contributing at a level not far below Germany, and higher than France, thereby reassuring the suspicious Germany, which in 1973 granted to Italy a loan guaranteed by her gold reserves.

This proposal was originally conceived in 2004 (Quadrio Curzio, 2004), specified five years later (Quadrio Curzio, 2009) and reformulated in precise way at the beginning of the current decade (Quadrio Curzio, 2011b) (see Section 15.7).

15.4 Stabilitybonds: The Role of EU Institutions

The years 2010–12, with some extensions into 2013, saw many analyses and discussions on Eurobonds. The quantity and quality of the contributions were such that it is impossible to do justice to this variety. Therefore, I focus on those that are, in my view, the most important ones: that of the European Commission (EC) in 2011–13, and that of the European Parliament (EP) in 2011–12. For the public opinion might be interesting also the two Ministers' (Juncker and Tremonti) proposal, published on a newspaper in 2010.

15.4.1 The Two Ministers' proposal

Jean-Claude Juncker, Eurogroup President and Prime Minister of Luxembourg, a country without a public debt problem, and Giulio Tremonti, Minister of Economy and Finances of Italy, a country with a large and dangerous public debt, made a proposal on 5 December 2010.[5] They 'informally' (Juncker and Tremonti, 2010) called for the issuance of 'Eurobonds' to be used for restructuring public debt in EMU member states. This would also function as a means for reducing speculative attacks.

The J-T proposal stated that sovereign bonds of many EMU member states were under pressure in spite of the fiscal and monetary measures taken by the EU and the EMU. Therefore, they argued that the EU/EMU should act more decisively to preserve the EMU and the Euro. In doing so a clear signal should be sent to both markets and European citizens. Accordingly, they advocated the issuance of 'European sovereign bonds' (which I term Stabilitybonds), to be issued by a European Debt Agency (EDA) also envisaged to replace the European Financial Stability Facility (EFSF) that had been active since August 2010 (see Section 15.6). According to the J-T proposal, the EDA (which should become complementary to the ECB) should place bonds on the market in an amount equal to 40 per cent of the GDP of the EMU and thus of the Eurozone member states. This would create a market for European sovereign debt securities with high liquidity and of size comparable to that of US public bonds (which have flooded international markets due to the absence of any comparable high-liquidity bonds). Using the liquidity created by such bond issues, the EDA should then purchase EMU member states' sovereign bonds, both at issuance and on the secondary market, thus becoming creditor to these states and thereby replacing the market itself.

---

[5] Even if the proposal was not analytically elaborated, the institutional role of the two authors made it an important statement in the EMU scenario

15.4.2 *The European Parliament's Proposal*

The role of the European Parliament (EP) was much more important, even if surprisingly disregarded by public opinion and also by governments. The starting point is the EP Resolution of 6 July 2011 on the financial, economic and social crisis: recommendations concerning the measures and initiatives to be taken, which states that the EP

[c]alls on the Commission to carry out an investigation into a future system of Eurobonds, with a view to determining the conditions under which such a system would be beneficial to all participating Member States and to the euro area as a whole; points out that Eurobonds would offer a viable alternative to the US dollar bond market, and that they could foster integration of the European sovereign debt market, lower borrowing costs, increase liquidity, budgetary discipline and compliance with the Stability and Growth Pact (SGP), promote coordinated structural reforms, and make capital markets more stable, which will foster the idea of the euro as a global 'safe haven'; recalls that the common issuance of Eurobonds requires a further move towards a common economic and fiscal policy; [s]tresses, therefore, that when Eurobonds are to be issued, their issuance should be limited to a debt ratio of 60% of GDP under joint and several liability as senior sovereign debt, and should be linked to incentives to reduce sovereign debt to that level; suggests that the overarching aim of Eurobonds should be to reduce sovereign debt and to avoid moral hazard and prevent speculation against the euro; notes that access to such Eurobonds would require agreement on, and implementation of, measurable programmes of debt reduction. (European Parliament, 2011) This statement and the invitation to the European Commission (EC) were and are very clear, and to that the EC answered with the publication of the 'Green Paper on the feasibility of introducing Stability Bonds' (European Commission, 2011) issued on 23 November 2011 (see par. 4.3). The EP examined the Green Paper in detail, first of all in the plenary session of 7 December 2012 on the basis of a report of its Committee on economic and monetary affairs presented by Sylvie Goulard. Finally on 16 January 2013 the EP adopted by 361 votes to 268 with 33 abstentions a resolution on the feasibility of introducing Stability Bonds (European Parliament, 2013), in response to the Commission Green Paper on the same subject.

The EP resolution touches upon a wide set of issues, and I shall focus on four crucial passages.

First: The report 'Towards a Genuine Economic and Monetary Union' presented by President Herman Van Rompuy to the European Council (28–29 June 2012), is seen as a good starting point in order to overcome the weakness of the EMU due to its lack of common budgetary policy and common bonds market.

Second: The measures to confront the crisis have been useful but do not represent 'a balanced approach that combines solidarity and responsibility within the euro area' that cannot 'rely solely on rescue mechanisms such as the ESM and the EFSF'.

Third: Recalling that 'the mutualisation of eurozone sovereign debt cannot in itself compensate for the loss of competitiveness of the euro area', Parliament believes that the prospect of common bonds may be a strong signal to financial markets, help to preserve the integrity of the EMU, underpin a return to economic stability and reduce uncertainty, provided that progress is made with EU financial and budgetary integration and supervision. Parliament considers that 'it is essential to establish a roadmap for finding, in the short term, an exit from the current crisis, and for moving, in the long term, towards a fiscal union by completing, strengthening and deepening the economic and monetary union'. It 'calls on the Commission as soon as possible to present a report to Parliament and the Council examining the options for, and – if appropriate – making proposals for a roadmap towards, common issuance of public debt instruments, taking into account financial, budgetary and legal aspects'.

Fourth: 'Common issuance of a genuine European debt in conjunction with an enhanced European budget involving a Treaty change: the Commission could put forward proposals for possible issuance of bonds to finance EU investments for EU public goods (infrastructure, research and development, etc.), to facilitate adjustments to country-specific shocks by providing for some degree of absorption at the central level, to facilitate structural reforms that improve competitiveness and potential growth in relation to an integrated economic policy framework.'

I believe this EP resolution was extremely important from both a political and institutional economy points of view and clearly in favour of the '[c]ommon issuance of a genuine European debt'.

15.4.3 *The European Commission's Proposal*

The European Commission (EC) also carried out an important work that I have partially considered in the previous section and that can be summarized in three steps: the 'Green Paper' (European Commission, 2011), the 'Blueprint' (European Commission, 2012) and the 'final comments' (European Commission, 2013).

I will concentrate on the third document, which makes clear the point of view of the EC and the latter's position vis-à-vis that of the EP. The European Commission sets its Green Paper in the context of the EP's resolution of 6 July 2011 (even if the EP resolution is only quoted in a footnote of the GP) and concludes its analysis on Stabilitybonds (SBs) by addressing itself directly to the EP. As a matter of fact, before the release of the EC Green Paper, other proposals regarding European bonds and stability or redemption funds had been advanced. However, the Green Paper is the fundamental contribution also because it gives a valuable summary of the other proposals.

In its final comments, the EC summed up at first its interpretation of the EP's position as follows: the necessity of the completion of EMU as the prerequisite to launch SBs; the possibility of issuing three types of SB proposed, that is, the European Redemption Fund and Eurobills (temporary instruments to be issued for the short term), blue-bonds (issued in the medium term) and genuine European SBs (as a long-term initiative to be taken in conjunction with an enhanced European budget[6]). The final conclusions are worth quoting because they have been practically and surprisingly disregarded by the governments of EMU countries.

The Commission presented a roadmap to this end in our 'Blueprint for a deep and genuine EMU' in late November, where the ideas of the profound

---

[6] It is also stated that 'In its resolution, the European Parliament asks the Commission to provide further clarification on the following aspects: (1) Conditionality related to Stability Bonds, (2) the upper limit of 60% of Stability Bond issuance in the 'blue/red' proposal in the context of the stability of the scheme, (3) legal aspects, such as legal restraints (article 125 TFEU), or the possible use of article 352/1 TFEU, (4) moral hazard problem, (5) criteria for the allocation of the loans, (6) exit and entry criteria, (7) options to establish a system of differentiation of the interest rates between Member States, (8) technicalities linked to any Stability Bonds Scheme (such as guarantees, tranching and pooling structures, potential collaterals, the balance between rule based and market based fiscal discipline, additional safeguards, restructuring, issuance, relations with existing mechanisms, the investor base, regulatory requirements, phase-in coverage of debt and maturity), (9) a legitimate and appropriate form for governance and accountability. Additionally the Commission is asked to present a report examining the different options and proposing a roadmap towards common bond issuance (with particular attention to a debt redemption fund and Eurobills), taking into account financial, budgetary and legal aspects. (European Commission, 2013, p. 1).

rebuilding of EMU were presented. In the Blueprint, common debt issuance was also included as a tool that can play an important role within the process of completing deepening the EMU. In this context the possibility of a European Redemption Fund and for Eurobills in the medium term, and building on that towards a more complete solution and a full fiscal and economic union in the long term were presented.

The objective and rationale of Stability Bonds would be the stabilization of sovereign debt markets and the creation of a new deep and liquid bond market. However, it is indispensable that the risks of moral hazard are addressed first.

As common issuance entails the risks of moral hazard, a further reinforced economic governance that would address these risks is necessary. This should involve enhanced budgetary surveillance and further sharing of fiscal sovereignty. The guiding principle remains: there can be no further mutualisation without deeper integration.

Moreover, progressive integration towards a full banking, fiscal and economic union will require parallel steps towards a political union with reinforced democratic legitimacy and accountability.

Most importantly, any progress or roadmap towards common issuance must obviously build on broad political acceptance and support by all participating governments and by civil society. Therefore, the Commission is of the opinion much more work would need to be done to credibly address the concerns of those governments and parts of the civil society that are currently not yet convinced of common debt issuance. (European Commission, 2013, p. 2)

This was effectively the last pronouncement on SBs by European institutions. German opposition blocked further discussion, as I highlight in the concluding remarks of this chapter.

15.5 RescueBonds: Temporary Help for the EMU[7]

From 2010 onwards, in order to tackle the crisis in some member states (EMU-MS) (Greece, Ireland, Portugal and later Spain), European institutions created in sequence two emergency funds – the European Financial Stability Facility (EFSF) and the European Stability Mechanism (ESM) – which I will call Rescue or Bailout Funds (RBFs). Their structures are well known, so I will consider only some of their most important features.

---

[7] This paragraph is an updated and modified version of parts of Quadrio Curzio (2012).

15.5.1 The EFSF Fund

The EFSF is a temporary fund and since June 2013 has not activated new assistance programmes. It will, however, continue to operate until it has fulfilled all of its commitments. Its goal is to preserve the financial stability of the EMU giving assistance to EMU member states that officially request assistance and accept severe adjustment programmes signing a 'memorandum of understanding'. Let us consider the key features of the EFSF fund.

1. *The start-up phases of EFSF.* The first phase was from May–August 2010, when the EFSF was set up, to the end of 2011. At the beginning, a 'framework agreement' among EMU-MSs was introduced, under which the EFSF, although a 'private' body incorporated under Luxembourg law, also took up a 'public' nature in regard to capital guarantees for the purpose of its operations. Its initial capital was €440 billion guaranteed by EMU member states that were shareholders paying in only a total of €30 million. The contribution of EMU member states to the EFSF capital was determined according to the shares of those countries in the ECB capital, adjusted to take account of countries that are not part of the EMU, being instead shareholders of the ECB. The guarantee commitments of the major EMU member states in accordance with their share (expressed in percentage as 'contribution key') are: Germany (27.06 per cent), France (20.31 per cent), Italy (17.86 per cent) and Spain (11.87 per cent), followed by the other Eurozone countries. In total, the main EMU member states guarantee 77.10 per cent of the EFSF capital. Countries receiving financial assistance step out from the EFSF, so that contribution keys may change.

2. *The second phase of the EFSF* began at the end of 2011. Several European Council meetings, with the contribution of the Economic and Financial Affairs Council (ECOFIN) and the Eurogroup, have widened and strengthened the Framework Agreement. In November 2011, the EFSF took its final configuration. To date it has worked quite actively. The capital of the EFSF is, according to the 'framework agreement', €780 billion and is guaranteed (not paid in) by EMU-MSs in proportion to exposure. Funds totaling €440 billion are available for direct intervention, on the basis of guarantees provided to the fund by the participating states having the highest credit ratings.

3. *The operations of the EFSF.* Let us consider two categories: resource mobilisation and instruments to support the beneficiary countries. With regard to funding, the EFSF can (and so it had done) issue bonds or other debt instruments placed in different ways, including syndications, competitive auctions and private placements. Its capability to intervene can be increased through the leveraged issue of 'partial protection certificates' on government bonds and the creation of co-financing funds in partnership with the private sector. Initially, the fund operated with a simple back-to-back funding strategy, issuing only what was needed in view of the borrowing request of a specific beneficiary state. Since November 2011, a diversified funding strategy has been adopted, establishing a liquidity buffer not immediately used but held in reserve as a guarantee or for an emergency. Funding operations have grown over time and have been diversified in terms of the financial instruments used. It is impossible here to analyse in detail all operations, but it is necessary to understand, at the aggregate level, the enhanced market appeal of EFSF. I will consider data (from 26 November 2013) concerning syndicated issues (placements by auction are not included). Clearly, the EFSF were welcomed by a diversified and solid group of investors. The geographical distribution of investors shows that nearly three-quarters of them were located in Europe and Asia: 52 per cent belonging to the Eurozone and 21 per cent to Asia. The United Kingdom and Switzerland accounted for 14 per cent with the remaining 13 per cent divided among other (European and not European) countries. Types of investors further illustrated the pattern of distribution: 28 per cent central banks, government funds and sovereign wealth funds; 39 per cent banks; 23 per cent fund managers; 9 per cent pension funds, insurance companies and corporations; and 1 per cent other.

Concerning coupons, yield was very low because of the high credit ratings and the high demand by investors that outpaced supply. For example, consider a transaction of 9 April 2013, in which the EFSF placed 'its largest ever bond': a five-year bond for a total of €8 billion and a coupon equal to 0.875 per cent (0.956 per cent re-offer yield). Investors who subscribed the security were geographically distributed as follows: 46 per cent euro area, 29 per cent Asia, 14 per cent United Kingdom and 11 per cent other. The involvement of central banks, government funds and sovereign wealth funds (37 per cent), asset managers (30 per cent) but also of banks (28 per cent) has been significant, while insurance companies, pension funds (in this case), corporations and others had a marginal role (5 per cent).

Therefore, the EFSF has been much welcomed by the market and could have increased the volume of issues to take advantage of this situation. In fact, the performance of the EFSF has led to a consolidation of its credibility, since long-term rates have declined over time. It is worth mentioning that its credit rating was triple A for a long time and now maintains a very good investment grade, being AA from Standard & Poor's, Aa1 from Moody's and AA+ from Fitch Ratings.

With regard to the types of instruments that the EFSF can use in its interventions, they include: (1) provision of loans; (2) interventions in the primary market for government bonds; (3) interventions in the secondary market for government bonds; (4) actions on the basis of a precautionary programme and (5) recapitalization of financial institutions through loans to governments. The analysis of each of these types of intervention is not feasible here, which is why I focus on the two already used: type (1) for Greece, Ireland and Portugal; and type (5) for the same three countries and even Spain (whose programme was nevertheless put in place by the ESM, as discussed later in the chapter).

Type (1) provision of loans consists of the following two phases: a request for help from the member state concerned; and a support programme processed by the European Commission, in collaboration with the IMF and in liaison with the ECB. Aid is conditional on a rigid stabilization programme to be implemented by the state requesting support. A Memorandum of Understanding (MoU) is negotiated, which sets out the terms of the loan between the beneficiary state, the European Commission and the IMF and which must be approved by the Eurogroup and eventually by the IMF Board; and the availability of loan disbursement, for which the EFSF determines the technical aspects (deadlines, interests, maturities, repayments); and the decision on the date when the EFSF makes the loan available to the borrower. I further investigate this type of support in Section 15.5.2.

It takes at least three to four weeks to carry out these steps, which must be added to the time needed for the actual EFSF funding. If, during the implementation of the support programme, the beneficiary state does not comply with the conditions laid down, the disbursement of the loan is suspended and new negotiations begin, as happened in the Greek case. The loans are repaid with interest rates that cover the financing costs plus a margin for the EFSF operational costs.

The procedure in type (5) is intended to allow recapitalisation of financial institutions of an EMU-MSs at an affordable cost and to limit the risk of contagion from the failure of such institutions. It can also be adopted for countries that have not activated a type (1) programme. Support is still subject to the signing of the memorandum of understanding that involves requirements at the level of the beneficiary financial institutions and at the state level.

My assessment of the EFSF is positive, in particular because creating and running such a complex fund is a very difficult task. Several problems remain, in particular concerning the accompanying accounting procedure, as Eurostat 'considers that the debt issued by the EFSF for each support operation for a member of the euro area must be reallocated to the public accounts of States providing guarantees, in proportion to their share of the guarantees for each debt issuing operation' (Eurostat, 2011). This is a choice that could attract substantial criticism.

15.5.2 Assistance by EFSF to Ireland, Portugal and Greece

The first EFSF support programme went out to Ireland and was launched on 28 November 2010 for a total of €85 billion, funded in the following way: €17.5 billion collected in Ireland from state funds and pension funds; €67.5 billion in external support from the IMF and European Financial Stabilisation Mechanism (EFSM) (€22.5 billion each); and €17.7 billion from the EFSF, plus loans from the United Kingdom, Sweden and Denmark. The programme ended successfully on 8 December 2013.

The support programme for Portugal was launched on 17 May 2011 for a total of €78 billion, funded in the following way: €26 billion each from the IMF, EFSM and EFSF (of which up to €12 billion were designated within the programme for the recapitalisation of the financial sector).

The support programme for Greece (also known by the acronym GLF, Greek Loan Facility) is much more complicated but is also another instance of EFSF's flexibility. In May 2010, Greece had benefitted from the first programme of bilateral loans of up to €110 billion, of which €80 billion and €30 billion were provided, respectively, by

EMU-MSs and by the IMF. The EFSF intervened only in the second programme, which has run since 21 February 2012. This programme amounts to €172.6 billion: the EFSF contributes approximately €109 billion (€24.4 billion collected through commitments made in the first EMU-MSs programme) of which up to a maximum of €48 billion can be used for the recapitalization of banks. A contribution by the IMF of €28 billion (including €10 billion from the first programme) should also be added and a 'haircut' loss for private holders of Greek government bonds amounting to €107 billion, later reduced by various contributions from the EFSF.

The total programme (public and private, direct and indirect) for Greece may have a final cost of approximately €330 billion, even if it is not easy to calculate the total figure, since all official sources refer to partial figures only. If these figures are correct, this would be of the same order of Greek government debt that was calculated at the end of 2010. The amount is enormous, and the question remains whether a quicker intervention might have been far less costly. Another debated issue deals with the entry of Greece into EMU in 2001, a wrong decision taken without an appropriate analysis of its heavily manipulated fiscal and budgetary situation, which have been disclosed by the Greek Prime Minister Papandreou at the beginning of 2009.

15.5.3 From the EFSF to the ESM

The EFSF ceased to activate new support programmes since July 2013 but continues to exist until all of those launched are completed. The European Stability Mechanism (ESM) is its successor and is a permanent institution with all the features of the EFSF in its enhanced version. It is thus not necessary to describe them here again, except for some fundamental distinctions.

(1) The ESM is an intergovernmental organization between EMU and member states. An international treaty to this effect was signed on 2 February 2012 after a consultative process that was begun in December 2010 by the representatives of the governments concerned. The ESM was ratified by the countries involved in the succeeding months and entered into force on 27 September 2012, just after the notification of ratification by Germany. This took place only after a judgment of the German Federal Constitutional Court. This pronunciation was politically relevant; if decided in the negative, it could have

prevented the launch of the ESM, as it would never have reached the threshold of 90 per cent of the capital required for entry into force. On 8 October 2012, the ESM began its work.

The ESM Treaty required an amendment to Article 136 (later integrated) of the Treaty on the Functioning of the European Union in order to state (clarify) that the ESM was necessary for safeguarding the stability of the Eurozone. The ESM is therefore fully institutional (while the EFSF was not) as an international treaty but not as a part of the European Treaties.

(2) The ESM Treaty, consisting of forty-eight articles, is of great interest and deserves a separate analysis; here, however, we will consider only some crucial elements.

The preamble states that all EMU-MSs become members of the ESM, and Article 3 states that the purpose of the ESM is to mobilize financial resources and implement actions for the stability of EMU-MSs who are or are likely to be in financial difficulties that could compromise the stability of the EMU and individual EMU-MS.

The subscribed capital of the fund is €700 billion, of which €620 billion is guaranteed and €80 billion paid in by EMU-MSs with proportions almost identical to those of the EFSF. Interest rates on loans are more flexible covering operating and financing costs (also with a margin). Deadlines for repayment will be up to thirty years. The conditionality in lending is very strict and this entails compliance with the 'fiscal compact' by any EMU-MS requesting assistance. Moreover, the treaty institutionalized the involvement of the private sector (as does the IMF in its support programmes), but on a case-by-case basis, in all the restructuring operations of public debt and also collective action clauses from 2013.

On 20 June 2013, the Eurogroup reached a political agreement on the main features of the ESM direct bank recapitalisation instrument with the condition of clear definition of precise rules of compliance. This tool is part of the Banking Union according to the legislation on bank resolution and deposit guarantee. The ESM has already been used to recapitalize, indirectly through loans to the government, the Spanish banks (and later for the restructuring of the financial system of Cyprus).

The programme of assistance to Spain is of great importance. In July 2012, the Eurogroup approved a package of financial assistance for

Spain of up to €100 billion. On 31 December 2013, the ESM financial assistance programme for Spain expired. The ESM disbursed a total of €41.3 billion (close to €39.5 billion in December 2012 and a further €1.8 billion in February 2013), and the programme has been accompanied by policy conditionality focused on the banking sector.

The loans (with an average maturity of approximately 12.5 years) were provided to the Fondo de Restructuración Ordenado Bancaria (FROB), the bank recapitalisation fund of the Spanish government, and then channelled to the financial institutions concerned. The operations were carried out with very competitive rates, more advantageous in respect to those of the market.

(3) The positive reaction, with which the operations of the ESM have been evaluated by the markets, is also evidenced by the first issues of short-term securities (an initial priority for the fund), but especially by the issues of bond in the long term. It is sufficient to consider the 'inaugural long term bond issue' which took place on 8 October 2013, exactly one year after the inauguration of the fund. A five-year bond was offered to the market, attracting a total of €7 billion (with orders from more than 200 investors worldwide), paying a coupon yield of 1.25 per cent (re-offer yield 1.288 per cent). The geographical and by-investor-type breakdowns are not too dissimilar to those of EFSF issues. In particular, orders have been made as follows: 39 per cent from the euro area and 38 per cent Asia (for a total of 77 per cent!), 16 per cent from the United Kingdom and Switzerland and 7 per cent from others. Bonds have been purchased mostly by central banks, government and sovereign funds (43 per cent), banks (32 per cent), assets managers (19 per cent) and insurance and pension funds and others (6 per cent). This transaction has been followed by a ten-year bond with an issue (12 November 2013) of €3 billion and a coupon yield of just 2.125 per cent (2.26 per cent reoffer yield). Also in this case, a great part (79 per cent) of the issue was purchased from the Eurozone (52 per cent) and from Asia (27 per cent); correspondingly, 30 per cent of the investors interested in this transaction were represented by central banks, government and sovereign funds (30 per cent) and especially banks (40 per cent).

Also due to the 'robust capital structure' and a pretty conservative strategy of funding and investment, the ESM has been assigned high-quality credit ratings reflecting strong shareholder support: Aa1 by Moody's and triple A by Fitch Ratings.

Despite the problems inherent in any launch, the two funds have consistently issued total transactions (according to publicly available data as of January 2014) of about €420 billion. Most has been issued by the ESFS (€356 billion), but the ESM also has been busy, in little more than a year issuing bills and bonds for a total of approximately €63 billion.

(4) It is possible to distinguish several aspects that differentiate the EFSF and the ESM, but I will only focus on two that allow us to speculate on how the new fund could be the embryo of a European Financial Fund which issues Eurobonds.

The first one relates to the ESM's highest governing body, the Council of Governors composed of the finance ministers of the Eurozone countries and chaired by the President of the Eurogroup or by another member of the board with the office having a duration of two years, though renewable. There is, therefore, an overlap of this governing body with the Eurogroup. In the event that the President of the Eurogroup is not in the Council, he/she has the right to participate as an observer at the meetings, along with the Commissioner for Economic and Monetary Affairs and the President of the ECB.

The second aspect concerns the non-accounting of EMU-MSs financial resources collected by the ESM on the public debt of EMU states which are the shareholders. This is due to the fact that the ESM is an international financial organization such as the IMF and not an intermediary between states shareholders (EMU-MSs), markets and beneficiary states.

My conclusion is that, after a few years of activity, the ESM could undertake the functions of and evolve into a European Financial Fund. I discuss this further in the next section.

15.6 EuroUnionBonds: Stability and Growth

15.6.1 *The Proposal: EUBs and the EFF*

In 2011 and 2012 I proposed, jointly with Romano Prodi, the issuance of EuroUnionBonds (EUBs). This proposal is further discussed and extended in this section.[8]

---

[8] I would like to express my thanks to Romano Prodi for some useful discussions both on these subjects and on wider topics concerning the EU and the EMU. Of

The stability and growth aims of EUBs may and should be combined, taking into account the following issues in order to strengthen the EMU and the EU.

First, without sustainable growth of the EMU (and the EU), stability is impossible, as convergence among EMU-MSs cannot be achieved only through the internal market, rigorous fiscal consolidation and the Multiannual Financial Framework.

Second, the EMU is backed by a strong structural economic system with one of the most powerful worldwide manufacturing bases and with a regular surplus in balance of trade. If this structure weakens as a result of fiscal consolidation, the consequences will be very serious for international European competitiveness.

Third, EMU-MSs have generally a good balance between private and public collaboration in many fields, including R&D and infrastructure. Meanwhile, the interconnections and networks linking European states must be improved.

Fourth, the fiscal situation of the EMU is much better than that of the United States and this should be better exploited and communicated to global financial markets.

The EMU obviously has many inherent weaknesses in comparison to the United States and among them three are particularly significant: the institutional environment, which does not encompass a political union; the fiscal environment without common debt bond issuance; and the monetary and currency environment, as the Fed is much more powerful than the ECB. Indeed the dollar is a strategic currency and a *numéraire* for almost all primary commodities, while the Euro is only an economic currency.

The crisis has aggravated some of the EMU's weaknesses, among which two deserve comment.

The first weakness is that the crisis has largely benefitted Germany, with very low interest rates on sovereign bonds due to the enormous inflows of capital. Other countries have been damaged, especially Italy and Spain, which suffered speculative attacks with severe consequences on their funding costs, public investments and growth. The gap between EMU-MSs has significantly increased, as a result of market pressures that continued until the ECB President Mario

course, responsibility for what here differs from the articles we jointly wrote is solely mine.

Draghi stated that the ECB was ready to intervene with a much more active monetary policy.

The second weakness is the widening gap between EMU-MSs and the United States in terms of growth. Let us consider the ten-year period between 2006 and 2015, which includes two pre-crisis years, two post-crisis years and six years of crisis. The cumulated growth of EMU-MSs' GDP was 7.4 per cent, while that of the United States was 16 per cent. Since before the crisis EMU-MSs were growing faster than the United States was, the main change took place during the crisis, during which the United States grew by 6 per cent whereas the EMU declined by 1.7 per cent. According to available data when writing, the forecast for 2014 and 2015 was for growth of 6 per cent in the United States and 3 per cent in the EMU.

The following proposal answers some of the previous issues and can be divided into four components:

1. The European Financial Fund (EFF), its capital and its governance
2. EuroUnionBonds (EUBs)
3. The EFF and EUBs for EMU-MSs sovereign debt
4. The EFF and EUB's for structural investments.

Here I present a more detailed version of the proposal bearing in mind that the proposal's aim is twofold: to attain a sustainable public debt to GDP ratio in the long run, and to increase investment in Eurozone material and immaterial infrastructure.

15.6.2 *The European Financial Fund's Structure*

This new entity should be equipped with capital composed of real assets supplied by the EMU-MSs in proportion to their shares in the European Central Bank, recalculated to exclude the non-EMU countries.

The main quotas will be allocated as follows: Germany (27.06 per cent), France (20.31 per cent), Italy (17.86 per cent) and Spain (11.87 per cent). In total, these countries will own 77.1 per cent of the overall fund's capital.

Let us suppose that a capital of €1 trillion would be paid in by the main EMU member states as follows: Germany (€270.6 billion), France (€201.3 billion), Italy (€178.6 billion), Spain (€118.7 billion). The total is €771 billion, while the remaining €229 billion would be paid by the other EMU countries.

It is reasonable to conjecture that with a capital of €1 trillion, the EFF will be able to issue 3 trillion EUBs and utilize financial resources in two ways: the restructuring of public debt of EMU-MSs, and the financing of investments in infrastructure.

Capital should be provided at the establishment of the EFF in order to avoid suspicions of doubtful promises by peripheral countries and fears of a possible subsequent bailout.

It is obvious that the structure of the EFF, the amount of its capital, the amount of bonds issues and the use of the financial resources raised are fundamental economic policy decisions that should be taken by the top-tier institutions of the EMU (and of its member states) and of the EU according to an international treaty, as it had happened with the ESM.

15.6.3 *The EFF and the Central Bank Gold Agreements*

The first and more important part of the paid-in capital of the EFF should be in the form of the official gold reserves owned by EMU-MS. These reserves are the largest in the world, amounting to 347 million ounces (the United States has approximately 260 million ounces), worth around €319 billion at a price of about €1,023 per troy ounce, which is the average price for the period 2009–13 and which is a reasonable hypothesis after a long depression of gold prices.

Endowing the EFF with gold is a proposal that deserves further comment.

The Central Bank Gold Agreements
The idea that gold is an untouchable official reserve in the EMU is a commonly held but inexplicable belief. In fact, this is contradicted by both facts and regulations, taking into consideration the Central Bank Gold Agreement (CBGA) that was promoted by the ECB itself. This agreement, which dates back to September 1999, states that gold remains an important element of global monetary reserves, and that the member banks will declare their intentions and will coordinate their gold-selling programmes in order to sell a maximum of up to 400 tons of gold reserves per year for a five-year maximum total of 2,000 tons (64 million ounces). The man reason behind the CBGA seems to be the aim to maintain an ordered gold market avoiding any downward pressure on prices.

The first Central Banks Gold Agreement (CBGA1) (1999–2003) was signed by fifteen European central banks (those of the then eleven Eurozone countries plus the European Central Bank and those of Sweden, Switzerland and the United Kingdom). The sales of EMU central banks were 485 tons (Austria 90 tons, Germany 35.2 tons, Netherlands 35.2 tons and Portugal 124.8 tons). In addition, the United Kingdom sold 345 tons and Switzerland sold 1,170 tons. The total sales of gold were 2,000 tons, in line with the ceiling provisions of the agreement.

The second agreement (CBGA2) (2004–08) was signed by the same countries (except for the United Kingdom, which did not adhere) and by the ECB as well as by Greece, Slovenia, Cyprus and Malta, the latter three countries having by then joined the euro. Maximum sales for each year were fixed at 500 tons for a five-year total of 2,500. The sales of EMU central banks were 1,443 tons (Austria 37.4 tons, Belgium 30 tons, France 572 tons, Germany 25.5 tons, the Netherlands 165 tons, Portugal 9.7 tons and Spain 241.8 tons). The ECB sold 271.5 tons. In addition, Sweden sold 60 tons and Switzerland 380 tons. The total sales of gold for the period were 1,883.9 tons.

The third agreement (CBGA3) (2009–14) was signed by all the central banks of the Euro system, including the ECB, plus Sweden and Switzerland. The maximum sales for each year were fixed at 400 tons for a five-year total of 2,000 tons. The sales of EMU central banks were 22.7 tons (Germany 20.6 tons, Greece 0.9 tons and Malta 0.4 tons).

It is worthwhile mentioning that neither the United States nor the IMF signed any of the three CBGAs. Nevertheless, the IMF between September 2009 and December 2010 sold 403.3 tons of gold, which remained within the limits of the CBGA3 as stated in a joint declaration between the subscribers of the CBGA and IMF of August 2009. The sales were 222 tons in off-market transactions (to the Reserve Bank of India – 200 tons; to the Central Bank of Sri Lanka – 10 tons; to the Central Bank of Bangladesh – 10 tons and to the Central Bank of Mauritius – 2 tons) while the remaining 181.3 tons were sold gradually on the market within the ceiling set by the CBGA so as to avoid any disordered effects on the gold market.

The Gold Sales of ECB and EMU-MSs

The total amount of gold sold by EMU-MSs during the three CBGAs was: France 572 tons, Netherlands 400.2 tons, ECB 271.5 tons, Spain

241.8 tons, Portugal 224.5 tons, Austria 127.4 tons, Germany 81.3 tons, Belgium 30 tons, Greece 0.9 tons and Malta 0.4 tons. A total of 1.8 tons could not be ascribed to a specific country. Italy (the second EMU-MS holder after Germany) sold nothing. Two other CBGA signatory countries sold gold: Switzerland 1,550 tons and the United Kingdom 345 tons.

The majority of the sales were realized during periods of comparative low gold prices. The average price in the 1999–2003 period was €311 per troy ounce and the average price in the 2004–08 period was €486 per troy ounce, while in the period 2009–13, when the average price was the highest (€1,023 per troy ounce), the sales dropped dramatically.

These sales can therefore be considered, in my opinion, as 'significantly discounted', for the following reasons. If we take into account the difference between the potential revenues if the sales had been realized at the average price during 2009–13 and the real revenues at the average prices of the period in which the sales took place, the result is the sellers suffering a potential loss of €36 billion. Among these losers is the ECB. This proves that gold management by EMU-MSs and by the ECB might be considered unsatisfactory. I do not think, in fact, that the potential sales during 2009–13 might have depressed gold prices in a dramatic fashion given that, in the midst of the Great Recession, gold was experiencing a bull market.

The Role of the ECB

Let us investigate further the role of the ECB.

First, gold of EMU-MSs cannot be considered as being under the ECB's control, otherwise it would have been unnecessary to have the Central Bank Gold Agreement. Furthermore, if the ECB were to be considered a 'supervisor' of the 350 million ounces of official reserves, its performance would have to be rated as very poor considering the average price at which gold was sold.

Second, the ECB's general objectives in managing official reserves are liquidity security and return on investments. The last two criteria appear to have been disregarded with respect to the ECB's official gold reserves that currently amount to only 16 million ounces after about one-third having been sold at very low prices. In March 2005, the ECB owned 24.7 million ounces of gold, while in April 2009 it only held 16.1 million ounces. Considering the five-year average price of gold (for the period between April 2005 and April 2009), which was approximately €517 per ounce, the ECB sold 8.5 million ounces for a total of €4.4 billion. If it had sold the same amount of gold in the following five years (2010–2014), the ECB could have earned double this amount![9]

Let us go back to the EMU member states' supply of capital to the EFF, part of which will be made up by gold reserves. Evaluating them at the mean price in 2009–13, the total value of gold reserves would be €355.5 billion, and each member state's contribution would be as follows in Table 15.1.

15.6.4 The EFF and 'In-In' Real Capital

Since gold alone will not cover all the capital needed by the EFF, other assets must be paid in. They may consist of shares in existing or new companies in sectors deemed acceptable by the EFF. These sectors should limited to industrial and infrastructural facilities. For this reason I label them 'In-In'.

---

[9] In view of this, it is difficult to understand the rationale behind a recent case in which the ECB vetoed the Italian government's proposal to reevaluate its gold reserves (a proposal that was also opposed by the Bank of Italy). We cannot exclude that in order to use gold as the EFF's capital, it may be necessary to change some national laws, but this does not seem unfeasible, as the Fund will have individual states (and possibly central banks) as shareholders, and gold will remain a 'reserve of last resort' for the EFF. What appears odd is to consider gold as an untouchable entity while it has been often sold by EMU member states and by the ECB (see Coltorti and Quadrio Curzio, 2013). In 2007, Romano Prodi, President of the EU Council, and Tommaso Padoa Schioppa, Italian Minister of Economy and Finances, hinted at the possibility of using gold reserves to reduce public debt. Their intention was not formulated as a project, because the reaction was harsh and the idea was shelved. In 2009, it was the turn of the new Minister of Economy and Finances Giulio Tremonti, who, through a decree, tried to impose a €300 million revaluation tax on the gold reserves of the Bank of Italy. The Bank, however, opposed this solution by appealing to the ECB, which confirmed the non-taxability of gold, as this would infringe on the autonomy of the central bank. Therefore, when the decree was converted into law in August of that year, Article 14 (relating to capital gains tax on non-industrial gold owned by companies and organizations) merely recorded, in paragraph 4, a rather cryptic possibility of taxing gold in official reserves. It is interesting to remember that in the postwar period, Italy between June 1974 and July 1978 gave up 540 tons of gold reserves as collateral for a loan from West Germany.

Table 15.1. *Contribution to EFF in terms of gold reserves (volume in billions of fine troy ounces)*

Euro area	347.1
Germany	109.3
France	78.4
Italy	78.8
Spain	9.1

As mentioned earlier, the total EFF capital will amount to €1 trillion, consisting of €355.5 billion corresponding to 347.1 million ounces of gold and €644.5 billion coming from other assets.

The main EMU member states should subscribe capital with a breakdown as follows:

- Germany: €270.6 billion, with €112 billion in the form of 109.3 million ounces of gold and €158.6 billion in other assets;
- France: €201.3 billion, with €80.3 billion in the form of 78.4 million ounces of gold and €121 billion in other assets;
- Italy: €178.6 billion, with €80.8 billion in the form of 78.8 million ounces of gold and €97.8 billion in other assets. These include shares in companies held by the Finance Ministry and by the 'Cassa Depositi e Prestiti' (CDP) (ENI, ENEL, Finmeccanica, SNAM, Poste, etc.);
- Spain: €118.7 billion, with €9.3 billion in the form of 9.1 million ounces of gold and €109.4 billion in other assets.

This implies solving two rather difficult issues. The first one concerns identification of the bodies that should confer the assets. Such bodies could be the state or legal entities in which the state is the majority shareholder (such as Kreditanstalt für Wiederaufbau [KfW] in Germany, Caisse des Dépôts et Consignations [CDC] in France, Cassa Depositi e Prestiti [CDP] in Italy and Instituto de Crédito Oficial [ICO] in Spain). In some cases (like that of CDP), these companies also have private shareholders who must be satisfied in terms of their property rights.

The second issue concerns the evaluation of the assets conferred. They should be evaluated at fair value on the basis of expertise of the highest international standard rather than at market prices, also because in many cases the EFF will become the main owner of companies belonging to homogeneous sectors such as energy, telecoms and transport. This procedure would be in line with the infrastructural and industrial aims of the EFF.

Concerning the EFF's possible recapitalization needs, these should always consist of proportional transfers from EMU-MSs in real capital rather than nominal warranties.

15.6.5 *The Issue of EUBs*

The EFF with €1 trillion of paid-up capital could issue 3 trillion EUBs with a leverage of a factor of 3 and a duration between twenty to thirty years. Looking at the European 'best bonds' of 2013 and 2014, we find the following examples: Bund 30Y issue of February 2014 – yield to maturity 2.53 per cent (historical minimum of 2.16 per cent in April 2013); BEI 30Y issue of September 2013 – fixed rate 3 per cent and yield to maturity in the first day of quotation 2.959 per cent; BEI 31Y issue of January 2013 – fixed rate 2.75 per cent and yield to maturity in the first day of quotation 2.81 per cent; EFSF 21Y issue of August 2013 – yield 3.043 per cent (fixed rate); EFSF 25Y issue of June 2012 – yield 3.420 per cent (fixed rate). On this basis, and taking into account the success of EFSF and ESM issues, which had a demand significantly higher than actual supply, I suppose that a coupon of about 3 per cent would be reasonable.

The total yearly amount of interest would be €90 billion, which is nearly 1 per cent of EMU-MSs' GDP. These financial resources should and could be collected by the EFF from many sources. Among them, there are the payments of the EMU debtor countries, which – of course – should not pay a premium over the market EFF rate of interest in view of the guarantees provided, and also in consideration of the fact that the programme is a solidarity component of a quasi-federation. If a premium must be paid, this should not form any part of the budget deficit compatible with compliance with EMU criteria.

Moreover, when EFF investments in In-In sectors generate profits, these must be proportionally deduced from the payment due by EMU-MSs. In other words, the EFF's profits will be distributed to EMU-MS shareholders only if they exceed the interests that the EMU-MSs must pay to the EFF holding their sovereign bonds.

The ratio of EFF debt – which in my hypothesis is €3 trillion – to the 2012 EMU GDP which is close to €9.5 trillion, will be 31.6 per cent and so by far the lowest ratio of the united debt of any quasi-federal entity.

As we will see in Section 15.6.7, the EFF should use EUBs for restructuring the EMU-MS public debts and financing infrastructural investment.

15.6.6 EFF Governance

The implementation of the EFF's aims will require strong governance, which can be similar to that of the ESM with some minor differences. The ESM (see Section 15.5) has a board of governors and a board of directors, as well as a managing director. The managing director of the ESM is appointed by the board of governors for a term of five years and chairs the board of directors' meetings. The board of directors ensures that the ESM is run in accordance with its Treaty and by-laws.

The board of governors is composed of one representative of each ESM country, which shall appoint as governor its minister of finance. So, there would be overlap between the ESM Council of Governors and the Eurogroup, because the Council, in accordance with the ESM Treaty, could be chaired by the President of the Eurogroup (alternatively by another member of the board) with the office term being two years, renewable.

The decisions of the board of governors and the board of directors shall be taken by mutual agreement, qualified majority or simple majority, depending on the importance of the decision. By way of derogation from standard rules, an emergency voting procedure may also be envisaged, requiring a qualified majority of 85 per cent of the votes cast.[10]

According to the ESM Treaty, the voting rights of each ESM member are equal to the number of shares allocated to it in the authorized capital stock of the ESM. If any ESM member fails to pay any part of the amount due in respect of its obligations in relation to paid-in shares or calls of capital, or in relation to the reimbursement of financial assistance, such ESM member shall be unable, for so long

---

[10] An emergency voting procedure shall be used where the Commission and the ECB both conclude that a failure to urgently adopt a decision to grant or implement financial assistance would threaten the economic and financial sustainability of the euro area.

as such failure to pay continues, to exercise any of its voting rights (the voting thresholds shall be recalculated accordingly). The EFF could have a similar governance structure and similar voting procedure.

15.6.7 EFF and EUBs for EMU-MS Sovereign Debt

The first utilization of EUBs should be in the restructuring of EMU-MS debts. The public debt situation of the EMU area and of its four main member states is as follows:

Let us consider the situations that would follow from the purchase by the EFF of the EMU-MS sovereign debt. The purchase from EMU-MSs should be of an amount between €1 trillion and €2 trillion and in the same proportion of the members states' quotas in the EFF. The difference between the total amount of EFF bond issues and the fund allocated to debt restructuring should be allotted to In-In investment purposes.

The amount of EMU-MS bonds bought by the EFF would correspondingly reduce the amount that EMU-Member States owe to markets. As a result, each country will have two types of debts and, consequently, two types of debt to GDP ratios. One type of debt will be the debt owed to markets, and the other the debt owed to the EFF, as shown in Tables 15.2 and 15.3.

Many problems need to be solved in order to implement this two-tier system of sovereign bond governance. We shall mention the most important ones.

Governments' consolidated gross debt (2012, billion euro), GDP (2012, billion euro) and debt/GDP ratio

	Debt	GDP	Debt/GDP	Quotas on EA debt
Euro area	8,596	9,484	90.6%	100%
Germany	2,160	2,666	81.0%	25%
France	1,834	2,032	90.2%	21%
Italy	1,989	1,567	127.0%	23%
Spain	885	1,029	86.0%	10%

Source: Elaboration of Eurostat data, January 2014.

Table 15.2. *Governments' consolidated gross debt (2012, billion euro)
and the split between the EFF and the market depending on the share
of resources allocated by the EFF for debt restructuring, under three
hypotheses: the EFF buying €1 trillion (column 3 and 4), €1.5 trillion
(column 5 and 6) and €2 trillion (column 7 and 8) of debt*

| | | €1 trillion | | €1.5 trillion | | €2 trillion | |
		EFF	Market	EFF	Market	EFF	Market
Euro area	8,596	1,000	7,596	1,500	7,096	2,000	6,596
Germany	2,160	271	1,890	406	1,754	541	1,619
France	1,834	203	1,631	305	1,529	406	1,428
Italy	1,989	179	1,811	268	1,722	357	1,632
Spain	885	119	766	178	707	237	647

Elaboration (with approximations) of Eurostat data, January 2014

Table 15.3. *Governments' consolidated gross debt/GDP ratio (2012, %)
and the split between the EFF and the market depending on the share
of resources allocated by the EFF for debt restructuring under three
hypotheses: the EFF buying €1 trillion (column 3 and 4), €1.5 trillion
(column 5 and 6) and €2 trillion (column 7 and 8) of debt*

| | | €1 trillion | | €1.5 trillion | | €2 trillion | |
		EFF	Market	EFF	Market	EFF	Market
Euro area	90.6	10.5	80.1	15.8	74.8	21.0	69.6
Germany	81.0	10.1	70.9	15.2	65.8	20.3	60.7
France	90.2	10.0	80.2	15.0	75.2	20.0	70.2
Italy	127.0	11.4	115.6	17.1	109.9	22.8	104.2
Spain	86.0	11.6	74.4	17.3	68.7	23.1	62.9

Elaboration of Eurostat data, January 2014

The EFF has to buy the sovereign bonds (SBs) of EMU-MSs through
a deal arranged with the treasury of each country, which would issue
the bonds with duration slightly shorter than that of the EUBs (as the
latter's duration should be between twenty and thirty years). This
duration can be considered a 'solidarity and restructuring period'.
The rate of interest paid by SBs to the EFF cannot be higher than the
rate paid by the EFF to the markets. The advantage of this situation

compared to the current one is that the rate of interest paid to the EFF will be on average lower than the market rate and that the EFF will keep the sovereign state bonds of EMU-MSs until maturity. This implies that the EFF issue of EUBs should be decided taking into account the EFF's programme of sovereign bonds purchase.

The EMU-MSs would find it easier to deal with sovereign debt, as their 'market' sovereign debt would be reduced by the SBs sold to the EFF. However, moral hazard should be avoided and the market debt-to-GDP ratio should converge to a target agreed by EMU-MSs.

This procedure would also reduce the pressure on bonds already on the market, and this will lower their interest rates. Under these conditions, market volatility would not increase, and would likely decrease, as the market would become less liquid. Indeed, the volume of the whole European sovereign bond market (EUBs plus EMU-MS sovereign bonds) will increase while the risk for each country's sovereign bonds will decrease. The longer the life of the EUBs issued, the better it will be for member states, as they would have more time to lower the debt-to-GDP ratio on their sovereign debt sold on the open market.

Many problems still need to be solved after splitting the aggregate debt of EMU-MSs. In particular, should the market debt ratio to which countries have to converge remain 60%? What ought to be the speed of convergence? What might be the penalties for countries that might not follow the prescribed convergence?

All these problems should be considered, along with the meaning of the debt ratio of 60 per cent. I remain unconvinced about the accurate meaning of such targets, for many reasons. Among them let us consider that the average debt-to-GDP ratios for the euro area over five-year cycles are as follows: 72.7 per cent (1995–99), 68.9 per cent (2000–04), 71.1 per cent (2005–09), 91.5 per cent (2010–14). In the period 1995–2014, which might be considered a long cycle, it is equal to 76.05 per cent, which means that the average was never close to 60 per cent. To judge the deviation of EMU-MSs from the 60 per cent debt-to-GDP ratio since 2016, when the fiscal compact enters into full force, seems to me unrealistic even in the long term.

Whatever might be the path of convergence of the debt ratio and the length of the period to be considered in order to assess the degree of convergence, there must be penalties for the countries that do not comply. A proposal to avoid the moral-fiscal hazard might consist of modifying the voting powers of each country inversely to the deviation from the prescribed debt-to-GDP ratio.

If a particular country that should reduce its debt ratio by 5 percentage points over a five-year period would not achieve the target ratio, its share of voting power and/or property rights (dividends) in the EFF should fall from 17.85 per cent to 12.86 per cent. The 5 percentage points of voting powers and/or the income from the property rights will be proportionally allotted to the countries that have satisfied the convergence path.

Other penalties could also be envisaged, such as levying a fine on countries that do not comply with the convergence path.

15.6.8 The EFF and EUBs for Structural Investment

Having assumed that the total financial resources of the EFF are €3 trillion, the 'take-out' remaining after debt restructuring should be devoted to investment in infrastructure (e.g. electricity grids) and industry (e.g. merging energy companies) (that I call the paradigm of '3i'). These investments should encompass the whole infrastructural network of EMU and EU, including energy, rail, info grids, joint centers of science and technology and so on.

Without exploring the details of EU infrastructure projects, it is worth mentioning that the EU, with Europe 2020, Horizon 2020 and the MFF 2014–2020, has planned public investment projects that are not supported by sufficient financial resources. For example, Europe faces enormous infrastructure investment needs in transport, energy and broadband networks.

To meet the policy goals of the Europe 2020 Strategy for smart, sustainable and inclusive growth and infrastructure development, the necessary investment in the above sectors is estimated between €1.5 trillion and €2 trillion, with a sectorial breakdown and time horizon as follows:

- Transport: Demand is estimated at more than €1.5 trillion for 2010–30 for the entire transport networks of the EU member states. The completion of the trans-European transport networks alone requires about €500 billion by 2020 (of which €250 billion would be needed to complete missing connections and remove bottlenecks in the core network).

- Energy: European networks as a whole would require investments of €1 trillion by 2020 (€200 billion of this investment for electricity and gas networks of European level importance alone).
- Broadband: Investment required to bring ultra-fast connections to all European households and businesses by 2020 is estimated at €270 billion (an investment gap of up to €220 billion).

The European Commission launched two initiatives of great importance: the Europe 2020 Project Bond Initiative (in liaison with the European Investment Bank) and the Connecting Europe Facility within the Multi-annual Financial Framework 2014–2020. But there is the risk that some investments in infrastructure will not take place or will be delayed far beyond 2020 because of insufficient financial means. Therefore, a significant funding contribution at the European level is needed.

The EU draws up ambitious plans, but in practice, there are not enough resources available to carry them out. The EU budget, for example, (the Multiannual Financial Framework 2014–2020) has been reduced for the first time in history. Total commitment appropriations (legal pledges to provide finance, provided that certain conditions are fulfilled) amount to €960 billion (just 1 per cent of the EU's Gross National Income), that is, approximately €137 billion annually. A programme that deserves particular attention is Horizon 2020, the EU Framework Program for Research and Innovation. But even in this case resources, with a total budget at current prices of about €80 billion, are insufficient (Quadrio Curzio, 2013a; 2013b).

15.6.9 The EFF and EUBs in the Very Long Run: Some Open Issues

The obvious final question is what happens when the EMU-MS bonds held by the EFF would reach their maturity (the restructuring and solidarity period) and would have to be repaid by the issuer state.

An obvious solution would be to renew fully or partially the initial purchase of EMU-MS bonds by the EFF. There is nothing wrong with these quasi-consolidation solutions if the EFF and EUBs work in favour of stability and growth.

Many other solutions could be devised, also depending on the length of the solidarity period, the convergence periods and the target debt-to-GDP ratio.

15.7 Conclusions

My conclusions concentrate on two issues of political and economic importance; there will be no further discussion of technical solutions for implementing the EFF and EUBs proposal or of any alternative proposals.[11]

The first issue is German opposition to EUBs; the second is the EUBs' advantages for all individual EMU member states, and for the EMU as a whole.

15.7.1 German Worries

German worries with any type of EB (with the exception of rescue bonds) have been constant in the past four years. They have been clearly expressed just after the Juncker-Tremonti proposal in 2010. Juncker accused Germany of refusing to consider the common problem of over-indebted states, of erecting taboo areas and thus of having an anti-European attitude. The German government replied that it was wrong to accuse them of being anti-European as they had studied in depth the problem of EBs, which was after all an old idea. In August 2011, when bond spreads began to increase rapidly, also involving Italy, mixed messages came from the ruling German coalition and the opposition, while the German government said firmly that the issue of EBs was not a viable solution. Chancellor Angela Merkel urged Europe to stand firm in the face of market pressure and of the 'dramatic crisis' gripping the Eurozone, but she also told German television: 'Solving the current crisis won't be possible with Eurobonds and that's why Eurobonds are not the answer.' (see Wiesmann, Thompson and Hope, 2011). The right answer was, on the contrary, to replace a 'debt union' with a 'stability union'.

When in November 2011 the European Commission released its Green Paper, the proposal for 'stability bonds' (see Section 15.4.2) drew a frosty reception from some of the 'most creditworthy Eurozone states'. The German chancellor remained resolutely unimpressed, describing the Commission's decision to propose Eurobonds as 'extra-ordinarily inappropriate' and 'troubling' in the midst of the crisis,

---

[11] Bibliography on different types of Eurobond is very wide. See, for instance, the contributions of Ashoka, Claessens and Vallée (2012), De Grauwe, and Moesen (2009), Delpla and von Weizsäcker (2010), Favero and Missale (2012).

arguing it was wrong to suggest that collectivization of the debt would allow the EU to overcome the currency union's structural flaws.

Finally, in June 2012, with negotiations in the European Council, and the presentation of the Van Rompuy report (European Council, 2012) ahead, Chancellor Merkel – speaking before the German parliament – held firm to her conviction that the Eurozone's next move should be to institute more central controls over European banks and national budgets. She said, 'I believe that Eurobonds, or mutualised debt, are the wrong way to go.' (see Spiegel, Peel and Carnegy, 2012)

I do not want to analyse in depth the many reasons for German and in particular Merkel's opposition, even if it has been observed that the most obvious one was that Germany might fear a worsening of the rates by which it currently finances its own public debt. Yet the reasoning behind this line of thinking is not fully convincing, as Germany would have to refinance only a relatively small amount of its own debt after the Eurobonds issue, and this might lower even more the interest rates on its market bonds. Another reason is the German electorate's fears to be burdened by the debt of the other EMU-MSs. This fear is not unfounded, but with the EuroUnionBond solution it could be overcome.

15.7.2 European Necessities

EUBs advantages have been discussed in the previous sections, but it may be useful to underline some of them again.

The first is that the EFF would not be an opportunistic, but rather a stabilizing factor in managing state treasury bonds by holding onto them for long periods up to maturity and therefore making speculation more difficult as the risk premium even of highly indebted countries will decline.

The second is that the average interest rates, especially of highly indebted countries, will decline, making it much easier to shift the debt dynamic towards a lower level.

The third is that a wide EUB market can compete with that of US Treasury Bonds and attract the financial resources available in global markets. Two figures must be kept in mind: the estimated dimension of sovereign wealth funds ($6.2 trillion at the end of 2013), the US public debt ($16.7 trillion at the end of 2013) and the amount of it held by foreign investors ($5.8 trillion at the end of 2013).

The fourth is that the EUB will promote EMU unification in two ways: (1) through convergence of the debt-to-GDP ratio of EMU-MSs to the agreed average ratio, thus balancing the fiscal strictness of some countries with expansionary policies in others; and (2) by enhancing European infrastructure and industrial networks (including techno-science).

The fifth is that two powerful instruments of economic policy are much better than one. In fact, under present conditions the only real but mainly short-term effective power within the EMU is the ECB, and the latter may be pushed to follow rather unorthodox policies that may be needed in the absence of EUBs but are certainly not in line with fiscal-strictness conditions. This expansion of the role of the ECB instead of the use of EUBs might in the end be ineffective, and under certain conditions even harmful, to EMU integration in regard to both the real (what I have called the 3i) economy and the fiscal economy as expressed by the convergence of the public debt-to-GDP ratio.

To conclude, in the preceding pages I have mainly quoted political and institutional opinions, but many distinguished economists and investors, such as George Soros (Soros, 2013), have expressed the view that the EMU will risk fracturing without some kind of EUBs. We cannot be sure whether this would be the final outcome, but we are confident that, without EUBs, the EMU will be an area of low growth and high unemployment. This would be exactly the opposite of EMU 'grand institutional design'.

In the meantime, the data, facts and EMU institutional setting are rapidly changing. The most striking change is the 'extreme' quantitative easing put in place by ECB that has taken many interest rates into negative territory. This is a situation without precedent in the history of the twentieth and twenty-first centuries and carries with it the danger of a new financial bubble and many other risk of further splitting between finance and the real economy (Hannoun, 2015). These events make EUBs more and more necessary to channel the enormous available liquidity to the real economy, and also in order to support and to strengthen the (weak) Juncker plan for infrastructural investment in Europe. In short, the decision not to innovate the policies of EMU and EU with the introduction of EUBs has been, and is, a wrong one. Both Juncker's plan and Draghi's quantitative easing would not be enough to trigger a new growth phase for Europe. EuroUnionBonds should be considered again as soon as possible.

Acknowledgements

Thanks are due to Roberto Scazzieri and Valeria Miceli for useful suggestions and to Andrea Sartori for his assistance. Thanks are due also to Seamus Taggart for the English revision. However, I am solely responsible for the views expressed in this essay.

References

Aliber, R. Z. (1982) 'Medium and Long Term Structural Aspects: Conclusions and Evaluations', in A. Quadrio Curzio (ed.) 1982a, pp. 181–83.

Ashoka, M., Claessens, S. and Vallée, S. (2012) 'Paths to Eurobonds', *IMF Working Paper* 12/172, July.

Boyer De La Giroday, F. (1982) 'The European Monetary System and Gold', in A. Quadrio Curzio (ed.) 1982a, pp. 205–26.

Coltorti F. and Quadrio Curzio A. (2013) 'Bankoro: The Plan to Use Gold Reserves', *Il Sole 24 Ore*, 16 April.

De Grauwe, P. and Moesen, W. (eds.) (2009) *Gains for All: A Proposal for a Common Euro Bond*, Brussels: CEPS Commentary.

Delpla, J. and von Weizsäcker, J. (eds.) (2010) *The Blue Bond Proposal*, Bruegel: Bruegel Policy Brief, Updated version of 21 March 2011.

Du Boulay, L. (1982) 'Medium and Long Term Structural Aspects: conclusions and Evaluations', in A. Quadrio Curzio (ed.) 1982a, pp. 173–81.

Du Boulay, L. and Fells, P. (1982) 'The Medium and Long Term Structural Aspects for Gold', in A. Quadrio Curzio (ed.) 1982a, pp. 85–100.

European Commission (ed.) (1993) *Growth, Competitiveness, Employment: The Challenges and Ways Forward into the 21st Century*. White Paper, COM (93) 700, 5 December.

European Commission (ed.) (2011), *Green Paper on the feasibility of introducing Stability Bonds*, COM (2011) 818 final, 23 November.

European Commission (ed.) (2012), *A Blueprint for a Deep and Genuine Economic and Monetary Union: Launching a European Debate*, COM (2012) 777 final/2, 30 November.

European Commission (ed.) (2013) *Follow up to the European Parliament Resolution on the Feasibility of Introducing Stability Bonds*, 24 April.

European Council (ed.) (2012), *Towards a genuine Economic and Monetary Union*, EUCO 120/12, 26 June.

European Parliament (ed.) (2010) *European Parliament Resolution of 6 July 2011 on the Financial, Economic and Social Crisis: Recommendations*

Concerning the Measures and Initiatives to Be Taken, 2010/2242 (INI), 6 July.

European Parliament (ed.) (2013) *European Parliament Resolution of 16 January 2013 on the Feasibility of Introducing Stability Bonds, 2012/2028 (INI)*, 16 January.

Eurostat (ed.) (2011) *The Statistical Recording of Operations Undertaken by the European Financial Stability Facility*, 13/2011, 27 January.

Favero, C. A. and Missale, A. (2012) 'Sovereign Spreads in the Eurozone: Which Prospects for a Eurobond?', *Economic Policy*, 70, pp. 231–71.

Hannoun, H. (2015) *Ultra-Low or Negative Interest Rates: What They Mean for Financial Stability and Growth*, Remarks at the Eurofi High-Level Seminar, 22 April 2015, Riga: Bank for International Settlements.

Juncker, J. C. and Tremonti, G. (2010) 'E-bonds Would End the Crisis', *The Financial Times*, 5 December.

Languetin, P. (1982) 'Medium and Long Term Structural Aspects: Conclusions and Evaluations', in A. Quadrio Curzio (ed.) 1982a, pp. 171–73.

Larre, R. (1982) 'National and Supranational Monetary Authorities Position: Conclusions and Evaluations', in A. Quadrio Curzio (ed.) 1982a, pp. 281–83.

Montefiori S. (2010) 'Eurobond per la crescita non solo contro il debito', *Corriere della Sera*, 21 Dicembre.

Prodi, R. and Quadrio Curzio, A. (2011) 'EuroUnionBonds, Here Is What Must Be Done', *Il Sole 24 Ore*, 23 August.

Prodi, R. and Quadrio Curzio, A. (2012a) 'EuroUnionBonds: Why Are We Proposing Them Again?', *Il Sole 24 Ore*, 23 August.

Prodi, R. and Quadrio Curzio, A. (2012b) 'Gold in the Past and Euro-UnionBonds for the Future', *Economia Politica: Journal of Analytical and Institutional Economics*, 29/3, pp. 295–303.

Quadrio Curzio, A. (ed.) (1982a) *The Gold Problem: Economic Perspectives*, Oxford: Oxford University Press.

Quadrio Curzio, A. (1982b) 'Gold Problems and a Conference on Gold', in A. Quadrio Curzio (ed.), *The Gold Problem: Economic Perspectives*, Oxford: Oxford University Press.

Quadrio Curzio, A. (1985) 'Dal rifiuto del numerario aureo ai prezzi quasi ufficiali dell'oro', *Rivista Internazionale di Scienze Economiche e Commerciali*, 10–11/32, pp. 965–986.

Quadrio Curzio, A. (2004) 'Una spinta dall'Europa', *Il Sole 24 Ore*, 28 novembre.

Quadrio Curzio, A. (2008a) Un Fondo sovrano con l'oro d'Europa, *Il Sole 24 Ore*, 5 febbraio, also translated into English and published as

A Sovereign-wealth Fund with Europe's Gold, in A. Quadrio Curzio (ed.) 2008b, pp. 376–78.

Quadrio Curzio, A. (2008b) 'Reflections on the Crisis 2007–2008', *Economia Politica: Journal of Analytical and Institutional Economics*, 3/25, pp. 369–80.

Quadrio Curzio, A. (2008c) 'I vantaggi dell'eurodebito', *Il Sole 24 Ore*, 8 maggio.

Quadrio Curzio, A. (2008d) 'L'Europa e le illusioni della finanza spericolata', *Il Sole 24 Ore*, 17 luglio.

Quadrio Curzio, A. (2008e) 'L'Europa non è solo BCE', *Il Sole 24 Ore*, 24 settembre, also translated into English and published as Europe Is Not Only The European Central Bank, in A. Quadrio Curzio (ed.) 2008b, pp. 378–80.

Quadrio Curzio, A. (2008f) 'Bruxelles diligente ma senza idee', *Il Sole 24 Ore*, 2 dicembre.

Quadrio Curzio, A. (2009) 'Per un Fondo di Euro-Sviluppo', *Corriere della Sera*, 28 febbraio.

Quadrio Curzio, A. (2011a) 'A proposito di bond europei', *il Mulino*, 2, pp. 282–90.

Quadrio Curzio, A. (2011b) 'On the Different Types of Eurobonds', *Economia Politica: Journal of Analytical and Institutional Economics*, 3/28, pp. 279–94.

Quadrio Curzio, A. (2012) 'I Fondi salva Stati europei: limiti, pregi, potenzialità', in *il Mulino*, 3, pp. 849–57.

Quadrio Curzio, A. (2013a) 'Un bilancio comunitario sempre più difficile', in *il Mulino*, 3, pp. 469–78.

Quadrio Curzio, A. (2013b) 'Un bilancio per l'Europa della crescita', *Il Sole 24 Ore*, 6 febbraio.

Quadrio Curzio, A. (2014) 'Eurobond for EMU Stability, Convergence, Growth', CRANEC Working Paper, Catholic University, Milan, Vita-Pensiero.

Quadrio Curzio, A. and Miceli, V. (2009) *I fondi sovrani*, Bologna: il Mulino.

Quadrio Curzio, A. and Miceli, V. (2010) *Sovereign Wealth Funds: A Complete Guide to State-owned Investment Funds*, Petersfield: Harriman House.

Schwartz, A. (1982) 'The Past, Current and Prospective Role of Gold in the US Monetary System', in A. Quadrio Curzio (ed.) 1982a, pp. 237–43.

Soros G. (2013), 'Germany's Choice', *Project Syndicate*, 9 April.

Spiegel P., Peel Q. and Carnegy H. (2012), 'Merkel digs in heels over action on euro', *The Financial Times*, 27 June.

Wiesmann G., Thompson J. and Hope K. (2011), 'Merkel defies pressure on debt crisis', *The Financial Times*, 21 August.

Wittich, G. (1982) 'The role of gold in the International Monetary Fund today', in A. Quadrio Curzio (ed.) 1982a, pp. 227–36.

Sitography

European Central Bank (ECB): www.ecb.europa.eu/
European Commission (EC): http://ec.europa.eu/
European Council: www.european-council.europa.eu/
European Parliament (EP): www.europarl.europa.eu/
European Financial Stability Facility (EFSF): www.efsf.europa.eu/
European Stability Mechanism (ESM): www.esm.europa.eu/
Il Sole 24 Ore: www.ilsole24ore.com/english-version/front-page.shtml[12]
World Gold Council: www.gold.org/

---

[12] All articles by Alberto Quadrio Curzio quoted in this essay are also published in English on this website.

16 | *How False Beliefs about Exchange Rate Regimes Threaten Global Growth and the Existence of the Eurozone*

WILLIAM R. WHITE

16.1 Introduction

The ongoing economic and financial crisis has raised many questions. How much do we really know about how the global economy operates and the Eurozone within it? Many people have "beliefs", but belief is not "knowledge". Knowledge is a belief that can be justified either through the force of logic or recourse to the facts, or preferably both. Unfortunately, a number of widely held beliefs about both the International Monetary System and the Eurozone seem to fail both tests. As Mark Twain said more than a century ago, "It ain't the things you don't know what gets you. It's the things that you know for sure, what ain't so". False beliefs about the operations of the International Monetary System and the Eurozone system constitute significant threats to the "strong, sustainable and balanced growth" desired by both the G20 and European political leaders. Indeed, they constitute a threat to the existence of the Eurozone itself.

Actually implementing policy solutions to deal with practical problems demands overcoming three sets of obstacles. These have been referred to since classical times as the "should, could and would" problems. More recently, Véron (2012) has referred to these same concerns by noting that the Eurozone has an analytical deficit, an executive deficit and a democratic deficit. The "should" problem (the analytic deficit) refers to getting agreement at the level of theory about what policy needs to do. The "could" problem (the executive deficit) refers to the issue of power and whether agents that need to act have the power to act. Finally the "would" problem (the democratic deficit) addresses the question of the will to act to do what needs to be done. Broadly speaking, these three obstacles respectively address economic, legal and political issues.

This chapter is primarily about "should" (analytical) issues, which logically precede the other concerns. If chosen policies are misguided to begin with, being based on false economic beliefs, then it is not at all clear that we would want them to be implemented effectively. Moreover, this essay is focussed on pointing out deficiencies in current beliefs rather than recommending alternatives. This approach is in the spirit of Hayek (1937, p. 94) who, seeking to improve the workings of the gold standard,[1] stated: "The most important step in this direction (improving the rules of the game) is that the *rationale* of an international standard and the true sources of the instability of our present system should be properly appreciated."

Section 16.2 identifies two fundamental analytical challenges. First, there are some important policy insights to be drawn from treating the economy as a complex adaptive system. Unfortunately, this way of looking at the economy is not yet typical for policymakers, whether at the global level or within Europe. Second, as a testimony to this complexity, there are a host of considerations to be taken into account in choosing an exchange rate regime. These choices do not always take into account all the relevant considerations, both short term and especially long term. The basic conclusion is that the "right answer" involves trade-offs, and these can change over time. In sum, it is not hard to make wrong decisions.

Against this background, Sections 16.3 and 16.4 are addressing current issues more specifically. Section 16.3 emphasizes a fundamental misapprehension that has shaped policies at both the level of the International Monetary System and within the Eurozone. This is the false belief that the achievement of CPI price stability would be sufficient to avoid broader macroeconomic problems, indeed systemic crises. Section 16.4 then turns to additional false beliefs that have contributed to suboptimal policy outcomes, first at the level of the International Monetary System and then at the level of the Eurozone. While these issues are treated separately, the interactions between them add an extra

---

[1] Hayek suggests that the failure of the gold standard was primarily due to an important false belief. Governments viewed it as a truly metallic standard that would ensure adjustment by both creditors and debtors when current account imbalances led to international gold flows. This belief was false because it failed to recognize the importance of the national credit structures (essentially fiat money) that had been superimposed on the gold standard over the course of the years.

layer of complexity. If false beliefs about how the International Monetary System works constitute a threat to global growth, they will surely have implications for the Eurozone in turn. Similarly, should false beliefs threaten to slow economic growth within the Eurozone, or even its continuing existence, this would undoubtedly have global implications.[2] Section 16.4 concludes with some alternative scenarios about how the Eurozone project might evolve. Evidently, this demands the reintroduction of the "could" and "would" issues that will also drive policies going forward. Section 16.5 draws together a few tentative conclusions.

16.2 Some fundamental analytical challenges

16.2.1 The Challenge of Complexity

The dominant school of economic thought, prior to the crisis, essentially modelled the national economy as a changeless machine.[3] Moreover, the machine always operated at its optimal speed, churning out outputs in an almost totally predicable (linear) way, under the close control of its (policy) operators. While the sudden and unexpected onslaught of the current crisis, to say nothing of its unexpected depth and duration, might have been expected to have put paid to this false belief, in practice it has not.[4] Nevertheless, the crisis has significantly increased interest in another viewpoint, as described in Haldane (2015). Rather than being a machine, the economy should instead be viewed as a complex adaptive system, like a forest, with massive interdependencies among its parts and the potential for highly non-linear outcomes. Such systems evolve in a path-dependent way,[5] and there is no equilibrium to return to. There are, in fact, many such systems in both nature and society,[6] and their properties have been well studied.[7] Economists could learn a great deal from these studies. Four points are essential and

---

[2] See OECD (2012).
[3] The dominant academic models are described as Dynamic Stochastic General Equilibrium Models.
[4] In fact, many if not most macro economists have not changed their views in any significant way. The difficulties in achieving paradigm shifts were well described in Kuhn (1962). For some more recent observations, see White (2013).
[5] David (2000).
[6] For example, traffic patterns, movements of crowds, the spread of crime and diseases, social networks, urban development and many more.
[7] For popular introductions, see Ball (2012), Buchanan (2000) and Beinhocker (2006). For a more rigorous analysis, see the many references in Haldane (2015).

contain lessons for national policymakers as well as those charged with overseeing the operations of the global economy.

First, all complex systems fail regularly; that is, they fall into crisis. Moreover, the literature suggests that the distribution of outcomes is commonly determined by a Power Law. Big crises occur infrequently while smaller ones are more frequent. A look at economic history indicates that the same patterns apply.[8] For example, there were big crises in 1825, 1873 and 1929, as well as smaller ones more recently in the Nordic countries, Japan and Southeast Asia. The policy lesson to be drawn is that if crises are indeed inevitable, then we must have ex ante mechanisms in place for managing them. Unfortunately, this was not the case when the global crisis erupted in 2007 and when the Eurozone crisis erupted in 2010.[9]

Second, the trigger for a crisis is irrelevant. It could be anything, perhaps even of trivial importance in itself. It is the system that is unstable. For example, the current global crisis began in 2006 in the subprime sector of the US mortgage market. Then Chairman of the Federal Reserve Ben Bernanke originally estimated that the losses would not exceed USD 50 billion and they would not extend beyond the subprime market. Today, eight years later and still counting, the crisis has cost many trillions of dollars[10] and has gone global. It seems totally implausible that this was "contagion". Similarly, how could difficulties in tiny Greece in 2010 have had such far-reaching and lasting implications for the whole Eurozone? The global crisis was in fact an accident waiting to happen, as indeed was the crisis within the Eurozone. The lesson to be drawn is that we must focus more on interdependencies and systemic risks both at the global level and within the Eurozone. If the timing and triggers for crises are impossible to predict, it remains feasible to identify signs of potential instability building up and to react to them.[11] In particular, economic and financial systems tend to instability as credit and debt levels build up.

---

[8] Economic history has become fashionable again after many years of neglect. See Kindleberger and Aliber (2015), Reinhart and Rogoff (2009) and Schularick and Taylor (2009).

[9] Sapir and Wolff (2015).

[10] The Federal Reserve Bank of Dallas recently estimated the costs to the United States alone would eventually cumulate to one full year of US production at the 2013 levels. See Atkinson, Luttrell and Rosenblum (2013).

[11] The Bank for International Settlements has written extensively on this over the years. See Borio and Lowe (2002) for a seminal example. More recent research

Third, complex systems can result in very large economic losses (often associated with political instability) much more frequently than a normal distribution would suggest. The lesson to be drawn is that policymakers should focus more on avoiding really bad outcomes than on optimizing good ones. We simply do not have the knowledge to do policy optimization.[12] Unfortunately, both at the global level and within the Eurozone, the focus prior to the crisis was almost totally on how well the economy was performing rather than on the dangerous "imbalances" building up under the surface. As a corollary, using policy levers to lean against growing "imbalances" should also help to lower the costs of crises.

Fourth, looking at economic and financial crises throughout history, there have been many similarities but also many differences. History does not repeat itself, but it does seem to rhyme. In part this is due to adaptive human behaviour, both in markets and on the part of regulators, in response to previous crises. While excessive credit growth might be common to most crises, both the source of the credit (banks vs. non-banks) and the character of the borrowers (governments, corporations and households) might well be different. Note too that such crises have occurred under a variety of exchange rate regimes. Moreover, prized stability in one area today (e.g. payment systems) does not rule out that area being the trigger for instability tomorrow. Changes in economic structure or behaviour can all too easily transform todays "truth" into tomorrow's "false belief". The lesson to be drawn is that policymakers need eternal vigilance and, indeed, institutional structures that are capable of responding to changed circumstances. Do not fight the last war.

Haldane (2015) notes that a national economy is a very complex system made up of three interconnected complex systems: individual financial institutions, the financial system and the real economy. He notes that each of the three can be influenced by government policies – micro prudential, macro prudential and monetary policies,

---

seems to indicate that property prices and housing finance are commonly implicated in big breakdowns. See Jorda, Schularick and Taylor (2014).

[12] This has been a long-held view of the Austrian school of economics. It is not surprising that Hayek's Nobel Prize lecture was titled "The Pretence of Knowledge"; see Hayek (1975). An excellent book drawing the link between the Classical economists and modern complexity theory is Simpson (2013). The primary link is through Hayek, especially Hayek (1967).

respectively. Haldane then documents how interactions between these national economies have grown rapidly in recent year, adding a fourth layer of complexity. Finally, he adds, "[I]t is here where the existing policy architecture may at present be most deficient" (Haldane 2015, p. 20). In this chapter, an attempt is made to identify some of these shortcomings both at the global level and at the level of the Eurozone.

16.2.2 The Challenge of Choosing an Exchange Rate Regime

The need to choose an exchange rate regime reflects the underlying reality of what is called the Impossible Trinity.[13] A country cannot simultaneously have highly mobile international capital flows, an autonomous monetary policy and a fixed exchange rate. For example, tighter monetary policy will attract capital inflows, which will threaten the fixed exchange rate. The practical question is which of the three elements policymakers choose to give up. At the level of the global economy, the G3 in particular, the choice has been to float – they have chosen to give up the fixed exchange rate. Conversely at the level of the Eurozone, the individual sovereign countries have given up their capacity to follow an autonomous monetary policy. In still further contrast, many emerging market countries have decided not to choose one of these corner solutions. Rather, they have taken measures (largely administrative) to constrain each element of the Impossible Trinity in the hope of producing a coherent policy package.[14]

Why do countries make the exchange rate choices they do? Each regime choice should be made on the basis of a long list of economic pros and cons. There is no "right answer". When political motivations enter in, as was the case leading up to the formation of the Eurozone,[15] this conclusion is suggested even more strongly. Moreover, even objective circumstances can change over time (e.g. the degree of wage flexibility), implying that the balance leading to a final decision can also change over time.

---

[13] Mundell (1963).

[14] The suggested constraints include the following. Use monetary policy in a rather cautious way. Constrain capital flows using capital controls and macro prudential policies. Use foreign exchange intervention to moderate exchange rate changes. It is far too early to say that these efforts have been successful.

[15] James (2012) argues that the political motivation behind the establishment of the Eurozone was less important than many think.

Evidently, in weighing up the balance of the arguments, trade-offs must be made. While some such trade-offs reflect objective assessments (albeit hard to measure) of the costs and benefits, others simply reflect national preferences. For example, some choose to float, arguing that this removes a constraint. Thus, it gives more freedom to policymakers in their pursuit of "strong" growth. Those choosing to fix often emphasize that it provides discipline for policymakers and contributes to more "sustainable" growth. Since "strong" and "sustainable" growth are both desirable, there is an obvious inter-temporal trade-off.

The United States is traditionally more in the former camp, while Germany and other core members of the Eurozone are in the latter. These preferences are often linked to what an individual country considers to have been its "defining historical moment"; the Great Depression in the case of the United States and the hyperinflation in central Europe following World War I.[16] The United States therefore has a bias towards growth as an economic objective, while central European countries have a bias towards stability.

It is often argued that countries should only fix their exchange rates if they constitute an optimal currency area. In particular, does each part of the area have susceptibility to the same shocks? If not, will highly adjustable wages, high labour mobility and the availability of fiscal transfers act to cushion asymmetric shocks? Unfortunately there is an inter-temporal complication here as well. Some would argue that, even absent these advantages, entering into a currency union would foster the required structural changes over time. Many took this line prior to the introduction of the euro. Others, however, took the opposite position, implying a greater chance that the euro construct would not survive.

This debate about the euro echoed the much earlier exchange between Keynes ("wages have become inflexible") and the UK Treasury ("wages will become flexible again") when Churchill was deciding whether to put the United Kingdom back on the gold standard at the pre-war parity. Britain lost a whole decade of growth because of the failure to follow Keynes' advice.[17] But was the real problem

---

[16] Also important was the stabilizing role played by the Bundesbank after the introduction of the Deutschmark in the wake of World War II.

[17] Keynes (1925).

one of "fixing" or of fixing at too high an exchange rate? Almost a century later, scholars are still debating the issue.

There is another indicator that there can be no right answer when it comes to the choice of currency regimes. Both sets of regimes have repeatedly broken down throughout history, or were replaced as experience indicated that their practical shortcomings overwhelmed their presumed advantages. Some transitions were quite orderly, as for example with the introduction of the euro and the breakup of Czechoslovakia. In contrast, other transitions were often quite disorderly, ending in deep recession, hyperinflation or often both. The breakup of the Hapsburg Empire, the Soviet Union and Yugoslavia provides three good examples of such developments.

There have been many transitions from fixed to floating. The gold standard broke down due to the exigencies of financing World War I. The gold exchange standard broke down in the 1930s as countries, particularly those accumulating gold, failed to follow the "rules of the game". The Bretton Woods system broke down when the United States failed to resist inflation as its European partners wanted. And the European Exchange Rate Mechanism proved incapable of dealing with international capital flows after administrative controls over such movements were lifted. While less likely, it is not impossible that the Eurozone could suffer the same fate. Were even one country to leave the Eurozone, it would clearly discredit the notion that this was impossible and possibly raise doubts about other countries as well.

Similarly, there have been many transitions from floating to fixed rate regimes. There was the return to gold after World War I and the introduction of Bretton Woods after World War II. In the middle to late 1980s, G7 policymakers concluded that the Plaza and the Louvre Accords were needed; the first to lower the value of the US dollar and then the latter to prevent it from falling too far.[18] As well, we have the example of many countries giving up entirely on their own currency and choosing to adopt the dollar, the euro or some other "stable" currency as an alternative. It is not impossible then that the current

---

[18] As part of that latter effort, Japan's easy money policies arguably contributed to the Japanese "boom and bust" of the 1980s and 1990s. Japan was faced with strong international pressure to keep interest rates low to restrain the rise of the yen and the fall of the dollar. Arguably, the fallout from this mistaken exchange rate policy is still being felt today.

dollar-based system might be replaced with a truly international currency, perhaps linked in some way to the price of something real.[19]

While it must be repeated that there are no "right answers" in this area, it is a simple fact that the G3 and the Eurozone have come to dramatically different conclusions. Unfortunately, both systems are now showing signs of great strain. It would be far too ambitious to give specific suggestions for improving these systems. Rather, the focus of this essay is on pointing out a number of "false beliefs" that are making it more difficult to prevent crises. Moreover, when crises do occur, false beliefs can also lead to policies that make them more difficult both to manage and to resolve. Shortcomings with respect to crisis management and resolution are more clearly evident in the Eurozone where the crisis is further advanced than at the global level. If policymakers could only be disabused of these false beliefs, the door would be open for the contemplation of policy actions that would be more successful than those followed to date.

16.2.3 The Shared False Belief That Price Stability Ensures Macroeconomic Stability

This belief was shared by all the major central banks, with the possible exception of the Bank of Japan, in the decades leading up to the crisis that began in 2008. Unfortunately, this belief is erroneous. History should have taught us that CPI price stability does not guarantee macroeconomic stability even in large countries. There was no inflation in the United States prior to the Great Depression. There was no significant inflation prior to the Japanese Great Recession, or in Southeast Asia prior to their crisis in the late 1990s. These crises were, in fact, all created by the excessive creation of credit and debt in an environment of very easy monetary conditions.

In the decades leading up to the onset of the current crisis, the global economy was characterized by very easy monetary conditions, directed by central banks to offsetting excessively disinflationary or even deflationary conditions. This pre-crisis policy was based on the false belief that all deflations are bad. In fact, deflations associated with positive supply-side shocks, such as those in recent decades associated with the return of China and other command-and-control economies into the

---

[19] See Pringle (2012) for some very practical suggestions.

world trading system, are not necessarily bad. Prices can go down even as profits and output levels rise. It is simply a fact that virtually all historical experiences of falling prices have been of this nature. For all practical purposes, the Great Depression was unique.[20] It is unfortunate then, to say the least, that this particular historical period became the pre-crisis template to guide policymakers about how to react to falling prices.

In the pursuit of price stability, the "financial rate of interest" in the advanced market economies was kept well below the "natural rate" of interest for many years prior to the onset of the crisis. Moreover, the former rate was also commonly held below the level recommended by a "Taylor rule".[21] By 2007 this had led to conditions in financial markets that the Bank of International Settlements (BIS) warned, rightly, were dangerously unbalanced even if there were no overt signs of consumer price index (CPI) inflation. The onset of the current global crisis then proved definitively the falseness of the belief that achieving price stability was a sufficient condition to avoid broader macroeconomic crises. The subsequent onset of the Eurozone crisis simply reinforced this point. Relatively easy monetary conditions in Europe prior to the crisis, induced by the global disinflationary pressures referred to earlier, contributed to the heavy borrowing by peripheral countries in the Eurozone and to the onslaught of the crisis itself. In this fundamental sense, the Eurozone crisis was a microcosm of the global crisis. As at the global level, aggregate CPI inflation in the Eurozone was well under control prior to the crisis.

Following the onset of the global crisis, financial markets in most advanced market economies seized up in a "Minsky moment" characterized by heightened counterparty risk. Central banks, led by the European Central Bank, responded appropriately with unprecedented and eventually successful efforts to restore market functioning. Subsequently, however, the objective of expansionary monetary policies reverted back to stimulating aggregate demand. This was because unemployment rose very sharply during the global recession of 2009 and inflation threatened to fall below 2 per cent, the generally accepted definition of "price stability".

---

[20] See Atkenson and Kehoe (2004); also Borio et al. (2015).
[21] This has been repeatedly documented in various publications of the BIS.

In pursuit of price stability, policy rates were essentially lowered to zero, the size of the balance sheet of the major central banks was massively expanded, and "forward guidance" was given concerning possible future policy actions. The Federal Reserve was the most active supporter of such expansionary policies, contending that they would work and that possible undesired side effects could be ignored. The ECB also participated, albeit much more reluctantly, while the Bank of Japan also reacted very aggressively, but only with a long lag and after the previous Governor of the Bank had been replaced.

Monetary stimulus of this sort is essentially "more of the same" policies that were followed prior to the crisis. Even after seven years, these policies have not succeeded in spurring "strong, sustainable and balanced growth" either at the global level or within the Eurozone. While previous easing cycles had succeeded in reducing unemployment and restoring price stability, these policies were at the same time encouraging the continuous growth of debt and financial leverage. In the English-speaking countries, not least the United States, growing debt levels eventually restrained spending by the household sector. In the Eurozone, the problem of excessive debt affected a variety of sectors in the peripheral countries in particular. Corporations almost everywhere in the advanced market economies also cut investment sharply. This could have reflected earlier over investment, uncertainty about future government policy as well as the unexpected interaction between low interest rates and corporate compensation practices.[22]

Other factors reducing the impact of monetary easing might also have been underestimated by conventional thinking and models. Very low interest rates in support of price stability redistribute income from the middle classes (who mostly hold interest-bearing accounts) to richer people (who hold more risky assets). If richer people have a lower marginal propensity to consume than poorer people do, the net

---

[22] From a Wicksellian perspective, setting the financial rate below the natural rate results in both too little saving and too much investment. After the onset of crisis, the saving rate tends to rise and the investment rate to fall. Put otherwise, why invest further in production capacity when consumption is likely to be restrained? A different argument is made by Andrew Smithers. In his Blog at the *Financial Times* he has repeatedly argued that low interest rates encourage corporate managers to buy back stock with borrowed money to push up the share prices to which their compensation is related. Cutting investment also frees up cash for similar purposes while raising profits through reduced depreciation. These arguments could be complementary.

effect might actually be to reduce consumption rather than increase it. Not surprisingly, this has been a very common theme in the German popular press. Further, low rates of return on financial assets imply the need for more savings, if a particular threshold level (e.g. for a retirement annuity) is to be achieved. Creditors also suffer losses from write-offs on bad credits, and financial intermediaries can suffer too. Europe's banks in particular are still not well capitalized, and lending to small and medium-sized enterprises (SMEs) everywhere has been restrained. Low interest rates squeeze bank margins and profits, as do negative interest rates on reserves with central banks. Similarly, the solvency of many pension funds and insurance companies is becoming increasingly questionable.[23] Finally, for all their longer-run benefits, regulatory regimes for the financial sector have become more restrictive virtually everywhere. This might also have impeded lending and near-term economic recovery.

If the efficiency of monetary easing in response to excessive disinflation might have been overestimated, the negative implications of the side effects might have been underestimated.[24] One particular side effect is that they have generated market conditions that seem very similar to those prevailing in 2007 prior to the onset of the crisis. As of mid-2015, very low bond rates, narrow high yield spreads, the continued rise in equity prices and the continued easing of credit standards[25] all indicate that the likelihood of a significant setback in global financial markets has become exceedingly great. Within the Eurozone, the spreads of peripheral sovereigns (excepting Greece) have fallen so sharply that a number of countries could borrow more cheaply than the US Treasury does. Moreover, through the various spill-overs described later in the chapter, the problem of excessive growth and associated imbalances is no longer confined to the advanced market economies, but has spread to the emerging markets as well. Whereas resilient emerging market economies were thought to be part of the solution to deficient global growth in 2009, by 2015 their domestic weakness has become part of the problem.

The spread of credit-driven imbalances to the global stage has in part been due to exchange rate considerations. Central banks in a fiat

---

[23] See Swiss ReGroup (2014) and Hofmann (2013).

[24] For a fuller assessment of both, see White (2012).

[25] The proportion of "cov-lite" bank loans in 2014 significantly exceeded those in 2007.

money world can print an infinite amount of money to resist currency appreciation or to encourage depreciation. Easy monetary policies in the United States first led to dollar depreciation and the onset of what the Brazilian Minister of Finance called "currency wars". Not only the emerging market economies but also the Bank of Japan and the European Central Bank responded with unprecedented monetary initiatives which had the effect of reducing the value of their currency against the US dollar. While this process of global liquidity generation was being increasingly monitored by the IMF, the BIS and others, there is no global body in charge of controlling this process. Nor were there any international rules in place, as under the gold standard or the Bretton Woods system, to enforce self-discipline on the part of the major players. Given the false belief that price stability guarantees macroeconomic stability, the process of global liquidity expansion has essentially been allowed to spin out of control. It threatens to become the "nightmare" outcome predicted by Hayek as far back as 1937, when he considered how the undisciplined use of national monies might lead to international financial instability.[26]

Looking forward, the global economic difficulties arising from the pursuit of price stability (excessive disinflation) seem more likely to worsen than to recede. Non-financial debt levels are almost 20 percentage points (of GDP) higher in 2015 than in 2007.[27] As a result, the possible onset of a Fisher-type "debt deflation" is increasingly being viewed as a serious problem.[28] On the one hand, it is being more widely recognized that this situation might have been a side effect of the earlier

---

[26] Among the many possible triggers for a global crisis, the situation in Japan as of mid-2015 raises the greatest concerns. The government deficit is about 7 per cent of GDP and government debt is already 230 per cent of GDP, the highest in the OECD. The Bank of Japan is currently purchasing government bonds at a rate that implies it is financing 40 per cent of the total expenditures of the Japanese government. The principal worry is that if an increase in inflationary expectations (or anything else) were to shock upwards the rates on government bonds, Japanese government debt would become unserviceable other than through further recourse to the Bank of Japan. History teaches us that such situations can culminate in a sudden shift from price stability (or even from deflation) into high inflation or even hyperinflation. See Bernholz (2015). Theory also supports this position. It is the interaction of bad fiscal and bad monetary policies that creates such problems, not monetary policy alone. See Sargent and Wallace (1981).

[27] McKinsey Global Institute (2015) and Buttiglione et al. (2014)

[28] Fisher (1933). If debts are fixed in nominal terms and prices (and the revenues of debtors) are falling, then debt service becomes more difficult.

attempts of central banks to resist excessively disinflationary tendencies. Very low rates for a very long time actively encouraged this debt accumulation. Recognition of this possibility might also call for a shift towards tighter monetary policy to resist further debt accumulation. On the other hand, with debt levels having already grown so high and deflation already threatening, there seems no alternative to keeping policy rates low enough that existing debts remain serviceable. A number of authors began to refer to this as a "debt trap", implying that (for them at least) the way out for the global economy was not obvious.[29]

The continued commitment of the ECB to aggregate CPI price stability within the Eurozone was made clear by the commitment to quantitative easing early in 2015. Whether it will be effective in stimulating aggregate demand remains highly problematic. What is more clear are the unwelcome side effects of monetary easing to date in the pursuit of price stability. Property prices in a number of European countries, both for houses and commercial property, have recently been under strong upward pressure. The price of financial assets, not least bonds and equity, has risen sharply. While there can be debate about the sustainability of the latter, negative yields on some relatively long-term European sovereign bonds must eventually be reversed. Further, it is notable that productivity growth in both France and Germany has been slowing in recent years. In part, this may be due to unusually easy monetary conditions which have allowed banks to support "zombie" companies that would otherwise have been forced into bankruptcy.

Finally, the pursuit of price stability in the Eurozone, post crisis, has some arithmetical implications as well. If prices and wages must fall in peripheral countries to restore competitiveness and reduce current account deficits, as discussed later in the chapter, then inflation must rise in core countries if the overall target is to be achieved. Core countries with a strong historical aversion to inflation, particularly in Central Europe, might find this prospect very unappealing. At a minimum, this might lead to efforts to prevent the ECB from engaging in policies that might have this outcome. At a maximum, it might lead to political agitation supporting the withdrawal of core countries from the Eurozone itself.

[29] Sinn (2014), Pringle (2012), Prasad (2014) and the BIS Annual Report for 2014 all refer to this "trap" phenomenon, albeit in different contexts. Also see Kotlikoff (2010) who suggests that the prospective debt problems faced by many governments are actually far worse than conventional accounting implies.

16.3 Different False Beliefs about the International Monetary System and the Eurozone

16.3.1 False Beliefs about the International Monetary System

In spite of the shrinking share of the United States in global production, the dollar continues to lie at the heart of the world economic and financial system. Mistakes made in Washington, on the basis of false beliefs, can thus have big implications everywhere. While Eurozone and Japanese policymakers often share these beliefs, fortunately, the domestic policies they follow in response are likely to affect other countries less.[30] The false beliefs referred to later in this section (advocated most vigorously by US policymakers) in effect support the continuation of the current dollar exchange standard from which the United States is thought to derive an "exorbitant privilege".

Largely due to the false beliefs identified in the following discussion, policymakers failed to *prevent* the current global crisis. Moreover, they also failed to put into place the institutional and other policy changes that would have allowed the crisis to be better *managed* and ultimately *resolved*. Absent that resolution, the crisis remains ongoing and could potentially culminate in a still more dramatic global downturn.

Belief 1: Floating Will Automatically Adjust Global Current Account Imbalances
Unfortunately, this proposition is not true, either for the United States or for other countries. Indeed Padoa-Schioppa has said this belief "is nothing but an illusion".[31] Why is this so? Frequently, the exchange rate simply does not move in the direction required to deal smoothly

---

[30] This is not to say there is no influence at all. For example, low policy rates in Japan led to decade-long "carry trade" investments pushing up exchange rates and asset prices in many other countries. More recently, the anticipation of quantitative easing in the Eurozone had a dramatic effect on the Swiss franc and some other currencies as well. The manifestation of these latter polices was not confined to small countries but could even be seen in the United States. Many commentators suggested that lower bond rates in the Eurozone in the first half of 2015 were driving down the rates on US Treasuries. This serves to underline the profound interdependencies that currently characterize the global economic and financial system.

[31] See Padoa-Schioppa (2010). The vigour with which he made this case against floating undoubtedly reflected his support for the fixing inherent in the introduction of the euro.

with an emerging current account problem. The increase in the value of the US dollar from mid-2014 is a case in point. Second, even if the exchange rate does move properly, the shifts in domestic production in response do not take place, or only with a long delay. Think of how little reaction there has been to the depreciation of the yen and the pound over the past few years.[32] Third, suppose an internal shift (say) towards tradables does occur. Then the government of the country with a current account deficit must improve its fiscal position to make room for this reallocation of real resources. However, this often does not happen, and domestic inflation then offsets the increase in "competitiveness" from depreciation of the nominal exchange rate.

An important corollary of this false belief is that countries can and have set domestic policies without worrying about their current account position. For example, when the crisis began, the fiscal stimulus provided to the US domestic economy (as a percentage of GDP) was by far the largest of the major OECD countries. Given the size of the US current account deficit, that seemed odd at best. Similarly, this false belief implies that currency areas with current account surpluses have not let this fact condition their domestic policies. There are many recent examples of this.

After the beginning of the crisis in the Eurozone, the peripheral economies in the Eurozone began to lower their current account deficits as required. However, with nothing forcing an offsetting contraction of the surplus in core Eurozone countries, the overall surplus of the Eurozone rose sharply. Moreover, in spite of this strengthening of the Eurozone surplus, the ECB subsequently embarked on a programme of quantitative easing. This pushed the euro down sharply against the dollar and should further increase the Eurozone surplus. Further examples would include "Abenomics" in Japan, which resulted in a significant weakening of the Yen in spite of Japan already

---

[32] There is a growing empirical literature on this. For some recent references, see Guigliano (2015). Some analysts suggest that this reflects the growing proportion of global trade that is accounted for by high-value-added products, often part of global value-added chains. Such producers prefer to allow exchange rate changes to affect margins rather than their share of global trade in the product. This phenomenon actually attracted attention many years ago. As globalisation was proceeding, the "law of one price" should have been ever more in evidence. The puzzle was that exchange rate pass-through was not rising, but was falling sharply. See Galati and Mellick (2006) and also White (2008).

having a massive net foreign asset position. Looking forward from early 2015, the domestic Chinese economy also seems to be slowing. Although China has already accumulated the world's largest (ever) stock of foreign exchange reserves, there is nothing to prevent the Chinese authorities from pursuing again an export-led growth strategy, perhaps by reversing the renmimbi's recent appreciation.

What should be better appreciated by creditor countries is that the pursuit of such policies could rebound negatively on the creditor countries themselves. More likely is that the resulting strength of the US dollar will weaken the US recovery and in turn weaken economies reliant on the United States for export demand. Less likely in the near term, but inevitable eventually, is that rising global current account imbalances will result in a dollar crisis that would affect everyone, not least Europeans with close economic and financial links with the United States. Admittedly, such concerns have been around for a long while[33] and have not yet fully materialized. The United States has not yet faced the "sudden stop" of capital inflows faced by debtor countries within the Eurozone. Yet, as the literature on complex systems reminds us, the future need not be like the past. Indeed, periods of great instability are often preceded by periods of great stability.[34]

Belief 2: If Countries Float Their Currencies, There Will Be No "Spill-Over" Effects from Monetary Policy in the United States

It does seem to be the case that US monetary policy has "spill-over" effects on other countries. Think back to the origins of the Eurozone. An important motivating factor was the recognition that monetary easing in the United States put huge upward pressure on the Deutsch-mark, in the context of the semi-fixed European monetary system, and

---

[33] In the 1960s, Robert Triffin gave his name to the "Triffin paradox". If other countries wished to use the dollar as an international currency, the United States would have to run current account deficits. In the end, however, the build-up of US foreign liabilities would destroy trust in the dollar and a crisis would ensue as holders of dollars tried to sell them. The first leg of this materialized in the early 1970s as declining confidence in the dollar led countries to demand gold in exchange for dollars. The Bretton Woods system subsequently collapsed. Nevertheless, and despite decades of large US current account deficits, the dollar has continued to be the world's primary reserve currency.

[34] Consider the period called "The Great Moderation" and the turmoil that followed. See also Taleb (2007). The thesis that stability breeds excessive confidence, and in turn lays the ground for subsequent instability, was central to the work of Minsky (2008).

created equally huge exchange rate tensions with other European countries. More recently, unusually easy monetary policies in the United States have led to large capital inflows into other countries, especially into emerging markets. Further, there has been a marked shift upwards in the correlation between the rates on long US Treasuries and longer-term rates in other markets. Capital inflows also led to larger central bank balance sheets and more available funding to support "imbalances" in the countries receiving the inflows.

Prior to the crisis, these capital inflows were largely generated by foreign banks. Subsequently, bonds issued (often offshore) by corporates in emerging markets replaced the banks.[35] Since most of these bonds were issued in dollars, many countries became exposed, not just to the usual problems of sudden capital outflows but also currency mismatch problems. Evidently, those who purchased the dollar bonds then became exposed to the possibility that the debts could not be serviced if the dollar rose in value.

More evidence of spill-over effects emerged in the spring of 2013 (the "taper tantrum") as the Federal Reserve began considering tightening policy after a long period of easing. Markets in many emerging market countries were severely affected, particularly those with fiscal and current account deficits. As of mid-2015, markets wait with apprehension for an actual increase in policy rates in the United States. Given low levels of liquidity in many markets, especially in emerging market economies, there are fears that the implications for the prices of financial assets could be substantial once capital outflows replace inflows.

It could, of course, be argued that all of these "spill-over" effects would have been avoided if other countries had been more willing to allow their exchange rates to rise in response to US easing. The difficulty with this argument is that, in addition to Dornbusch (1976) overshooting, there is ample evidence that the theory of uncovered interest parity only holds over very long time periods. Thus, exchange rates can move very long ways from levels justified by fundamentals, causing all sorts of domestic problems in consequence. To some degree, then, the "fear of floating" is justified. Rey (2013) goes even further. She suggests that "spill-over" effects, not least the high correlation of international bond yields, seem essentially unrelated to the exchange

---

[35] Bank for International Settlements (2015).

rate regime being pursued by the recipient country. Her final conclusion is that countries can pursue an autonomous monetary policy only if they bring in capital controls.

Belief 3: If Floating and Price Stability Rule Out Future Crises, Policymakers Need Not Prepare to Manage and Resolve Them

Everything just said indicates this belief too is untrue. Moreover, even countries like the Nordics, Canada and New Zealand (and many others) that seemed to have come through the crisis essentially unscathed have become more vulnerable to future crises. In these countries, property prices and household debt levels had "boomed" to record levels by 2015, evoking a commensurate rise in concern on the part of national authorities about a subsequent "bust".[36]

If future difficulties seemed increasingly likely, policymakers across the globe remain largely unprepared to deal with another serious downturn. Both monetary and fiscal stimulus has effectively reached its limits as a crisis prevention measure. As for crisis management, there was and is no international lender of last resort. The resources of the IMF would be too small to handle a number of small sovereigns in difficulty, much less a few (or even one?) large ones. Of particular concern would be a sharp increase in demand for dollar funding, as occurred in 2008 after the failure of Lehman Brothers. Only the Federal Reserve could provide such liquidity. While the Fed has established swap lines (first temporary but now permanent) with a number of central banks, including the European Central Bank, they exclude a number of countries that might well face liquidity problems. As well, it remains problematic whether Congress would in the end accede to the Fed lending vast sums of money to foreigners, in the middle of a crisis, without the compulsion of an international treaty to which Congress itself had agreed.

Nor are policymakers better prepared globally to preside over a process of crisis resolution. By this is meant a process of writing off losses, recapitalizing financial institutions and establishing new opportunities for profitable lending. At the global level, there are still no commonly agreed insolvency procedures for globally active banks

---

[36] In Sweden the Riksbank raised interest rates to slow the housing market and debt accumulation, but other parts of the economy slowed more. Faced with global deflationary pressures arising from the drop in commodity prices, the Riksbank then switched tack and introduced a negative policy rate.

(including many European banks) and no agreement on the international burden-sharing of losses. In effect, the problem of "too big to fail" banks lingers on, as does the associated moral hazard.

16.3.2 False Beliefs about the Eurozone

One way to begin reflections about the future of the International Monetary System might be in evaluating the success and failures of the Eurozone. There they have introduced not just a fixed rate system but one that was intended to be immutably so. There is no provision for adjusting currency values within the system. To do so, countries must leave the system, and there are no provisions for that either. Worse, since leaving the Eurozone is effectively illegal, exit could imply expulsion from the EU as well. This is truly a Hotel California in the heart of Europe, where "you can check out any time you like, but you can never leave". Should a country find itself, like Greece, with a sovereign debt level so high as to be unserviceable, some (or perhaps a number) of the rules embodied in the Maastricht Treaty will have to be broken or else rewritten. Evidently this will raise political concerns everywhere, but especially in Germany, where respect for the rule of law is of a particularly high order.

Unfortunately, in addition to these original institutional shortcomings, it is also possible to identify a number of false beliefs that have contributed both to the onset and to the continuation of the Eurozone crisis. With respect to *crisis prevention*, the false beliefs in the Eurozone essentially mirrored those at the international level. In addition to the false belief that price stability within the Eurozone guaranteed macroeconomic stability, there was the pre-crisis belief that current account imbalances need not be of concern to European policymakers. A number of other false beliefs have also misguided Europeans in their efforts at *crisis management*, with policymakers in core countries advocating these views with the greatest vigour. Arguably, worries about "moral hazard" and future imprudent behaviour on the part of peripheral debtor countries have unduly constrained the process of crisis management. Similarly, excessive worries about "contagion" and financial instability have led to forbearance concerning bad loans in the banking system. The result has been the failure of *crisis resolution*. As with the global crisis, it cannot then be ruled out that the worst is yet to come.

Belief 1: Current Account Imbalances Are Not a Source of Concern within an Immutable Currency Union

Dating from the mid 1990s, well before the introduction of the euro itself, capital flows from the core Eurozone countries into peripheral countries began to increase sharply. Interest rates on sovereign bonds in peripheral countries began to converge towards sovereign rates in core countries until, by the turn of the century, the differentials had almost totally disappeared. This implied that at the respective debt levels, neither sovereign nor international net foreign liabilities were playing any role in the determination of relative interest rates.[37] At the same time, current account imbalances began to rise sharply, with core countries running large surpluses and the peripheral countries (with Italy an exception) generally running increasingly large deficits.

In spite of these developments, both policymakers in Europe and financial markets seemed to conclude that balance-of-payments crises could not happen in the new Eurozone. Policymakers often made reference to the absence of such problems in the United States. Moreover, they were comforted by this belief since they no longer had to debate the contentious issue of the respective role of debtors and creditors in the adjustment process.[38] The absence of concern by participants in financial markets is harder to justify. On the one hand, it might be described as a huge market failure, a shortcoming in particular of risk assessment at banks in Northern Europe, which provided much of the financing. On the other hand, some argue that the markets understood the dangers but believed that, in the event of a crisis, they would be bailed out by the government, as indeed they were. Baer (2014) notes some regulatory considerations that might have encouraged such beliefs.[39] If this latter explanation is true, it also implies that that the "no bailout" provisions in the Maastricht Treaty were never taken seriously.

---

[37] McCauley and White (1997) noted that the convergence of Italian and Belgian sovereign bond rates towards German rates seemed odd given the much lower government debt ratio in Germany. The willingness of both the markets and the rating agencies to overlook this fact conflicted with prior experience in Canada, where provincial bond issues had spreads against the sovereign debt that were closely related to provincial debt levels.

[38] On this issue, see James (2012).

[39] For example, the zero-risk weighting of sovereign debt under the Basel capital standards, and the equal treatment of sovereign debt used as collateral at the ECB.

Whatever its origins, we now know that this was a false belief. The analytical failure was simple. While foreign exchange risk within the Eurozone was evidently no longer a problem, everyone failed to appreciate that counterparty risk remained a serious concern. Moreover, the longer that current account imbalances were sustained, the greater the stock of accumulated international indebtedness. In addition, a further effect of the inflows was to allow domestic prices and wages in the peripheral countries to rise significantly faster than in core countries, reducing their competitiveness. Taken together, the implication was that these inflows left the peripheral countries exposed to a "debt-deflation" problem of the type described by Fisher (1933). In effect, introduction of the euro replaced the danger of recurrent small crises associated with currency changes with the danger of a much larger and longer-lasting crisis.

This in fact materialized in 2010, with a "sudden stop" in private sector capital inflows to peripheral countries, followed by significant outflows. Absent continued external financing for large current account deficits, domestic spending (absorption) would have had to fall massively to reduce imports to the level that could be financed. In these circumstances, public-sector support programmes for a number of peripheral countries were organized by the so-called Troika,[40] significantly alleviating these external liquidity problems. This issue is discussed further later in the chapter. In spite of this support, all the peripheral countries suffered serious recessions and massive increases in unemployment, especially for younger workers. The resulting fall in domestic absorption, and increased competitiveness in some cases, did have the beneficial effect of reducing the current account deficits of the peripheral countries. However, many commentators suspect this improvement will not be sustained once an economic recovery is under way.[41]

The private-sector capital exodus which triggered the crisis was made worse by four other considerations. None of the four have subsequently been addressed in any significant way. Indeed, in many respects these constraints on cross-border investments in the Eurozone have grown worse due to policies introduced to manage the crisis.

---

[40] The Troika is made up of the European Commission, the ECB and the IMF.
[41] See Sinn (2014) who refers to studies by Goldman Sachs and others.

First, there is the issue of the so-called bank-sovereign nexus. Troubled banks can traditionally turn to their sovereigns for support. Similarly, troubled sovereigns could borrow from their domestic banks. However, the rapidly increasing debts of the peripheral sovereigns eventually began to raise doubts about their capacity to support their banks. At the same time, the purchases of doubtful sovereign debt by domestic banks were increasingly seen as a threat to the bank's own solvency. In effect, what had been the hope of mutual support turned into fears of mutual insolvency. Since the crisis, the holdings by peripheral banks of their own sovereign's debt (as a proportion of total assets) have in fact risen sharply.

Second, creditors who had previously entertained few doubts about their own solvency increasingly began to have such worries. This implied a general tightening of credit conditions, even in creditor countries, but eventually an effective collapse of cross-border lending. As is also typical, lenders overreact in both the boom and the bust phases of a financial cycle. As discussed later here, this issue of the adequacy of capital levels for core banks has never been totally resolved. Indeed, successive and successful "stress tests", subsequently followed by disastrous bank failures, have further undermined credibility.

Third, capital repatriation seems to have been actively encouraged by domestic regulators in creditor countries.[42] While this might have seemed prudent and sensible from a purely domestic viewpoint, from the systemic perspective of the Euro area as a whole, it made little sense. Of course, regulators and central banks working at cross purposes is hardly a new phenomenon.

Finally, domestic depositors in peripheral countries began to withdraw deposits from domestic banks, given the absence of euro-denominated deposit insurance. This phenomenon was clearly seen in Ireland, Greece and, for a time, Spain just after the crisis began. Fortunately, these withdrawals never reached significant proportions, not even in the immediate wake of the imposition of losses on depositors[43] in Cyprus and the introduction of capital controls.

---

[42] See Monet, Pagliari and Valéé (2014), in particular section 4 on "The euro crisis and the recomposition of national ecosystems"

[43] The original Troika proposal to deal with the crisis in the banking system of Cyprus was to force losses on all deposit holders, even small ones. While this proposal was quickly withdrawn, deposit holders in other peripheral countries must at least have become sensitized to their possible future exposure.

Nevertheless, concerns about prospective deposit flight remained "the elephant in the room", given the continued unwillingness of core countries to countenance cross-border guarantees in the context of banking union.[44] By the summer of 2015, deposit withdrawals from Greek banks had risen to the point that a bank holiday had to be declared and capital controls were also imposed in Greece.

Belief 2: In Avoiding and Managing Problems in a Currency Union, Only Borrowers Need to Modify Their Behaviour

This too is false. Whenever a loan is made, there are a lender and a borrower, both of whom might well be acting imprudently. Both the banks themselves and the Eurozone authorities should have been monitoring from the start, not only current account imbalances but also the character of the real and financial flows associated with those imbalances.

The original expectation was that loans from savings in core countries would finance sustainable and profitable capital deepening in the south. However, far from that, loans were actually being made imprudently for purposes that were simply not sustainable. In Ireland and Spain, foreign money helped to finance a housing boom. In Italy and Portugal, the finance allowed the governments to avoid needed structural reforms.[45] In Greece, capital inflows both helped to impede structural reforms and contributed to a massive increase in government deficits and debt. Policymakers should have been reacting negatively to these developments, but instead they focussed on the associated narrowing of sovereign spreads within the euro area, which they interpreted as a sign of the euro's success.

Nor was running a large current account surplus to generate these capital outflows in the best interests of Germany and other surplus countries. First, it implied that living standards in lending countries were lower than they might otherwise have been. Second, because

---

[44] Deposit insurance is guaranteed by each national sovereign. The depth of suspicion as to whether these guarantees will be honoured is indicated by a remarkable phenomenon. German depositors can receive significantly higher interest rates by booking deposits at foreign branches of German banks (say, in Spain or Italy). There has been no transfer of deposits sufficient to remove these interest rate differentials.

[45] In Italy, the current account deficit never rose sharply. For many years, the government debt-to-GDP ratio was also declining steadily.

savings could be invested abroad, it implied a lower rate of domestic investment than otherwise. Third, as foreign investments turned sour and the euro rose in value against other currencies, losses in euros had to be accepted by the lenders. Ma and McCauley (2013) suggest that Germany has lost almost one-third of the assets accumulated through current account surpluses over the last fifteen years.

Had slower growth in peripheral countries been accompanied by faster growth in the core, this too might have helped to avoid the crisis. As Keynes argued at Bretton Woods,[46] more symmetry in demand management across countries can play a useful role in many circumstances. Further, there might have been more symmetry in structural reforms as well.[47] In the process of implementing a single European market and an "optimal currency area", wages in the core countries should have been encouraged to rise more than they did. As well, deregulating the services sectors in those countries[48] would have increased profit opportunities and reduced the reliance on exports to maintain full employment.

All of these arguments for more policy symmetry across Eurozone countries, to help to prevent a balance-of-payments crisis, should have applied even more strongly in helping to manage the crisis. In fact, new measures were introduced by the European Commission to ensure that all members of the Eurozone were monitoring their current account position. However, the standards applied continued to be asymmetric, with deficits constrained at 4 per cent while surpluses could rise to 6 per cent. Moreover, as the German current account surplus hit 7.5 per cent of GDP in 2014, without a restrictive response from Brussels, a sense emerged that the Commission was becoming more lenient in enforcing the rules on some countries than on others.

---

[46] Steil (2013). In the negotiations leading up to the agreements at Bretton Woods, the United States (then the surplus country) advocated a fixed exchange rate system that would help it to preserve that surplus.

[47] See Legrain (2014), especially chapter 8, on why Germany is not a role model for the rest of Europe. He notes that German growth since 2000 has been about the same as France's, that both public and private investment have been particularly weak, and that "Germany's cosy corporatism also privileges insiders, restricts competition and impedes change" (p. 265).

[48] For example, according to the OECD, the regulation of professional services In Germany is stricter than in twenty-two of the twenty-seven countries covered by their survey.

This was unfortunate, since such perceptions help to destroy cross-border trust on which the whole euro construction is based.

Looking back, however, it is crucially important to recognize that the absence of symmetry reflected a kind of political game as well. Core countries were not prepared to move until they saw clear evidence that peripheral countries were doing "the right thing". Patently, in the lead-up to the crisis, they were not. However, the failure of both Germany and France in the early years of this century to respect the Maastricht criteria for fiscal deficits actively encouraged bad behaviour on the part of others. Since the crisis, most of the peripheral countries have taken painful steps, both fiscal and structural, to improve the functioning of their economies and reduce current account deficits.[49] The stronger these measures become, the greater the argument for a more symmetric response – and the greater the argument for explicit debt reduction, as discussed later here. Conversely, as shown in 2015 in the case of Greece, the failure of countries to introduce required structural reforms could strengthen the case for intransigence at the core as a bargaining ploy.

Belief 3: Fiscal Excess Caused the Crisis, and Fiscal Austerity Is the Solution

As emphasized earlier, the Eurozone crisis was a balance-of-payments crisis rather than a fiscal crisis. Initially, the fiscal position of countries such as Spain and Ireland were significantly better than that of Germany. It was therefore problematic to demand deep fiscal cuts in peripheral countries in the first place. De Grauwe and Ji (2013) go further in suggesting that the interest rate backup in the peripheral countries was actually induced by the relentless focus in the core countries on the need for fiscal restraint everywhere. In effect, everyone was tarred with the Greek brush, when Greece's overall economic performance was actually uniquely bad. Whatever the cause, when the financial markets did finally lose confidence in the debt-servicing capacities of peripheral countries, a degree of fiscal austerity became necessary to help to restore that confidence.

---

[49] Greece continues to be a worrisome exception. While many structural reforms were supported by legislation in the post-crisis period, implementation was generally inadequate.

What is less arguable is that the Troika seriously underestimated the size of the fiscal multipliers associated with restraint.[50] In spite of significant efforts to reduce deficits, economic activity fell away so sharply that debt-to-GDP levels generally rose rather than fell. Indeed, a recent study by the McKinsey Global Institute (2015) shows (Executive Summary, p. 2) that of the forty-seven countries considered, Greece, Ireland, Portugal and Spain were among the six countries that recorded the largest increases in their debt-to-GDP ratio between 2007 and 2014Q2. As for suggestions that austerity would quickly restore confidence, investment and growth in the peripheral countries, this has proved to be equally illusory.

Moreover, if the Eurozone crisis was at heart a balance-of-payments crisis, then reducing the deficits of some countries implies reducing the surpluses of others. From this perspective, it was not appropriate for countries with large trade surpluses, above all Germany, to impose significant fiscal restraint on themselves. Indeed, a number of countries took pride in hitting fiscal targets even earlier than domestic legislation demanded. This could not have been helpful to the peripheral countries trying to increase their exports.

Belief 4: Further Debt Restructuring Is Not an Option

The arguments for explicit, albeit conditional, debt reduction in Greece and potentially other small peripheral sovereigns are quite compelling. First, as noted earlier, debt levels are very high. In Greece, in spite of write-offs in 2012 amounting to almost three-quarters of the outstanding debt in private hands, the IMF has recently stated that the "debt sustainability" is not possible without explicit debt relief.[51] Elsewhere, "debt sustainability" conditions demand running very high primary surpluses for many years,[52] even under very optimistic assumptions

---

[50] The fiscal multipliers were vastly underestimated, as the IMF itself eventually agreed. The chief economist of the IMF has suggested that this error was due to underestimating the impact of the zero lower bound on interest rates and the fact that many countries were tightening simultaneously. This is likely the case. However, there were also fundamental shortcomings in the forecasting models themselves (no banks, no debt, no confidence factors etc.). Arguably, these played a much bigger role in explaining forecast errors.

[51] With most of Greek sovereign debt now in the hands of the public sector, any future restructuring would be at the explicit cost to taxpayers, largely in core countries.

[52] See OECD (2015).

about economic outcomes. Second, as just noted, fiscal austerity actually seems to have worsened the problem of debt sustainability, and the prospect of outright deflation would make it worse still.[53] Third, structural reforms are also threatened by very high debt levels. Why undertake painful structural reforms if only the creditors benefit through enhanced debt service payments? Finally, the political dimension must be explicitly recognized. If all a country can look forward to is decades of penury, directed by foreigners, it is inevitable that radical parties with better promises will arise and flourish.[54] This would constitute an existential threat to the Eurozone itself.

Unfortunately, the arguments against writing down the face value of sovereign debts cannot be easily ignored. First, there is the legitimate concern that debt relief will weaken rather than strengthen the resolve to carry out needed structural reforms. Second, there is the concern that relief granted to one small country might spread to demands for similar treatment for other, larger countries. Moreover, in the case of peripheral countries whose sovereign debt remains largely in private hands, fears about prospective debt relief could result in a destructive rise in interest rate spreads. Third, it is argued that debt relief can be provided in a variety of more subtle ways, and indeed already has been.[55] Finally, there is an important political dimension. Ordinary citizens in the core countries seem unalterably opposed to using "yet more" taxpayer money to support peripheral countries.[56] While political leaders could admit that, in fact, public-sector funds were largely used to benefit core banks that wished to repatriate funds lent to peripheral countries, this narrative would not likely contribute to their re-election.

---

[53] In the global system, nominal exchange rates can move to facilitate adjustment. While the exchange rate can for a time move in the wrong direction, in the end (likely in the context of a crisis) it will move in the right direction. Within the Eurozone, this is not possible. Domestic deflation must then substitute for nominal depreciation.

[54] Friedman (2014) refers to this process as "A Predictable Pathology".

[55] Hidden debt relief can be provided by extending maturities, by charging minimally low interest rates and by deferring interest rate charges. In the case of Greece, for example, debt was 109 per cent of GDP in 2008 versus around 175 per cent in 2014. Nevertheless, debt service as a percentage of GDP was actually lower in 2014.

[56] In fact, however, much of the public-sector funds were actually used to finance outflows of funds by core banks from peripheral countries.

Perhaps conditionality would be the best way to square the circle. Debt forgiveness could follow agreed and implemented policy measures, primarily structural ones. However, this brings us back to the "political game" referred to under Belief 2 above. Ordinary citizens in creditor countries clearly have their minds set firmly against such possibilities. It will take significant political courage to suggest such an option. Should politicians nevertheless decide to strike such a bargain, this will only deepen the "democratic deficit" from which the Eurozone already suffers.

Belief 5: The Banking System in Core Countries Is Healthy and There Is No Need for Explicit Bank Resolution

Insistence on this point serves to obscure a fundamental choice made by governments themselves early in the crisis. It was decided not to resolve the crisis by forcing lenders in the core to recognize losses (both sovereign and private), to write them off and then to face the need for recapitalisation or closure. In effect, "bail-out" replaced "bail-in". Presumably this was due primarily to fears of contagion, and of inadequate fiscal room to support recapitalisation. However, a further consideration is that many of the banks that would have been affected were variously either "national champions", actually owned by the state, or positioned politically to have significant influence over government decisions.[57] Whatever the reasons, it is remarkable how few of the costs of imprudent lending have been borne by the lenders themselves. However compelling at the time, the downsides of this choice are now becoming increasingly evident.

First, by absolving the lenders, this has meant potential losses can only be avoided through debtor adjustment or through taxpayers in creditor countries accepting losses. If the latter is ruled out politically, then austerity in peripheral countries has had to be much more stringent than would otherwise have been the case. Worse, by absolving the lenders, a sharply adversarial approach has been fostered

---

[57] For a fuller examination of these kinds of linkages, see Monet et al. (2014). They note that, unlike in the United States, European banks do not exert their influence through lobbying and the regular transfer (the "revolving door") of senior individuals between the financial industry and the government. In Europe, there are a variety of "formal and informal ties between the political system and the banking system". See also Haring and Douglas (2012), especially chapter 2, "Money is Power".

between the citizens of debtor and creditor countries. This is the very opposite of the cross-border trust that will be needed to make the difficult, longer-run reforms required to ensure the viability of the Eurozone over time.

Second, by leaving banks fearful about their own survival, lending in the Eurozone has been held back, as described earlier. SMEs in peripheral countries have been particularly affected. This is very unfortunate, since the economies of virtually all European economies are much more reliant on SMEs than are, say, the economy of the United States or the United Kingdom. Moreover, given relatively underdeveloped financial markets, again relative to the United States and the United Kingdom, SMEs' reliance on bank financing is also much greater.

Belief 6: Cross-Border Burden Sharing Must Be Avoided

The belief that all debts must be serviced, so that taxpayers in core creditor countries can be sheltered, points to a much more broadly held false belief. The popular perception in core countries is that burden sharing (cross-border fiscal transfers) in the Eurozone can and should be avoided. Indeed, this arises directly from Article 125 of the "European Treaty on the Functioning of the European Union" which states that countries should not take on the debts of other countries. The principal motivation appears to have been fear in core Europe of moral hazard. It is alleged that even temporary cross-border transfers would induce backsliding on fiscal and structural reforms and transform the Eurozone into a permanent "transfer union". For better or worse, there continues to be considerable debate about how Article 125 should be interpreted. Recent decisions by the European Court of Justice (including on Outright Monetary Transactions by the ECB) imply a greater tolerance for cross-border burden sharing than might previously have been supposed. Clarity on this issue is crucial if respect for the "rule of law" is to be maintained.

Yet, burden sharing, in the interests of the system as a whole, would seem to be inherent in the very concept of a currency union.[58] Indeed,

---

[58] In an early statement on monetary union, in September 1990, the Bundesbank spoke of the need for full burden sharing under a "solidarity committee". According to David Marsh, the absence of political union implied to the Bundesbank that other means would have to be found to bind the members together (see Marsh, 2013).

one important criterion for an optimal currency area is the ability of fiscal transfers to respond to asymmetrical shocks. In the United States, automatic stabilizers linked to a large federal government budget (in particular unemployment insurance) ensures that this happens automatically. Indeed, this feature is generally considered to be a highly desirable aspect of US fiscal arrangements. Further, the explicit recognition of possible fiscal risks (e.g. the resolution of cross-border European banks) and the need for ex ante arrangements for sharing those risks would also seem to have a lot to recommend it.[59] Absent such arrangements, suboptimal arrangements will be negotiated as national officials serve their own national interests. The risks of systemic financial problems might then be increased at great cost to everyone.

This aversion to burden sharing, which runs very deep in core countries, has already had important implications. First, it has led to resistance to the idea of jointly issued or guaranteed sovereign bond issues. Second, banking union began with supervisory reform since it had fewer cost implications than bank resolution[60] and the introduction of deposit insurance. Third, deposit holders in Cyprus, including businesses and their working capital, were forced to take large domestic losses, which will inhibit growth going forward. Fourth, the recently announced program of quantitative easing (bond buying) by the ECB has been structured so that sovereign risk remains with the national central banks. This will encourage rather than discourage the sovereign-bank nexus referred to earlier.

In spite of this inherent aversion to burden sharing, the crisis has in fact already led to substantial cross-border transfers. Many countries have received support packages (not least effective debt relief) in the context of Troika programs. Moreover, a number of facilities have been set up to ensure cross-border support for both banks and sovereigns in the future. Finally, when private-sector capital flows out of peripheral countries, the TARGET system automatically records an increase in the liability (to the ECB) of the peripheral country and an equal increase in the assets of the country receiving the funds. Broadly

---

[59] See Goodhart and Schoenmaker (2009)

[60] Recently agreed-upon bank resolution measures, with "bail-in" provisions for losses, apply only to loans made after the bank comes under the supervision of the ECB. Heritage loan losses continue to be the responsibility of the national authorities.

put, core shareholders at the ECB are already significantly exposed, even if the exact exposure is subject to much debate.[61]

Perhaps the fundamental problem is that what has been done to date, constrained by the "no burden sharing" principle, has simply not been enough. It might be contended that, in addition to resolving Eurozone banking problems, it would have been better to take stronger measures, including more policy symmetry and cross-border debt reduction, to help the Eurozone emerge more quickly from the crisis. The legality of such actions, under Article 125 of the Maastricht Treaty, would, of course, have had to be determined ex ante. Whatever the cause, the upshot has been that there has been no effective crisis resolution in the Eurozone, and the crisis therefore continues.

Finally, it must be emphasized that increased cross-border burden sharing to help to resolve the current crisis need not lead to moral hazard and a permanent transfer union. Recall that the crisis had its roots in excessive private-sector borrowing rather than fiscal profligacy. Moreover, these flows were a by-product of errors associated with the introduction of the euro, in particular the initial compression of spreads between the core and peripheral countries. By definition, the introduction of the euro was a one-off event. It will not happen again.

Of course, once the crisis has been resolved, it will be essential to have much more rigorous enforcement of the "rules" than has been the case to date.[62] Moreover, this enforcement should apply equally, and be seen to apply equally, to all members of the Eurozone. What will be required is more fiscal disciple, more attention to current account and other imbalances, sounder bank supervision and sound structural reforms.[63] This will help to ensure that temporary cross-border supports do not turn into permanent transfers. Indeed, albeit belatedly,

---

[61] German commentators often leave the impression that the exposure amounts to the full amount of Germany's TARGET surplus. Whelan (2013, p. 2) suggests that "the underlying costs to German taxpayers will be far lower."

[62] Even the new Fiscal Compact of 2012 has not been respected. The Compact required that all countries would reduce their debt ratios to 60 per cent of GDP, with the speed of convergence each year being one-twentieth of the distance to be covered. In fact, the government debt ratios in the crisis countries have all subsequently increased. However, this may have had more to do with negative fiscal multipliers than the absence of fiscal restraint.

[63] Sapir and Wolff (2015) suggest that Europe's institutional apparatus for governance would benefit from the introduction of a Competitiveness Council and a Fiscal Council. Similar suggestions have been made for a variety of countries by the OECD.

many such measures are now being introduced into the Eurozone. They constitute part of the broader journey towards fiscal, economic, banking and political union in the Eurozone discussed further here. One important side effect of these institutional developments is that they might in the end lead to a form of burden sharing acceptable to all.[64]

Belief 7: Actions Taken by the European Central Bank Will Suffice to Maintain Confidence in the Integrity of the Eurozone

As in many other parts of the world, the European Central Bank responded to the onset of the global crisis with unprecedented measures of monetary expansion. As described in Section 16.2, the ECB has become (albeit reluctantly) part of the global effort to maintain price stability and avoid deflation. More specifically, the ECB responded vigorously to the malfunctioning of global financial markets after the bankruptcy of Lehman Brothers. Subsequently, they took many steps to ease monetary conditions, not least a series of *long-term refinancing operations* (LTRO), culminating with the announcement of quantitative easing early in 2015. Even before its introduction, the euro and longer-term interest rates everywhere (except Greece) fell sharply and stock prices soared.

However, in the Eurozone as elsewhere, central bank policies can only "buy time" for governments to do what is required to finally resolve the crisis.[65] At its heart, the crisis has to do with debt and insolvency issues. These problems cannot be resolved by the provision of liquidity by central banks. This simply encourages more debt accumulation of the sort that caused the problems in the first place. Unfortunately, governments everywhere have proved extremely reluctant to do what only they can do. In large part this reflects concerns (the "would" problem) about the political costs of such government actions. A further problem in the Eurozone (the "could" problem) is

---

[64] On this, see the last chapter in Sinn (2014), in which he recommends a US- or Swiss-type federation for the Eurozone. Note that this combines automatic burden sharing with a "no bailout" policy for sub-federal levels of government.

[65] Countries with room for fiscal expansion, especially those with large current account surpluses, should use it. Public-sector investment, especially in infrastructure, should be encouraged. Systematic debt write-offs, accompanied by measures to recapitalize financial institutions, should be pursued more vigorously. Structural reforms to raise potential growth rates should be carried out.

getting the agreement of the governments in all the member countries to act in appropriate ways and to avoid the temptation of free-riding.

If the ECB shares some problems with other central banks – how to avoid deflation, for one – it also faces a problem which is unique: How to maintain investor confidence in the integrity of the Eurozone? This confidence was shaken in 2010 by the crisis in Greece and then aggravated by a number of policy missteps, largely based on the false beliefs described earlier in the chapter. A crucial and added mistake was the suggestion made publically by Chancellor Angela Merkel and President Nicolas Sarkozy that it might be no bad thing were Greece to leave the Eurozone.[66] This encouraged speculation that others might leave and even raised questions about the integrity of the European structure as a whole. Discussions in 2015 about a possible "Grexit" have worked in the same direction, though, thus far, to a markedly less degree than seen earlier.

In the interval, the ECB has played a crucial role (again "buying time") in maintaining confidence in peripheral countries. The ECB has done this in a variety of ways. First, individual banks from peripheral members have had direct access to lender-of-last-resort financing, subject to the provision of appropriate collateral. The standards defined for that collateral have, moreover, been declining steadily throughout the crisis period.[67] In addition, banks without adequate collateral can still borrow from their national central banks. Given a guarantee of repayment by the national sovereign, the central bank can then borrow in turn from the ECB. Third, the ECB for a time bought the bonds of peripheral sovereigns in the secondary market, under the Securities Market Program. However, it then chose to curtail these purchases, since they were viewed by some as financing fiscal deficits, a procedure explicitly ruled out by the Maastricht Treaty.

Finally, in the summer of 2012, President Mario Draghi of the ECB made a promise "to do whatever it takes", within the legal mandate, and then added, "And trust me, it will be enough." He then outlined the conditions under which support would be provided by the ECB to peripheral sovereigns. This supposed open-ended commitment led to a

---

[66] This was after the infamous "Walk at Deauville".

[67] See Sinn (2014) who notes that the "one state, one vote" principal gives Germany the same weight in decision-making at the ECB as Malta. Evidently, a large number of smaller countries have habitually voted for easier lending standards.

rapid stabilization of market sentiment with yield spreads falling rapidly. As with the QE program more recently, the benefits were received well before any specific action was taken. Indeed, no action has in fact ever been taken. This is fortunate in that a request for ECB support had to be made by a sovereign that was already receiving support from the EMS. This left open the danger, still extant, that a country under market attack would fail to meet the preconditions for ECB support. If the ECB therefore felt it could not intervene, the whole exercise might be revealed as a sham inviting still more dangerous market speculation.

As time goes on, market attention is likely to shift to the more fundamental reforms required to ensure the integrity of the Eurozone over time. The belief that the ECB can maintain confidence on its own is very likely to fade, particularly if CPI inflation begins to deviate from the ECBs own target.[68] Legal uncertainties as to what the ECB can and cannot legally do will further limit confidence, though recent decisions by the European Court of Justice have not supported the predominant German position opposing recent ECB actions.[69] As well, it must be noted that the market's renewed willingness to finance peripheral sovereigns at very low rates, after the introduction of OMT, might also have reflected the extraordinarily easy monetary policies being followed at the global level in response to the global crisis. Were rates to back up at the global level, the ECB's promise "to do whatever it takes" could well be tested. In sum, it is a false belief to assume that ECBs actions alone will suffice to maintain confidence in the integrity of the Eurozone. Much else needs to be done and many risks remain.

Belief 8: Ample Time Is Available for Institutional and Structural Reforms

In June 2012, a document was circulated by Herman Van Rompuy that finally articulated clearly the need for institutional reforms to improve the governance of the Eurozone. The crisis had shown that the original framework was fundamentally flawed, and would lead to a

---

[68] Critics of the ECB contend that its sole concern should be maintaining CPI inflation in the Eurozone at under, but close to, 2 per cent. This focus on near-term price stability seems to ignore the fact that a breakup of the Eurozone would likely lead to very unstable prices in many countries. This is discussed further later in the chapter.

[69] Sinn (2014), especially chapter 8. For a contrasting view, see Munchau (2015).

permanent "transfer union" that no one wanted. Fiscal and financial oversight had to move to the centre if the Eurozone was to be properly governed.

Van Rompuy's vision implied the need for three sets of institutional reforms to support longer-term confidence in the integrity of the Eurozone. First, efforts had to be made to establish a fiscal union, with much stronger rules for domestic fiscal positions and potentially even a much larger centralized budget. Left unstated were prospects for jointly guaranteed euro bond issues. Second, efforts had to be made to establish a banking union, comprising centralized supervision and joint resolution procedures along the lines described earlier in the chapter. Third, there would have to be significant steps towards political union, with more sovereignty ceded to central institutions like the European Commission or the European Parliament. If one can trust the argument that a problem recognized is a problem half-solved, then acceptance of Von Rompuy's vision constituted a major step forward.

Yet, implementation of each individual form of union will be very tough in the face of the "should, could, and would" arguments referred to previously. The chosen approach to banking union (joint supervision first) could be just a sign of the difficulties to come. Moreover, there are interlinkages between these reforms that will make their implementation even harder. As noted earlier, how can there be banking union without some form of fiscal union that involves cross-border burden sharing? In turn, how can there be fiscal union without a commensurate transfer of political power to ensure the appropriate degree of governance?[70] Distributional issues are, after all, quintessentially political. Harold James has noted that the need for the different forms of "union" was recognized by some as far back as the 1980s.[71] Unable to bring others along with them at the time, those wanting stronger governance processes took comfort in the thought that future difficulties would make further reforms more likely. It still remains a hope and not yet a certainty, a quarter of a century later, that the current crisis will provide sufficient political motivation to complete the process of institutional reform.

A further and equally difficult requirement to support longer-term confidence is that the individual members of the Eurozone carry out

---

[70] Baer (2014) puts it nicely "No taxation without representation"
[71] James (2012).

significant structural reforms. Taken all together, these reforms constitute the pursuit of an "economic union" to go along with the three other "unions" just noted. One reason for wanting this economic union is that national rules and practices in the economic (and financial) spheres still differ widely. After all the decades that have passed since its foundation, the European Union is in fact very far from being a single market with all the benefits it might provide.

Yet, as with the longer-run institutional challenges, structural reforms also face challenges from the "should, could and would" problems. Effective structural reforms demand a planning process that sets out economic priorities and an implementation strategy that considers issues of sequencing and timing, especially with respect to legislation. It is also important that reforms are consistent with any need for future fiscal consolidation. Perhaps even more important, successful structural reforms demand broad political support. In gaining such support, national governments must convince the population of the need for change. As well, they must use available carrots (an enhanced status within Europe?) and sticks (failure could lead to chaotic outcomes?) to get the public on their side.

Finally, it is also crucially important that suggested structural reforms are seen as fair, and that vested interests are confronted in the best interests of the country as a whole. Trust in the integrity of national governments is essential in such circumstances to avoid fears of one set of vested interests simply being replaced by another. Unfortunately, in many euro area countries today, survey evidence indicates that such trust is conspicuous by its absence. The imposition by core countries of "technocratic" governments in a number of the peripheral countries of the euro area may have had many benefits, but national trust building was likely not one of them.

Cross-border trust is also important in pursuing institutional and structural reforms. As noted earlier, the decision to bail out core banks and allow bigger countries easier terms of surveillance than smaller ones has already eroded that trust to some degree. Developments surrounding the prospective Grexit problem in 2015 also seem to have worsened the cross-border trust problem by fostering the view that reforms were being imposed by foreign (essentially German) overlords. In contrast, it is significant that the governments of all the other peripheral countries, who had themselves made difficult internal adjustments, also supported the German bargaining position.

This could imply that popular mistrust, rooted in fears of German dominance, are less widespread than some suggest. Alternatively, it could be that the governments of the peripheral countries are simply out of touch with the popular mood.

Subject to all these constraints, the process of institutional and structural reform has since 2010 proceeded very rapidly by the standards of previous history. Nevertheless, it is still proceeding absolutely slowly. Moreover, progress seems to be moving in fits and starts. Whenever market pressures recede, and yield differentials between core and peripheral countries narrow, both institutional reforms (at the level of the Union as a whole) and structural reforms (in national capitals) slow down. This must throw doubts on the commitment to the final destination, thus inviting further market speculation. As well, the overall timidity of the governments' policy response, likely constrained by fears of burden sharing, has also raised fundamental questions about the political capacity of European policymakers to keep the Eurozone intact.[72] A perception of "timidity" is a further invitation to a loss of confidence and speculative attacks.

Such hesitation and timidity resonate, not only in markets but also at the level of ordinary citizens. Absent a clear vision of what the Eurozone and the EU are to become, debate intensifies on the advantages provided by both projects. Radical parties wishing to strengthen national sovereignty, rather than subsume it in a European construct, have in recent years gained ground in most European countries. Whereas radical parties in the peripheral countries feel the core has done too little to support them, radical parties in the core feel the core has already done far too much. In short, it is a false belief to suppose that both financial markets and ordinary citizens will provide ample time for the institutional and structural reforms required to support the Eurozone project.

Given the complexity of the situation, both economic and political, a wide variety of outcomes for the Eurozone are conceivable. In the discussion that follows they are described as orderly, disorderly and very disorderly. Key to achieving more desirable outcomes will be resolving the "should and would" problems in the creditor countries. Both the governments and the voting public must agree that the

---

[72] Marsh (2013, p. 2) alludes to the same policy problem when he says, "There is a hole in the heart of the currency. No one is in charge."

heritage problems of excessive debt cannot be dealt with without more debt write-offs and some degree of cross-border burden sharing. The recent treatment of Cyprus was a step forward concerning the former issue, but certainly not the latter. Looking forward to preventing further crises, there must also be institutional and structural reforms within the euro area. Crucially, they must be sufficient to convince the citizens of core countries that this restructuring was truly a "one-off" and not the beginnings of a permanent transfer union from the centre to the periphery. In Germany in particular, still bearing the scars and the costs of German reunification, this will be a tough sell.

The most optimistic possibility, an "orderly outcome", is that the state of market confidence prevailing in 2015 (with the important exception of Greece) continues and strengthens. The European authorities have made a lot of policy changes; indeed, many great sacrifices have been made in a number of peripheral countries. This might suffice to attract increasing levels of private-sector capital back into peripheral countries as well as to restart bank lending more generally. Ongoing discussions about various longer-term reforms might be judged promising in themselves, and indicative of a capacity to produce still more reforms going forward. This orderly outcome might even survive a Greek exit, presuming that Greece was thought to have "uniquely severe problems" compared to other peripheral countries. Indeed, there are reasonable grounds for believing this to be the case.[73]

Unfortunately, a second scenario, a "disorderly outcome" is also possible. The Eurozone could prove vulnerable to a further lack of confidence that could be triggered by a wide variety of economic or political events. Credit spreads would widen and bank funding become more difficult. This would demand and, by assumption for this scenario, get a policy response. Should more effective policies then be implemented forcefully, confidence would be more likely to return and the euro area would also be much better placed to sustain

---

[73] See Acemoglu and Robinson (2012) who emphasize how "extractive" economic and political institutions prevent countries from achieving sustainable growth. Moreover, the introduction of so-called democratic processes commonly only transfers the extractive powers from one elite to another. Greece, having been part of the Ottoman Empire for four hundred years, is uniquely badly placed in this regard.

confidence going forward. It is of particular importance that the new policies put in place would give hope to peripheral countries for an eventual resolution of their difficulties. Austerity policies that are "more of the same" could temporarily reassure financial markets, but only at the price of growing social and political unrest. This would be a recipe for the "permanent transfer union" that no one wants and that would inevitably explode.

The third possibility is for a "very disorderly outcome", in which countries decide to leave the euro area. This could be due to a sudden loss of market confidence and the drying up of euro funding needed to pay salaries, pensions and the normal business of government. This would demand an early introduction of an alternative currency, which would be fraught with risks.[74] Alternatively, the decision could be the result of a rational evaluation of the costs and the benefits of leaving. Whatever the trigger, there would be a tendency for currency appreciation and deflation in creditor countries and depreciation and potentially high (or even very high) inflation in debtor countries. Some banks would likely fail everywhere, perhaps even in the creditor countries, as debtors failed to meet their debt service obligations. Two versions of this very disorderly outcome can be suggested.

On the one hand, debtor countries could choose to leave. This could well spark contagion, would likely incite hard feelings with creditors, and would also lead to enormous legal uncertainties about the status of debts denominated in euros that countries with new (and depreciating) currencies could no longer service. On the other hand, creditor countries could choose to leave. Historically, when currency unions have broken up, this has often been the route chosen.[75] In a recent article, George Soros has actually called on Germany to "Lead or Leave".[76] Were creditors to leave, and establish a new currency, this would obviate the legal uncertainties, since the debtors would continue to have service obligations in their own currency, the euro. Further, creditor countries would have an incentive to cooperate with the

[74] A problem, which has received little attention, is how the payments and settlement systems would work in a country leaving the Eurozone. National systems have now been replaced by the fully centralized Target system, which has facilities at the Bundesbank, the Bank of France and the Bank of Italy. An economy simply cannot function without both a medium of exchange and a system for making payments.
[75] See Aslund (2012).   [76] Soros (2013).

debtors to avoid large exchange rate changes that would increase the creditors' losses. As the English might put it, "It's the best of a bad job." But of course it would be a terribly "bad job" nonetheless.

16.4 Conclusions

The belief system that says "all is well" because price stability has been maintained is seriously flawed. Preventing excessive disinflation through the expansion of money, credit and debt can lead to a wide range of other problems, whether at the level of the whole global economy or within the Eurozone.

In addition, the International Monetary System has many fundamental shortcomings that threaten global growth prospects. Unfortunately, because of widely held false beliefs about the functioning of the system, these shortcomings are unlikely to be addressed. Had there been an alternative International Monetary System in place that imposed some international discipline on the behaviour of countries (particularly the United States but also China, Germany and Japan), the global economy would not have become so seriously unbalanced and exposed to future shocks. Reforming the International Monetary System should then be given a much higher priority than it has been.

In this context, an important procedural initiative would be for individual European countries to give up their current status at the IMF ("chairs and shares") and agree to a reassignment to countries whose influence at the IMF is not commensurate with their economic importance. This would curry a great deal of favour with such countries. Moreover, if European countries were then to merge their "chairs and shares" and speak with a single voice, the influence of Europe within the Fund would be appreciably greater than it is at the present time.

Similarly, some of the false beliefs held by many policymakers within the Eurozone also need to be reassessed. The onset of the crisis has put paid to the belief that said such a crisis could not happen in a currency union. Yet, other false beliefs have led to the Eurozone crisis being both badly managed and, in the end, left unresolved. There needs to be more symmetry between debtors and creditors in the adjustment process, and less reliance on fiscal austerity. There should be a greater willingness to recognize that some debts, both sovereign and private, have become unserviceable and should be written off. Lenders should be held more accountable for the bad loans they have made in the past, not just those they might make in the future. Burden sharing should be embraced within the Eurozone, subject to legal authority, as well as much more strongly enforced rules about national behaviour likely to contribute to future crises. Finally, it should be recognized that the current calm in financial markets is likely to be temporary. Indeed, actions taken by the ECB that have so far contributed to that calm might also lead to still more disorder over time. Therefore, the longer-term structural and institutional reforms required to stabilize the Eurozone should be vigorously pursued.

These prescriptions "should" and "could" be acted upon. Perhaps the greatest danger is that the "would" problem remains insurmountable. Sir Arthur Salter (1932), the UK finance sherpa, addressed a recommendation to Germany's creditors after World War I (especially the United States) when he said, "What this apprehensive and defensive world needs now, above all, are the qualities it seems for the moment to have abandoned: courage and magnanimity." It is ironic that the same words might be addressed to the creditor countries of the Eurozone today. As proved to be the case in Sir Arthur's time, the costs of failure could be high, with implications extending well beyond the realm of economics.

References

Acemoglu, D. and Robinson, J. A. (2012) *Why Nations Fail: The Origins of Power, Prosperity and Poverty*, New York: Crown Publishers; London: Profile Books.

Aslund, A. and Peterson Institute for International Economics (2012) 'Why a Breakup of the Euro Area Must Be Avoided: Lessons from Previous Breakups', Washington, DC: Peterson Institute for International Economics. *Policy Briefs PB12*, 20.

Atkenson A. and Kehoe, P. J. (2004) 'Deflation and Depression: Is There an Empirical Link?', *American Economic Review, Papers and Proceedings*, 94 (2, May), pp. 99–103.

Atkinson T., Luttrell, D. and Rosenblum, H. (2013) 'How Bad Was It? The Costs and Consequences of the 2007–2009 Crisis', *Federal Reserve Bank of Dallas Staff Papers*, n. 20 (July).

Baer, G. D. (2014) 'More Effective Management of the Euro Area', in Shigehara, K. (ed.), *The Limits of Surveillance and Financial Market Failure*, Houndmills, Basingstoke, UK and New York: Palgrave Macmillan, pp. 163–69.

Ball, P. (2012) *Why Society Is a Complex Matter: Meeting Twenty-First Century Challenges with a New Kind of Science*, Berlin: Springer Verlag.

Bank for International Settlements (2015) *Annual Report*, Basel.

Beinhocker, E. (2006) *The Origins of Wealth: Evolution, Complexity, and the Radical Remaking of Economics*, Boston, MA: Harvard Business Press.

Bernholz, P. (2015) *Monetary Regimes and Inflation: History, Economic and Political Relationships*, Second edition, Cheltenham, UK; Northampton, MA: Edward Elgar Publishing.

Borio, C., Erdem, M., Filardo, M. A. and Hofman, B. (2015) 'The Costs of Deflation: A Historical Perspective', *Bank of International Settlements Quarterly Review*, March, pp. 31–54.

Borio, C. and Lowe, P. (2002) 'Asset Prices, Financial and Monetary Stability: Exploring the Nexus', *Bank of International Settlements Working Papers*, 114 (July).

Buchanan, M. (2000) *Ubiquity: The Science of History ... or Why the World is Simpler Than We Think*, London: Weidenfeld & Nicolson.

Buttiglione, L., Lane, P. R., Reichlin, L. and Reinhardt, V. (2014) 'Deleveraging? What Deleveraging?', *Geneva Reports on the World Economy*, International Center for Monetary and Banking Studies (ICMB), 16.

David, P. A. (2000) 'Path Dependence, Its Critics and the Quest for "Historical Economics"', in P. Garrouste and S. Ioannides (eds.), *Evolution and Path Dependence in Economics*, Cheltenham, UK; Northampton, MA: Edward Elgar Publishing, pp. 15–40.

De Grauwe, P. and Ji, Y. (2013) 'Panic Driven Austerity in the Eurozone and Its Implications', *Vox CEPR Policy Portal*, 21 February.

Dornbusch, R. (1976) 'Expectations and Exchange Rate Dynamics', *Journal of Political Economy*, 84 (6, December), pp. 1161–76.

Fisher, I. (1933) 'The Debt Deflation Theory of Great Depressions', *Econometrica*, 1 (4, October), pp. 337–57.

Friedman, B. M. (2014) 'A Predictable Pathology', Keynote Address prepared for the Bank of International Settlements (BIS) Conference, Conference on 'Debt', Lucerne, 26 June 26.

Galati, G. and Mellick, W. (2006) 'The Evolving Inflation Process', *Bank of International Settlements Working Papers*, n. 196 (February).

Goodhart, C. A. E. and Schoenmaker, D. (2009) 'Fiscal Burden Sharing in Cross Border Banking Crises', *International Journal of Central Banking*, 5(1), pp. 141–65.

Guigliano, F. (2015) 'Dispiriting Narrative That Shows Devaluation Does Not Always Work', *Financial Times*, 10 March.

Haldane, A. (2015) 'On Microscopes and Telescopes', Speech given at the Lorentz Centre Workshop on Socio-Economic Complexity, Leiden, 27 March.

Haring, N. and Douglas, N. (2012) *Economists and the Powerful: Convenient Theories, Distorted Facts, Ample Rewards*, London, New York and Delhi: Anthem Press.

Hayek, F. A. (1937) *Monetary Nationalism and International Stability*, Publications of the Graduate Institute of International Studies (Geneva), n. 18, London: Longmans, Green.

Hayek F. A. (1967) 'The Theory of Complex Phenomena', in F. A. Hayek, *Studies in Philosophy, Politics and Economics*, London: Routledge and Kegan Paul, pp. 22–42.

Hayek, F. A. (1975) 'Full Employment at any Price?', London: The Institute for Economic Affairs, Occasional Paper 45.

Hofmann, D. (2013) 'The Poisonous Prescription of Low Interest Rates – Were Banks Rescued at the Expense of the Insurance Industry?', *Insurance Economics Newsletter*, n. 68, The Geneva Association, 2 July.

James, H. (2012) *Making the European Monetary Union*, with a foreword by M. Draghi and J. Caruana, Cambridge, MA; London: Belknap Press.

Jorda, O., Schularick, M. and Taylor, A. M. (2014) 'Betting the House'. *Hong Kong Institute for Monetary Research Working Papers*, n. 31.

Keynes, J. M. (1925) *The Economic Consequences of Mr Churchill*, London: L. and V. Woolf at the Hogarth Press.

Kindleberger, C. P. and Aliber, R. Z. (2015) *Manias, Panics and Crashes: A History of Financial Crises*, seventh edition, Basingstoke, Hampshire: Palgrave Macmillan.

Kotlikoff L. (2010) "The US Is Bankrupt and Doesn't Even Know It", *Bloomberg Business*, 10 August.

Kuhn, T. S. (1962) *The Structure of Scientific Revolutions*, Chicago: University of Chicago Press.

Legrain, P. (2014) *European Spring: Why Our Economies and Politics Are in a Mess – and How to Put Them Right*, London: Curtis Brown.

Ma, G. and McCauley, R. N. (2013) 'Global and Euro Imbalances', in M. Balling and E. Gnan (eds.), *50 Years of Money and Finance: Lessons and Challenges*, SUERF – The European Money and Finance Forum, Brussels: Larcier.

Marsh D. (2013) *Europe's Deadlock: How the Euro Crisis Could Be Solved and Why It Won't Happen*, New Haven and London: Yale University Press.

McCauley, R. N. and White, W. R. (1997) 'The Euro and European Financial Markets', in P. R. Masson, T. H. Kreuger and B. G. Turtelboom (eds.), *EMU and the International Monetary System*, Washington: International Monetary Fund.

McKinsey Global Institute (2015) *Debt and (Not Much) Deleveraging*, Washington DC: McKinsey and Company.

Minsky, H. (2008 [1986]) *Stabilizing an Unstable Economy*, foreword by H. Kaufman, New York: McGraw Hill .

Monet, E., Pagliari, S. and Vallée, S. (2014) 'Europe between Financial Repression and Regulatory Capture', Bruegel Working Paper, n. 8.

Munchau, W. (2015) 'The Make Believe World of Eurozone Rules', *Financial Times*, 27 July.

Mundell, R. A. (1963) 'Capital Mobility and Stabilisation Policy Under Fixed and Flexible Exchange Rates', *The Canadian Journal of Economics and Political Science / Revue canadienne d'Economique et de Science politique*, 29 (4, November), pp. 475–85.

OECD (2012) *Economic Outlook*, December.

OECD (2015) 'Government Debt and Fiscal Frameworks', paper prepared for WP1, March, Paris.

Padoa-Schioppa, T. (2010) 'The Ghost of Bancor: The Economic Crisis and Global Monetary Disorder', Lecture, Louvain-la-Neuve, 25 February.

Prasad, E. S. (2014) *The Dollar Trap: How the U.S. Dollar Tightened Its Grip on Global Finance*, Princeton and Oxford: Princeton University Press.

Pringle, R. (2012) *The Money Trap: Escaping the Grip of Global Finance*, Houndmills: Palgrave Macmillan.

Reinhart, C. and Rogoff, K. S. (2009) *This Time Is Different: Eight Centuries of Financial Folly*, Princeton and Oxford: Princeton University Press.

Rey, H. (2013) 'Dilemma Not Trilemma: The Global Financial Cycle and Monetary Policy Independence', Paper prepared for a Symposium Organized by the Federal Reserve Bank of Kansas City, Jackson Hole, Wyoming, August.

Salter, A. (1932) *Recovery: The Second Effort*, London: G Bell and Sons.

Sapir, A. and Wolff, G. (2015) 'Euro Area Governance: What to Reform and How to Do It', Bruegel Policy Brief, 1 February.

Sargent, T. J. and Wallace, N. (1981) 'Some Unpleasant Monetarist Arithmetic', *Reserve Bank of Minneapolis Quarterly Review*, 5(3, Fall), pp. 1–17.

Schularick, M. and Taylor, A. M. (2009) 'Credit Booms Gone Bust: Monetary Policy, Leverage Cycles and Financial Crisis 1870–2008', *NBER Working Paper Series*, n. 15512, Cambridge, MA.

Simpson, D. (2013) *The Rediscovery of Classical Economics: Adaptation, Complexity and Growth*, Cheltenham, UK; Northampton, MA: Edward Elgar.

Sinn, H.-W. (2014) *The Euro Trap: On Bursting Bubbles, Budgets, and Beliefs*, Oxford and New York: Oxford University Press.

Soros, G. (2013) 'Why Germany Should Lead or Leave', Project Syndicate 8 September, www.project-syndicate.org.

Steil, B. (2013) *The Battle of Bretton Woods: John Maynard Keynes, Harry Dexter White, and the Making of a New World Order,* Princeton: Princeton University Press.

Swiss ReGroup (2014) *Financial Repression: Quantifying the Costs*, Zurich: Asset Management Group.

Taleb, N. (2007) *The Black Swan: The Impact of the Highly Improbable*, London: Allen Lane.

Véron, N. (2012) 'The Challenges of Europe's Fourfold Union', Bruegel Policy Contribution, 13 August.

Whelan, K. (2013) 'TARGET 2 and Central Bank Balance Sheets', New Draft, University College, Dublin, 17 March.

White, W. R. (2008) 'Globalisation and the Determinants of Domestic Inflation', Bank of International Settlements Working Papers, n. 250, March.

White, W. R. (2012) 'Ultra Easy Monetary Policy and the Law of Unintended Consequences', Globalisation and Monetary Policy Institute, Federal Reserve Bank of Dallas, Working Paper Series, n. 126.

White, W. R. (2013) 'What Has Gone Wrong with the Global Economy? Why Were the Warnings Ignored? What Have We learned From the Experience?', The Official Monetary and Financial Institutions Forum (OMFIF), Golden Lecture Series, London, 24 October.

PART IV

Framing the Eurozone

17 | Framing the Political Economy of the Eurozone

Structural Heuristics for Analysis and Policy

IVANO CARDINALE, D'MARIS COFFMAN
AND ROBERTO SCAZZIERI

17.1 Introduction

This volume has characterized the political economy of the Eurozone as a domain straddling multiple layers of economic and political inter-dependencies. This characterization has far-reaching implications, especially for what concerns the crisscrossing of group and sectoral interests within and across member states, and the constraints and opportunities shaping different, and often overlapping, policy domains. Such interdependencies call for new tools of political economy, in so far as it becomes necessary to overcome established dichotomies (such as markets versus state, or macro versus micro relationships) and to focus on multiple, partially overlapping spheres of interest and policy domains.

This characterization highlights two key features: (1) the multiple layers of interdependencies, spanning supranational, national, regional, and sectoral levels and (2) the overlaps between the economic and political spheres. It has been argued throughout the volume (see, e.g., chapters by Cardinale, Pabst, Scazzieri and White) that the current thinking on the Eurozone struggles to cope with those features. This chapter draws together the contributions of the chapters in the volume and takes a step further, systematizing the contribution of the volume as a whole. In particular, it aims to provide analytical tools that are able to address the multiple layers of interdependencies and overlaps between the economic and political spheres. In this way, this chapter aims to lay the foundations for a new research programme on the political economy of the Eurozone.

This is done in three steps. The first is internal to the history of economic analysis. Using John Hicks's (1982) distinction between *catallactics* (the study of coordination of individuals and groups through market exchange) and *plutology* (the study of coordination requirements for the production of national income), we reconstruct the different ways in which economic analysis has dealt with interdependencies and addressed the overlap between the economic and political spheres. We find that, despite profound differences, both traditions assume interdependencies but do not analyse them explicitly, and both tend to dichotomize the economic and the political, often subordinating the latter to the former. We then show that this reconstruction can help to systematize current thinking about the Eurozone and take steps towards overcoming its limitations.

The historical reconstruction also provides the starting point for this chapter's contribution. In fact, this chapter builds upon a strand of economic analysis that has explicitly represented interdependencies between intermediate levels of aggregation. The further step is to use those models not only for studying economic interdependencies but also as heuristics for interdependencies that are potentially both economic and political. In this sense, the research programme advocated here can be seen as compatible with approaches outside economic analysis that do address intermediate levels of aggregation such as sectors (e.g. Scitovsky, 1958; Hirschman, 1981a; McCormick, 2007) but are not based on explicit models of interdependencies.

Doing so requires a conceptual shift, which is performed through the second and third analytical steps of the chapter. In particular, the second step has to do with tracing back the idea that division of labour can provide a fundamental structuring principle for society. Starting at least from Durkheim, division of labour in society has been seen as a fundamental principle structuring society into groups. This idea provides the foundation for using models of interdependencies, which provide alternative representations of division of labour as heuristics that go beyond the economic sphere strictly conceived, and that can be used more flexibly to provide insights on the polity more generally.

The third step briefly introduces alternative representations of productive interdependencies (circular interdependencies in the Quesnay-Leontief tradition and vertical integration in Pasinetti's and Quadrio Curzio's versions). It then shows how they can be used for the kind of political-economic analysis advocated here. Alternative models of interdependencies highlight different possibilities to aggregate economic activities, and hence different representations of division of labour in society. As a result, they highlight different constellations of interests at different levels of aggregation. They can, therefore, be used as a heuristic for the 'material constitution' of the Eurozone, by which we mean the set of relatively persistent interdependencies among its units, which span the economic and political spheres.

We bring the chapter to a close by providing some new research questions about the Eurozone, which illustrate the research programme that this volume advocates.

17.2 How Should We Think about the Eurozone?

17.2.1 Towards a Structural Analysis of European Monetary Integration: Lessons from History, Economics and Politics

This volume has examined the political economy of the Eurozone from the vantage points of comparative history, economic theory, and institutional analysis. Taken in their unity, the contributions in the volume highlight the historical recurrence of problems and solutions to the coordination issues arising in a monetary union. They also point to the *multi-dimensional character of coordination* (say, on commodity and service markets, public budgets, arrangements for the provision of liquidity) within monetary unions in general and within the European Monetary Union in particular. Such coordination is associated with multi-level interdependencies. For example, the European Single Market has created (or strengthened) cross-country interdependencies at the sectoral level, and coordination of public budgets has heightened the effects of macroeconomic interdependencies across countries.

The consequence of multi-dimensionality of coordination and inter-dependencies is twofold. On the one hand, the need to achieve a *degree of coordination* along multiple dimensions makes coordination complex and lack of coordination more costly. On the other hand, the very multidimensionality of coordination points to *multiple ways* in which different, but mutually compatible, coordination criteria for different domains may lead to systemic coordination outcomes. A lesson from the historical and comparative institutional analysis of chapters in Part I is that the decomposability of coordination arrangements (i.e. the presence of partial arrangements involving only a limited number of policy dimensions) may be an opportunity (a condition making coordination easier) more than a constraint (a condition making coordination more difficult) whenever a monetary union is introduced between greatly differentiated countries or areas. The chapter by James Macdonald brings to light that the emergence of federal systems in the United States and Germany is evidence of decomposability achieved through a combination of autonomy and central control. In either case, funding independence of member states was granted on a selective basis (purpose-oriented borrowing for investment projects in the United States, strict brakes on overall Länder borrowing in Germany), and systemic coordination was achieved either through default insulation and bailout avoidance (United States) or through introduction of a legal 'debt brake' for Länder borrowing (Germany after 2009). As Luca Einaudi shows in his chapter, a decomposition criterion was clearly at work also in the Latin Monetary Union, although on an entirely different basis. For in this case decomposability was achieved through radical decoupling of participating countries (countries could opt in and out of the Union depending on circumstances), while an external standard (the gold standard) allowed systemic coordination.

Contributions in Part I also highlight the close relationship between the complex internal dynamics of integration processes and the plural triggers that may impact those dynamics determining a speeding up or slowing down of integration. Duncan Needham in his chapter brings to light the interplay of speeding-up and slowing-down factors in the lead-up to the European Monetary System and the Eurozone. His discussion concentrates on the role of convergence between French interest in European-level monetary policy, protection against exchange rate volatility and capital availability for the modernization of French industry on the one hand, and the German drive for political reunification, independent European Central Bank and free capital mobility on the other hand. The role of convergence of French and German interests draws attention to the importance of *relatively independent* but mutually consistent triggers in making the cumulative process leading to monetary unification possible. Coşkun Tunçer describes a paradoxically similar mechanism at work in his chapter on the sovereign bond crises of Egypt, Ottoman Empire, Serbia and Greece of the late nineteenth century. In these cases, the containment of crises entailed insulating the disturbance within the country of origin through policies such as the centralization of its tax collection system or the direct control of debtors' state finances by creditor countries. These means avoided the spread of disturbances within a larger set of interdependent economies. The insight from Needham's and Tunçer's chapters is that decomposability may either facilitate the build-up of structural changes leading to the emergence of an integrated system (as in the process leading to European monetary unification) or thwart the spread of disturbances that might disrupt the existence of a given system of interdependencies (as with late nineteenth-century sovereign bond crises). Sovereign borrowing is also central to D'Maris Coffman's exploration into the historical sociology of the fiscal state. Her contribution is a plea for investigating any historical integration process (such as the formation of the modern fiscal state) by setting it within the context of the social interdependencies that make the 'target process' feasible under existing constraints.

Multi-level interdependence and decomposability (i.e. partial integration) are thus the two fundamental historical lessons provided by the chapters in Part I. Decomposability allowed distinct processes, not necessarily coordinated with each other, to be independently at work in different domains, and made it possible to have cumulative structural changes under certain conditions and crisis containment policies under different conditions. On the other hand, interdependence triggered spill-over effects from one domain to another, so that processes initially circumscribed to a particular domain could sometimes trigger the transformation of a whole system of coordinated monetary and financial arrangements. This set of contributions calls attention to the causal mechanism at the root of the historical institutional changes under consideration, and to the *plural causal paths* compatible with any such mechanism.[1]

The contributions in Part II of the volume outline a theoretical framework for the structural analysis of the Eurozone. These contributions explore the analytical implications of interdependencies between economic activities when activities are grouped into *relatively resilient* subsets (such as sectors or industries), and those subsets are in turn connected to one another by *relatively persistent* linkages, both at any given time and across different time periods. The aim of chapters in Part II is to facilitate the conceptual leap that is necessary (to

---

[1] Wesley Salmon (1984, 1998) defines 'causal mechanism' in terms of an invariance criterion compatible with a variety of causal paths. For a discussion of causal mechanisms from a plural causality point of view, see Pearl, 2000; Galavotti, 2008.

economists but also to other social scientists) to move beyond the conventional dichotomy between micro and macro analysis. The chapter by Roberto Scazzieri outlines a conceptual framework for investigating a system of interdependent activities characterized by mutual input requirements imperfectly synchronized over time. This synchronization problem brings to light a structural liquidity condition for the viability of the integrated system of interdependent activities, and draws attention to the requirements for a monetary and credit policy compatible with that condition. In particular, this chapter emphasizes the potentially integrative role of liquidity policy if the provision of liquidity meets the structural liquidity needs. Conversely, monetary and credit policies incompatible with the structural liquidity condition are likely to have a disruptive effect on the viability of the integrated system. This chapter considers Leontief-type interdependencies between economic units at intermediate levels of aggregation (such as sectors or industries), and explores the liquidity needs arising within this system of interdependencies when there are Hicks-type 'complementarities over time' between imperfectly synchronized activities. The chapter draws attention to the liquidity arrangements needed for the viability of an integrated economy consisting of any such system of interdependent processes, and brings to light the different liquidity conditions that would allow, respectively, the structural stability of the existing system or successful trajectories of structural change within the integrated economy.

The internal structure of an integrated economic system is rooted in interdependencies that go beyond the domain of production technology. This suggests addressing interdependencies in the social domain. Ivano Cardinale in his chapter develops an analytical framework based on intermediate levels of aggregation and examines opportunities and constraints arising from the relationships among socio-economic groups beside material interdependencies among productive sectors. This contribution builds upon François Quesnay's analysis of the interdependence between social classes in the *Tableau Économique* (Quesnay, 1758) with the aim of disentangling structural conditions for viability and growth in a system of interconnected social groups. This chapter focuses on the relation between sectoral interdependence and 'systemic interest', where the latter is the condition by which an integrated system of interdependent components (such as Quesnay's social classes, or the sectoral interests of a modern industrial economy) is capable of maintaining its fundamental structure from one period to another. The chapter highlights that manifold possible criteria of systemic interest may be compatible with the maintenance of a given integrated system, and discusses the alternative dynamic trajectories that may be open to the system depending on which criterion of systemic interest is adopted. The maintenance of any integrated system presupposes that one of the manifold criteria of systemic interest compatible with the fundamental structure of the system is actually satisfied. However, more than one criteria of systemic interest may be compatible with that structure (which suggests a conflict between alternative specifications of systemic interest for the integrated economy under consideration). There may also be specifications of systemic interest incompatible with the existing system but compatible with the integration of some of its elements with other elements external to the system (which suggests a conflict between the given integrated economy and other systems alternative to it).

The relationship between viability of an integrated economy and systemic interest brings to light the political dimension of integration. Adrian Pabst in his chapter draws attention to the concept of 'constitution' as a central tool in the analysis of systemic interest. In particular, Pabst outlines a conceptual framework for analysing the constitutional arrangements of an integrated economy. In his view, the constitution of an integrated economy is best reconstructed by avoiding identification of the constitutional settlement with a formal-legal order that subordinates social interdependencies to the normative conditions of public and private law (and, in particular, the law of contract). In fact, the constitution of an integrated economy goes beyond the 'framework conditions' (*Rahmenbedingungen*) for the competitive process to work and presupposes recognition of a complex hierarchical structure of political domains and sub-domains, in which alternative ways of identifying systemic interest may co-exist without necessarily leading to irreconcilable conflicts and disruptive tensions. This approach brings to light the relational structure of systemic interest and sees it as the result of the multi-layered positioning of specific interests that may be convergent or divergent at different levels. There may be manifold ways of identifying systemic interest, but differences are often 'contained' within specific sub-domains and do not necessarily extend to the whole range of the interdependent activities in the integrated economy. This point of view leads Pabst to criticize the neo-functionalist approach to Western European integration (economic integration by convergence leading to political integration), and to argue that integration by distinct sub-domains is a more effective way to identify systemic interests and to allow for compensation mechanisms that would be defective, or altogether missing, if a purely neo-functionalist approach were followed.

Part III of the volume has examined the emergence of different *asymmetries* and *imbalances* between sectors and/or member states or regions within the Eurozone, or between the Eurozone and the rest of the world. The need to address these asymmetries and imbalances provides the context of the policy scenarios discussed in this part of the volume. The chapter by Finn Marten Körner and Hans-Michael Trautwein examines to what extent the continuity in export orientation of the German economy may have been conducive to tensions within the international monetary system from the breakdown of the Bretton Woods system in the early 1970s to the present. This chapter emphasizes the central role of neo-mercantilism and ordo-liberalism in defining the post–World War II economic policy model, in spite of the different policy contexts respectively associated with the Bretton Woods system, the European Monetary System (EMS) and the European Monetary Union (EMU). Körner and Trautwein argue that during the 1950s and 1960s, fixed exchange rates according to the Bretton Woods rules allowed a systematic undervaluation of the D-mark, which supported the West German export-led growth but eventually led to imported inflation triggering D-mark revaluations. The subsequent EMS regime overcame the constraints and volatility of the Bretton Woods regime and buttressed Germany's export-led growth thanks to the regional undervaluation of the D-mark and to the liquidity premium on the D-mark leading to relatively low interest rates relative to other EMS economies. However, asymmetric policy objectives between member countries (with Germany giving priority to internal stability in terms of low inflation, and the other countries trying to stabilize their exchange rates relative to the D-mark) again made the system unstable, leading to its demise in the early 1990s. The EMU regime reproduced conditions favourable to the continuation of the neo-mercantilist/ordo-liberal economic policy in Germany while breeding asymmetries such as persistent foreign account deficits and surpluses, and rising interest rate spreads within the Eurozone. Körner and Trautwein bring to light the ineffectiveness of available policy tools under the EMU regime, noting in particular the persistence of trade surpluses under irreversibly fixed exchange rates, and that a common monetary policy adopting a uniform standard may face impossible tasks in the case of asynchronous business cycles across member states.

The chapter by Ivano Cardinale and Michael Landesmann draws attention to the relationship between units of analysis and forms of interdependence within the Eurozone and the European Union at large. This chapter highlights that different types of interdependence may arise between different units of analysis (such as regions, nation states, industrial sectors), and that different cleavages may arise in each case. Interdependence brings to light both potential alliances and potential conflicts, as a 'systemic interest' is not always visible and may be identified differently by alternative constellations of socio-economic groups. Building on this analytical framework, the chapter discusses two issues facing policy-making in the Eurozone and the two corresponding cleavages. One is the cleavage between tradable and non-tradable sectors with respect to external account imbalances; the other is the cleavage between real and financial sectors with respect to potential sovereign debt write-off. In a two-country case, the appreciation of the real exchange rate will differently affect the tradable and non-tradable sectors of each country, while also making the tradable sectors of the two countries opposed to one another (appreciation may be seen as a zero-sum game making one tradable sector better off and the other tradable sector worse off). In the case of potential sovereign debt write-off (if one considers the case in which the write-off is borne by the debtor country), there will be a cleavage between sectors favouring the write-off (the financial sectors of both countries) and sectors against it (the real sector of the debtor country). The chapter brings to light that a further differentiation of sectors (acknowledging 'within sector' heterogeneity) may make visible cleavages and alliances other than those discussed above. Crucially, the relative weight of integrationist forces relative to triggers of potential breakup depends on the configuration of cleavages and alliances both between sectors as well as across intra-sectoral groups belonging to different member states.

Cleavages may reveal conflicts of interests within the Eurozone but may also conceal the existence of potentially strong systemic interests across countries. This is especially the case as cleavages and potential alliances may be different depending on whether we focus on short-, medium-, or long-term time horizons. The chapter by Marco Fortis brings to light the deep interconnectedness between the Eurozone's principal manufacturing economies (Germany, Italy and France), the long-term conformity of their dynamics and the long-term systemic losses that would derive from exclusive concentration of attention on export-led growth to the disadvantage of internal Eurozone demand. This argument emphasizes the complementarity between external and internal demand and highlights the negative feedback of internal demand contraction on the growth of the Eurozone as a whole as well as on that of its most successful export-led economy (Germany). Sluggish competitiveness cannot explain the economic contraction that has taken place in all most important Eurozone economies except Germany. For example, Italy, France, Spain and Portugal all had significant positive trade balances in exports of manufactured goods with extra-EU countries in the recent past. Crucially, competitiveness indicators for industrial systems (such as UNIDO's Competitive Industrial Performance Index, and the indicators provided by the International Trade Centre of UNCTAD and WTO) show many Eurozone member countries having a strong competitive position on world markets. For example, Italy is second only to Germany in the International Trade Centre's competitiveness line-up of export market position, and again second only to Germany in the EU and in the world in terms of foreign trade surplus in manufactured goods. This chapter exposes 'the false myth of lost competitiveness' as the root cause of Eurozone's negative macroeconomic performance. The chapter also emphasizes the negative medium-term feedback of sluggish internal Eurozone demand on the macroeconomic performance of Eurozone export-led economies (including the German economy in times of extra-EU market turbulence), and brings to light the long-term systemic interest of Eurozone member countries in preserving the integrity and cohesion of the Eurozone internal market.

The intertwining of national and systemic interests is also central in the chapter by Alberto Quadrio Curzio, who discusses to what extent Eurobonds may be a liquidity instrument that makes it possible to alleviate macroeconomic pressures bound to lead to asymmetric developments across the Eurozone. Eurobonds may achieve this by allowing a differentiated liquidity provision both between sectors and between national economies at different phases of the cycle. Liquidity provision through Eurobonds would lead to a decline in average interest rates on the sovereign debt of highly indebted countries while at the same time attracting financial resources from global markets at a manageable cost. These developments would make it possible to achieve stabilization goals at the level of the Eurozone as a whole by reducing, in the medium term, the Eurozone-level ratio of sovereign debt to GDP. Macroeconomic stabilization at the Eurozone level would be compatible with differentiated macroeconomic policies at the level of the different member countries. The advantage provided by Eurozone-level stabilization would allow countries to pursue expansionary or contractionary policies depending on the phase of the economic cycle (which is likely to be different for different countries). Finally, liquidity provision through Eurobonds would target specific needs of the real economy, such as infrastructural investment, and particularly investment in European-level infrastructure supporting the cohesion of the European economy. In this way, liquidity provision would avoid the danger of a purely macroeconomic governance of monetary supply, which may in turn increase the likelihood of financial bubbles and jeopardize the stability of the whole system. Quadrio Curzio outlines the details of a Eurobond architecture that would allow differentiated liquidity provision adjusted to the structural needs of the real economy, both in terms of its long-term prospects (infrastructural investment) and medium-term macroeconomic policy (differentiated macro policies adjusted to cycle phase in each member country). This approach to Eurozone liquidity is contrasted with European Central Bank's quantitative easing, which is thought to be a potential source of market speculation and instability. In particular, Quadrio Curzio calls attention to lack of synchronization between the short-period time horizon of ECB's quantitative easing and the long-period time horizon implicit in the convergence goal of public debt over GDP ratio. A range of differentiated policy instruments is necessary to achieve the long-term convergence objective without jeopardizing Eurozone's systemic coherence.

Yuning Gao's chapter further explores the interdependence between financial flows and structural transformation by examining the character of China's investments in the Eurozone. This chapter points to the increasing role of Eurozone investment as a share of both outward direct investment and portfolio investment from China. Gao' s reconstruction calls attention to the specific direction of Chinese direct

investment, which shows a clear preference for 'giant investment projects' such as the investment by China's sovereign fund (CIC) into GDF
Suez and the investment by China's Three Gorges into Energias de
Portugal. Involvement in manufacturing activities also features prominently among Chinese investments in the Eurozone, as shown by the
acquisition of Volvo and of the three German manufacturing firms,
Putzmeister, Schwing and Kion. The Chinese thirty-five-year lease of the
main dock at Piraeus (Greece), with the associated pledge to finance the
construction of a new pier and the upgrading of existing docks, signalled
a strong interest in European logistic infrastructure. Infrastructure investment of this kind has also shown another feature of Chinese involvement
in the Eurozone, since a consortium of Chinese banks (China Development Bank, Export Import Bank of China, Bank of China and China
Construction Bank) has pledged to finance Greek merchant shipping
industry in order to back Greek demand at Chinese dockyards. This
combined strategy calls attention to the nexus between infrastructural
investment and export-support investment, and highlights the critical role
that a resilient structure of interdependencies can play in supporting
lasting trade arrangements. Chinese involvement in the European Financial Stability Facility (EFSF) follows a similar logic as far as Chinese
foreign investment looks more interested in pursuing the consolidation
of interdependencies between trade partners rather than in the maximiza-
tion of short-term gains. This approach is coherent with Chinese interest
in large construction projects that would not yield any return before
completion, as it is projects of this type that are most likely to generate
stable trade and financial relationships over the long term.

Finally, the chapter by William White calls attention to the 'analytical deficit' that makes it difficult to understand the dynamics of
the Eurozone and to address its problems effectively. In White's
view, the root of the difficulty is the representation of the economic
system as a 'changeless machine' rather than 'as a complex adaptive
system ... with massive interdependencies among its parts and the
potential for highly nonlinear outcomes'. Because of that, a number
of 'false beliefs' have dominated discussions about the Eurozone and
the International Monetary System. This attitude, from economists
and policymakers alike, has led to disregard the role of interdependencies, to overlook the cumulative dynamics of imbalances and to
rely on ineffectual policy tools (such as inflation targeting)
as instruments towards macroeconomic stability. The consequences

of this analytical deficit are far-reaching. Lack of understanding of the architecture of the Eurozone as a complex system has triggered ad hoc crisis management interventions (quantitative easing) that could make future financial crises more likely. White's chapter emphasizes the need for crisis prevention mechanisms based on explicit recognition of the interdependent character of imbalances, and on effective precautionary measures that would counter the cumulative dynamics of imbalances. This systemic approach entails consideration of interdependencies within and across different levels of aggregation and moves beyond the conventional micro-macro dichotomy. Because of this, crisis management turns into crisis prevention through policies reducing the asymmetry between debtors and creditors on the adjustment traverse. These policies would generally require the introduction of burden sharing between debtors and creditors, and of buffers countering otherwise unavoidable spill-over effects. Both inflation targeting through price index stabilization and contraction prevention through monetary expansion can lead to further imbalances in the Eurozone and/or in the global economy. Avoidance of disruption requires stakeholders to remove the analytical deficit due to false beliefs concerning the relationship between price stability and macroeconomic stability, as well as the self-regulating character of international trade and monetary flows. Recognition of the nature of the Eurozone and of the International Monetary System as complex adaptive systems suggests a shift from crisis management to *crisis prevention*, and highlights the need of effective institutional mechanisms improving the governance of global economic imbalances (such as pooling of European IMF shares and reassignment of IMF shares to countries in proportion to their actual importance in the world economy).

The contributions in Part III emphasize the complex internal structure of the Eurozone. In particular, these contributions highlight the need to distinguish between the formal institutional arrangements of the Eurozone and the actual patterns of interdependence that have emerged behind formal rules and procedures. The implementation of effective policies at the level of the Eurozone presupposes the recognition of emerging imbalances and the introduction of policy instruments sensitive to specific conditions and contexts. A common lesson of these analyses is that the different Eurozone countries and regions are likely to follow *differentiated and diverging trajectories* in the absence of structurally effective countervailing policies. Contributions in this part highlight the need to identify a systemic interest criterion as a condition for effective policy action at the level of the Eurozone. They also emphasize the need of effective institutional means by which to channel liquidity flows into structural investment funds capable of consolidating a systemic view of the interdependencies across the Eurozone.

Taken in their unity, the contributions in the three parts of the volume bring to light the need to address the internal structure of the Eurozone's political economy as a complex arrangement of multiple domains of interdependence and interaction. This internal structure presupposes a constellation of relative positions among stakeholders at sub-national, national, cross-national, and supra-national levels. Opportunities and constraints for the Eurozone, and conditions for effective policy action at Eurozone level, reflect the configuration of this internal structure and the range of different dynamic trajectories feasible within that structure. This point of view calls for a radical departure from current approaches to the Eurozone's political economy. In particular, it highlights the need to overcome the micro-macro dichotomy and calls for explicit recognition of the linkages between stakeholders *within* and *across* different levels of aggregation. A substantial conceptual shift is necessary to fully grasp the distinctive character of a political economy research programme based on a plurality of aggregation levels and the overlap between the economic and the political spheres. The first step towards such a shift requires a historical excursus, in order to facilitate identification of the specific features of such a research programme and to compare it to other approaches to the political economy of the Eurozone.

17.2.2. *Political Economy of Interdependence: An Historical Excursus*

A central theme of the volume is that, in dealing with the political economy of the Eurozone, one cannot circumscribe the space of possible outcomes by analysing the economic and political domains separately. In fact, the space of possible outcomes derives from the overlap of economic and political opportunities and constraints. This means it would not be sufficient to address specific features of the Eurozone (such as the crisis of the 2010s) by simply looking at economic concepts and techniques. However, it would also be insufficient to see the

Eurozone crisis purely in political terms without considering how economic conditions may critically circumscribe the set of options open to political decision-makers. This set of considerations, and the shifting confines between economic and political spheres, point to the need for a *political economy of interdependence* that does not take the distinguishing line between economics and politics for granted. A historical excursus may clarify this issue (see also Cardinale and Scazzieri, 2014).

The expression 'Political Economy' initially referred to 'the economy of the state' or to 'public policies of an economic nature' (Schumpeter, 1972 [1954], p. 21). This was especially the case in German economic literature, where the term used to denote 'political economy' ('*Staats-wissenschaft*') points to the narrowing down of the political domain from the body politic at large to the specific configuration of the body politic in the age of the modern nation-state. Economics as 'political economy' was often considered a particular sphere of political science, that is, that sphere of political science dealing with the provision of necessaries and 'all the economic problems of the nation' (Schumpeter, 1972 [1954], p. 197). On the other hand, 'Economics' (as distinct from 'Political Economy') is initially conceived as a general discipline investigating 'what are the best methods of a broad policy devoted to that end' rather than 'those exigencies of party organization, and those diplomacies of home and foreign politics of which the statesman is bound to take account in deciding what measures that he can propose will bring him nearest to the end that he desires to secure for his country' (Marshall, 1961 [1890], p. 43). This point of view led Marshall to argue that the study of economic matters 'is better described by the broad term "Economics" than by the narrower term "Political Economy"' (Marshall, 1961 [1890], *ibid*). Joseph Alois Schumpeter came close to Marshall when maintaining that 'all the facts and tools relevant to the analysis of the behavior of individual firms, past and present, come within our meaning of economics just as much as do the facts and tools relevant to the analysis of the behavior of governments' (Schumpeter, 1972 [1954], p. 22). In short, 'Economics' came to be seen as a discipline dealing with the formal aspect of human dispositional activity, independently of the economic units under consideration. The relationship with political science became a relationship between general (formal) conditions for the identification of 'best methods' (that would be the proper sphere of 'Economics') and the application of 'best methods' to decision-making concerning the economic configuration of the body politic. This intellectual development within economic studies led John Hicks to suggest the distinction between two separate sub-disciplines, which Hicks respectively calls 'Plutology' and 'Catallactics'. Hicks describes the former ('Plutology') as the study of national wealth, principally in its association with the flow of production, and under the assumption that the flow of production 'is so far homogeneous that it can be greater or less' (Hicks, 1976, p. 210; see also Hicks, 1976, pp. 215–16; Hicks, 1982). On the other hand, Hicks describes the latter ('Catallactics') as the study of dispositional activity bringing individuals (or social groups) to substitute one collection of goods for another, as characteristically occurring in exchange (Hicks, 1976, p. 212; see also Hicks, 1982).

In the Plutology tradition, there is a concentration of attention on the systemic requirements for the reproduction and expansion of the overall system. This emphasis expresses itself in the analysis of the system's net product (Physiocrats, Classical Political Economists) and in the consideration of the macroeconomic relationship between the net product and the amount of resources employed in its formation (Pigou, 1912, 1920; Keynes, 1936). On the other hand, Catallactics concentrates on the systemic requirements for the coordination of rational choices in view of exchange. This concentration of attention expresses itself in the analysis of the conditions for market clearing (Walras, 1874–77), in the identification of criteria for the efficient allocation of resources in a multi-agent setting (Pareto, 2014 [1906]; de Finetti, 1952) and in the analysis of the relationship between market clearing and efficient allocation (Arrow, 1951; Debreu, 1954).

Both the Plutology and the Catallactic traditions *presuppose* the existence of interdependencies between individuals and/or social groups determined by their relative positions within the social sphere. In fact, there are contributions in both traditions that bring light on specific patterns of interdependence, and on their influence on the working of the overall system. The English Political Arithmeticians of the seventeenth century and the French Physiocrats emphasize the internal structure of the economic system seen as a system of relative positions and relationships between a finite numbers of principal sectors of economic activity. Political Arithmeticians stressed the role of productive funds in the formation of national wealth (Graunt, 1665; Petty, 1691; Davenant, 1701; King, 1936 [1696, 1697]). The relationship between 'productive funds' is central to that objective. Physiocrats, starting with François Quesnay's *Tableau économique* (Quesnay, 1758) called attention to inter-sectoral flows of products as a structural prerequisite for society's maintenance and possible expansion. Already at the end of the seventeenth century, Pierre de Boisguillebert (1695) had emphasized the role of 'proportions' in the formation and maintenance of national wealth.[2] Shortly after Quesnay, Cesare Beccaria called attention to the 'hierarchy of arts' (that is, the hierarchy of productive activities) within the economic system. According to Beccaria, this hierarchy is the fundamental set of relative positions determining both the specific character of wealth formation in any economic system and the way in which the productive apparatus of that system connects with the productive apparatuses of other economies (Beccaria, 1971 [1769]; see also Audejean, 2010; Scazzieri, 2014b). Contributions in the Catallactic tradition provide a different focus, as their primary attention is on the original distribution of primary resources and their reallocation (by means of exchange or otherwise) between individuals and/or social groups. However, in this case, too, there are contributions that bring to light relative positions and interdependencies as a central characterizing feature of any given economic system. Research into the asymmetries between economic agents are relevant in this connection (Edgeworth, 1881; Pantaleoni, 1898), as are contributions emphasizing the role of 'power' in economic interdependence (Wieser, 1983 [1926]; Rothschild, 1947) and the influence of asymmetric positions in determining the character of strategy and the nature of conflict (Schelling, 1960).

However, the structure of relative positions, though implicit in both the Plutology and the Catallactic traditions, has seldom been a central object of direct investigation in either tradition. The political economy of interdependence that this volume brings forth highlights intermediate levels of aggregation and thus the internal structure of the economic system. These levels organize according to complex hierarchies, and it is within these hierarchies that the multi-layered relationship between the economic and the political domain comes fully into view. Intermediate levels of aggregation bring to light the multiple

---

[2] According to Boisguillebert, 'it is thus proportions that make all wealth' (Boisguillebert, as quoted in Lutfalla, 1981, p. 29).

interfaces between the economic and the political domain, make visible alternative criteria of systemic congruence, and highlight plural conditions that may lead to compromise or conflict.

Before developing this line of reasoning in the remainder of this chapter, it is important to discuss the relationship between the economic and political spheres which is implicit in the Plutology and Catallactics approaches. In the Plutology perspective, reciprocal arrangements of a material kind (i.e. flows of commodities) between social classes and/or productive sectors are a prerequisite for wealth formation at the level of the overall economic system. These arrangements also involve government (and the political sphere) both in the sense of an external guarantee of the circular flow *and* in the sense of a direct participation of the public sector in the production and circulation of the social product. Similarly, but in a different perspective, Catallactics views economic life from the standpoint of a system of interdependencies between acts of exchange, such that the 'political element' becomes part of the market organization of society. Interdependencies presuppose the existence of a series of acts of exchange of the individuals among themselves as well as between the individuals and the state (or other public bodies). As a result, the 'political' element is itself embedded within the system of market transactions, and the postulate of exchange becomes the general condition ensuring the mutual compatibility of choices concerning resource allocation, for both private and public actors.[3]

Therefore, in both Plutology and Catallactics, the political sphere is assimilated into the economic sphere, although the criterion of inclusion is different and reflects the different standpoints of the two approaches. In fact, both Plutology and Catallactics presuppose a historical condition of *structural differentiation* in society, that is, a society in which an advanced division of labour has developed. In a society of this type, it is possible to visualize economic interdependencies independently of political relationships, and ultimately the political sphere appears as embedded within the economic sphere itself (although in two different ways). Nicola Matteucci describes this historical condition as follows:

---

[3] According to the postulate of exchange, no transaction is possible for any pair of actors unless as a result of the transaction both actors are better, or at least one actor is better while the other is not worse.

First, it is necessary to have, from the structural point of view, a highly segmented and fragmented social system, with the co-existence of different institutional orders, which would be shared by different social groups and would be centered on different problems. Second, from the historical point of view, it is necessary to have a process of institutional or structural differentiation of human aggregates, in which different spheres of action become distinct from one another, as was the case in the history of modern Europe. (Matteucci, 1979, p. 20)

This process follows the dual track of institutional fragmentation and activity differentiation, and makes it possible to single out economic interdependencies as a relatively independent sphere of social relationships. These relationships may in turn encompass the political sphere as a component either of the circular flow of production and consumption (as in Plutology) or as a component of the system of interdependent acts of exchange (as in Catallactics). In the former case, the public sector is part of the system of sectoral interdependencies and may be a factor influencing the overall coherence of that system, both within the single period and across a sequence of periods.[4] In the latter case, the public sector is itself part of the system of interdependencies among acts of exchange and follows the same principles governing the exchange of goods in the private economy.[5]

Hence, both Plutology and Catallactics reduce the sphere of politics either to the reproduction prerequisites of sectoral interdependencies (this is done in the classical formulations of Plutology) or to the coordination prerequisites of an economy of markets (this is done in Catallactics). We may wonder to what extent this reduction is justified,

[4] In a single-period perspective, the coherence of a system of structural interdependencies including a public sector must be assessed by considering to what extent the public sector can influence the 'viability' of the overall system, that is, the ability of that system to reproduce, within any given period, the initial conditions of that period. In a multi-period perspective, the inclusion of a public sector may influence the possibility of the system of structural interdependencies to allow certain dynamic paths (sometimes to the exclusion of others).

[5] This entails the 'reduction' of the political sphere to the sphere of exchange, that is, a 'reduction' of politics to Catallactics. Antonio de Viti de Marco was among the first to call attention to this analytical possibility: 'Our conclusion, then, is that fiscal phenomena belong to the theory of the demand and supply of public goods, just as private – economic phenomena belong to the theory of the demand and supply of private goods. For the individual supplier we substitute the State and for the individual wants we substitute collective wants' (de Viti de Marco, 1928, in Kayaalp, 1998, p. 100).

and whether the interface between the economic and the political sphere does not require a more comprehensive assessment of the relationship between the two spheres.

A way to address this question is to revisit historical situations in which the identity of the relationship between the economic and the political domain was explicitly addressed and changes in the character of that relationship recognized or even fostered. These were often periods of discontinuity and crisis that called conventional categories into question[6]. The very beginning of 'Political Economy' as a distinct field of investigation bears the mark of the discontinuity associated with the consolidation of the early modern nation-state (Montchrétien, 1999 [1615]; see also Lavalley, 1903). Awareness of the need to overcome the traditional separation between the domains of state sovereignty and household sovereignty is at the root of the new terminology. This terminology reflected the increasing dependence of political authority on resources *external* to the sovereign household, and therefore the increasing need to bring provision and distribution of 'private' material resources under political control (see, for example, Brunner, 1968). The turning of economic activities into means for political objectives is apparent in Johann von Justi's claim that 'from the necessity and unavoidability of the expenses which a state has to meet for its maintenance, it does not follow directly ... that the subjects must contribute the necessary funds from their private means; but this follows only in the case where a state has no direct and special property, or where this is inadequate for the state's necessary expenses' (Justi, 1951, p. 382; 1st edn 1766). One can identify another, even if different, discontinuity when considering the shift, in the latter part of the eighteenth century, from a 'Political Economy' of administrative governance to one of formal rules and freedom of trade among contracting agents. In this case, 'Political Economy' is primarily the set of administrative arrangements and policy decisions that allow to employ 'the inhabitants [of any given state] (supposing them to be free-men) in such a manner as naturally to create reciprocal relations

---

[6] Radical economic and political transformations often affect precisely the interfaces between conventional domains of inquiry and bring to the fore the need for new distinctions, classifications and categories. John Hicks made a similar point when arguing that '[m]onetary theories arise out of monetary disturbances' (Hicks, 1967, p. 156).

and dependencies between them, so as to make their several interests lead them to supply one another with their reciprocal wants' (Steuart, 1966 [1767], p. 17). Even later developments such as the 'Keynesian revolution' of the mid-twentieth century and the neo-liberal policy agenda in the latter part of that century are instances of the shifting boundaries between the economic and the political domains, with Keynesians urging expansion of the state into the economic sphere and neo-liberals advocating its withdrawal from that sphere.

In order to conceptualize such shifting boundaries, we need heuristics that can help us to make sense of the relative autonomy *as well as* interdependence between the economic and the political spheres. This is because the effectiveness of political economy as heuristic presupposes its ability to deal with 'interfering concepts', that is, with concepts covering the intersection between the economy and the polity and taking on a different structure depending on the shifting configuration of either sphere (on this point, see Ornaghi, 2012; Sella, 1904).[7]

17.2.3. The Eurozone in Economic and Political Thinking

The distinction between Plutology and Catallactics provides a fruitful lens to understand the debates on the Eurozone. In fact, economic and political discussion of the Eurozone can be seen as concentrating around two principal focal points. On the one hand, there are economists, and to a lesser extent political scientists, who see the monetary union primarily through the lenses of market coordination and its prerequisites. On the other hand, many studies of the Eurozone share with the plutology tradition an interest in the congruence between different parts of society (e.g. sectors) and its implications for systemic viability.

The former approach is rooted in the theory of customs unions and its emphasis on 'trade creation' through the lowering of tariffs and the

---

[7] This point of view suggests that identifying structurally grounded economic opportunities and constraints is necessary to the determination of effective legal and administrative criteria (Quadrio Curzio, 2007, pp. 43–44). The same approach calls attention to the political and institutional conditions for effective use of economic opportunities (Hont, 2005; Reinert, 2011).

reduction of transaction costs (Viner, 1950). Indeed, economists have often seen trade creation as the fundamental trigger of spill-over effects affecting institutional and socio-economic structures, and leading to convergence around a common benchmark defined by competitive pressure (Haas, 1958; Scitovski, 1958; Casella, 1994, 1996). Economists' beliefs in the welfare-enhancing effects of competitive pressure and convergence have been an important intellectual root of the drive towards the European single market and European monetary unification. Much of this intellectual drive goes back to the prerequisites for market coordination in a Catallactic economy. In the absence of double coincidence of needs, money is a necessary condition for market clearing (Jevons, 1875).[8] This point of view gives prominence to money as unit of account and means of payment facilitating spot transactions, without directly addressing the role of money as standard in terms of which debts are expressed. This approach goes hand in hand with the assignment of a primary coordinating function to rules and normative benchmarks when it comes to features of monetary coordination that a purely 'spot transaction' view of money cannot address. Inflation targeting and state budget discipline are instruments by which Eurozone governance tackles the coordination issues inherent to the structure of exchanges once 'forward transactions' are allowed.[9] More specifically, inflation targeting aims at making market coordination reliable in a world in which spot payments are the exception rather than the rule.[10] This is because excessive

---

[8] This is because '[i]In the presence of double coincidence [of needs], barter exchange can take place in a fully decentralized way. Given double coincidence, execution of a given redistribution of goods requires traders to consult only their own and their current trading partner's excess supplies and demands and then trade so as to yield up their excess supplies and fulfill their excess demands. In the absence of double coincidence such a trading rule will achieve an inefficient allocation far from competitive equilibrium ... If the trading rule is relaxed to permit sellers to accept payment in commodities for which they have no excess demand, there is always a centralized rule but, in general, no decentralized rule which guarantees full execution in a limited number of trades. Full and decentralized execution is achieved through monetary exchange' (Ostroy and Starr, 1974, p. 1111).

[9] We may take forward transactions to include both payments for future delivery and delivery in view of future payment.

[10] John Hicks noted that payment in settlement of a debt 'should be taken as the general form of a transaction (of sale or purchase); it covers the case of the spot transaction, when the debt is settled immediately; but there are many more complicated transactions it also covers' (Hicks, 1989, p. 41).

price volatility would disrupt intertemporal transactions by introducing uncertainty into future payment and/or future delivery. On the other hand, budget discipline aims at achieving convergence and uniformity in the field of debt-credit relationships, which would be disrupted by excessive interest rate volatility and/or persistent deficits or surpluses in national accounts. This approach looks at the two principal features of European monetary governance (inflation targeting and budget discipline) as responses to the needs of market coordination in a world of intertemporal transactions (Mundell, 1969; Maes, 1992; Jones and Underhill, 2014). This point of view is apparent in Robert Mundell's remark that '[t]he expectations of exchange rate changes greatly unsettle the money markets, make planning difficult, and in the long run weaken the control a government has over economic policy' (Mundell, 1969, p. 4). Years later, Mundell maintained that '[i]n the euro area, every household has a world-class currency, every firm has a continental capital market and every country has a better policy mix. Inflation throughout the euro has been rubbed out, transaction costs associated with currency-changing have been eliminated, and information costs have been reduced to a minimum' (Mundell, 2006, p. 5). Mundell's classic paper on optimum currency areas highlights the broadly Catallactic foundation of his view of monetary integration:

Any given money qua numeraire or unit of account fulfills this function less adequately if the prices of foreign goods are expressed in terms of foreign currency and must then be translated into domestic currency prices. Similarly, money in its role of medium of exchange is less useful if there are many currencies; although the costs of currency conversion are always present, they loom exceptionally large under inconvertibility or flexible exchange rates. (Indeed, in a hypothetical world in which the number of currencies equaled the number of commodities, the usefulness of money in its roles of unit of account and medium of exchange would disappear, and trade might just as well be conducted in terms of pure barter.) Money is a convenience and this restricts the optimum number of currencies. (Mundell, 1961, p. 662)

The Catallactic view of economic coordination is the dominant intellectual influence behind this point of view, which focuses on ability to adjust towards equilibrium as the most important requirement for effective monetary arrangements. In this connection, a number of recent assessment of the Eurozone crisis bring to light structural problems arising from the inadequacy of Eurozone architecture in overcoming disequilibria through mechanisms of competitive market adjustment (Feldstein, 2005, 2012; Goodhart and Lee, 2013; Basevi and D'Adda, 2014; Goodhart, 2014).[11]

Other economists, social scientists and legal scholars distance themselves from the Catallactic tradition and look at the Eurozone from a systemic (and broadly political or constitutional) point of view. This approach has led to a joint focus on the institutional dynamics triggered by the Maastricht Treaty and on the asymmetries generated by free trade and free capital movements under Treaty rules. Central to this line of investigation is comparison between the (formal) economic constitution of the Eurozone and the (informal) constitutional realignments triggered by the Eurozone crisis as from 2010.[12] This approach moves from consideration of the implicit political character of seemingly technical economic policy rules (Jones, 2002)[13] and emphasizes the dual character of Europe's economic constitution, based as it is on a *microeconomic constitution* enshrining free trade principles and a *macroeconomic constitution* centred on aggregate policy objectives such as inflation targeting and fiscal budget discipline. In this connection, the discrepancy between integration processes in the economic and in the political domains (Rodrik, 2011) has led scholars to address the drifting away of Eurozone's governance and institutions from other constitutional principles in the social and political spheres (Scharpf, 2010b; Habermas, 2012; Chiti and Teixeira, 2013; Streeck and Elsässer, 2014; Streeck, 2015).[14] Eurocrisis management has called attention to

---

[11] Giorgio Basevi and Carlo D'Adda note that 'the absence of an instrument for making final settlements of balance of payments disequilibria among the Euro-area countries implies economic transfers among the countries that are in a direction opposite to those that would naturally follow from the classical adjustment of the balance of payments' (Basevi and D'Adda, 2014, p. 19).

[12] The concept of 'realignment' of constitutional principles in the framework of Europe's responses to the crisis is discussed in Tuori and Tuori (2014, pp. 180–204).

[13] According to Eric Jones, '[t]he political act of selecting the rules of economic policy is a problem because the selection process necessarily remains open to contestation on technical as well as political grounds. Put another way, the differences between schools of economic thought may not be so much analytical and empirical as they are political' (Jones, 2002, p. 24).

[14] Friedrich Scharpf emphasized that '[a]s long as the asymmetry between political immobilism and judicial activism persists, progress [towards further integration] is mainly achieved by non-political action, which – since the judicial power to destroy far exceeds its capacity to create-is bound to favour negative integration' (Scharpf, 2010b, p. 311). In a similar vein, John P. McCormick had argued that

the variety of responses to crisis in different Eurozone countries in the light of differences between their respective social fabrics (Hall, 2012, 2014) and has highlighted the resurgence of a broad interest in the specific character of the national political economies making up the Eurozone system (Iversen and Soskice, 2013).

This broadly institutionalist line of investigation into responses to the Eurozone crisis differs markedly from the view of researchers following the Catallactic view of markets and states. Scholars adopting an institutionalist point of view express dissatisfaction with concentration of attention on market coordination and institutional developments ascribed to adoption of uniform market standards. They rather address requirements for congruence between different social spheres and between their distinct modes of governance. Interest for systemic viability is central to this point of view, which shares some of the features of the classical political economy tradition in its concern for the conditions ensuring the viability (reproducibility) of the socioeconomic system as an integrated whole of economic and social activities.

However, both the Catallactic and the systemic-institutionalist approaches fall short of addressing a key aspect of the Eurozone, which this volume has highlighted, that is, its productive interdependencies at intermediate levels of aggregation within and across national political economies. A first utilization of intermediate levels of aggregation in the analysis of European integration can be found in Tibor Scitovsky's attempt to move beyond the Catallactic framework in order to correct the likely asymmetries arising from free trade: '[C]ertain forms or aspects of integration would at least provide scope and the machinery for bargaining among governments that might well accomplish some form of compensation. One of these is integration by sectors' (Scitovksy, 1958, pp. 148–49). For example, 'the effect on the balance of payments of the reallocation of coal production might conceivably be offset by a compensatory reallocation of steel capacity' (Scitovsky, 1958, p. 149). A similar attention for sectoral interests may

'European law effectively dismantles market-correcting institutions within the member states that the Council of Ministers, as a result of near unanimity requirements, will block reconstruction of at the EU level' (McCormick, 2007, p. 252). The clash between financial stability measures and Maastricht Treaty rules has also been emphasized (de Gregorio Merino, 2012; Scharpf, 2010a, 2012).

also be found in Albert Hirschman's analysis of the politics of economic integration, in which he emphasizes the trade diversion effect of integration due to 'discrimination against non participants' (Hirschman, 1981a, p. 271). In particular, Hirschman argued that 'in view of its political benefits, it may well be desirable to arrange for some trade diversion so as to make use of interest group support for the union in its difficult formative years. The policy problem then becomes that of keeping trade creation to politically safe limits while providing for a vitally needed minimum of trade diversion' (Hirschman, 1981a, p. 272). Hirschman's approach to European integration makes use of a conceptual framework he had previously developed in his analysis of divergent sectoral interests as fundamental explaining factor of political attitudes towards trade tariffs or inflation (Hirschman, 1968, 1981a; see also Furtado, 1967; Mamalakis, 1969; O' Donnell, 1977). In Hirschman's view, the relationship between trade creation and trade diversion is a major factor influencing the constellations of interests that may either support or oppose the integration process.[15] A recent development of Scitovsky's and Hischman's sectoral approaches is John P. McCormick's analysis of the EU as a *Sektoralstaat*, which 'accentuates deliberation among interested parties in microspheres of transnational policy making, but also insulates these spheres from public and governmental oversight and regulation through which the *Sozialstaat* attempted to guarantee the equity of negotiation, if not always deliberation for all participants affected' (McCormick, 2007, p. 9). This point of view not only acknowledges the influence of differentiated sectoral interests in policy formation but also emphasizes the existence of policy domains *separate from each other*, and such that the interplay of sectoral interests would be different as one moves from one policy domain to another. The *Sektoralstaat* will be 'fundamentally fragmented by the increased number of smaller policy-making

---

[15] Hirschman argued that 'in view of its political benefits, it may well be desirable to arrange for some trade diversion so as to make use of interest group support for the union in its difficult formative years. The policy problem then becomes that of keeping trade creation to politically safe limits while providing for a vitally needed minimum of trade diversion' (Hirschman, 1981a, p. 272). Hirschman's approach to European integration makes use of a conceptual framework he had previously developed in his analysis of divergent sectoral interests as fundamental explaining factor of political attitudes towards trade tariffs or inflation (Hirschman, 1968, 1981a, 1981b; see also Furtado, 1967; Mamalakis, 1969; O' Donnell, 1977).

spheres, the more rigid boundaries between macropolicy alignments, and the lack of an overarching political enforcement mechanism holding the different pieces together or at least serving as quasi-objective monitor of them' (McCormick, 2007, p. 23). This process brings to light 'the issue of dissonance between the functioning of multifarious policy sub-groups and the rights and interests of the larger public in a way perhaps never before observed in European democratic theory and practice' (McCormick, 2007, p. 23). This fragmentation of the European public sphere has attracted the attention of constitutional scholars who have addressed the split between policy domains in terms of 'an inverse relationship between rights-related principles and economic policy factors' (Tuori, 2010, p. 29). The sectoral view of policy formation highlights that systemic interest may be difficult to materialize across different policy domains, and that this may hinder the achievement of systemic objectives. In this connection, Giandomenico Majone has argued that resumption of a political integration process may be a way to introduce a degree of systemic coherence at the Eurozone (and EU) level. However, in his view, systemic integration should avoid assuming 'unilinear development from the nation state to something fulfilling much the same functions, on a grander scale and allegedly more effectively' (Majone, 2014, p. 322). This approach views integration in functional, rather than territorial, terms (Dahrendorf, 1973; Frey and Eichenberger, 1999) and leads to acknowledgement that 'top-down harmonization may be desirable when the market is relatively small and homogeneous. In a large market, on the other hand, harmonization tends to be brought about by the recognition of similar demands, rather than by a policy imposed from the top' (Majone, 2014, p. 18).[16]

To summarize, economic and political writings on the Eurozone (and on the EU at large) have moved between Catallactic, systemic and sectoral approaches to the integration process and have emphasized in different ways the opportunities and constraints associated with monetary, economic and institutional integration. Catallactic approaches have focused on market coordination requirements and have seen monetary and institutional developments as conditioned

---

[16] Majone calls attention to James Buchanan's (1965) theory of clubs and Mancur Olson's (1971) theory of collective goods as possible analytical foundations of this approach.

upon, or triggered by, developments in the market sphere. Systemic approaches emphasize coordination requirements between different domains (such as the economic, social and political spheres) and see institutional developments as a way to overcome asymmetries and mismatches between those domains (and especially as a way to overcome asymmetries triggered by developments in the market sphere). Sectoral approaches address integration as a process responding to needs and objectives arising at different intensities and speeds in different domains, and leading to differentiated patterns of integration depending on which domain is considered.

Interdependencies at different levels of aggregation and overlaps between the economic and political spheres, which this volume has highlighted, underlie the Catallactic, systemic, and sectoral perspectives on integration, because all these perspectives address opportunities and constraints arising from existence of relatively persistent patterns of interdependence between socio-economic interests within and across member states, and are sometime aimed at transforming existing interdependencies. By making interdependencies and overlaps explicit, the research programme advocated here complements the aforementioned perspectives and opens up new ways of framing the Eurozone. The remainder of this chapter aims to lay the foundations for such a programme.

17.3 The Eurozone as a Political Economy Field

17.3.1 Exploring the 'Material Constitution' of the Eurozone

Historical research provides a cue into the multi-layered structure of interdependencies from which European monetary cooperation has emerged. The interface between the economic and the political domain has been central to the unfolding of interdependencies within and across member states. In the years leading to the introduction of the European Monetary System (EMS), its political dimension was 'so strong that it managed to create the perception over the long run that the EMS was a truly new and innovative mechanism' (Mourlon-Druol, 2012, p. 261). Indeed, the introduction of the EMS is a characteristic instance of interdependence straddling across multiple domains, as it has been described as the product of 'the interaction of transnational, supranational, and intergovernmental phenomena' (Mourlon-Druol,

2012, p. 268). Multi-domain interdependence and interaction led to distinct developments in different domains that sometime (but not always) proved to be mutually consistent with each other. One such development was the formation of a technical élite of monetary economists and policy practitioners who, while often starting from different theoretical premises, ended up acquiring the features of an epistemic community marked by strong commitment to monetary and budgetary stability. A parallel development was the emergence of the European Council as an intergovernmental governance tool and the practice of monetary coordination involving some but not all EEC member states. This paved the way to the possibility of institutional developments that could take place within the European institutional framework without involving all EEC (or EU) member states. In particular, as Mourlon-Drüol argues,

[t]he corollary to British non participation in the [European Exchange Rate Mechanism] and, more generally, to the difficulties encountered in trying to apply a single monetary scheme to all EEC member states contributed to the emergence of the more general theme of a "two-tier Europe" ... This would remain a constant feature of the development of the EEC in the following years: belonging to the EEC/EU does not necessarily mean belonging to the EMS/Euro. (Mourlon-Druol, 2012, p. 277)

However, one cannot take mutually consistent developments for granted. For example, the push towards European monetary coordination as expressed in the making of the EMS had already weakened by the end of the 1970s due to an increasing wedge between the macroeconomic policy goals of different countries (Ludlow, 1982). If one considers the interests of relevant social groups (in our case, EEC member states) as given, conflict may be as likely as agreement. Multi-domain interdependence suggests that when a clash of interests is likely at given level of interdependence (e.g., at the level of monetary or budgetary coordination), convergence of interests may still be possible provided attention shifts to other dimensions of the political economy domain. Peter Ludlow, who was writing just after the introduction of the EMS, noted that

[t]he most promising point of departure for any really serious attempt to extend the scope and scale of European cooperation at the present juncture is almost certainly in the defence and foreign policy fields ... [U]nless there is an advance in this direction, the impetus towards and therefore the

likelihood of gains in other spheres, including the monetary system, will be much less strong. (Ludlow, 1982, p. 298)

Subsequent developments in the monetary field leading up to the introduction of the single currency and to the vicissitudes of the Eurozone in the second decade of its existence provide further evidence of multi-domain interdependence triggering monetary cooperation (or lack of it) as a response to developments in other dimensions of the political-economy field. The co-evolution of German political unification and European monetary unification is a striking instance of this. Indeed, the management of the subsequent Eurozone crisis suggests that, in the absence of strong links between the different dimensions of the Eurozone political-economic field, focusing on monetary and economic issues alone may not be a viable route to coordination, and might indeed trigger further distancing between different member states' policy objectives. Here we find an instance of the role complementarities may play in triggering policy action by shifting the focal point of coordination from one domain of interdependence to another or, vice versa, in blocking that shift through coordination constraints acting within interdependence domains different from the one at which policy formulation is envisaged. 'Nexus of complementarities' are central to the working of interdependencies within the political economy field (Hall and Soskice, 2001). However, a complementarity nexus in a certain domain may prove to be an obstacle in view of effective policy coordination in a different domain.[17] This possibility calls attention to the plurality of complementarity nexus existing within the political economy field, and to the fact that, in general, the working of any particular complementarity nexus becomes fully visible by looking at the way in which that nexus influences the relationship between *different* domains of interdependence – for instance, by considering how a complementarity nexus at the national level may influence the working of interdependencies at the sub-national or supranational level. The relationship between interdependencies at the regional, national and supra-national levels is inherently dynamic, and this dynamic results from the different degrees of resilience of the complementarity nexus at those levels. In the European integration experience, there were cases in which national complementarity nexus

---

[17] This possibility points to the dysfunctional character of complementarities under certain conditions (see Soskice, 2007, p. 90).

were stronger than complementarity nexus at the sub-national or supra-national levels (as when conflicting macroeconomic policy goals weakened supra-national coordination in the monetary field). But there were also cases in which supra-national or sub-national complementarity nexus were stronger and significantly affected the way in which the whole (multi-layered) complementarity system reacted to triggers of change (as when complementarities in the foreign policy field made monetary integration easier to achieve). Here we find an instance of the criterion of *relative structural invariance*, by which the overall dynamics of a system of interdependent components reflects *both* the character of triggers of change affecting those individual components and the degree to which any such component reacts to those sources of change (what we may call the 'distribution of resilience' across the different components of the system).[18] One important consequence of relative structural invariance is that any system of interdependent components would normally react to internal or external triggers of change by following a trajectory characterized by asymmetries and imbalances across the individual dynamic tracks of those components.[19] As we have seen, both the more distant history of European monetary cooperation and the process leading to the introduction of the monetary union result from interdependence and interaction across mutually related domains (such as the economic, monetary and strategic domains). This dynamics results from a differentiated pattern of motions (or blockages) characterizing specific sub-fields and eventually determining the dynamics of the overall system.[20] Analysing this type of process requires consideration of

[18] The criterion of relative structural invariance entails that 'any given economic system subject to an impulse or force is allowed to change its original state by following an adjustment path that belongs to a limited set of feasible transformations. In fact, the set of feasible transformations is the consequence of both the characteristics of certain elements of an economic system that are taken as constant and certain patterns of interrelationships among the different components that are assumed as invariant in the structural specification of the system' (Landesmann and Scazzieri, 1990, p. 96).

[19] The economic theory of 'traverse' embeds the relative invariance criterion as a tool for analysing the differentiated dynamics of the sub-units of a system subject to dynamic impulses (Hicks, 1973a, 1973b; Hagemann and Scazzieri, 2009).

[20] Different degrees of resilience may reflect the different strength of complementarity at one level of interdependence relative to other levels of interdependence. However, resilience is not always an obstacle to structural transformation. In certain cases, the relative resilience of certain structural

multiple levels of aggregation as both resilience and change may differently affect different parts of any given political-economic system.
Any political economy – including the Eurozone as a political economy
field – is subject to the criterion of relative structural invariance.
In particular, structural invariance may take a different character
depending on which level of aggregation is considered. For example,
the complementarity nexus would normally be different depending on
whether we consider the sub-national, national, or supra-national
levels. However, to fully analyse the internal structure of any political
economy requires moving beyond conventional units of analysis (such
as nation states, sub-units within nation states or the Eurozone as a
whole) so as to allow identification of the *plurality of domains* in which
complementarity nexus may arise. This task requires a new set of
concepts and tools. In particular, it is necessary to look behind macro
units without falling back to a plurality of micro units without stable
mutual linkages. Intermediate levels of aggregation are central to this
purpose because they allow flexible use of decomposition and aggregation techniques, and thus the identification of nexus of complementarities that might otherwise go unnoticed.

To focus on *intermediate levels of aggregation*, and to approach
interdependencies by adopting a *plurality* of decomposition and aggregation techniques, provides a radically distinctive viewpoint on the
political economy of the Eurozone. In particular, decomposition and
aggregation techniques across different levels of aggregation allow
viewing the Eurozone as an economic-political domain in which different nexus of interdependence may arise along different axes, thus
giving support to alternative patterns of coordination. This approach
provides a cue into the *material constitution* of the Eurozone, which
may be defined as the relatively persistent set of interdependencies
among its constituent units, together with the relative weights attached

elements of the political-economic system may simply direct structural change
along a certain trajectory to the exclusion of others (Rosenberg, 1969, 1976).
Resilience is an important prerequisite for the identification of determinate paths
of structural dynamics: '[T]he economic system may or may not be mutable
under a number of structural descriptions, but it needs to be invariant with
respect to at least one type of structural characterization. The property of
invariance inherent in such a characterization identifies the dynamic structure in
terms of which the analysis of structural change may be carried out'
(Landesmann and Scazzieri, 1990, p. 98).

to those units.[21] The material constitution of the Eurozone, hence its political economy, is rooted in the existence of multiple nexus of interdependencies within and across different levels of aggregation. Decomposition and aggregation techniques are needed to detect alternative, and often co-existing, nexus of interdependencies. This makes it possible to identify alternative possibilities for coordination or conflict depending on which type of interdependence is more effective in any given situation.

17.3.2 Aggregation Levels and Complementarity Nexus: Structural Heuristics for the Eurozone

The Eurozone is a complex political-economic field embedded in a larger political-economic domain (the EU). It also encompasses a multi-layered plurality of other political-economic domains at lower levels of aggregation (such as nation states, Länder, and regions). Cross-level political-economic domains also exist, as stakeholder groups may cross over national boundaries and/or the boundaries between Eurozone and non-Eurozone members of the EU. Investigating the political economy of the Eurozone presupposes analytical tools which are able to capture different patterns of interdependence and their mapping onto varying patterns of interest aggregation/disaggregation.

A multi-level political economy encompasses different systems of complementarities among its components at different levels of interdependence as well as *between* those levels. This configuration highlights that different specifications of unit of analysis (say, firms, constellations of firms, industries) may be conducive to detection of different types of interdependence at any given level of aggregation, as well as of different connections between those levels. For instance, the types of interdependence between sub-national units may be remarkably

---

[21] The legal scholar Costantino Mortati considered a 'material constitution' to be the foundation of any formal constitutional arrangement, and thought of it as deriving from 'social forces, historically determined, which provide a sufficient guarantee that limitations [in the exercise of power] will be met' (Mortati, 1998, p. 204). Mortati also maintained that, whenever 'the fundamental law arises from compromises between opposing principles ... the prevalence that either force gains over the other, and the resulting change in the working of the original constitution, cannot be reduced to the latter, but must be considered as the expression of the introduction of a different constitutional arrangement' (Mortati, 1998, p. 207).

different, depending on whether we consider units within individual nation states or units belonging to a variety of nation states. In addition, the connections between sub-national and supra-national levels are likely to be different depending on whether sub-national units can only relate to other sub-national units of the same state, or also to sub-national units of states different from their own.

A socio-economic system of interdependent components is conducive to a plurality of aggregation criteria depending on the analytical purpose at hand (Simon, 1962). In particular, different aggregation criteria call attention to different ways in which relative structural invariance affects the different components of the system under consideration. Moreover, each configuration of relative structural invariance highlights a specific dynamic mode that is likely to be different from the dynamic modes associated with alternative configurations of invariance. We may also note that, for any given configurations of invariance, dynamic triggers and bottlenecks may affect in different ways different parts of the system at different levels of aggregation. For instance, there could be industries or other subsystems of economic activities with different degrees of resilience to internal or external factors of change. The investigation of this type of system requires levels of aggregation intermediate between that implied by macro analysis and that implied by analysis of the microeconomic type.[22] Indeed, it would generally require the ability to switch from one intermediate level of aggregation to another in order to follow the complex and varying pattern of interdependence among the different parts of the socio-economic system.

Previous chapters of this volume have discussed analytical tools built on intermediate levels of aggregation and conducive to a heuristic of

---

[22] Intermediate levels of aggregation are necessary in order to disentangle the web of asymmetric relationships that characterize any socio-economic system subject to time-differentiated constraints across its different components. A case in point is the formation of stocks and the relationship between product stocks and flows in a system of interdependent activities. This is because stocks result from coordination mismatches along the time dimension (no stocks would arise in a production system consisting of fully synchronized and interdependent activities). This structural property in turn calls attention to aggregation criteria as the central heuristic for stock-flow analysis: what are stocks at a certain level of aggregation may be flows at a different level, and vice versa. (See Lowe, 1976, for a discussion of stock-flow relationships in relation to aggregation criteria; see also Baranzini and Scazzieri, 1990, pp. 312–15).

multiple-level interdependence (see, in particular, the contributions by Cardinale, Pabst and Scazzieri). The analysis of multi-level interdependence presupposes identification of appropriate levels of aggregation/disaggregation and the selection of the corresponding units of analysis. In the following subsection we discuss economic theories based on the explicit consideration of interdependent units of analysis (such as socio-economic groups or productive sectors) at different levels of aggregation. These theories provide a conceptual framework to the structural analysis of interdependence, which we extend to the study of interdependencies between the economic and the political spheres. But before introducing those theories, we shall reconstruct the rationale for using models of interdependencies between economic activities as a structuring principle for society.

17.3.3 Group Affiliations, Interdependence and Cleavages

Group affiliations are central to the fabric of society and to the very identity of its constitutive units. Georg Simmel provided a classic statement of this property as follows: '[t]he groups with which the individual is affiliated constitute a system of coordinates, as it were, such that each new group with which he becomes affiliated circumscribes him more exactly and more unambiguously' (Simmel 1955 [1922], p. 140). Simmel also noted, in the same passage, the relationship between the increasing complexity of social structure and the size of fields in which social actions take place: 'To belong to any one of these groups leads the individual considerable leeway. But the larger the number of groups to which an individual belongs, the more improbable is it that other persons will exhibit the same combination of group-affiliations, that these particular groups will intersect once again [in another individual]' (Simmel, 1955 [1922], p. 140).

Interdependencies in the production sphere are fundamental to the way in which group affiliations take shape in modern society. This feature characterizes a socio-economic system in which production activity depends on extensive division of labour (Durkheim, 1902). In that system, group affiliations reflect the complementarity and coordination requirements of production processes of increasing complexity, rather than other dimensions of social life (such as reproduction and kinship). Increasing division of labour is associated with manifold crisscrossing interdependencies between specialized activities.

(For example, productive task *i* may be required for performing tasks *j* and task *k* but not task *z*, while task *z* may be required for performing task *i* but not task *j*.) This characteristic of division of labour is inherently associated with a configuration of social connectivity in which manifold group affiliations are possible. Georg Simmel called attention to this structural plurality of group affiliations as a distinctive feature of modern society: '[As] the individual leaves his established position in one primary group, he comes to stand at a point at which many groups "intersect". The individual as a moral personality comes to be circumscribed in an entirely new way, but he also faces new problems. The security and lack of ambiguity in his former position gives way to uncertainty in the conditions of his life' (Simmel, 1955 [1922], p. 141).[23] Division of labour makes intersections between activities a structural characteristic of the socio-economic system. However, these intersections do not fully determine which connections between activities are most important at any given time: '[T]he objective structure of a society provides a framework within which an individual's non-interchangeable and singular characteristics may develop and find expression depending on the greater or lesser possibilities within that structure' (Simmel, 1955 [1922], p. 150). This argument applies to groups and sectors as well as to individuals. For example, a productive sector (or social group) *i* may be necessary for the activity performed by productive sectors (or social groups) *j* and *k*, but not for the activity performed by sector (or social group) *z*. On the other hand, sector (or social group) *z* may be necessary for the activity performed by sector (or social group) *i* but not for the activity performed by sectors (or social groups) *j* and *k*. In this case, the intensity of connectivity between sectors (or groups) at any given time would ultimately reflect (1) the structure of connections that are feasible under the given division of labour and (2) the pattern of interaction that is dominant under given circumstances. For example, the indirect connection between sector (or group) *z* and sectors (or groups) *j* and *k* may or may not be active depending on whether there is in the economy an actual need for the commodities or services that activities *j* and *k* provide.

---

[23] Ernest Gellner expressed a similar view in his analysis of social modularity (Gellner, 1994; see also Kallinikos, 2003).

Division of labour thus provides an objective structure in which social groups can develop connections, alliances and cleavages. For this reason, alternative decompositions of the interdependencies associated with a given division of labour may give a cue into the types of group affiliations that can materialize under specific circumstances. Decomposition techniques such as the ones discussed in this section provide analytical tools for the identification of the social affiliations/cleavages that are *possible* under given structural conditions. They also provide a heuristic for identifying which degrees of fragmentation, cleavage overlap and cleavage crosscutting are *most likely* under those conditions.[24] In the next section, we shall propose criteria for group affiliation that allow identification of special interests at varying levels of aggregation. This makes analysis of the 'objective structure' of interdependence an important condition for assessing which coalitions and conflicts are possible given that structure, and is a necessary step for evaluating which coalitions or conflicts are *likely* in any given situation.

17.3.4 *Schemes of Interdependence and Analysis of Linkages*

Economic analysis provides a variety of tools to represent division of labour in society, starting with François Quesnay's *Tableau économique* (Quesnay, 1758). Quesnay's approach consisted in focusing on a small number of socio-economic groups (in his case, agriculture, manufacturing and the 'classe stérile' of rentiers) so as to disentangle relationships (*sectoral interdependencies*) deemed to be relatively stable and conducive to the discovery of important structural properties for the system as a whole.

Quesnay's approach led to the first analytically explicit representation of the socio-economic system as a 'circular system' of interdependent

---

[24] Given a set of group affiliations leading to social cleavages, the *fragmentation* associated with any particular cleavage may be defined as the degree to which 'this cleavage [sets] the members of the community against each other', or in terms of 'how many pairs of members find themselves at odds over any other cleavage' (Rae and Taylor, 1970, p. 3). Given a set of cleavages, their *overlap* is the extent to which 'the crystallized portion of the community on one cleavage [is] the same as the crystalized portion on another' (Rae and Taylor, 1970, p. 4), while *crosscutting* between any two cleavages is the extent to which 'pairs divided by one cleavage [are] united by another and vice versa' (Rae and Taylor, 1970, p. 4).

product flows transferred from one social group (or 'social class') to another. This point of view led to the formulation of the concept of 'net product' (*produit net*) and the identification of conditions for the sustainability of any such economy in terms of proportionality requirements to be satisfied by those product flows. Modern formulations along this line of research improved on the conceptual structure of Quesnay's framework while retaining his core set of ideas. The most important innovations have been the following: (i) the substitution of productive sectors (or 'industries') for Quesnay's social classes (Leontief, 1991 [1928], 1941; Sraffa, 1960); (ii) the comparative analysis of the different types of sectoral interdependence that can be detected by adopting, respectively, a horizontal (circular flow) representation of the economy or a representation of the economy in terms of 'subsystems' such as vertically integrated sectors (Sraffa, 1960, Appendix 'On Sub-Systems'; Pasinetti, 1973); (iii) the investigation of which price ratios may be consistent with the systemic congruence (viability) requirements associated respectively with a 'horizontal' circular-flow economy or with an economy of vertically integrated subsystems (Sraffa, 1960; Quadrio Curzio, 1967; Pasinetti, 1973, 1977; Seton, 1992 [1985]); (iv) the identification of systemic conditions for the expansion of the economy along a proportional path of maximum growth (von Neumann, 1935–37), or along a non-proportional path of structural dynamics at full employment and full utilization of productive capacity (Pasinetti, 1965, 1981; Leon, 1967; Quadrio Curzio, 1975; Lowe, 1976). These analytical developments afford a better understanding of the plurality of linkages that may arise within any given system of production interdependencies depending on which criterion of aggregation and/or disaggregation is adopted. This heuristic of linkages may also provide analytical tools for the investigation of multi-layered connectivity beyond the production sphere narrowly defined. Wassily Leontief's contribution (presented as a modern 'Tableau' of the American economy) provides the conceptual backbone of a structural heuristic aimed at exploring interdependencies in the economic-political system at large. Table 17.1 shows Leontief's representation of horizontal interdependence between simultaneous product flows.[25]

---

[25] This formulation of horizontal interdependence is due to Luigi Pasinetti (1977, Chapter III). Its original statement and discussion are in parts I and II of Leontief's *Structure of the American Economy* (Leontief, 1941, pp. 9–65).

Table 17.1 *A scheme of horizontal interdependence*

Inputs	Outputs			
	Industry 1	Industry 2	Industry j	Final Sector (consumption)
Commodity 1	$q_{11}p_1$	$q_{12}p_1$	$\cdots$ $q_{1j}p_1$	$\cdots$ $q_{1n}p_1$
Commodity 2	$q_{21}p_2$	$q_{22}p_2$	$\cdots$ $q_{2j}p_2$	$\cdots$ $q_{2n}p_2$
Commodity i	$q_{i1}p_i$	$q_{i2}p_i$	$q_{ij}p_i$	$q_{in}p_i$
Final sector (value added)	$q_{n1}p_n$	$q_{n2}p_n$	$\cdots$ $q_{nj}p_n$	$\cdots$ $q_{nn}p_n$

Table 17.1 describes '[t]he economic activity of the whole country ... as if covered by one huge accounting system' (Leontief, 1941, p. 11). In particular, the element $q_{11}p_1$ shows the expenditure by industry *1* for the commodity produced in industry *1*, $q_{ij}p_i$ the expenditure by industry *j* for commodity *i*, and $q_{1n}p_1$ the expenditure by the final sector (the aggregate of final consumers) for purchases from industry *1*. The same is true for all other entries in the table.[26]

A central feature of the scheme of horizontal interdependence is the *proportionality condition* that must be satisfied if the set of interlocking product flows is to reproduce itself from one period to another. This condition is that, with given production techniques, the interlocking product flows should be consistent with each other. Consistency requires that any one industry should be able to secure its own intermediate inputs from other industries within the system. As industries can supply their respective intermediate inputs' requirements through product transfers from one industry to another, interlocking product flows may generate a set of exchange ratios (*structural prices*) that would assure the consistency (reproducibility) of the whole system.[27]

---

[26] As Leontief noted, 'this type of account is related not to a single instant but rather to a period of time, say a year, a month, or a week' (Leontief, 1941, p. 11).

[27] The Hawkins-Simon condition for the viability of an economy of inter-industry product flows expresses the consistency requirement in terms of the zero-determinant condition for the system of production equations to generate a set of non-negative structural prices (see Pasinetti, 1977; Seton, 1992 [1985]).

A scheme of horizontal interdependence presupposes the decomposition of the political-economic system into industries that are transferring positive product quantities to each other within the same accounting period. In the formulation of Table 17.1, there is neither a negative nor a positive balance, as overall supply equals overall expenditure for each product within the period under consideration.[28] Horizontal decomposition may be applied both to a system with given production techniques and to a system with changing techniques. In the latter case, the viability condition for systemic congruence would still be relevant, even if it may be necessary to drop the one-to-one correspondence between production techniques and produced commodities to allow for the simultaneous utilization of different techniques in the production of a given commodity. (This is a common case when the substitution of the most effective technique for the old technique takes place along a traverse requiring time to work itself out; see Hicks, 1973a; Hagemann and Scazzieri, 2009.)

However, there are dynamic issues that call for utilization of a different type of decomposition, thereby suggesting a different criterion for systemic congruence. For example, a process of technical change may disrupt the existing dividing lines between industries to such an extent that it becomes difficult to single out a coherent and complete system of interlocking product flows. In this case, a vertical decomposition technique may be more appropriate than a horizontal scheme of interlocking product quantities flowing from one industry to another. The horizontal system of inter-industry product flows splits into a number of self-contained subsystems, where each subsystem contains only the quantities of primary and intermediate inputs necessary to the attainment of an objective that is external to the subsystem itself. Different types of vertical decompositions are possible. Luigi Pasinetti proposes to split a circular system of interdependent industries into subsystems delivering different components of the vector of net outputs produced in the complete system (Pasinetti, 1973). In his approach, any vertically integrated subsystem includes all intermediate and labour inputs needed for the delivery of a particular component of the net output vector. In formal terms, any subsystem of this type is

---

[28] The cases of purchases made on credit or of the accumulation of purchasing power over and above expenditures may be compatible with the scheme of horizontal interdependence but would require a special treatment of structural liquidity provision (see Cardinale and Scazzieri, 2013, 2016).

associated with a labour quantity v_i (the vertically integrated labour coefficient corresponding to subsystem i) and a vector of intermediate inputs $\mathbf{h}_i$ (Pasinetti's 'unit of vertically integrated productive capacity' corresponding to subsystem i).[29] A remarkable feature of this decomposition is that the overall interdependence of intermediate product flows is set aside, and that it is possible to visualize objectives specific to particular subsystems *independently* of the nexus of complementarities between different subsystems within the structure of inter-industry flows. In a subsequent formulation of his vertical decomposition technique, Pasinetti includes in each vertically integrated subsystem also the labour and intermediate inputs needed for that subsystem to grow at its own rate g_i (Pasinetti, 1988). The latter generalization makes it possible to describe the structural dynamics of growing economic systems subject to technical change without addressing transformations that may entirely upset existing industrial structures. Vertical decomposition makes this result possible by making it redundant to follow the consequences of technical changes through the whole set of relations characterizing inter-industry product flows. The reason for this is that

essential though these complicated relations are for any analysis concerning the interrelations of the circular (expanding) process at any given time, they become irrelevant for all those dynamic analyses that concern the movements through time of the final consumption goods and of the corresponding physical quantities of labour, as well as for all those relations that follow therefrom ... As far as the analyses of those problems are concerned, complete emancipation is obtained from the constraints of fixed technical coefficients. The analysis is open to the assumption of technical progress in whatever form it may take place. (Pasinetti, 1988, p. 134)

---

[29] In Pasinetti's formulation, '[e]ach coefficient v_i ... expresses in a consolidated way the quantity of labour directly and indirectly required in the whole economic system to obtain one physical unit of commodity i as a final good. We shall call it the *vertically integrated labour coefficients* for commodity i ($i = 1$, $2,...,n$). Likewise, each column vector $\mathbf{h}_i$ [...] expresses in a consolidated way the series of heterogeneous physical quantities of commodities $1,2,...,n$, which are directly and indirectly required as stocks, in the whole economic system, in order to obtain one physical unit of commodity i as a final good ($i = 1, 2,...,n$). This is another particular composite commodity which we shall call *a unit of vertically integrated productive capacity* for commodity i ($i = 1,2,...,n$)' (Pasinetti, 1973, p. 6).

In a further development of this approach, Pasinetti has concentrated on the case of an economy in which there are no capital goods and the production of all commodities requires labour alone. The production and consumption structure of that economy at any given time is described by labour and consumption coefficients that reflect, respectively, the technology in use for production of any commodity and the corresponding per capita consumption of that commodity. In this economy, '[t]he activity of production is carried out with extensive division of labour, and thus with a marked specialization', while each individual 'will ... need to obtain all the consumption goods he/she needs through exchange' (Pasinetti, 1986, pp. 421–22). The specialized processes of production and consumption are connected with one another by the very existence of human beings in their dual character of workers and consumers. A 'fundamental macroeconomic condition' ensures consistency of production and consumption activities under conditions of full employment (Pasinetti, 1993, p. 18).

Alberto Quadrio Curzio has proposed a different type of vertical decomposition by focusing on cases in which the system of inter-industry flows derives from the joint activation of two or more complete sets of production techniques.[30] This analytical scheme leads to distinguishing between two alternative ways of representing the technical structure of an economic system in which there is no one-to-one correspondence between commodities produced and techniques of production. (Quadrio Curzio considers situations in which there are more techniques in use for producing one or more commodities.) One way of representing this type of technical structure is that of *global technologies*, in which the circularity of inter-industry flows in maintained by introducing 'splitting coefficients' that allow distinguishing between the different supply sources of any intermediate product produced in the economy. Another way is that of *compound (or composite) technologies*, in which there is no longer complete circularity of intermediate product flows, and technical structure consists of a collection of self-contained subsystems such that each subsystem is capable of supplying its own needs for intermediate products. This decomposition technique preserves circularity within individual

---

[30] Any complete set of techniques is able to supply the intermediate products requirements of each technique in the set by means of products delivered by other techniques in the same set.

subsystems but connects different subsystems with one another via vertical linkages that work through the accumulation of capital *across* the different subsystems. This may happen when the net output vector of a given subsystem (say, subsystem I) is wholly or partially invested into another subsystem (say, subsystem II), and the latter subsystem's net output vector is in turn invested into another subsystem (say, subsystem III) according to a sequence triggered by the scarcity of a given resource or the 'structural scarcity' of a particular technique (Quadrio Curzio, 1990; Quadrio Curzio and Pellizzari, 1999; see also Scazzieri, Baranzini and Rotondi, 2015, pp. 427–46).[31] Differently from Pasinetti, Quadrio Curzio preserves a degree of horizontal inter-dependence (between the interlocking processes within any given sub-system) while bringing to view the one-way relationship between sub-economies that are structurally separate but connect dynamically along the *same* expansion path. This decomposition technique calls attention to the asymmetric linkages across sub-economies contribut-ing to the process of accumulation and growth, while acknowledging the persistence of circular interdependencies within each one of those sub-economies.[32]

---

[31] Any given technique may be *structurally scarce* if there are technological or organizational conditions making it possible to activate that technique at certain scales of production but not at others. The law of multiples requiring scale expansion by integer multiples of the minimum scale at which a given technique is feasible is an important factor of structural scarcity, for it makes any such technique to be, respectively, feasible or unfeasible depending on which scale range is considered (Scazzieri, 1993, 2014a). A case in point is that of infrastructures whose operation may be impossible below or above certain scales due to the indivisibility of certain components.

[32] This decomposition calls attention to the rigidities associated with technological dynamics due to the compatibility requirements that need to be satisfied in order to activate combinations of different techniques. In the technological setting described above, the structural dynamics of technology reflects 'not only ... the degree of internal efficiency of each of the single techniques available, but also ... the compatibility of the structures of the various techniques, which will be put successively into operation on account of the constraints imposed by the non-produced means of production' (Quadrio Curzio, 1986, p. 336). Indeed, 'technical progress in the individual techniques cannot be transformed ipso facto into an increase in the efficiency of those technologies that use several techniques; this is due to the problems arising from the different production structures of the techniques and from the possibility that the residuals [that is, intermediate products delivered by certain subsystems and not usable in other subsystems] will reduce or eliminate the effects of the technical progress' (Quadrio Curzio, 1986, p. 336). The above process of technological

The decomposition and aggregation techniques outlined above point to manifold ways in which activities are materially connected with one another at any given time and across different time periods. They provide a heuristic for identification of possible complementarities between the different components of any given socio-economic system. As we have seen, production interdependencies provide a blueprint for group affiliations in societies characterized by extensive division of labour. This makes decomposition and aggregation techniques an invaluable tool for analyzing the structuring of interests in societies of that type.

Alternative criteria for the aggregation/disaggregation of units of analysis within a particular political economy lead to the identification of distinct ways in which the elementary components of that political economy may cluster together or getting apart from each other. For example, aggregating productive activities within the Eurozone by commodity (or commodity basket) produced would lead to productive units such as cross-national industries different from productive units obtained if we aggregate activities across the Eurozone by the vertical integration of processes directly or indirectly responsible for delivering different commodities (or commodity baskets) as final products. As we have seen in the previous subsection, the structural analysis of economic systems leads to alternative representations of the economy depending on the aggregation/disaggregation criterion adopted. Horizontal aggregation of activities by homogeneous commodities (or commodity baskets) delivering intermediate inputs to each other brings to light a decomposition of the economy in which fragmentation is the principal feature of the production system. This means that the production of each commodity (or commodity basket) is distinct from the production of any other commodity (or commodity basket). As a result, the coordination of productive activities needed to produce any given commodity is *external* to the corresponding unit of analysis

differentiation modifies the internal structure of the production system, which will come to consist of a number of distinct production subsystems. These subsystems are distinct from each other from the *analytical* point of view, even if under certain technological conditions each process in either subsystem could use intermediate inputs delivered by one or the other subsystem. This decomposition splits the production system into separate subsystems that may be subject to *different* scarcity constraints. In this case, vertical integration calls attention to bottlenecks within the structure of the production system and to the possibility or mismatches *or* complementarities between the different components of the system.

(the corresponding industry) and presupposes a set of interdependencies across the set of inter-industry relationships (as in the Leontief model discussed in the previous subsection). On the other hand, the vertical aggregation of activities by heterogeneous commodities directly or indirectly needed to deliver a particular commodity (or commodity basket) as final product brings to light a different type of decomposition. Here the merging of a plurality of heterogeneous activities into a finite set of processes (vertically integrated sectors) is the principal feature of the economy. The production of any given commodity combines with the production of other commodities in order to define any given vertically integrated sector. As a result, the coordination of productive activities needed to deliver any given commodity is *internal* to the corresponding unit of analysis (the vertically integrated sector) and presupposes interdependencies within a particular subsystem of the economy (the corresponding vertically integrated sector). In addition, this type of decomposition highlights the possibility of a plurality of coordination criteria, as interdependencies may exist both *within* any given vertically integrated sector (see above) and *across* those sectors. This is shown, respectively, by Pasinetti's fundamental macroeconomic condition under producers' and consumers' learning (Pasinetti, 1981, 1993), and by Quadrio Curzio's maximum-growth condition under structural scarcity (Quadrio Curzio, 1986). Decomposition of a political-economic system into distinct vertically integrated subsystems brings to view the fact that interdependence of activities *within* individual subsystems is not necessarily the same as interdependence *between* different subsystems. For example, the type of coordination between productive units within a given vertically integrated subsystem is different from the type of coordination between vertically integrated subsystems that would be compatible with full employment and full capacity utilization (Pasinetti, 1981, 1988). In addition, coordination between productive units within a vertically integrated subsystem making use of a particular primary resource is distinct from coordination between resource-using subsystems to meet the maximum growth target for the economic system as a whole (Quadrio Curzio, 1986; Quadrio Curzio and Pellizzari, 1999).

Alternative decomposition techniques bring to light alternative sub-units within the economic system, and alternative patterns of interdependence between those sub-units (see discussion earlier in the chapter). Fragmentation into subsystems may be necessary to make coordination possible. However, 'fragments' may be of different types and may require different means of coordination. For instance, interdependence among production units within a subsystem making use of a particular natural resource (say, a particular 'land' or 'oil field') t_h ($h = 1,\ldots, k$) is distinct from interdependence among subsystems making use of *different* natural resources t_i and t_j ($i, j = 1,\ldots, k$). Interdependence of the former type reflects the structure of intermediate input requirements within any given subsystem, whereas interdependence of the latter type results from linkages *across* different subsystems.

The above property suggests that different patterns of interdependence may intersect each other. Horizontal interdependencies resulting from intermediate input requirements within any given 'circular' economy may co-exist with the vertical interdependencies resulting from the arrangement of activities according to some 'final objective' (such as attainment of a particular output level for a specific commodity, or group of commodities). In the former case, the analytical representation of the economic system brings to light complementarities among production activities without emphasizing the existence of a hierarchy among potentially competing objectives, as a viable economic system may require outputs from all industries as intermediate commodities. In the latter case, the analytical representation emphasizes *distinct* sets of complementarities corresponding to the different vertically integrated sectors one has identified. This type of decomposition brings to light a possible trade-off between complementarity requirements for different vertically integrated sectors, as under certain conditions one may secure the intermediate inputs required for sector i only at the expense of intermediate inputs required for sector j. This may be the case if production of intermediate inputs in both subsystems i and j requires inputs of the same non-produced resource and the latter's availability is limited (see Quadrio Curzio and Pellizzari, 1999, chapter VI, which discusses the 'non-equiproportional' dynamics generated in a collection of subsystems subject to the same scarcity constraint).

17.4 The Variable Geometry of Interests: Multiple Objectives and Reduction of Diversity

Aggregation/disaggregation criteria are an important condition for the identification of relevant interests and their association with particular units of analysis. The concept of 'interest' as disposition to achieve objectives is central to the political economy of disaggregation and interdependence. It is also central to the exploration of the ways in which multiple co-existing patterns of interdependence may aggregate into a general goal or disaggregate into a variety of fractional objectives. The intellectual history of the concept of 'interest' in early modern Europe is evidence of the close relationship between those criteria and the way in which the consideration of 'interest' may occur along a divisive or an integrating dimension. For instance, political thinking in this period makes the sovereign's 'particular, concrete interest' coincide with 'the general interest, and welfare, of the community' (Ornaghi, 1990, p. 29; see also Meinecke, 1924). On the other hand, the existence of different spheres of interest within the same social structure could make the same groups opposed to one another or, vice versa, mutually supportive depending on which particular cleavage is considered. For example, Hirschman, when discussing Latin American inflations, points out that the macroeconomic cleavage between wages and profits was overshadowed by cleavage concerning 'the intersectoral income distribution' since 'inflation often favored one group of property holders or entrepreneurs at the expense of another' (Hirschman, 1981b, p. 189).

As we have seen, the objective structure of complex societies reflects a complex division of labour, and thus a crisscrossing web of interdependencies between individuals and between groups makes a plurality of group affiliations possible (see previous subsection). However, group affiliations in a particular society *may or may not* follow the crisscrossing configuration of the objective structure. This may have important consequences for the configuration of group interests that is likely to arise, and for the type of systemic interest that it would be possible to identify on its basis. James Madison's discussion in the *Federalist Papers* provides an early argument for the view that crosscutting linkages are a major factor leading to cohesion in a fragmented social space.[33] Simmel's later work on the multiple group affiliations

---

[33] Madison developed his argument while discussing the governance features of small and large republics: 'The smaller the country, the fewer probably will be the distinct parties and interests composing it; the fewer the distinct parties and interests, the more frequently will a majority be found of the same party; and the smaller the number of individuals composing a majority, and the smaller the compass within which they are placed, the more easily will they concert and

consistent with the objective structure of modern society triggered research on the relationship between multiple affiliations and cleavages and on the condition for cleavages and conflicts to be compatible with systemic resilience. Edward Alsworth Ross provided a classical statement of that condition:

Every species of social conflict interferes with every other species in society ... save only when lines of cleavage coincide; in which case they reinforce one another ... A society, therefore, which is ridden by a dozen oppositions long lines running in every direction may actually be in less danger of being torn with violence or falling to pieces than one split just along one line. For each new cleavage contributes to narrow the cross clefts, so that one might say that *society is sewn together* by its inner conflicts. (Ross, 1920, pp. 164–65; emphasis in the original)

Later work emphasized that multiple group affiliations are not sufficient to produce social congruence. For this outcome to be possible, it is necessary to exclude situations in which 'the members of a society [...] have mutually reinforcing interests' as in this case 'multiple affiliations, instead of crisscrossing each other, would eventually consolidate into basic cleavages' (Coser, 1956, p. 78). If this condition is satisfied, 'the multiple group affiliations of individuals make for a multiplicity of conflicts criss-crossing society' (Coser, 1956, p. 79). Crisscrossing makes conflicts cancel each other out and serves to bind society together, thus preventing 'disintegration along one

---

execute their plans of oppression. Extend the sphere and you take in a greater variety of parties and interests; you make it less probable that a majority of the whole will have a common motive to invade the rights of other citizens; it will be more difficult for all who feel it to discover their own strength, and to act in unison with each other' (Madison, 1787; also published as Federalist 10, see Hamilton, Madison and Jay, 2003). Interestingly, Madison linked his crosscutting argument to the view that federal systems may be more effective than centralized systems in achieving social cohesion: 'The influence of factious leaders may kindle a flame within their particular States, but will be unable to spread a general conflagration through the other States. A religious sect may degenerate into a political faction in a part of the Confederacy; but the variety of sects dispersed over the entire face of it must secure the national councils against any danger from that source. A rage for paper money, for an abolition of debts, for an equal division of property, or for any other improper or wicked project, will be less apt to pervade the whole body of the Union than a particular member of it; in the same proportion as such a malady is more likely to taint a particular county or district, than an entire state (Madison, 1787; also published as Federalist 10, see Hamilton, Madison and Jay, 2003).

primary line of cleavage' (Coser, 1956, p. 80). For this reason, con-flicts may be compatible with the 'interdependence of antagonistic groups' (Coser, 1956, p. 80). Indeed '[w]hen close relationships are characterized by frequent conflicts rather than by the accumulation of hostile and ambivalent feelings, we may be justified, given that such conflicts are not likely to concern basic consensus, in taking these frequent conflicts as an index of the stability of these relationships' (Coser, 1956, p. 85). Similarly, '[i]n secondary relationships ... the presence of conflict may be taken as an index of the operation of a balancing mechanism' (Coser, 1956, p. 85).[34] Subsequent research has called attention to further conditions for multiple group affili-ations to generate a stable system of social interdependencies. In particular, Douglas Rae and Michael Taylor have emphasized that crosscutting can be an effective binding device provided fragmenta-tion (the degree to which cleavages set individuals or groups against each other) is neither too low or two high (Rae and Taylor, 1969, 1970). The rationale of this property is that crosscutting membership is ineffective when cleavages are little noticeable, as in this case it would not be easy to determine clear-cut group affiliations. On the other hand, crosscutting membership may also be ineffective when, say, fragmentation on one particular cleavage is so high that alterna-tive group affiliations by other cleavages become irrelevant[35].

Interdependence through differentiation of production (division of labour) makes the objective structure of society compatible with mul-tiple social cleavages and a plurality of group affiliations. However, differentiation may lead to different types of interdependence depending on the decomposition technique adopted (see discussion earlier in the chapter). This structural variety makes decomposition techniques of central relevance when examining whether existing cleavages and group affiliations are compatible with the internal consistency requirements of any given system of interdependence, for

---

[34] A balancing mechanism allows conflict settlement without disrupting the consensual foundation of the corresponding social arrangement.

[35] This intermediate fragmentation condition is a reason why, in a situation of extreme fragmentation, 'self-containment and mutual isolation' may be more effective routes to systemic cohesion than 'a high incidence of overlapping affiliations' (Lijphart 1968, p. 200; see also Lijphart, 1977). This may also be a reason why, in certain historical situations, it has been possible to achieve systemic congruence thanks to common secondary traits rather than through primary group affiliations (see Scazzieri, 2008; Pabst and Scazzieri, 2012).

alternative decompositions are possible for the same system, and different consistency conditions may be relevant in each case. In addition, different aggregation/disaggregation criteria may correspond to alternative ways of identifying group affiliations (spheres of interest) within the social structure.

Cleavages that appear at a given level of aggregation may altogether disappear when we consider unit of analysis at a different level, and crosscutting cleavages may alternatively *appear or disappear* depending on which aggregation level is considered. For example, the cleavage between rich and poor speakers of a particular language (say, English) may recede to the background in a multilingual society. In a society of this type, the crosscutting between cleavage A (English speaking vs. non-English speaking) and cleavage B (rich vs. poor) may be visible or invisible depending on whether the society under consideration gives salience to the crosscutting of cleavages involving particular groups of speakers (in this case, English vs. non-English speakers).

The political economy of the Eurozone is rooted in interdependencies existing both *within* and *across* levels of aggregation. For example, the relative positions and corresponding interactions between sub-national actors across member states may be as important as the relative positions and interactions between sub-national actors within member states. This consideration highlights the need of a multi-level heuristic allowing detection of alternative aggregation/disaggregation criteria for the elements of the political economy under consideration. This heuristic should allow identification of alternative decompositions of the Eurozone, and alternative ways of assessing the possibilities for the convergence or divergence of interests at the different levels of interdependence.[36] The previous section of this chapter examined a variety of decomposition techniques by which a system of interdependent activities may be split into a number of sub-units, which can at the same time be re-assembled in different ways depending on the type of

---

[36] Aaron Vildavsky noted the inherent flexibility of a system of multi-level interdependence when discussing H.E. Brady and P.M. Sniderman's theory of attitude attribution: 'The more people are able to choose sides – ours versus theirs – the more they appreciate the differences between the issue positions of the sides. What counts, then, is not how people feel toward groups, one by one; rather it is how they feel toward pairs of opposing groups' (Brady and Sniderman, 1985, p. 1075). It is precisely this pairing or, more accurately, this triangulation of rival cultures, I believe, that enables people to position themselves in political life' (Vildavsky, 1987, p. 9).

systemic congruence that any given decomposition technique implies. As we have seen, horizontal and vertical decomposition techniques imply not only different criteria for splitting the political-economic system into sub-units but also different ways of re-assembling those sub-units into a coherent whole. In addition, it is possible to apply decomposition techniques at different levels of interdependence (say, at sub-national, national and supra-national levels). In a political economy built upon manifold co-existing levels of interdependence, systemic congruence may be *possible* (or, respectively, *impossible*) depending on which particular level and type of interdependence one is considering. For instance, there may be cases in which it is possible to achieve horizontal congruence (as expressed by the viability condition for the set of inter-industry product flows) at the sub-national or national level but not at the supra-national level. There may also be cases in which it is possible to achieve vertical congruence consistent with full employment and full utilization of productive capacity at the supra-national level but not at the national or sub-national levels. Systemic congruence may alternatively be difficult or easy to achieve depending on the degree of 'completeness' we require from it. Thus, it may be that a given political economy meets systemic congruence from the point of view of horizontal viability without fulfilling the vertical condition for full employment. Alternatively, it may be that the system meets the vertical full employment condition but not the condition for maximum growth compatible with existing technology.

The above conceptual framework calls attention to the internal structure of a political economy seen as a system of interdependent activities. These activities are normally associated with social groups, although the relationship between activities and social groups may vary considerably within the same political economy. Thus, one may have a one-to-one relationship (one distinct social group for any activity), a one-to-many relationship (a plurality of social groups for any given activity) and a many-to-one relationship (a plurality of activities for any given social group). The plurality of decomposition techniques makes it possible to identify a plurality of system-subsystem configurations for any given political economy. Therefore, it may be necessary to switch from one structural representation of that system to another depending on which set of characteristics is prominent. For example, the horizontal scheme of interdependence al the national level may recede to the background if attention shifts to horizontal or vertical interdependencies *at the supra-national level*. In this case, we may want to aggregate the different manufacturing activities of a particular national economy into a single 'manufacturing sector' to emphasize the interdependencies between that manufacturing sector and the other sectors of the supra-national economy. Alternatively, we may focus on a particular industry in a given national economy and identify the interdependencies between that industry and the aggregate manufacturing sector of the supra-national economy. For example, we may single out the steel-making industry of country A and determine the degree to which demand for that industry comes from the aggregate manufacturing sector of the Eurozone. Finally, we may want to identify the interdependence between a particular industry in a given national economy and the aggregate final sector of the supra-national economy as a whole. For example, we may single out the textile-making industry of country B and determine the degree to which demand for that industry comes from the aggregate final demand of the Eurozone. The *horizontal approach* allows analysis of interdependencies across different levels of aggregation within the supra-national economy provided we differentiate among the national sectors delivering a particular commodity, so that we may also be able to distinguish between the *different* national sources of intermediate inputs entering particular sectors of the supra-national economy (for example, different components entering a car assembled by the automotive industry in Germany may have been delivered by metalworking industries in the Czech Republic, Italy and Poland).[37] If, instead, we adopt a framework that focuses on vertical interdependencies, the relevant political economy divides into a number of vertically integrated sectors that cut across the boundaries of different national economies (here metalworking industries in the Czech Republic, Italy and Poland would be considered parts of the same vertically integrated European sector delivering assembled cars as final output). Each subsystem includes the activities directly and indirectly necessary to the attainment of a particular objective (such as the production of a specific element of the final output vector, or the delivery of a sectoral element of the value added vector). The activities belonging to any given subsystem are subject to a condition of 'internal' subsystemic congruence ensuring

---

[37] Quadrio Curzio's 'global technology' framework provides a useful analytics for discussing this case (Quadrio Curzio, 1996).

that the proportions and interdependencies of activities within the subsystem are compatible with the objective of that subsystem. In addition to the congruence conditions for individual subsystems, the vertical decomposition technique also allows identification of congruence conditions at the level of the whole economy. In particular, it is possible to identify a macroeconomic condition by which certain combinations of vertically integrated sub systems (but not others) are compatible with full employment and full capacity utilization (Pasinetti, 1981, 1993). It is also possible to identify systemic conditions determining (i) which rates of capital accumulation for the different subsystems are compatible with growth at an exogenously given rate g (Pasinetti, 1988) or (ii) which proportions between subsystems using different techniques are compatible with maximum growth (Quadrio Curzio, 1986, 1990; Quadrio Curzio and Pellizzari, 1999). It is important to note that it is seldom possible to satisfy different congruence conditions at the same time. For example, the structural macroeconomic condition for full employment may require combinations of productive sectors incompatible with growth at the maximum rate for the whole economy, and expansion at the maximum 'internal' growth rate for *some* vertically integrated sectors may not be compatible with growth at the maximum rate for the whole economy.

Vertical decomposition techniques do not directly consider interdependencies of the horizontal type. However, horizontal interdependencies still exist behind the arrangement of the economy by vertically integrated subsystems. As we know, the viability (sustainability) of any given system of inter-industry product flows expresses the horizontal congruence condition for a corresponding political-economic system at a given time. However, a collection of vertically integrated subsystems may or may not satisfy dynamic efficiency across the whole range of its components and across different time periods. This may happen, for example, when vertical subsystems associated with different production techniques exist side by side and there is not a perfect match between the structures of the two techniques.[38] Here, vertical and horizontal decomposition techniques bring to view *different* conditions for systemic congruence and the potential mismatches that may arise because, under certain circumstances, fulfilling both the horizontal and

---

[38] This is the 'residuals' case considered in Quadrio Curzio, 1986, 1990, and discussed in subsection 17.3.4.

vertical conditions for congruence may be impossible. The plurality of decomposition techniques makes it possible to identify a plurality of interdependence levels and to assess the extent to which congruence at one level of interdependence may co-exist with lack of congruence (and, possibly, conflict) at another level. Decomposition techniques highlight a host of trade-offs between *different conditions* for systemic congruence. In this way they bring to light that the same political-economic system is compatible with alternative constellations of interests, and therefore with alternative patterns of alliances and conflicts.

17.5 Framing Questions for the Eurozone

The foregoing discussion of decomposition and aggregation techniques calls attention to the internal structure of the Eurozone as a multi-layered political-economic domain, and suggests new questions for the political economy of the Eurozone. This may be seen in a number of crucial policy objectives that have characterized policy-making in the Eurozone and EU more broadly in recent years.

First, at the level of aggregation of the EU as a whole, competition policy, which aims to introduce a level playing field through purely catallactic measures, may be seen as increasing EU-level growth potential. However, attention for lower levels of aggregations reveals that competition policy could reinforce asymmetries at the sectoral, regional and national levels. For example, it may trigger the concentration of industrial activities in certain regions and countries while leading to de-industrialization of other parts of the EU. This is consistent with an infant industry argument, as competition policy would force competition between areas at different stages of development, which would lead to de-industrialization of the less developed areas. Therefore, divergence rather than convergence could follow from attempts to introduce a level playing field across the EU.

Second, monetary policy may have different effects depending on the structure of the economic system at the sectoral level. Liquidity contraction or expansion is likely to have a different impact on industrial sectors depending on the capital intensity of each sector (and of individual production units within it). Processes of high capital intensity are likely to respond positively to monetary expansion (due to lower borrowing cost of loanable funds) and negatively to monetary contraction (due to higher borrowing cost of loanable funds). On the other hand, monetary expansion is unlikely to significantly affect processes of low capital intensity unless lower interest rates are associated with a significant increase in internal demand for final consumption goods.

Third, alternative decomposition techniques draw attention to alternative adjustment paths ('traverses') that the economic system may follow in response to policies. The different adjustment paths may entail different time profiles of adjustment along the traverse and eventually lead to significantly different outcomes. Hence, the effectiveness of any given policy stimulus is crucially dependent on the transmission traverse specific to that stimulus. One case of immediate relevance to the Eurozone is that of fiscal policy as compared to structural funds policy. Fiscal policy (budgetary measures) presupposes the view of the European economy as a collection of vertically integrated sectors constructed from macroeconomic impulses to macrosectoral employment levels, without directly addressing the intersectoral transmission mechanism of policy. On the other hand, structural funds policy entails the view of the European economy as a collection of vertically integrated subsystems constructed through forward linkages from basic infrastructure (such as railway networks, airports, pipeline networks) to aggregate income and employment levels. Attention for different disaggregation techniques highlights the character of different traverses. For example, a traverse initiated by a fiscal stimulus may lead to an immediate increase of final demand without necessarily inducing a significant boost of productive potential, while a traverse initiated by a structural funds stimulus would lead to a direct increase of productive potential, which may lead to a later increase in demand for final consumption.

The decomposition and aggregation techniques discussed above provide heuristics to study the interests of political economy actors at different levels of aggregation. They also make it possible to think about the different kinds of systemic interest associated with national and supranational patterns of coordination, as well as the likelihood that one or the other prevails in a given situation. For example, it has been discussed in the volume that crisis resolution is less urgent for surplus countries than it is for deficit countries. However, in order to understand whether surplus countries will support coordinated measures of crisis resolution, such as those which would allow real devaluation in deficit countries relative to surplus countries, we need to look at the relative weight of interdependencies within and outside the EU, both for countries and for relevant sectors. For example, a country may be highly integrated in the EU, thus benefitting from crisis resolution even if this entails a loss of competitiveness vis-à-vis extra-EU countries. However, within the country there could be sectors whose interdependencies mostly lie outside the EU; if they are particularly influential in the national political sphere, the national government might decide not to support measures to solve the problem of external imbalances between Eurozone member states. In addition, such political decisions depend not only on the 'objective' relative strength of interdependencies within and outside the EU, but also on how key political economy actors visualize those interdependencies, and hence which systemic interest is more salient. It has been highlighted throughout the volume that such salience also depends on actors' categories of analysis, which often derive from prevalent analytical frameworks and policy traditions.

A general message from this volume is that combined utilization of decomposition and aggregation techniques is needed to single out the specifications of economic structure attached to different policy objectives and measures, and to identify their respective trade-offs. Moreover, the detection of structural opportunities and constraints is a necessary condition for recognising alternative coalitions of interests that may facilitate or hinder policy implementation in each case. This heuristic points to a field of new and fundamental questions for the political economy of the Eurozone.

References

Arrow, K.J. (1951) 'An Extension of the Basic Theorems of Classical Welfare Economics, in J. Neyman (ed.), *Proceedings of the Second Berkeley Symposium on Mathematical Statistics and Probability*, Berkeley and Los Angeles: University of California Press, pp. 507–32.

Audejean, P. (2010) *La philosophie de Beccaria: Savoir punir, savoir écrire, savoir produire*, Paris: Vrin.

Baranzini, M. and Scazzieri, R. (1990) 'Economic Structure: Analytical Perspectives', in M. Baranzini, and R. Scazzieri, (eds.), *The Economic Theory of Structure and Change*, Cambridge: Cambridge University Press, pp. 227–333.

Basevi, G. and D'Adda, C. (2014) 'Overview: Analytics of the Eurozone Crisis', in D. Daianu, G. Basevi, C. D'Adda and R. Kumar (eds.), *The Eurozone and the Future of Europe: The Political Economy* of *Further Integration and Governance*, Houndmills: Basingstoke, Palgrave Macmillan, pp. 9–22.

Beccaria, C. (1971 [ms. circa1769]) *Elementi di economia pubblica*, in C. Beccaria (ed.), *Opere*, a cura di S. Romagnoli, Firenze, Sansoni, vol. I, pp. 383–649.

Boisguillbert, P. Le Pesant, sieur de (1695) *Le détail de la France; la cause de la diminution de ses biens et la facilité du remède*.

Brady, H.E. and Sniderman, P.M. (1985) 'Attitude Attribution: A Group Basis for Political Reasoning', *The American Political Science Review*, 79 (4, December), pp. 1061–78.

Brunner, O. (1968) 'Das "ganze Haus" und die alteuropaische "Okonomik"', in O. Brunner (ed.), *Neue Wege der Verfassungs – und Sozialgeschichte*, 2nd edition, Gottingen: Vandenhoek and Ruprecht, 1968, pp. 103–27.

Buchanan, J.M. (1965) 'An Economic Theory of Clubs', *Economica*, 32 (1), pp. 1–14.

Cardinale, I. (2017) 'Sectoral Interests and "Systemic Interest": Towards a Structural Political Economy of the Eurozone', in I. Cardinale, D. Coffman and R. Scazzieri (eds.), *The Political Economy of the Eurozone*, Cambridge: Cambridge University Press.

Cardinale, I., Coffman, D. and Scazzieri, R. (2017a) 'Framing the Political Economy of the Eurozone: Structural Heuristics and Policy Analysis', in I. Cardinale, D. Coffman and R. Scazzieri (eds.), *The Political Economy of the Eurozone*, Cambridge: Cambridge University Press.

Cardinale, I., Coffman, D. and Scazzieri, R. (2017b) (eds.) *The Political Economy of the Eurozone*, Cambridge: Cambridge University Press.

Cardinale, I., Coffman, D. and Scazzieri, R. (2017) 'Towards a Political Economy of Industrial Fluctuations', introductory essay in A. Aftalion, *Periodic Overproduction Crises*, London: Anthem Books.

Cardinale, I. and Scazzieri, R. (2012) '*Macroeconomía y política económica*', *Diario Clarín*, 27 May, Buenos Aires: Argentina.

Cardinale, I. and Scazzieri, R. (2013) 'Money, Industry and Structural Liquidity: A Theoretical and Policy Framework', Keynote Lecture, Deuxième colloque sur 'les relations entre la finance et l'industrie', Université Lumière Lyon 2, jeudi 17 et vendredi 18 octobre.

Cardinale, I. and Scazzieri, R. (2014) 'The Political Economy of the Eurozone: Crisis and Prospects', *Rendiconti della Classe di Scienze Morali*, Accademia delle Scienze dell'Istituto di Bologna, pp. 151–60.

Cardinale, I. and Scazzieri, R. (2016) 'Structural Liquidity: The Money-Industry Nexus', *Structural Change and Economic Dynamics*, 39 (December), pp. 46–53.

Casella A. (1994) 'Trade as an Engine of Political Change: A Parable', *Economica*, 61 (243, August), pp. 267–84.

Casella, A. (1996) 'On Market Integration and the Development of Institutions: The case of International Commercial Arbitration', *European Economic Review*, 40 (1, January), pp. 155–86.

Chiti, E. and Teixeira, G.P. (2013) 'The Constitutional Implications of the European Responses to the Financial and Public Debt Crisis', *Common Market Law Review*, 50 (3), pp. 683–708.

Coser, L. (1956) *The Functions of Social Conflict*, London: Routledge and Kegan Paul Ltd.

Dahrendorf, R. (1973) *Plaedoyer für die Europaische Union*, Munich: Piper.

Daianu, D., Basevi, G., D'Adda, C. and Kumar, R. (eds.) (2014) *The Eurozone and the Future of Europe: The Political Economy of Further Integration and Governance*, Houndmills, Basingstoke: Palgrave Macmillan.

Davenant, C. (1701) *Essays upon 1. The ballance of power. 2. The right of making war, peace, and alliances. 3. Universal monarchy. To which is added, an appendix containing the records referr'd to in the second essay*, London, printed for James Knapton, at the Crown in St. Paul's church-yard.

Debreu, G. (1954) 'Valuation Equilibrium and Pareto Optimum', *Proceedings of the National Academy of Sciences of the United States of America*, 40 (7, July), pp. 588–92.

de Finetti, B. (1952) 'Sulla preferibilità', *Giornale degli Economisti*, XI, pp. 685–709.

de Gregorio Merino, A. (2012) 'Legal Development in the Monetary and Economic Union During the Debt Crisis: The Mechanism of Financial Assistance', *Common Market Law Review*, 49 (5), pp. 1613–45.

de Viti de Marco, A. (1928) *I primi principii dell'economia finanziaria*, Roma: Sampaolesi.

Durkheim, E. (1902) *De la division du travail social*, 2nd ed. augmentée d'une preface sur les groupements professionels, Paris: Alcan.

Edgeworth, F.Y. (1881) *Mathematical Psychics*, London, C.K. Paul & co.

Eichengreen, B. (2015) 'The Next Financial Crisis', *Economia Politica*, 32 (1, April), pp. 53–66.

Feldstein, M. (2005) 'The Euro and the Stability Pact', *The Journal of Policy Modeling*, 27 (4, June), pp. 421–26.

Feldstein, M. (2012) 'The Failure of the Euro', *Foreign Affairs*, 91 (1, January–February), pp. 105–16.

Frey, B.S. and Eichenberger, R. (1999) *The New Democratic Federalism for Europe: Functional, Overlapping and Competing Jurisdictions*, Cheltenham: Elgar.

Furtado, C. (1967) 'Industrialization and Inflation', *International Economic Papers*, 12, pp. 101–19.

Galavotti, M.C. (2008) 'Causal Pluralism and Context', in M.C. Galavotti, R. Scazzieri and P. Suppes (eds.), *Reasoning, Rationality and Probability*, Stanford: CSLI Publications, pp. 233–52.

Gellner, E. (1994) *Conditions of Liberty: Civil Society and Its Rivals*, London. Hamish Hamilton.

Goodhart, C.A.E. (2014) 'Lessons for Monetary Policy from the Euro-Area Crisis', *Journal of Macroeconomics*, 39 (Part B), pp. 378–82.

Goodhart, C.A.E. and Lee, D.J. (2013) 'Adjustment Mechanisms in a Currency Area', *Open Economies Review*, 24 (4), pp. 627–56.

Gossling, W.F. (1972) *Productivity Trends in a Sectoral Macro-Economic Model: A Study of American Agriculture and Supporting Industries 1919–1964*, London: Input-Output Publishing Company.

Graunt, J. (1665) *Natural and Political Observations mentioned in a following index, and made upon the Bills of Mortality by Capt. John Graunt, Fellow of the Royal Society. With reference to the Government, Religion, Trade, Growth, Air, Diseases, and the several Changes of the said City*, the 4th impression, Oxford, printed by William Hall for John Martyn, and James Allestry.

Haas, E. (1958) *The Uniting of Europe*, London: Stevens and Sons Ltd.

Habermas, J. (2012) *The Crisis of the European Union: A Response*, translated by C. Cronin, Cambridge, Polity.

Hagemann, H. and Scazzieri, R. (2009) 'Capital Structure and Economic Transitions: An Introductory Essay', in H. Hagemann and R. Scazzieri (eds.), *Capital, Time and Transitional Dynamics*, Abingdon, Oxon, and New York: Routledge, pp. 1–39.

Hall, P. (2012) 'The Economics and Politics of the Euro Crisis', *German Politics*, 21 (4), pp. 355–71.

Hall, P. (2014) 'Varieties of Capitalism and the Euro Crisis', *West European Politics*, 37 (6), Special Issue: 'Europe's Crisis: Background, Dimensions, Solutions', pp. 1223–43.

Hall, P. and Soskice, D. (2001) (eds.) *Varieties of Capitalism: The Institutional Foundations of Comparative Advantage*, Oxford: Oxford University Press.

Hamilton, A., Madison, J. and Jay, J. (2003). *The Federalist with Letters of "Brutus"*, ed. T. Ball. Cambridge, Cambridge University Press, (1st edn 1788).

Hancké. B., Rhodes, M., and Thatcher, M. (2007) 'Introduction: Beyond Varieties of Capitalism', in B. Hancké, M. Rhodes and M. Thatcher (eds.), *Beyond Varieties of Capitalism: Conflict, Contradictions and Complementarities in the European Economy*, Oxford: Oxford University Press, pp. 3–38.

Hicks, J. (1967) *Critical Essays in Monetary Theory*, Oxford: Clarendon Press.

Hicks, J. (1973a) *Capital and Time: A Neo-Austrian Theory*, Oxford: Clarendon Press.

Hicks, J. (1973b) 'The Mainspring of Economic Growth', *Swedish Journal of Economics*, 75 (December), pp. 336–48.

Hicks, J. (1976) 'Revolutions in Economics', in S. Latsis (ed.), *Method and Appraisal in Economics*, Cambridge: Cambridge University Press, pp. 207–18.

Hicks, J. (1982) 'The Scope and Status of Welfare Economics', in J. Hicks, *Collected Essays on Economic Theory*, vol. I, *Wealth and Welfare*, Oxford: Basil Blackwell, pp. 218–39.

Hicks, J. (1989) *A Market Theory of Money*, Oxford: Clarendon Press.

Hirschman, A. (1968) 'The Political Economy of Import-Substituting Industrialization in Latin America', *The Quarterly Journal of Economics*, 82 (1, February), pp. 1–32.

Hirschman, A. (1980) *National Power and the Structure of Foreign Trade*, expanded edition, Berkeley and Los Angeles: University of California Press.

Hirschman, A. (1981a) 'Three Uses of Political Economy in Analyzing European Integration', in A. Hirschman, *Essays in Trespassing: Economics to Politics and Beyond*, Cambridge: Cambridge University Press, pp. 266–84.

Hirschman, A. (1981b) 'The Social and Political Matrix of Inflation: Elaborations on the Latin American Experience', in A. Hirschman, *Essays in Trespassing: Economics to Politics and Beyond*, Cambridge: Cambridge University Press, pp. 177–207.

Hont, I. (2005) *Jealousy of Trade: International Competition and the Nation-State in Historical Perspective*, Cambridge, MA and London: Belknap Press of Harvard University Press.

Iversen, T. and Soskice, D. (2013) 'A structural-institutional explanation of the Eurozone crisis', paper presented at the Political Economy Workshop, London, London School of Economics, 3 June.

Jevons, W.S. (1875) *Money and the Mechanism of Exchange*, London: D. Appleton and Co.

Jones, E. (2002) *The Politics of Economic and Monetary Union: Integration and Idiosyncrasy*, Lanham, Boulder, New York, Oxford: Rowman & Littlefield.

Jones, E. and Underhill. G. (2014) 'Theory of Optimum Financial Areas: Retooling the Debate on the Governance of Global Finance', SWIFT Institute, SWIFT Institute Working Paper No. 2014-XXX.

Justi, J.H.G. von (1766) *System des Finanzwesens*, Halle: Zu finden in der Rengerischen Buchhandlung.

Kallinikos, J. (2003) 'Work, Human Agency and Organization Forms: An Anatomy of Fragmentation', *Organization Studies*, 24 (4), pp. 595–618.

Kayaalp, O. (1998) 'Antonio De Viti de Marco', in F. Meacci (ed.), *Italian Economists of the 20th Century*, Cheltenham, UK and Northampton, MA: Edward Elgar, pp. 95–113.

Keohane, R.O. (1984) *After Hegemony: Cooperation and Discord in the World Political Economy*, Princeton: Princeton University Press.

Keohane, R.O. and Nye, J.S. (1977) *Power and Interdependence: World Politics in Transition*, Boston: Little Brown.

Keohane, R.O. and Nye, J.S. (1987) 'Power and Interdependence Revisited', *International Organization*, 41, pp. 725–53.

Kerr, P. and Scazzieri, R. (2013) 'Structural Economic Dynamics and the Cambridge Tradition', in G.C. Harcourt and P. Kriesler (eds.), *The Oxford Handbook of Post-Keynesian Economics*, Oxford and New York: Oxford University Press, vol. I, pp. 257–87.

Keynes, J.M. (1936) *The General Theory of Employment, Interest and Money*, London: Macmillan.

King, G. (1936) *Two Tracts by Gregory King (a) Natural and Political Observations and Conclusions upon the State and Condition of England [1696]. (b) Of the Naval Trade of England Ao. 1688 and the National Profit then arising thereby [1697]*, edited with an introduction by George E. Barnett, Baltimore: Johns Hopkins Press.

Landesmann, M. and Scazzieri, R. (1990) 'Specification of Structure and Economic Dynamics', in M. Baranzini and R. Scazzieri (eds.), *The Economic Theory of Structure and Change*, Cambridge: Cambridge University Press, pp. 95–121.

Landesmann, M. and Scazzieri, R. (1993) 'Commodity Flows and Productive Subsystems: An Essay in the Analysis of Structural Change', in M. Baranzini and G.C. Harcourt (eds.), *The Dynamics of the Wealth of Nations. Growth, Distribution and Structural Change (Essays in Honour of Luigi Pasinetti)*, Houndmills, Basingstoke, London and New York: St. Martin's Press, pp. 209–45.

Lavalley, P. (1903) *L'oeuvre économique de Antoine de Montchrétien*, Caen, E. Adeline (Thèse pour le doctorat soutenue publiquement dans la Salle des actes de la Faculté de droit le mercredi 1. juillet).

Leon, P. (1967) *Structural Change and Growth in Capitalism*, Baltimore, Johns Hopkins University Press.

Leontief, W.W. (1941) *The Structure of the American Economy, 1919–1929*, Cambridge, MA, Harvard University Press.

Leontief, W.W. (1991 [1928]) 'The Economy as a Circular Flow', *Structural Change and Economic Dynamics*, 2 (1), pp. 181–212.

Lijphart, A. (1968). *The Politics of Accommodation: Pluralism and Democracy in the Netherlands*, Berkeley and Los Angeles: University of California Press.

Lijphart, A. (1977). *Democracy in Plural Societies: A Comparative Exploration*, New Haven, CT: Yale University Press.

Lowe, A. (1976) *The Path of Economic Growth*, Cambridge: Cambridge University Press.

Ludlow, P. (1982) *The Making of the European Monetary System: A Case Study of the Politics of the European Community*, London, Boston, Sydney, Wellington, Durban and Toronto: Butterworth Scientific.

Lutfalla, M. (1981) *Aux origines de la pensée économique*, Paris: Economica.

McCormick, J.P. (2007). *Weber, Habermas and Transformations of the European State: Constitutional, Social, and Supranational Democracy*. Cambridge: Cambridge University Press.

Madison, J. (1787) 'The Utility of the Union as a Safeguard Against Domestic Faction and Insurrection', *Daily Advertiser*, Thursday, 22 November.

Maes, I. (1992) 'Optimum Currency Area Theory and European Monetary Integration', *Tijdschrift voor Economie en Management*, 37 (2), pp. 137–52.

Majone, G. (2014) *Rethinking the Union of Europe Post-Crisis: Has Integration Gone Too Far?*, Cambridge: Cambridge University Press.

Mamalakis, M. (1969) 'The Theory of the Sectoral Clashes', *Latin American Research Review*, 4 (Fall), pp. 9–46.

Marshall, 1961 [1890] *Principles of Economics*, ninth (variorum) edition with annotations by C.W. Guillebaud, vol. I, London: Macmillan for the Royal Economic Society.

Matteucci, N. (1979) 'La pensabilità dell'economico ovvero delle strutture della prassi', in R. Crippa (ed.), *La dimensione dell'economico*, Padova: Liviana Editrice, pp. 5–27.

Meinecke, F. (1924) *Die Idee der Staatsräson in der neureren Geschichte*, München: Oldenbourg.

Milner, H.V. (2009) 'Power, Interdependence, and Nonstate Actors in World Politics: Research Frontiers', in H.V. Milner and A. Moravcsik (eds.), *Power, Interdependence, and Nonstate Actors on World Politics*, Princeton: Princeton University Press, pp. 3–27.

Milner, H.V. and Moravcsik, A. (eds) (2009) *Power, Interdependence, and Nonstate Actors on World Politics*, Princeton: Princeton University Press.

Montchrétien, A., Sieur de Watteville (1999 [1615]) *Traicté de l'oeconomie politique,* édition critique par François Billacois, Genève: Droz.

Mortati, C. (1998) *La Costituzione in senso materiale*, reprinted with preface by G. Zagrebelsky, Milano: Giuffrè (1st ed. 1940).

Mourlon-Druol, E. (2012) *A Europe Made of Money: The Emergence of the European Monetary System*, Ithaca and London: Cornell University Press.

Mourlon-Druol, E. (2014) 'Don't Blame the Euro: Historical Reflections on the Roots of the Eurozone Crisis', *West European Politics*, 37, pp. 1282–96.

Mundell, R.A. (1961) 'A Theory of Optimum Currency Areas', *American Economic Review*, 51 (4, September), pp. 657–64.

Mundell, R.A. (1969) 'A Plan for a European Currency', paper prepared for discussion at the American Management Association Conference on Future of the International Monetary System, New York, 10–12 December, mimeo.

Mundell, R.A. (2006) *Acceptance of an Honorary Degree from the University of Bologna*', Bologna: University of Bologna.

Neumann, J. von (1935–37) 'Uber ein Okonomisches Gleichungs-System und eine Verallgemeinerung des Brouwerschen Fixpunktsatzes', in *Ergebnisse eines Mathematischen Kolloquiums*, Vienna, VIII, pp. 73–83. (English translation: 'A Model of General Equilibrium'. *The Review of Economic Studies*, 9, pp. 1–9.)

O'Donnell, G. (1977) 'Estado y Alianzas en la Argentina 1956–1976', *Desarollo Económico*, 16 (January–March), pp. 523–54.

Olson, M. (1971) *The Logic of Collective Action*, Cambridge, MA: Harvard University Press.

Ornaghi, L. (1990) 'Economic Structure and Political Institutions: A Theoretical Framework', in M. Baranzini and R. Scazzieri (eds.), *The Economic Theory of Structure and Change*, Cambridge: Cambridge University Press, pp. 23–44.

Ornaghi, L. (2012) 'Sui "problemi terminali" dell'economia e della politica', in G. Antonelli, M. Maggioni, G. Pegoretti, F. Pellizzari, R. Scazzieri and R. Zoboli (eds.), *Economia come scienza sociale: teoria, istituzioni, storia. Studi in onore di Alberto Quadrio Curzio*, Bologna, Il Mulino, pp. 397–416.

Ostroy, J.M. and Starr, R.M. (1974) 'Money and the Decentralization of Exchange', *Econometrica*, 42 (6, November), pp. 1093–1113.

Pabst, A. and Scazzieri, R. (2012) 'The Political Economy of Civil Society', *Constitutional Political Economy*, 23, pp. 337–56.

Pantaleoni, M. (1898) 'An Attempt to Analyze the Concepts of "Strong" and "Weak" in their Economic Connexion', 1898, *The Economic Journal*, 8, pp. 183–205.

Pareto, V. (2014 [1906]) *Manual of Political Economy: A Critical and Variorum Edition*, eds. A. Montesano, A. Zanni, L. Bruni, J.S. Chipman and M. McLure, Oxford: Oxford University Press.

Pasinetti, L.L. (1965) *A New Theoretical Approach to the Problems of Economic Growth*, Vatican City, Pontificiae Academiae Scientiarum Scripta Varia.

Pasinetti, L.L. (1973) 'Vertical Integration in Economic Theory', *Metroeconomica*, 25, pp. 1–29; reprinted in Pasinetti, L.L. (ed.), *Essays on the Theory of Joint Production*, London, Macmillan; New York: Columbia University Press, 1980.

Pasinetti, L.L. (1977) *Lectures on the Theory of Production*, London, Macmillan; New York: Columbia University Press.

Pasinetti, L.L. (1981) *Structural Change and Economic Growth: A Theoretical Essay on the Dynamics of the Wealth of Nations*, Cambridge: Cambridge University Press.

Pasinetti, L.L. (1986) 'Theory of Value – A Source of Alternative Paradigms in Economic Analysis', in M. Baranzini and R. Scazzieri (eds.), *Foundations of Economics: Structures of Inquiry and Economic Theory*, Oxford and New York: Basil Blackwell, pp. 409–31.

Pasinetti, L.L. (1988) 'Growing Subsystems, Vertically Hyper-Integrated Sectors and the Labour Theory of Value', *Cambridge Journal of Economics*, 12, pp. 125–34.

Pasinetti, L. L. (1993) *Structural Economic Dynamics: A Theory of the Economic Consequences of Human Learning*, Cambridge: Cambridge University Press.

Pearl, J. (2000) *Causality: Models, Reasoning, and Inference*, Cambridge: Cambridge University Press.

Petty, William, (1691) *Political Arithmetick: or A discourse concerning the extent and value of lands, people, buildings ... as the same relates to every country in general, but more particularly to the territories of His Majesty of Great Britain, and his neighbours of Holland, Zealand, and France*, London: printed for Robert Clavel ... and Hen. Mortlock.

Pigou, A.C. (1912) *Wealth and Welfare*, London: Macmillan.

Pigou, A.C. (1920) *The Economics of Welfare*, London: Macmillan.

Pisani-Ferry, S. (2014) *The Euro Crisis and Its Aftermath*, Oxford: Oxford University Press.

Quadrio Curzio, A. (1967) *Rendita e distribuzione in un modello economico plurisettoriale*, Milan: Giuffrè.

Quadrio Curzio, A. (1975) *Accumulazione del capitale e rendita*, Bologna: Il Mulino.

Quadrio Curzio, A. (1980) 'Rent, Income Distribution, Order of Efficiency and Rentability', in L.L. Pasinetti (ed.), *Essays on the Theory of Joint Production*, London: Macmillan, pp. 218–40.

Quadrio Curzio, A. (1986) 'Technological Scarcity: An Essay on Production and Structural Change', in M. Baranzini and R. Scazzieri (eds.), *Foundations of Economics: Structures of Inquiry and Economic Theory*, Oxford and New York: Basil Blackwell, pp. 311–38.

Quadro Curzio, A. (1990) 'Rent, Distribution and Economic Structure: A Collection of Essays', Milano: Consiglio Nazionale delle Richerche–CNR, *Quaderni IDSE*. n. 1.

Quadrio Curzio, A. (1996) 'Production and Efficiency with Global Technologies', in M. Landesmann and R. Scazzieri (eds.), *Production and Economic Dynamics*, Cambridge: Cambridge University Press, pp. 105–39.

Quadrio Curzio, A. (2003) 'Europa: economia e istituzioni', in *Rendiconti della Classe di Scienze morali, storiche e filologiche della Accademia Nazionale dei Lincei*, series IX, vol. xiv, n. 3, pp. 501–26.

Quadrio Curzio, A. (2007) *Economisti ed economia. Per un'Italia europea: paradigmi tra il XVIII e il XX secolo*, Bologna: Il Mulino.

Quadrio Curzio, A. (2012) 'Cambridge e l'Eurozona: Superare le dicotomie', *Il Sole 24 Ore*, 7 October, p. 35.

Quadrio Curzio, A. and Pellizzari, F. (1999) *Rent, Resources, Technologies*, Berlin: Springer.

Quadrio Curzio, A. and Scazzieri, R. (1983) *Sui momenti costitutivi dell'economia politica*, Bologna: Il Mulino.

Quesnay, F. (1758) *Tableau économique*, Versailles.

Rae, D.W. and Taylor, M. (1969) 'An Analysis of Crosscutting between Political Cleavages', *Comparative Politics*, 1 (4, July), pp. 534–47.

Rae, D.W. and Taylor, M. (1970) *The Analysis of Political Cleavages*, New Haven and London: Yale University Press.

Reinert, S. (2011) *Translating Empire: Emulation and the Origins of Political Economy*, Cambridge, MA and London: Harvard University Press.

Rodrick, D. (2011) *The Globalization Paradox*, Oxford: Oxford University Press.

Rosenberg, N. (1969) 'The Direction of Technological Change: Inducement Mechanisms and Focusing Devices', *Economic Development and Cultural Change*, 18 (1): pp. 1–24.

Rosenberg, N. (1976) *Perspectives on Technology*, Cambridge: Cambridge University Press.

Ross, E. A. (1920) *The Principles of Sociology*, New York: The Century Company.

Rothschild, K.W. (1947) 'Price Theory and Oligopoly', *The Economic Journal*, 47 (September), pp. 299–320.

Salmon, W. (1984) *Scientific Explanation and the Causal Structure of the World*, Princeton: Princeton University Press.

Salmon, W. (1998) *Causality and Explanation*, New York: Oxford University Press.

Scazzieri, R. (1993) *A Theory of Production: Tasks, Processes and Technical Practices*, Oxford: Clarendon Press.

Scazzieri, R. (1998) 'Hierarchy of Production Activities and Decomposition of Structural Change: An Essay in the Theory of Economic History', in H. Hagemann and H.D. Kurz (eds.), *Political Economy in Retrospect: Essays in Memory of Adolph Lowe*, Cheltenham UK and Northampton, MA: E. Elgar, pp. 195–207.

Scazzieri, R. (2008) 'Context, Congruence and Co-ordination', in M.C. Galavotti, R. Scazzieri and P. Suppes (eds.), *Reasoning, Rationality and Probability*, Stanford, CA: CSLI Publications, pp. 187–207.

Scazzieri, R. (2009) 'Traverse Analysis and Methods of Economic Dynamics', in H. Hagemann and Scazzieri, R. (eds.), *Capital, Time and Transitional Dynamics*, Abingdon, Oxon, UK and New York: Routledge, pp. 96–132.

Scazzieri, R. (2012a) 'Structural Economic Dynamics: Methods, Theories and Decisions', in H.M. Kramer, H.D. Kurz and H.-M. Trautwein (eds.), *Macroeconomics and the History of Economic Thought: Essays in Honour of Harald Hagemann*, Abingdon, Oxon, UK and New York: Routledge, pp. 314–28.

Scazzieri, R. (2012b) 'Dinamiche strutturali e idee cardine: prospettive di ricerca sulla teoria economica del Novecento', in G. Antonelli, M. Maggioni, G. Pegoretti, F. Pellizzari, R. Scazzieri and R. Zoboli (eds.), *Economia come scienza sociale: teoria, istituzioni, storia. Studi in onore di Alberto Quadrio Curzio*, Bologna: Il Mulino, pp. 417–34.

Scazzieri, R. (2014a) 'A Structural Theory of Increasing Returns', *Structural Change and Economic Dynamics*, 29 (2), pp. 75–88.

Scazzieri, R. (2014b) 'L'illuminismo delle riforme civili: divisione del lavoro, commercio, produzione della ricchezza', in P.L. Porta and R. Scazzieri, (eds.), *L'illuminismo delle riforme civili: il contributo degli economisti lombardi*, Milano, Istituto Lombardo di Scienze e Lettere, Incontro di studio n. 64, pp. 13–38.

Scazzieri, R. (2017) 'Liquidity Architectures and Production Arrangements: A Conceptual Scheme', in I. Cardinale, D. Coffman, and R. Scazzieri (eds.), *The Political Economy of the Eurozone*, Cambridge: Cambridge University Press.

Scazzieri, R., Baranzini, M. and Rotondi, C. (2015) 'Resources, Scarcities and Rents: Technological Interdependence and the Dynamics of

Socio-Economic Structures', in M. Baranzini, C. Rotondi and R. Scazzieri (eds.), *Resources, Production and Structural Dynamics*, Cambridge: Cambridge University Press, pp. 427–84.

Scharpf, F.W. (2010a) 'The Asymmetry of European Integration, or Why the EU Cannot be a Social Market Economy', *Socio-Economic Review*, 8 (2), pp. 211–50.

Scharpf, F.W. (2010b) *Community and Autonomy. Institutions, Policies and Legitimacy in Multilevel Europe*, Publication Series of the Max Planck Institute for the Study of Societies, Frankfurt and New York: Campus Verlag.

Scharpf, F.W. (2012) *Legitimacy Intermediation in the Multilevel European Polity and Its Collapse in the Euro Crisis*, Cologne: Max Planck Institute for the Study of Societies.

Schelling. T.C. (1960) *The Strategy of Conflict*, Cambridge, MA: Harvard University Press.

Schumpeter, J.A. (1972 [1954]) *History of Economic Analysis, edited from manuscript by Elizabeth Boody Schumpeter*, London: Allen and Unwin.

Scitovsky, T. (1958) *Economic Theory and Western European Integration*, London: Allen ad Unwin.

Sella, E. (1904) 'Della natura logica dei problemi terminali dell'economia politica', in *Giornale degli economisti*, series II, vol. xxix, pp. 401–26.

Seton, F. (1992 [1985]) *Cost, Use and Value: The Evaluation of Performance, Structure and Prices across Time, Space, and Economic Systems*, Oxford: Clarendon Press.

Shepsle, K.A. (1979a) 'The Role of Institutional Structure in the Creation of Policy Equilibrium', in D.W. Rae and T.J. Eismeier (eds.), *Public Policy and Public Choice*, Beverly Hills and London: Sage Publications, pp. 249–81.

Shepsle, K.A. (1979b) 'Institutional Arrangements and Equilibrium in Multi-Dimensional Voting Models', *American Journal of Political Science*, 23 (February), pp. 23–57.

Simmel, G. (1955) 'The Web of Group-Affiliations', in G. Simmel, *'Conflict' and 'The Web of Group Affiliations'*, New York: The Free Press; London: Collier-Macmillan, pp. 125–95. (First German edition 1922.)

Simmel, G. (1968) 'The Conflict in Modern Culture', in G. Simmel, *The Conflict in Modern Culture and Other Essays*, New York: Teachers College Press, pp. 11–26.

Simon, H. (1962) 'The Architecture of Complexity', *Proceedings of the American Philosophical Society*, 106 (6), pp. 467–82.

Soskice D. (2007) 'Macroeconomics and Varieties of Capitalism', in B. Hancké, M. Rhodes and M. Thatcher (eds.), *Beyond*

Varieties of Capitalism: Conflict, Contradictions and Complementarities in the European Economy, Oxford: Oxford University Press, pp. 89–121.

Sraffa, P. (1960) *Production of Commodities by Means of Commodities: Prelude to a Critique of Economic Theory*, Cambridge: Cambridge University Press.

Stein, J.L. (2014) 'The Diversity of Debt Crises in Europe', in D. Daianu, G. Basevi, C. D'Adda, and R. Kumar (eds.), (2014) *The Eurozone and the Future of Europe: The Political Economy of Further Integration and Governance*, Houndmills, Basingstoke: Palgrave Macmillan, pp. 25–39.

Steuart, Sir J. (1966 [1767]) *An Inquiry into the Principles of Political Economy*, Edinburgh and London: Oliver and Boyd for the Scottish Economic Society.

Streeck, W. (2015) *The Rise of the European Consolidation State*, Discussion Paper 15/1. Köln: Max Planck Institute for the Study of Societies.

Streeck, W. and L. Elsässer (2014) *Monetary Disunion: The Domestic Politics of Euroland*, Discussion Paper 14/17. Köln: Max Planck Institute for the Study of Societies.

Tuori, K. (2010) 'The Many Constitutions of Europe', in K. Tuori and S. Sankari (eds.), *The Many Constitutions of Europe*, Farnham, Surrey, and Burlington, VT: Ashgate Publishing Company pp. 3–30.

Tuori, K. and Tuori, K.K. (2014) *The Eurozone Crisis: A Constitutional Analysis*, Cambridge: Cambridge University Press.

Truman, D.B. (1951) *The Governmental Process*, New York: Knopf.

Véron, N. (2012) 'The Challenges of Europe's Fourfold Union', Bruegel Policy Contribution. Statement delivered at the hearing on *The Future of the Eurozone: Outlook and Lessons* at the Subcommittee on European Affairs of the US Senate Committee on Foreign Relations, in Washington, DC on 1 August.

Vildavsky, A. (1964) *Politics of the Budgetary Process, 1964*, New York: Little, Brown.

Vildavsky, A. (1987) 'Choosing Preferences by Constructing Institutions: A Cultural Theory of Preference Formation', *The American Political Science Review*, 81 (1, March), pp. 3–22.

Viner, J. (1950) *The Customs Union Issue*, London: Stevens for the Carnegie Endowment for International Peace.

Walras, L. (1874–77) *Eléments d'économie politique pure, ou théorie de la richesse sociale*, Lausanne, Corbaz & Cie; Paris: Guillaumin & Cie; Bâle, Georg.

Wieser, F. von (1983 [1926]) *The Law of Power*, translated into English by W.E. Kuhn, edited with an introduction by W. J. Samuels, Lincoln: Bureau of Business Research, University of Nebraska.

Young, B. (2014) 'The Power of Ordoliberalism in the Eurozone Crisis Management', in D. Daianu, G. Basevi, C. D'Adda and R. Kumar (eds.), *The Eurozone and the Future of Europe: The Political Economy of Further Integration and Governance*, Houndmills, Basingstoke: Palgrave Macmillan, pp. 126–37.

Index[1]

---

[1] The index does not include references to this volume's contributors.

Lightning Source UK Ltd.
Milton Keynes UK
UKHW022051270322
400701UK00018B/389